To
Janice Kamrin

For all the good work
she has done
for Egypt

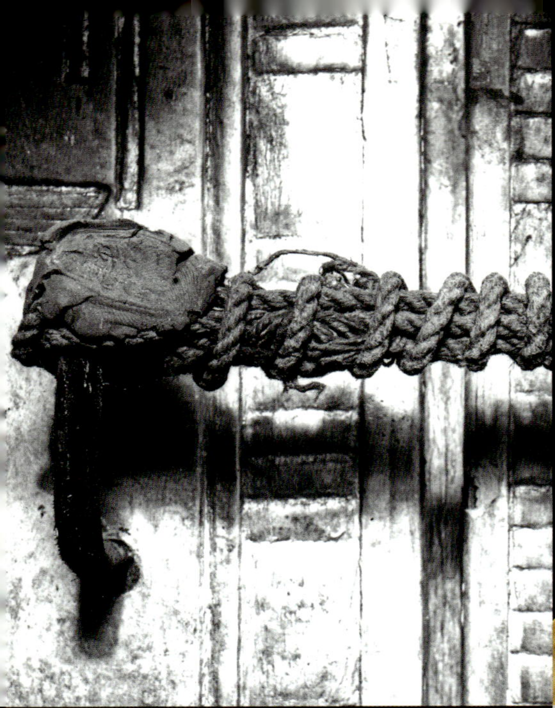
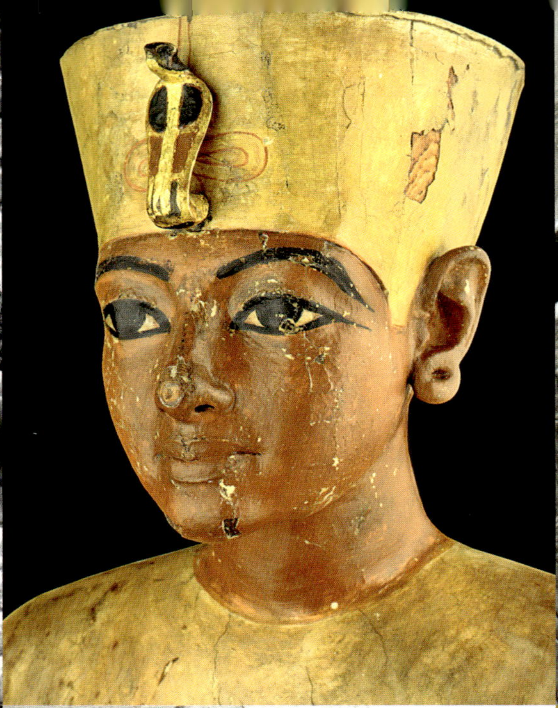
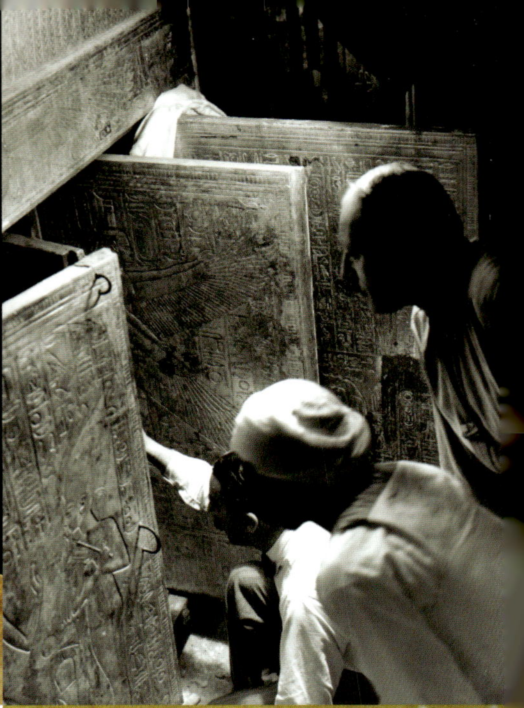
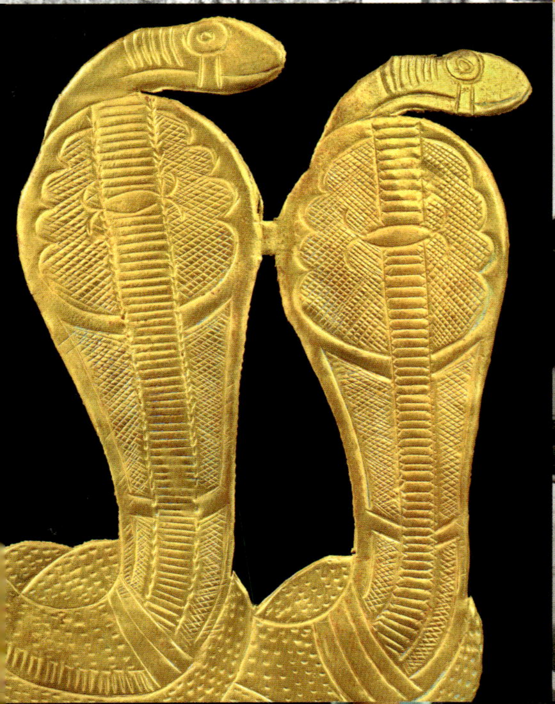
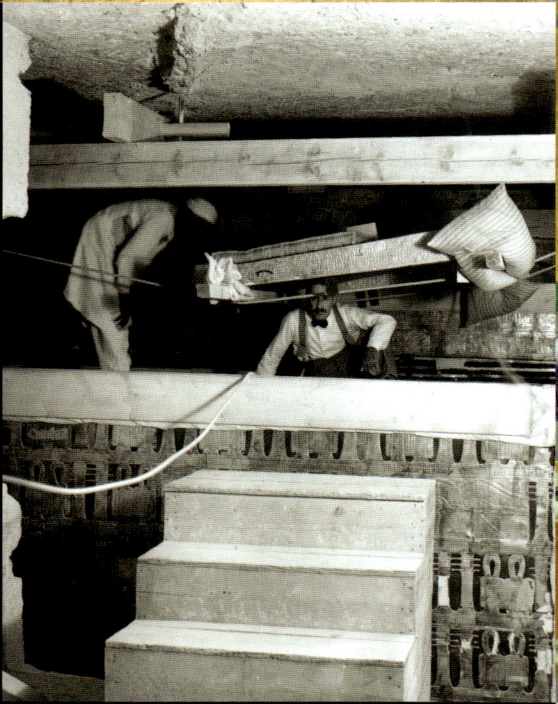
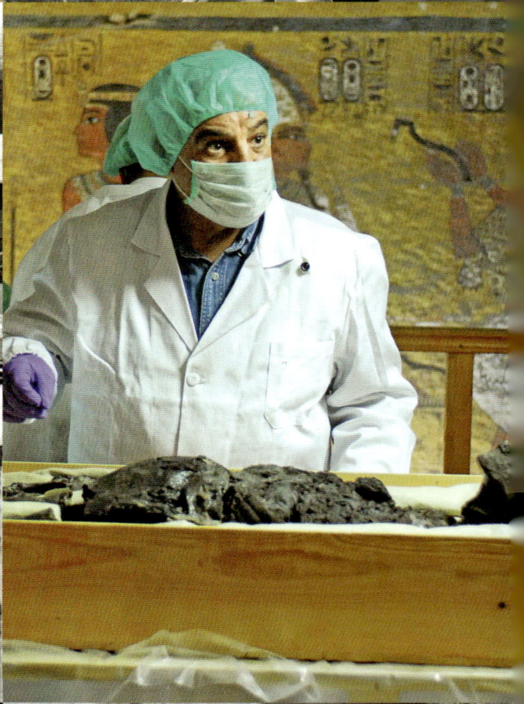
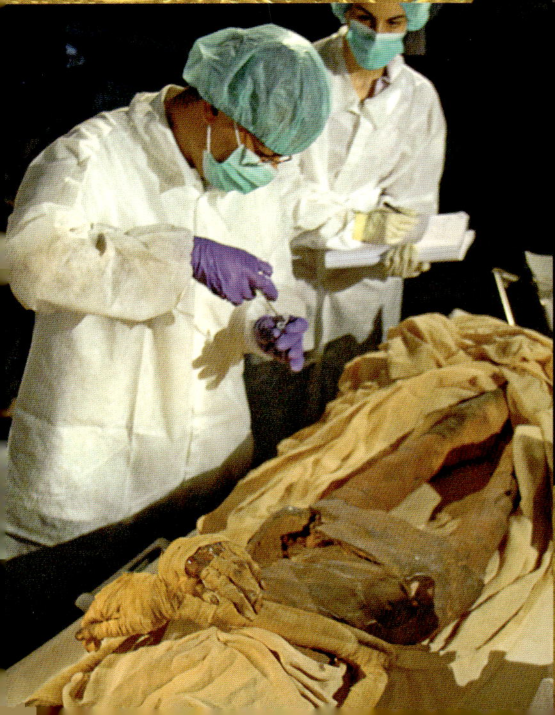
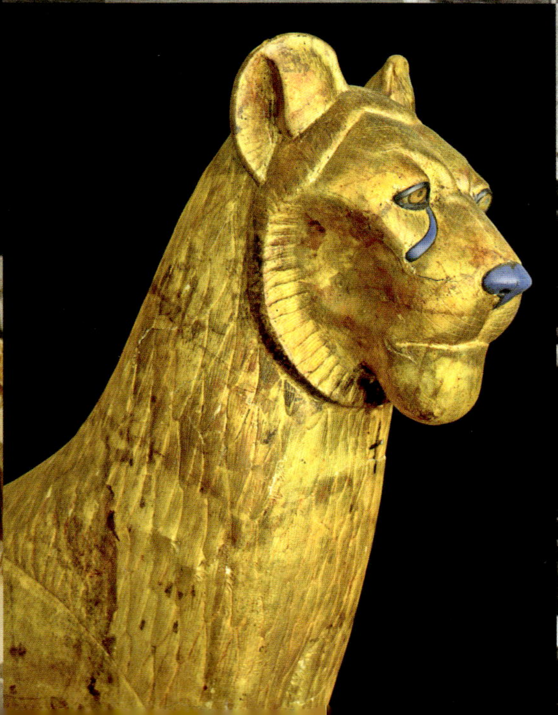
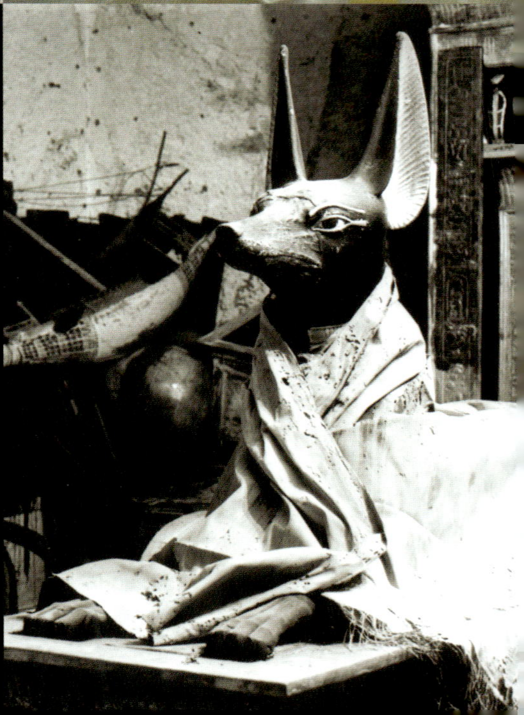

ZAHI HAWASS

DISCOVERING TUTANKHAMUN

FROM HOWARD CARTER TO DNA

ACKNOWLEDGMENTS

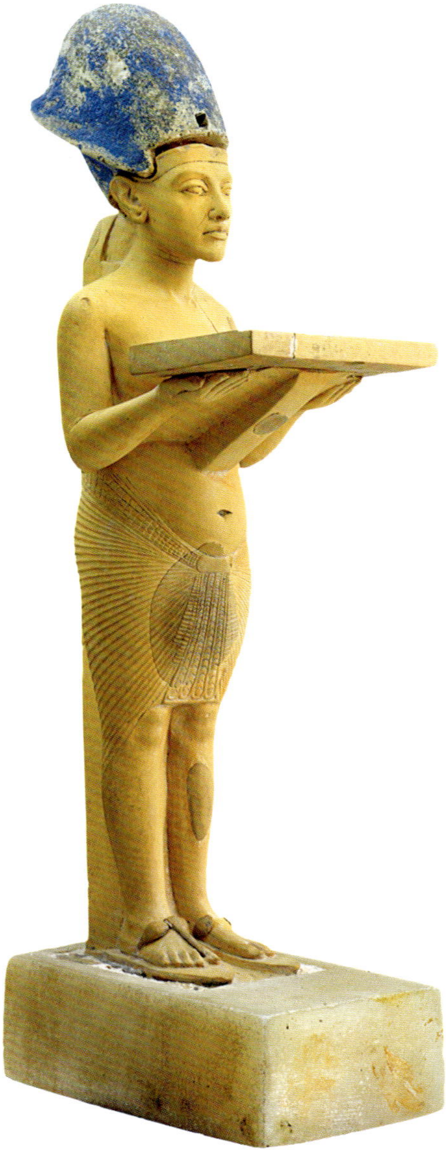

I would like to thank the many people and friends who helped me to finish this book. First, I would like to thank Yasmin El Shazly and Marwa Abdel Razek from the Egyptian Museum in Cairo, and Sana Mohamed Ali from the Luxor Museum, who provided me with lists of Tutankhamun's objects in storage. Also, I express my gratitude to Mansour Boraik for reading the text and also for giving me a list of objects in storage.

Further thanks go to Tom Campbell, director of the Metropolitan Museum of Art, and Dorothea Arnold, who as curator of Egyptian Art at the Metropolitan Museum of Art returned to the Egyptian Museum 19 objects from the MMA collection that belonged to Tutankhamun. I would also like to thank Brando Quillici, who played an important role in the construction of the DNA Labs and supported the Egyptian Mummy Project.

Thanks also to Ray Johnson, Tarek El Awady, Janice Kamrin, Edward Brovarski, John Darnell, Otto Schaden, Omar Abu Zeid, Oliver Rosenwald, Aleksandra Fuhrer, Stefan Fuhrer, Luisa Franz Kleopatra and Manfred Kostal for reading this manuscript and having prepared it for publication.

Last but not least I would like to thank Noreen Doyle for her good work in editing the English of this book.

ZAHI HAWASS

TABLE OF CONTENTS

4 ACKNOWLEDGMENTS
8 FOREWORD
12 INTRODUCTION
14 CHRONOLOGY

16 CHAPTER I
17 THE GOLDEN AGE OF EGYPT: DYNASTY 18
18 Egypt before Tutankhamun
21 Founding the Empire: Ahmose and the Kings of the Early New Kingdom
24 Amenhotep III and Tiye
26 Amarna: Akhenaten and Nefertiti
30 Tutankhamun: Boy and King
31 Cities Loved by the King
33 The King and His Court
36 The End of Tutankhamun's Reign

38 CHAPTER II
39 RELIGION AND LIFE AFTER DEATH
40 Inspiration
41 The Afterlife
42 Mummification
44 The Funeral
45 The Royal Tombs: Pyramids
46 The Valley of the Kings: Architecture for the Afterlife
48 Burial Equipment
49 Religious Texts

54 CHAPTER III
55 ROBBERS IN THE VALLEY OF THE KINGS
56 The Later New Kingdom and the Third Intermediate Period
57 Early Excavations in the Valley
58 Howard Carter and Lord Carnarvon
60 The People around Carter
61 The Day of the Discovery
62 The Legend of the Boy Who Found the Tomb
63 Trouble in Paradise: Carter and the Antiquities Service
64 Aftermath: Carter after Tutankhamun

66 CHAPTER IV
67 THE TOMB AND ITS TREASURES
68 THE STAIRWAY AND ENTRANCE CORRIDOR
69 THE ANTECHAMBER
74 Ritual Beds
83 Golden Throne
88 THE BURIAL CHAMBER
92 The Second Shrine
94 Fan
95 Cartouche
96 THE DECORATION OF THE BURIAL CHAMBER
98 THE COFFINS
103 THE GOLDEN MASK
104 THE TREASURY
105 Inlaid Pectorals
108 Canopic Chest and Canopy
110 The Human-Headed Stoppers
111 Canopic Coffinettes
112 The Name Pendant of Tutankhamun
112 Coronation Pectoral
114 Necklaces
116 Box with Delicate Contents
117 Crooks and Flails
118 Mirror Cases
119 Scribal Kit
120 Ritual Figures
124 Zoomorphic Deities and Osiris
124 Nest of Coffins
126 King on a Bier
126 Model Boats
128 *Shabtis*
130 THE ANNEXE
131 Furniture
132 Shields
133 Headrests
134 Games
135 Vases and Vessels
138 Model Boats

140 CHAPTER V
141 TUTANKHAMUN'S MUMMY
142 Howard Carter and the Mummy
143 THE JEWELRY OF THE MUMMY
144 Collars
145 Rings
145 Bracelet
146 Daggers and Sheath
146 Necklace
149 Amulets
152 Golden Protection
154 X-rays of the Mummy
154 The Mystery of the Mummy's Head
154 CT Scan of the Mummy
157 The King's Diet
158 DNA and Other Modern Tests
159 How Tutankhamun Died

160 CHAPTER VI
161 THE DISCOVERY OF THE FAMILY OF TUTANKHAMUN
162 The Family of the Boy-King
165 The Problem of Ancient DNA
165 DNA Now and the CT Scan
166 The Mummies
167 The Results
168 The Two Fetuses
169 Searching for Nefertiti
170 The Search for Nefertiti's Sister
171 King Tutankhamun's Pedigree (based on DNA analysis)

172 CHAPTER VII
173 THE VALLEY OF THE KINGS AND FINDS AFTER THE DISCOVERY OF TUTANKHAMUN
174 The Story
175 The Rediscovery of KV 5
181 The Discovery of an Embalming Cache in the Valley of the Kings (KV 63)
184 The Discovery of KV 64
186 The Secret Tunnel of Seti I Is Revealed
190 The Search for the Tomb of Rameses VIII
191 Excavation in Front of the Tomb of Tutankhamun
197 Excavation in the Valley of the Monkeys
198 The Rediscovery of KV 53 by the Egyptian Expedition
199 The Rediscovery of the Missing Pieces of the Colossal Statue of Amenhotep III and Queen Tiye at the Egyptian Museum
204 The Excavation of the German Expedition at Amenhotep III's Temple
206 The Discovery of the Cache of Statues of Amenhotep III by the Egyptian Expedition
209 Tutankhamun's Statues Stolen from the Egyptian Museum
210 Protecting the Valley of the Kings

212 CHAPTER VIII
213 THE CURSE OF TUTANKHAMUN

218 CHAPTER IX
219 TUTMANIA

224 CONCLUSION

226 APPENDIX 1
List of Objects Found in KV 62 Based on a Handlist to Howard Carter's Catalogue of Objects in Tutankhamun's Tomb, compiled by Helen Murray and Mary Nuttall
226 Stairway and Entrance Corridor
227 Antechamber
231 Burial Chamber
233 Treasury
235 Annexe

239 APPENDIX 2
Objects of Tutankhamun in Museums Worldwide
239 KV 62 Valley of the Kings, Theban Necropolis
Egyptian Museum, Cairo
Agricultural Museum, Cairo
240 Kasr el Aini Hospital, Cairo
Objects in Storage in the Egyptian Museum, Cairo
Objects in Storage at the Grand Egyptian Museum, Cairo
241 Objects in the Luxor Museum, Luxor
Objects in Storage in the Luxor Museum, Luxor
Objects in Storage on the West Bank of Luxor
242 Objects Returned by the Metropolitan Museum of Art (MMA), New York
Objects Outside of Egypt
243 Monuments Connected with King Tutankhamun

244 APPENDIX 3
Tutankhamun's Tours

249 APPENDIX 4
Royal Tombs of Kings and Queens Still to be Discovered

250 APPENDIX 5
The Official Request for the Return of Nefertiti's Bust

253 SOURCES OF QUOTATIONS
254 BIBLIOGRAPHY
259 INDEX
264 Imprint

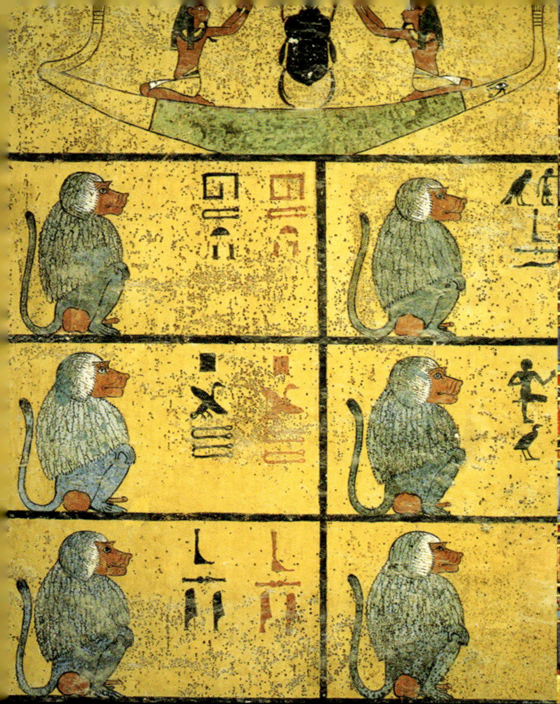
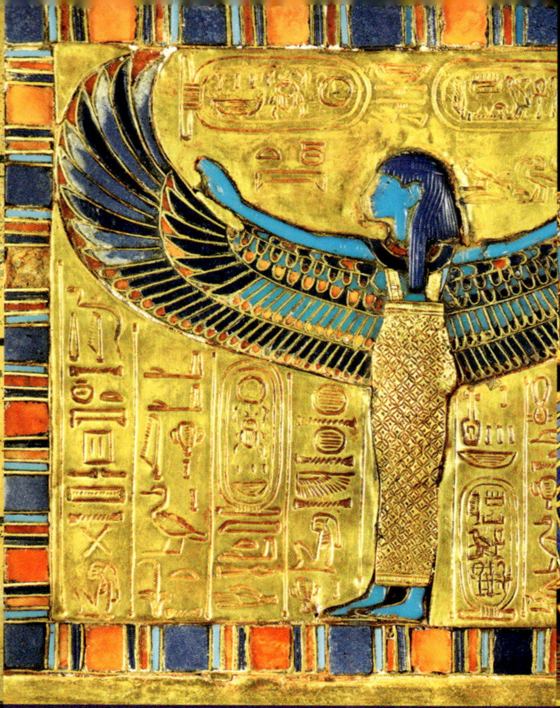
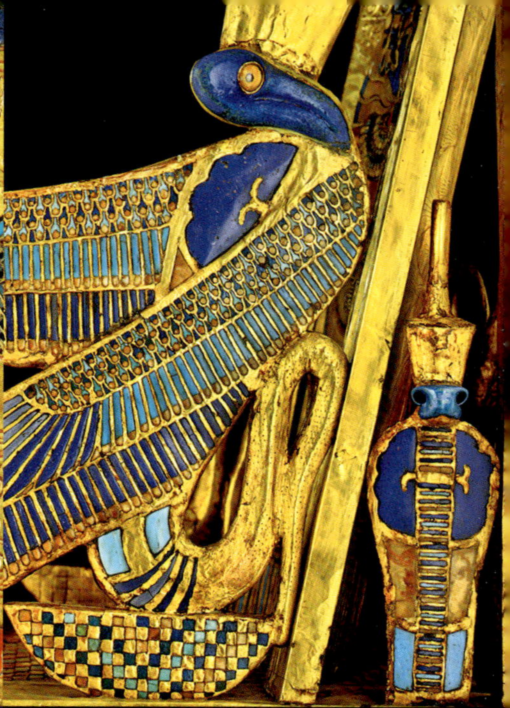
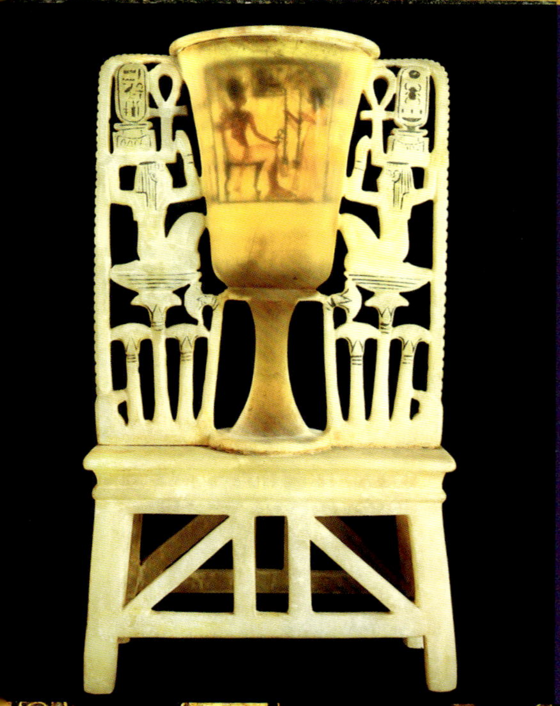

FOREWORD

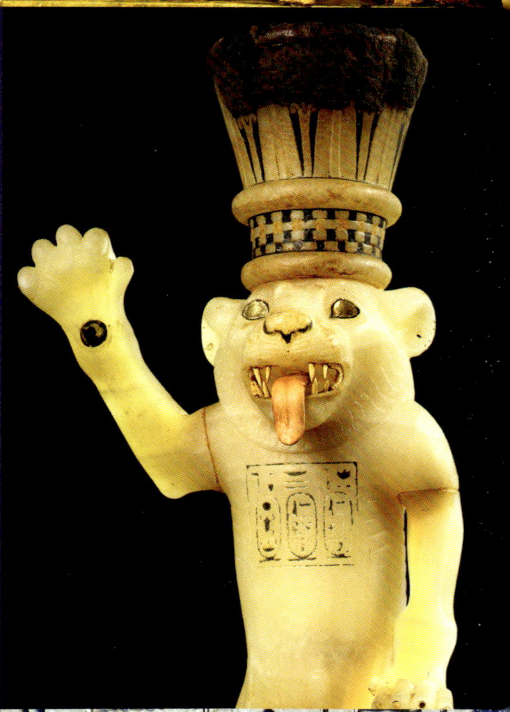
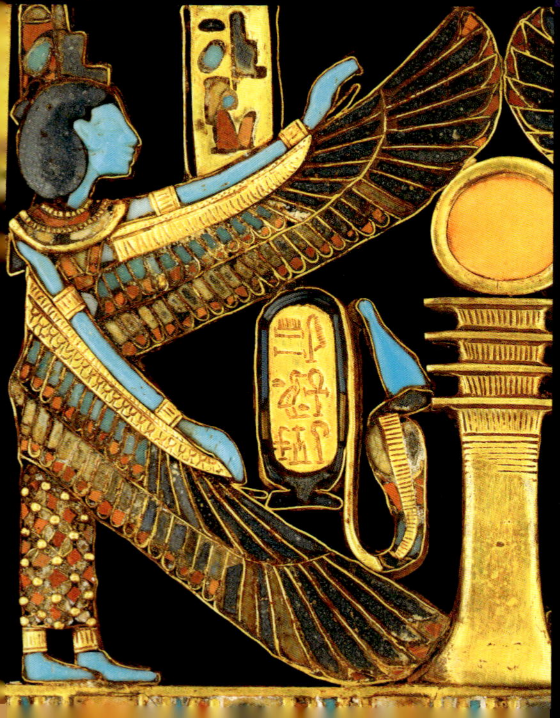
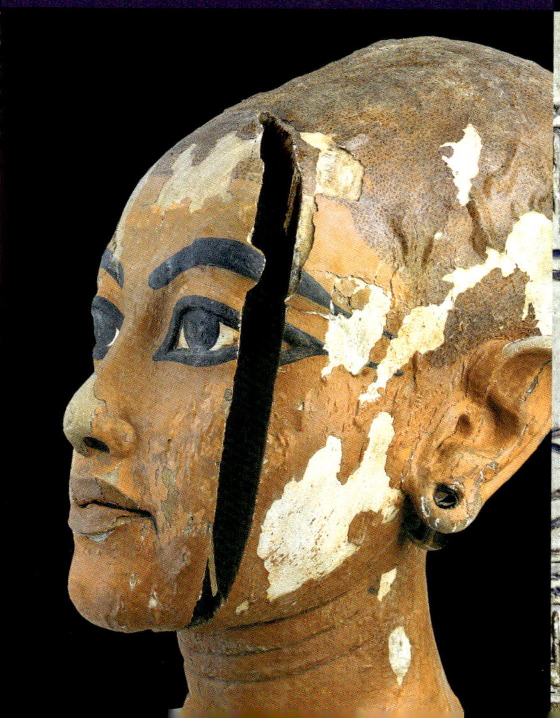
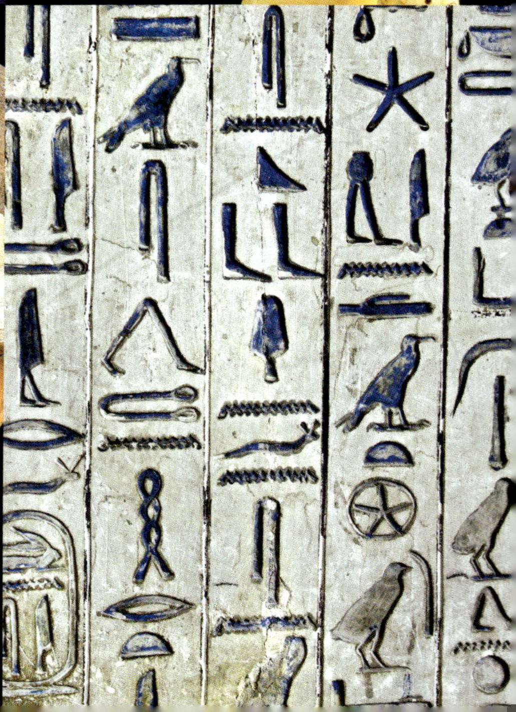

The discovery of the tomb of Tutankhamun by Howard Carter in November 1922 profoundly affected Egyptian archaeology, as well as high and low cultures world-wide, and gave birth to a legend. Even now, more than ninety years later, we are struggling to come to terms with its significance and still await a comprehensive study of objects found in the tomb. This book has been penned by a scholar who, as former Secretary General of the Supreme Council of Antiquities and later Minister of State for Antiquities, was personally involved in research into this enigmatic young king and his intriguing tomb in the Valley of the Kings, in the southern part of Egypt opposite modern Luxor.

The book provides a complete package of information for those interested in Tutankhamun and his tomb. Dr Zahi Hawass places the King in the broader context of Egyptian history. He unravels the intricate and still much debated relationship between various members of the royal family and their entourage, and the delicate circumstances surrounding the turbulent Amarna period and the revolutionary reign of Akhenaten, Tutankhamun's father. He also succinctly explains the religious background and complex beliefs in the afterlife, which defined and underlay many features of Tutankhamun's tomb. The history of the exploration of the Valley of the Kings is discussed, as well as the background and mutual relationships of the main protagonists. Howard Carter's early work and the initial discovery of items bearing the name of Tutankhamun are considered, as is the much disputed original ownership of the tomb. Carter's sometimes stormy relationship with the authorities throughout the decade of his work in the tomb is outlined in absorbing detail. It is interesting to read how Zahi Hawass the archaeologist can relate to another archaeologist, Howard Carter, when describing the pressures upon the excavator who has made a great discovery.

The tomb and the most important finds are described and illustrated and the modern X-raying and CT scanning of the King's mummified body are presented in detail. The description of the latest DNA examination of the mummies of Tutankhamun and several members of his family is one of the most absorbing parts of the book and demonstrates that scientific methods may produce results which cannot at present be paralleled by traditional Egyptology.

Dr Hawass's account does not stop at the discovery of the tomb of Tutankhamun, but continues with the recent exploration of the Valley of the Kings and of other monuments on the Theban west bank by Egyptian archaeologists, often under his direction, as well as by several expeditions from abroad. The book is fully up to date and does not shirk from outlining the sad episode of the robbery which took place in the Egyptian Museum in Cairo on 28th January 2011 during the heady days of the Egyptian Revolution when fifty-four items, including some from the tomb of Tutankhamun, were taken. Several of these are still missing. Hawass also expounds his views on how to protect the Valley of the Kings for posterity and how to reconcile any such measures with the need for allowing access to monuments for visitors.

The author provides an interesting overview of the persisting legend of 'the curse of Tutankhamun' and recounts some amusing personal remembrances and anecdotes connected with Tutankhamun exhibitions sent abroad. He concludes with the rather sad statement 'I do not think that anyone will be able to make Tutankhamun's treasures travel again'. He also reproduces the text of his famous letter requesting the return of Nefertiti's bust from Berlin.

This is a work by a man who passionately loves Egypt's past and is not afraid of controversy. There is nothing like reading a book which contains first-hand recollections and impressions, bringing to life an exacting academic topic. Dr Hawass does this in masterly fashion.

Jaromir Málek
Oxford
15th June, 2013

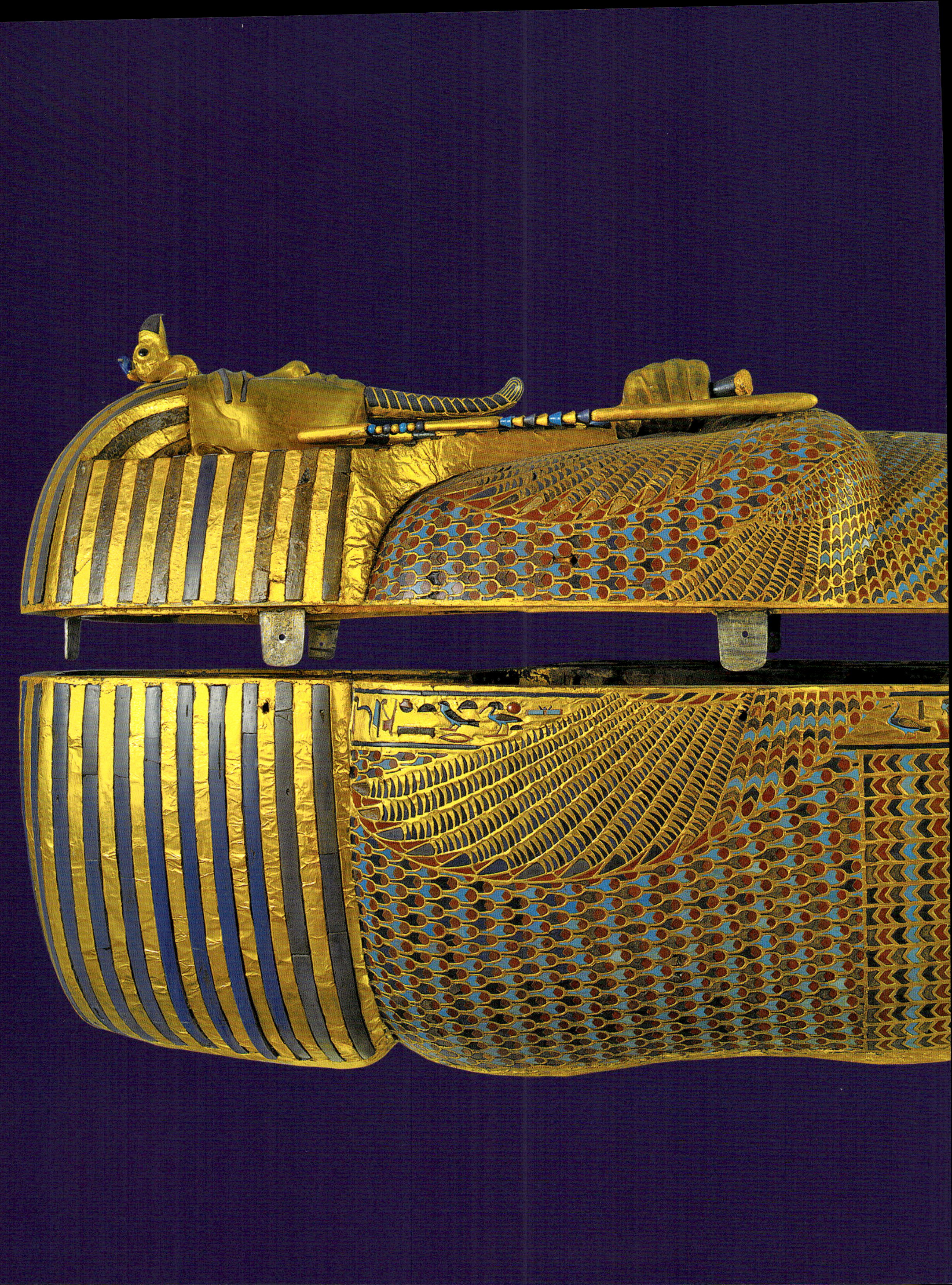

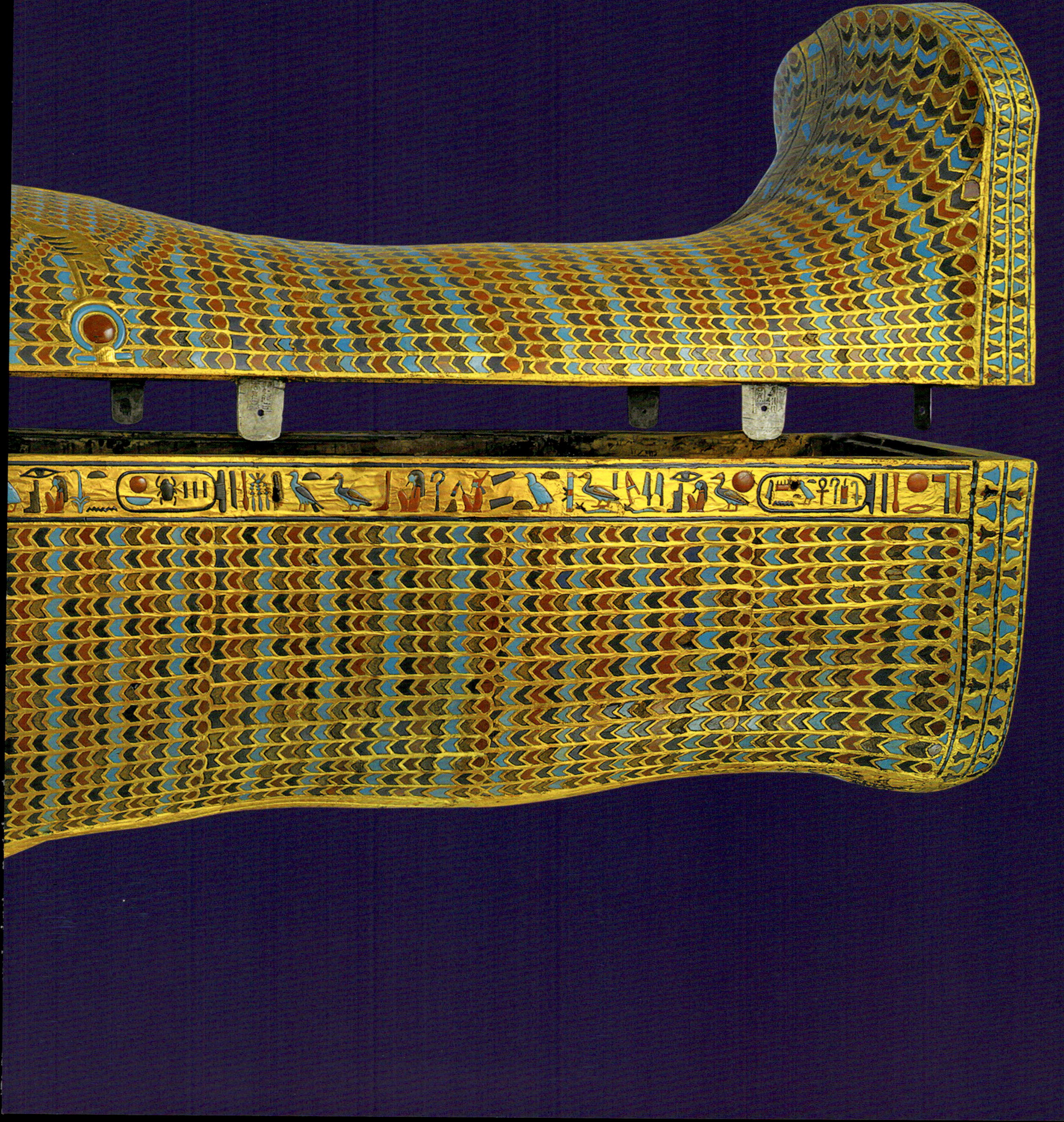

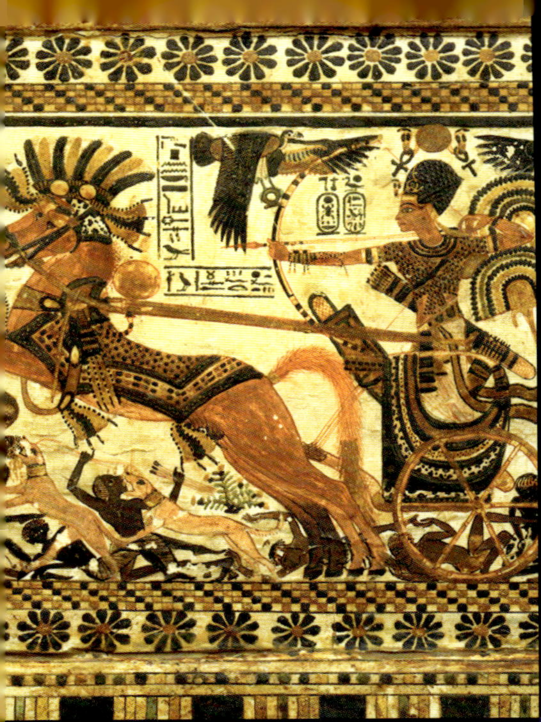
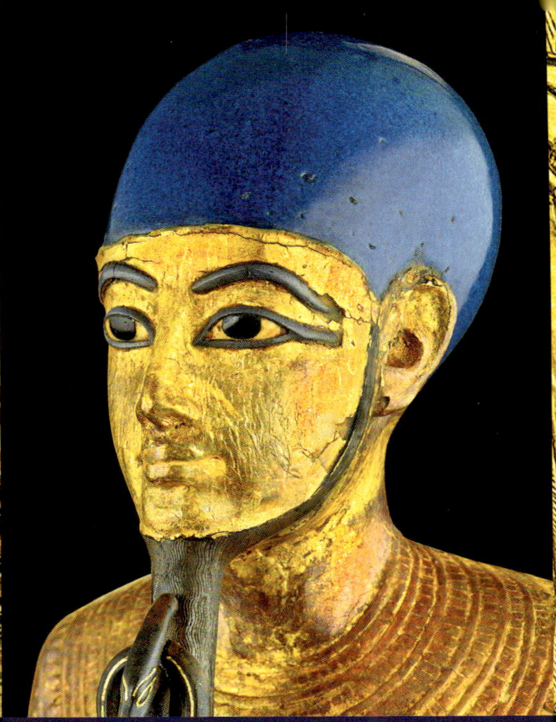
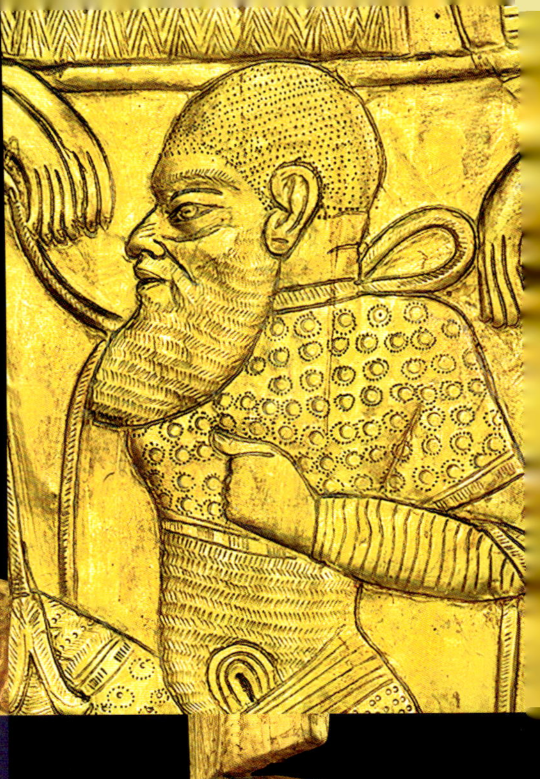
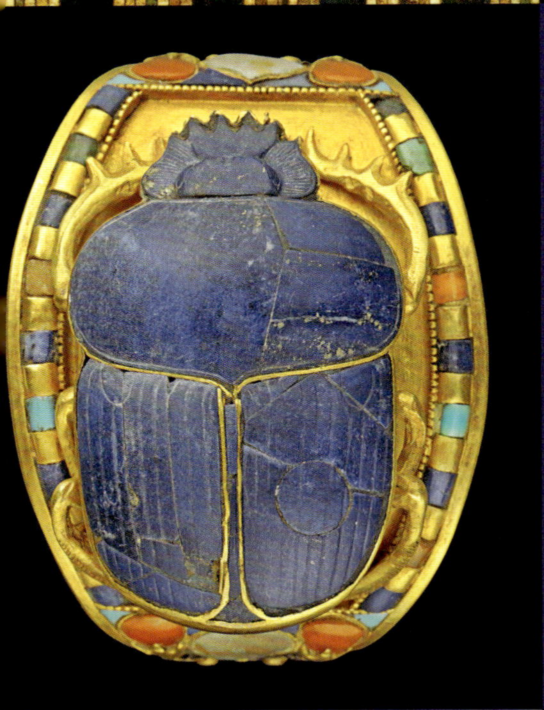

INTRO-DUCTION

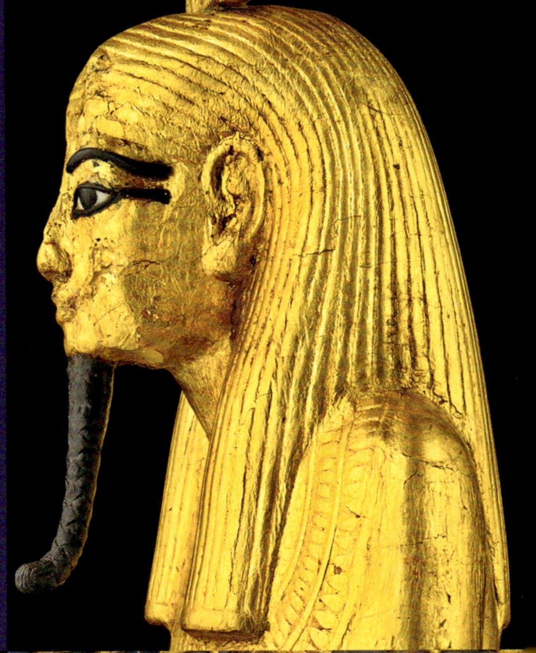
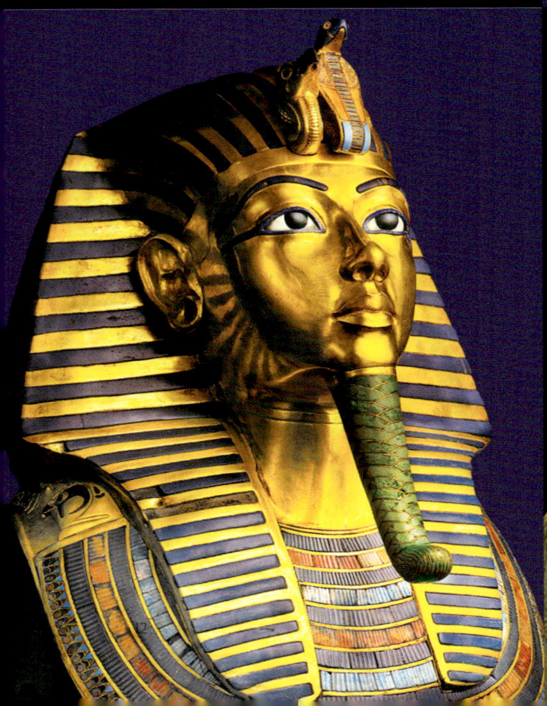
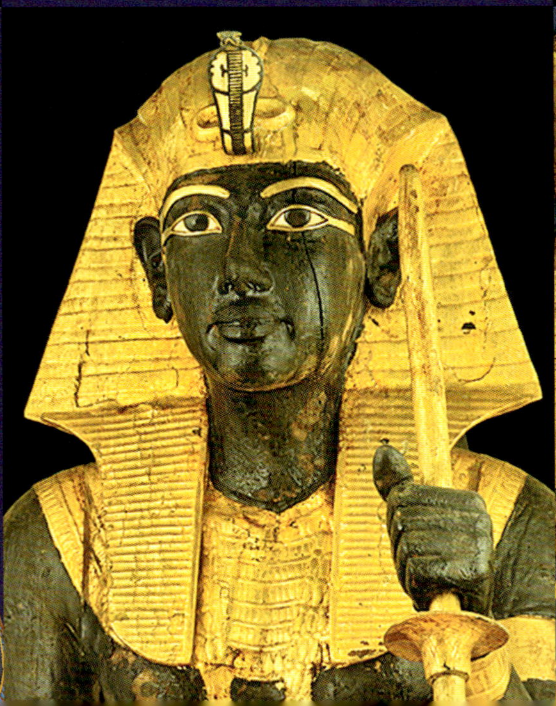
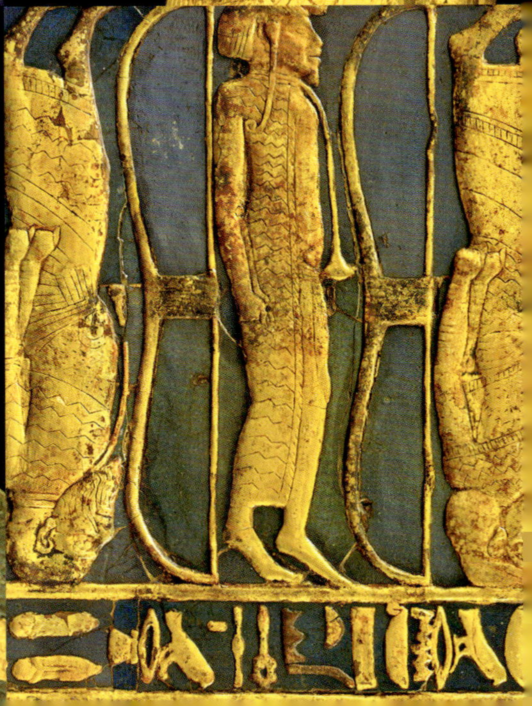

When Christoph Scholz asked me to write this book, I told him that I had already written six others on Tutankhamun and the discovery of his tomb. Three were catalogs for the exhibits of Tutankhamun in the United States and Japan, and one was about the "golden boy." Two more books focused on the discovery. I even re-excavated the tomb (imitation), which you can read about in *King Tutankhamun: The Treasures of the Tomb*, and found out that I could not do anything better than Howard Carter. He was a great archaeologist.

Scholz then said to me that there was no book that included the new information about the king and also what has been found in the Valley of the Kings after Carter.

I thought about that and realized that this is true. So in this book I concentrated on the history of Egypt before the golden king and also the history of his time, along with the discovery of the tomb and the objects.

But what is especially interesting for me about this book is being able to introduce new people in the life of Tutankhamun, such as Maia, the wet nurse whose tomb has been found at Saqqara, a man named Sennedjem, buried near the city of Sohag, who might have been the boy-king's tutor, Parennefer, called Wenennefer, who lived in his time. There are also newly discovered scenes from his reign found at Memphis, and what they can show about the king's life.

Many people thought that this tomb of Tutankhamun might be the last treasure to be discovered in the Valley of the Kings, but many important things have happened since Howard Carter, such as the rediscovery of KV 5 and KV 53, and the truly new discoveries of KV 63 and KV 64. There has been an Egyptian expedition working in the Valley of the Kings now for the first time, searching for missing tombs there and in the Valley of the Monkeys. We have found important things about how the ancient Egyptians tried to protect the royal necropolis. and we have revealed the secret of the mysterious tunnel in the tomb of Seti I, which has puzzled archaeologists since the tomb was first found in 1817.

Not all the work has been out in the field. Using forensic techniques such as CT scanners and DNA we are working to uncover secrets of the mummies. You will read elsewhere in this book about what science has told us about the family of Tutankhamun and about how the young king died, but I will tell you here a little bit about what we have learned about three other mummies. We have been able to identify the mummy of an unknown woman found in KV 60 as Queen Hatshepsut. This happened thanks to CT scans and a tooth found in a wooden box containing a liver and stomach and inscribed with the queen's name, which was found in the mummy cache at Deir el-Bahari in 1871. CT scans also revealed that Rameses III was murdered with a sharp knife, a fact not mentioned in the ancient papyri recording the trials of the people involved in the harem conspiracy. With DNA analysis, we realized that a famous mummy in the Egyptian Museum known as Unknown Man E is Rameses III's son, Pentawere, who worked with his mother Tia to murder the king.

King Tutankhamun's artifacts began touring again in 2004, visiting many cities in Europe, North America, Australia, and Japan. With the selection of 50 small objects from the tomb, we have been able to raise more than $120 million for the construction of the Grand Egyptian Museum, which is being built within view of the Giza pyramids. When this museum is complete, all the beautiful artifacts from Tutankhamun's tomb will be moved from the Egyptian Museum on Tahrir Square to the Grand Egyptian Museum.

I do not think that anyone will be able to send an exhibit of Tutankhamun's objects abroad again. But through this book you will feel the magic of the great discovery and read how Tutmania has entered the hearts of people all over the world.

What is even more interesting is that I will take you on a great adventure through all the new discoveries about this great king and his time.

I hope you will follow along with me as we explore all about the legend and the mysteries of Tutankhamun.

Zahi Hawass
Cairo
31st January 2013

CHRONOLOGY

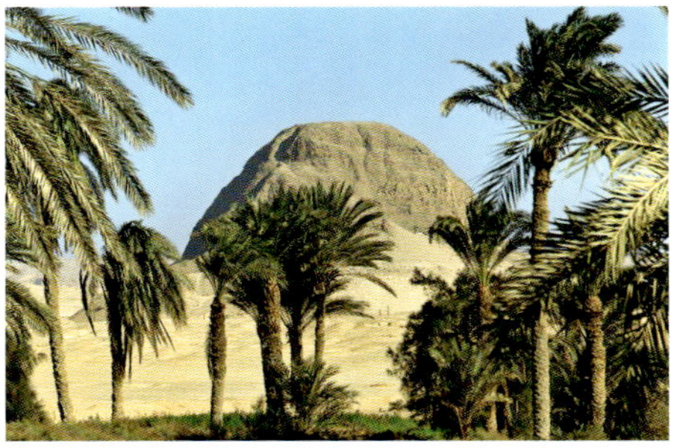

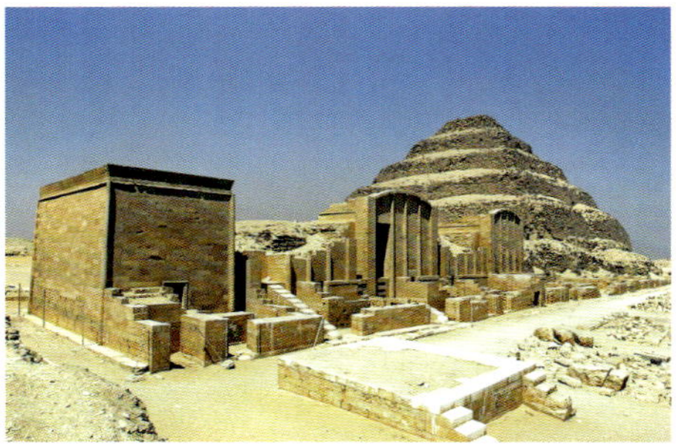

EARLY DYNASTIC PERIOD

0 – 2nd dynasties

c. 3050 — c. 2650 BC

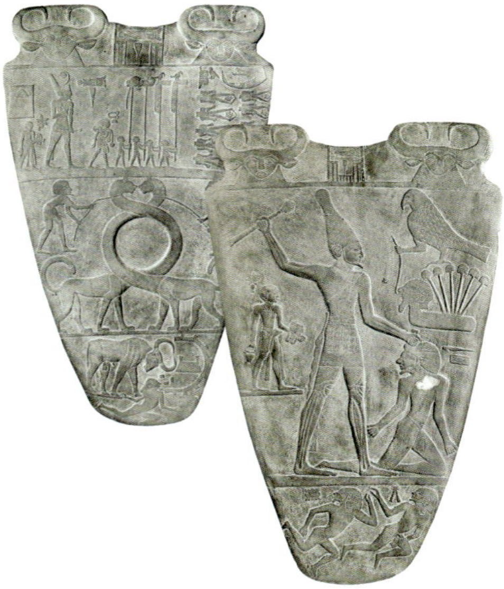

OLD KINGDOM

3rd – 6th dynasties

c. 2650 — c. 2175 BC

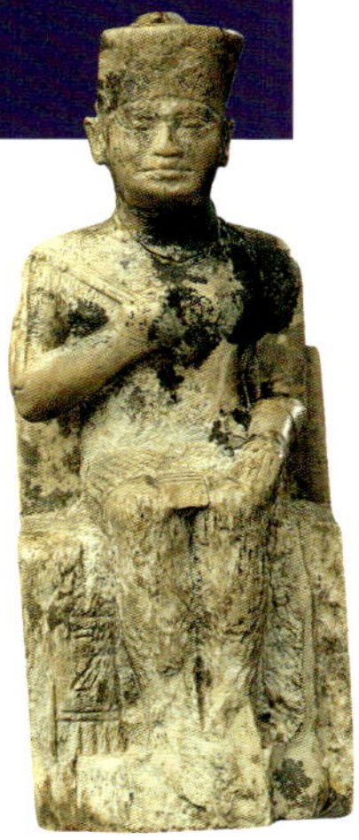

FIRST INTERMEDIATE PERIOD

7th – 11th dynasties

c. 2175 — c. 2080 BC

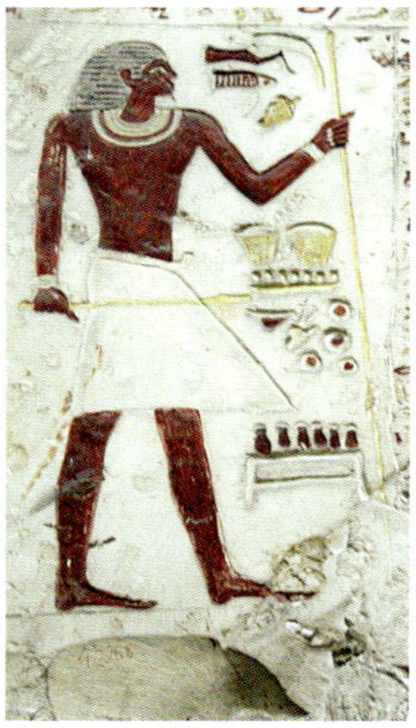

MIDDLE KINGDOM

11th – 13th dynasties

c. 2080 — c. 1630 BC

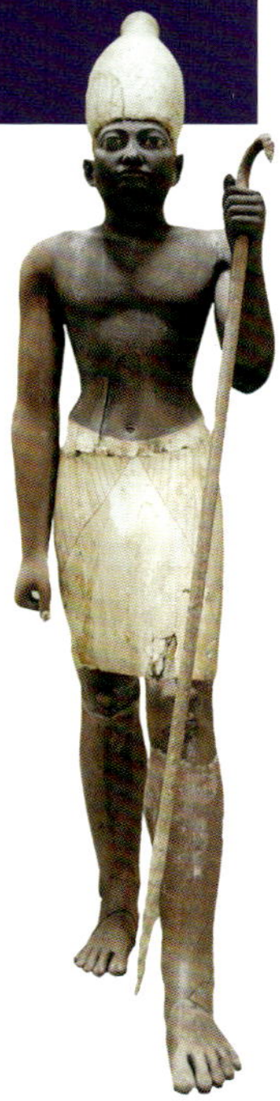

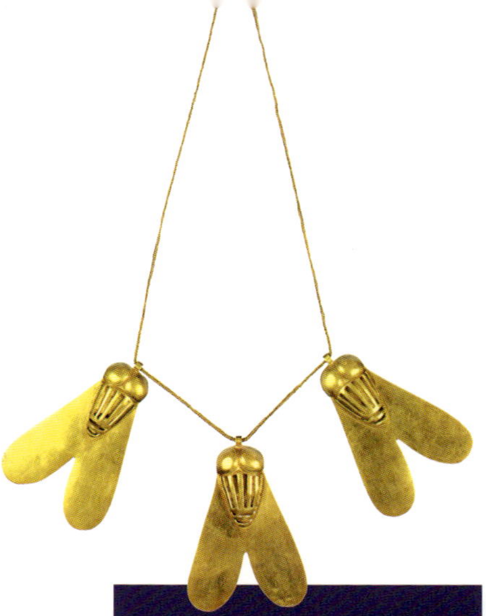

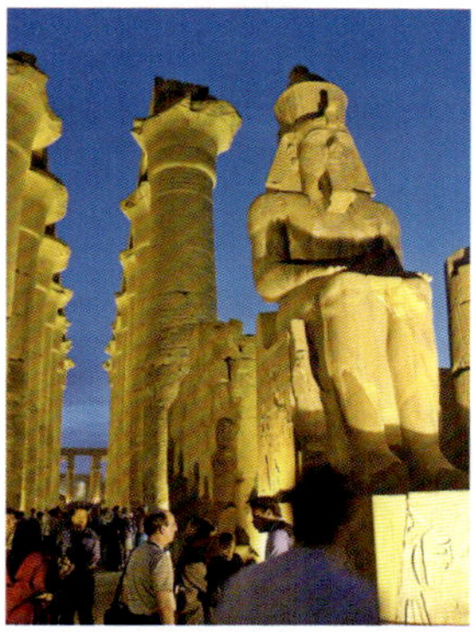

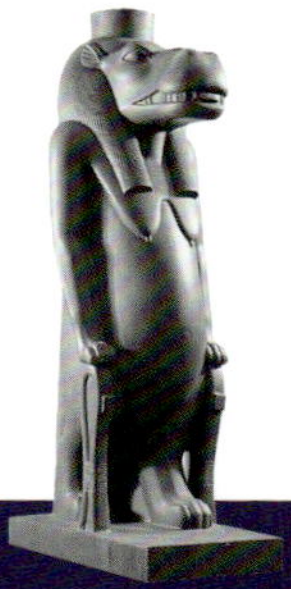

SECOND INTERMEDIATE PERIOD

14th – 17th dynasties
c. 1630 — c. 1539 BC

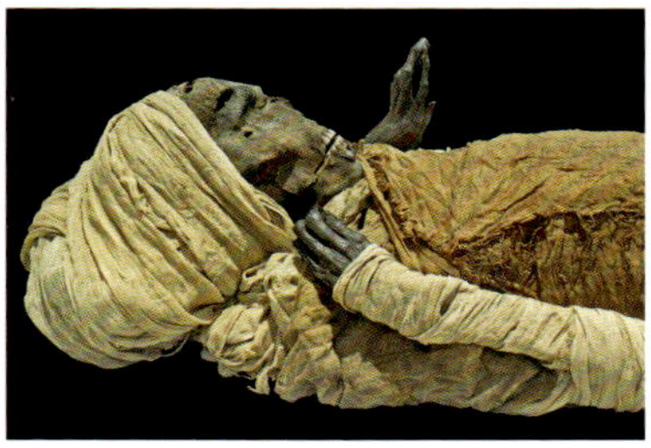

NEW KINGDOM

18th – 20th dynasties
c. 1539 — c. 1069 BC

18th Dynasty
c. 1539 — c. 1292 BC

19th Dynasty
c. 1292 — 1186 BC

20th Dynasty
c. 1186 — 1069 BC

THIRD INTERMEDIATE PERIOD

21st – 25th dynasties
c. 1069 — 657 BC

LATE PERIOD

26th – 31st dynasties
664 — 332 BC

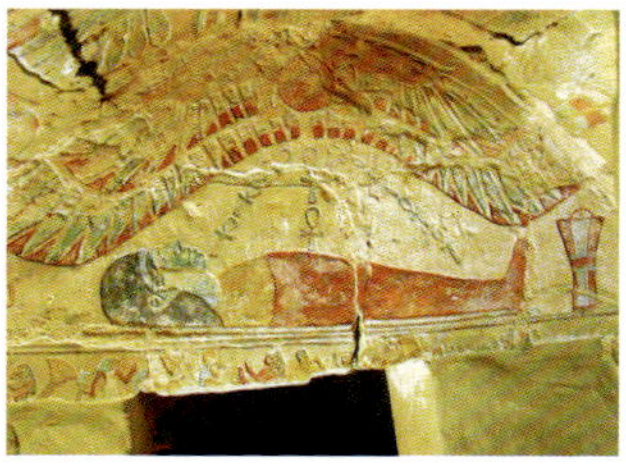

Ahmose
c. 1539 — c. 1514 BC

Amenhotep I
c. 1514 — c. 1493 BC

Thutmose I
c. 1493 — c. 1481 BC

Thutmose II
c. 1481 — c. 1479 BC

Thutmose III
c. 1479 — c. 1425 BC

Hatshepsut
c. 1473 — c. 1458 BC

Amenhotep II
c. 1426 — c. 1400 BC

Thutmose IV
c. 1400 —c. 1390 BC

Amenhotep III
c. 1390 — c. 1353 BC

Amenhotep IV (Akhenaten)
c. 1353 — c. 1336 BC

Smenkhkare
c. 1335 — c. 1332 B

Tutankhamun
c. 1332 — c. 1323 BC

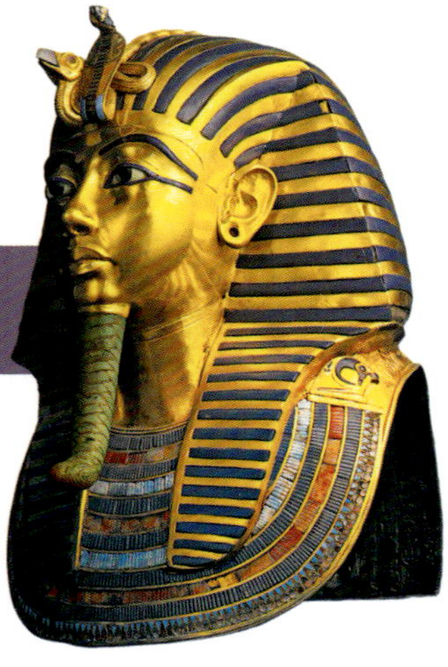

Ay
c. 1323 — c. 1319 BC

Horemheb
c. 1319 — c. 1292 BC

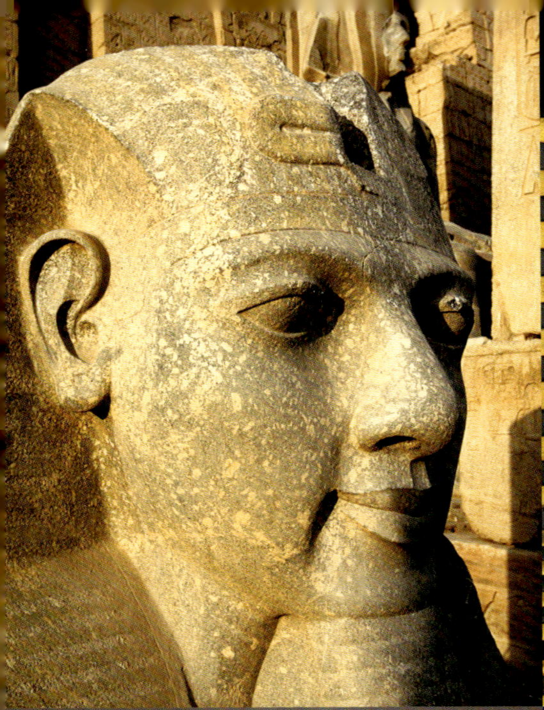
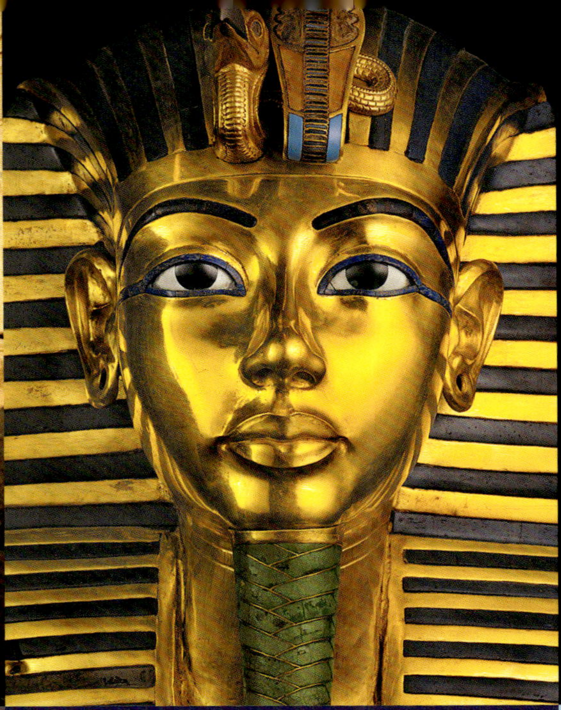
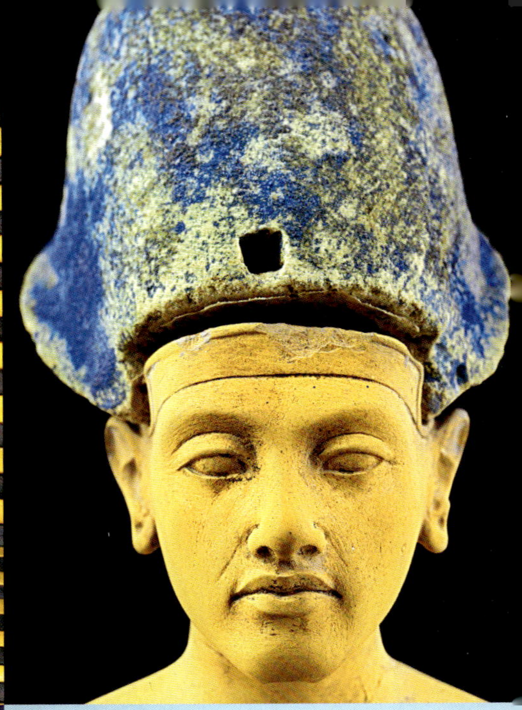
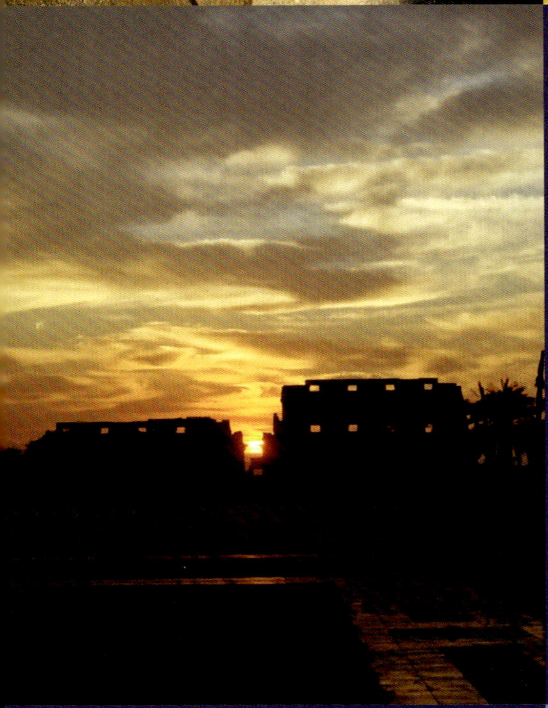

CHAPTER I

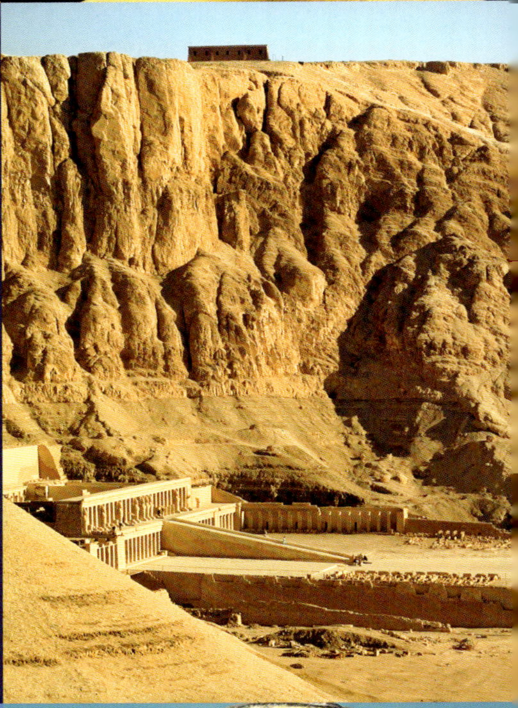
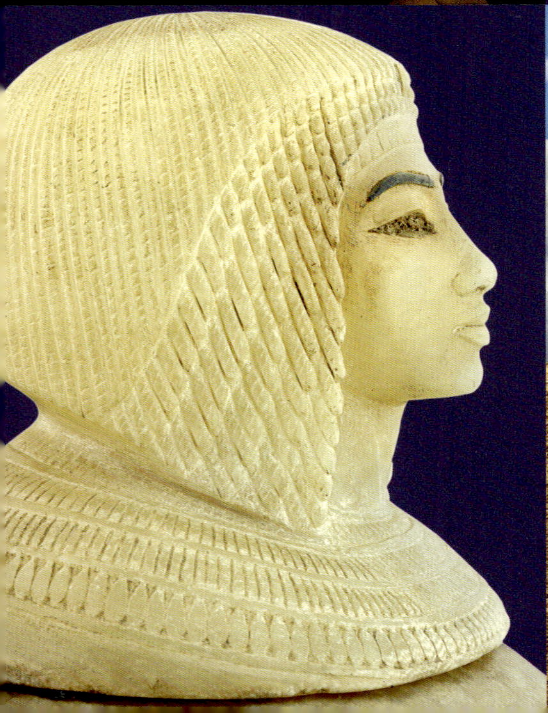
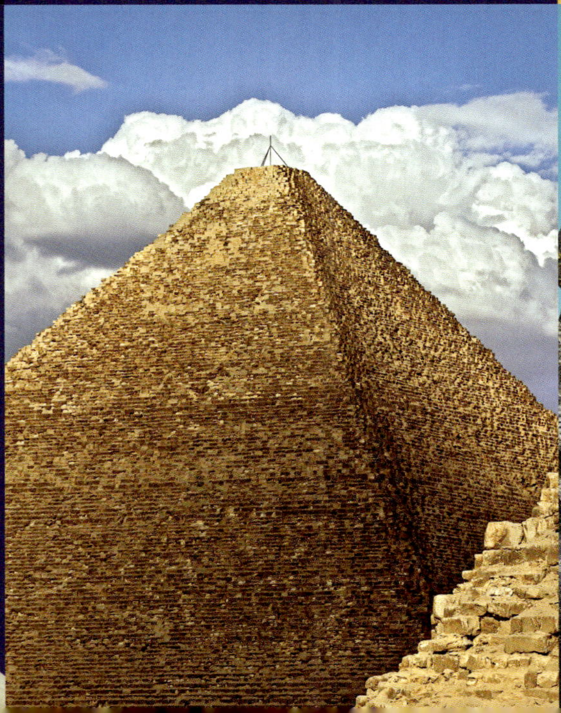
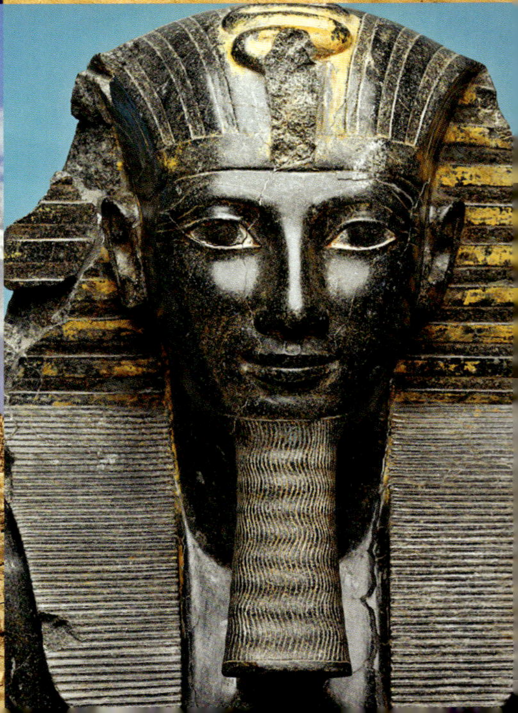

THE GOLDEN AGE OF EGYPT: DYNASTY 18

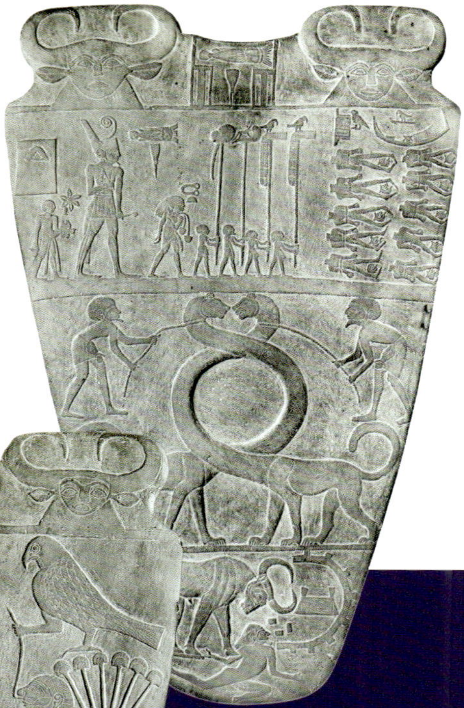

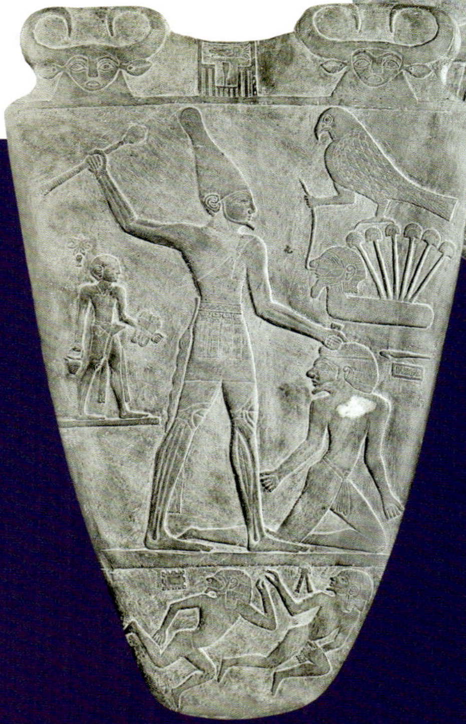

Narmer Ceremonial Palette
from the temple of
Horus at Hierakonopolis.
Siltstone
Early 1st Dynasty
Egyptian Museum in Cairo

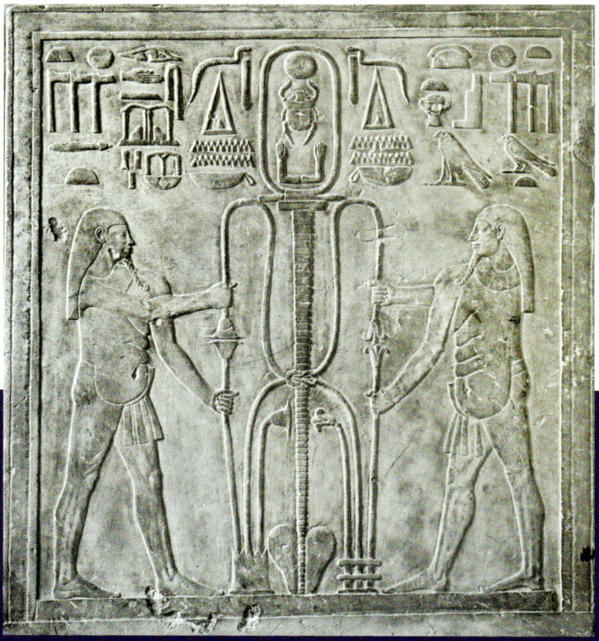

Bas-Relief on the throne of the
statueof Senwosret I from Lisht.
The unification of the Two Lands
of Egypt performed by
two representations of Hapi,
god of the Nile flood.
Limestone
12th Dynasty
Egyptian Museum in Cairo

EGYPT BEFORE TUTANKHAMUN

In about 3050 B.C., the civilization of the pharaohs arose from the Predynastic cultures that had grown up along the Nile River. It was during that time that the whole of Egypt became united under a single king of the 1st Dynasty, whose home city was in the south, Upper Egypt. Despite this unification, the Egyptians imagined their country as consisting of two distinct halves, Upper and Lower Egypt, which joined together as one.

Each retained its own symbols and patron gods. The cobra goddess Wadjet was the patron goddess of the Delta. Her counterpart for the south was a vulture, Nekhbet. There were pairs of plants (papyrus/lotus) and crowns (red/white). These pairs, and various combinations of them, frequently appear in art, symbolizing the union of the Two Lands. They represented the vast geographic spread that the Egyptian king ruled, an accomplishment made possible by the development of a highly organized bureaucracy, aided by the invention of the distinctive Egyptian hieroglyphic writing system.

By the Old Kingdom, which began with the 3rd Dynasty, the rulers of the Nile Valley had enough resources at their disposal to create truly monumental works of architecture, the first pyramids and their surrounding complexes. These were tombs for the highest members of society – the king, his family, and members of the court – as will be discussed later. The largest of these were erected at Giza, near the ancient city of Memphis and modern Cairo.

Egypt's first capital was a city known first as "White Wall," which has recently been identified with the site of North Saqqara. It later shifted to Memphis, modern Mit Rahina.

Both North Saqqara and Mit Rahina are in the vicinity of modern Cairo, a strategic location that facilitated exchanges with major trading partners in the north, the civilizations that occupied cities such as Byblos and others in the Levant. Kings had to maintain strong armies against foreign rivals not only to the north but also to the south, in Nubia, and to the west, in Libya.

The cults of certain gods flourished during this time. Osiris, god of the dead, became important, and so did worship of the sun god Re. Starting with Djedefre, son of Khufu, in the 4th Dynasty, kings began to call themselves "Sons of Re." They endowed temples with estates to provide for their functioning, turning them into powerful economic institutions.

Slowly, starting with the late 5th Dynasty, the centralized power of the government began to slip from the hands of the king and his court out to the provinces. Eventually the central government collapsed, ushering in the First Intermediate Period. During this time, which lasted about a century, nomarchs (governors) became like local kings. Other privileges also spread to even lower members of society. The idea that anyone might aspire to an afterlife with the gods, an honor once reserved for royalty, spread to people of every social class.

By the end of the 11th Dynasty, a line of ambitious rulers arose in Thebes, a city in Upper Egypt. Under the kings of the 11th and 12th Dynasties, a period known as the Middle Kingdom, Egypt became reunited again. This resulted in a promotion for Amun, patron god of the region. Soon the Egyptians considered him king of the gods and associated him with the earthly king. Despite the dynasty's close connections with Amun of Thebes, a capital for the newly reunited Egypt was founded farther north, at Lisht, where the Nile branched off to a large lake called the Faiyum. Like Memphis, Lisht was reasonably close to their trading partners, and potential enemies,

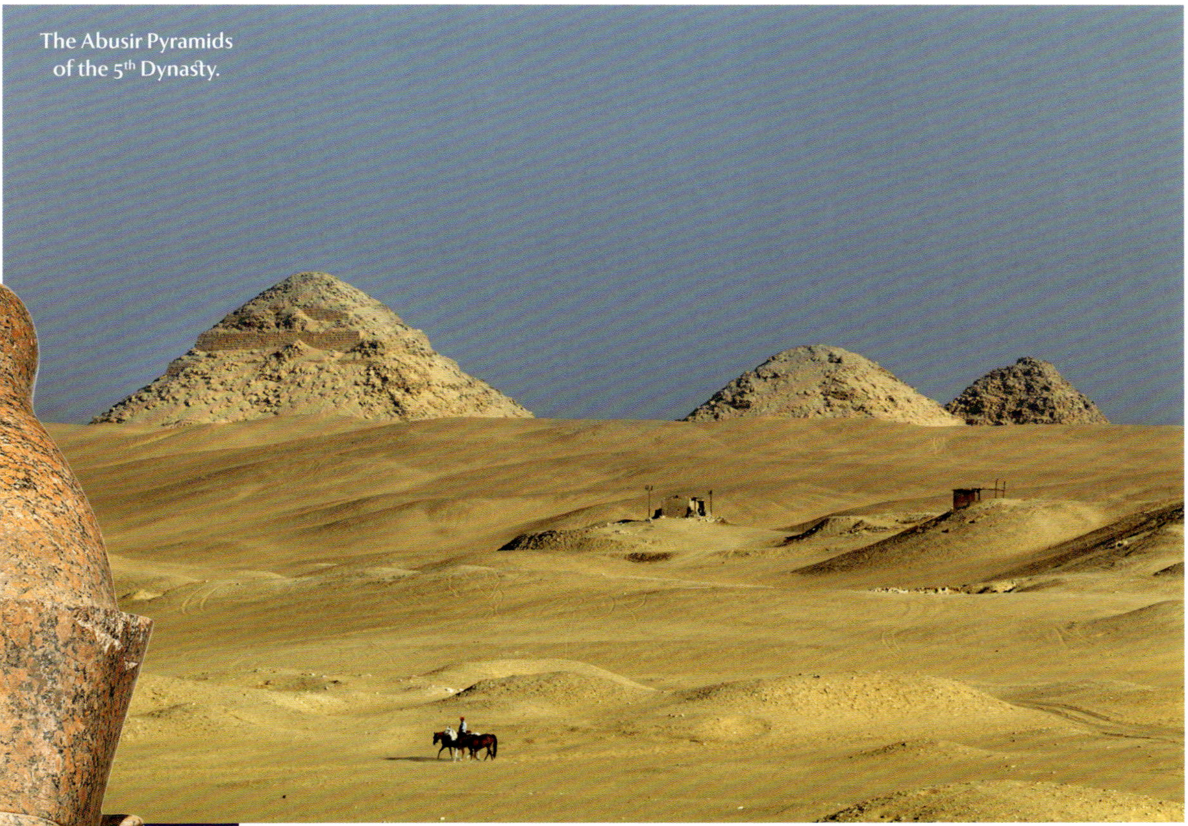

The Abusir Pyramids of the 5th Dynasty.

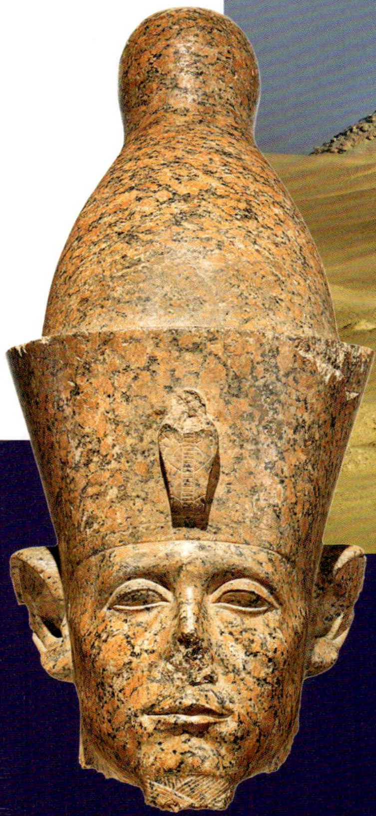

Head of Senwosret III wearing the double crown.
Red granite
12th Dynasty
Luxor Museum

in western Asia. These kings also constructed enormous fortifications to control trade in Nubia, far to the south. Egypt began to expand its influence into distant regions, even more so than during the Old Kingdom. At home, kings finally reconsolidated the power of the government into their own hands. The days of the once-powerful nomarchs came to a final end during the reign of Senwosret III. This was a time of cultural flowering in Egypt.

Some of the best-known works of Egyptian literature were written at this time: the *Tale of the Eloquent Peasant*, the *Story of Sinuhe*, the *Tale of the Shipwrecked Sailor*, and others. Goldsmiths produced stunning works of jewelry. Kings commissioned ambitious building projects of temples throughout the country and had the resources to construct large pyramids.

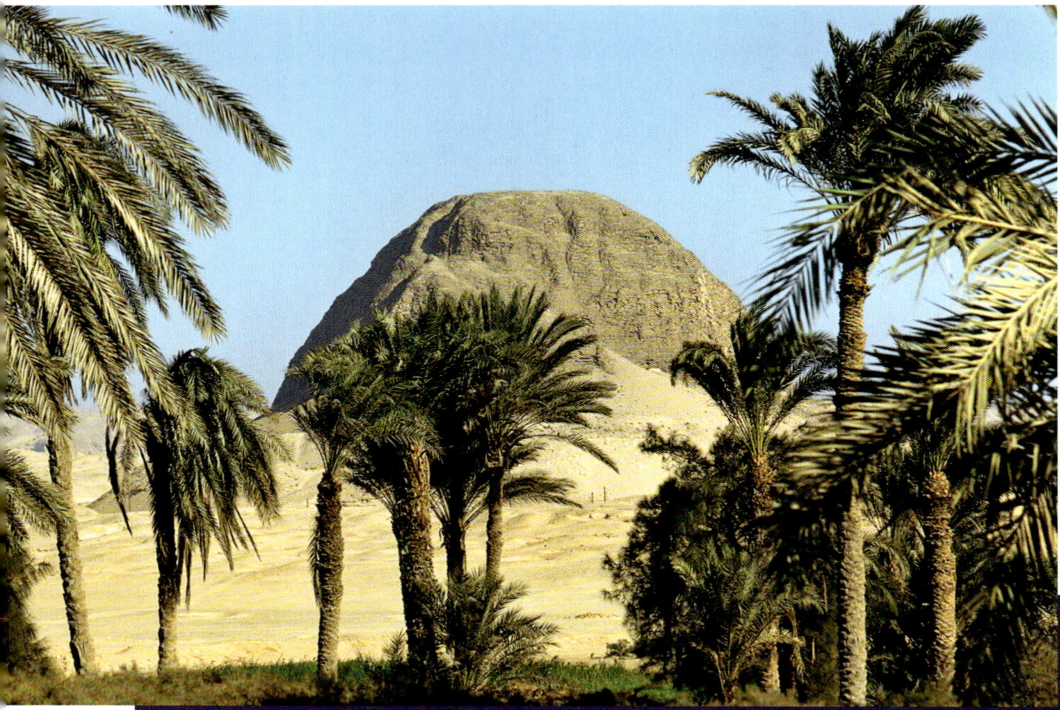

The Pyramid of Amenemhat III. It was built of mud brick with a limestone outer casing, which is now entirely lost.
Hawarah

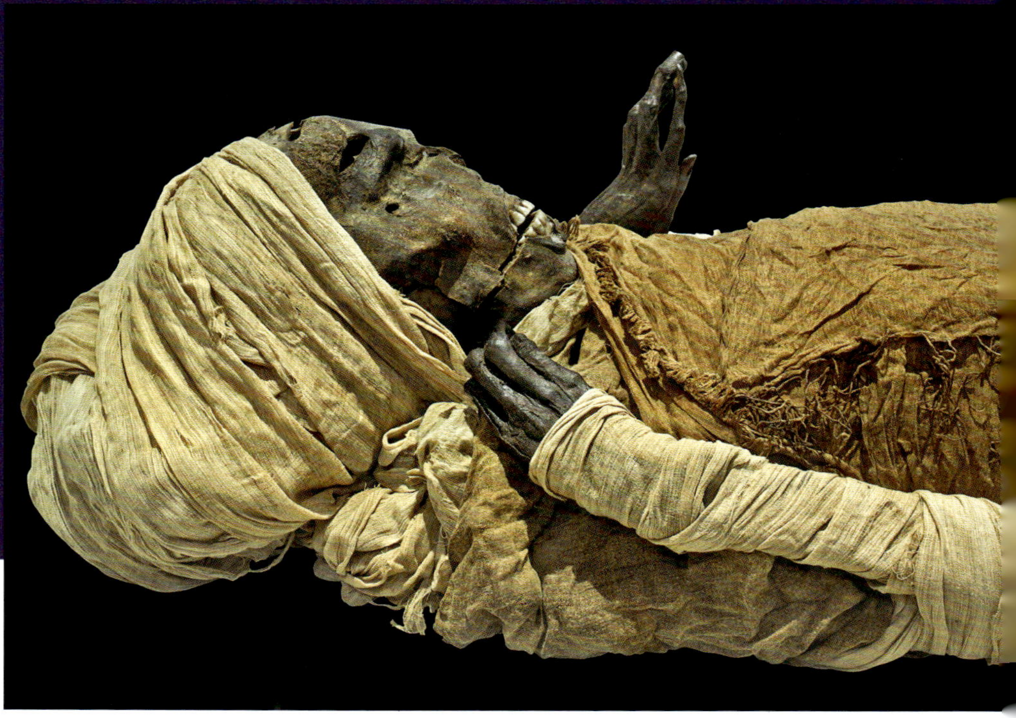

The mummy of Seqenenre Tao.
17th Dynasty
Egyptian Museum in Cairo

However, the power of the great Egyptian kings waned once again. The rulers of the 13th Dynasty were weak. Foreigners from the Levant, known as the Hyksos, had settled in the eastern Delta. Although they had come in peacefully, they, or perhaps new immigrants, took advantage of the situation and proclaimed their own kingdom with the city of Avaris as the capital. By about 1650 BC., they controlled the north and a considerable part of the south. Egypt entered its Second Intermediate Period.

Native Egyptian kings ruled the southern region of Upper Egypt from their capital at Thebes. An alliance between the Hyksos and the Nubians trapped the Theban kingdom in the two critical directions of upstream and downstream, cutting them off from many important resources, such as gold mines. King Seqenenre Tao of Thebes fell in battle against the Hyksos, as suggested by the multiple wounds found on his mummy. The first of these, a blow to his head, was probably delivered by a Hyksos ax.

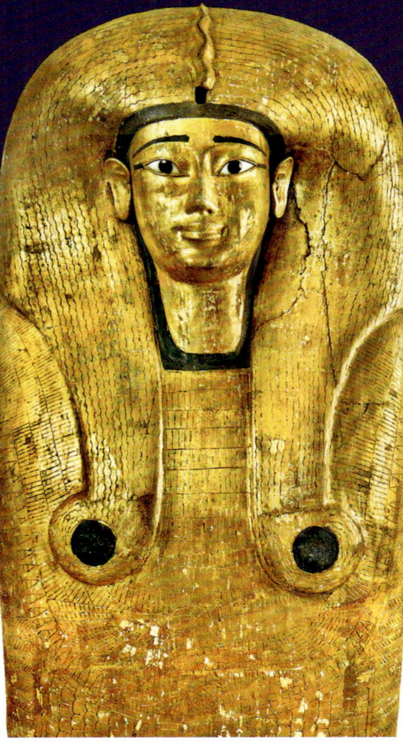

The upper part of the anthropoid coffin of Queen Ahhotep.
Gilded wood, calcite (Egyptian alabaster) and obsidian
18th Dynasty
Egyptian Museum in Cairo

FOUNDING THE EMPIRE: AHMOSE AND THE KINGS OF THE EARLY NEW KINGDOM

Seqenenre Tao's two sons, Kamose and Ahmose, and his wife, Ahhotep I, kept up the fight. Kamose, who became king, made significant strides against the enemy. By the time of his death he had beaten the Hyksos back to the north, to Avaris, and seized a portion of Nubia. Ahhotep may have served as regent for a time and possibly also went to war, but it was Ahmose who finally ousted the Hyksos from Egyptian soil.

With his wife, a woman named Ahmose-Nefertari, Ahmose founded the 18th Dynasty. He erected monuments throughout Egypt, including Karnak, Abydos (sacred to Osiris), and Avaris. Thebes became the religious center of Egypt, but, yet again, the Egyptian king knew that the city lay too far south to serve as the political capital. The seat of government had to be closer to their potential enemies, but the borders of Egyptian influence also needed to be pushed outward. Being ruled by foreigners had a deep effect on Egypt. Egyptians now acknowledged that it was not enough to simply maintain its borders against the "chaos" of the world beyond. Nubia was conquered not only for security, but for its rich goldmines. Nubians had long served as mercenaries for Egyptian kings, and they continued to do so in the New Kingdom. To the north, cities in the Levant would become clients of Egypt. The royal treasury grew, and so did Egyptian political might.

Internally, Egyptian kings concentrated the power of the royal family by marrying a princess of their own royal house. Seqenenre Tao and Ahhotep, for example, were not merely husband and wife, but also brother and sister. Royal women helped to maintain the cosmic order, which the Egyptians called *maat*. The king served as representative of Amun, king of the gods, on earth and was identified as his son. This may have been why, beginning with Queen Ahmose-Nefertari, some queens and royal daughters of the 18th Dynasty were given the title "God's Wife of Amun," about which little is known. God's Wives were, however, active in temple ritual and possibly performed rites intended to stimulate the god's fertility and thus his power to maintain the cosmos.

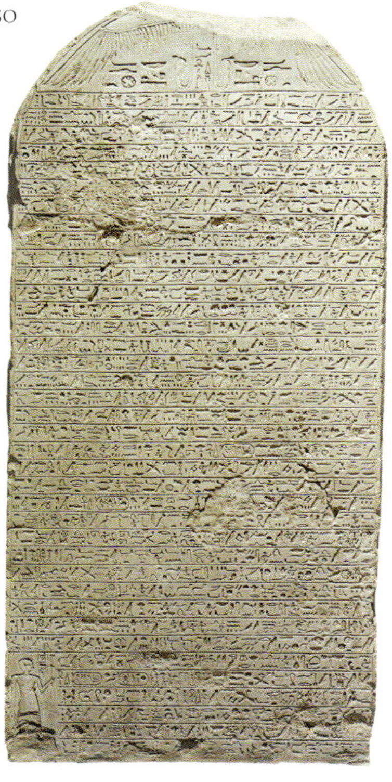

The so-called Victory Stela of Kamose commemorating his triumph over the Hyksos.
Limestone
Late 17th Dynasty
Egyptian Museum in Cairo

The son of Ahmose and Ahmose-Nefertari, named Amenhotep I, succeeded his father as king. He ruled for two decades – when he was younger, with the aid of his mother – and campaigned not only in Nubia but westward, in Libya, too. He had buildings erected at Karnak, Abydos, and at the Nubian border. He died apparently without a son who could inherit the throne from him. Instead, the kingship passed to Thutmose I, who seems not to have had any connection to the royal family. His wife, however, could have been a royal relative. Her name was Ahmose, which suggests she was related to Ahmose-Nefertari. Thutmose expanded Egypt's southern sphere of influence by defeating the Nubian kingdom of Kerma and installing a viceroy to oversee Nubia. In the north, he campaigned to the Euphrates River in a not entirely successful attempt to curtail the influence that the kingdom of Mitanni was exerting in Syria. He was active at home as well, adding to the monuments at Karnak with monumental gateways (pylons), obelisks, halls, and figures of Osiris, and dedicating buildings at Giza and at Osiris's cult center at Abydos.

Thutmose I did have a son to succeed him, a boy also named Thutmose, but he was born of a minor wife. His child by his chief queen, Ahmose, was a daughter named Hatshepsut, who was a God's Wife of Amun. Hatshepsut and Thutmose II married, but another wife of Thutmose II gave birth to a son, likewise named Thutmose. When his father died after a reign of perhaps only three years, this boy, Thutmose III, was too young to rule independently, so Hatshepsut served as his regent.

Hatshepsut exercised kingly powers by her own hands. At some point between the second and third years of the coregency, she took on the titles and power of a king. In order to ensure the legitimacy of her claim to the throne, she had herself depicted as a king, not as a queen, and even had inscriptions refer to her as "he." Amun himself, she declared, had created her specifically for the kingship. The god, disguised as Thutmose I, had visited her mother and impregnated the queen. The gods had personally crafted her body and her soul.

Like male kings before her, Hatshepsut initiated building programs at various temples. Her architect, Senmut, oversaw projects at several locations in Thebes, including Luxor and Karnak. Senmut also tutored Hatshepsut's daughter, Neferure, who also became a God's Wife of Amun. (After Neferure, the power that accompanied this title seems to have faded, and during some reigns there was no God's Wife of Amun at all.)

Thutmose III disappeared from the historical record for a while, but after two decades of "joint" rule, he reappears as his coregent's equal. Not long afterward it was Hatshepsut's turn to disappear, this time for good. It has often been suggested that Thutmose III had her murdered. However, in 2007 the Egyptian team of the Egyptian Mummy Project, which I headed, was able to identify the unknown mummy of KV 60 as the mummy of Hatshepsut. Examination of her mummy suggests that cancer claimed her life. Thutmose III was now king without a regent or co-ruler.

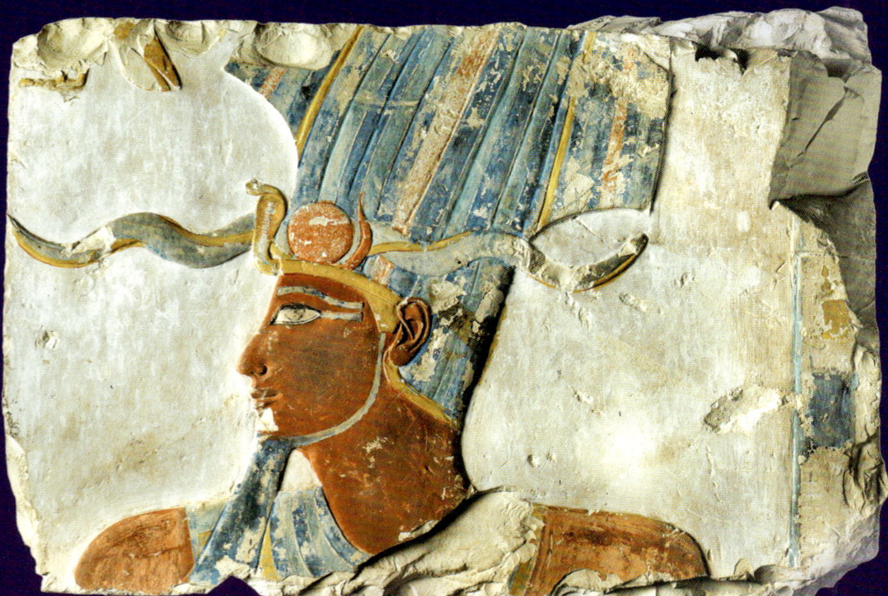

Relief of Thutmose III wearing the *atef* crown from Deir el-Bahari.
Limestone
18th Dynasty
Luxor Museum

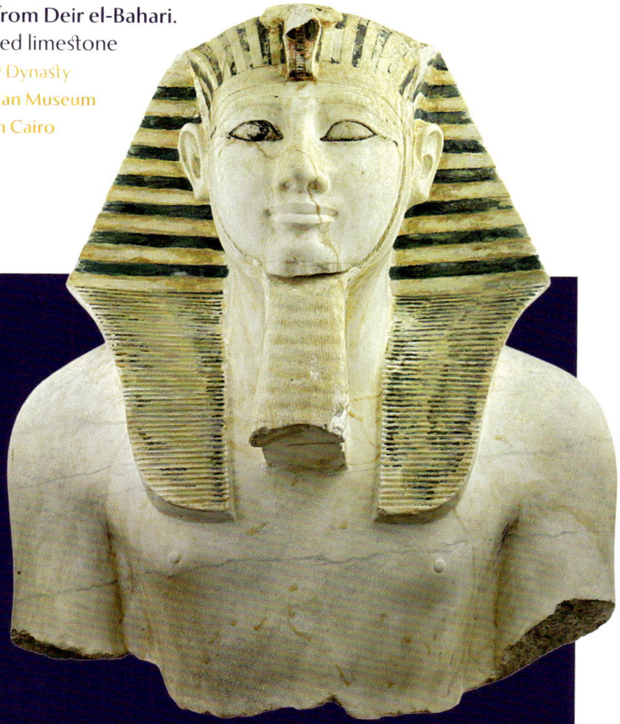

Upper part of a statue of Thutmose III from Deir el-Bahari.
Indurated limestone
18th Dynasty
Egyptian Museum in Cairo

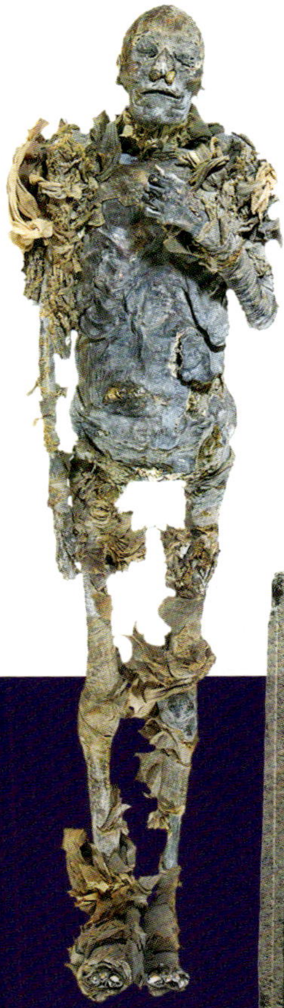

Mummy of Queen Hatshepsut.
Egyptian Museum in Cairo

He was more than capable of ruling on his own. Through 16 foreign campaigns, he proved his worth as a military leader, and he also showed himself to be interested in intellectual pursuits. He brought with him artists who recorded the unfamiliar plants and animals of the Levant, as did Napoleon when he brought the French army to Egypt 3,000 years later. The temple of Amun grew wealthy from the offerings with which Thutmose III returned, and he initiated the construction of temples throughout Egypt and in its new vassal states.

Thutmose III was succeeded by his athletic son, Amenhotep II, who may have been responsible for the desecration of Hatshepsut's monuments, a deed that is so often attributed to his father. Because people could not accept the existence of a female pharaoh performing the functions that the Egyptian religion assigned to a male king, her name and images were chiseled away to erase her from the historical record. Amenhotep continued his father's campaigns, putting down rebellions and forging new alliances. He had as many as ten sons, one of whom, Thutmose IV, ultimately succeeded him, though he may not have been the intended heir.

Thutmose IV claimed that, while he slept in the shade of the Great Sphinx at Giza, the god Horemakhet ("Horus in the Horizon") appeared in a dream to tell him that he would become king if he cleared the sand away from the great monument. (The prince's father had built a temple beside the Great

Amenhotep II in his chariot as an archer, from the Temple of Amun.
Red Granite
Luxor Museum

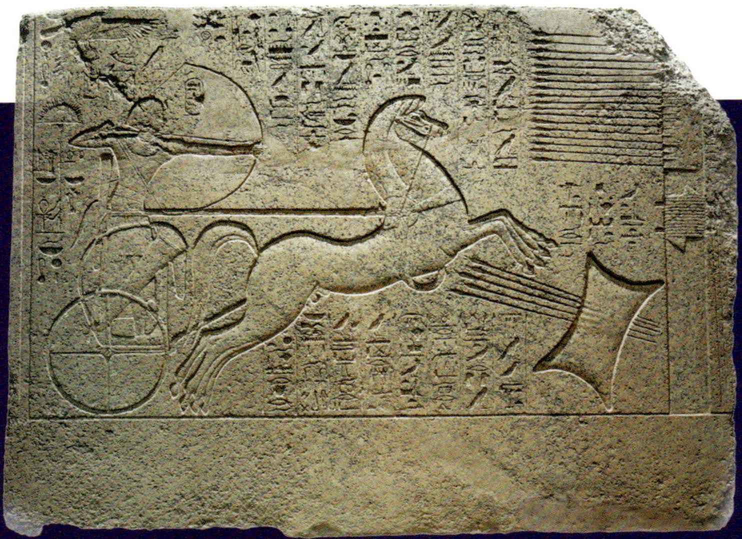

Drawing of Senmut from his tomb at Deir el-Bahari.
Thebes

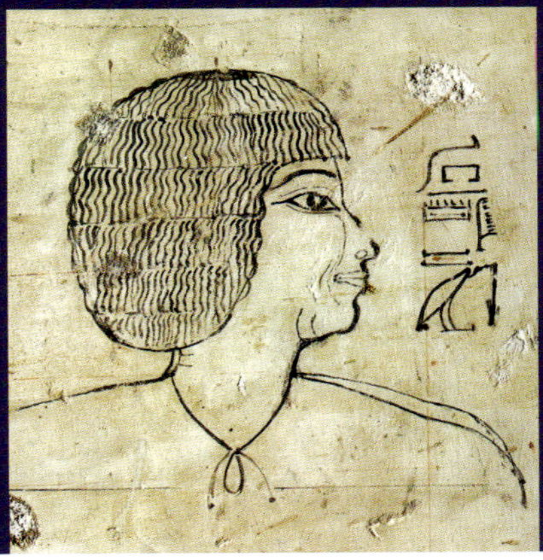

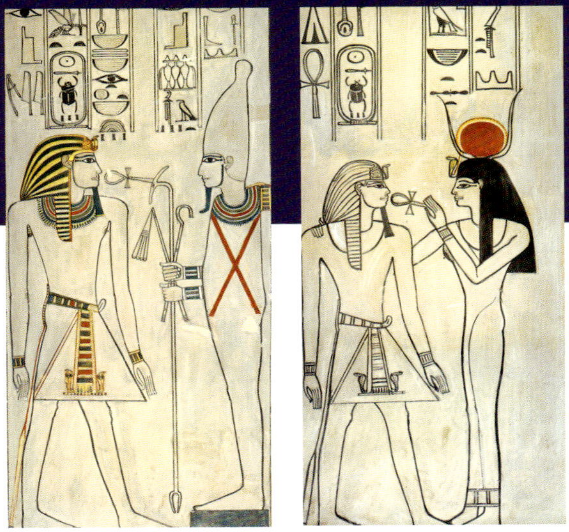

Amenhotep II receiving an *ankh* (life) from Osiris, Lord of the Netherworld, and Hathor, Mistress of the West.
18th Dynasty
Thebes, Valley of the Kings

Votive Statue of Amenhotep III from Karnak.
Steatite
18th Dynasty
Egyptian Museum in Cairo

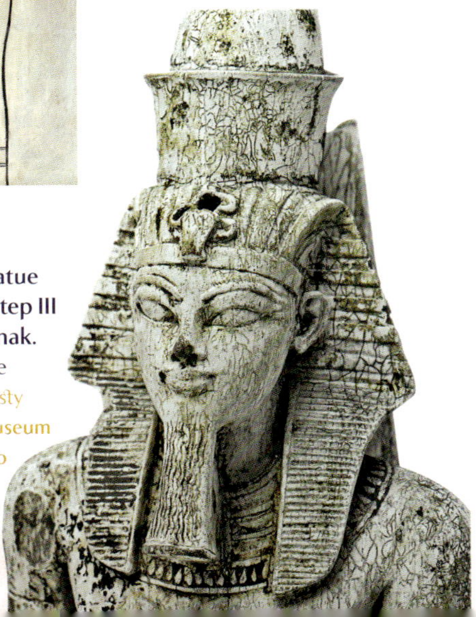

Sphinx.) Perhaps Thutmose IV was offering an explanation for some "irregularity" – perhaps even a murder – that occurred before his accession to the throne.

One of Thutmose IV's minor wives was a woman named Mutemwia, who might have been the daughter of King Artatama I of Mitanni. Wherever she came from, she was the mother of Thutmose IV's successor, Amenhotep III. When Thutmose IV died and was buried, this boy, perhaps 12 years old, inherited a wealthy kingdom at its peak.

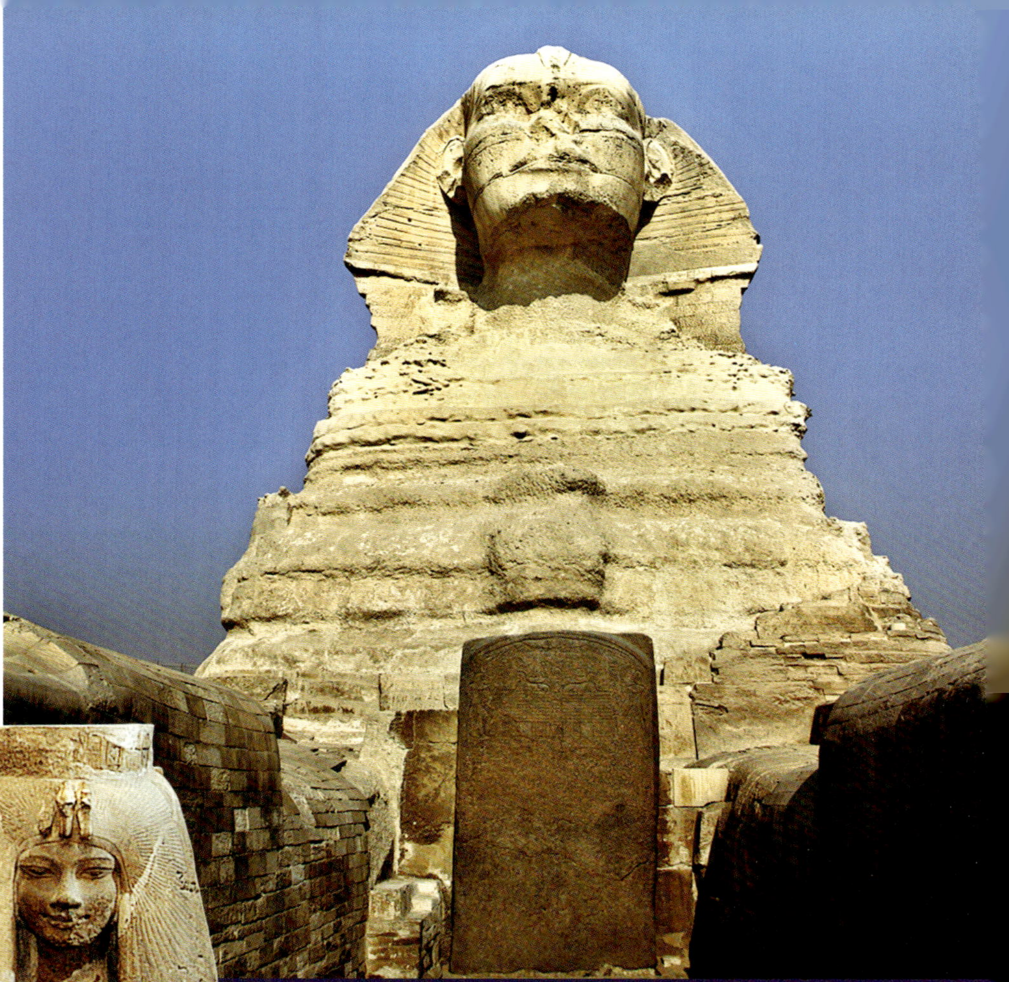

The Dream Stele erected by Thutmose IV between the two paws of the Sphinx.
Red granite
18th Dynasty
Giza

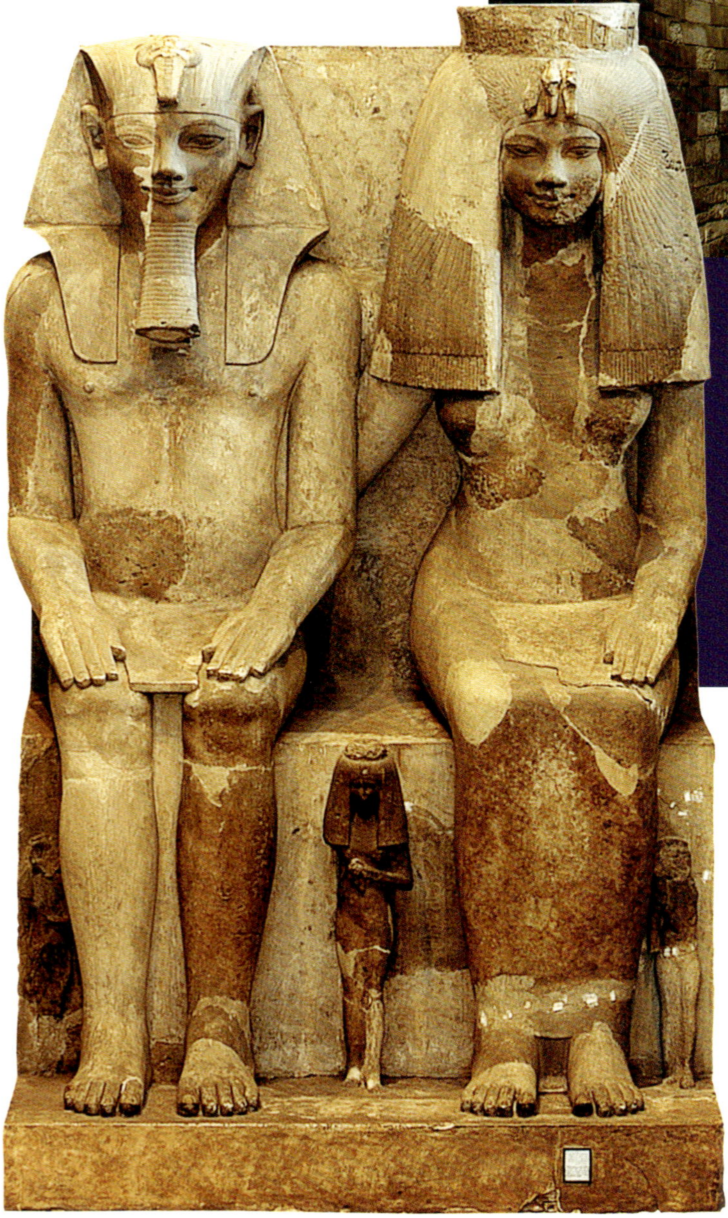

Collossal Statue of Amenhotep III, Queen Tiye and three daughters.
Sandstone
18th Dynasty
Egyptian Museum in Cairo

AMENHOTEP III AND TIYE

Even at such a young age, Amenhotep III had a wife named Tiye, who was the daughter of high-ranking commoners named Yuya (priest of the god Min) and Tjuya. Tiye had one brother named Aanen, who served the god Re as high priest, and possibly another brother named Ay, who would serve their son and grandson as a high official and then go on to even higher office. At the end of their lives, Yuya and Tjuya were granted burial in the Valley of the Kings, an honor not often permitted for commoners. It is thought that Amenhotep III and Tiye's marriage was not merely one of convenience but of love. The frequent mention of her and her parents on commemorative scarabs even when the occasion was the king's marriage to a foreign princess does seem to support this.

Although in monumental sculpture Tiye usually appears tiny compared to her husband, as was the Egyptian convention, she appeared equal in size beside him on a colossal statue from his funerary temple at Kom el-Hitan on the west bank of Luxor. Her name was written in a cartouche, something usually reserved for certain names belonging to the king. She was given other royal iconographic prerogatives as well, even appearing as a female sphinx overcoming enemies. Frequently, she wore a crown with tall cow horns and the solar disk between them, like Hathor, a goddess intimately connected with kingship.

The reign of Amenhotep III was a period of great wealth and power for Egypt. It was also a period of important developments in religion, including the deification of the living king. At Soleb, in Nubia, Amenhotep III founded a temple devoted not only to the god Amun, but also to Amenhotep himself. Queen Tiye was also deified and worshiped as a goddess at Sedinga, a site nearby. The king added "the Dazzling Aten" to his epithets, equating himself directly with the solar disk. Although the king was considered a god, he was not immortal. The many statues of Sekhmet, the lioness-headed goddess of healing, that the king erected (see Chapter VII) could indicate that the king was ill toward the end of his reign. Amenhotep III reigned perhaps into his 39th year and might have shared the last few years with his son, named Amenhotep like his father. The length of the coregency between Amenhotep III and Amenhotep IV – and even if there was a coregency at all – is a matter of scholarly debate. Some believe that father and son may have shared the throne for as long as 12 years. When Amenhotep III finally died, Egyptian history took an unexpected turn.

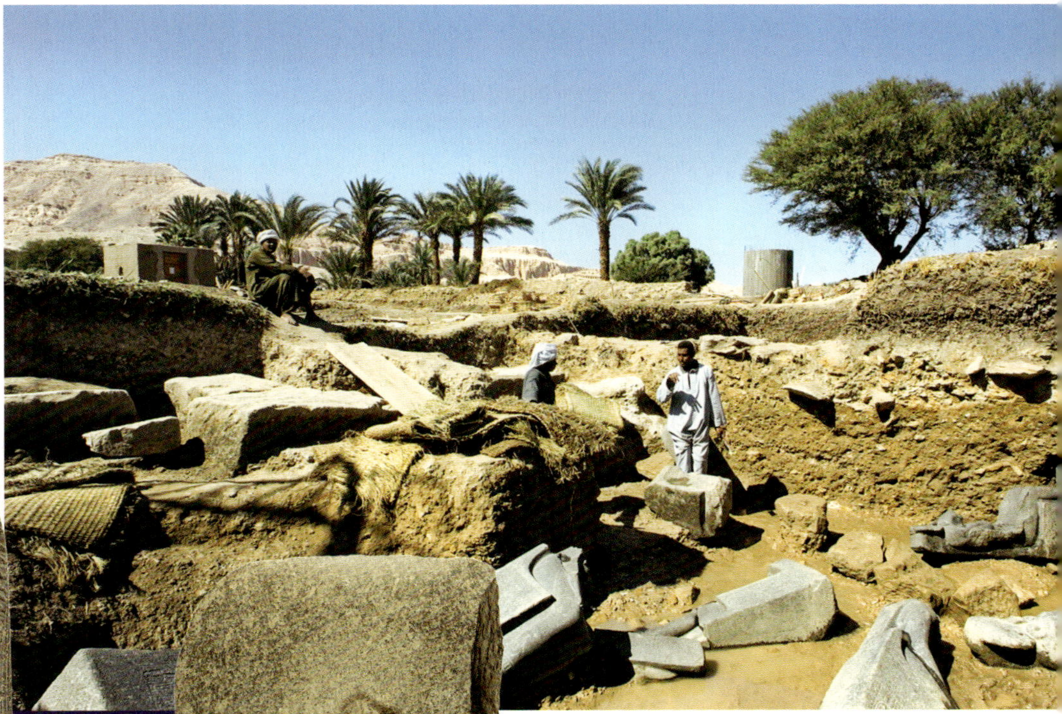

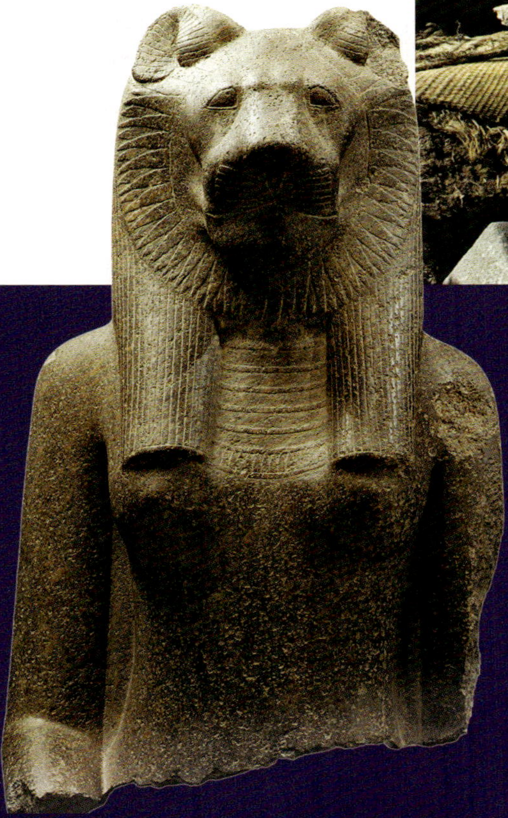

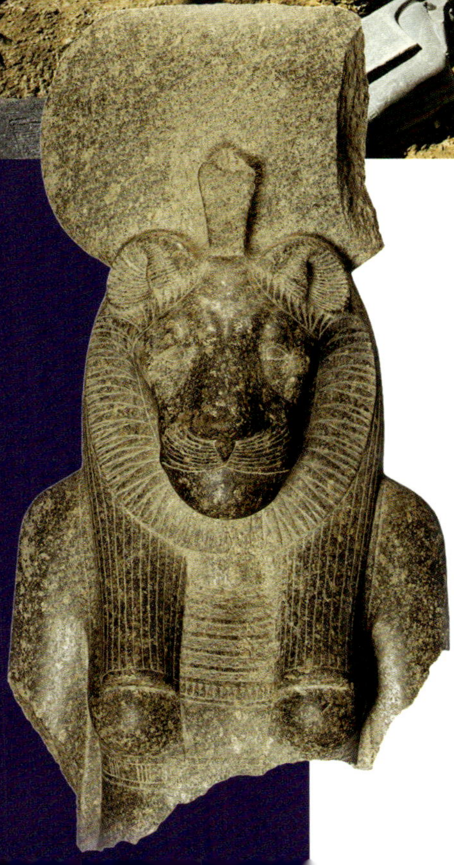

Sekhmet: The patron goddess of healing shown as a woman with a lioness head, was depicted in many statues erected by Amenhotep III.
Granite
18th Dynasty
Thebes, Kom el-Hitan

The cache of Sekhmet statues at the site of the mortuary temple of Amenhotep III.
Thebes, Kom el-Hitan

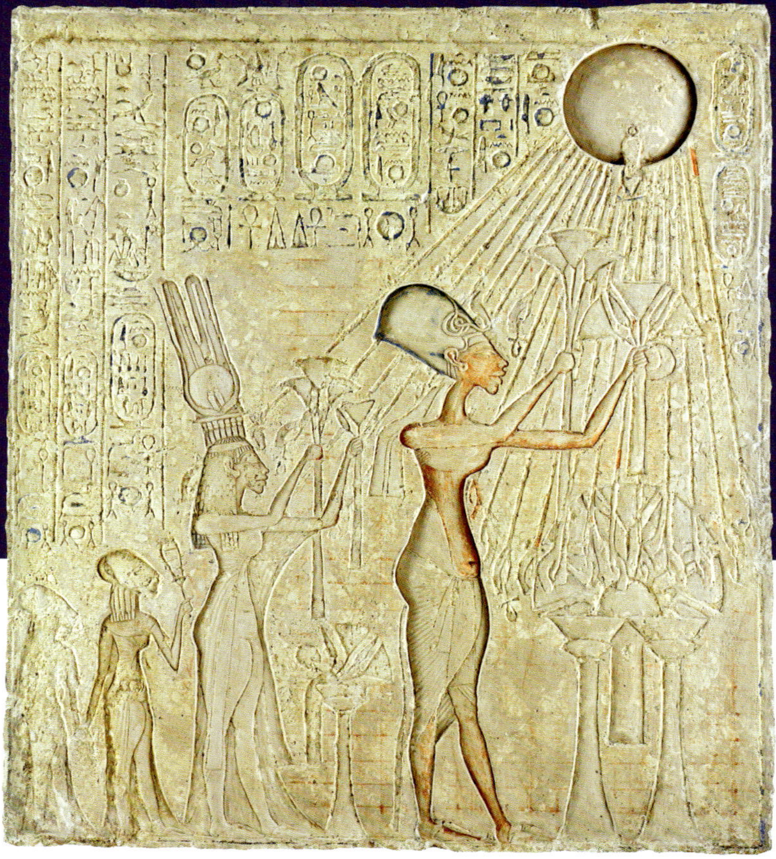

Akhenaten with his wife, Nefertiti and two of their daughters making offerings to the Aten.
Limestone
18th Dynasty
Egyptian Museum in Cairo

AMARNA: AKHENATEN AND NEFERTITI

The kings of the 18th Dynasty owed much to the god Amun and his temples at Luxor and Karnak, which had become enlarged by generations of rulers. When Amenhotep IV began building at Karnak, however, he did not dedicate his temple to Amun. He dedicated it to the Aten.

The Aten was an ancient aspect of the Egyptian sun god, who could take many forms. Known since the Old Kingdom, the Aten was the god in his most abstract manifestation, the visible disk of the sun in the sky with virtually no anthropomorphic characteristics except for the symbolic hands that appear at the ends of the solar rays, giving life to the royal family. Possibly, Amenhotep IV was worshiping his dead father, who had, after all, been called the Dazzling Aten.

Several tombs dating from his reign contain a hymn to the Aten that the king himself may have composed. The longest version of this hymn, known as the "Great Hymn to the Aten," occurs in the tomb of Ay. In it, the king praises the solar disk as it first rises at dawn:

"You fill every land with your beauty.
You are beauteous, great, radiant,
High over every land."

In the hymn, the Aten is not just the god of Egypt. The Aten is a universal god, father of the king. Nighttime is like a time of death, when evil roams, but the Aten's rays during daylight give life and activity to all things. Everything from a chick in its egg, to the fish in the sea, to the birth of a baby, to differences between human races, occurs because of the god. The only one who knows the Aten is his son, the king.

Early in his reign, the king acknowledged other forms that the sun god took, most notably the hawk-headed Re and Re-Horakhety, and he and his wife, a woman named Nefertiti, played the roles of Shu and Tefnut, deities of air and moisture who were the first offspring of the creator god.

But Amun, the king's own namesake, was a different matter. The exact cause of the rift between the king and this god's priesthood is not known. Possibly the priesthood had, in Amenhotep IV's eyes, grown too wealthy and influential due to the gifts his predecessors had lavished on the temples. Sometime after his fifth year, Amenhotep IV changed his name from "Amun is Satisfied" to "He who is Effective for the Aten"-Akhenaten. Nefertiti added Neferneferuaten, "Beautiful are the Beauties of the Aten," before her name.

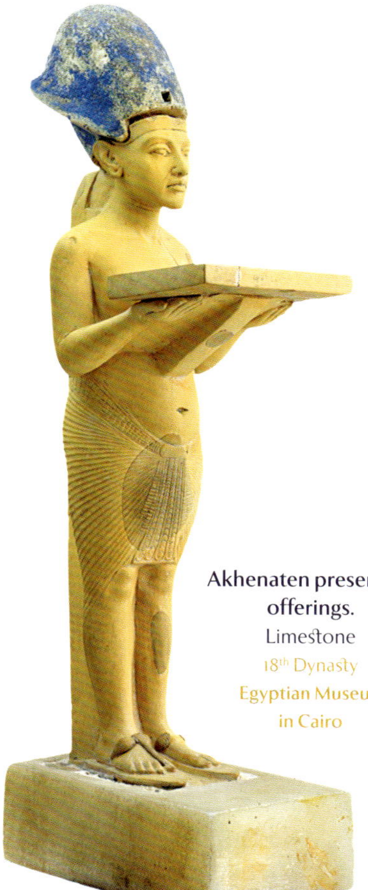

Akhenaten presenting offerings.
Limestone
18th Dynasty
Egyptian Museum in Cairo

Akhenaten commissioned temples dedicated to the Aten at other sites in Egypt and Nubia, including Memphis and the ancient center of the solar cult, Heliopolis. But people could not worship the Aten directly. Under the old religion, there were divine families of gods: Ptah, Sekhmet, and Nefertem at Memphis, and Amun, Mut, and Khonsu at Thebes, for example. Under Akhenaten's new religion, the royal family – Akhenaten, Nefertiti, and their daughters, shown receiving the sign of life from the Aten – took the place of these divine triads. This later proved to be a mistake, because upon the king's death, there was no way for the people to communicate with his god.

He personally developed a new artistic canon, changing the proportions of the human figure and having himself depicted with curious features: an extremely long face and feminine body. Colossal statues found at Karnak showing the king in this way have inspired many to think that he had a disease of some kind, perhaps Marfan syndrome. His mummy, however, shows no sign of deformity. The new artistic style was the king's expression of his new religion, dedicated to the androgynous Aten, which was responsible for the creation of the universe. The sculptor Bak left an inscription specifying that the king had taught him. Unusually for Egyptian history, several other artists are also known, including Thutmose, who created the famous bust of Nefertiti, and Yuti, who served as "chief artist" for Queen Tiye. These sculptors worked at the king's most ambitious building project, at a virgin site known in modern times as Amarna.

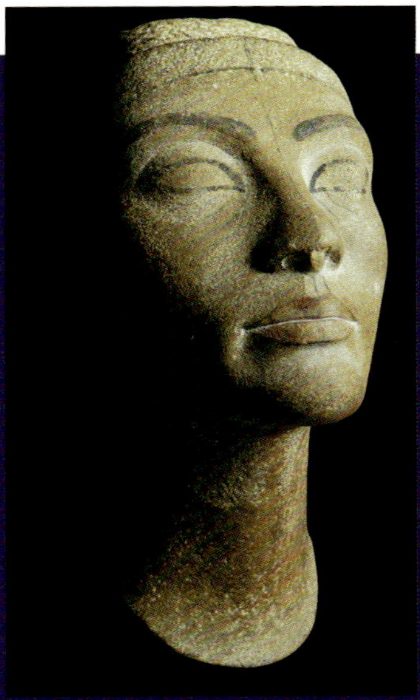

Unfinished head of Queen Nefertiti from Amarna.
Quartzite
18th Dynasty
Egyptian Museum in Cairo

Colossus of Akhenaten from the temple of the Aten at Karnak.
Sandstone
18th Dynasty
Egyptian Museum in Cairo

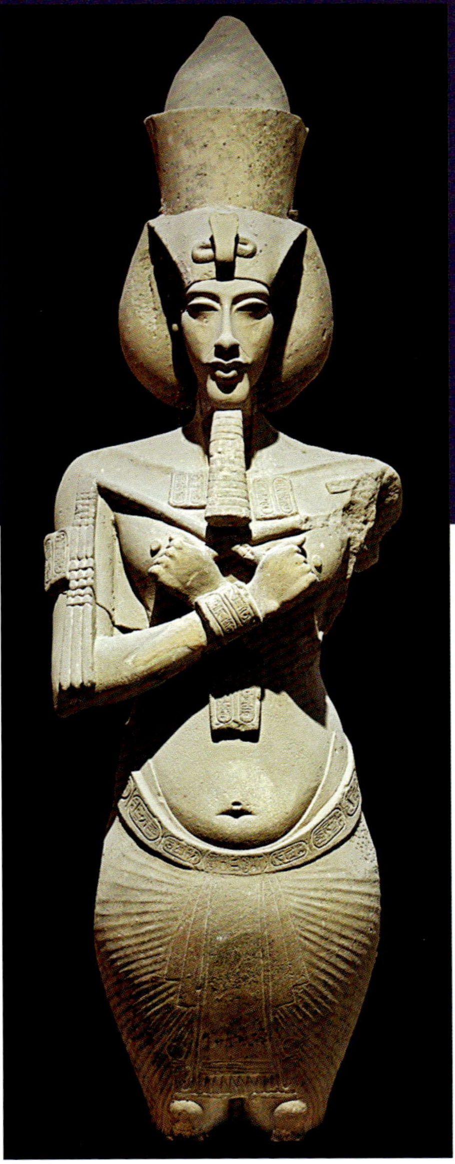

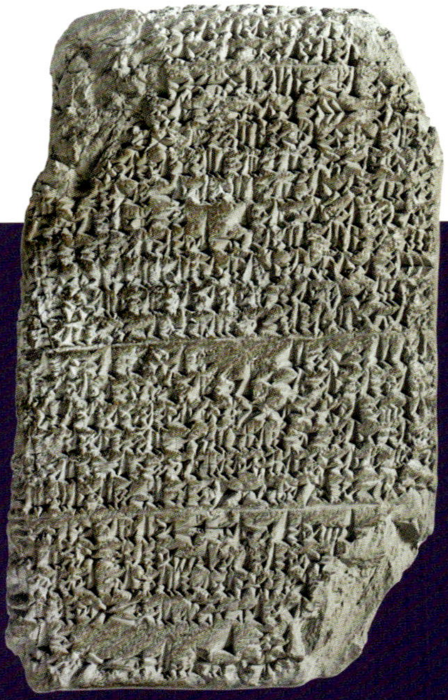

One of the Amarna Letters official correspondence written in the Akkadian language on clay tablets.
Clay
18th Dynasty
Egyptian Museum in Cairo

Here, in Middle Egypt, he constructed an entire new city, called Akhetaten, "Horizon of Aten," which would serve as the capital during his reign. It took the form of a large crescent about 13 km long from north to south and 5 km from east to west. At its peak it was inhabited by as many as 20,000 people. The central part of the site was occupied by an immense temple to the Aten. This "Great Temple" covered an area roughly 750 m by 250 m. It had a huge court open to the sky and the sunlight streamed down by the god. Near this temple was a formal reception palace where the king could meet his officials and foreign dignitaries. Nearby were administrative buildings, including the royal archives.

South of the Great Temple and west of the Royal Road that ran north to south was an enormous palace built of limestone. Another royal enclosure, with gardens, pools, storerooms, and a king's house, stood across the Royal Road. This dwelling may have had a "window of appearances" from which the king and queen could greet their subjects and bestow such high rewards as golden *shebyu* collars. Nearby was also the Small Temple to the

Aten, and there were also temples for the use of specific royal women.

North of the Great Temple were two more royal palaces, known today as the North Palace and the North Riverside Palace. The latter was most likely the principal home of the royal family.

It is known that Tiye joined her son at Amarna. In the tomb of Huya at Amarna (EA 1), Tiye appears dining with Akhenaten and Nefertiti, and elsewhere in this tomb there is a scene in which Akhenaten conducts his mother to a sunshade temple erected for her. Huya's own title, "steward in the house of the king's mother, the Great Royal Wife Tiye" indicates that she had a residence in the new city, although it remains unknown if she resided there or merely visited and lived at Thebes or perhaps at the "harem town" of Medinet el-Ghurob.

Foreign vassals and other great kings sent ambassadors to this new city of Akhetaten, bearing letters not only for the king but for his mother, Tiye, as well. She remained influential, or so the foreigners hoped. Foreign kings demanded gifts from Egypt. Egypt's own client states begged for gold, weapons, and soldiers so they could defend themselves from their enemies. The Hittites, whose kingdom occupied parts of what is now Turkey, were taking lands in Syria that had belonged to Mitanni, an Egyptian ally. Letters found at Amarna present evidence of a politically and diplomatically complex landscape.

In Akhenaten's 12th year as king, vassals poured into Akhetaten for an elaborate ceremony of tribute. The exact nature of this ceremony is often debated. Some believe that Akhenaten and his father shared a long coregency and that this occasion marked the younger king's "promotion" to senior. Others suggest that it was a kind of jubilee, a

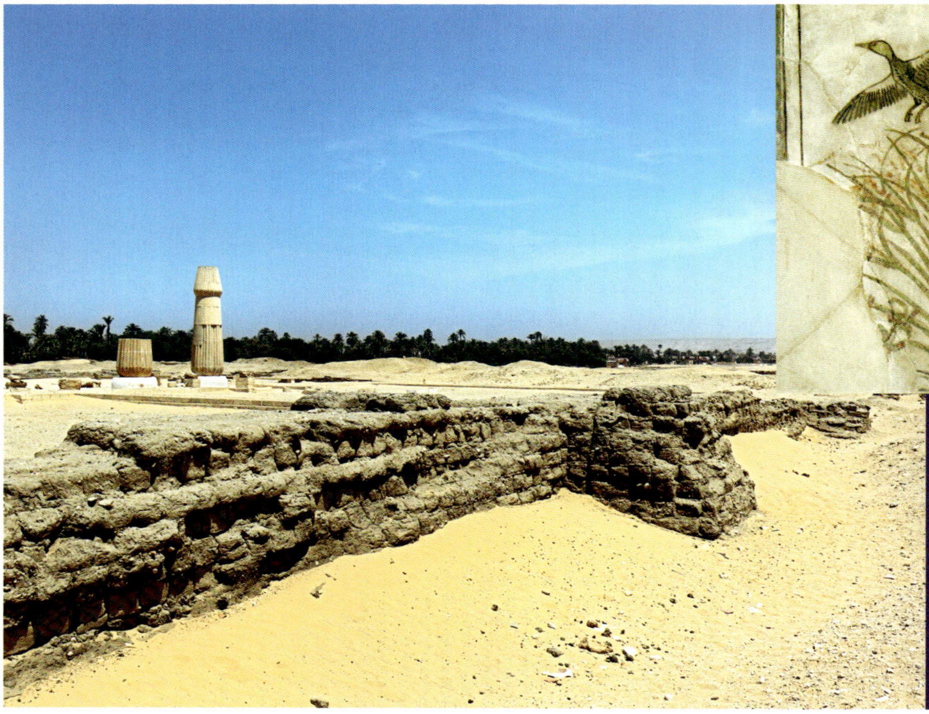

Ruins of Akhenaten's palace at Amarna.
18th Dynasty

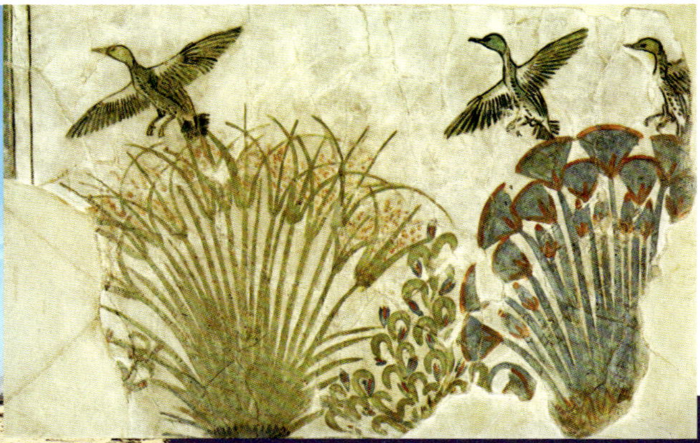

Wild birds in the marshes a fragment of paving recovered from the Southern palace at Amarna.
Plaster
18th Dynasty
Egyptian Museum in Cairo

sed-festival, although that was not normally celebrated until a king's 30th year of reign. Not long after this grand event, several key players disappear from the stage.

Akhenaten and Nefertiti had produced, by this time, six daughters. Four of them died, along with their grandmother, Tiye. The princesses and Tiye were buried in a tomb Akhenaten was preparing for himself in the Great Royal Wadi, in the hills east of Amarna. Akhenaten's minor – but prominent – wife, a woman named Kiya, also passed away. Kiya seems to have been given a lavish burial, presumably also within the royal tomb. Objects from this tomb were moved from Amarna to Thebes, probably during the reign of Tutankhamun. Kiya's four canopic jars, which would have contained certain internal organs, and a shrine made for Queen Tiye, as well as other Amarna Period objects – including a mummy – were found in a curious tomb in the Valley of the Kings known as KV 55.

Some scholars suggest that a plague was responsible for these losses among the royal family. It was often thought that Nefertiti disappeared, too, but very recently an inscription was found at a limestone quarry at Deir el-Barsha, mentioning Nefertiti as Akhenaten's wife, along with a date in Year 16. Clearly Nefertiti was still alive one year before Akhenaten's own reign ended.

Things more curious than death were going on during the final few years of the reign. Akhenaten and Nefertiti's eldest daughter, Meritaten, had survived whatever tragedy claimed the lives of so many of her sisters. Her image was carved over that of Kiya, she took the title of "Great Royal Wife," and she seems even to have supplanted her mother.

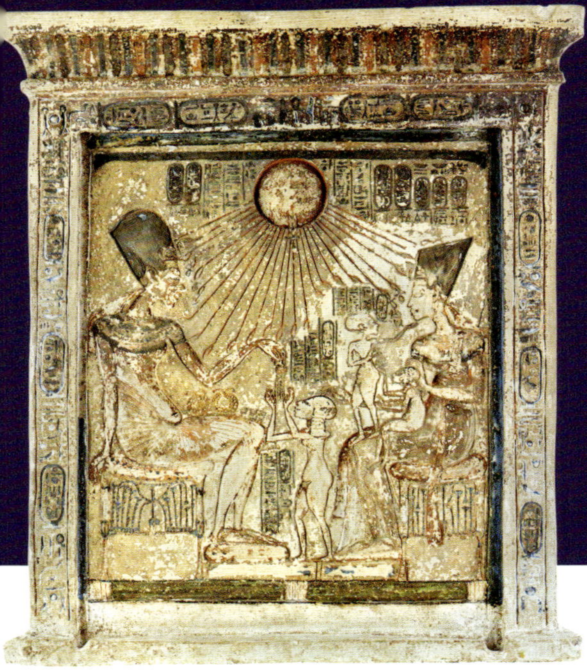

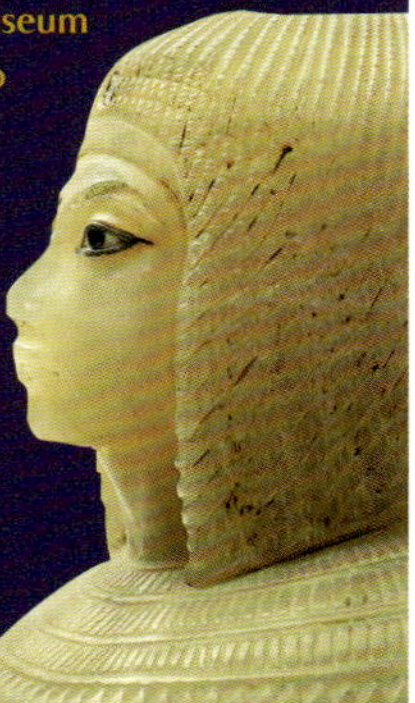

Canopic jar of Queen Kiya (?) from tomb KV 55 in the Valley of the Kings.
Calcite (Egyptian alabaster)
18th Dynasty
Egyptian Museum in Cairo

Akhenaten and Nefertiti playing with their daughters under the rays of the Aten.
Limestone
18th Dynasty
Egyptian Museum in Cairo

Was "Great Royal Wife" just a title, taken for ceremonial purposes? Maybe, but the appearance of a child named Meritaten-the-Younger suggests incest within the family.

Nefertiti was extremely prominent throughout Akhenaten's reign. She accompanies her husband when he offers to the Aten, serving in effect as the Aten's high priestess. Like Tiye before her, she sometimes appears in feminine versions of kingly roles. A relief depicting a royal boat shows that its decoration included a scene of Nefertiti smiting a foreign (female) foe, just as kings are shown to do. Another relief shows her sitting with her husband, wearing the double crown. Adding to the mystery is the appearance of an apparent co-ruler with the name Ankhkheperure, which was sometimes spelled in the feminine form, Ankhetkheperure. Who Ankh(et)kheperure was remains elusive. This person also used the name Neferneferuaten, as did Nefertiti. In fact, some scholars think that Ankh(et)kheperure was none other than Nefertiti under another name.

After beginning his 17th year as king, Akhenaten died. He was buried in the royal tomb in the Great Royal Wadi, alongside his mother. His body would later be moved to KV 55 in the Valley of the Kings.

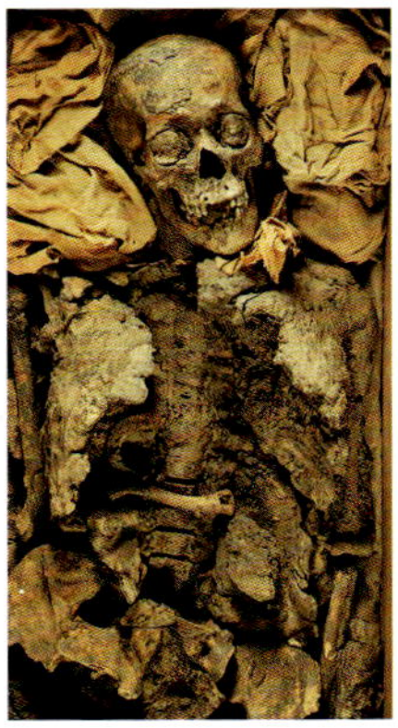

Mummy from KV 55 recently identified as that of Akhenaten.
18th Dynasty
Egyptian Museum in Cairo

His successor was the shadowy Ankh(et)kheperure. Could this have been Nefertiti, ruling independently as female pharaoh, like Hatshepsut generations before her? There may be a clue in the tomb of Meryre, high priest of the Aten. One scene in this tomb shows a procession and ceremony performed in the second month of Akhenaten's 12th year of rule. According to Eptologist James Allen, this scene illustrates the royal family as it existed at that time. This included Nefertiti and six daughters: Meritaten, Meketaten, Ankhesenpaaten, Neferneferuaten-the-Younger, Neferneferure, and Setepenre. The king and queen are shown seated next to one another so closely that one is drawn virtually atop the other, so they seem almost to share the same outlines. Nicholas Reeves, founder of the Amarna Royal Tombs Project, thinks that at the time when this scene was carved Nefertiti was beginning to be considered to be Akhenaten's co-ruler. This may be why she seems to disappear from the records and changed her name, as part of her elevation in rank.

After Ankh(et)kheperure, for a year or two there appears to have been yet another king, this time a man named Djeser-Kheperure Smenkhkare, whose name appears on a few inscriptions. Meritaten appears to have been his wife. Norman de Garis Davis, the Egyptologist who published Meryre's tomb in 1906, believed that this tomb was finished during the reign of Smehkhkare. Another scene here shows this king with Akhenaten's eldest daughter as his chief queen. Perhaps Smenkhkare was a brother of Akhenaten, but there is simply no evidence for who he might have been. It was long believed that his body was found in KV 55, but this has been proven to be Akhenaten himself. Some propose that Smenkhkare is none other than another guise for Nefertiti, or perhaps even Meritaten.

It is possible that Nefertiti (by whatever name we should call her at this time) wrote the famous letter making a very unusual request of the Hittites. This letter, which is usually attributed to Tutankhamun's widow, Ankhesenamun, says,

> *My husband has died and I have no sons. They say that you have many sons. You might give to me one of your sons and he might become my husband. I would not want to take one of my servants. I am loathe to make him my husband. I am afraid.*

We know that the king of the Hittites, Suppiluliumas, did not believe the queen, whoever she was. Although Egyptian kings married foreign princesses, an Egyptian queen marrying a foreigner was unheard of. Finally satisfied that the request was genuine, Suppiluliumas sent one of his sons to Egypt. The prince died en route, perhaps murdered by the Egyptian general Horemheb.

No matter who wrote this letter and when, no matter who Ankh(et)kheperure and Smenkhkare really were, we know with certainty one thing. The next king was a nine-year-old Egyptian boy, "the king's son of his body," Tutankhaten.

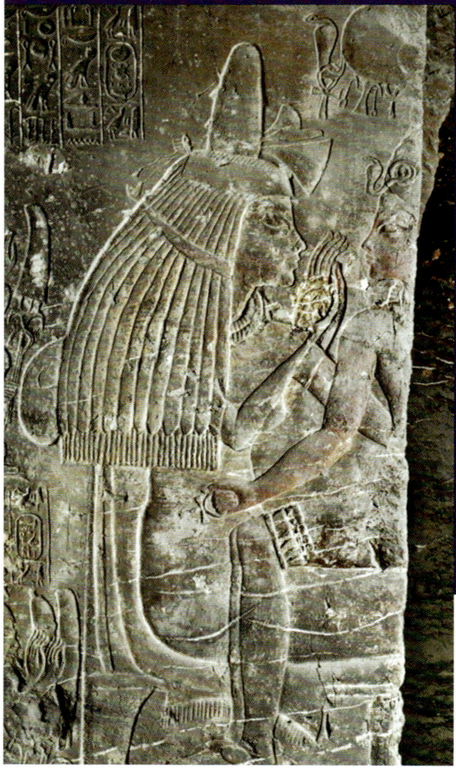

Tutankhamun in full regalia as the king of Egypt sitting on the lap of his wet nurse, Maia.
18th Dynasty
Tomb of Maia, Saqqara

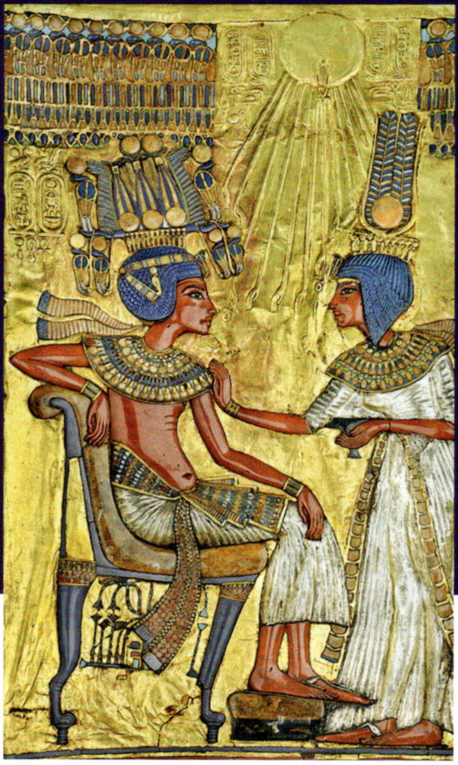

Under the rays of Aten, Tutankhamun relaxing on his throne with his queen, Ankhesenamun, rubbing his body with scented oil.
Gilded wood with semiprecious stones
18th Dynasty
Egyptian Museum in Cairo

TUTANKHAMUN: BOY AND KING

This boy named Tutankhaten, the "Living Image of Aten," was likely born in Year 11 of the reign of Akhenaten, who was probably his father. Although artists portrayed Akhenaten's daughters prominently, royal sons do not appear in art of the period. Tutankhaten might, however, be shown as an infant in his father's tomb. In one scene a woman stands holding a baby, who is shaded by a fan, an image that some believe to be Tutankhaten with his mother or wet nurse.

He was brought up in Amarna and perhaps also at Memphis, which remained an important city through the Amarna Period. He may have lived in the large palace built there by Thutmose I. The tomb of his wet nurse, a woman named Maia, has been found at Saqqara, the Memphite necropolis, near other tombs of important officials of the late 18th and 19th Dynasties. The tomb is devoted to Maia, which is unusual because most women were secondary figures in the tombs of their husbands. The substructure of Maia's tomb goes down into the bedrock. Above is a temple-like structure, with rooms dedicated to the deceased. Most of the decoration is badly damaged, but one scene that in part survives, on the eastern wall of the first room in the chapel, shows Maia sitting on a chair with the very young king, who wears the blue crown with protective uraeus, on her lap. Behind her is a hieroglyphic inscription giving the name of Tutankhamun. Other scenes in the tomb are devoted to religious themes, including Maia as a mummy and standing before the god Osiris.

Maia was not the only woman intimately connected with the young king. An inscribed block found at Ashmunein, near Amarna but on the west bank of the Nile, names not only the "king's son of his body," Tutankhaten (spelled here "Tutankhuaten"), but also a "king's daughter of his body." Much of the name of this daughter is missing, but it seems to have been Ankhesenpaaten. This princess, third of Akhenaten and Nefertiti's six daughters, was his wife even before he became king. No doubt raised together, they would have had time to know each other very well and to become fond of each other in the palace. For children who did not have to contend with diplomacy, life at Amarna was a time of pleasure and ease. The young couple would have played board games in the garden beside a pool, and they were no doubt taught not only to read and write, but also all about their father's religion. From the game boards found in his tomb, we know that he enjoyed these pastimes. Even though their marriage may have been for political reasons, it is easy to imagine them together at the palace, genuinely in love. Objects from the tomb give the impression of this, as she sits in his company or offers him jewels or flowers. These things had ritual meaning, but that need not mean that they also did not signify that real love grew between the king and his queen during their days in their father's palace.

It was a beautiful place to live, with scenes of ponds filled with fish and marsh plants. Egyptian artists, especially during the Amarna Period, gave movement and liveliness to their subjects. These scenes of nature were not only beautiful, but probably also symbolized the creations of the Aten. The palace also had an open-air court with altars where the royal family worshipped the solar disk.

When Tutankhaten took the throne, he was only nine years old, and possibly he was even as young as eight. His young age at his coronation is made touchingly evident by the number of child-sized objects from his tomb: crook and flail, furniture, even weaponry, sized for a child. Some are inscribed with the name he was given at birth, "Tutankhaten."

He changed his birth name, or it was changed for him, just a few years into his reign. "Tutankhaten" became "Tutankhamun," "Living Image of Amun," the god his father had hated so much. At the same time, Ankhesenpaaten was renamed "Ankhesenamun," "She Lives for Amun." Perhaps at the beginning of his reign the king was under the control of the priests of Amun, who could have forced him to restore the old cults and reject worship of his father's god, the Aten. He may have been selected to reign because priests, and perhaps Smenkhkare, decided that they needed a malleable young boy who could be turned from his father's religion.

The name that changed was not his only one. Like other kings of this period he had five names. His Horus name was "Strong Bull, of Perfect Birth." His Two Ladies name, which offered him protection by the patron goddesses of Upper and Lower Egypt, translates as "He Whose Beneficent Laws Pacify the Two Lands," while his Golden Horus name meant "He Who Wears the Crowns, Who Satisfies the Gods." The names by which we know him best are his throne name, Nebkheperure, "Re is the Lord of Manifestations," and his birth name, "Tutankhaten, "Living Image of Aten" or Tutankhamun, "Living Image of Amun". It is these last two, the throne and birth names, that occur on most of his monuments, written in cartouches. His birth name was followed by the title Heqa-Iunu-shema, "Lord of Southern Heliopolis" or "Lord of Thebes," an interesting choice of epithet because it links the southern city of Thebes with Heliopolis, the ancient center of the solar cult in the north, near Memphis.

Both Thebes and Memphis would serve as primary residences for the king and his wife.

Sunrise at Karnak Temple in Thebes.

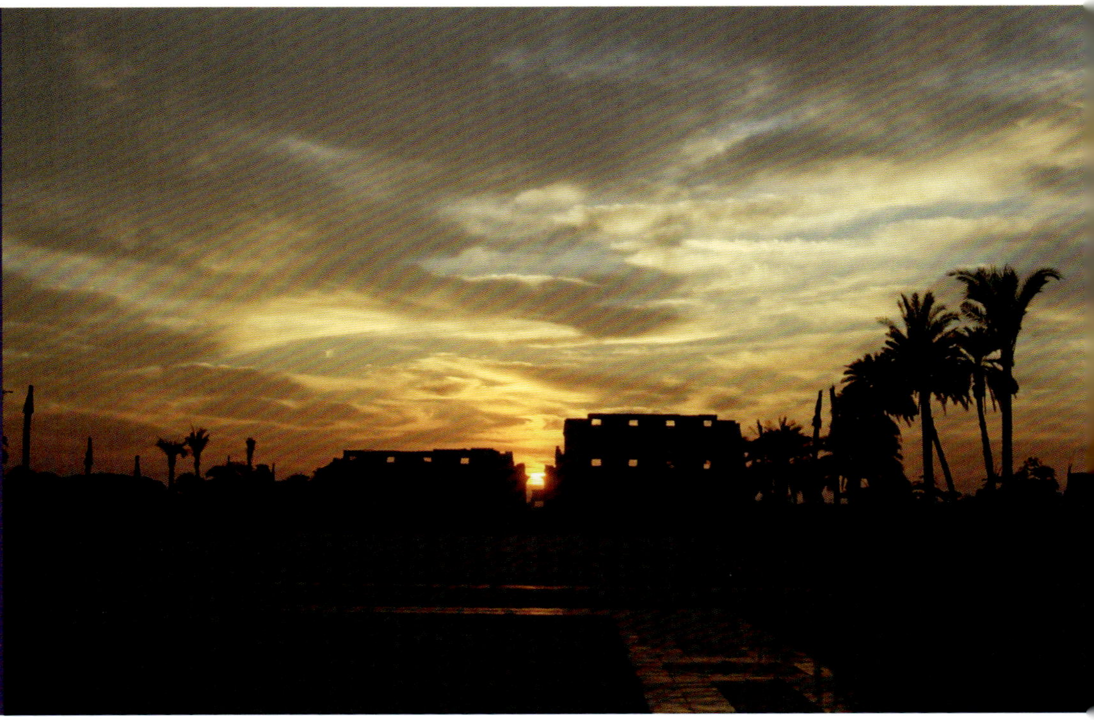

CITIES LOVED BY THE KING

Early in the reign, the royal court abandoned Amarna. Priests of Amun-Re performed the young king's coronation at Karnak, and it was from Karnak that the announcement went out that Egypt had a new king, with the blessing of the god Amun-Re. We have noticed that on 21st December each year, sunlight enters the interior of the temple sanctuary for a period of three days and then went out to the pylon, which represents the hieroglyphic sign for "horizon." The sun appearing between the two pylons occurs on the day of the birth of Re, the winter solstice, when the growing of wheat and barley began. The sun also enters the temple at the summer solstice, 21st June. This was when the Beautiful Feast of the Valley took place, when the divine family of Thebes – Amun, Mut, and their son Khonsu – would visit the temples on the west bank of Thebes. Festivities such as this, and the even grander Festival of Opet, were banned under Akhenaten.

No doubt all of this happened under the influence of the priests of Amun, with the blessings of the two most important courtiers of his reign, Horemheb and Ay. This change in religion seems to have begun even before the court abandoned Amarna. A stela from Amarna shows the king, called "Tutankhaten," with Amun and Amun's wife, Mut. Such a thing would have been unthinkable under the reign of his father.

The royal court moved to Memphis. The presence of the court there is indicated by the tombs of Maia, the king's wet nurse, and Maya, his treasurer. Although it is known that the king occupied the palace of Thutmose I, he may also have built a palace of his own at Memphis. Evidence for this comes from two important blocks found by accident under the foundation of a house in a small village near Abusir, in the region of the ancient city.

It seems to me that these are palace scenes and may have come from the royal house he used during his stays at Memphis. One shows Tutankhamun smiting a Nubian and an Asiatic. The other block shows him sitting and shooting an arrow at an animal while his wife Ankhesenamun sits at his feet. This last scene is similar to a scene on the Small Golden Shrine (Carter No. 108, in Chapter 4).

In 1920, the royal rest house he built near Memphis was uncovered south of the valley temple connected to the pyramid of Khafre at Giza. It might have been here that he learned to drive a chariot, a vehicle that had been introduced to Egypt during the Second Intermediate Period.

Several types of chariot were found in his tomb. He would have also been taught the skills needed to be a military leader. Although it was used for hunting, this rest house also had a religious role. It was located near the Great Sphinx, worshipped as the god Horemakhet. Unfortunately, the rest house was not well recorded during its excavation so we do not have a good idea of its appearance, but we can imagine it would have reflected his father's palace at Amarna and his grandfather's palace at Thebes: many large rooms and columned halls, surrounded by suites of smaller ones, all of mud brick (as palaces ordinarily were). The largest would have been for the king, whose throne room would be approached through a series of large halls. The walls would have been painted with colorful, naturalistic scenes, perhaps of marshlands and gardens with flowers and birds. As at Amarna, the rest house would have gardens and pools designed to soothe and delight the royal eyes and ears.

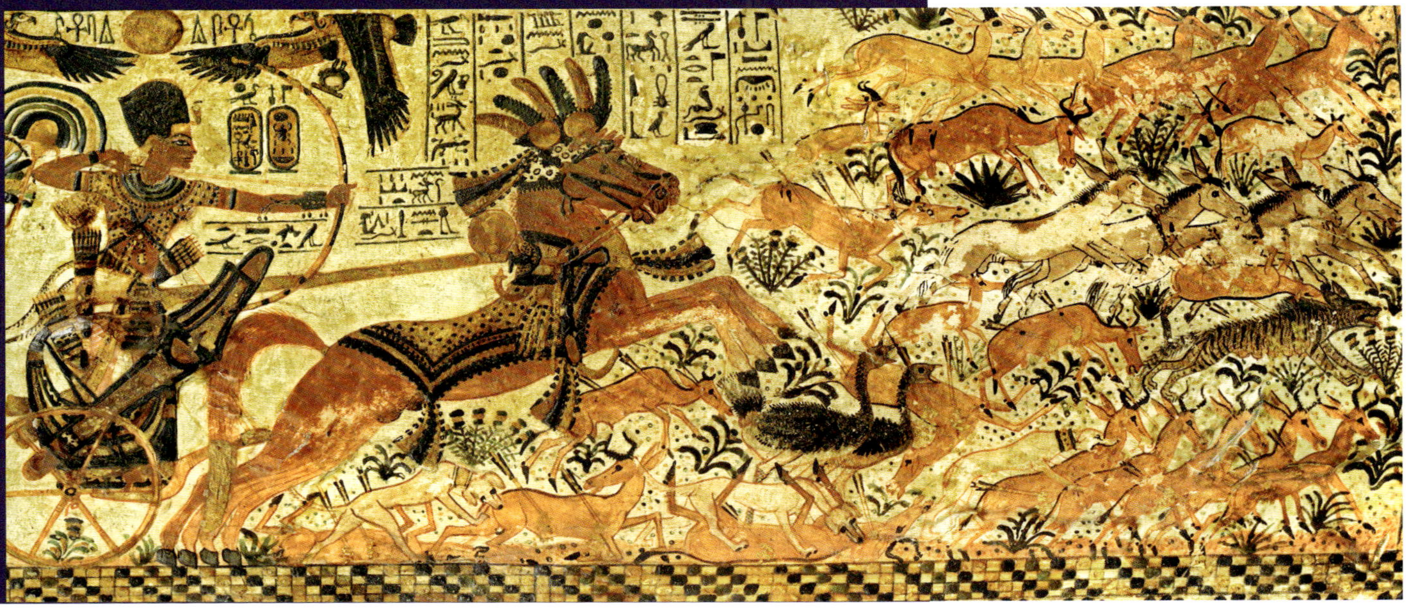

TUTANKHAMUN IN HIS CHARIOT, HUNTING DESERT ANIMALS
War chest
Egyptian Museum in Cairo
Carter 21

It was from the palace of Thutmose I in Memphis that Tutankhamun issued a decree recorded on a monument that has become known as the Restoration Stela. The inscription describes the state of the country when Tutankhamun, "the son of Amun," was crowned. From the far south, at Elephantine, to the Delta, the temples and their estates were in ruins, no more than overgrown rubble. The world was in chaos because the gods had turned their backs on Egypt. No prayers were answered, and people despaired. According to the stela, Tutankhamun took upon himself responsibility for restoring the temples. He did what needed to be done for the country, and then thought about what had to be done to please Amun. He settled on a new cult statue of electrum (an alloy of silver and gold), with inlay of lapis lazuli, turquoise, and other semiprecious stones. He did this for other gods, too, taking metals from the treasury to do so. He restored the priesthoods, as well, and endowed the temples with great wealth out of the royal treasury. This great burst of building and craft activity described by the Restoration Stela left its mark on the archaeological evidence. Although much of his work was usurped or built over by later kings (and the wonderful gold statues of the gods were no doubt melted down in antiquity), monuments from his reign have been found at a number of important sites, especially Thebes. A significant number of stone statues with the face of the young king have survived the millennia. During Tutankhamun's reign an Apis bull, sacred to the god Ptah, was buried at the Serapeum. His grandfather, Amenhotep III, had been the first to do this.

He also added an inscription to the temple of Thutmose III at Medinet el-Ghurab, the "harem-town" at the entrance to the Faiyum.

Garments and other objects found in his tomb show that Tutankhamun participated in all the religious activities of a king, even at a young age. He restored one of the most elaborate of all Egyptian ceremonies, the Festival of Opet, a grand procession, largely river-borne, of the images of the divine Theban family of Amun, Mut, and their son Khonsu, between the great temples at Luxor and Karnak. Tutankhamun dedicated his reliefs in the Great Colonnade Hall at the temple at Luxor to show this great occasion, and also the festival of Min, the god of male fertility and the Eastern Desert. Perhaps Tutankhamun stayed at the palace at Malqata, on the west bank, for such religious festivals. And, of course, it would be at a royal workshop in the west bank of Luxor that the king would be mummified, and from here his body be moved in ceremony to his tomb in the valley.

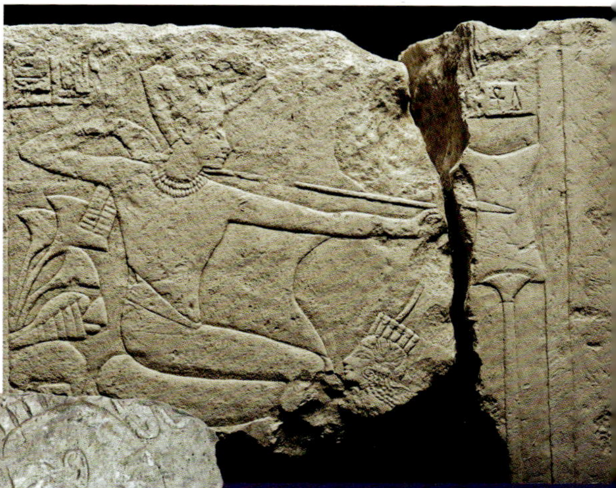

Tutankhamun seated firing arrows at a target.
Relief on limestone blocks from Memphis, Saqqara
Archive Zahi Hawass

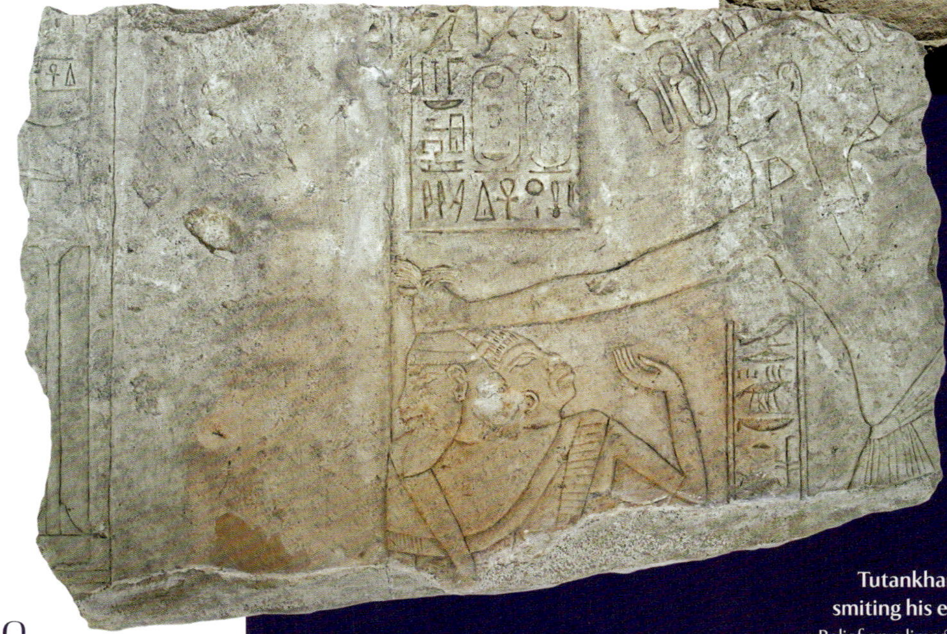

Tutankhamum smiting his enemies.
Relief on a limestone block from Memphis.
Saqqara

THE KING AND HIS COURT

By the time Tutankhamun came to the throne, the golden days of the Egyptian empire were gone. The Restoration Stela claims that if the army was sent to Djahy (a region in the Levant) to widen the borders of Egypt, it had no success. The rise of the Hittite kingdom had shattered the delicate peace that two generations of kings had maintained. Egypt even lost some of its vassal states. A campaign undertaken to retake the key city of Qadesh either late in Akhenaten's reign or during the reign of his immediate successor apparently ended in defeat. A stalemate had been reached between the two great powers, Egypt and the Hittites, and it remained that way until the ninth year of Tutankhamun's reign.

In that year, the Egyptian army attacked Qadesh, most likely under Tutankhamun's commander of the army, Horemheb. But again, the army met defeat. The Hittites took advantage of the situation and attacked the kingdom of Mitanni, Egypt's old ally. The result was a decisive defeat that wiped the Mitanni empire off the map.

Despite this setback, Horemheb was the most important individual near the king. In addition to being general, he held the titles of "deputy of the king in the entire land," and "overseer of all works," as well as "crown prince." No doubt he was the real ruler of the country.

He built a wonderful tomb for himself at Saqqara, where the remaining decoration hints at military conflict during Tutankhamun's reign. Fragmentary battle scenes from Thebes, studied recently by Ray Johnson of the University of Chicago, suggest that the young king did in fact participate in at least one major battle. But, as will be seen in more detail later, his health meant that he could never become a

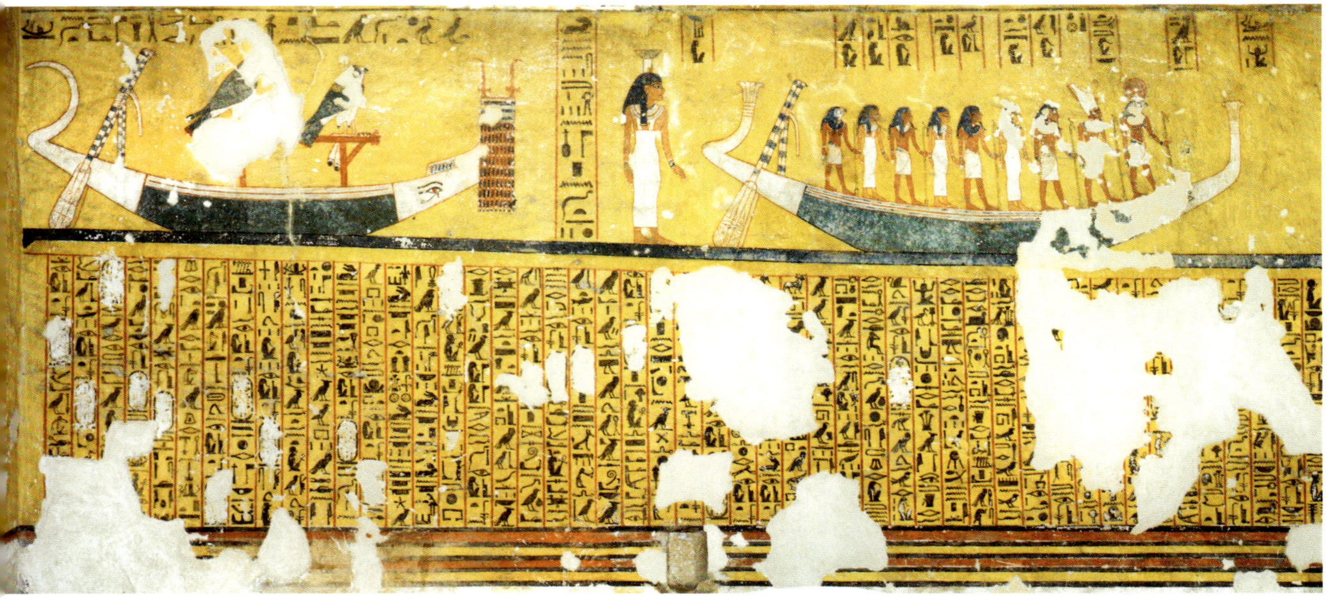

The night journey of the sun god and spells from the *Book of the Dead* (nos. 130, 141 and 142).
Tomb of Ay (KV 23)
18th Dynasty
Thebes, Valley of the Kings

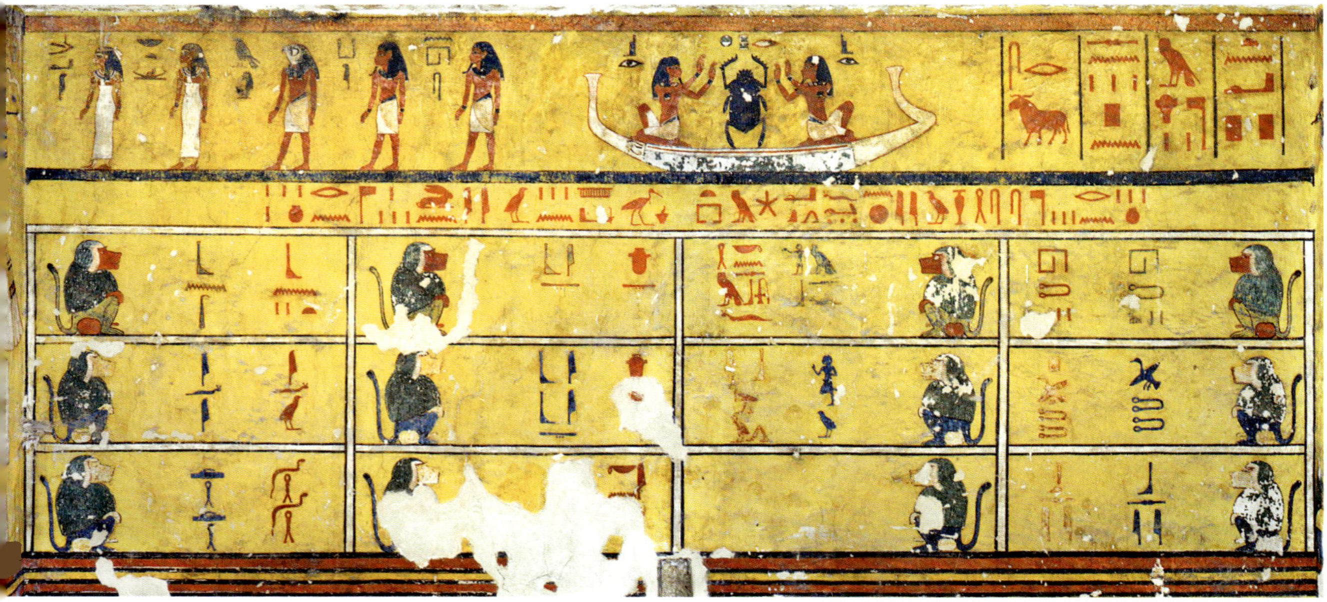

The baboons and a barque with scarab from the First Hour of the *Book of the Amduat*.
Tomb of Ay (KV 23)
18th Dynasty
Thebes, Valley of the Kings

warrior king. But that did not stop Tutankhamun from learning to drive a chariot (even though he would have had a charioteer with him) and to handle weapons. Horemheb's own career must have begun during the Amarna Period, but nothing is known of it.

Tutankhamun was surrounded by other powerful men in the royal court. The second most influential, after Horemheb, was Ay, who bore the title "God's Father," which seems to refer to the king's father-in-law. He may have been Nefertiti's father, and thus a son of Yuya and Tjuya, but the connection between them remains uncertain. Ay had served as a priest and military officer under Akhenaten. Ay may have been the father of another important general, Nakhtmin, who was close enough to Tutankhamun to have commissioned five *shabtis* for the king's tomb. Another *shabti*, and another funerary figure (Carter No. 331a), was donated by Maya, Tutankhamun's treasurer and "overseer of works in the Place of Eternity," as the royal necropolis was known. As such, he seems to have been responsible for the young king's burial and was probably involved with restoring the tomb after the robberies. Maya and his wife, Meryet, had a tomb near Horemheb's in Memphis, splendidly decorated.

Not all of the royal courtiers chose to build tombs at Memphis. Boyo Ockinga of Macquarie University published a tomb dated to the reign of Tutankhamun at Akhmim (Sohag). The owner of this tomb, a man called Sennedjem, was a royal tutor. The tomb contains several cartouches of Tutankhamun and is decorated in the Amarna style. It is suggested that this man likely lived early in Tutankhamun's reign. Therefore, he could have been Tutankhamun's tutor when the king was a young boy. It is also interesting that the tomb of Sennedjem is the only tomb that has been found at the site. Why Sennedjem – a royal tutor – would choose not to be buried within a major necropolis remains unknown.

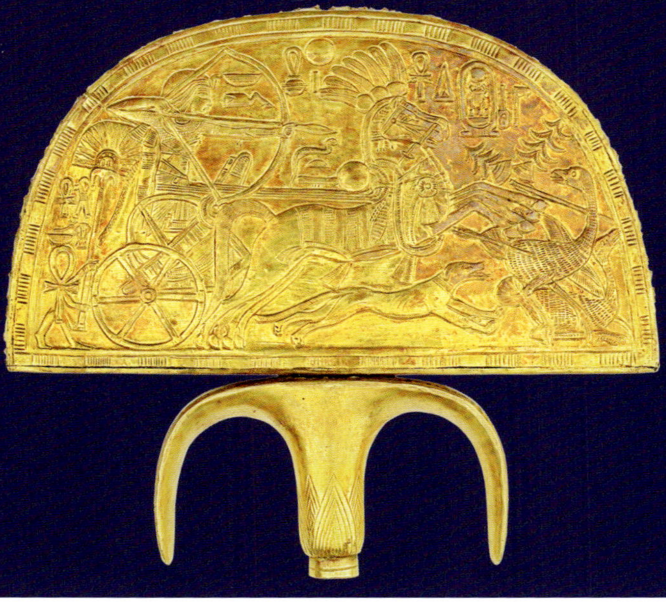

Base of Tutankhamun's ostrich feather fan: the king in his chariot, hunting ostriches.
Gilded wood
Egyptian Museum of Cairo
Carter 242b

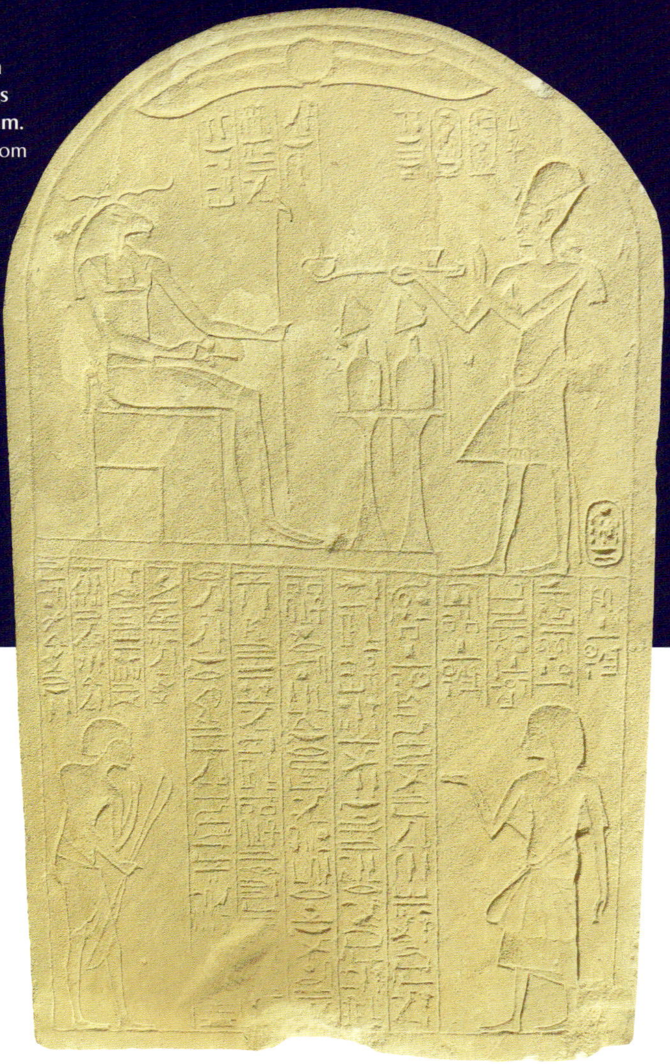

Tutankhamun giving offerings to the god Khnum.
Sandstone stela from Aswan.
Luxor Museum

Another person who could have been a part of Tutankhamun's court is a man named Parenefer, called Wenenefer, the high priest of Amun. His tomb at Thebes (TT 162), which was partly published by Friederike Kampp (who is now director of the Egyptian Museum in Berlin), has reliefs in the Amarna style fused with traditional (non-Amarna) iconography.

Two high officials who perhaps played some part in Tutankhamun's burial are Pentu and Usermont. They were viziers, two heads of the civil administration of the country, which was divided into Upper and Lower Egypt. Two unnamed viziers appear in the decoration of the burial chamber as members of the funerary party dragging Tutankhamun's mummy; they could have been Pentu and Usermont.

Another high official, a viceroy, oversaw the governance of Nubia. During the reign of Tutankhamun, this was a man named Huy (or Amenhotep), whose wife, Taemwadjsi, held the title "chief of the harem of Tutankhamun." Huy was responsible for bringing gold from Nubia's rich mines and other forms of tribute from the south. Huy left inscriptions at Biga and Faras in Nubia, and statues at Abusir and El Kab.

One of the deputies who served under Huy left a unique stela at the Kurkur Oasis, which lies southwest of Aswan. His name was Penniut, and one of his titles was "deputy of Wawat" (northern Nubia). Artists portray him a bit earlier in his career in Huy's tomb, when he commanded the fortress at Faras. The stela shows Tutankhamun offering incense to the ram-headed god Khnum. Below this is a text that preserves words exchanged between Penniut and a Nubian policeman, or Medjay, who served the king. Both men appear on the lower part of the stela. The Medjay, whose name is not given, bows before his superior. Penniut scolds him for being late to receive an official seal. This would have been an important object proving that he was acting legitimately for the king, much like a police badge today. Penniut also reminds him of something that Huy said: the man who does not have the king in his heart will die. The Medjay explains his tardiness by the great length of his daily patrol route, which was about 42 km up and down hills. The Medjay asks Penniut that he be allowed to keep his job, but the stela does not record his fate.

Other officials who served Tutankhamun were Seba, the mayor of Thinis, Governor Panakht of Kawa, the chief steward Ipy, and a high priest of Ptah named Ptahemhat-Ty. In addition to a scattering of other names of private individuals, there was also a Nubian chieftain with the Egyptian name Heqanefer, who was buried in Nubia.

Although Heqanefer's tomb has been excavated, most of these men are known from just a few inscriptions. Little is otherwise known about them, but in Tutankhamun's day they, and many other officials and functionaries, were well known and responsible for the operation of the civil, military, and religious branches of the government. The king, as a boy, could have had virtually no real power of his own, although he sat at the top of the pyramid of Egyptian society. Like other boy-kings, such as his grandfather Amenhotep III, he would have to grow into his power.

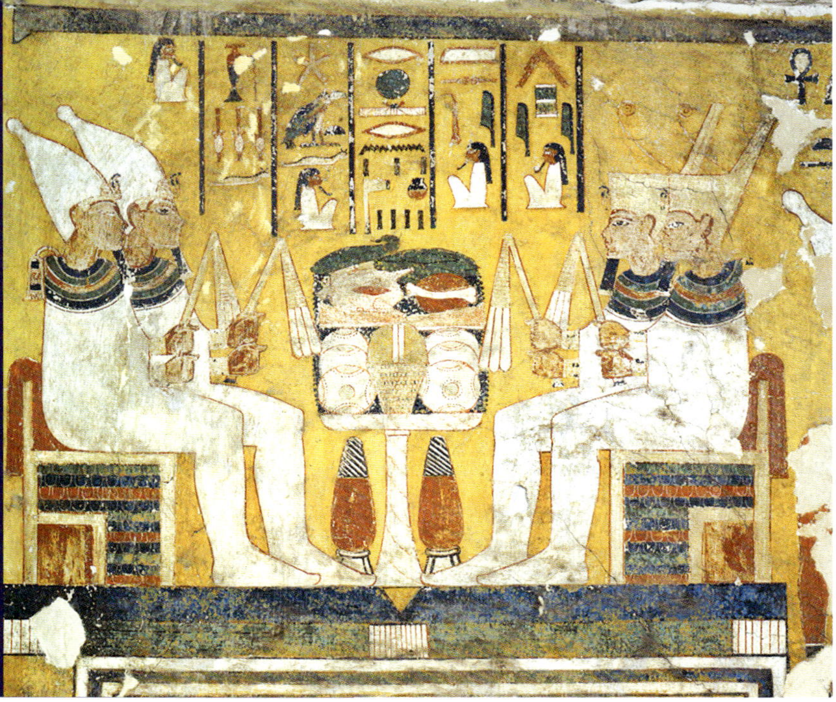

The four sons of Horus, guardians of the mummified internal organs of the deceased.
Tomb of Ay (KV 23)
18th Dynasty
Thebes, Valley of the Kings

THE END OF TUTANKHAMUN'S REIGN

There were probably concerns for the dynasty's survival even when Tutankhamun was young. The king had disabilities, as we will later see. Ankhesenamun, the young wife he seemed to love so much, may have become pregnant at least twice, but these pregnancies ended prematurely. Perhaps this is why Horemheb, a vigorous military man, was appointed to be heir. When the king died, in January of perhaps 1327 BC, likely no

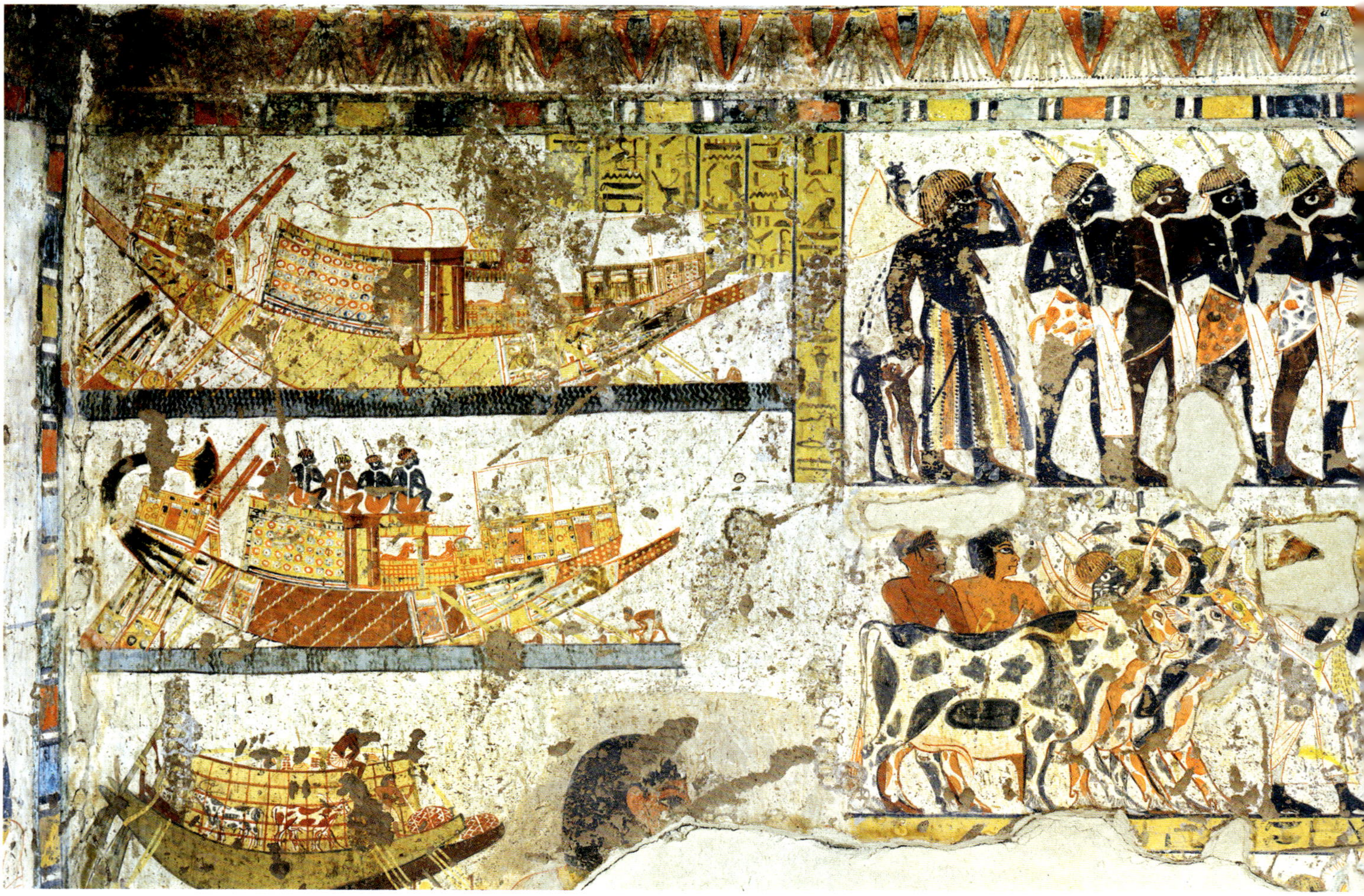

one was ready. Horemheb must have been out of the country on campaign, because otherwise he would have performed the Opening of the Mouth on Tutankhamun's mummy, a ceremony traditionally undertaken by a son or heir to secure his father's position. Instead, the decoration in the burial chamber shows that Ay did this honor. It is also known that Ay married Ankhesenamun, his own granddaughter, and had a tomb built for himself as king in the Valley of the Monkeys (KV 23).

Craftsmen had to work quickly to prepare objects for the young king's tomb. Some, like the Golden Mask (**Carter No. 256a**), were made for Tutankhamun, but other items were pressed into service from at least one other burial. These included "heirlooms" that might have been the king's personal possessions, such as a scarab and calcite (Egyptian alabaster) vessels with the name of Thutmose III, but others were critical elements of the burial, including the king's canopic jars (**Carter No. 266c-f**), the second gold coffin (**Carter No. 254**), and the second gold shrine (**Carter No. 237**). Some of these had been made for the burial of Ankh(et)-kheperure.

And what about the tomb itself? It is thought that a larger tomb (KV 23) was being prepared for the young king in the Valley of the Monkeys and, because it was unfinished, KV 62, perhaps originally intended for a private person (maybe even Ay), was used for him instead.

However, seals were found with the name of Tutankhaten and Tutankhamun, indicating that the tomb was, at some point, sealed during his reign. This was almost certainly originally the burial place of his mother or Nefertiti. But, of course, what Howard Carter would find in it was the boy-king himself and all his treasures.

Tutankhamun's death left a widowed queen. I mentioned earlier a letter that either she or Nefertiti might have written to the king of the Hittites, asking for a royal son to marry. When the skeptical Hittites eventually sent their prince, he was killed along the way, perhaps by Horemheb. However, we do see Ankhesenamun was close to Ay. Some say that she married Ay so that he could legitimately become king of Egypt while Horemheb was on campaign outside of Egypt. There is a ring with twin cartouches, giving the names of Ay and Ankhesenamun, that prove that she kept her title as the royal wife of the king of Egypt. The aged king Ay ruled for only four years. Upon his death, the throne went smoothly to Horemheb, but what happened to Ankhesenamun is still a mystery.

Tribute from Nubia coming to Tutankhamun.
Tomb of Huy (TT40)
18th Dynasty
Thebes

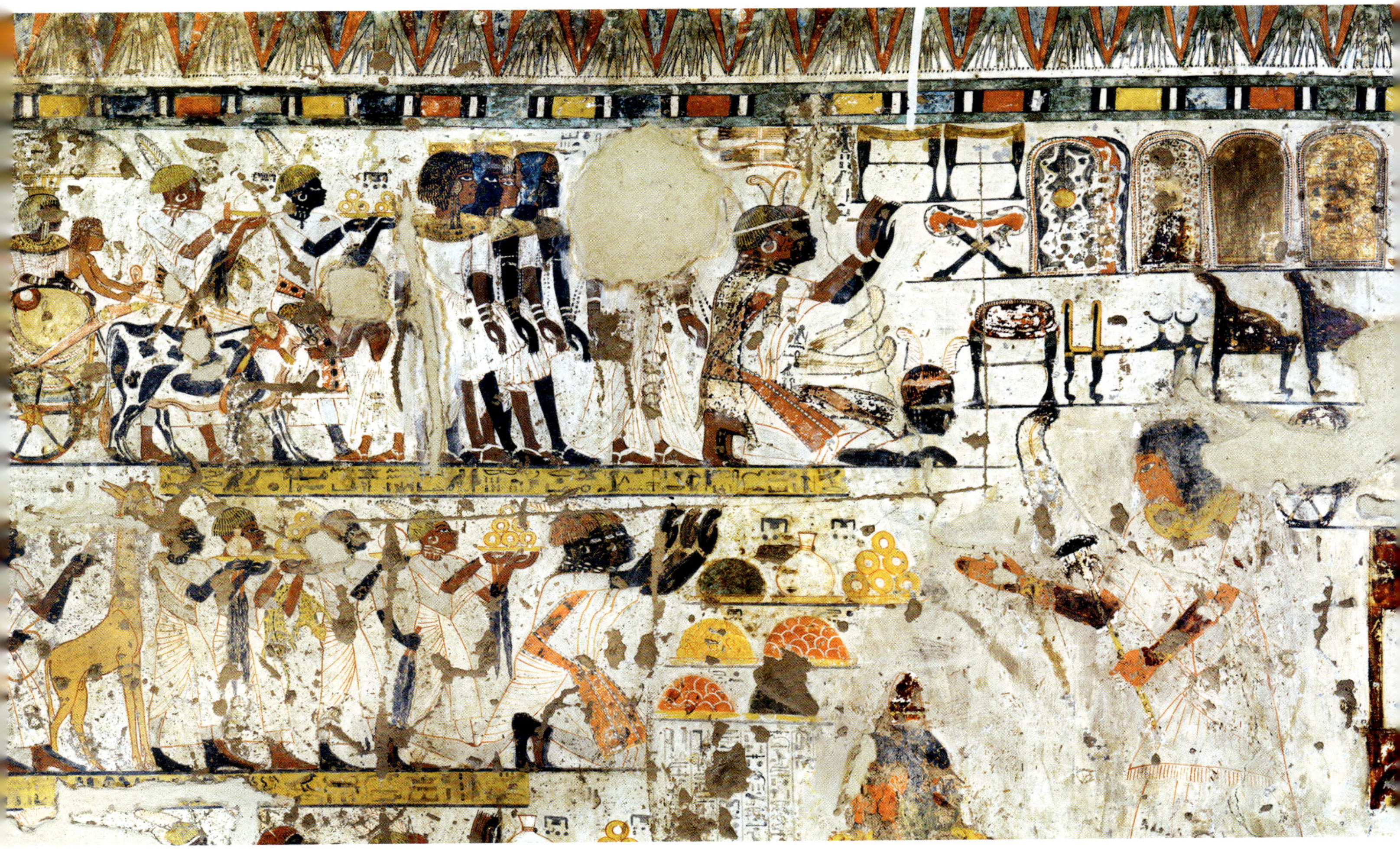

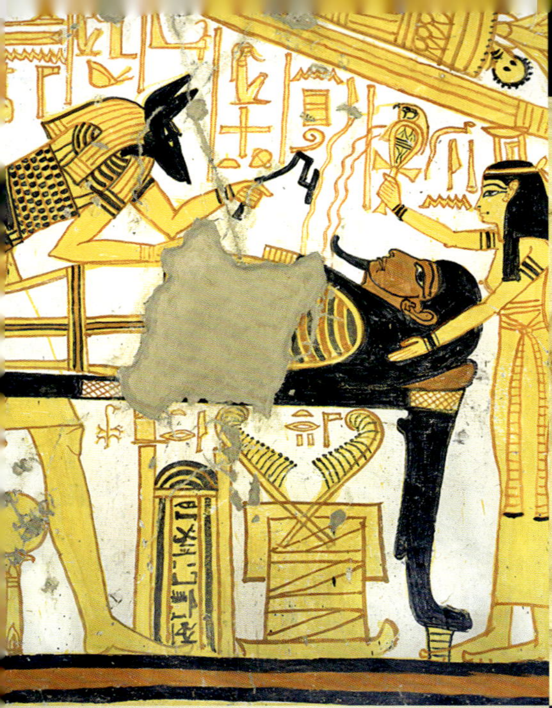
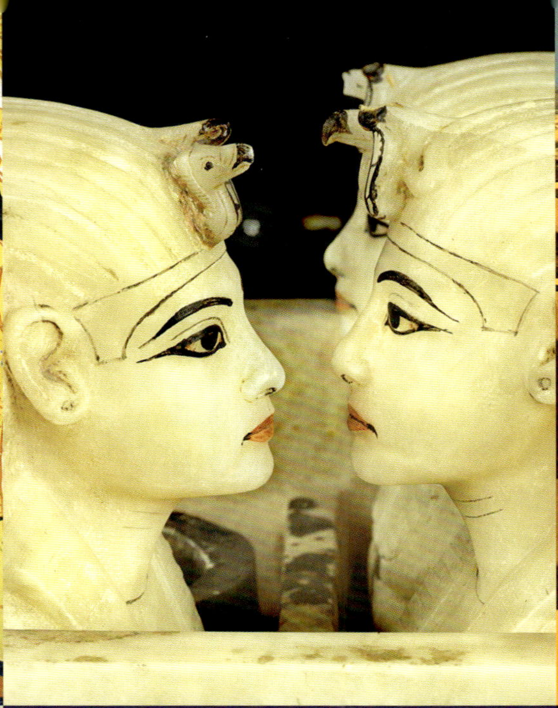
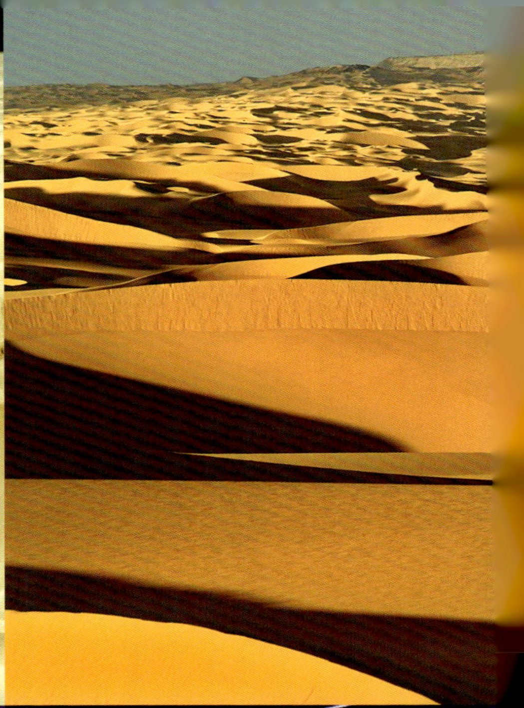
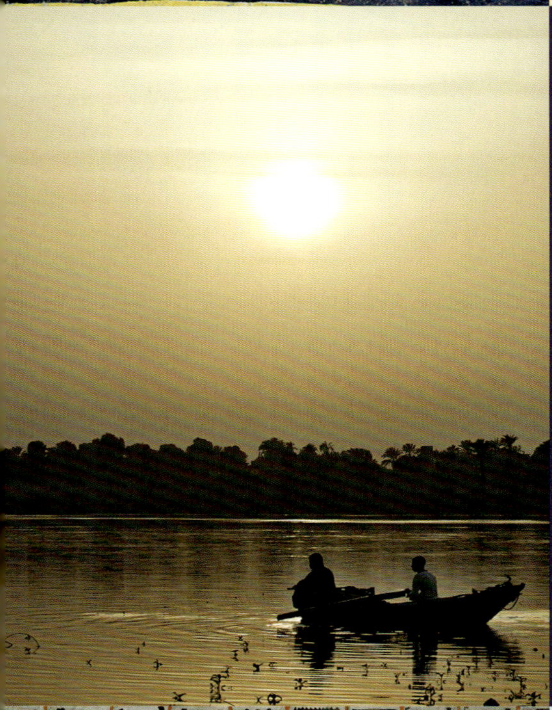

CHAPTER II

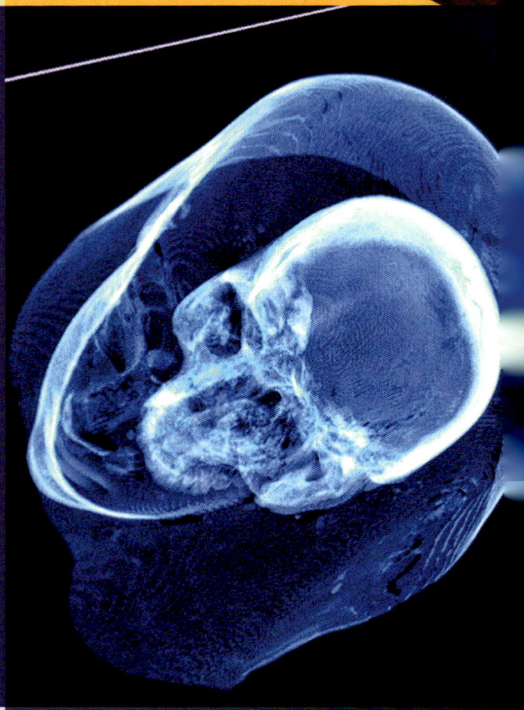
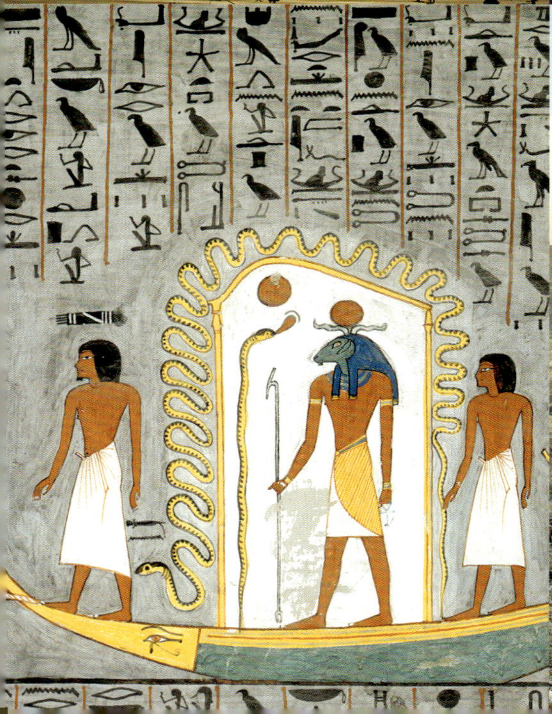
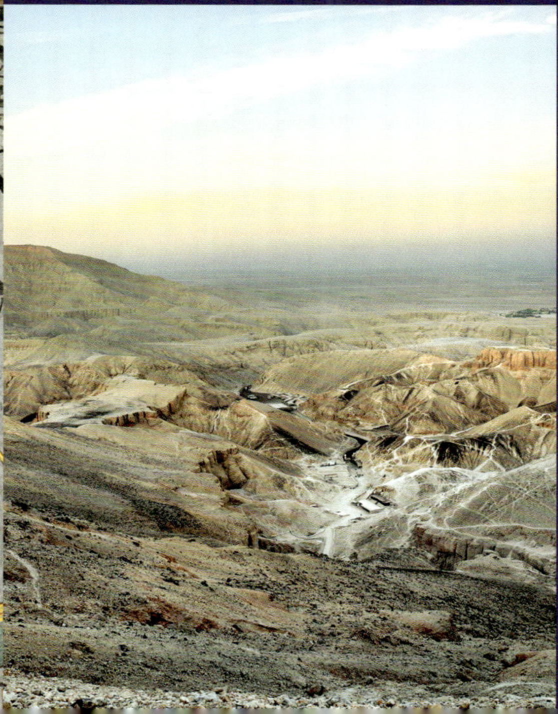
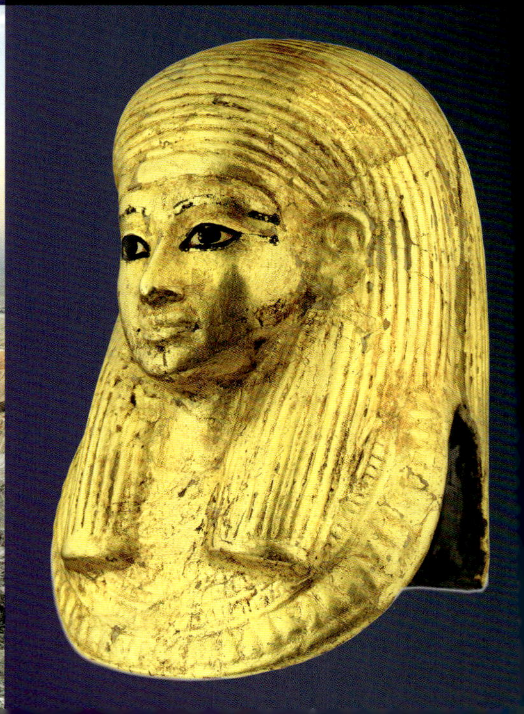

RELIGION AND LIFE AFTER DEATH

INSPIRATION

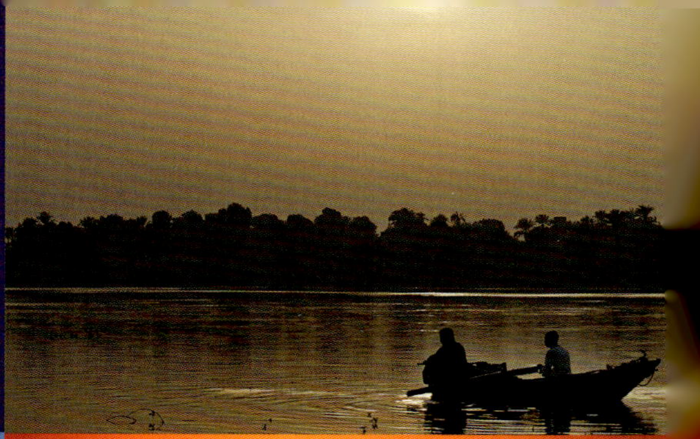

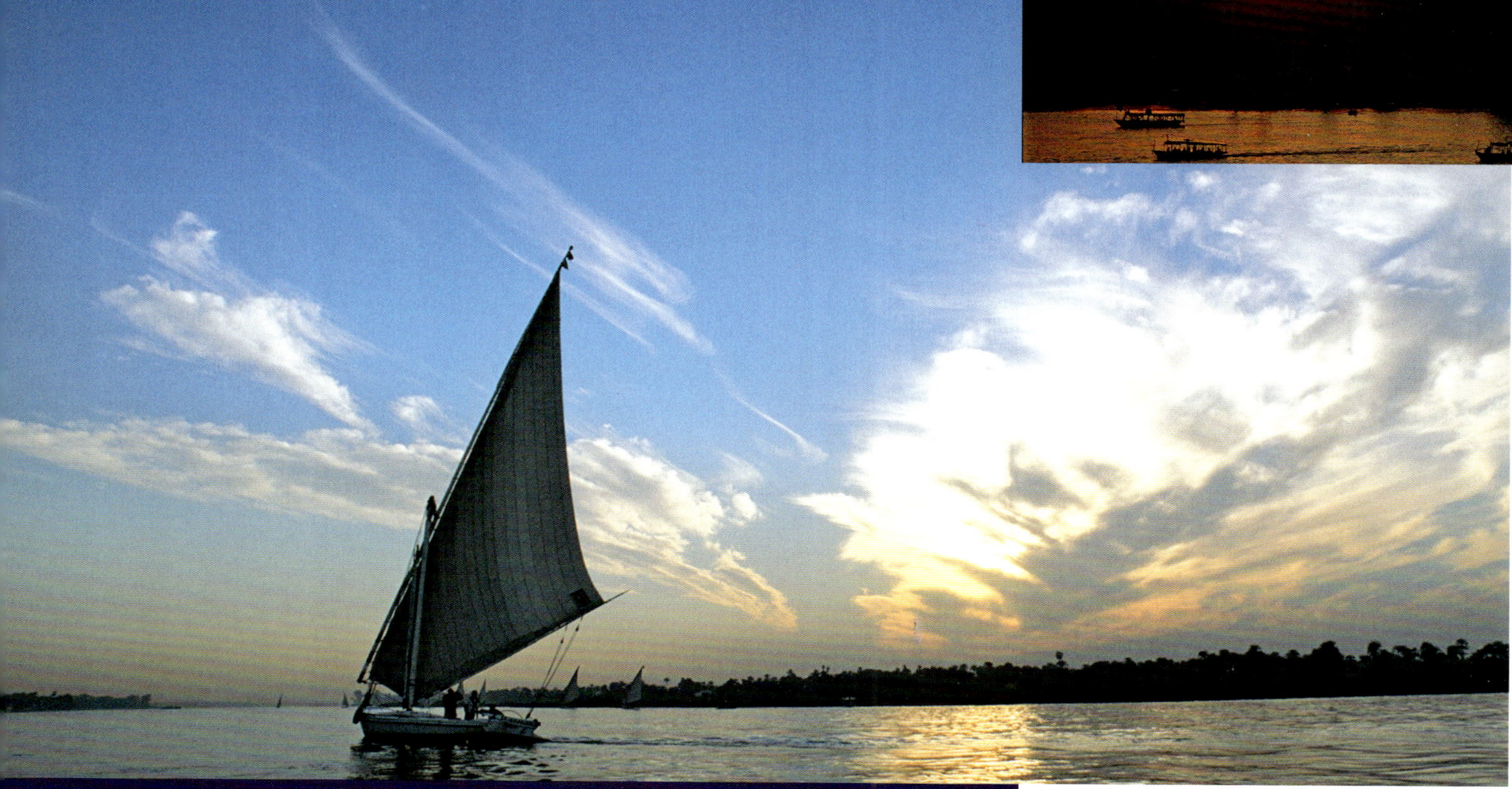

Egyptian religion, with its pantheon of hundreds of gods, sprang from the environment along the Nile River and the deserts around it. Plants, animals, and geography provided the Egyptians with the visual and literary symbolism to express sophisticated ideas about the world and the broader cosmos. The annual inundation of the valley by the river was virtually as regular as the sun rising each morning. Both of these cycles inspired the patterns of Egyptian religious thought, including the belief that human life might be cyclical, as well, and that, like sunset, death provided a passage to another stage in existence that would ultimately result in rebirth.

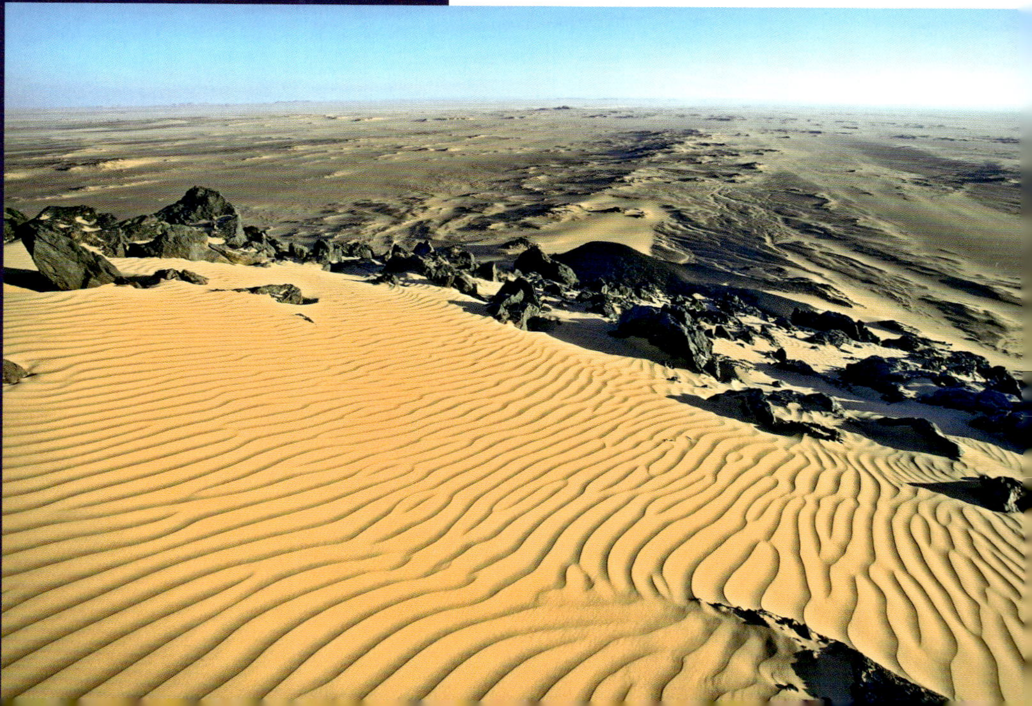

THE AFTERLIFE

By the time of the New Kingdom, an afterlife among the gods was available to all. Early in Egyptian history, this had been a royal privilege, but through the Old Kingdom and First Intermediate Period, this belief – as well as the spells required to achieve it – spread to other classes of society. Everyone was now thought to have a ***ka***, a life-force or protective spirit created at the moment of birth, that needed to be sheltered and nurtured after death. The tomb served as a place for the ***ka*** to dwell and for the living to present it with offerings, especially food and drink. The ***ba*** was another aspect of the deceased, usually depicted as a bird with a human head. As a ***ba***, the dead could depart from the tomb and visit the living, and also travel to the celestial realm and the netherworld.

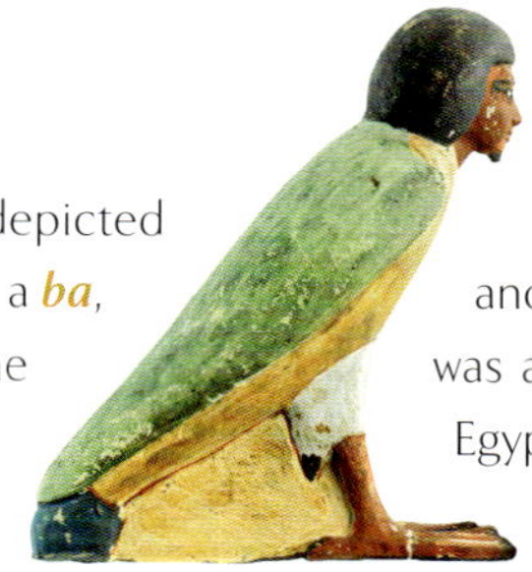

Statuette of the *ba* of Yuya
Painted wood
18th Dynasty
Egyptian Museum in Cairo

After death, the first task of a ***ba*** was to find its way to the Judgment Hall of Osiris. For most of Egyptian history, Osiris was considered the supreme god of death, king of the netherworld, but once, they believed, he had been king of the living. As the first-born offspring of the earth god Geb and the sky goddess Nut, Osiris was appointed by his father to rule Egypt. In a fit of envy, Osiris's younger brother Seth murdered him and scattered the pieces of the corpse. Osiris's sister Isis, who was also his wife, went in search of him. Once she had retrieved Osiris's body, with the help of the jackal god Anubis and other deities, Isis brought about Osiris's resurrection. Osiris became king of the dead and held court to judge each soul that reached his realm, to determine if they were worthy of an eternal afterlife or of a second, final death.

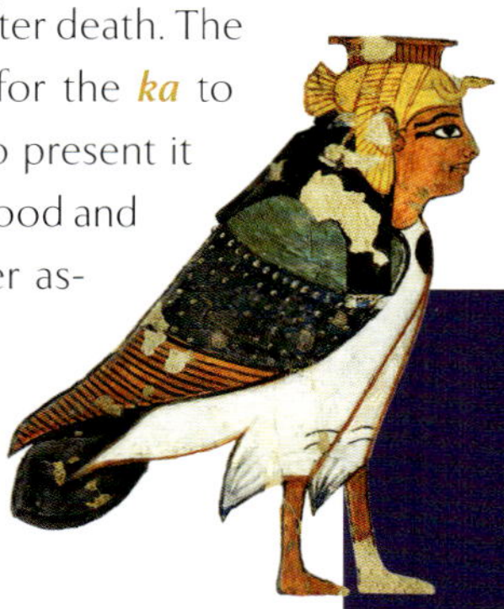

The depiction of Queen Nefertari's *ba* in her tomb (QV 66).
19th Dynasty
Thebes, Valley of the Queens

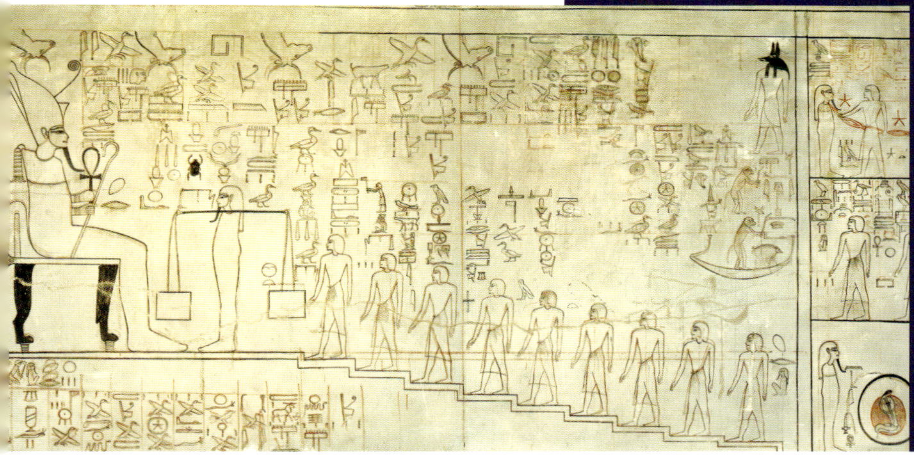

The Judgment Hall of Osiris, Lord of the Afterlife from the tomb of Horemheb (KV 57).
18th Dynasty
Thebes, Valley of the Kings

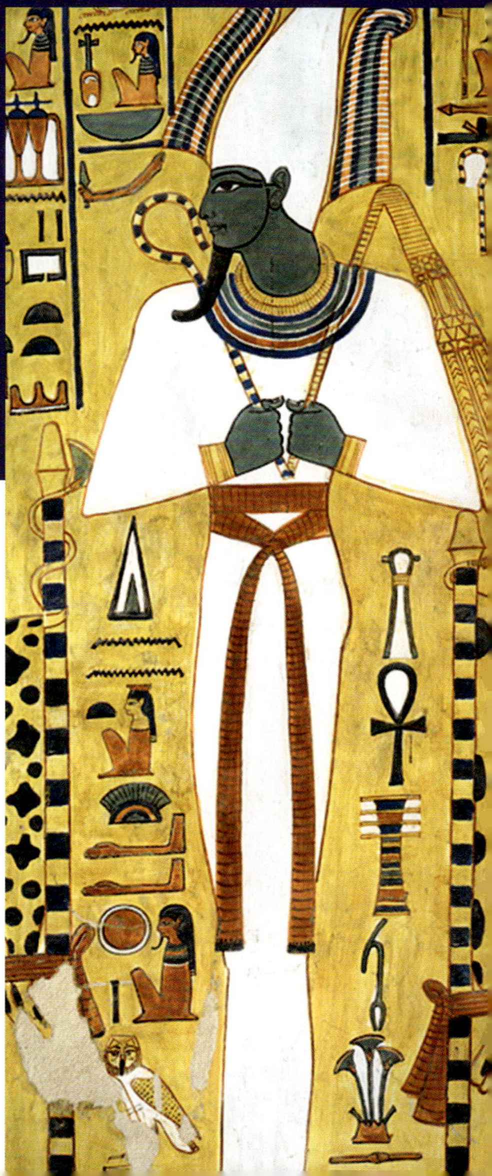

Depiction of Osiris, Lord of the Afterlife from the tomb of Queen Nefertari (QV 66).
19th Dynasty
Thebes, Valley of the Queens

Osiris did not do this alone. Forty-two divine judges sat nearby to receive a "negative confession" from the deceased, who would declare that he (or she) had not committed a list of crimes. Anubis tended the scales where the heart of the dead was weighed against Maat, the goddess of truth and cosmic order, often represented as an ostrich feather. Thoth, the divine scribe and god of wisdom, who appeared as a baboon or an ibis-headed man, recorded the judgment. Anyone who failed this test was denied entry into the Blessed Fields and met some terrible, ultimate end, such as being devoured by a female monster named Ammut, "Eater of the Dead."

This transition from life to afterlife did not happen on its own. The Egyptians prepared elaborate rituals to facilitate this process and to unite the ***ka*** and the ***ba*** after death so that the deceased could become an ***akh***, a transfigured spirit who would have a place in the netherworld. This required the preservation of the body, accomplished by mummification.

MUMMIFICATION

The CT Scan of the mummy of Tutankhamun confirmed the existence of the brain in the skull.
Archive Zahi Hawass

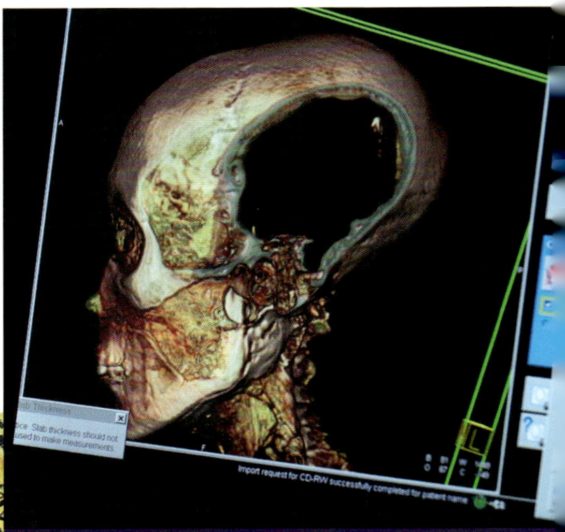

Natural mummification inspired the Egyptians to mummify their dead. During the Predynastic Period (4800–3050 B.C.), before Egypt was unified, a corpse was covered with a reed mat or animal skin and laid in a shallow grave in the desert, positioned to face the rising sun. The heat and aridity of the desert desiccated the body, preserving its features. When the higher classes of society developed new burial customs that placed the body in a wooden coffin, it was necessary to preserve the body through artificial means. The first attempts were made by the 2nd Dynasty, or perhaps even earlier.

The mummies themselves provide us with the most valuable information about how the ancient embalmers went about creating them. There are some ancient written sources and a very few ancient images of the process. Archaeology has revealed some of the equipment, from beds to tools, used in the processes. Modern experimentation has also yielded insights.

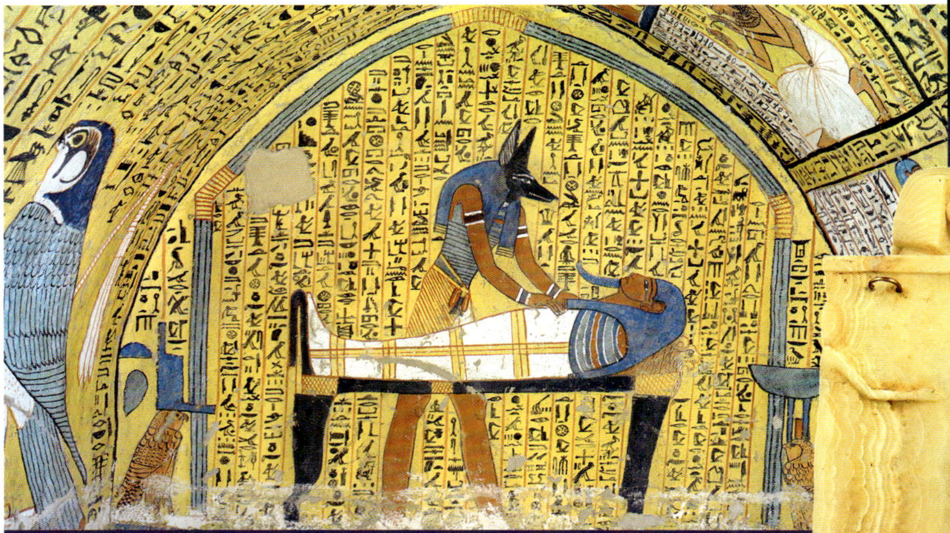

Anubis, Lord of the necropolis and mummification, finishing his work on the tomb owner's mummy.
Tomb of Khaemteri (TT220)
19th Dynasty
Thebes, Deir el-Medina

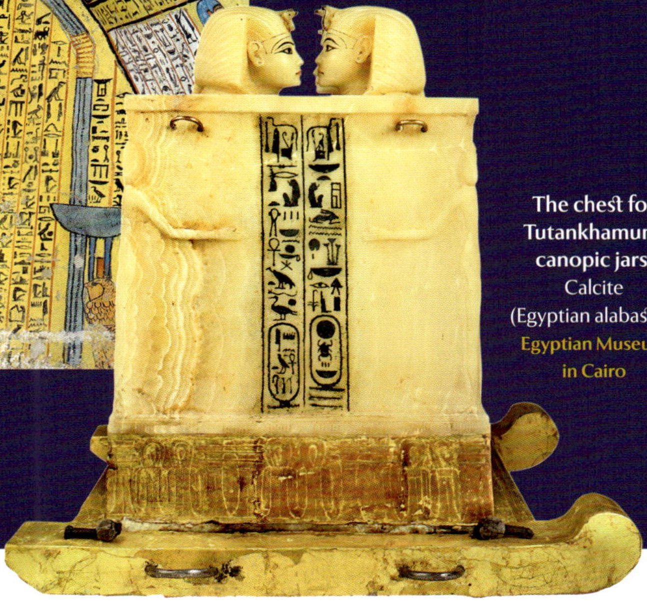

The chest for Tutankhamun's canopic jars.
Calcite
(Egyptian alabaster)
Egyptian Museum in Cairo

The ancient embalmers had to experiment, as well. In the Old Kingdom, a body was wrapped in linen bandages and covered with plaster, which was then "molded" and painted to create the appearance of the body. The art evolved, but of course not everyone could afford the best mummification available, and most people could not afford to be mummified at all. By the time of the New Kingdom, the well-to-do of society would have their body preserved much as I am about to describe.

The body, once it was cleansed, was brought to the embalming workshop, which was called, somewhat euphemistically, either the "pure place" or the "good house." The brain was removed usually by breaking the ethmoid bone (between the brain and the nasal cavity) and inserting a tool through the nose. This tool of either metal or wood was swished around vigorously inside the skull. The embalmers then tipped the body so that the liquefied brain ran out through the nose. This was done because the brain decayed easily and, protected by the skull, would not be dried out by the mummification process. Nonetheless, it was not always performed, even on kings. A recent study of the royal mummies performed with CT scans revealed that several kings, including Thutmose II and Thutmose III, still had brain tissue in their skulls after they were mummified. There was no indication that any attempt had been made to remove this organ.

To facilitate removal of internal organs from the torso, the embalmers made an incision in the abdomen. (The exact location varied in time.) The stomach, intestines, lungs, and liver were removed through this slit. All these organs were dried with natron (a natural mixture of hydrated sodium carbonate, sodium bicarbonate, and some other salts), wrapped, and either put back into the body or placed in canopic jars to be included in the burial.

One organ that was always left in the chest (sometimes after having been embalmed) was the heart. This was considered to be the most important organ, the seat of intelligence.

After the removal of the organs, the body was ready for the next step. The eviscerated corpse was washed out with water and wine. Then the embalmers filled up the cavity with linen, natron, frankincense, and myrrh. These helped the body to dry out while also recreating some of its bulk, so that it would emerge from the desiccation process appearing somewhat more lifelike. Artificial eyes of stone, glass, or wood were sometimes inserted, and the body was sometimes given cosmetic treatments. The hair might receive henna dye, for example. Arms were set in certain positions, depending on if the body was royal or not. Then the embalmers heaped natron on the body, which dried for another 40 or so days.

At this point, the embalmers began to wrap the mummy in linen bandages. This was a highly ritualized process that took place over 15 days. Arms were wrapped separately. Each finger was bandaged and, for royalty, covered in a stall made of gold. Legs were individually wrapped, too, before being bound together. Embalmers enveloped the head and the entire body in many meters of linen strips. Throughout the process, amulets

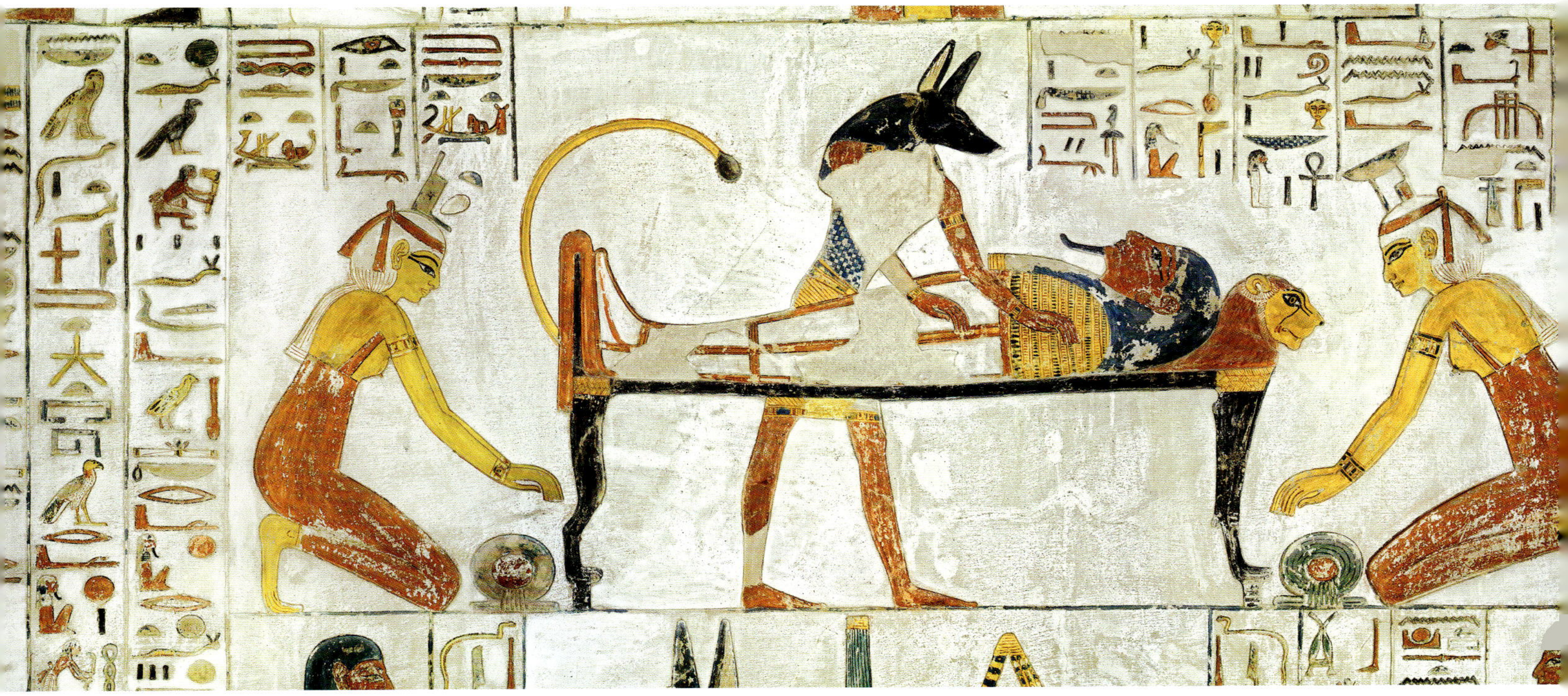

Anubis embalming a king with the godesses Isis (left) and Nephthys (right).
Tomb of Siptah (KV 47)
19th Dynasty,
Thebes, Valley of the Kings

and other forms of protective jewelry, often made of gold with semiprecious stones, were included among the wrappings at specific points. Finally, for royalty or other wealthy members of society, a gold or gilded mask encased the head.

The entire procedure took 70 days. This may have been less a matter of practicality and more a matter of ritual, associated with the 70 days when the star Sirius disappeared below the horizon. The Egyptians believed that during this time the star, known to them as the goddess Sopdet and to the Greeks as Sothis, was immersed in the primordial waters known as Nun. Sopdet's reappearance was timed with the beginning of the Nile's annual flood.

Mummification was, in fact, an extremely elaborate ritual during which spells were read aloud. Embalmers were priests, and at times procedures were carried out by an embalmer wearing a mask in the shape of a jackal's head, so that he could act as Anubis. With mummification complete, the body was ready for a new set of rituals.

THE FUNERAL

A proper funeral was so important to the Egyptians that it is mentioned as a reward for the hero in the Middle Kingdom *Story of Sinuhe*:

"A funeral procession is made for you on the day of the burial; the mummy case is of gold, its head of lapis lazuli. The sky is above you as you lie in the hearse, oxen drawing you, musicians going before you. The dance of the muu-dancers is done at the door of your tomb; the offering is read to you, sacrifice is made before your offering stone."

The mummy was placed in its coffin and dragged on a sledge either by oxen or by men to the tomb, along with the goods that were to be interred with the body. Relatives attended the procession. Women acted as mourners, tearing at their clothing, throwing dust on their heads, and collapsing in grief. These might have been genuine emotions, but some of them were professional mourners, hired to intensify the display. A pair of women played the part of Isis and Nephthys, Osiris's divine sisters who were responsible for finding his body and achieving his resurrection.

A priest performed the complex rituals of the Opening of the Mouth ceremony at the entrance of the tomb. This was, at least in the ideal case, the eldest son of the deceased, acting as Horus, the son of Osiris and Isis, who inherited the crowns of Egypt

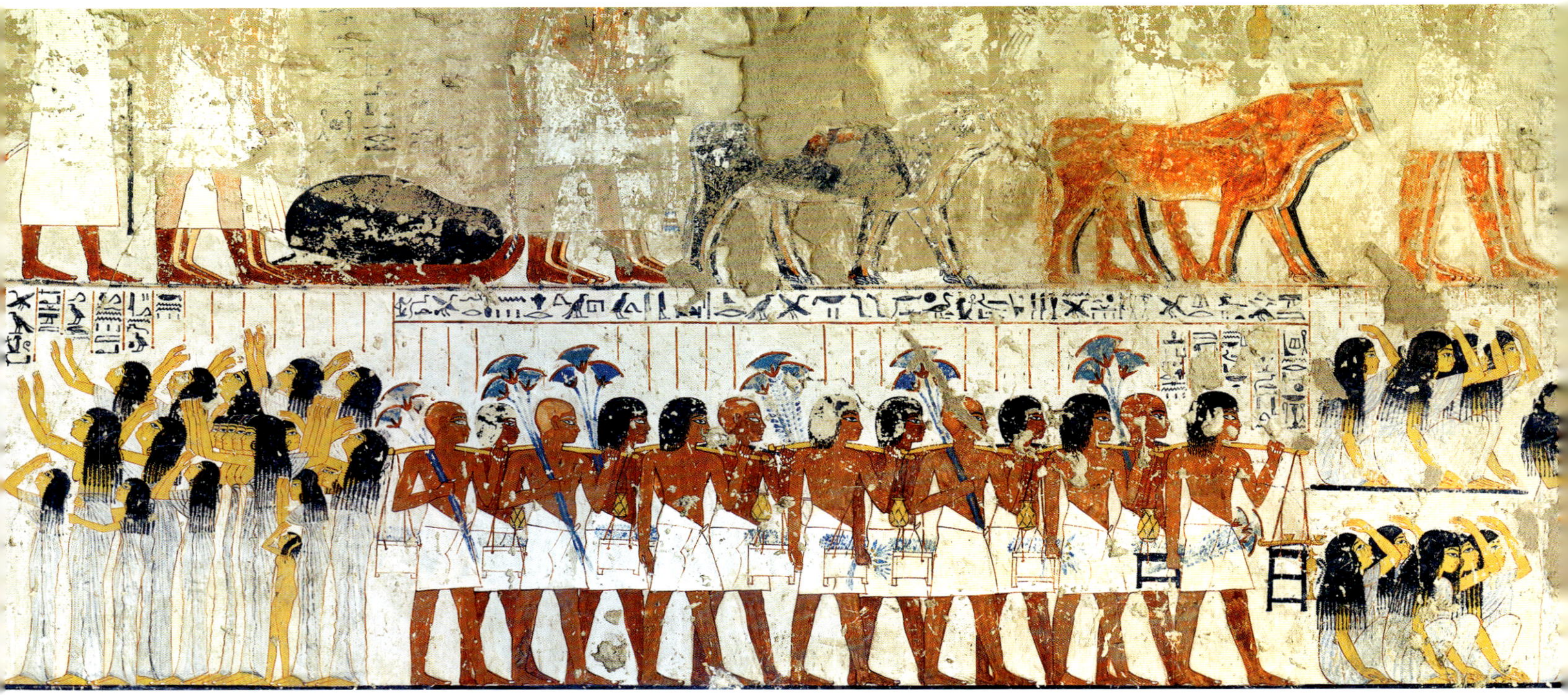

Funeral of the vizier Ramose accompanied by a group of professional mourners.
Tomb of Ramose (TT55)
18th Dynasty
Luxor

from his father only after he overthrew a usurper, his father's brother, Seth. When the mouth, eyes, nose, and ears of the mummy, or other images of the deceased, were touched with certain implements, the deceased regained these senses and the *ba* could return. The mummy and the grave goods were taken into the tomb. When all was complete, the tomb was sealed and its shaft or entrance corridor was blocked with rubble and dirt to deter thieves.

There then followed a funerary feast enjoyed not only by the living, but the dead as well. This would not be the last time the family would visit the tomb. At various times of the year, the tomb chapel was the site of celebration and sharing meals with the souls of the dead, who remained part of the family. The dead were expected to help the living who provided for their needs by interceding with the gods or unfriendly spirits. To keep the dead properly equipped, the wealthy might endow land to support a funerary priest (often one of their relatives, so the property remained in the family) to perpetuate their cult and provide them with offerings, hypothetically forever.

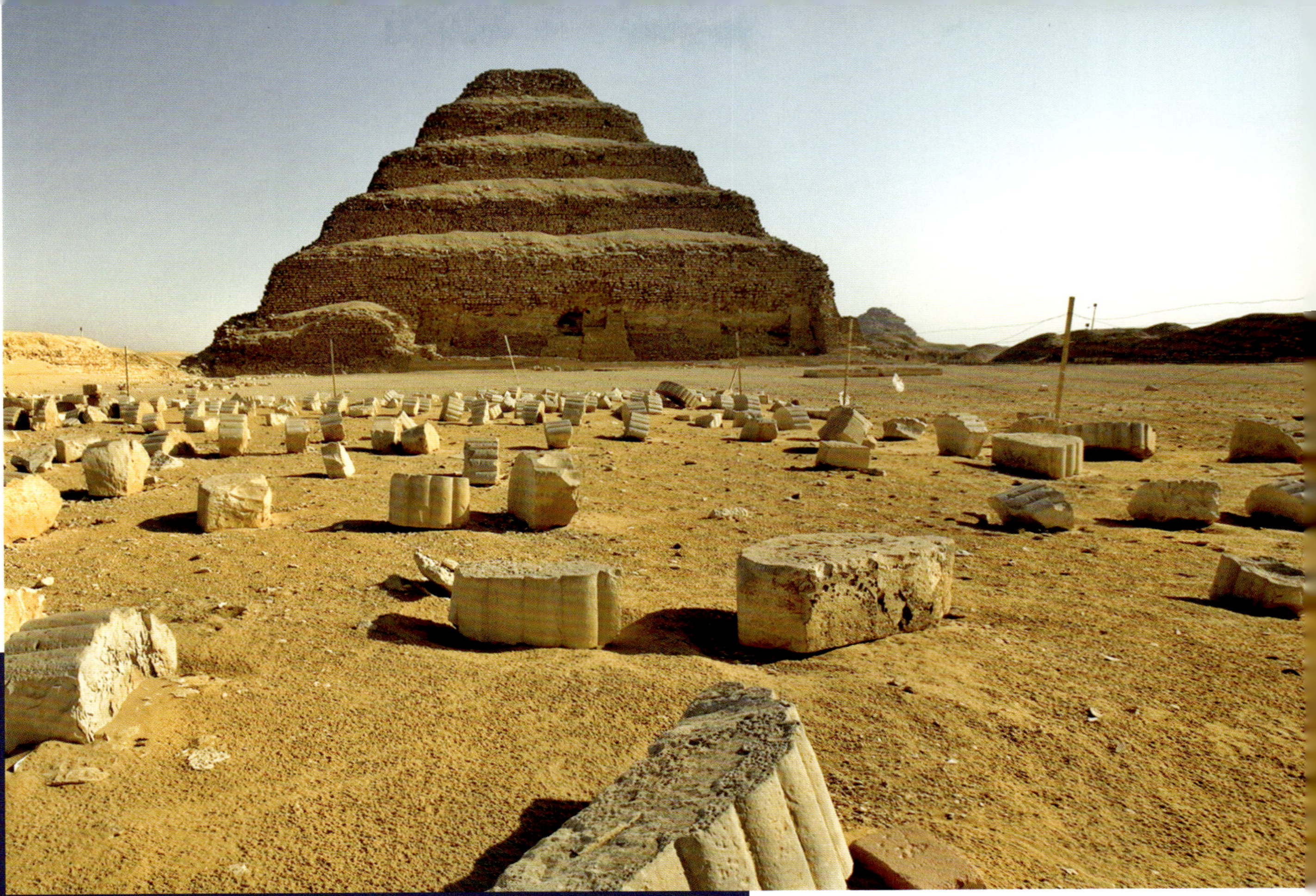

The Step Pyramid of Djoser.
3rd Dynasty
Saqqara

THE ROYAL TOMBS: PYRAMIDS

The tomb was, of course, a vital part of the equipment that the deceased needed to arrive in the afterlife. This was perhaps particularly important for kings, whose tombs went through dramatic developments throughout Egyptian history.

In the earliest dynasties, the tombs of kings at Abydos evoked the primeval mound, the first bit of land that arose from the watery chaos at the time of creation. These royal tombs were brick-lined pits covered by a mound of sand. At Saqqara, flat-topped mud-brick tombs known as mastabas ("benches") mimicked the royal palace, where the deceased could dwell.

From these relatively simple tombs, truly monumental pyramid complexes evolved in the 3rd Dynasty, giving rise to the Pyramid Age. Like the funerary mounds at Abydos, these pyramids symbolized the primordial mound, the *benben*.

The first of these was the Step Pyramid, designed by the architect Imhotep for his king, Djoser (2687–2667 BC). The first true pyramids followed soon thereafter. About a hundred years after Djoser, Khufu constructed the Great Pyramid, largest of them all, at Giza.

Pyramids of the Old Kingdom were constructed of stone. Kings of the Middle Kingdom made theirs mostly of mud brick. They learned hard-won lessons from their predecessors. They knew that the pyramids of the earlier dynasties had been robbed too easily, so they set about thwarting the thieves by hiding the entrances and constructing passages that would be filled by enormous blocks after the burial party had left.

THE VALLEY OF THE KINGS: ARCHITECTURE FOR THE AFTERLIFE

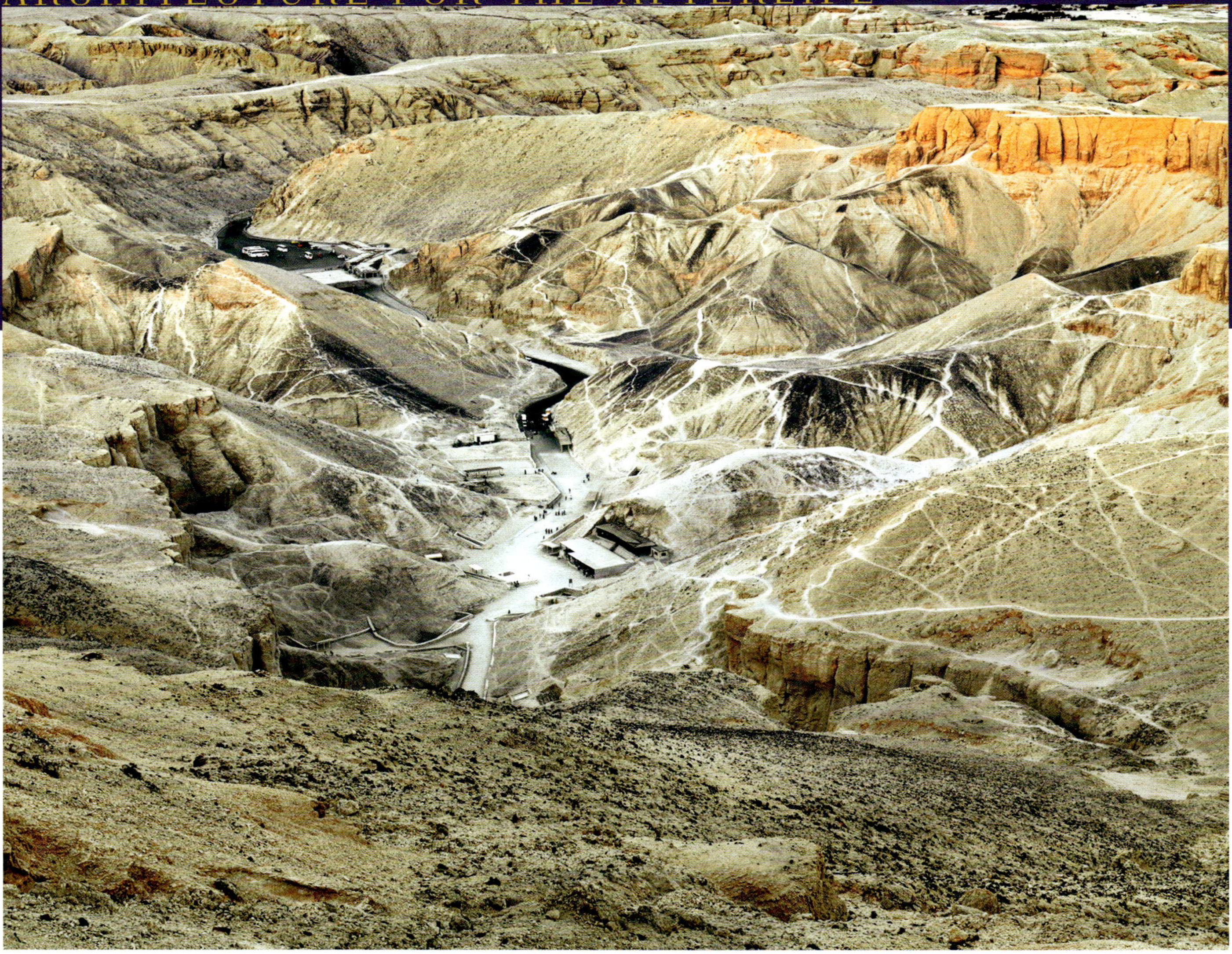

Thebes, the Valley of the Kings.
The final resting place of Egypt's pharaohs of the New Kingdom, represents the largest royal cemetery in the world.

By the New Kingdom, kings knew that even the elaborate precautions used to safeguard the Middle Kingdom pyramids were not enough. A monumental tomb was simply too obvious a target for tomb-robbers. So they instead elected to hide their tombs in the desert hills that lay to the west of Thebes, which was the center of the cult of Amun, chief god of the state. There was even a pyramid-shaped hill, known today as el-Qurn, "the Horn," and nearby peaks were reminiscent of a recumbent cow, suggesting the great goddess Hathor, who was closely connected with kingship and the afterlife. This area remained the royal necropolis from the 18th through the 20th Dynasties, with the exception of the reign of Akhenaten, who rejected all things connected with Amun.

The tombs of the royal Theban necropolis (which includes the Valley of the Kings, the Valley of the Queens, and the Valley of the Monkeys or Western Valley) were quarried into the hillsides, either high up a cliff face or at the valley floor. No two are alike, but each was carefully designed, running more or less from east to west, mirroring the daily passage of the sun. Every corridor and room had a special purpose. As a whole, the tomb offered the king a path or gateway to the afterlife.

Archaeologists have numbered the tombs in the order in which they were found. The earliest constructed was probably KV 20, a fairly simple tomb consisting of a long shaft ending in a burial chamber with some roughly hewn side chambers and three storerooms. This was created for Thutmose I or perhaps for his daughter, Hatshepsut. This queen's coregent, Thutmose III, had a far more elaborate tomb, KV 34, with descending stairways, a ritual well shaft, a pillared hall, and a pillared burial chamber shaped like a cartouche (the oval coil of rope in which royal names were written). Its route is not straight but angles down, and its axis turns 90 degrees at the first pillared chamber.

Some tombs have provisions for the burial of other royal family members. Amenhotep III's tomb (KV 22) had rooms for his daughter Sitamun and wife Tiye. (However, when Tiye died, she was buried in the tomb of her son Akhenaten at Amarna.)

A few tombs in the Valley of the Kings were not occupied by royalty. Tiye's parents, Yuya and Tjuya, were given KV 46, a small tomb with no decoration. The tomb occupied by Tutankhamun, KV 62, was built for someone other than the young king, who was probably intended to be buried in KV 23, which was not yet ready at the time of his death. KV 62 has very little decoration, which is unusual for its time. Early in the 18th Dynasty, decoration was confined to the burial chamber, but this had changed by the reign of Thutmose III, when other chambers were adorned with scenes of gods and sacred texts. Some tombs had a chamber with an image of the night sky.

KV 23 was occupied by Tutankhamun's successor, Ay. Ay's tomb has features that are unusual for a royal tomb of the period. One is the unique inclusion of a scene of marsh hunting. Also, unlike most earlier royal tombs in the valley, Ay's has a straight axis. In this respect it resembles the tomb of Akhenaten at Amarna, and this trait was adopted for all other royal tombs in the valley. Ay's successor, Horemheb, also had a tomb in the Valley of the Kings, although he had another grand tomb built at Saqqara when he was still just a courtier of Tutankhamun. Horemheb's tomb in the valley has brightly painted relief.

Through the 18th Dynasty, these tombs had hidden entrances. After that time, the tomb builders no longer took the trouble. However, unlike private tombs, the cult of the dead king was celebrated not at the tomb itself but in a temple near the floodplain. The Egyptians called these "temples of millions of years," and here the king was worshipped not only after death but during life. The remains of most of the 18th Dynasty funerary temples have all but disappeared, but Hatshepsut's at Deir el-Bahari remains a spectacular example.

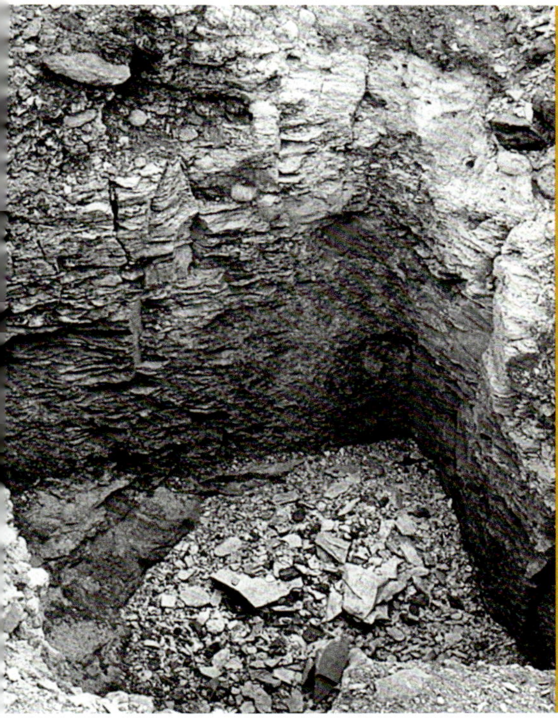

Archival photograph of KV 54: Thebes, the Valley of the Kings.
Zahi Hawass Photo Archive

In 1907, a British archaeologist named Edward Ayrton discovered a small "tomb," the 54th to be discovered in the Valley of the Kings. It was an open pit about 1.5 m deep that measured 1.25 m × 1.9 m. It contained no mummy and no objects of precious materials. Instead it held storage jars that were found to contain bits and pieces of other pottery vessels, fragments of animal bones, linen bags of natron, elaborate collars of flowers and leaves, and a miniature mask made of gilded cartonnage (a sort of ancient papier-maché made of papyrus and plaster). There were also pieces of linen dating to the sixth and eighth year of Tutankhamun.

These objects were of no real interest to Ayrton or his patron, the American millionaire Theodore Davis. But H. E. Winlock, of the Metropolitan Museum of Art, recognized their importance. Winlock suggested that the pit contained the remains of Tutankhamun's mummification and the funerary banquet, things that he believed needed to be buried away from the tomb because they were ritually dangerous.

It is now known that these objects had originally been buried very close to Tutankhamun's tomb – at the entrance. After robbers broke into the tomb, officials of the necropolis decided to remove these objects and bury them elsewhere before blocking the tomb entrance with debris.

BURIAL EQUIPMENT

The effectiveness of mummification and tomb architecture were further supplemented by the inclusion of objects in the tomb. Most of these did not survive the looting of tomb robbers and other intruders. Of all the royal tombs, only Tutankhamun's survived intact with most of its equipment, although pieces from others demonstrate that they, too, once included such treasures. Each king's would have been a little different, designed for his specific use.

These included the nest of coffins, sarcophagus, and shrines that surrounded and protected the king's body. Tutankhamun's were particularly spectacular, as will be seen in Chapter 4. Compared to his, those of other kings can be disappointing. Neither the coffin of Thutmose III nor the finely carved one used by later priests for the rescued mummy of Rameses II (which was probably made for Horemheb or Ay) retains any of the original gilding. These had been stripped of their gold in antiquity.

The dead king's mummified organs were placed in the tomb so that his body would be complete and he would have use of their functions. Servant statues (***shabtis***) would allow him to avoid being called to labor in the afterlife, while other statues – either of the gods or of the king – performed protective functions. Objects from the king's daily life, ranging from clothing to games to chariots to food and drink, would give him access to all the necessities of life in the netherworld.

Tutankhamun's antechamber with its precious funerary equipment.
Harry Burton / Griffith Institute

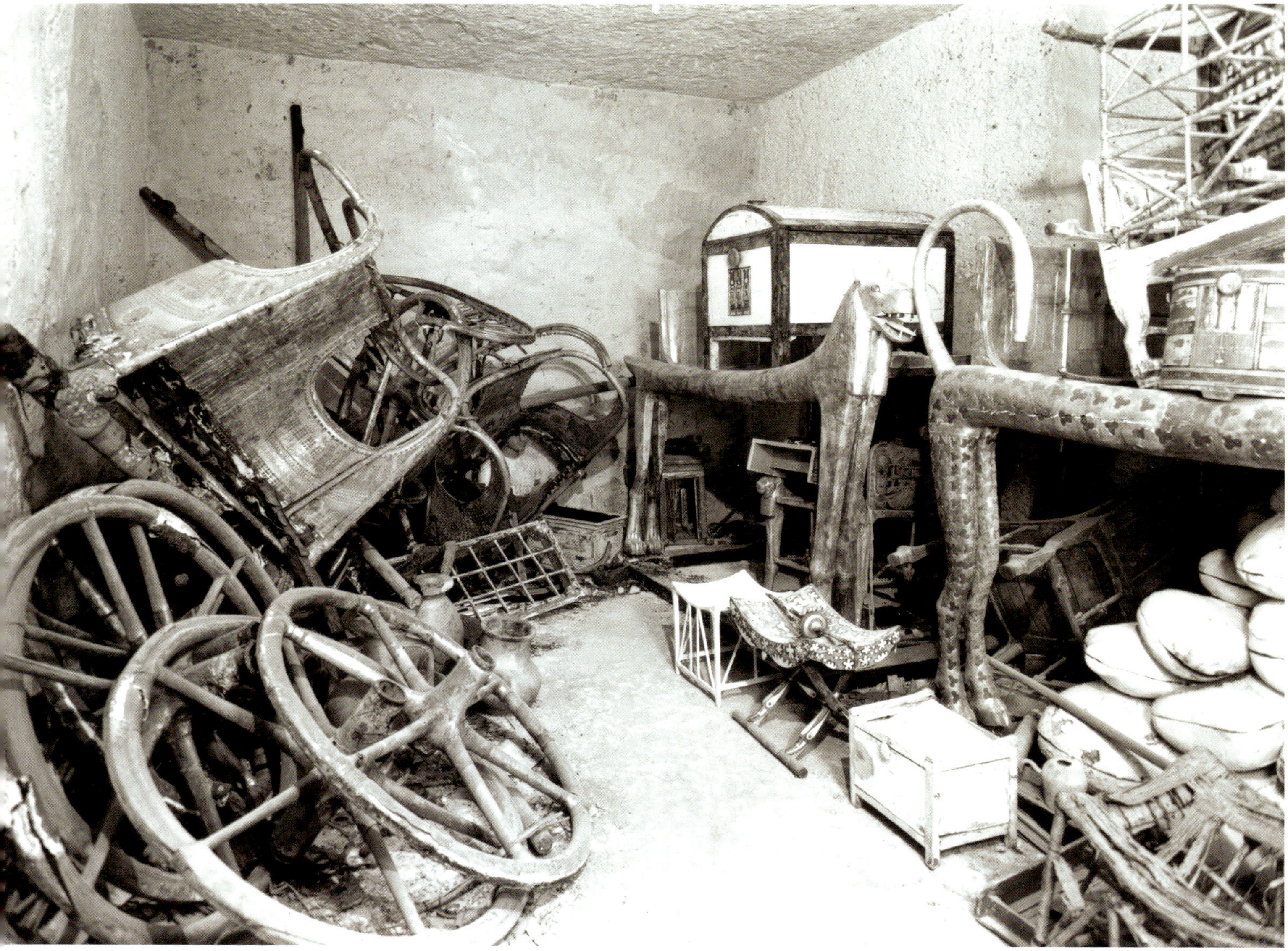

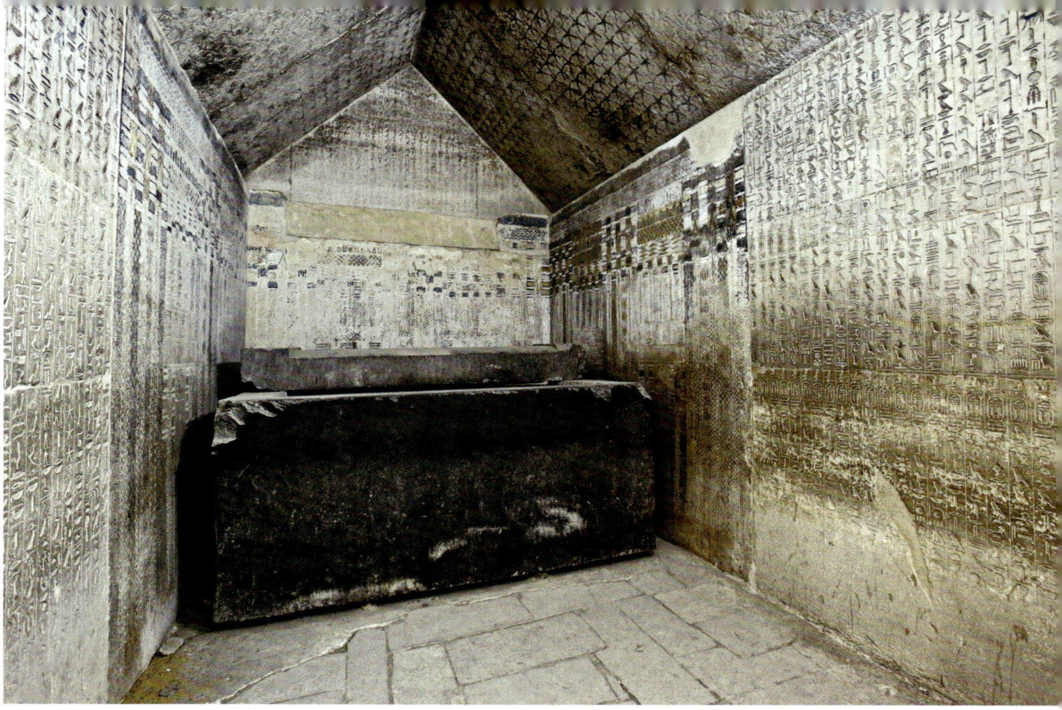

The burial chamber of King Unas adorned with the Pyramid Texts.
End of 5th Dynasty
Saqqara

RELIGIOUS TEXTS

Religious texts provided the king with one more resource to achieve his eternal life.

The earliest preserved examples come from the 5th and 6th Dynasties: the Pyramid Texts, inscribed on the interior walls of the royal tombs to help the king's soul join the gods in the sky and navigate the dangers of the netherworld. These passed into the hands of private persons to become the Coffin Texts of the First Intermediate Period and Middle Kingdom. Now, it was not just the king who could identify himself with the sun god Re and become Osiris after death.

By the New Kingdom these had become spells popularly known today as the ***Book of the Dead***, but known to the Egyptians as the ***Chapters of Coming Forth by Day***. These were written on papyri, the walls of tombs, coffins, and other objects. Some texts, depicting the nocturnal voyage of the sun god Re through the netherworld, were largely reserved for royal tombs.

The ***Imy Duat***, or ***Amduat*** (the ***Book of What is in the Netherworld***), describes the nightly journey of the sun god Re through the 12 hours of night, a voyage also undertaken by the king.

The west wall of Tutankhamun's burial chamber is decorated with an abbreviated version of the first hour of night. In the upper register, Khepri (the sun in the form of a scarab) is in the morning barque, preceded by five deities: Maat, the "Mistress of the Barque," Horus, Kashu, and Nehes. Below are 12 baboons rejoicing at the appearance of the sun. These animals were sacred to Thoth in his guise as a lunar god and were connected with the sun by their well-documented habit of turning to face the sunrise and barking at dawn. The second and sixth divisions of night (and other spells) appear on the walls of the

The great royal wife, mistress of the two lands Nefertari asks the god Thoth for the mysterious equipment.
Tomb of Nefertari (QV66).
19th Dynasty
Thebes, Valley of the Queens

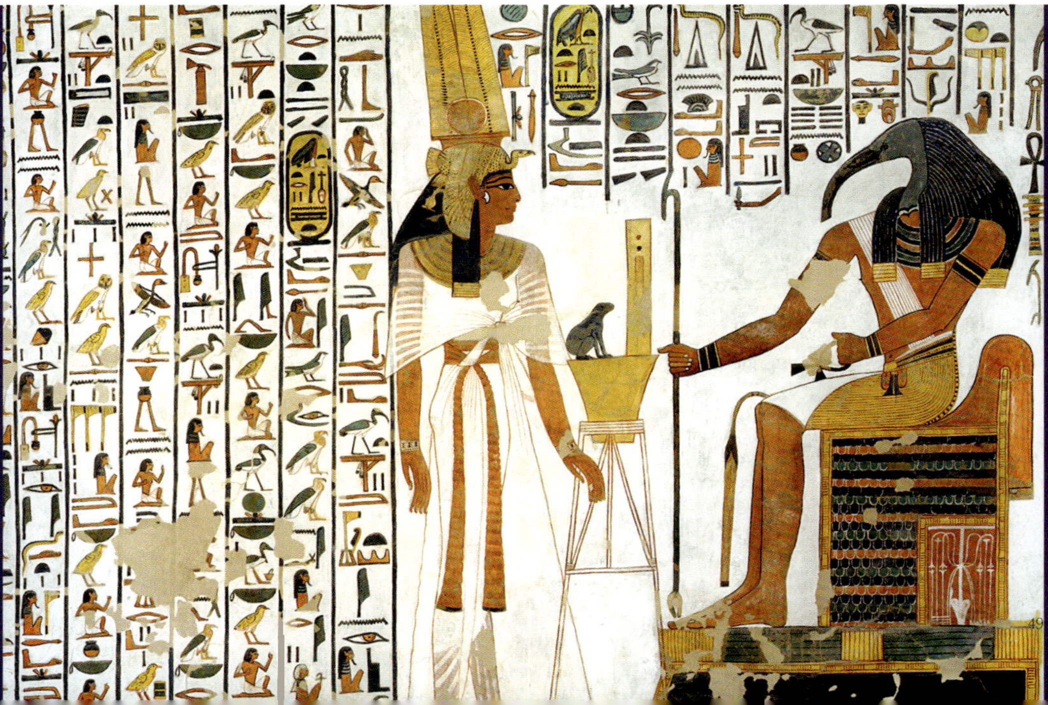

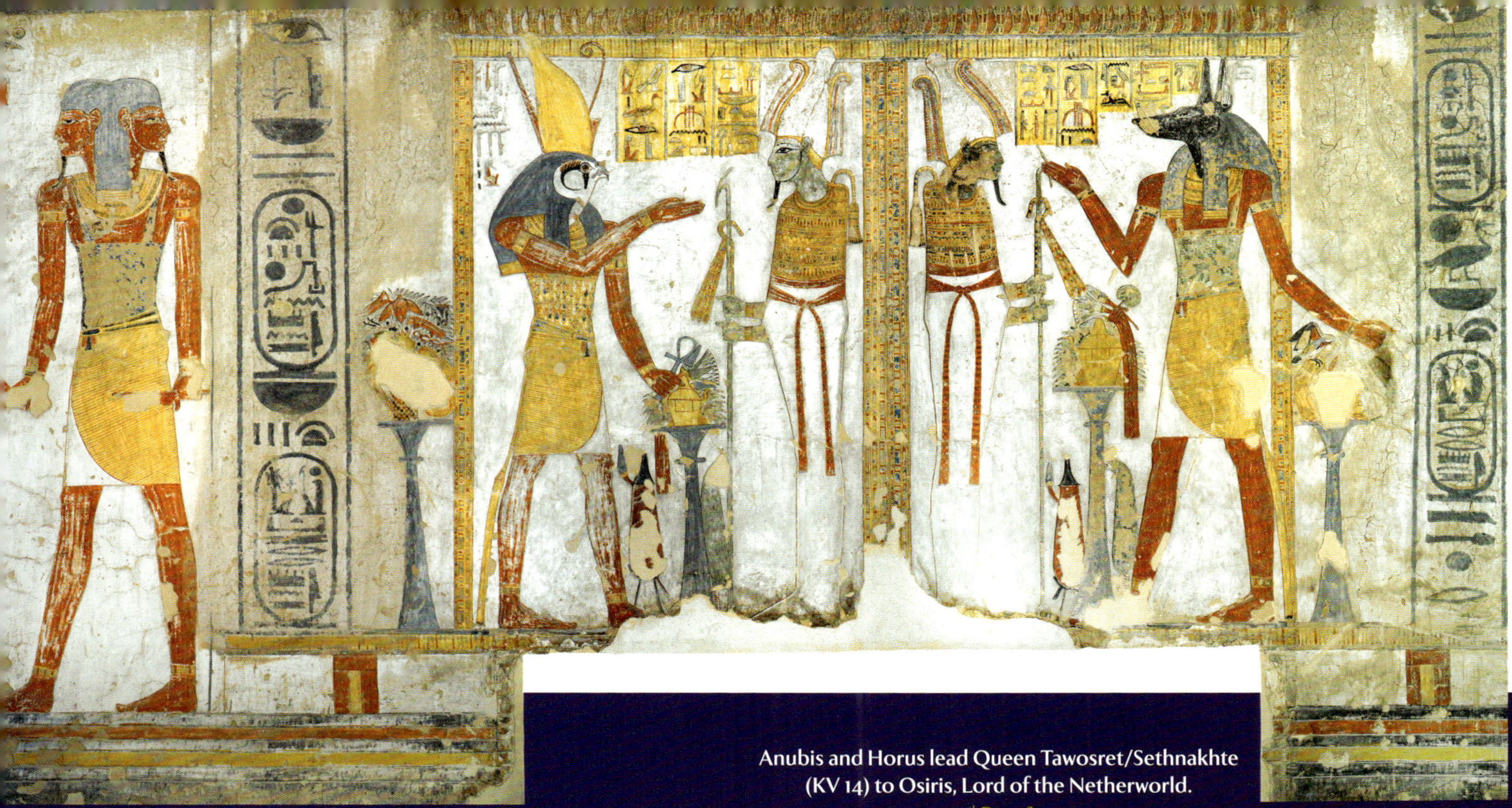

Anubis and Horus lead Queen Tawosret/Sethnakhte (KV 14) to Osiris, Lord of the Netherworld.
19th Dynasty
Thebes, Valley of the Queens

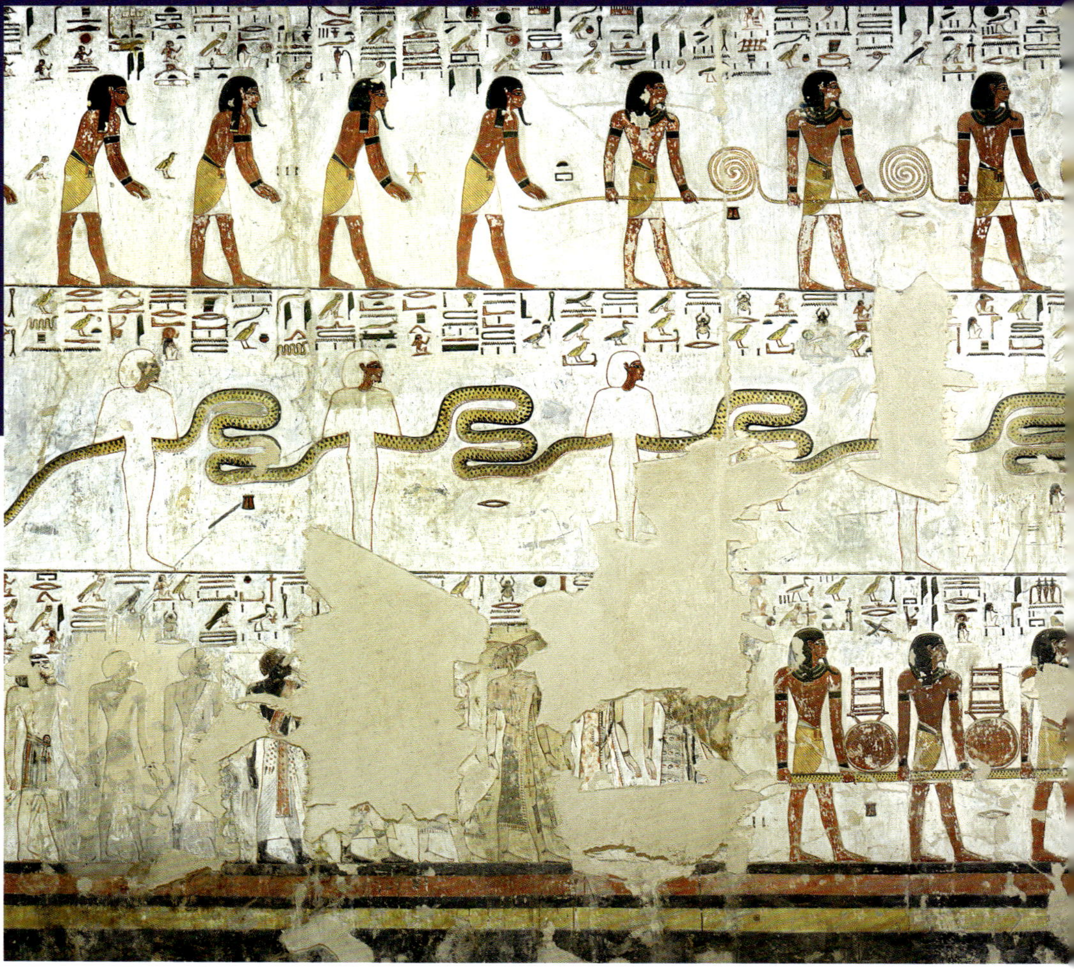

The fifth hour of the *Book of Gates*.
Tomb of Seti I (KV 17)
19th Dynasty
Thebes, Valley of the Kings

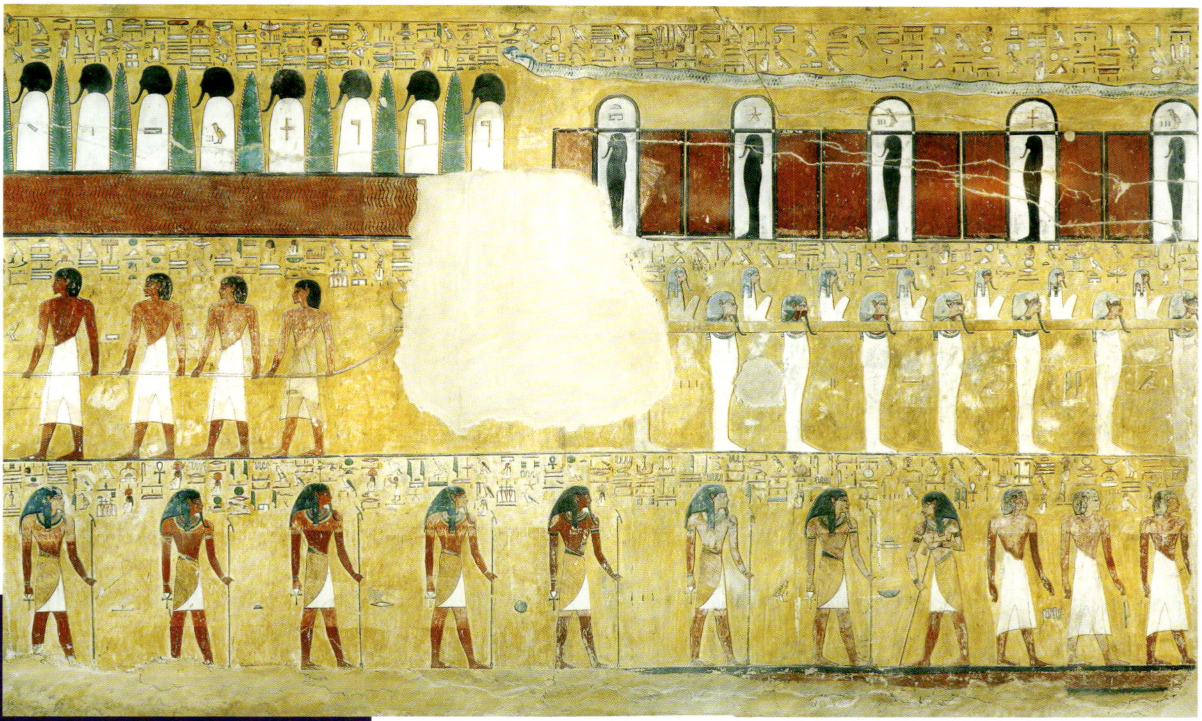

The third hour of the *Book of Gates*.
Tomb of Seti I (KV 17)
19th Dynasty
Thebes, Valley of the Kings

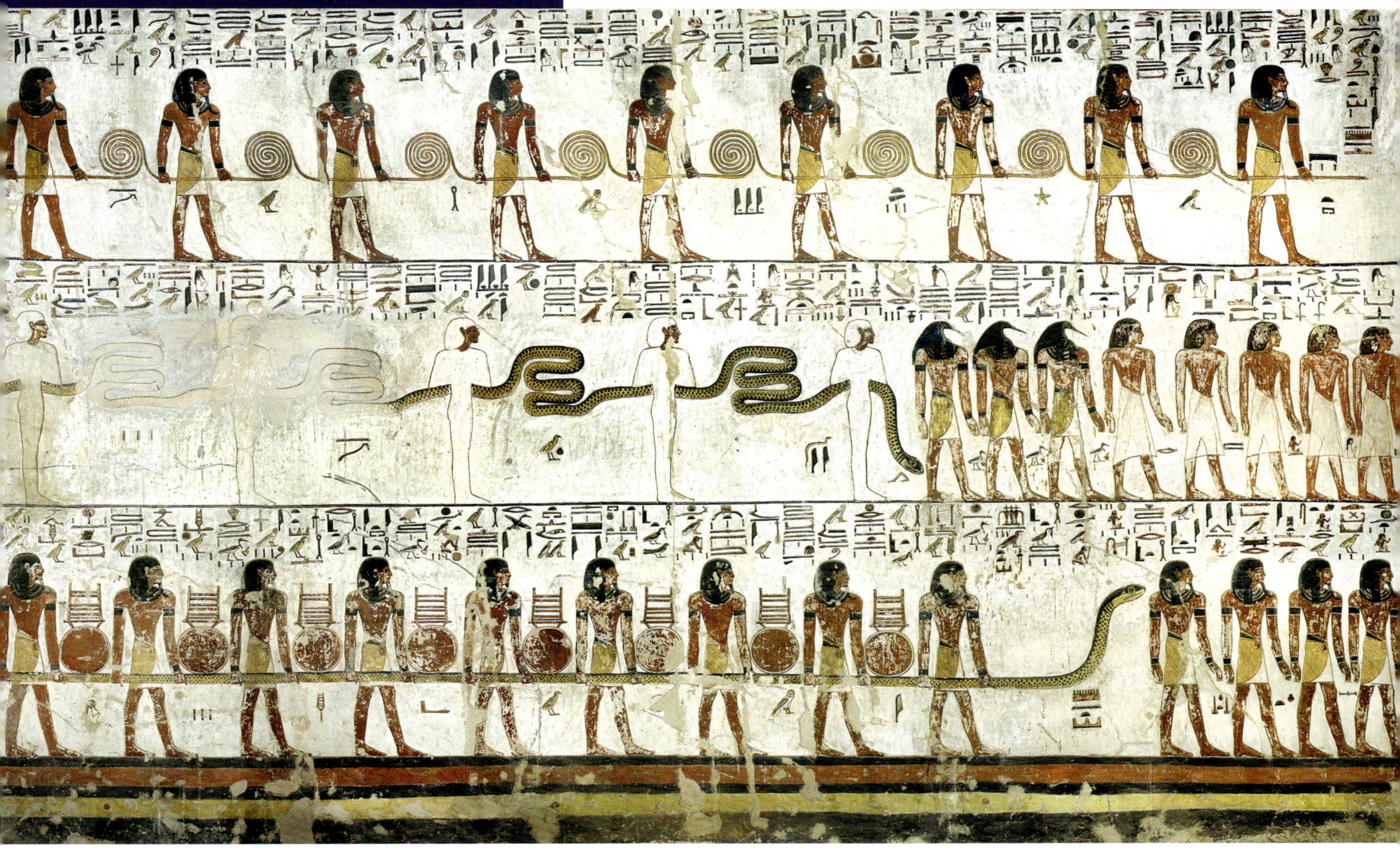

golden shrines that surrounded Tutankhamun's sarcophagus.

The first hour of the night was known as the "one who destroys the enemies of Re" or the "beginning of the western horn, the far border of the thick darkness." Its description illustrates the passage of the god through a transitional zone, the Valley of Re, and ends with his arrival in the Duat (netherworld) proper. During this hour, the sun god crosses 120 ***iteru*** (Egyptian miles, equaling about 700 English miles or a little more than 1,126 km). The night-barque of Re, the Mesektet, travels alongside the day-barque or Mandjet, in which the god appears in his morning form, the scarab beetle Khepri. Both boats are preceded by various netherworldly inhabitants who clear the way for the god.

During the second hour in the Duat, the solar barque is joined by a small fleet of other vessels, traveling for 309 ***iteru*** through the watery landscape known as Wernes. These waterways continue for 309 ***iteru*** spanned by the third hour, but in this case the river is called the "waters of Osiris."

Next, the fourth hour takes the sun from the watery landscape of the second and third hours to the severe desert landscape of Rosetau, the "cemetery," or underground tunnel. Here is the hill of the god Sokar. The cavern of Sokar is encountered in the fifth hour. This cavern is depicted as an oval area in which Sokar stands holding the wings of a four-headed serpent.

In the sixth hour, halfway through the night, the union of Re and Osiris is achieved. This is when the solar barque reaches the waters of the moon.

The defeat of Apophis, a powerful serpent who tried to swallow the sun each night, takes place during the seventh hour, in the cavern of Osiris. There is no water because a great snake has drunk it all. Having arrived at the eighth hour, the barque of the god has reached the land where the mummified dead reside. At the ninth hour, Re and his crew arrive at their rest house where they have a moment of respite.

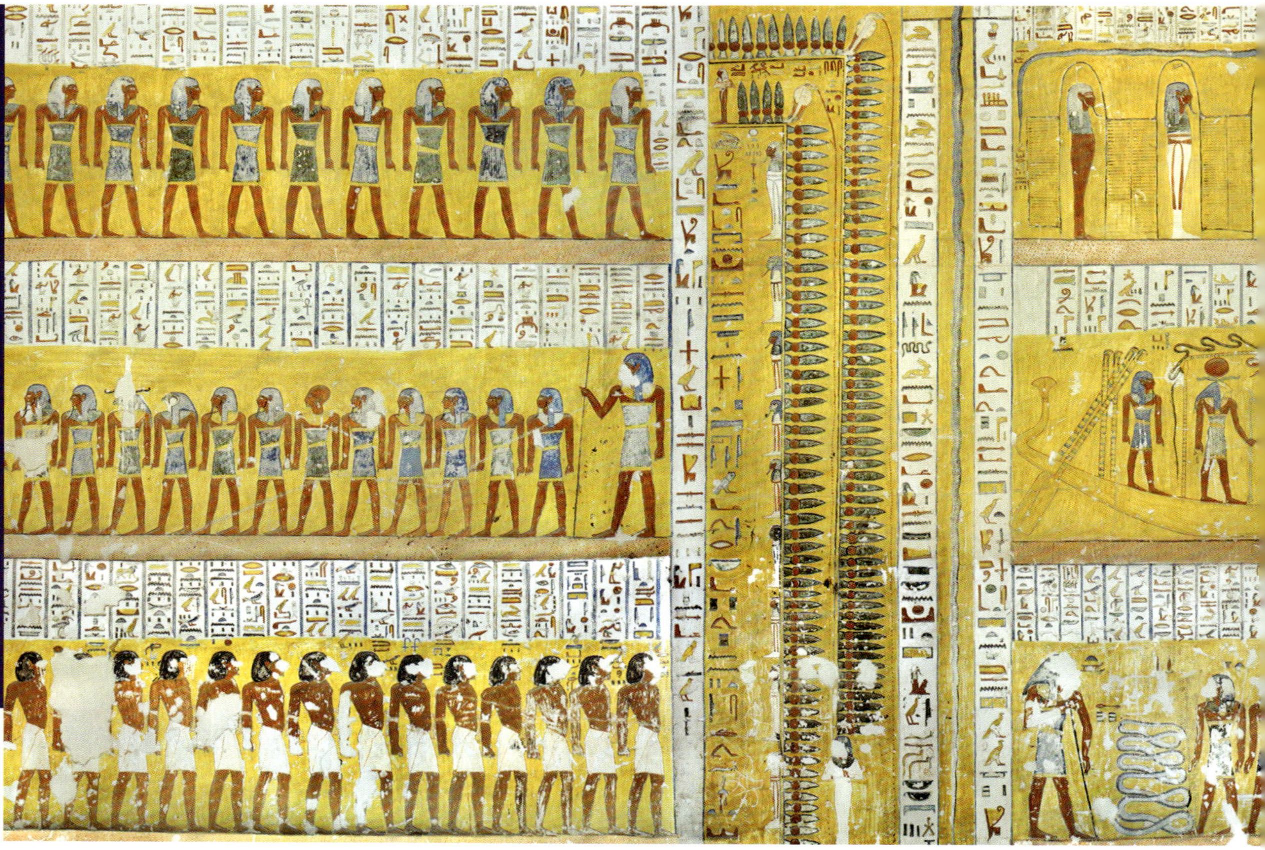

The second and the third hours from the *Book of Gates*: the sun god's barque is in the middle register, blessed souls are in the top register, and the damned are depicted in the bottom register.
Tomb of Rameses IV (KV 2)
20th Dynasty
Thebes, Valley of the Kings

The tenth hour sees the barque of Re pass through deep water with high banks into the eleventh hour, when preparations are made for the sun to rise.

The twelfth hour represents the successful completion of the sun's arduous journey, when the sun god and the deceased king are both reborn at dawn.

Another funerary text describing the sun's nocturnal voyage appeared in the 18th Dynasty. ***The Book of Gates*** debuted just after the Amarna Period. The first king to use this composition for the decoration of his tomb was Horemheb, last ruler of the dynasty. He selected the second, third, fourth, fifth, and sixth of the twelve nightly hours for inclusion on the walls of his burial chamber.

Why did the Egyptians create a second book of netherworldly descriptions? Was the ***Amduat*** not sufficient to guide the king safely into the afterlife?

Some Egyptologists believe that the ***Book of Gates*** was offered by the priests of

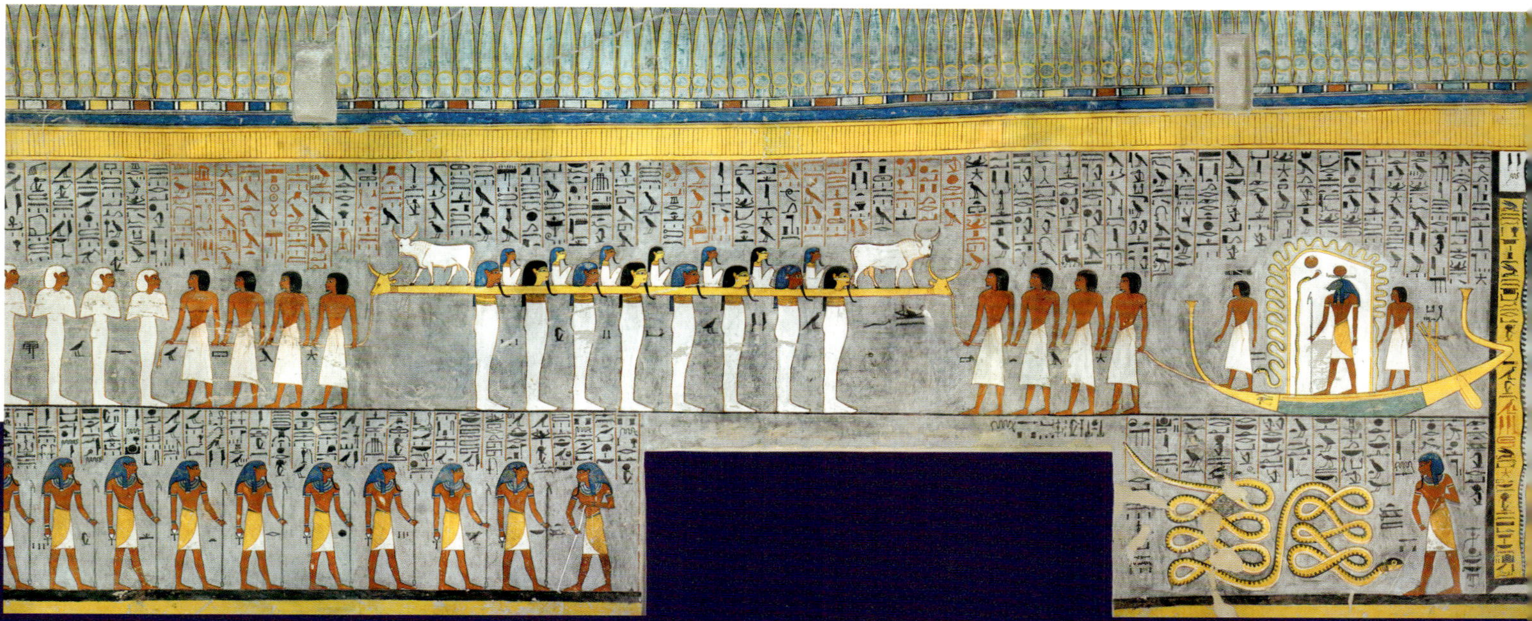

Second division of the *Book of Gates*: Eight mummified figures carrying the pole through which the rope of the sun barque passes. In the bottom register, Atum smites the snake of chaos, Apophis.
Tomb of Rameses I (KV 16)
19th Dynasty
Thebes, Valley of the Kings

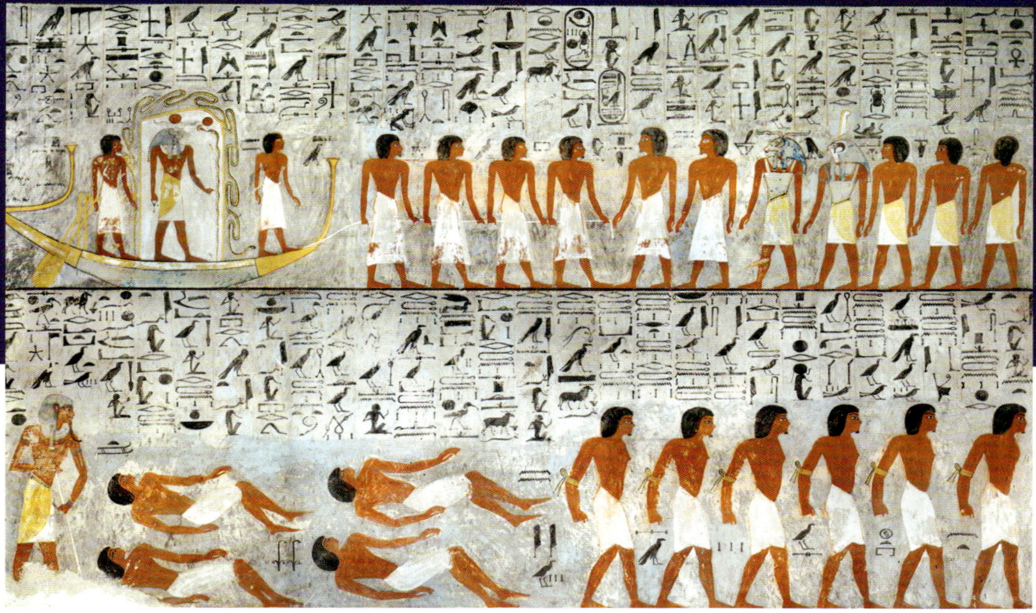

The second hour of the *Book of Gates*: The sun god's barque is being received by divinities, while, god Atum smites the enemies of the sun god.
Tomb of Horemheb (KV 57)
18th Dynasty
Thebes, Valley of the Kings

Amun-Re as an alternative to the *Amduat*. The focus of the *Amduat* was Osiris and his kingdom, and the text was composed to emphasize that he is the great god. The *Book of Gates* seeks to preserve the primacy of Amun-Re and perhaps expand this god's control over all the earth, the sky, and even the netherworld.

Not all of the religious texts that appeared in the royal tombs were funerary in nature. In fact, one of the earliest compositions to appear in the Valley of the Kings was the "Great Litany of Re." The rise of the solar god Re began in the 3rd Dynasty, and he appears in the Pyramid Texts composed later in the Old Kingdom. Portions of the litany appeared first on the pillars of Thutmose III's burial chamber, and the entire text was found on a shroud from the tomb. This text was not a guide through the netherworld. Instead, it describes the various forms of the sun god, beginning with a list of his 75 names. The litany specifically identifies the deceased king with Re and links his *ba* with Osiris. The principal purpose of these texts was the symbolic union of Re and Osiris and their identification with the dead king in order to achieve his resurrection.

The *Book of the Dead* was also one of the most popular funerary texts during the New Kingdom. It can be found in both private and royal contexts. The earliest examples appear on coffins of the 17th Dynasty, and excerpts are found on mummy shrouds and coffins of the early 18th Dynasty, but none appears in a royal tomb until Amenhotep II buried his father Thutmose III. The entire corpus consists of nearly 200 spells or chapters. Some of these spells allowed the deceased to take on new forms, such as plants or animals, so that he could move easily through the darkness protected by light and continue through to rebirth. They also allowed him to traverse the Fields of the Blessed to join Osiris, as well as to go forth from the tomb during the hours of daylight. The shrines of Tutankhamun were decorated with more than a dozen spells from the *Book of the Dead*.

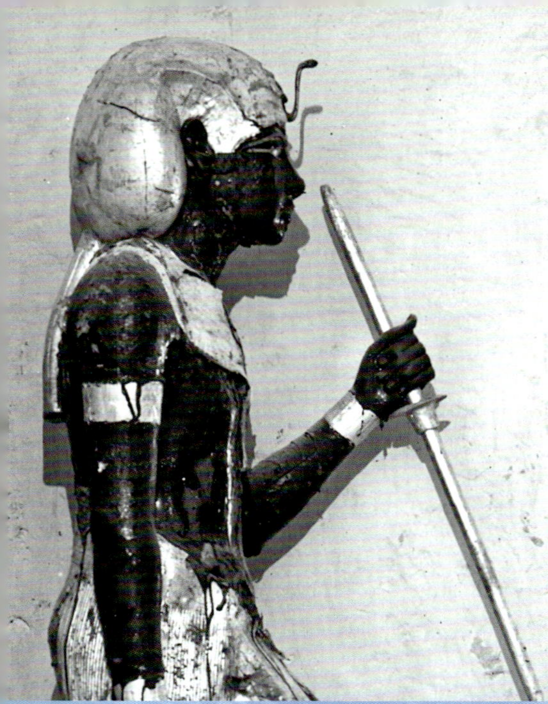

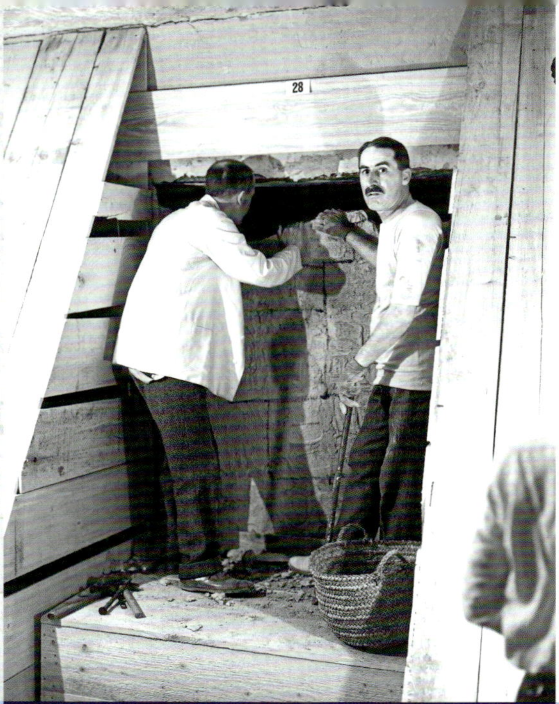

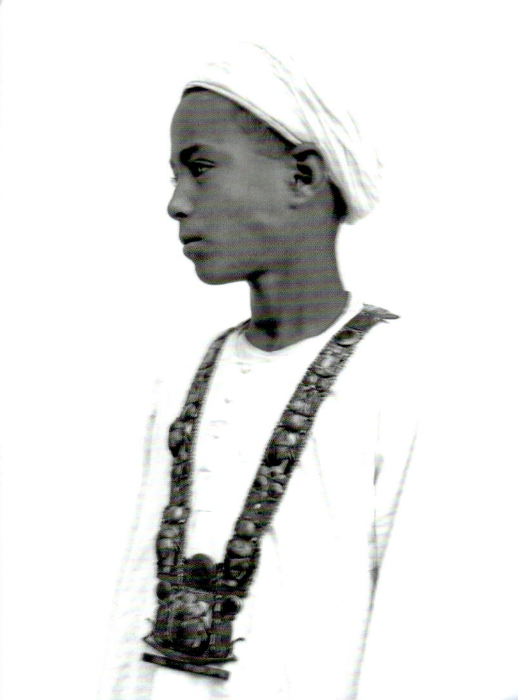

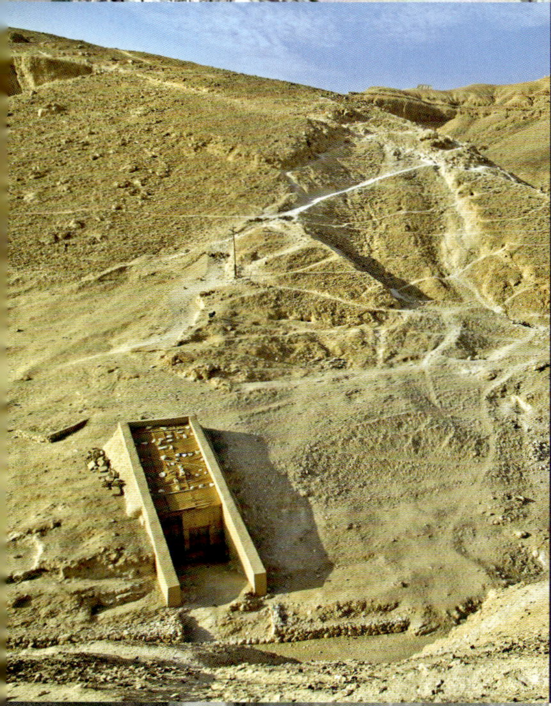

CHAPTER III

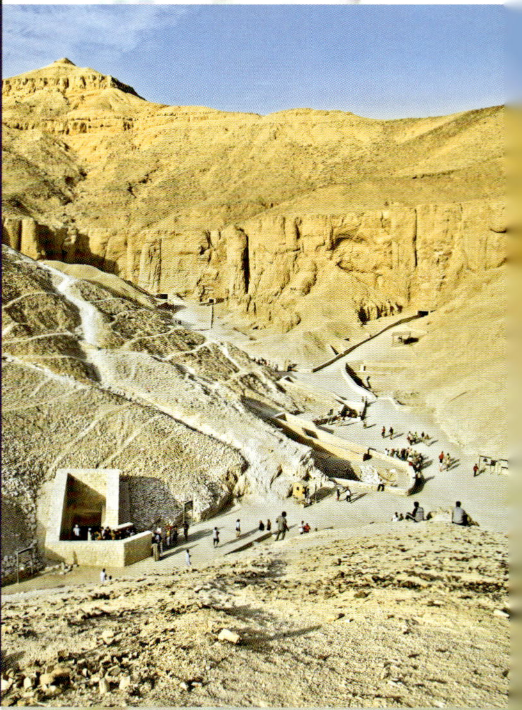

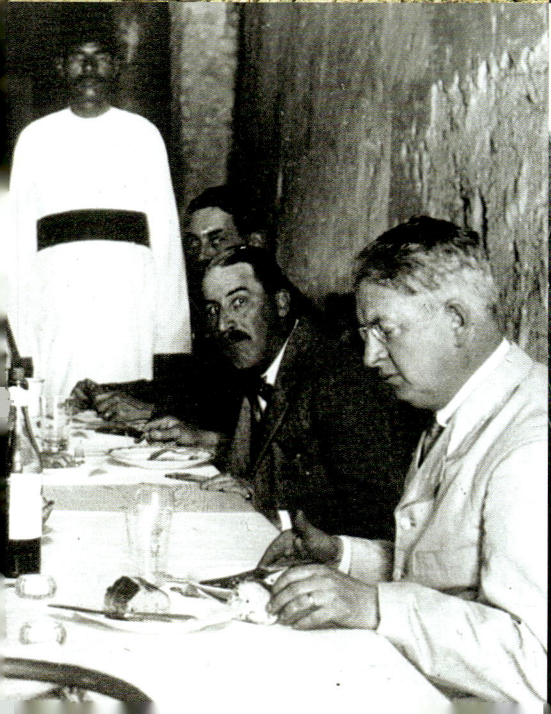

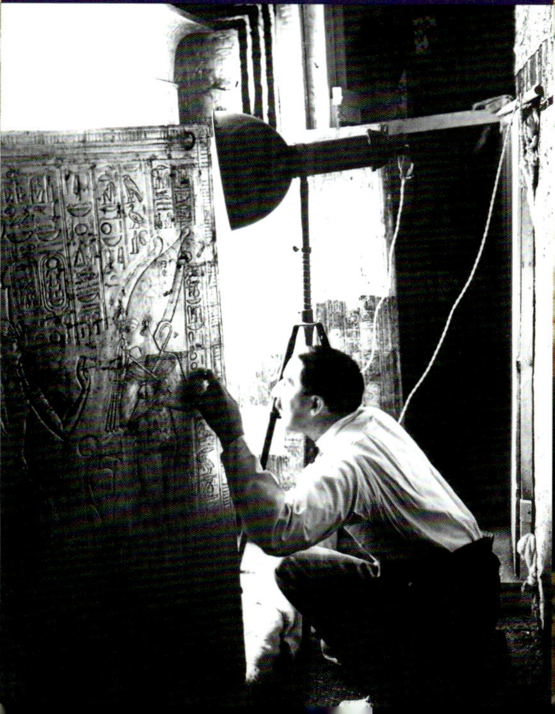

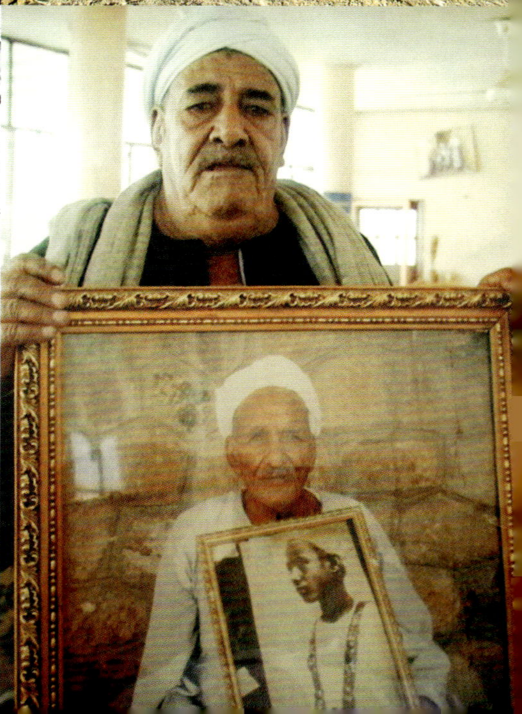

ROBBERS IN THE VALLEY OF THE KINGS

THE LATER NEW KINGDOM AND THE THIRD INTERMEDIATE PERIOD

The Valley of the Kings is considered to be one of the most romantic and exotic place in the world.

"Valley" is actually a misnomer. In reality, it is a complex of wadis, dry streambeds that cut into the cliffs lining the low desert that borders the west bank of the Nile at Luxor. Some Egyptologists propose that Thutmose I was the first king to be buried in the Valley of the Kings. His mortuary temple was built in the desert, close to the floodplain. Others believe that the first tomb was built in the valley for Hatshepsut, whose mortuary temple is located at the base of the cliffs at Deir el-Bahari.

In the New Kingdom, the Egyptians chose not to follow the pattern of their Old and Middle Kingdom predecessors, who connected the royal tomb with its mortuary temple. Instead of coming up with a new innovation, they reached back to the idea of the 1st Dynasty royal tombs at Abydos, where the royal tombs were located at Umm el-Qaab, while the associated temples were about 2.5 km away at Shonet el Zibieb. Likewise, the New Kingdom royal tomb was completely separated from its temple, hidden away in what turned out to be a vain attempt to foil ancient tomb robbers. Besides using the Early Dynastic idea of separating temple and tomb, Ineni also used the Old Kingdom idea of a pyramid. Rather than construct one, the Egyptians made use of a distinctive peak at top of the valley, known as al-Qurn, so that kings continued to be buried in a natural feature resembling the primordial mound.

The architect Ineni, who built the first tomb in the valley for the burial of Thutmose I, thought that he had protected the tomb. He inscribed this text on the wall of his tomb: "I built the tomb of my majesty... No one sees, no one hears..."

For many centuries, the 64 tombs that have been discovered so far in the valley were hidden. Twenty-six belonged to kings, and others were made for relatives and officials who were close to the king. At the end of the 19th Dynasty, queens began to be buried in a neighboring locale called the Valley of the Queens. Officials were also buried in other cemeteries nearby.

Despite attempts to hide the tomb, robberies began soon after a royal burial. This is an old practice, dating back thousands of years. The pyramids of the Old Kingdom were among the first targets. We can see that the tomb of Tutankhamun was broken into twice after it was sealed. Fortunately, the necropolis police were able to save the tomb and much of its contents both times, blocking up and sealing the robbers' entrance holes. Some scholars believe that more than 80% of the original treasures once hidden in the Valley of the Kings might have been stolen in antiquity.

Attacks on the tombs, both private and royal, became more frequent during the Ramesside Period, the 19th and 20th Dynasties. The culprits were people who lived on the west bank, supported by corrupt officials. Papyri dated to the 20th Dynasty (1187–1064 BC) provide us with important information about such robberies. We see the struggle between a man called Paser, who was the mayor of the east bank, and Pawera, mayor of the west bank, who was responsible for the protection of the royal tombs.

According to the report that Paser wrote to the vizier, Pawera was involved with looting the royal tombs. The vizier opened an in-

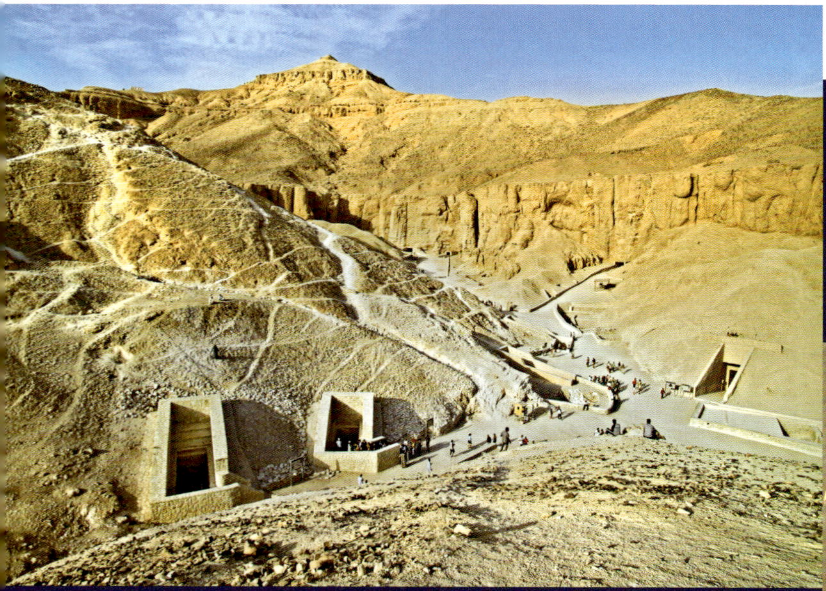

Sixty-four royal and non-royal tombs were cut into the rocks of a complex of ancient, dry riverbeds or wadis, known as the Valley of the Kings.

The Abbott Papyrus
one of the Tomb Robbery Papyri
20th Dynasty
British Museum [no. 10221]
The Trustees of the British Museum

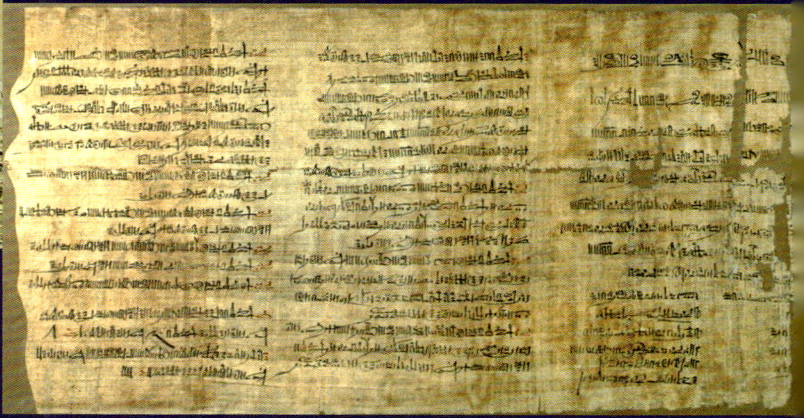

vestigation and appointed a committee to investigate the case. But the committee wrote a report in Pawera's favor. They examined nine tombs in the royal cemetery and found all in good condition, but objects had been taken from some of the nobles' tombs. The committee accused Paser of being a liar.

That report, of course, pleased Pawera, and we can see how he collected his men and crossed to the east bank to scream in the face of Paser and celebrate his victory in the streets of Thebes, with fighting and shouting in front of Paser's house.

Then Paser went to the vizier again and wrote another report and reopened the investigation. This time the thieves and the people who were on the side of Pawera began to declare the truth. All the evidence was collected and recorded in a group of papyri, which list by name the looted tombs and even the number of artifacts taken. It is recorded that the high priest of Amun received three men who were convicted of robbing the tomb of King Sobekemsaf (a king of the 17th Dynasty) and another man guilty of robbing private tombs. The high priest was also responsible for catching the thieves who had gotten away. All were to be held in the temple of Amun to await their punishment, which would be decided by the king. The penalty these men received may have been remembered years later, when the fate of "the thieves in the time of the vizier Khaemwaset" was used as a warning for those who wished to take up tomb robbery.

Tutankhamun was perhaps the eighth king to be buried in the valley, and Rameses X was the last. With the end of the 20th Dynasty came the end of the use of the Valley of the Kings for royal burials. Policing the area had probably become increasingly difficult and looting too frequent. But the valley was still used for burial. Recently, an 18th Dynasty tomb was discovered to have been re-used in the 21st Dynasty. In the 21st Dynasty, priests and kings authorized a final disturbance. They ordered that the royal mummies be gathered up, stripped of some of the jewels they retained, rewrapped, tagged with names, and hidden in caches. Although they may have been motivated by concern for their predecessors, the gold on the mummies was probably an additional lure, desired for the treasury. Even if greed was a factor, this "robbery" no doubt preserved these mummies for us today.

But even caching the bodies for safekeeping did not end thievery in the valley. Stealing from tombs remains an active criminal undertaking even today. People must realize that pieces of the past are more valuable to the world when they are used to understand history than when they are simply owned by individuals as beautiful or interesting objects. Until the day comes that everyone believes this, we will always have to fight tomb robbers.

EARLY EXCAVATIONS IN THE VALLEY

When Howard Carter, an English archaeologist, worked as chief inspector for the Theban area, he directed the attention of Theodore Davis to the Valley of the Kings. Davis was a wealthy American businessman who, Carter hoped, would fund Carter's own excavations in exchange for the portion of the finds that the government considered to be duplicates of what the Egyptian Museum held. This division of finds was the standard practice at the time. Hoping to locate the tomb of Thutmose IV, Carter began work in January 1902. Initially, the team uncovered two small non-royal tombs, including that of Maiherpri (KV 36), who had been raised in the royal nursery and might have been a contemporary of Thutmose IV. Soon, Carter found hollows containing foundation deposits, which are ritual caches of objects associated with the creation of a royal tomb. He also found the steps leading to KV 43, the tomb of Thutmose IV.

This whetted Davis's appetite for more. Their next target was a tomb known as KV 20, which had been located, but never properly excavated. This proved to be a difficult task because of the debris that occasional floods had packed in. Their hard work yielded material inscribed for Hatshepsut, the great female pharaoh, and for years it was thought that this was her tomb. However, in the 1970s, John Romer proved that this was a tomb that she had instructed Ineni to create for Thutmose I, her father. Most likely, this is the oldest tomb in the valley.

A new appointment as Chief Inspector of Lower Egypt drew Carter away from Luxor, so Davis partnered with British Egyptologist James Quibell for the next excavations. This team found a rare private tomb in the valley, hidden beneath the rubble from two 20th Dynasty tombs. Quibell and Davis found a door still blocked with stones that had been plastered and impressed with the seals of the royal necropolis: nine prostrate captives beneath a jackal representing Anubis, one of Egypt's most important funerary gods. There was also a robber's hole, not only in the outer door, but the inner door as well. The tomb was not intact, but Davis and Quibell hoped that some large pieces of the funeral equipment might remain inside.

And indeed, they were right. Peering into the chamber beyond the corridor they saw elegant furniture. Most everything of value that was portable had been removed. This included jewelry and other metal objects, as well as perfumes and other cosmetics. What remained behind, from boxes to the mummies themselves, had been disturbed by robbers looking for smaller treasure. That oils and other precious perishables had been stolen indicated a robbery not long after burial. Later sealings suggested that other thieves had entered during the reign of Rameses III.

Despite these intrusions, valuable objects remained. Quibell and Davis discovered chairs, beds, sandals, stone and pottery vessels, a chariot, canopic jars, coffins, the mummies themselves, and much else. All of these belonged to Yuya and Tjuya, the great-grandparents of Tutankhamun. A quarrel ended the partnership of Quibell and Davis. Arthur Weigall, another British Egyptologist, worked in the valley with Davis for a brief while, until archaeologist Edward Ayrton, who was known to be methodical in his work, took over. Ayrton's excavations revealed not only private tombs, but the royal tombs of Horemheb, last king of the 18th Dynasty, and Siptah, of the 19th Dynasty. He also found KV 55, a tomb containing a mix of objects from the Amarna Period, including a mummy we have recently determined to be that of the "heretic king," Akhenaten.

In 1906, Ayrton had found a faience cup with the name of Tutankahmun buried 3.7 m below ground level. The next year, not far from the find spot of the cup, Ayrton excavated a small pit, KV 54, with a variety of pottery vessels, some inscribed with "Nebkheperure," the throne name of Tutankhamun. There was also a miniature gilded mask, and a piece of linen cloth with an inscription calling him "beloved of Min" (god of the eastern Desert and of fertility) and dated to his sixth year of reign. Some of the pottery had been stamped with a seal from the necropolis. Years later, the American Egyptologist H. E. Winlock suggested that these were the remains of a funerary feast and the king's mummification.

Davis's refusal to publish these finds properly prompted Ayrton to retire in 1908. Davis replaced him with Ernest Harold Jones, a young archaeologist. In 1909, in a small rock-cut chamber, Jones found some pieces of gold foil from chariot fittings. One of these was decorated with a scene of Tutankhamun shooting arrows at a copper target. Others had the name of Ay. Three years later, Jones died and was replaced by Harry Burton, an English Egyptologist who would later work for the Metropolitan Museum of Art, but Burton had no luck making any major finds.

Davis declared that the little chamber that Jones had found was the tomb of Tutankhamun. It was thought at the time that this king's tomb would be found near the tomb of Amenhotep II. Horemheb had destroyed it, the theory ran, and priests loyal to Tutankhamun had gathered up what remained and hidden them from further harm. However, the objects that Jones excavated probably came from the tomb of Ay. Nonetheless, Davis was satisfied and gave up his concession in the valley in 1912. He died in 1915, never knowing that only two meters separated his excavations from the real tomb of Tutankhamun.

HOWARD CARTER AND LORD CARNARVON

Opening the burial chamber of Tutankhamun: Lord Carnavon looks inside the burial chamber while Howard Carter takes a rest.
Harry Burton / Griffith Institute

Next the concession for the Valley of the Kings came into the hands of George Herbert, better known as the 5th Earl of Carnarvon, and Howard Carter.

Carter had been born in 1874 into the family of an artist who already had 10 other children. Trained by his father, who recognized his son's artistic talents, Carter was introduced to Egyptologist Percy Newberry by Lord Amherst, who was interested in ancient Egypt. Newberry took Carter to Egypt to work as a copyist on the Middle Kingdom tombs at Beni Hasan. Carter then worked for a season with William Flinders Petrie, the "father of modern Egyptology," at Amarna. By 1899, Carter had worked his way up to appointment as Chief Inspector of Upper Egypt, stationed at Luxor.

One of his first important discoveries occurred entirely by accident. He was riding his horse near the temple of Hatshepsut at Deir el-Bahari one day in 1898 when the animal's hoof fell into a hole. When this hole was excavated in January 1900, it led to the discovery of a painted statue and sarcophagus of Mentuhotep II, first ruler of the 11th Dynasty. In memory of Carter's mount, this location has been ever since known as Bab el-Hosan, the "door of the horse."

Carter was moved to Saqqara in 1904 because of troubles with Davis, who was notoriously difficult to work with. By the next year, however, he was back in Luxor again, selling his paintings and antiquities to tourists. Difficulties with the Antiquities Service (he had sided with Egyptian guards in a dispute with a party of French tourists) caused him to quit his position in the north. Weigall introduced Carter to Lord Carnarvon in 1908. The fabulously wealthy Carnarvon, an Egyptological hobbyist, was in search of a "learned man" to excavate with him. He took Carter on, and after working elsewhere in Egypt, Carter convinced him to apply for a concession in the Valley of the Kings. Carter was sure that they would be able to locate an intact royal tomb. The next years of excavation, 1915–1919, were frustrating ones. With

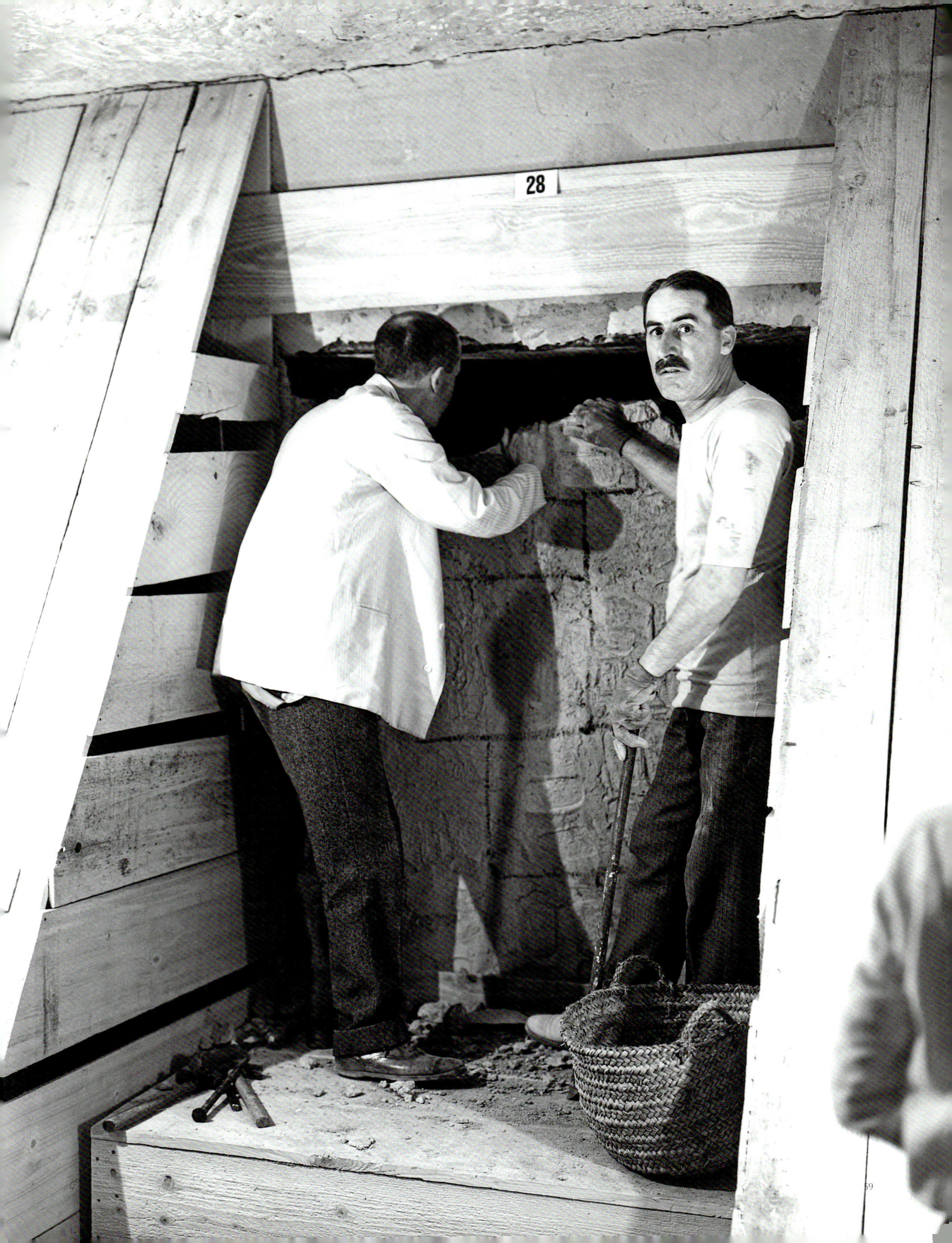
28

Carnarvon's funds, Carter was able to hire large crews of over a hundred men for each winter season. However, by the summer of 1922, Carnarvon had grown tired of fruitless investments. He called Carter to Highclere Castle in order to discuss whether it was worthwhile to continue. Carter asked him to fund one more season in the field. If Carnarvon failed to, Carter would fund the season himself because he was utterly certain that the valley held at least one more undiscovered royal tomb. He showed Carnarvon a map and detailed the area that had to be cleared before excavation in the Valley of the Kings could be considered genuinely complete. Carnarvon agreed, so in late October 1922, while the earl remained at Highclere, Carter was at work again in the Valley of the Kings, clearing a triangular area below the tomb of Rameses VI (KV 9).

At the time, this was considered to be the only area left unexplored in the valley. It had been covered by a bed of limestone chips from work on the tomb above and by ancient workmen's huts. Carter recorded the huts on November 1st. He then ordered his men to dig directly through these ancient remains.

THE PEOPLE AROUND CARTER

Great discoveries are seldom made by just one man. As is the case with every other archaeological expedition, Carter had a number of people assisting him. The head of a team cannot work alone, but he (or she) must have hardworking, skilled people working under him. When I excavated in the Valley of the Golden Mummies at Bahariya Oasis and the tombs of the pyramid builders at Giza, I had groups of people who helped me. But it is the head of the dig whose name everyone remembers with the discovery.

So although everyone associates the discovery of Tutankhamun's tomb with

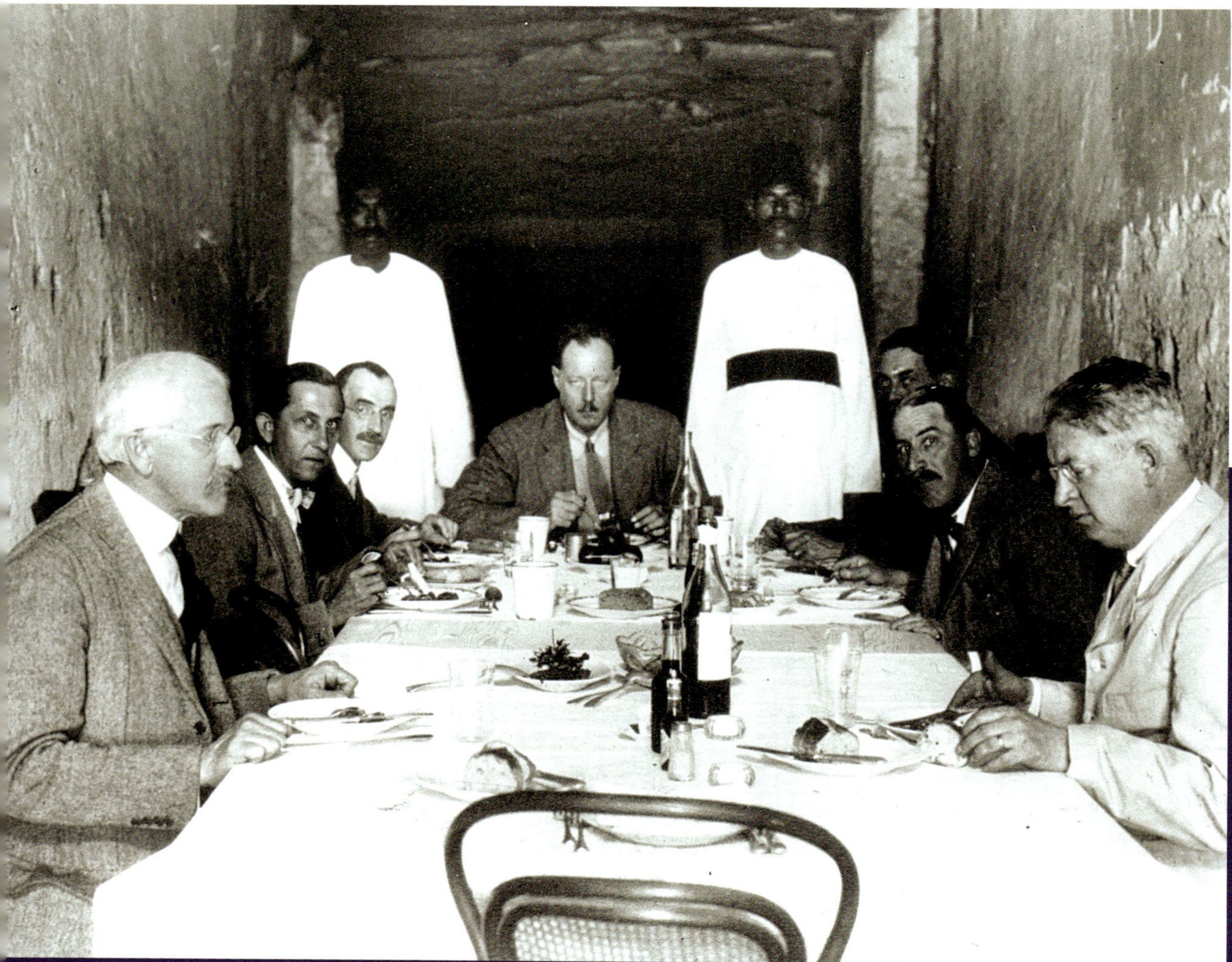

The Tutankhamun Team at lunch in the tomb of Rameses XI (KV 4). From left to right: J. H. Breasted, H. Burton, A. Lucas, A. R. Callender, A. Mace, H. Carter and A. Gardiner
Harry Burton / Griffith Institute

Howard Carter (and his sponsor, Lord Carnarvon), the names of the team members who assisted Carter are seldom mentioned.

You see them in photographs, at work in suit and tie, which seems very strange to me working as an archaeologist today. Lord Carnarvon took this particular photograph, catching everyone at lunch in the tomb of Rameses XI.

From the left we can see some of them: Breasted, Burton, Lucas, Callender, Mace, Carter, and Gardiner. It is worth knowing at least a little something about the members of Carter's team, who contributed so much to the excavation.

Alfred Lucas (1867–1945) worked as a chemist for the Antiquities Department. He became the foremost conservator in Egypt and was responsible for the conservation of all the artifacts from the tomb. Even today, his book *Ancient Egyptian Materials and Industries*, first published in 1926, is a key reference for Egyptology.

A retired engineer, Arthur Callendar (died 1936) was a friend of Carter's. His background made him especially helpful with the logistics of dismantling the shrines in the Burial Chamber.

Arthur Mace (1874–1928) was a curator of the Egyptian Department of the Metropolitan Museum of Art. He had excavated at Dendera, Abydos, Giza, and Naga el Deir. He co-authored the first of Carter's three volumes describing the excavation of Tutankhamun's tomb.

Another member of the Metropolitan's Egyptian Expedition was Harry Burton (1879–1940), who became the official photographer for Carter's excavation.

A veteran of Egyptian archaeology who had first brought Carter to Egypt, Percy Newberry (1869–1949) served as a professor of Egyptology at Liverpool University. His particular interest in Tutankhamun's tomb was the botanical specimens.

Alan H. Gardiner (1879–1963), a philologist, is best known today as the author of *Egyptian Grammar*, which remains one of the most important sources for learning to read ancient Egyptian. He was responsible for the translation of the hieroglyphic texts found in the tomb.

Sergeant Richard Adamson (1901–1982) served as a guard for the expedition over the course of seven years.

Lindsley Foote Hall (1883–1969) and Walter Hauser (1893–1959) were both draftsmen who worked for the Metropolitan Museum of Art. Hauser was also an architect and taught at the Massachusetts Institute of Technology.

James Henry Breasted (1865–1935) was the founder and director of the Oriental Institute of the University of Chicago. He is perhaps the best American historian of Egypt, and his books *History of Egypt from the Earliest Times Down to the Persian Conquest* (1905) and *Ancient Records of Egypt* (1905–1906) are remarkable, regularly consulted even today.

Carnarvon's daughter, Evelyn Herbert (1901–1980), was also present for some of the excavation.

And of course, we must mention the hundreds of workmen and their foremen who worked closely with Carter.

THE DAY OF THE DISCOVERY

This is Carter's description of how 4th November 1922 began for him:

"Hardly had I arrived on the work next morning than the unusual silence, due to the stoppage of the work, made me realize that something out of the ordinary had happened, and I was greeted by the announcement that a step cut in the rock had been discovered...
This seemed too good to be true..."

After the waterboy, Hussein Abdel Rasoul, told Carter what he had found (see sidebar), Carter ordered workmen to clear the sand away from the area. This uncovered a stairway with steps each about 1.68 m wide. By sunset, excavation revealed an entrance that had been blocked with stone, plastered, and impressed with necropolis seals. Evidently the entrance had been violated by robbers in antiquity, but this robbers' hole had been sealed up in antiquity as well. Even if the tomb was not truly intact, it was likely to contain something, just as the tomb of Yuya and Tjuya had.

Carter telegraphed Carnarvon: "At last have made wonderful discovery in valley; a magnificent tomb with seals intact; recovered same for your arrival; congratulations."

Lord Carnarvon and his daughter Evelyn traveled from Highclere Castle to Luxor, a journey that brought them by ferry, then by train, by ship, then another train, followed by another ferry, then, in the end, by donkey.

As we will explore in the next chapter, Carter opened the tomb with Carnarvon and a few others in attendance on 27th November 1922. But swirling around the spectacular archaeological events were difficult political ones.

THE LEGEND OF THE BOY WHO FOUND THE TOMB

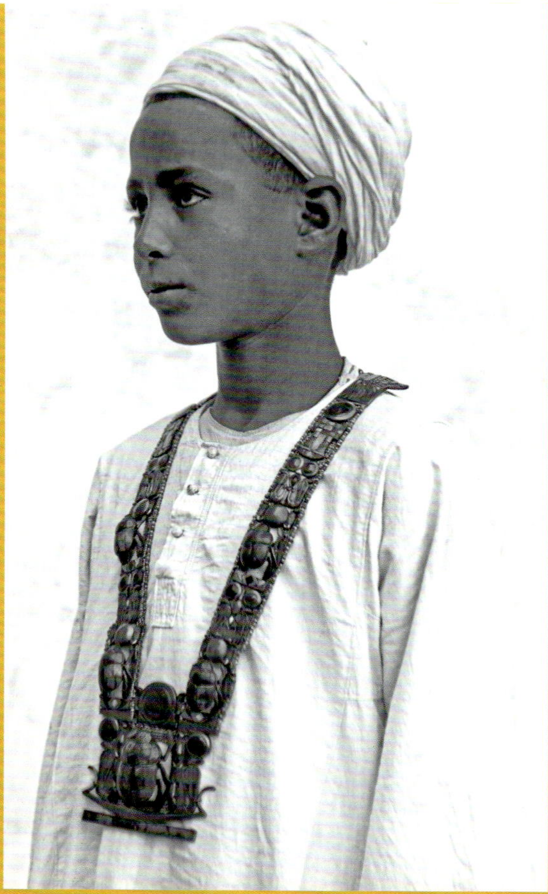

HUSSEIN ABDEL RASOUL WEARING THE NECKLACE OF TUTANKHAMUN, 1925
Carter 267G
Harry Burton / Griffith Institute

In his old age: Hussein Abdel Rasoul is carrying his own photograph commemorating the discovery of Tutankhamun's tomb.

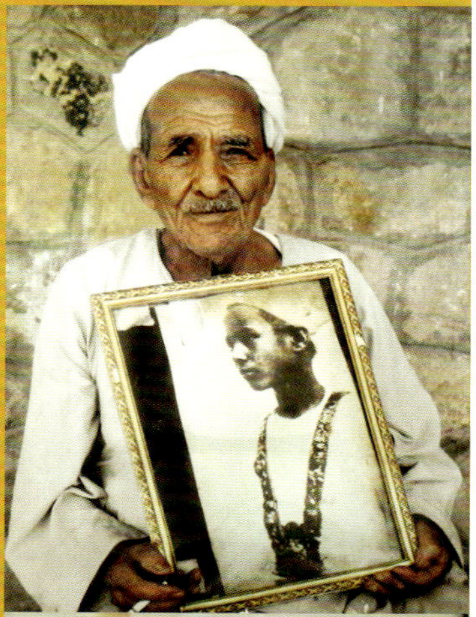

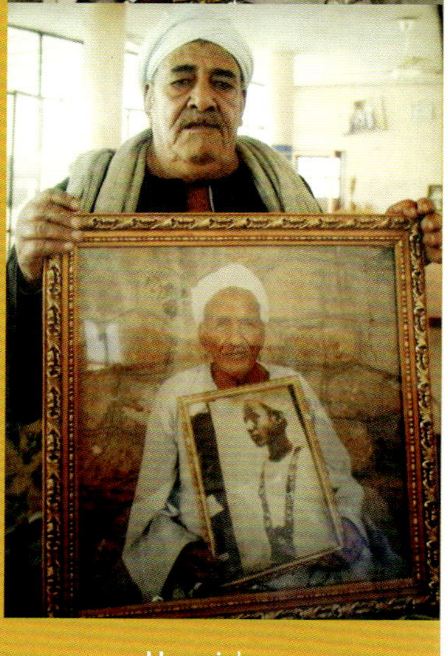

Hussein's son holds the photograph of his father in his youth and as an old man.

A young boy named Hussein Abdel Rasoul was hired by the overseer (*reis*) of Carter's workmen to bring water to the site, which he did in one or two trips each day. The water came in large pottery jars tied with ropes and set on the back of a donkey. Things have not changed much today. We used to do the same thing during my excavation at the Valley of the Golden Mummies.

On the morning of 4th November 1922, Hussein arrived as usual. Before he could set the jars on the ground he had to excavate a small hole because the bottoms were pointed. This time, Hussein's digging brought to light a flat patch of stone – the first step down to the tomb.

A photograph shows the boy wearing an elaborate necklace with a scarab and sun disk flanked by cobras, which was found in 1924 in the chamber known as the Treasury. Only Carter could have allowed such a privilege. He certainly put the necklace on Hussein himself as a reward for the discovery. I am sure that this was only for the purpose of taking the photograph.

This is not the only photograph of Hussein Abdel Rasoul at the site. The wife of the 7th Earl of Carnarvon, Jean Margaret Herbert, has said that among the photos of Lord Carnarvon's collections she found a photograph of this boy on the steps of the tomb.

A German reporter went to Qurna on the west bank of Luxor in search of the former waterboy. He met Hussein Abdel Rasoul at the rest house of the Ramesseum, the mortuary temple built for Rameses the Great. When Hussein met the journalist, he brought with him photographs taken with him in the necklace. There are two interesting photographs, one of Hussein as an old man of 70, and another of his son. In each photograph they are holding an old photograph of Hussein as a boy wearing the jewel of the boy-king. Sheikh Ali Abdel Rasoul, a descendent of a famous family of tomb robbers (see Chapter 7), told me that the waterboy was his cousin.

TROUBLE IN PARADISE: CARTER AND THE ANTIQUITIES SERVICE

Although Arthur Merton, a journalist with the *Times* of London, attended the official viewings over the next few days, the first official media event was not held until 22nd December. The public was wildly eager for news – Tutmania had taken hold of the world. Early in January, hoping to gain financially and to minimize disruption to the excavation by intrusive reporters, Carnarvon signed a contract with the *Times*, granting this newspaper a monopoly on news coming from the excavation. This exclusivity prompted an outcry not only from other foreign media, but from the Egyptian press as well. Even they would have to rely on the *Times*. Naturally, this generated a good deal of political ill-will and even suspicion. The British had been a military presence in Egypt since 1882, and in 1914, as a result of World War I, Britain declared a protectorate over Egypt. This had come to an end in April 1922. Egypt adopted a new constitution and so, at the time of Carter's excavation, Egyptian nationalism had come to the fore of the political scene.

Although he had not signed the *Times* contract, Carter had to handle the difficulties it caused largely alone. By February of 1923, Carnarvon had become ill, so he and his daughter Evelyn headed north to Cairo on 14th March to talk to Pierre Lacau, the French Egyptologist who was head of the Egyptian Antiquities Service, about an equitable division of the finds from the tomb. The law at that time stated that 50% of the objects were given to the excavator and 50% were given to the Antiquities Service. (In 1983, the law was changed to give the excavator only 10%, and I had the law changed in 2010 so that no finds were given to the excavator.) This division would take place only if there were objects already well represented in the collections of the Egyptian Museum in Cairo. Additional finds were considered to be "duplicates." But such a division between the Egyptian government and the excavator would not take place if the objects came from an intact royal tomb. Although Tutankhamun's tomb had been robbed twice in ancient times, the government regarded it as intact. This decision greatly displeased Carter and Carnarvon, who had hoped to recoup the investment of time and money they had made on their excavations in the Valley of the Kings.

But only a few days after arriving in Cairo, Carnarvon fell seriously ill with a fever and swollen glands. He had been bitten on the cheek by a mosquito, and this had become infected. With Carnarvon already unwell, the infection spread. It developed into blood poisoning, and early in the morning of 5th April, Lord Carnarvon died. After a farewell from Carter, his body was returned to England for burial. The following summer, Carter would convince his widow to continue to hold the concession.

Carter had an ingenious solution to the problem of the press: he added Arthur Merton, the *Times* journalist, to his staff. Merton would issue press bulletins each evening to the *Times* and then, in the next morning, to the Egyptian newspapers.

Visitors of any sort presented obstacles. Because Carter objected to the disruption of the team's "scientific work" by outsiders, he wished to limit when others could enter the tomb. He proposed the issuance of official passes when it was convenient for the excavation to receive guests. Lacau pressured James Quibell, who was now secretary-general of the Antiquities Service, to agree to this plan. Quibell did so reluctantly, as he did to Carter's solution to the press problem.

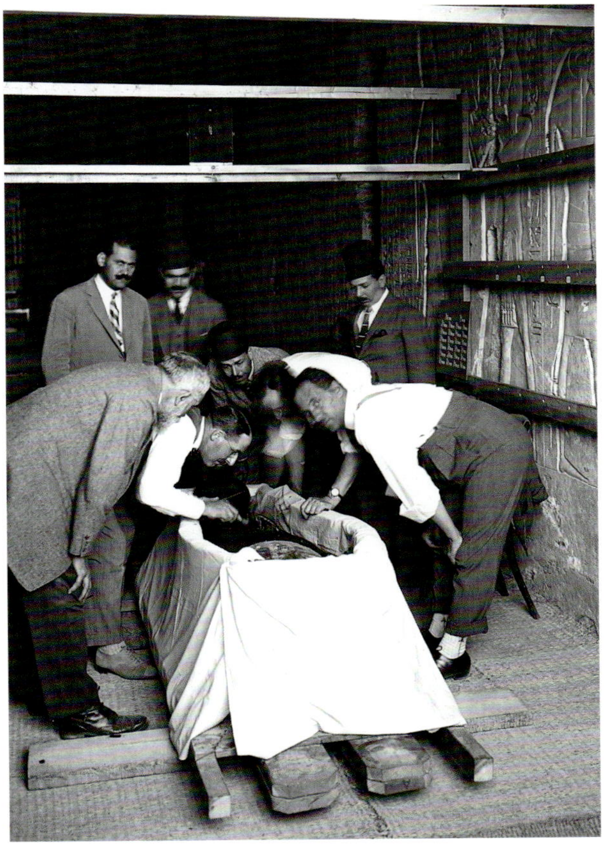

On 11th November 1929, Carter examining the mummy of Tutankhamun in the presence of the officials from the Egyptian Antiquities Service
Harry Burton / Metropolitan Museum of Art

Even when the next field season arrived, in October 1923, points of contention remained. The Antiquities Service informed Carter that he would have to work in the presence of an inspector. This greatly displeased Carter, although this is standard practice today. But through these difficulties, Carter and his team continued to excavate.

By early January 1924, the Antechamber had been cleared and work had begun on the Burial Chamber, which was dominated by a set of gilded shrines, one nested inside another. Carter opened the doors of the innermost shrine revealing the quartzite sarcophagus on 3rd January, and two days later received congratulations from Lacau and complaints from the Ministry of Public Works. This ministry, which oversaw the Antiquities Service, alleged that Carter had allowed another journalist from the *Times* to attend the opening without the appropriate permit while at the same time there had been no Egyptian inspector present. Carter denied both charges, although it was true that the inspector was informed to attend only an hour after the doors had been opened.

Despite continued disagreements regarding press coverage, Carter, Lacau, and Morcos Bey Hanna, the Minister of Public Works, agreed to open the sarcophagus on 12th February. Carter invited the Minister to attend, but when he was told that the opening of the sarcophagus would reveal a nest of coffins and not the king's mummy, Hanna declined. A delegate would attend instead.

The day after the sarcophagus lid was raised, revealing Tutankhamun's gleaming outer coffin wrapped in linen shrouds, a group of women, most of them wives of Carter's team members, was scheduled to see the Burial Chamber after a press viewing. That very day, 13th February, at 6:40 in the morning, Carter received word denying him permission to admit his guests into the tomb. The situation worsened: Carter next learned that, unless they were journalists authorized by the Ministry of Public Works, women were barred from the tomb. Carter had had enough. This "insult," as he called it, was the final straw in an enormous bundle of difficulties that Carter had been having with the government. So Carter and his team went on strike.

At 12:30 in the afternoon, he posted the following notice:

"Owing to impossible restrictions and discourtesies on the part of the Public Works Department and its Antiquities Service, all my collaborators in protest have refused to work any further upon the scientific investigations of the discovery of the tomb of Tut.ankhamen. I therefore am obliged to make known to the public that, immediately after the Press view of the tomb this morning, between 10 am and noon, the tomb will be closed, and no further work can be carried out."

And so it was closed, with the heavy sarcophagus lid still suspended over the king's coffins by pulleys.

The government could play this game, too. Instead of giving Carter the apologies he demanded, Hanna locked him out of the tomb and revoked Lady Carnarvon's concession. In order to preserve the safety of the artifacts, he ordered Lacau to reopen Tutankhamun's tomb and the others being used as work places by Carter's team. Carter declined Lacau's offer to help supervise the work.

Prime Minister Saad Zaghlul berated Carter in a telegram, reminding him that the tomb was not his property. Furious, Carter brought two court cases against Zaghlul's government in attempts to be given a half share of the antiquities in the tomb and for the right to restore the artifacts. He accused Hanna of being a thief and even employed a lawyer who had formerly tried to get Zaghlul convicted for treason. Carter came under further scrutiny when inspectors found an uncataloged object – a sculpture depicting Tutankhamun as the god Nefertem (**Carter No. 8**, in Chapter 4) – that they thought Carter might be trying to smuggle out of Egypt. Other Egyptologists intervened to bring the crisis to an end. Hanna relented but imposed new conditions on Carter: Carter had to apologize, relinquish any claim to the artifacts for himself and Lady Carnarvon, and issue a written document agreeing that the clearance of the tomb was rightfully under the supervision of the Ministry of Public Works.

A change in Egyptian administration and Carter's eventual agreement to their terms allowed him to return to work in the tomb. He and Lady Carnarvon relinquished any claim on their finds, and in return Lady Carnarvon would be amply rewarded by the government.

He returned to work on 22nd January, 1925, finding a great deal of damage. Sunshine had caused the linen pall, which had been left lying in the open, to decay beyond any hope of conservation. Wooden objects were deteriorating too. Even the jewelry was beginning to show signs of chemical change. Restoring order and conservation became the focus of that season's work.

The next season, the winter 1925–1926, more progress was made in the excavation of the tomb itself. In the Burial Chamber, the royal coffins were opened.

The boy-king was there within them, his mummy intact – for the time being.

AFTERMATH: CARTER AFTER TUTANKHAMUN

By the end of the excavation in 1926, a total of 5,398 objects had been brought out of the chambers of the tomb. This meant there was still much work to be done. The 1927–1928 season was devoted to conserving and photographing each treasure.

With the artifacts removed from the tomb, it could be opened to the public, which it was on 8th January, 1928.

For Carter, this season was eaten up by negotiation meetings with the Egyptian government. Lady Carnarvon had abandoned her concession to the tomb in October 1929, which meant that Carter lost his official access to it. Unable to continue his scientific work, he resumed his attempts to gain compensation for the Carnarvon estate, which had invested so much in locating and excavating the tomb. He finally met with success. Lord Carnarvon's heirs received a payment of more than £35,000 Sterling. Carter received a percentage of this sum, about £8,500.

In October 1930, the start of the next season, Carter was back at work in the tomb, but only under close supervision by an Antiquities Service inspector. The inspector kept the keys to the tomb and to the laboratory – and he kept a constant eye on Carter. He was not pleased, but Carter worked at the tomb until February 1932.

He had spent nearly 10 years of his life bringing the boy-king back from the dead.

They were not easy years. Whether he agreed with it or not, he paid the price for his patron's decision to sign an exclusive contract with the *Times* and had to cope with the political and media fallout. He had to cope, also, with the consequences of his success. He had, after all, made the most important discovery in Egyptology, an intact royal tomb, and both Egypt and the world wanted to share in it. The result was a seemingly endless stream of visitors, Egyptian and foreign, that wore away at the time he should have been spending on his scientific work. And, of course, there was a threat to the security of the tomb.

I know what this kind of pressure is like. When I discovered the Valley of the Golden Mummies at the Bahariya Oasis in Egypt's Western Desert, the site became a magnet for the press. The whole world came to know about it. As happened with Tutankhamun's tomb, all kinds of visitors came in droves. Some were foreign, some were Egyptian. Everyone wanted to see these fabulous treasures I had found. While it is good for people to be fascinated by the past, it is not good if they interrupt the careful work required to bring the past to light. And so many visitors were a risk to the tombs and to the mummies. They do not always understand the dangers that they bring to artifacts. Even a simple thing like a camera flash can be harmful. I argued with a member of the foreign press about that. They became very short-tempered when I forbade them from using flash photography inside a tomb. I know very well what kind of problems Carter had to deal with.

I also know that Carter overcame these challenges well enough to do extremely good scientific work on the tomb. He had only a small team to contend with an enormous, diverse array of artifacts. They had to be cleaned, consolidated, conserved, photographed, described, and understood. This was his work. He was an archaeologist, and this is what drove him to fight for limitations to visitors. Whatever difficulties arose, he did what he had to do to keep on with his work, this most important Egyptological task. As a fellow archaeologist, I can vouch for how great Carter's accomplishment was. The task of recording and conserving more than 5,000 artifacts, so many of them elaborate and delicate, and all of them precious to history, would have overwhelmed many others. Carter had the right experts with him, like Alfred Lucas, a chemist who had expert knowledge of these kinds of materials, everything from textiles to stone, from wood to gold. Lucas literally wrote the book on ancient Egyptian materials, which has only recently been succeeded by a more modern work.

After he had finished with Tutankhamun's artifacts, Carter's life became quiet. Although he published three volumes for a popular audience, he never realized his ambitions to do a full, scholarly publication of the tomb. When asked about his plans for the future, Carter replied that he would search for the tomb of Alexander the Great! Unfortunately, although he would live for another seven years, Carter's health was poor. Splitting his years between Luxor and London, he would accomplish little else of note. Hodgkin's disease set in and by 1939 had confined Carter to bed. He died on 2nd March of that year. He was buried in England, privately and quietly.

But Carter's story does not end with his death. After he died, his executors found a number of objects from the tomb in his possession. Either Carter or Carnarvon may have taken them early in the clearance, before they realized that there would be no division of the finds. Or possibly Carter stole them later. When they were found, it was decided immediately that these would be returned to Egypt. World War II interfered with this plan, but eventually these pieces were returned and are now part of the Tutankhamun collection housed in the Egyptian Museum in Cairo.

However much I identify with Carter, this is something that I cannot truly comprehend. Taking objects from the tomb and placing them into a private collection strips the artifacts from their context. An artifact without its context is an artifact less valuable. And an object in a private collection, although beautiful, is no longer available for study by scholars. We risk losing it as a way to understand the past.

Taking artifacts from the tomb was the biggest mistake Carter ever made. Defying the Egyptian government's decision to declare the tomb intact made him a thief. Many times people come up to me after I have given a lecture to tell me that someone in their family, or a friend of their family, visited Tutankhamun's tomb when Carter was excavating. Sometimes they tell me that they have small artifacts from the tomb. I must wonder what little treasures, and what bits of history, have been lost by the giving of such gifts.

How different Carter's actions were from those of George Andrew Reisner. Reisner was an American Egyptologist who, in 1925, discovered the tomb of Queen Hetepheres, mother of Khufu, the king who built the Great Pyramid. Like Tutankhamun's, it had been robbed in antiquity. The queen's mummy was even missing. But it contained beautiful objects that any museum would want: fabulous pieces of gilded furniture, a canopic box, and a sarcophagus carved of calcite (Egyptian alabaster). Reisner cooperated with the Egyptian Antiquities Service. As a reward, the Egyptian government gave his sponsor, the Boston Museum of Fine Arts, an exquisite gift: the bust of the vizier Ankhhaf, a masterpiece of Old Kingdom sculpture.

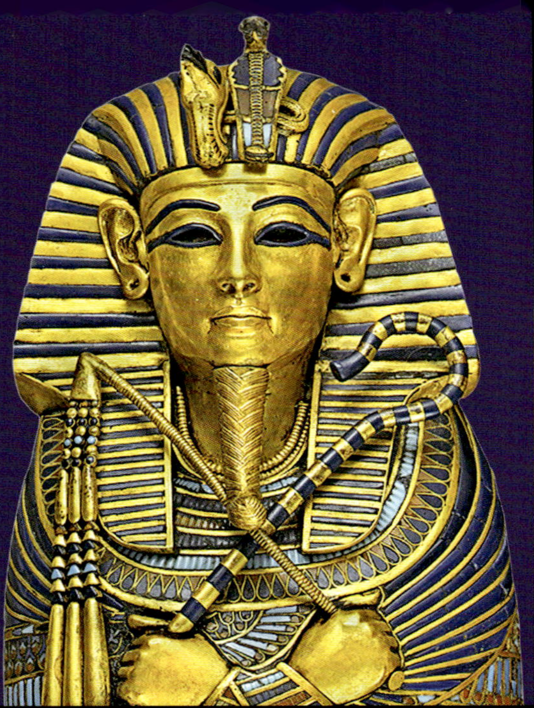
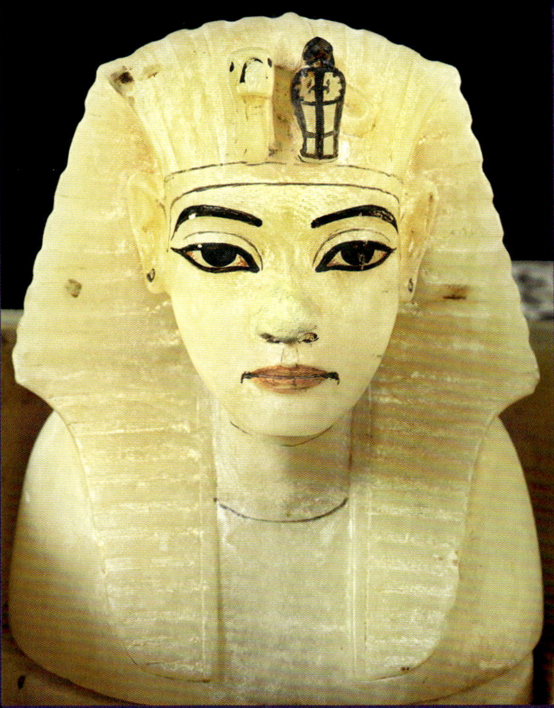
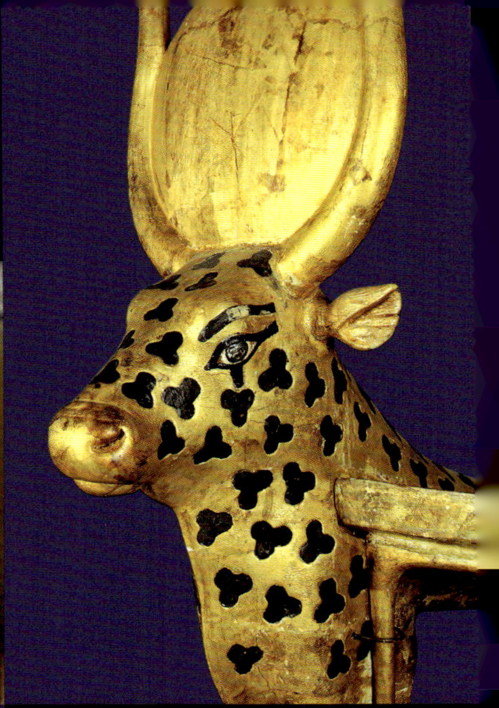
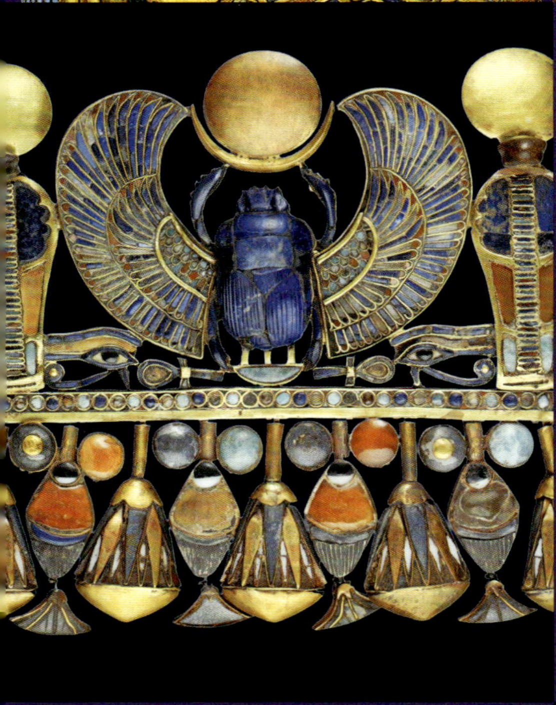

CHAPTER IV

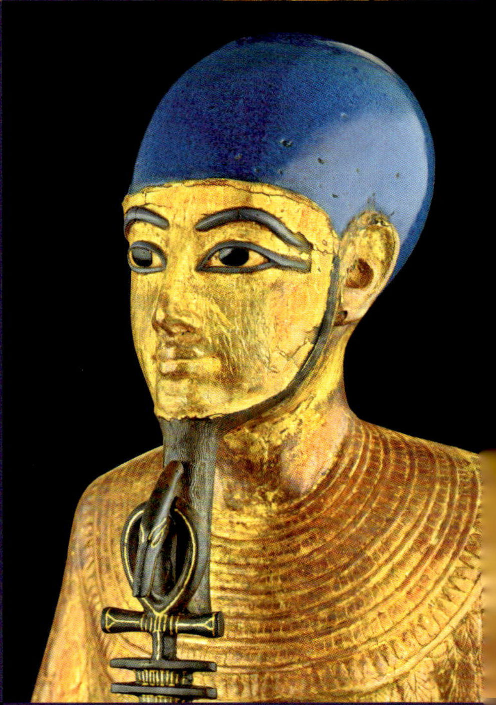
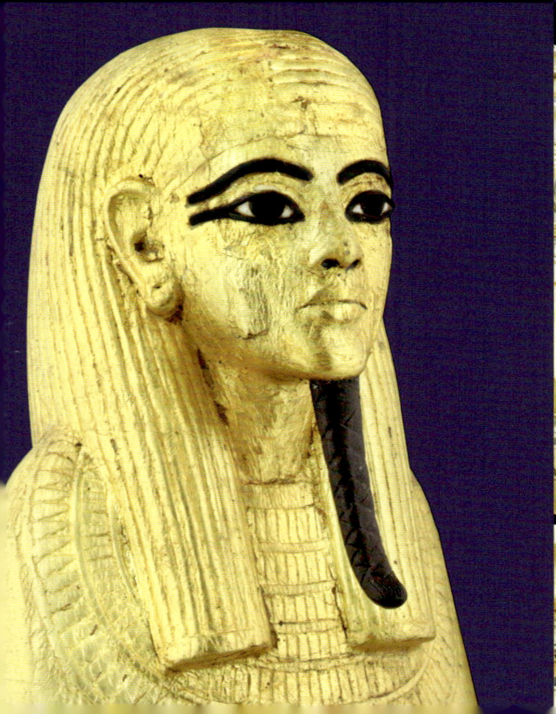
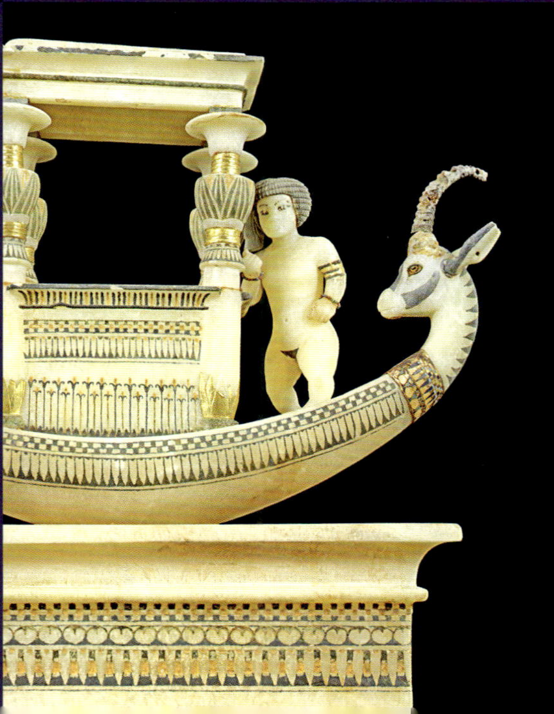
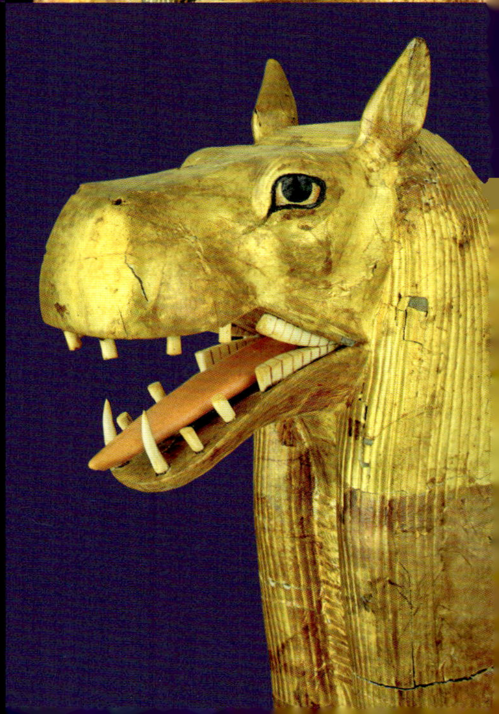

THE TOMB AND ITS TREASURES

THE STAIRWAY AND ENTRANCE CORRIDOR

On 24th November, four days after Lord Carnarvon arrived in Luxor, Carter's team resumed work on the tomb, intent on clearing the remainder of the stairway. These efforts paid off with the discovery of seals on the lower part of the doorway. They were those of Tutankhamun: whatever lay beyond, the tomb at least dated to his era. The digging also uncovered fragments of objects. Carter described their position: "Helter skelter in rubbish covering the last few steps and threshold of the doorway, as if dropped or cast away." The "rubbish" included bits of wood, resin, ivory, glass, dockets and jar sealings, reeds, potsherds, fragments of stone vessels, and even a scarab of Thutmose III. The cartouches of Akhenaten and Ankhkheperure Neferneferuaten, as well as the name of Meritaten, Akhenaten and Nefertiti's eldest daughter, were found on parts of a box. According to an inscription, this box had contained fine linen. Another box – likewise broken and empty – had once contained silver vessels belonging to Tutankhamun. A fragment of something with the name of Amenhotep III, who was very likely Tutankhamun's grandfather, was also alleged to have been found, but the object, whatever it was, has vanished.

Carter worried about these finds. Could all these royal names – Thutmose III, Akhenaten, Ankhkheperure, Amenhotep III– point to a king's tomb or to just another reburial of disturbed tombs that Tutankhamun's officials had overseen? Such a cache, also from the Amarna Period, had been found 15 years before by Theodore Davis and Edward Ayrton in the Valley of the Kings, KV 55. Carter suspected he would find, as in KV 55, more material from Amarna. After all of his hard work, what would Carter find here, beyond Tutankhamun's seals, in KV 62?

He would soon have his answer.

On 25th November, Carter's team recorded and dismantled the blocking at the foot of the stairway. This removal left them confronting a mass of rubble. Obviously in ancient times robbers had tunneled through here, in the upper left-hand corner. This area had been refilled with rocks larger than the limestone chips of the rest. More bits and pieces from the tomb were coming to light: more fragments from stone vessels and objects made of gold, ivory, ebony, and faience, sealings, and splinters of wood. There was even some dried fruit.

Carter claimed that he found this wonderful head of Tutankhamun among the rubble of the stairwell, in the entrance corridor beside a pile of waterskins. Made of wood that was covered with gesso and painted in realistic colors, it depicts the king as a boy, rising out of a lotus blossom in the role of the god Nefertem, who often appears as a god with a lotus blossom on his head, was the god of perfume and an incarnation of the sun god at dawn. The lotus flower opens in the morning and closes at night, suggesting the day-passage of the sun and the idea of rebirth. One of Egypt's many creation myths describes how the infant sun god appeared from a lotus blossom that rose out of the primordial waters, and it is this initial act of creation, with its implication of resurrection, that Tutankhamun's image represents.

Carter's notes from the excavation of the stairway and entrance corridor do not substantiate his claim of having found it there. They mention the skins, jars, and vases, but there is no trace of the king's fabulous head. When and where was it found?

Representatives of the Antiquities Service found it months after the tomb was first opened, in the tomb of Rameses XI, which by that time (30th March, 1924) Carter's team was using for storage. The object had been carefully wrapped and packed in a wooden wine crate, ready for shipment. Carter was not in Egypt at the time; he was lecturing in the United States.

Circumstances did not look good for Carter. The Egyptians suspected that he had intended to smuggle this wonderful image out of the country. Herbert Winlock, an Egyptologist with

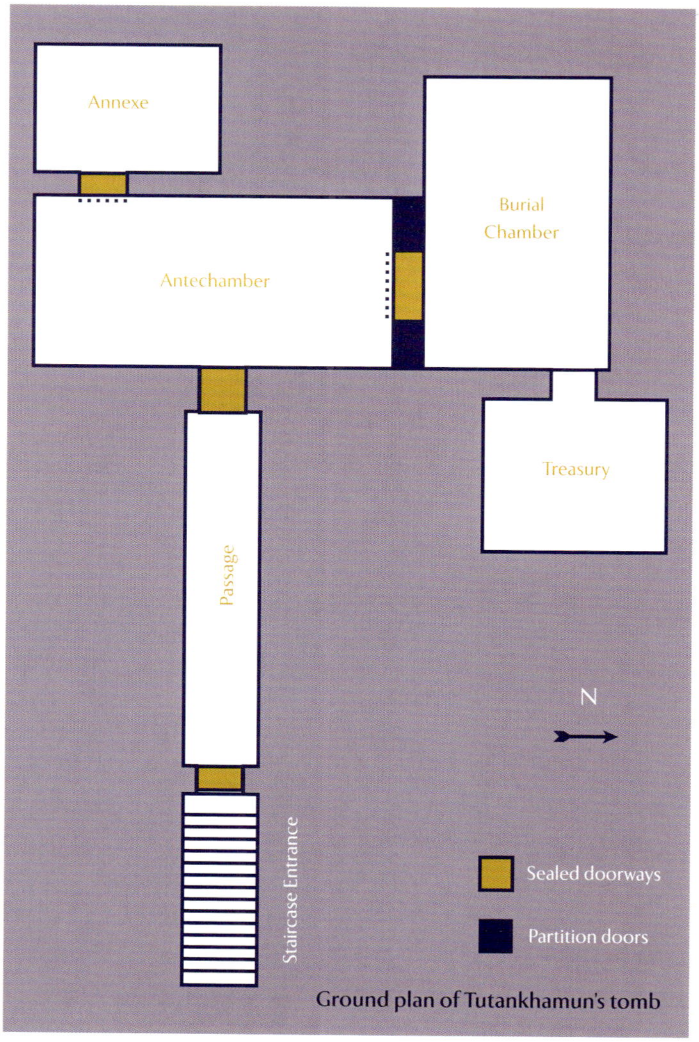

Ground plan of Tutankhamun's tomb

the Metropolitan Museum of Art in New York, tried to deflect such accusations by suggesting that Carter had purchased it legally for Lord Carnarvon from excavations at Amarna in 1923, but Carter denied this. He had found it in the corridor, he insisted, and it was packed so that it could be sent to Cairo.

The truth of the matter is elusive. If the head was indeed found in the corridor, what might it have been doing there? It might have been dropped there by tomb robbers. The wooden head itself would be of no value to them, but it had once been adorned with gold jewelry; none of this remains anymore except the back and post of an earring that once hung from the piercing in the king's left ear. And if that were the case, why hadn't the priests who sealed up the violated tomb placed this beautiful object in one of the chambers? Possibly it had been placed in the corridor deliberately as a magical artifact that would allow the king to leave the tomb each morning, to be reborn with the rising sun.

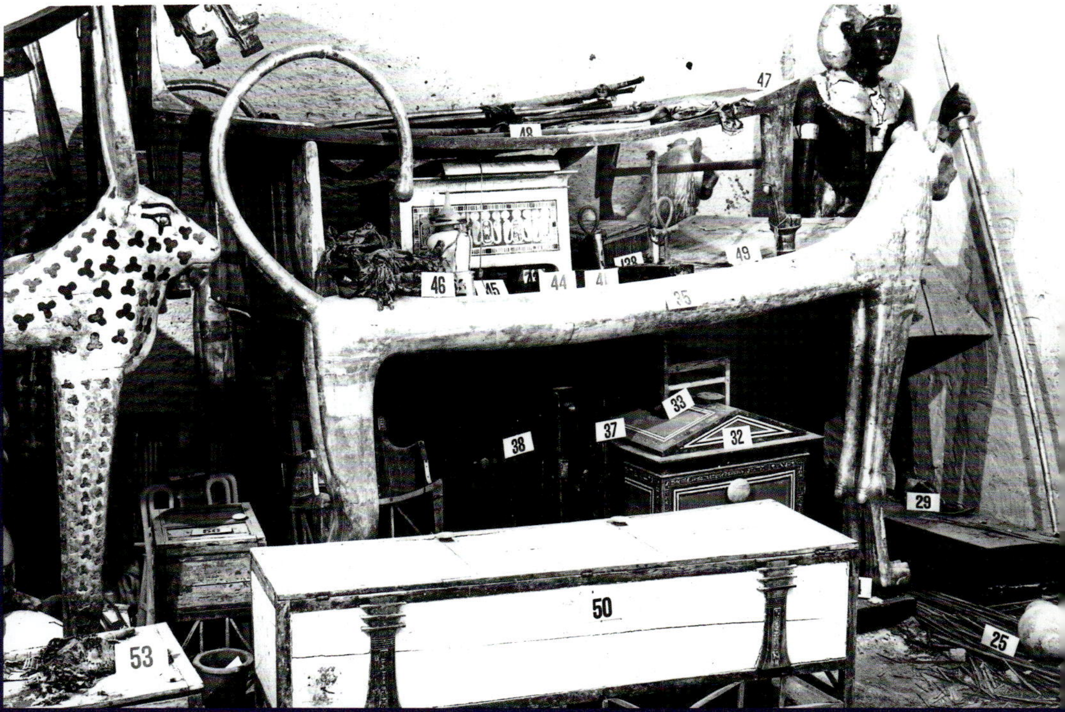

Part of the treasues of Tutankhamun as found in the Antechamber. Harry Burton / Griffith Institute

THE ANTECHAMBER

At 4:00 in the afternoon of 26th November, 1922, Howard Carter made a "tiny breach" in the blocked doorway at the end of the Entrance Corridor. After checking for noxious gases with a candle, he widened the hole a little more. An iron rod inserted into it met with no resistance. There was empty space, perhaps even a room, beyond the doorway.

Carter was not alone at the time. Lord Carnarvon and his daughter Lady Evelyn attended this event, as did Carter's friend and assistant, Arthur Callender. Carter inserted a candle into the hole and looked in.

Carter recollected: "Lord Carnarvon said to me 'Can you see anything'. I replied to him 'Yes, wonderful things'. I then with precaution made the hole sufficiently large for both of us to see. With the light of an electric torch as well as an additional candle we looked in. Our sensations and astonishment are difficult to describe as the better light revealed to us the marvellous collection of treasures: two strange ebony-black effigies of a King, gold sandalled, bearing staff and mace, loomed out from the cloak of darkness; gilded couches in strange forms, lion-headed, Hathor-headed, and beast infernal; exquisitely painted, inlaid, and ornamental caskets; flowers; calcite (Egyptian alabaster) vases, some beautifully executed of lotus and papyrus device; strange black shrines with a gilded monster snake appearing from within; quite ordinary looking white chests; finely carved chairs; a golden inlaid throne; a heap of large curious white oviform boxes; beneath our very eyes, on the threshold, a lovely lotiform wishing-cup in translucent calcite (Egyptian alabaster); stools of all shapes and design, of both common and rare materials; and, lastly a confusion of overturned parts of chariots glinting with gold, peering from amongst which was a mannikin. The first impression of which suggested the property-room of an opera of a vanished civilization. Our sensations were bewildering and full of strange emotion..."

I can understand, from my own experiences in archaeology, what Carter surely felt and thought in these moments. No language has sufficient words to express such things. The intensity of emotion that arises within me when I open a tomb for the first time, or gaze upon a statue that has not been seen by human eyes for millennia, defies adequate description. Anything we say or write about it is understatement.

After this initial exploration, it was decided that the official opening of the tomb would take place on 29th November. Egyptian government officials, in addition to foreign archaeologists and dignitaries, were in attendance.

This was only the beginning of a flood of visitors. By 1st December, Carter was forced to close the tomb. The great influx of "Egyptian notables of Luxor" who wanted to see the tomb caught him by surprise. He had to deny them the privilege until steps could be taken to ensure the security of the artifacts. He had the entrance fit with a steel door and assembled a team of experts to excavate the tomb. Key members of this team included Carter's own assistant, Arthur Mace; Harry Burton, photographer for the Metropolitan Museum of Art's Egyptian Expedition; Alfred Lucas, a chemist who worked for the Antiquities Service; and Arthur Callender, a retired engineer. More than two weeks later, on 16th December, Carter reopened the tomb.

Now the real work of his career began. "One of the greatest artistic treasures of the tomb," as Carter called it, was the first object removed from the tomb.

On one long side, a horde of Nubian soldiers falls in a terrified, disordered heap before Tutankhamun, trampled by the king's horses and bitten by his dogs. On the other side, the foes have Semitic features, indicating that they are from the Levant and Syria. Behind Tutankhamun, in an appropriately orderly fashion, comes his army of charioteers and foot soldiers; a team of fan-bearers runs behind the king. On the vaulted lid, the king and his hounds chase down lions, gazelles, wild asses, and ostriches, creatures of the desert savannah. In image and inscription, Tutankhamun is identified as brave and strong, slayer of all foes.

This was one of the king's most important ritual functions, insuring defeat of the chaos (foreign people and wilderness) that continually threatened Egypt. Images of such triumph, whether on small objects, such as this chest, or large monuments, such as a temple pylon, were instrumental in achieving this through magical means. In these scenes, too, the king is identified as a god.

They need not depict reality, although the large number of weapons, such as bows and arrows, found in the tomb indicate that Tutankhamun had interest in martial activities and hunting. At Giza, near the Valley Temple of King Khafre of the 4th Dynasty (c. 2500 BC), Tutankhamun had a hunting lodge or rest house. This region was a favorite hunting ground during the New Kingdom. Whether Tutankhamun ever participated in battle is less certain. It is generally believed that the boy-king never led his army, which instead fought under the command of Horemheb, Tutankhamun's commander-in-chief. But recently reconstructed fragments of relief at Luxor that suggest the king may have seen combat.

The contents of the chest, however, were not connected with war. Inside the box was clothing, including the costume of a priest, elaborate robes, sandals, slippers, and a gilded headrest. Some of the clothing was made for a child and surely belonged to Tutankhamun when he first became king as a boy of merely nine.

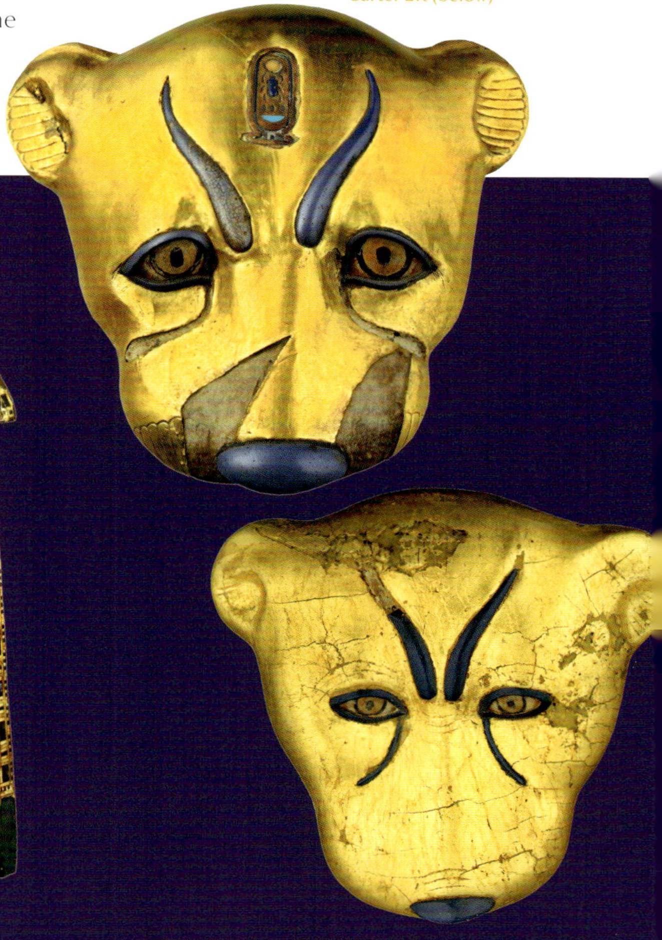

TWO LEOPARD HEAD APPLIQUÉS
Plastered and gilded wood, crystal, glass, calcite (Egyptian alabaster), bronze
Heights 17.5 cm (Carter 44q); 13 cm (Carter 21t)
Carter 44q (above) and Carter 21t (below)

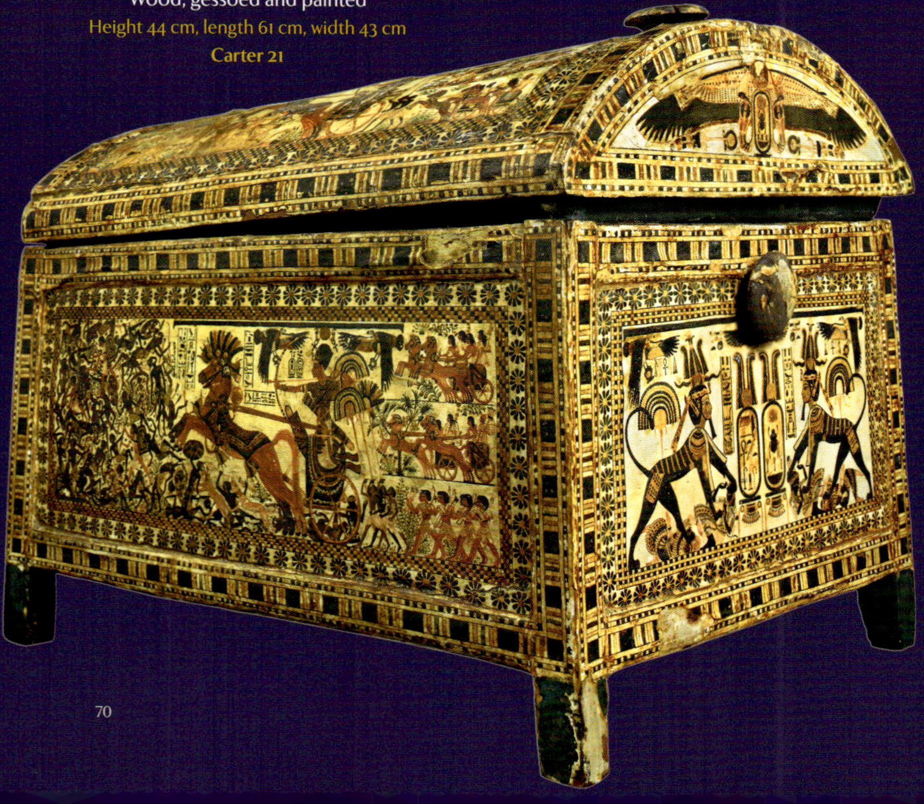

PAINTED CHEST
Wood, gessoed and painted
Height 44 cm, length 61 cm, width 43 cm
Carter 21

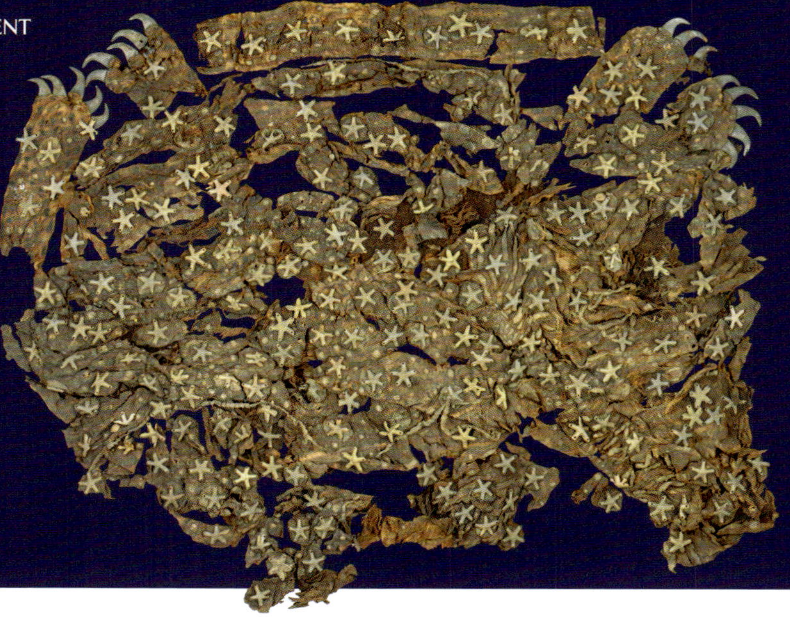

TEXTILE FRAGMENT
Cloth, silver, gold
Carter 21t

These items represent the remains of two priestly robes made to resemble leopard skins. The textile fragment and the smaller of the two leopard heads came from the Painted Chest (**Carter No. 21**). The small size may indicate that Tutankhamun wore this robe when he was a child. Carter found the larger head in a gilded and inlaid casket found elsewhere in the Antechamber.

Each leopard head was carved from wood, coated with plaster, then gilded and given inlay of crystal and glass. The king's throne name, Nebkheperure, is inlaid in colored glass and calcite (Egyptian alabaster) into the forehead of the larger.

Small bronze rings allowed each to be sewn to a cloth robe. The tapestry-woven textile here is a fragment of such a garment. Small five-pointed gold stars with holes in their points have been attached to the fabric. Not only does this suggest the starry night sky, but they also echo a leopard's spots. The four "legs" of the robe, which are hard to see now because the textile has so greatly decayed, once had silver claws. Robes such as this were worn over one shoulder, two claws hanging in the front and two down the back.

The pharaoh was the chief priest of the gods. Even as a young boy, Tutankhamun would have had to perform this role, hence the smaller, child-sized robe. In particular, this garment was worn by a ***sem*** priest, who had the duty of performing the ceremony of the Opening of the Mouth. Through this funerary ritual, the mummy and images of the deceased were given the powers to speak, hear, breathe, and perform other functions in the afterlife. Possibly the young Tutankhamun – perhaps while still named Tutankhaten – wore the small robe while performing the ritual for his predecessor.

One of the most exquisite of the artifacts from the tomb, this goblet was found just beyond the inner blocking of the doorway to the Antechamber, where perhaps thieves had dropped it. The cup takes the form of an open blossom of a white lotus, with other blossoms and buds at its sides. On each side, Heh, the god of infinity, kneels on a basket while holding ***ankhs*** (signs of life) and a notched palm rib signifying "millions of years." The palm ribs rest on tadpoles, the hieroglyph for "one hundred thousand."

The titles and names of the king, called "beloved of Amun," are incised onto the cup and painted in blue. The inscription around the rim says, "May your life-force (***ka***) live, may you pass (live) one million years, one who loves Thebes and dwells in it, your face towards the northern wind: may your eyes see the good place." This inscription has earned the goblet the nickname "Wishing Cup." The king probably drank wine or water from this vessel. Its symbols – from the flowers, associated with rebirth, and the symbols indicating great lengths of time – made this object a powerful symbol that magically offered the king rebirth and everlasting existence.

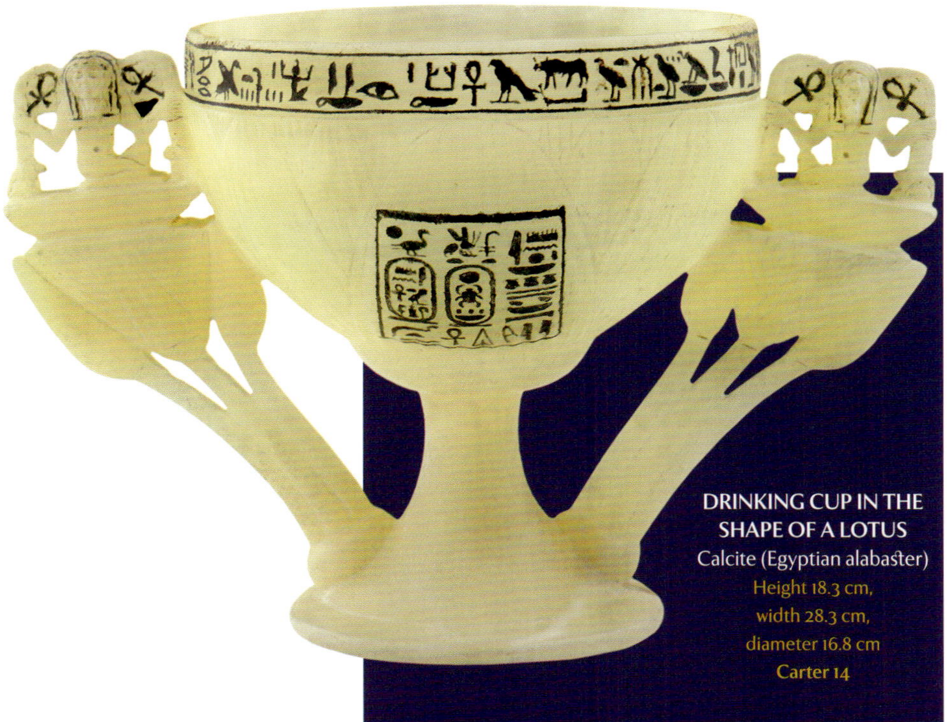

DRINKING CUP IN THE SHAPE OF A LOTUS
Calcite (Egyptian alabaster)
Height 18.3 cm,
width 28.3 cm,
diameter 16.8 cm
Carter 14

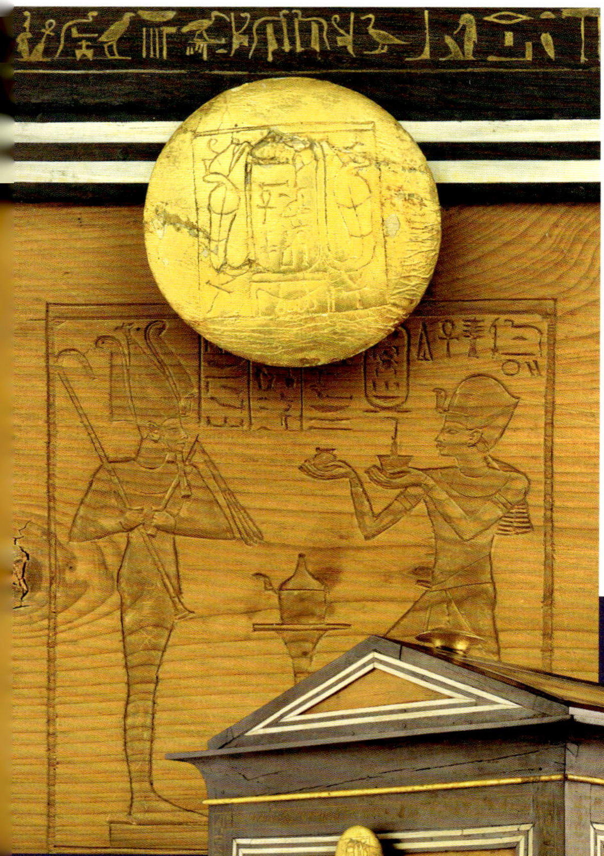

Made to be carried on poles by two porters, this is the only known example of a type of portable chest used in Egypt since the Old Kingdom. Found under one of the ritual beds in the Antechamber, the chest is made of cedarwood with ebony veneer. These were valuable, imported woods. Cedar came from the area of modern Lebanon, while ebony reached Egypt from lands to the south, deeper into Africa.

The use of such wood testifies to the importance of its contents. A figure of the king offering jars of water, wine, and incense to Osiris appears on one end. This, too, reflects some of the objects found in the box: stone knives, vessels made of glass and stone, pieces of incense, garlic cloves and dried fruit and ostrich feathers. Most of these can be associated with the Opening of the Mouth ceremony, which was performed on the mummy and images of the deceased, so that they could function in the afterlife. The hieroglyphic text on the chest contains spells from the ceremony, so its original contents were almost certainly the implements required to perform its complicated rituals.

TRAVELING CHEST WITH CARRYING POLES
Wood, ebony, ivory, gold leaf, copper alloy
Length 83 cm, width 60.5 cm, height 63.5 cm
Carter 32

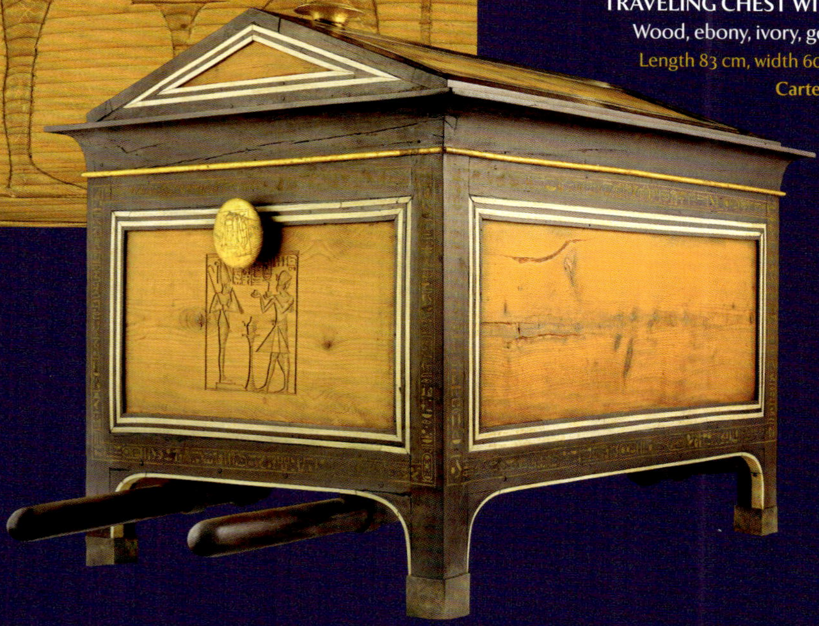

CARTOUCHE BOXES
Wood
Length 12.2 cm, width 5.5 cm
(Carter 14b)
Length 11.2 cm, width 4.6 cm
(Carter 367k)
Length 12 cm, width 5.4 cm
(Carter 620(95))
Carter 14b (right); Carter 367k (center); Carter 620(95) (left)

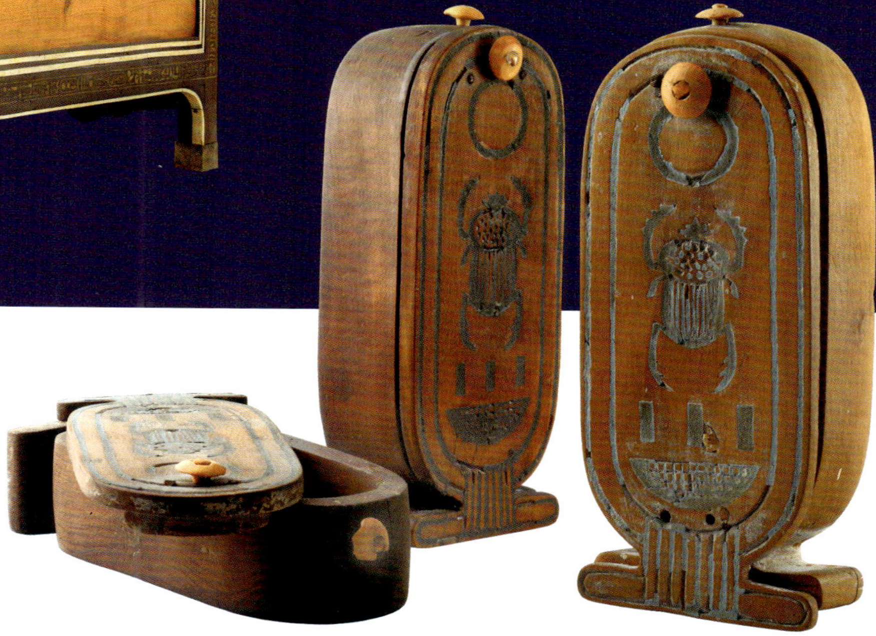

Carter found these small boxes scattered around the tomb, one (Carter No. 14b) in the Antechamber. Made of reddish wood with ivory knobs, each box has the form of a cartouche, the rope that enclosed two of the king's five names, his birth name (Tutankhamun, originally Tutankhaten), and his throne name (Nebkheperure). Taken at coronation, the king's throne name was chosen with care. "Nebkheperure," meaning "Re is the Lord of Manifestations," was written with the solar disk (*Re*), a scarab with plural strokes (*kheperu*), and a basket (*neb*).

The cartouche itself is a stylized circle of rope closed with a knot. It is an elongated form of the hieroglyphic sign *shen*, meaning "eternity." It protected his name, gave it long life, and indicated the king's dominion over everything. As the name was protected and given long life, so was the king himself.

Carter discovered six chairs in the tomb, including this one, made for the king when he was still a child.

Natural scenes embossed into gold foil ornament the armrests: plants (bordered by rectangles) on the interior faces and recumbent antelopes, positioned to fill the frames with running spirals, on the interior. These details show Syrian and Aegean influences in the art of the period. Each leg has a lion's paw with inlaid ivory claws.

The footrest seen here was found near the golden throne (**Carter No. 91**), but its geometric designs and materials coordinate well with the smaller chair.

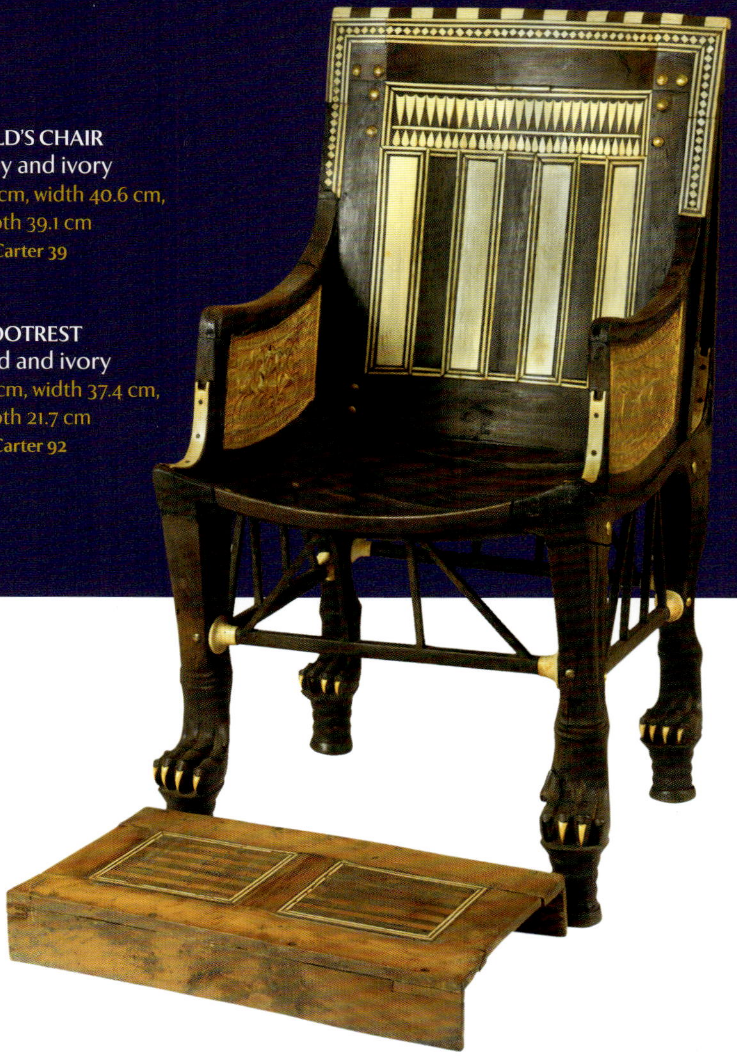

CHILD'S CHAIR
Ebony and ivory
Height 71.5 cm, width 40.6 cm, depth 39.1 cm
Carter 39

FOOTREST
Wood and ivory
Height 5.8 cm, width 37.4 cm, depth 21.7 cm
Carter 92

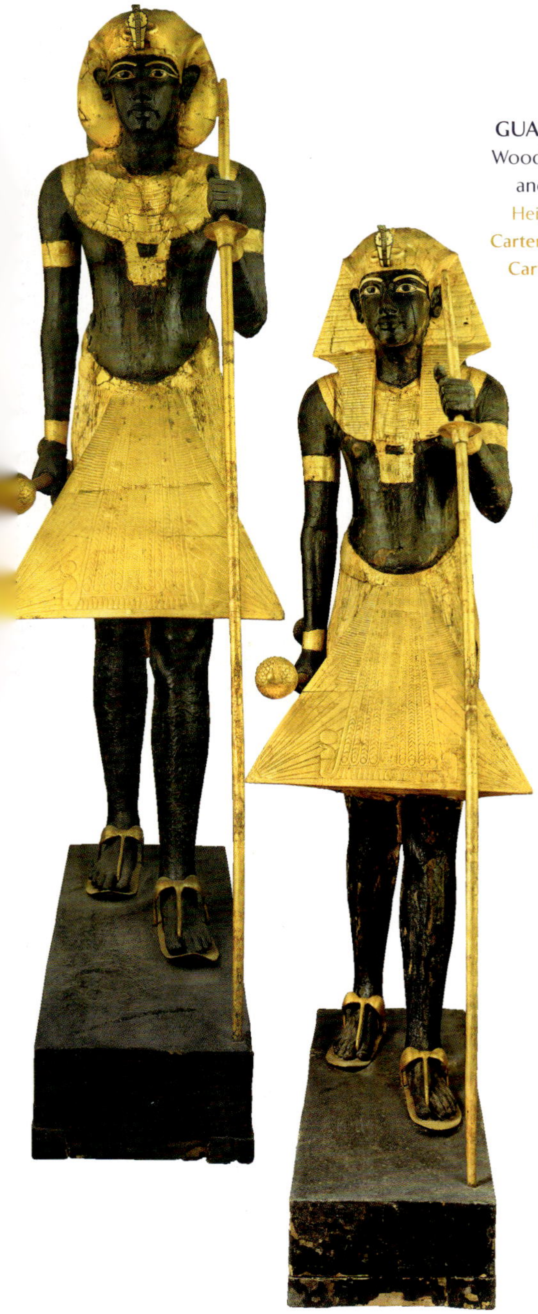

GUARDIAN STATUES
Wood, gessoed, painted, and gilded, bronze
Height 190 cm (both)
Carter 22 (*nemes*; left) and Carter 29 (*khat*; right)

This pair of life-sized wooden statues of the king stood beside the wall, at either side of the entrance to the Burial Chamber. The king's jewelry and clothing are gilded to identify the king with the sun, but the king's skin is painted black, a color associated with dark, fertile soil and with resurrection.

Each figure holds a papyrus staff in his left hand and, in his right, a mace. One figure wears the ***nemes***, a striped cloth, tied in a pigtail at the back, with lappets that hang down over the shoulders. This is the headdress seen on Tutankhamun's famous golden mask (**Carter No. 256a**), and also on another icon of pharaonic Egypt, the Great Sphinx. It was probably associated with Re-Khepri, the god representing the sun at dawn. The ***nemes*** also identified the king with Horus, both as the son of Osiris and in his form as the great sky god.

The other wears the ***khat***, or ***afnet***, also known as the bag wig. This headdress rarely appears outside of a funerary context and appears to be associated with the night and the passage through the Netherworld. An inscription on this statue identifies this image of the king as "the ***ka*** of Horakhty, the Osiris, King, Lord of the Two Lands, Nebkheperure, true of voice." By calling the king "the Osiris" and "true of voice," the inscription refers to Tutankhamun in a netherworldly context. So the figure here is Tutankhamun's ***ka***, or life-force, an aspect of his being that survived death and could receive offerings.

Together this pair of statues might represent Tutankhamun in both nocturnal and diurnal phases of the sun god's existence.

RITUAL BEDS

RITUAL BEDS
Gilded wood, glass, semiprecious stones, ivory

LION BED
height 161 cm,
length 228 cm, width 91 cm
Carter 35

COW BED
height 187 cm,
length 223 cm, width 128 cm
Carter 73

AMMUT BED
height 141 cm,
length 234 cm, width 91.3
Carter 137

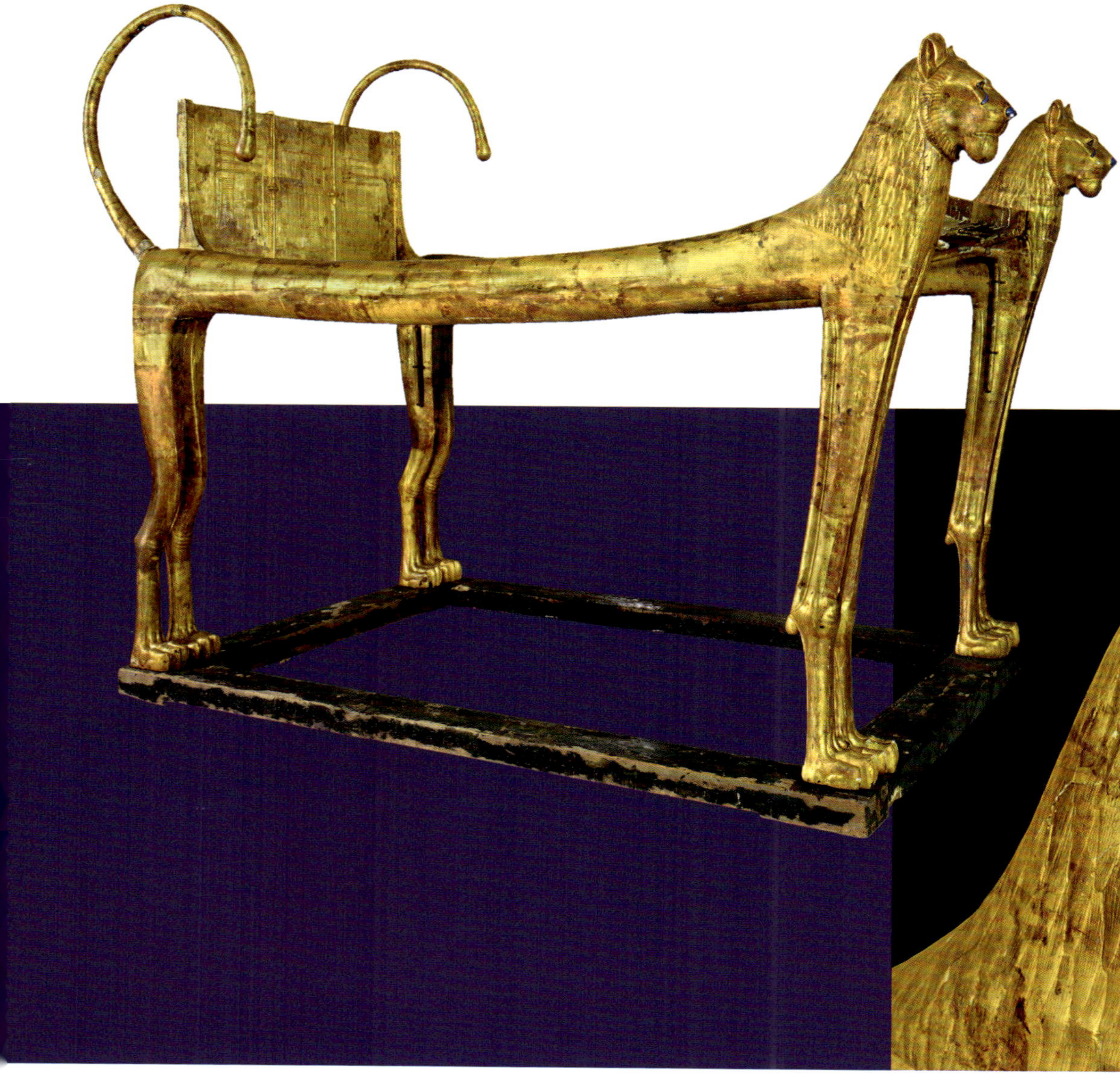

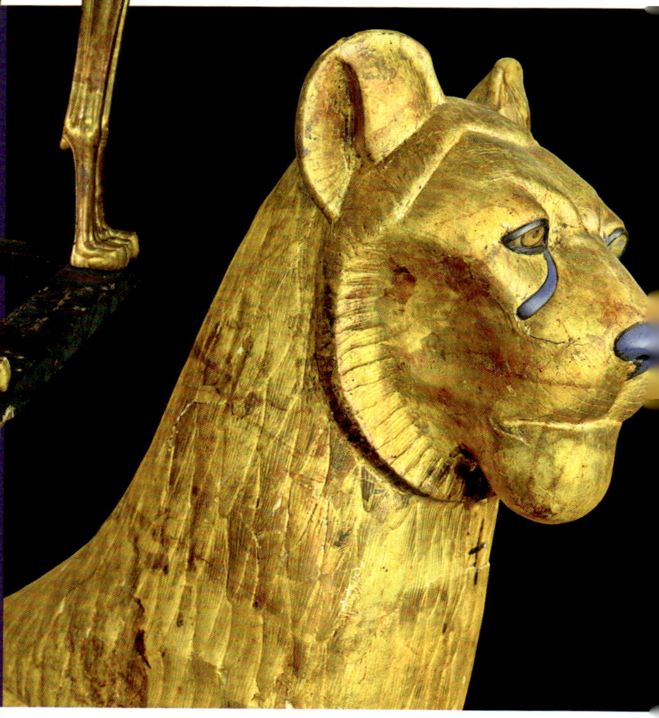

The purpose of these pieces of furniture is not entirely clear, but it seems likely that they were used during the mummification process and the funeral. Possibly the king's mummy was placed on each one to receive certain rituals.

One bed represents a lion deity; another, a cow goddess; and the third, Ammut, a mythical hybrid of lion, hippopotamus, and crocodile. When the beds were assembled, it seems that either the workmen or a scribe made a mistake. The cross-rail of the lion bed gives the name "Mehit-weret," a goddess typically depicted as a cow. The name of a lioness-goddess, Isis-Mehtet, is written on the cow bed. However, the name, as written here, does include a cow's head as its last hieroglyph.

The Egyptians visualized the horizon as two lions seated back-to-back, between which the sun rose in the morning. This idea of rebirth and resurrection could be at work here. However, although the lions of this bed have manes, indicating that they ought to be male, the inscription identifies one of the beds as Isis-Mehtet, a goddess. Perhaps the great cats on this bed are intended to be female.

The cow is probably Mehit-weret, the "Great Flood," a goddess closely linked with creation of the world. Between her tall horns sits the solar disk. In Egyptian mythology, she carried the sun from the primordial mound to the horizon at the time of creation and on each day thereafter. The spots on her hide are stars; Mehit-weret was associated with the night sky. The eyes have the falcon-markings of the ***wedjat***, or Eye of Horus, the

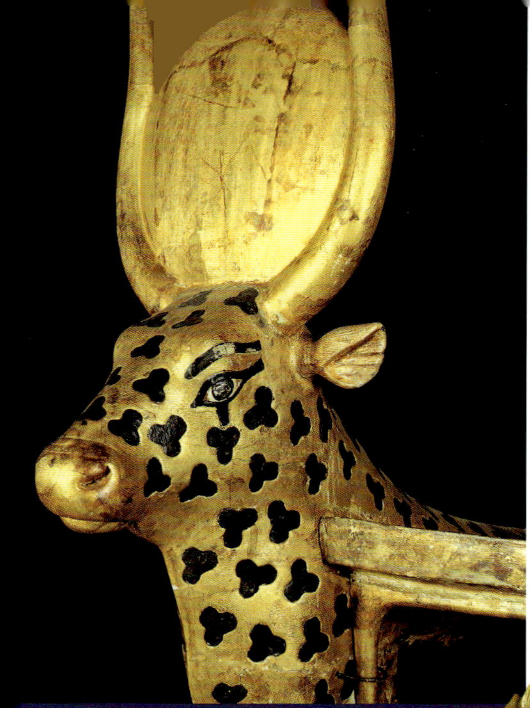

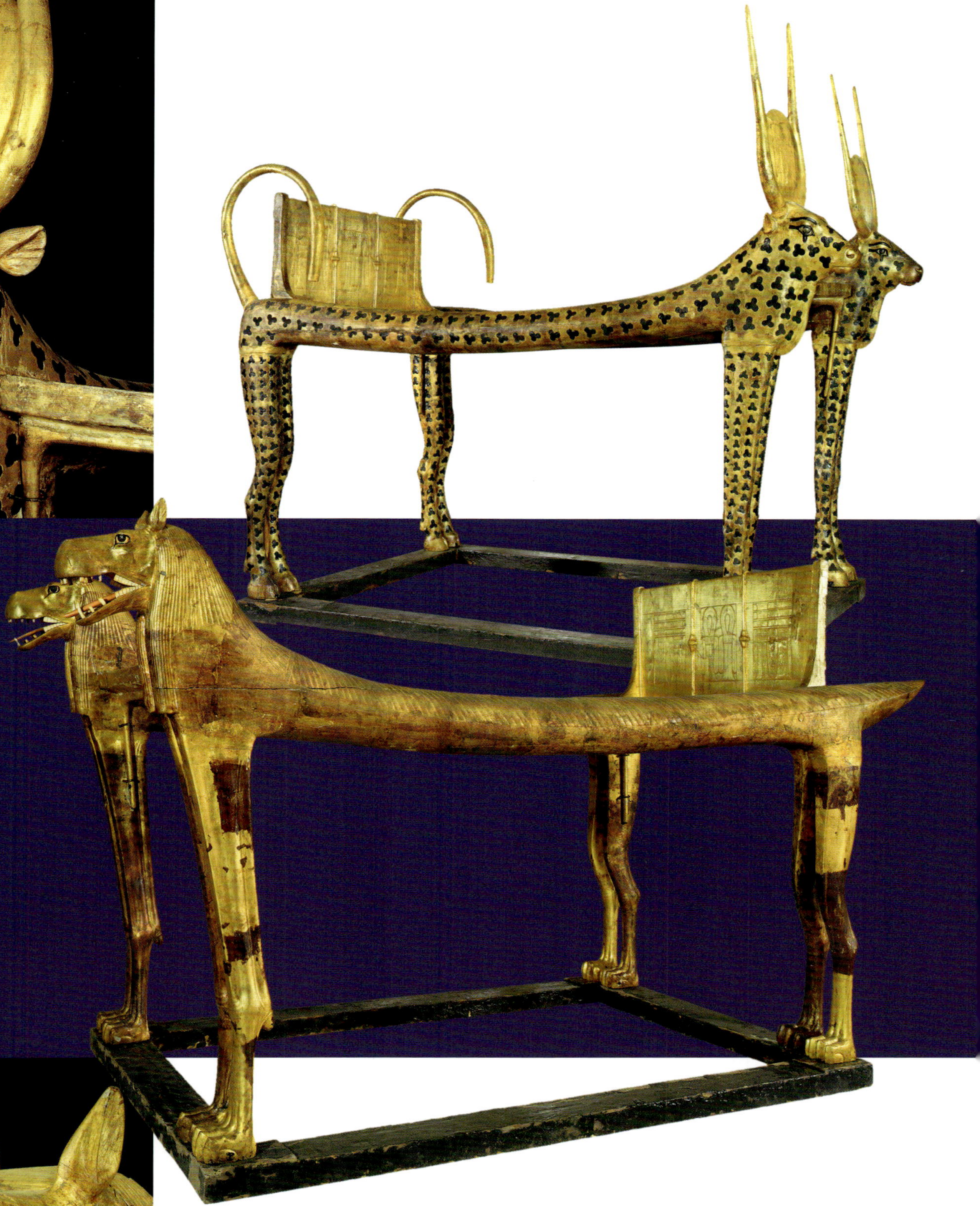

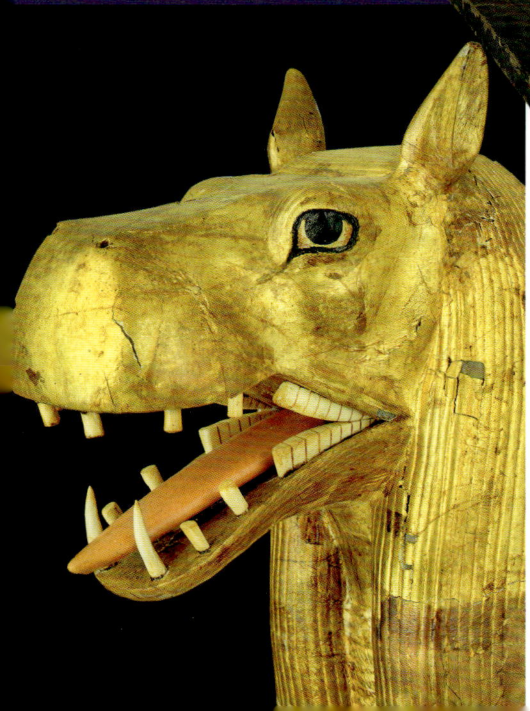

sky god. She is thus closely connected with the king, whose resurrection in the netherworld she would help to achieve.

The last bed is labeled correctly as "Ammut." Even without the text, there would be, in any case, no mistaking goddess, with her hippopotamus head, crocodile body, and lion's legs and mane. She appears in vignettes in the *Chapters of Coming Forth by Day*, in the judgment scene before Osiris, when the heart of the deceased is weighed against the feather of truth (*maat*, universal order). If the arms of the scale balanced, the deceased entered into Osiris's kingdom as one of the blessed dead. But if the heart outweighed *maat*, Ammut was there to devour it. The soul would perish forever.

The leather and metal chest protector that the king would have worn into battle or while hunting served as the model for this remarkable piece made of gold, which would have been worn on ceremonial occasions. It is often seen in art, including on other objects from the tomb, but no other example survives. The king wears such a corselet while hunting, as seen on the painted chest (Carter No. 21). It also appears on the king while he is presented to the deities Ptah and Sekhmet on the so-called coronation pectoral (Carter No. 267q). Amun, king of the gods and patron of the New Kingdom pharaohs, often wears such a garment. By wearing it, the king would associate himself with this god.

On the front, the pectoral shows Tutankhamun among the gods. Amun-Re, king of the gods, presents Tutankhamun with a palm rib signifying millions of years. From it hangs the image of a pavilion with two thrones. Together, these symbols signify a lengthy reign for the young king. The falcon-headed deity standing behind Tutankhamun is Atum, a creator-god; he is accompanied by his consort, Iusaas.

It seems to me that the craftsman, or craftsmen, were truly inspired and allowed their imagination to devise this wonderful object with painstaking care.

Carter found most of the corselet in Box 54, but elements from it were found scattered around the floor, and the broad collar was found in the small golden shrine (Carter No. 108). A feather inlay was found with the pieces of the royal chariot, and another bit was found in a dish of dates.

CORSELET
Gold, semiprecious stones, glass
Height 40 cm, length 85 cm
Carter 54k

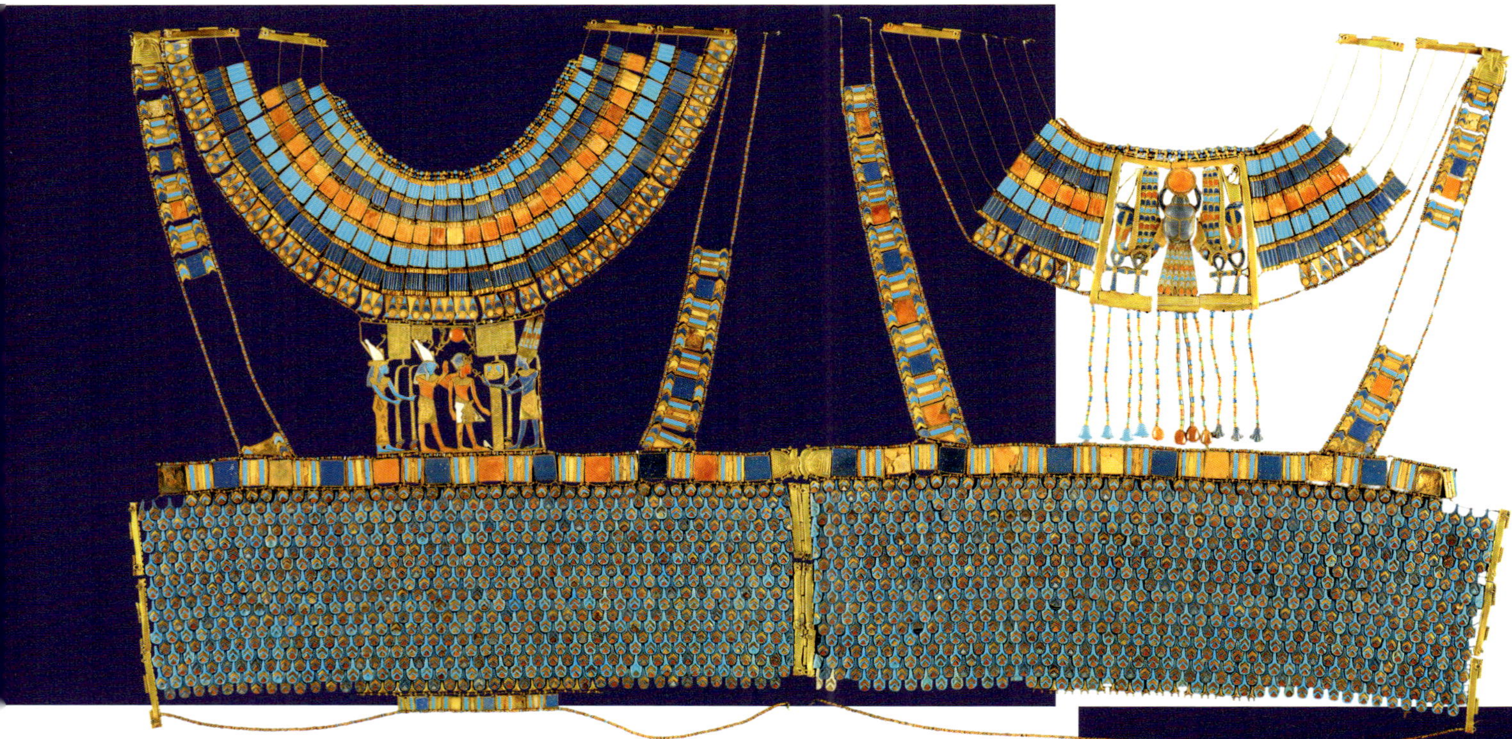

Carter found four of these clever lamps atop the lion bed (Carter No. 35), though he believed they had been stored in a box in the Treasury that happened to be the right size and had traces of varnish that might have come from the base of these lamps.

Anthropomorphized ***ankhs*** such as this appear occasionally in Egyptian art (for example, on the king's ostrich hunt fan, (Carter No. 242), but they are uncommon in three dimensions. The arms stretch out to hold little cups, though some of these are missing. The cups would have been filled with oil. A wick of twisted flax (one of which survived) would soak up the oil; this would keep the lamp burning. Carter suspected that two of the lamps, including this one, had cups of gold, which were stolen by thieves.

TORCH HOLDER
Bronze and wood
Height 23.8 cm
Carter 41c

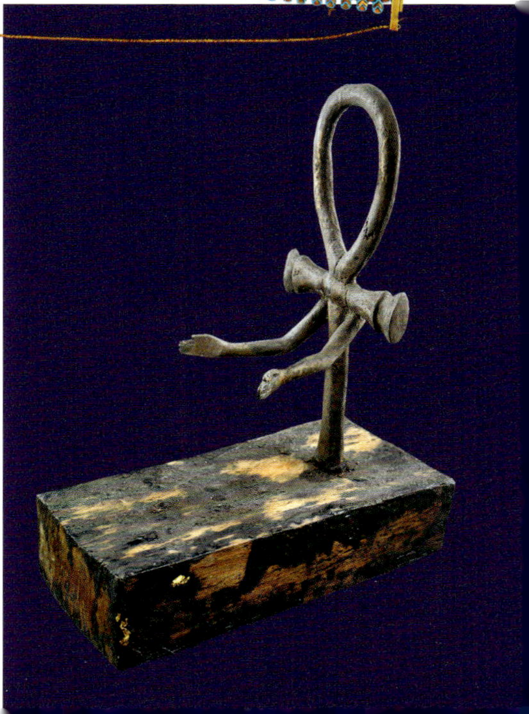

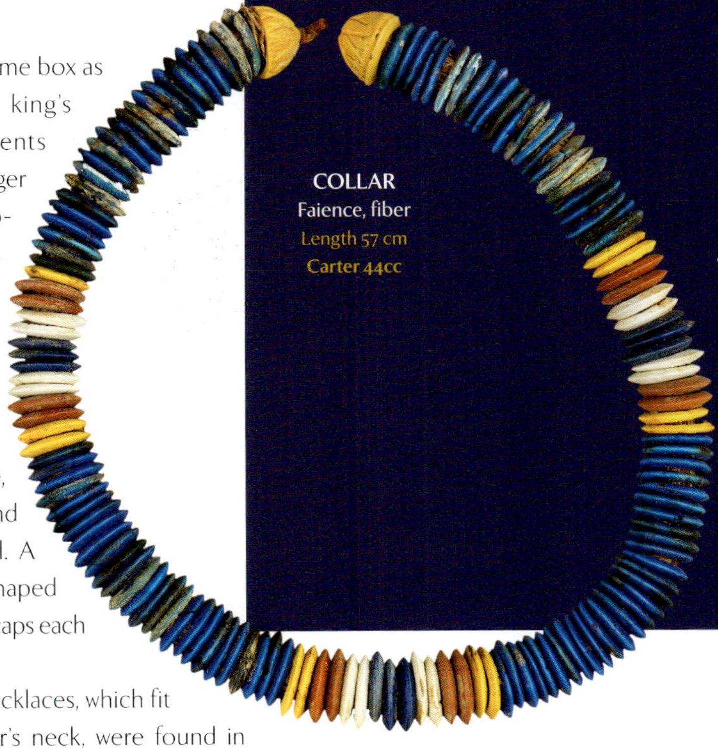

COLLAR
Faience, fiber
Length 57 cm
Carter 44cc

Found in the same box as some of the king's priestly garments (for example, the larger leopard head appliqué, **Carter No. 44q**), this collar is made of faience beads shaped like disks, strung on a cord. Most of the beads are bright blue, with yellow, red, and white beads as well. A larger yellow bead shaped like a lotus blossom caps each end.

Other similar necklaces, which fit close to the wearer's neck, were found in the box. They could have been worn together. These faience necklaces resemble a kind of necklace called the ***shebyu***, which became popular during the reign of Amenhotep III, perhaps because of an association with the sun god. ***Shebyu***-necklaces made entirely of gold disk-shaped beads served as an official reward from the king for some exceptional service, whether military or civil. Tomb owners sometimes had scenes of their reception of this "gold of honor" recorded on their tomb walls. Ay received this kind of collar from Akhenaten, and Horemheb received them from Tutankhamun.

These choker necklaces signified a promotion in status for the recipient. When worn by kings, they indicate that he has been elevated to the divine.

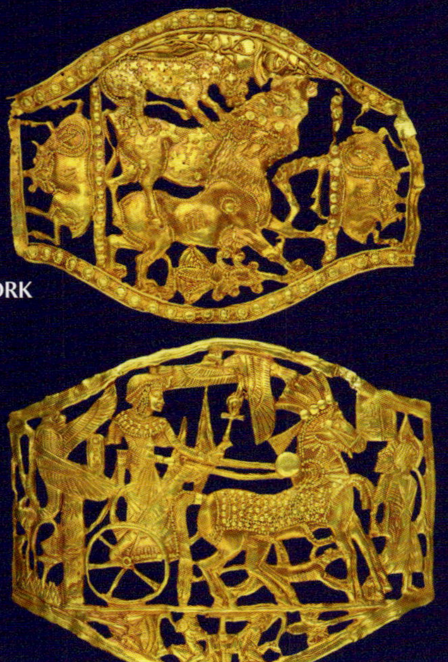

TWO OPENWORK PLAQUES
Gold
Length 9 cm
Carter 44a(1) (above), Carter 44a(2) (below)

When the tomb was breached in antiquity, the robbers probably tore these gold plaques from textiles, intending to melt them for scrap. Stripped from their original context, it is not certain what they were except that they are not "buckles," though they are often identified as such. When the necropolis officials returned them to the tomb, they threw them into a gilded and inlaid box (**Carter No. 44**), with a number of other artifacts. King Farouk donated a similar plaque to the Egyptian Museum in 1946. Carter had apparently given it to him as a gift during one of his visits to the tomb.

Similar in shape, the plaques are made from gold with a high iron content that gives it a distinct reddish tinge. One shows a leopard and a lion attacking a bull. This kind of imagery was popular in the ancient Near East. Here it may represent order, in the form of the lion, overcoming the forces of chaos, depicted here in the form of a wild bull.

The second plaque depicts Tutankhamun riding triumphantly in a chariot, protected by the vulture of Nekhbet, goddess of the south, and the winged cobra of Wadjet, goddess of the north. A royal hound runs alongside the chariot (appearing as though beneath the horses).

The king drives bound enemies before him, and beneath the entire scene are two kneeling and bound enemies.

NEMSET VESSEL ON A STAND
Calcite (Egyptian alabaster)
Height 29.5 cm
Carter 45

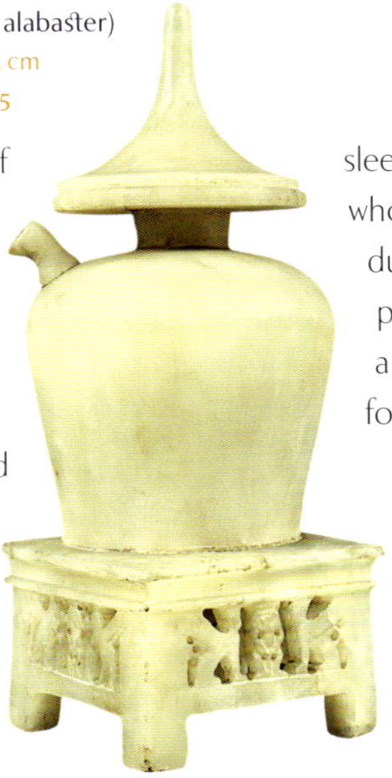

Most examples of this kind of vessel, which the Egyptians called a ***nemset***, are made of faience and are no more than half the size of Tutankhamun's fine example, carved from calcite (Egyptian alabaster). They were used to pour libations of water or other liquids to the gods or to the deceased. The lid, which rises to a peak, sits atop a flat rim. The vessel has a square stand carved of the same material.

The dwarf god Bes appears on two of the sides, between winged creatures with ***ankhs***. Bes's duty was to protect the vulnerable, particularly children, pregnant women, and sleepers. He was a popular deity, whose worship continued even during the Amarna Period. His protective nature made him a common decorative motif for household objects.

This is one of 80 vessels carved of calcite (Egyptian alabaster) Carter found in the tomb. Twenty-five of them were inscribed, including a number of heirlooms, which have the names of some of Tutankhamun's forbearers, including Thutmose III (his great-great-great grandfather) and his father, Akhenaten.

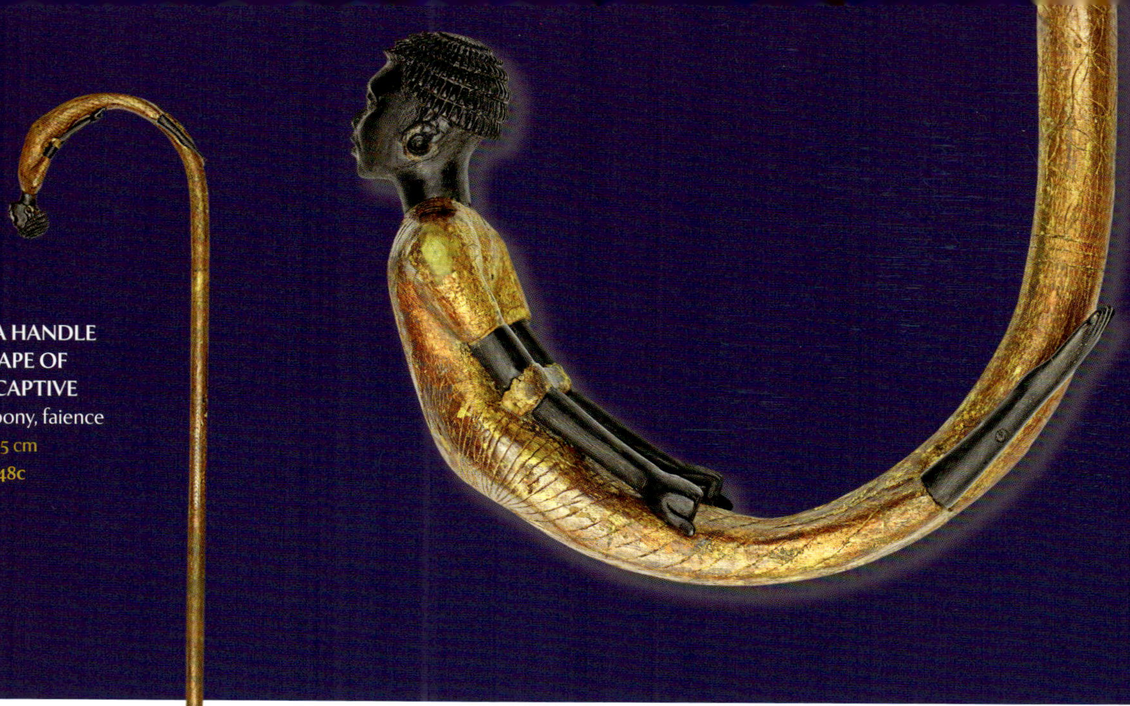

STAFF WITH A HANDLE IN THE SHAPE OF A NUBIAN CAPTIVE
Gilded wood, ebony, faience
Length 115 cm
Carter 48c

This staff, with an image of a Nubian bound as a captive, is among the most magnificent of the approximately 130 sticks and staffs found in the tomb. Some were ceremonial staffs, like this one. Others were fighting batons or sticks used to kill snakes, and yet others were walking sticks. The large number of them led Carter to suggest that the young king was "an amateur collector." The object here served a ceremonial or symbolic purpose. It is one of a set of four, each depicting either a single Nubian captive or, in one case, a Nubian captive paired with an Asiatic.

The handle takes the form of a Nubian man whose arms have been pinned behind his back at the elbows. His slender body is curved so that his head is pointed downward, rendered entirely helpless.

By using this staff, the king grasped Nubia and its people in his hand. This was a symbolic expression of a political fact, because Nubia was firmly in the Egyptian "empire" at this time. Perhaps even more importantly, this was an expression of universal order, the triumph of ***maat*** (orderliness, in the form of Egypt and the king) over chaos (in the form of foreign lands and peoples). Tutankhamun had to maintain order not only in the here-and-now of everyday life but also, as an incarnation of the creator god, on a cosmic level.

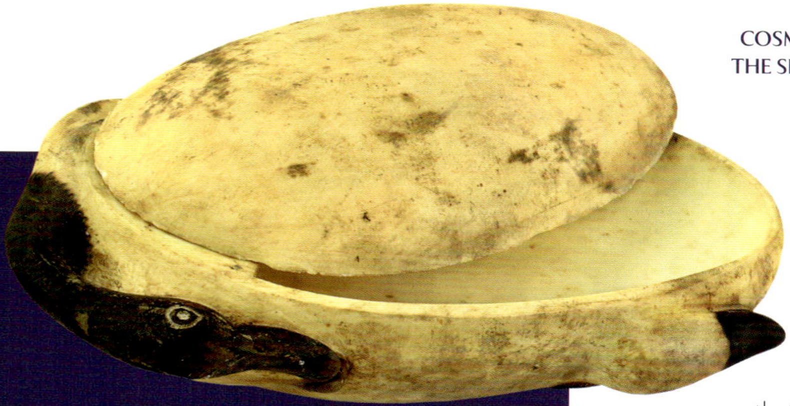

COSMETIC CONTAINER IN THE SHAPE OF WATERFOWL
Ivory
Length 9.8 cm
Carter 54s

Carter found this little ivory cosmetic container in Box 54. The back of the bird is cleverly crafted so that it can swivel on a peg to allow the inner cavity to be revealed.

Excavation reports make no mention of any residue having been found within the box, but it was probably intended to be a container for some kind of cosmetic, perhaps ointment. Perfumes and other cosmetics had religious significance, and they were practical as well, warding off bad smells and eye infections.

A number of small cosmetic boxes that generally resemble this one were reported to have been found in Carter's home after his death. Two were, like this one, shaped like waterfowl. Another was in the form of a grasshopper with wings that swiveled. Carter's notes reveal no trace of these objects, nor was there any evidence that he purchased them on the antiquities market. It seems, therefore, that he appropriated them from among the finds in Tutankhamun's tomb.

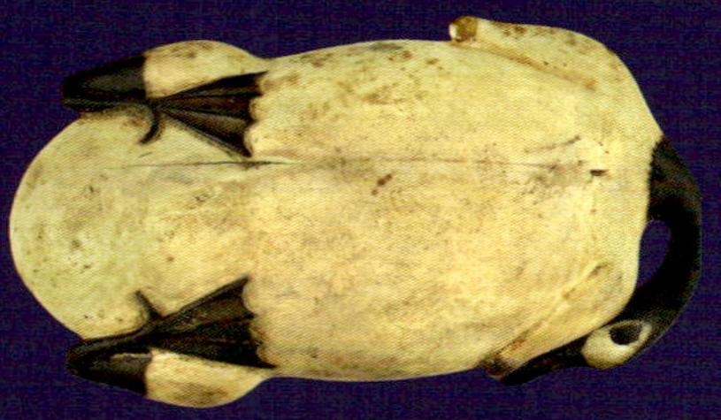

The underside

BLUE GLASS ROYAL FIGURE
Glass
Height 5.8 cm
Carter 54ff

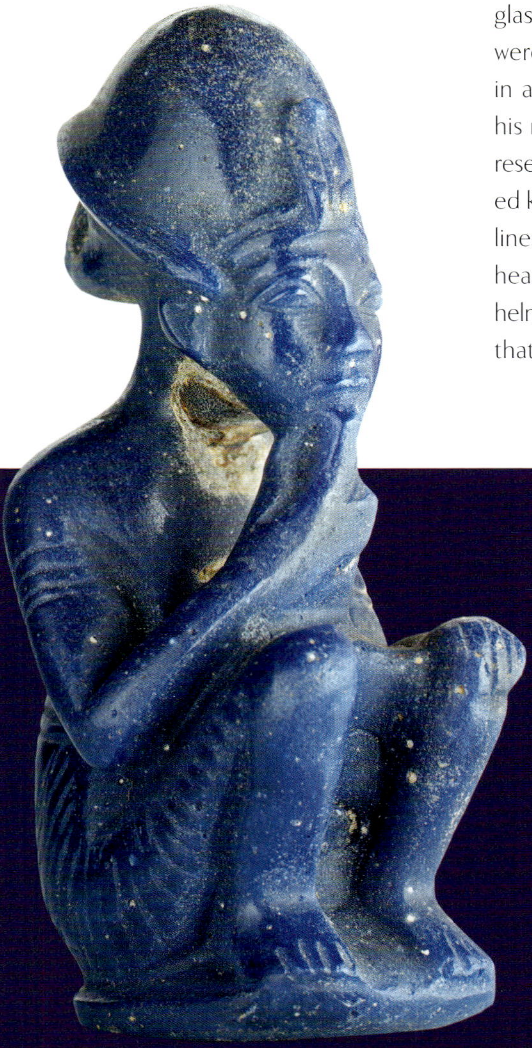

Glass was a new material for Egyptian artisans of the 18th Dynasty. They were, nonetheless, already experts at making glass vessels, but three-dimensional figures were rare. This little amulet represents a king in a squatting position, holding a finger to his mouth, which was a convention for representing childhood. The figure wears a pleated kilt and tunic, the garments suggested by lines molded onto the body. On the king's head is the so-called blue crown or battle helmet, which some scholars believe indicated that the figure was a war leader.

The amulet represents Horus the child, son of Osiris, with whom Egyptian kings were identified from very early times. However, which king is being portrayed as Horus here is a matter of debate. Carter believed that this represented Akhenaten, who is now known to be Tutankhamun's father. Although the face does seem long, as Akhenaten's sometimes is, and the crown is elongated (another Amarna trait), in Amarna Period sculpture the neck is longer and thinner. I believe that the amulet represents Tutankhamun himself.

RING BOX
Ivory
Height 13.1 cm, width 15.7 cm, depth 12.6 cm
Carter 54ddd

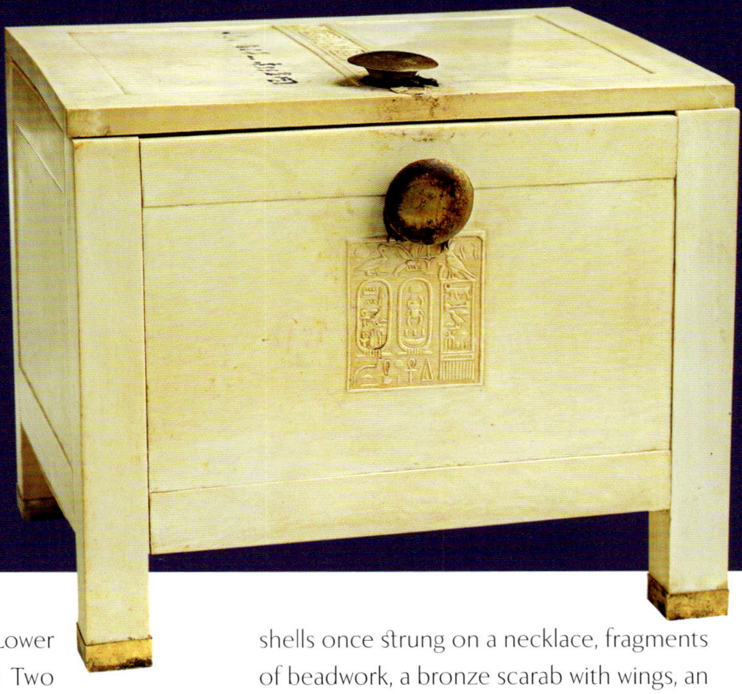

Ten pieces of very fine ivory from a large elephant tusk make up this lovely little box. Ivory appears in scenes of tribute being brought from Africa to the king or his officials.

An inscription on the front of the casket presents three of Tutankhamun's five names: "The Horus, Strong Bull, of Perfect Birth; the King of Upper and Lower Egypt Nebkheperure; and son of Re, Tutankhamun, ruler of Thebes, given life like Re forever." The top gives his two most commonly used names in cartouches, with variations on the epithets: "King of Upper and Lower Egypt, Lord of the Two Lands, Lord of Appearances, Nebkheperure, son of Re of his body, Tutankhamun, living forever." A column shaped like a lily, the floral symbol of Upper Egypt, has been carved in high relief on the back of the box.

There is also a hieratic (cursive) inscription on the lid, written in black ink. It says that the box was intended to hold "Gold rings for the funeral procession." Carter did not find rings in the box. Instead, he encountered a random mix of small objects: seven small shells once strung on a necklace, fragments of beadwork, a bronze scarab with wings, an ivory mirror handle, and damaged ornament. Carter did find a collection of eight gold rings, which might have been the original contents of this casket, knotted in a cloth inside another box in the Antechamber. It could be that the robbers took the rings from the tomb in the cloth and that the necropolis officials, rather than try to find their proper box, stuffed them where they could and used this now-empty box for other objects at hand.

Carter found this ritual ***nemset*** ewer in the box intended to hold it. The docket on box Number 54, which was made of painted wood and ebony, listed the contents as "17 blue faience ***nemset*** ewers," 16 of which remained, along with 17 lids. Other contents had been added to the box, including three gold sequins, "oddments of cloth," a scarab, a woven robe, the waterfowl box (**Carter No. 54s**), most of the corselet (**Carter No. 54k**), the amulet representing a king as Horus the child (**Carter No. 54ff**), the ivory ring box (**Carter No. 54ddd**), and two throw sticks. Carter referred to "the casual nature of the repacking" of objects in this box. Most likely Box 54 happened to be a convenient container for stray bits the necropolis officials found in the wake of the robberies.

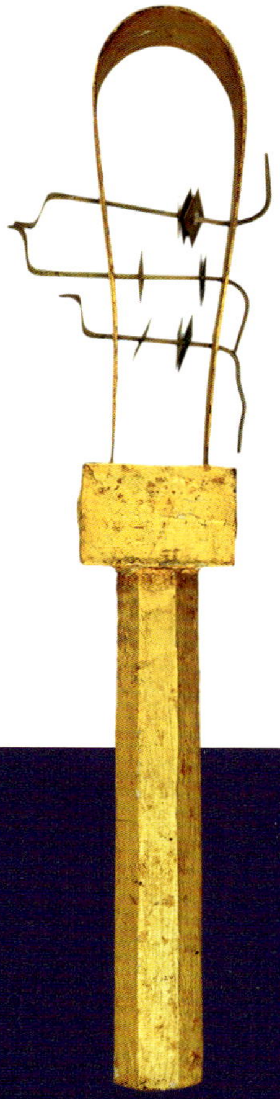

SISTRUM
Gilded wood, gold, copper, and bronze
Height 51.5 cm, width 7 cm
Carter 76

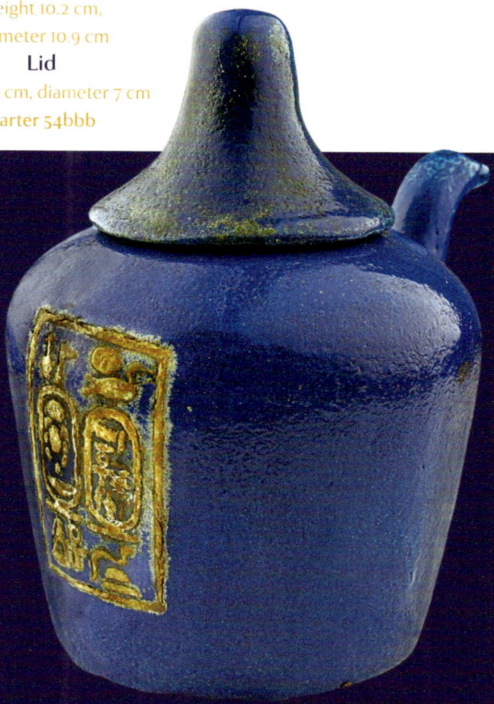

RITUAL VESSEL
Faience
Vessel
Height 10.2 cm, diameter 10.9 cm
Lid
Height 6 cm, diameter 7 cm
Carter 54bbb

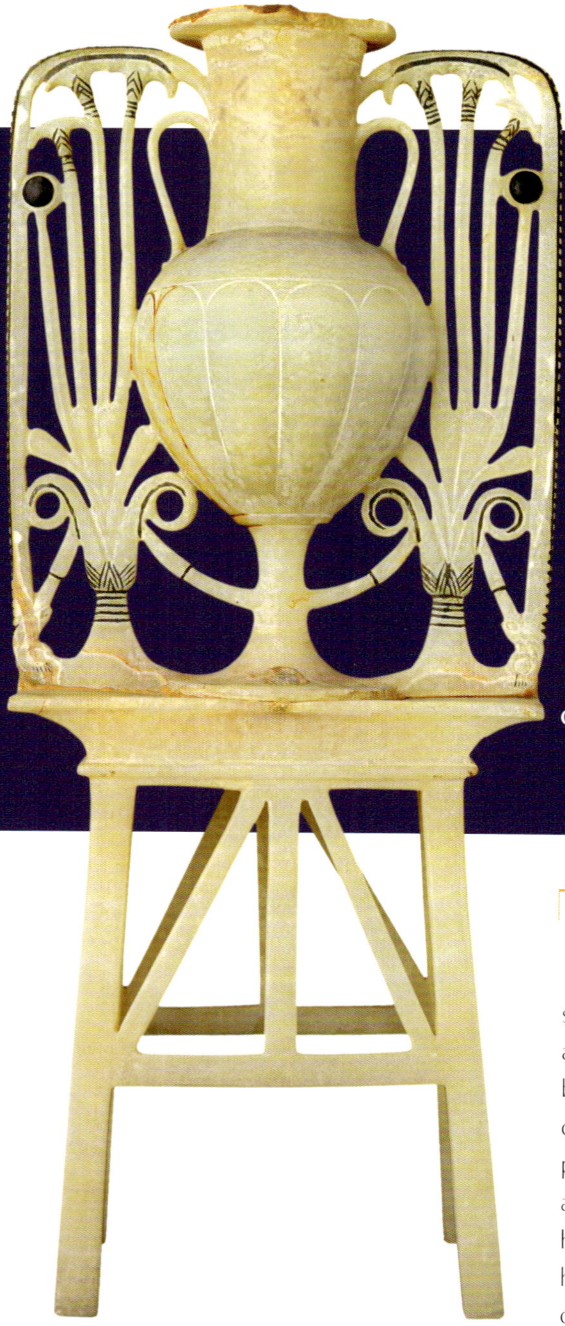

OVOID VASE WITH STAND
Calcite (Egyptian alabaster)
Overall height 65.5 cm
Carter 58

This elaborate vase, carved from a single piece of calcite (Egyptian alabaster) and set upon a calcite (Egyptian alabaster) stand, abounds with symbolism. Elegant arrangements of floral forms flank the ovoid body of the vase. On each side, from an opened lily bud, a plant associated with Upper Egypt, springs the plant of Lower Egypt, a clump of papyrus in bloom. The outer handless are given the form of palm ribs that have been notched to record individual years of a king's reign. Each palm rib stands on the back of a tadpole, the sign for "100,000," which in turn sits atop a ***shen*** ring, the hieroglyph representing "eternity." The entire arrangement signifies a wish for the unification of Upper and Lower Egypt to endure infinitely.

This symbolism might be magically passed to the contents of the vase, which the king would receive in the afterlife. Within the body of the vase, Carter found a brownish residue, all that remained of some kind of perfumed unguent. It was the contents of vessels such as this, not the beautiful vase itself, that would have attracted tomb robbers.

This distinctive rattle, known as a sistrum, appears being used in ceremonies throughout Egyptian history. Most often seen in the hands of priestesses, the metal disks of these rattles produce a gentle tinkling sound reminiscent of the wind passing through stands of papyrus. They were sacred to Hathor and are sometimes decorated with images of the goddess's human face with the ears of a cow. Rattling the sistrum pleased the gods and revived the souls of the deceased. In one of the scenes on the small golden shrine (**Carter No. 108**), Queen Ankhesenamun wears Hathor's horns and solar disk while shaking a sistrum for her husband Tutankh-amun. The sistrum also had connections with fertility.

Carter found this instrument and another one just like it on the cow bed (**Carter No. 73**). They were made during the Amarna Period, when the more elaborate form showing the goddess Hathor was evidently banned under Akhenaten's "heresy."

Both of the simple sistra show sign of use. Members of the funeral party, perhaps the queen herself, probably used these two sistra before they were abandoned on the ritual bed that is also appropriately associated with Hathor.

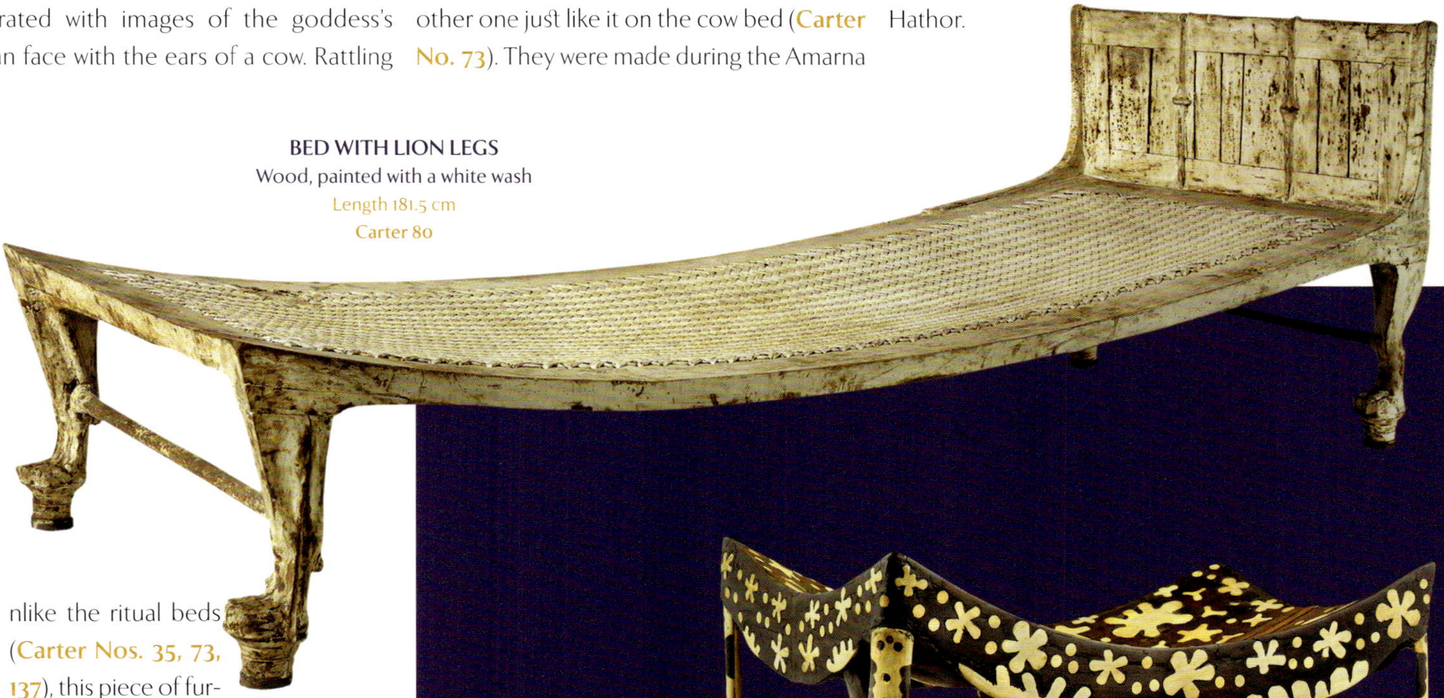

BED WITH LION LEGS
Wood, painted with a white wash
Length 181.5 cm
Carter 80

Unlike the ritual beds (**Carter Nos. 35, 73, 137**), this piece of furniture was made for the living. Carter found it carelessly left on the cow bed (**Carter No. 73**), with one of the cow's horns sticking through the linen bands woven across its frame – "obviously not in original position," he wrote. These bands, each 8 cm wide, would have supported a mattress made of linen. A headrest would have supported the sleeper's head at the open end, while the feet would have been pointed toward the footboard.

The legs are shaped like those of a lion, a common motif in Egyptian furniture perhaps intended for protective symbolism, as well as aesthetics. The bed was equipped with a wooden object found slung between two curved slats running between the sides of the bed, beneath the woven linen mat. Carter thought that this might be an accessory that allowed one end or the other of the bed to be raised, so the sleeper could choose to have either head or feet elevated.

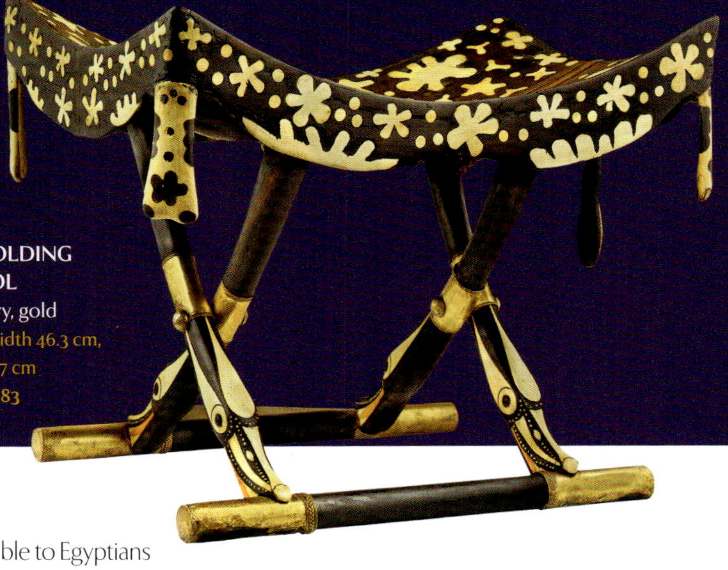

DUMMY FOLDING STOOL
Wood, ivory, gold
Height 37.5 cm, width 46.3 cm, depth 31.7 cm
Carter 83

A variety of seats were available to Egyptians wealthy enough to afford furniture, and Tutankhamun was provided with a number of them, including 12 stools. This one was made to imitate a camp stool, which would have had a collapsible leather or hide seat and pivoting legs so that the stool could be folded for easy transport or storage.

The seat of this stool is of wood grown in Egypt, but painted dark brown to look like ebony, an exotic imported timber from the south. It has been inlaid with ivory to resemble the spotted hide of cow or goat, down to the inclusion of "legs" dangling from each corner. A "tail" with an ivory tuft hangs down one side and lighter wood has been inlaid down the middle of the seat to suggest a "backbone." The crossed legs terminate in the heads of ducks or geese with mouths open to bite the stretchers at the base. The waterfowl motif is also seen on the real camp stools that were found in the tomb.

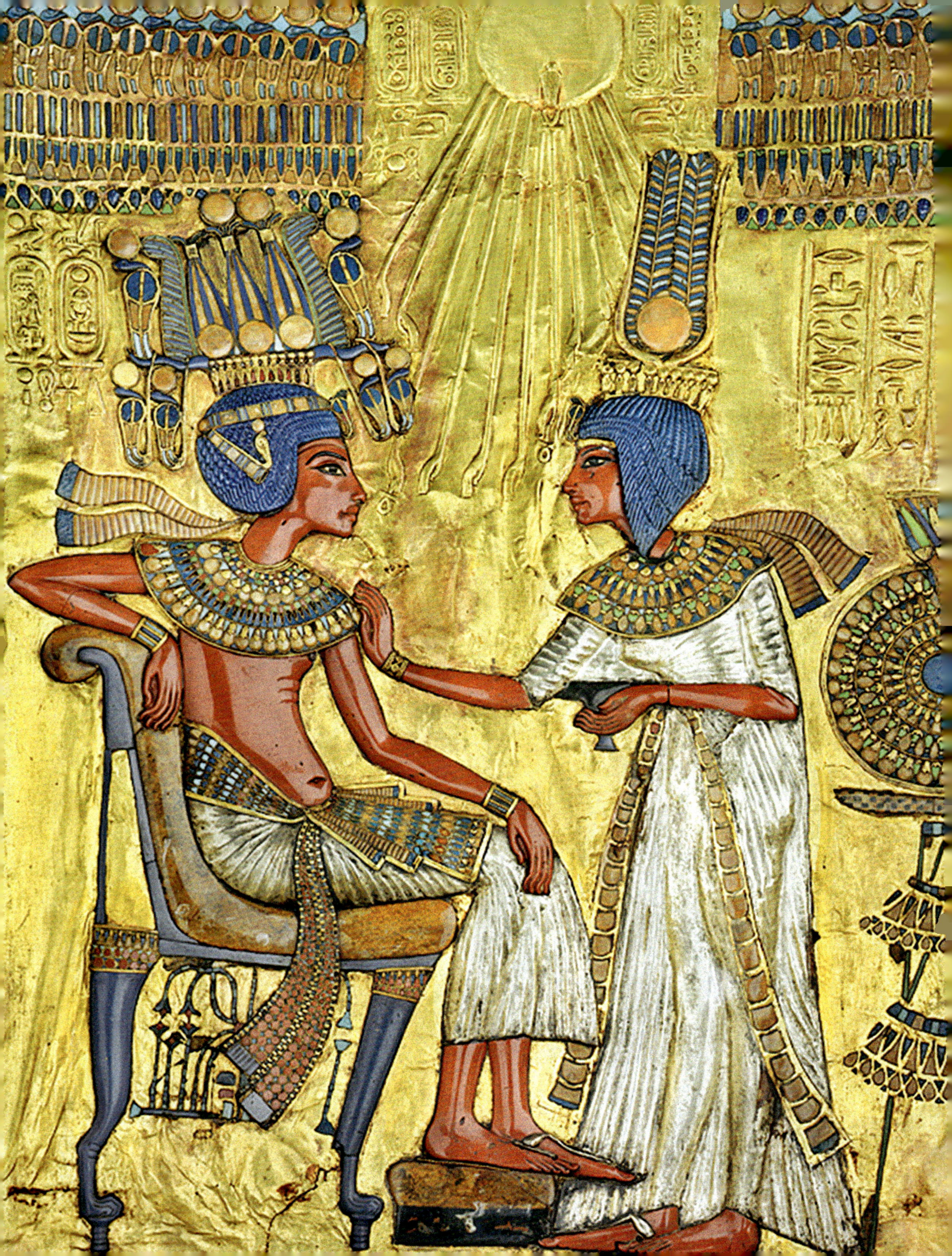

THE GOLDEN THRONE

This astonishing golden throne is among the great masterpieces to come from the tomb. Carter himself said, "I have no hesitation in claiming for it that it is the most beautiful thing that has yet been found in Egypt."

When first discovered, the back of the chair had bands of linen, perhaps for protection while it was carried into the tomb. No doubt the throne needed protection. Made of wood and gilded or sheathed in sheets of gold, the chair is covered in intricate decoration, chased into the gold and inlaid with colored glass and semiprecious stones. Thieves apparently broke the struts that once decorated the spaces between front and back legs, to strip them of their gold, or perhaps they were simply lost, broken in the move. Why they are missing is one of the mysteries of the tomb.

Each arm is made in the form of a divine cobra wearing the double crown and stretching its wings forward. At the wingtips are cartouches with the king's name.

The back of the throne shows a scene taking place in a pavilion with an open roof, through which the Aten extends his rays. The king sits casually on an armless chair, resting one arm against its back while the queen attends anoints him with perfumed oil from a silver cup. On her head is a "Nubian" wig, a short hairstyle brought into Egypt by Nubian mercenaries, which became popular among royal women during the Amarna Period.

The throne dates to early in Tutankhamun's reign and possibly before. On the back of the chair, the names given for the royal couple are "Tutankhaten" and "Ankhesenpaaten." Their names were changed to "Tutankhamun" and "Ankhesenamun" after about the second year of the young king's reign, and these are the names visible elsewhere on the throne.

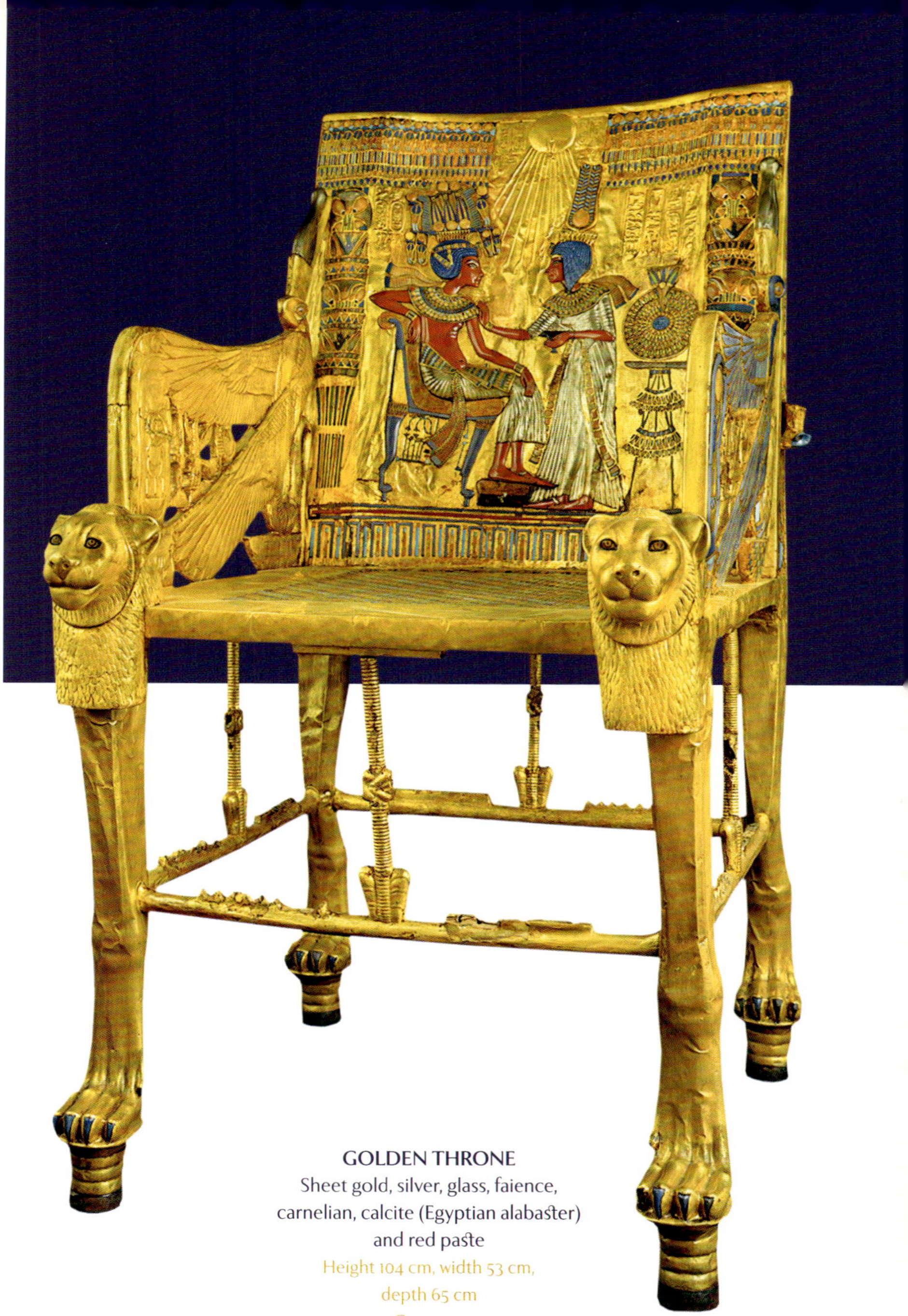

GOLDEN THRONE
Sheet gold, silver, glass, faience, carnelian, calcite (Egyptian alabaster) and red paste
Height 104 cm, width 53 cm, depth 65 cm
Carter 91

I can easily imagine Tutankhamun sitting on this astonishing throne, receiving dignitaries from foreign countries in a stately manner. But I can also see him reclining in it, relaxing a little, while his wife stands before him, just as the image on the back portrays. The imagery of the scene reflects the deep love that existed, I think, between king and queen in life, not just in official iconography.

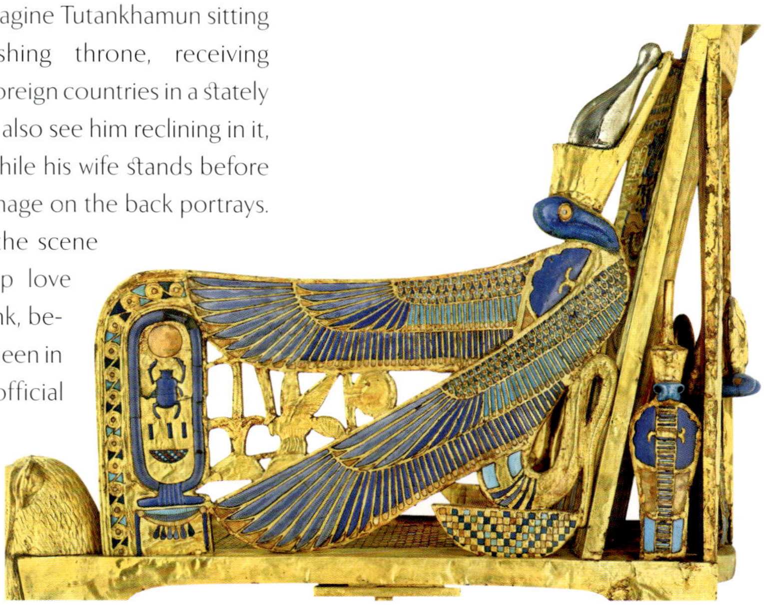

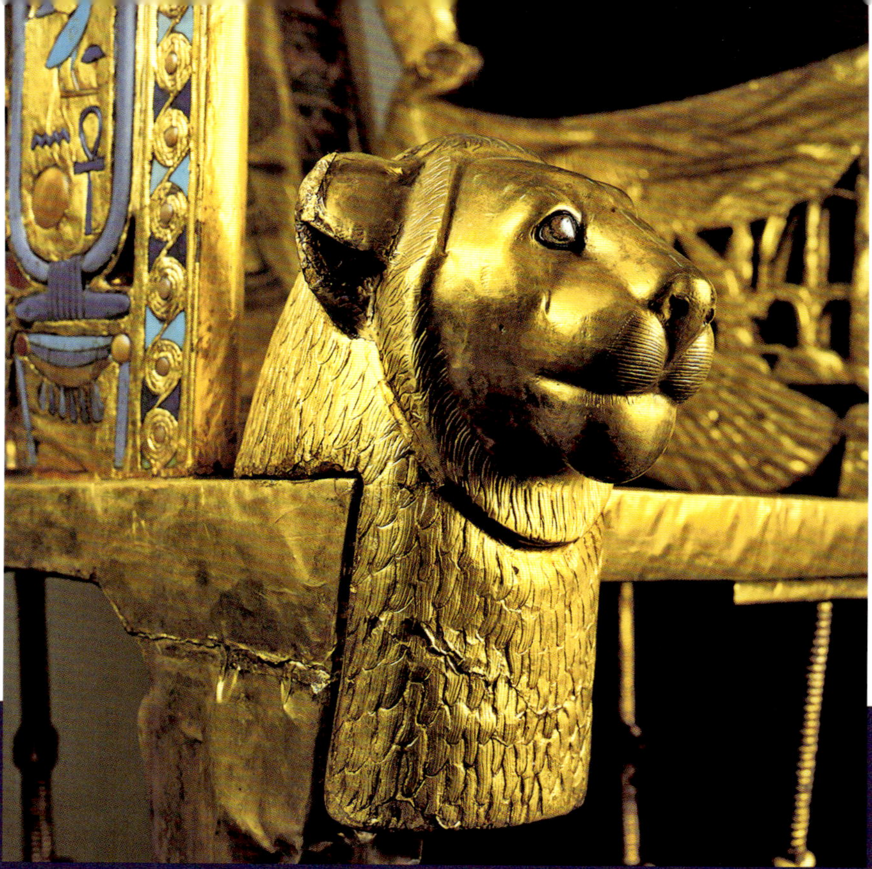

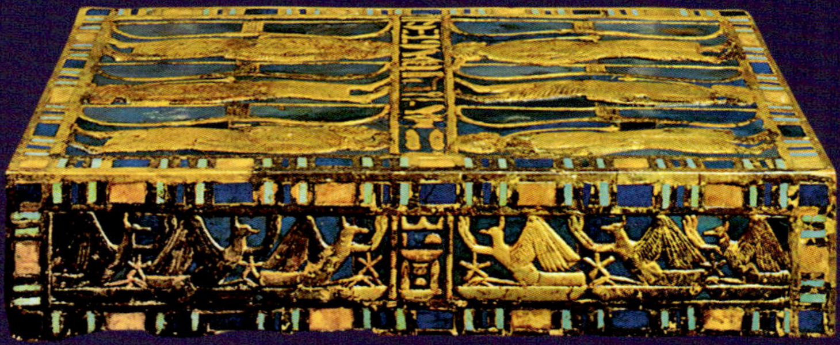

THE THRONE'S FOOTREST
Wood, gessoed, gilded, blue faience and yellow ston
Length 63.5 cm
Carter 90

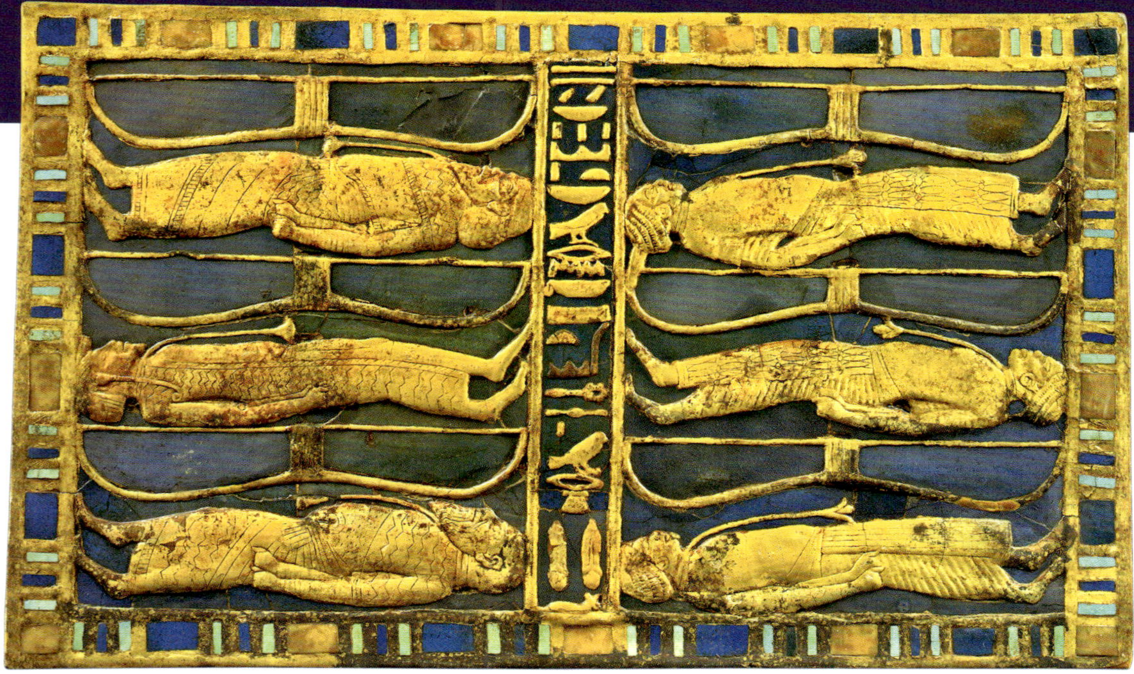

THE SMALL GOLDEN SHRINE

Carter found this small shrine beneath the Ammut bed (**Carter No. 108**) in the southwest corner of the Antechamber, near the entrance to the Annexe. Some suspect that Carter placed it there so that he and Lord Carnarvon could gain access to the Annexe during a surreptitious investigation of the tomb in November 1922.

This little shrine sits on a wooden sledge encased in silver. Inside Carter found some pieces of jewelry, including part of the royal corselet (**Carter No. 54k**) but it was perhaps made to contain a statuette. This is suggested by the small gilded pillar also found within the shrine. Such pillars commonly appear behind figures. This one gives the king's names and epithets, along with wishes for eternal life and health. However, there is no statue to accompany it, only the base for a statue, made of ebony. This base contains the suggestion of a figure: tiny engraved sandal-prints. A statue might have stood here, or perhaps the footprints magically represented the presence of one.

It is the outside of the shrine, not its contents, that makes this one of the most

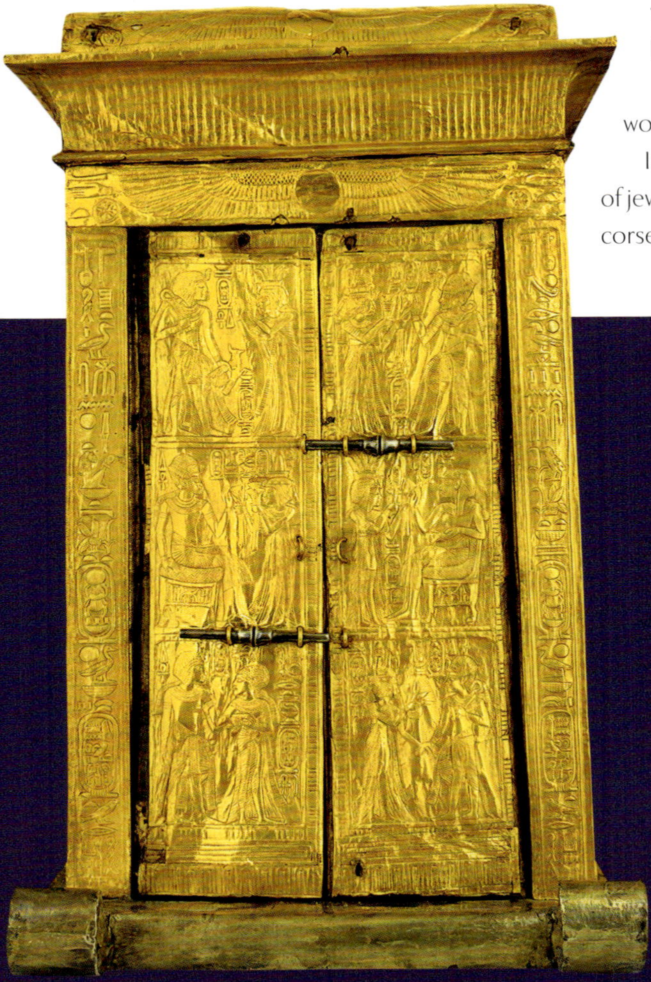

SMALL GOLDEN SHRINE
Wood and gold foil, silver
Height 50.5 cm, width 26.5 cm, depth 32 cm
Carter 108

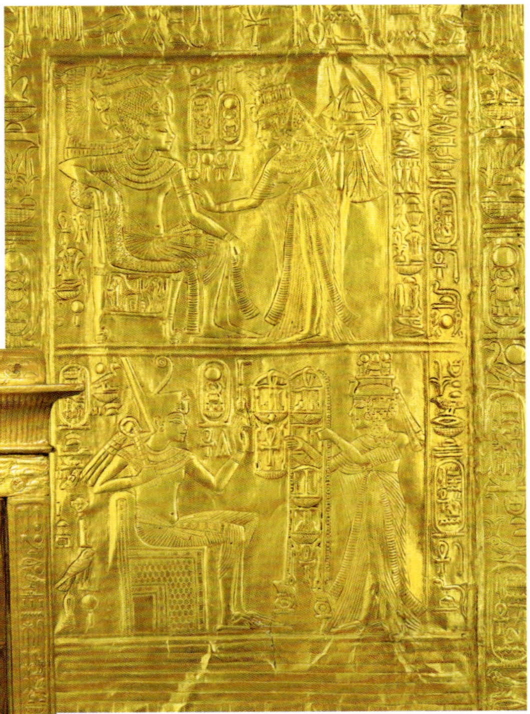

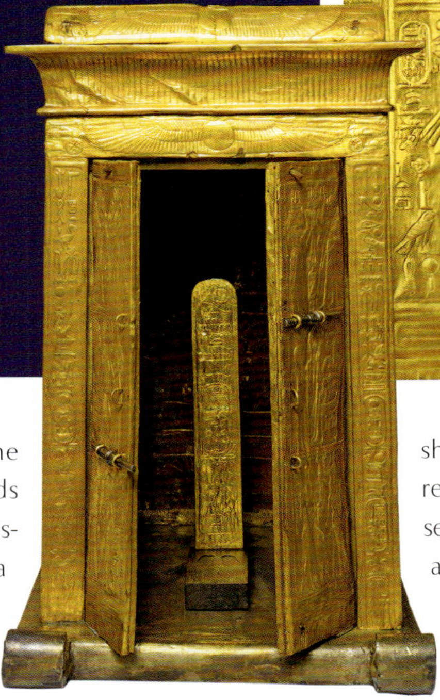

fascinating artifacts from the tomb. Like the golden throne (**Carter No. 91**), its scenes testify to the depth of love between Tutankhamun and his wife, Ankhesenamun. This bond was not merely romantic as any man and woman might have. In the Egyptian world view, the relationship between king and queen was necessary for the proper functioning of the cosmos.

In some scenes, the queen presents her husband with a broad-collar or receives a liquid that he pours into her hand. In others, the royal couple participates in hunting and fishing: the queen stands behind her husband aboard a papyrus raft as he hunts birds with a throwing-stick, or she hands him arrows while he shoots. Sexual imagery lurks behind this domestic and sporting imagery. Ducks, papyrus, lotus, oils, and necklaces are all erotic symbols. Even the words for many of the actions performed by the young couple – shooting, pouring, throwing – are related to sexual terms. Although seldom displayed explicitly in Egyptian art, sexuality was fundamentally related to regeneration and resurrection. Thus the representations here would help Tutankhamun and Ankhesenamun achieve their immortality in the afterlife. Simultaneously, Tutankhamun serves in these scenes as a representative of the sun and creator god, so his actions here also, once again, serve to maintain cosmic order.

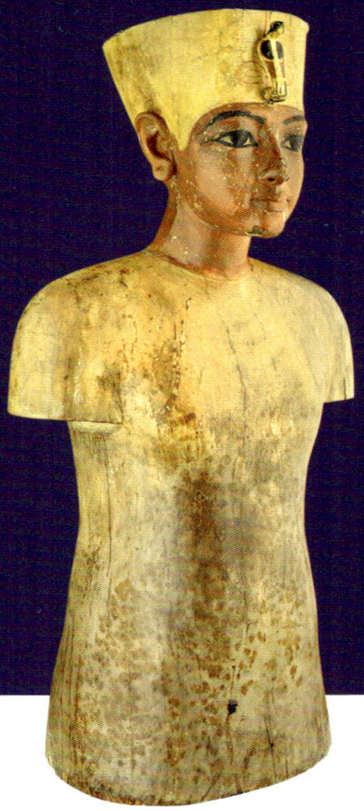

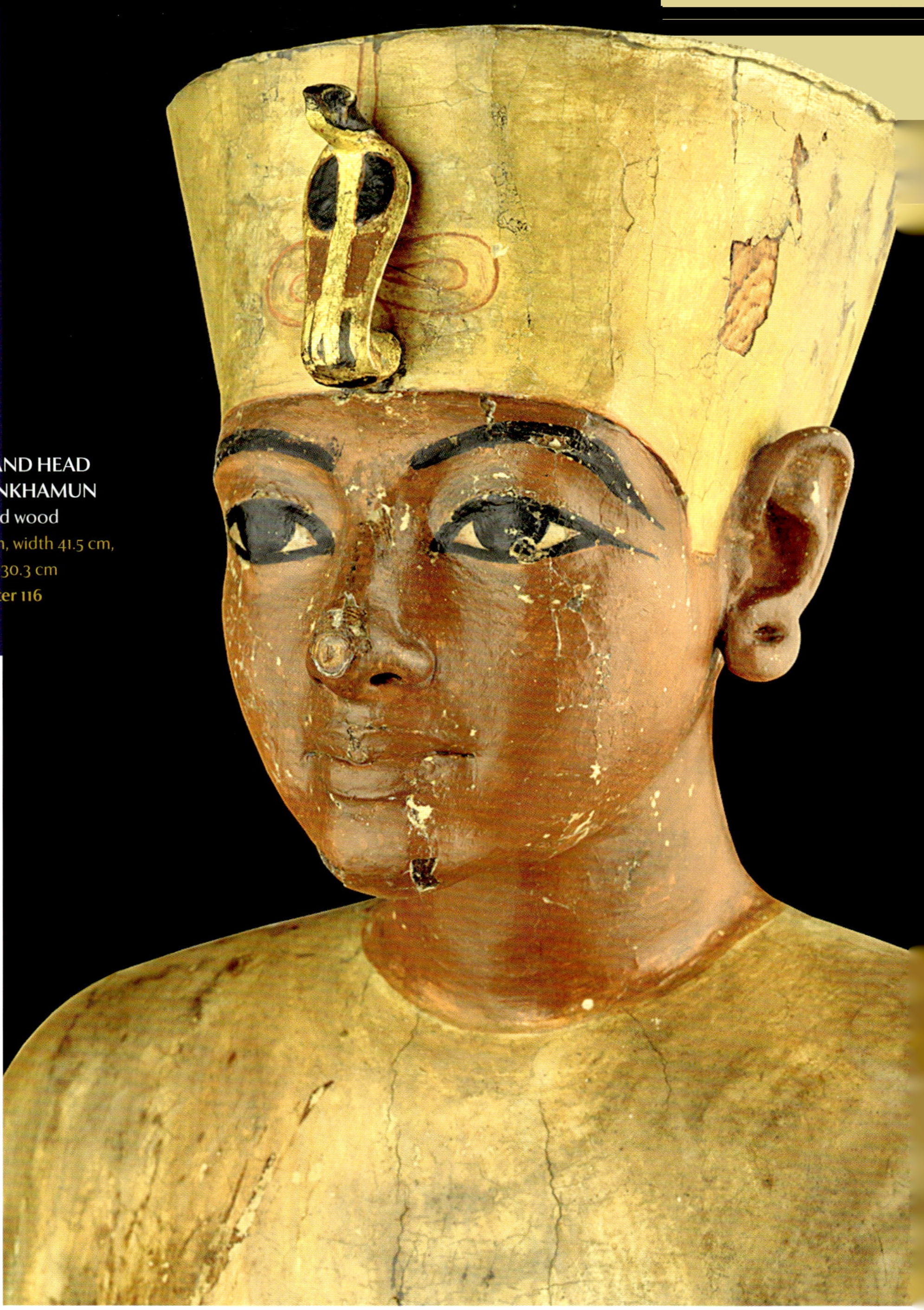

TORSO AND HEAD OF TUTANKHAMUN
Painted wood
Height 73.5 cm, width 41.5 cm, depth 30.3 cm
Carter 116

Looking at this object, which was found below one of the chariots (see Carter No. 120), makes me feel that I am in the presence of the king himself and am staring at the face of Tutankhamun. Even though it is not made of gold or any other precious material, it is, to my mind, one of the most beautiful objects that Carter found in the tomb. It is a life-size model of the head and torso of the king, carved in wood that has been covered in gesso and painted in natural hues: a pale yellow shirt, like aged or dyed linen, the dark reddish-brown of his face, the details of the uraeus on the front of his crown, lend an extraordinary, lifelike appearance.

Scholars remain perplexed as to what this object was made for. Carter suggested it was a mannequin on which the king's robes and jewelry would be hung in preparation for ritual occasions, or perhaps it was a dress-maker's dummy, used for making the king's clothing. Marks on its surface that seem to match a corselet like Carter No. 54k, lending evidence to these general ideas, but that leaves the question of where was it placed: in the royal palace? Perhaps in a temple? However, I do not believe that this is the case. It seems to me that a mannequin is a European notion, not something that the Egyptians would have devised.

Instead, perhaps, it might have been a ritual figure, like the Nefertem head. Its lack of arms means, however, that it cannot have been a *ka* figure, which would have been given arms to receive offerings. It does bear a resemblance to ancestor busts found in private homes during the New Kingdom, but it is still quite different from these. Egyptian sculptors often created statuary in more than one piece, often from more than one material. I suspect that it was meant to be part of a life-size statue of the king's entire body.

The crown is another unusual feature of this object. Although it looks like the flat leather bonnet of Amun, king of the gods, Amun's headdress does not have a uraeus, as this one does. The lack of a divine beard also suggests that this is not, really, the king appearing as Amun. A similar crown appears worn by Akhenaten in many scenes, but its significance is unknown.

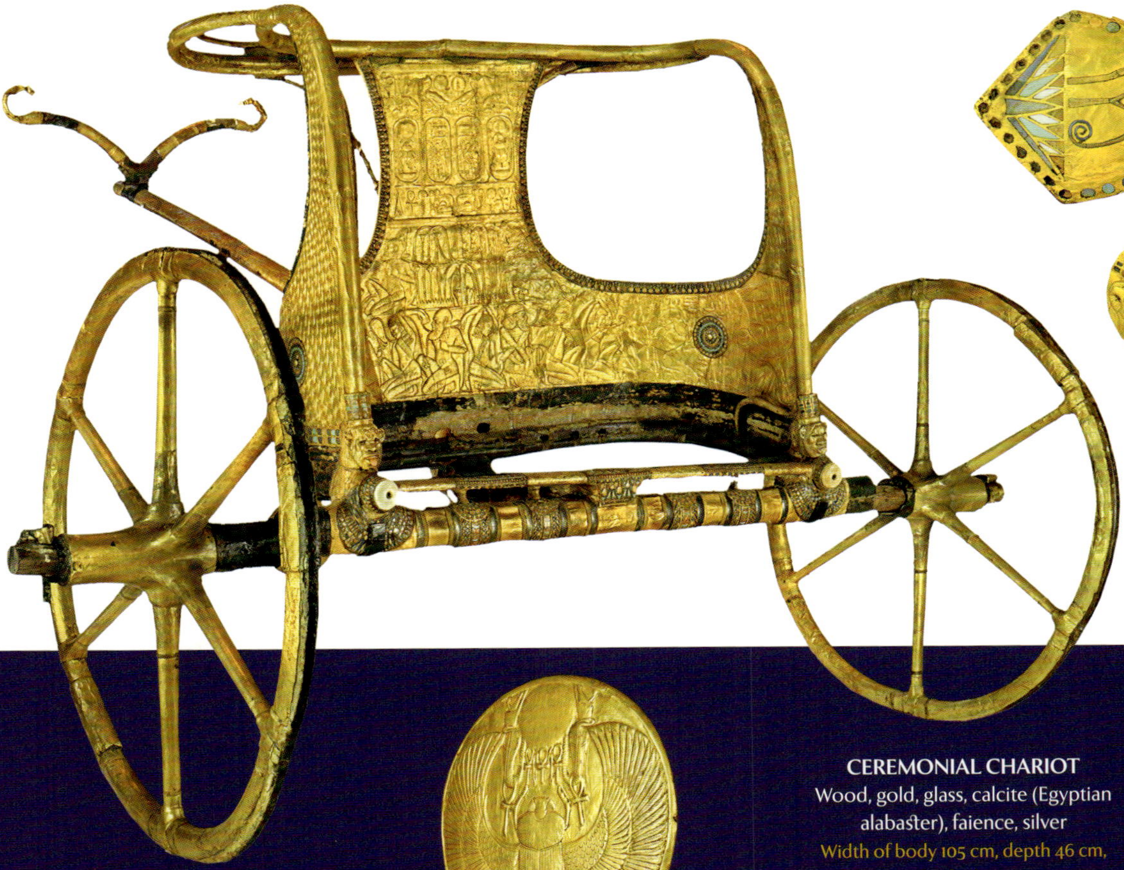

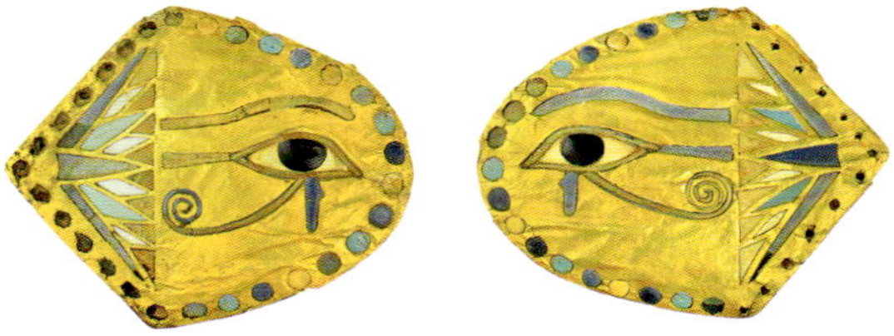

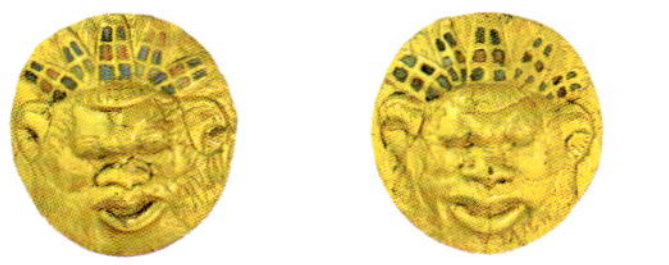

CHARIOT FITTINGS
Gilded wood, glass
BLINKERS
Length 13 cm, height 10 cm
Carter 122i
BES-HEAD DISKS
Gilded wood, glass
Carter 122l

CEREMONIAL CHARIOT
Wood, gold, glass, calcite (Egyptian alabaster), faience, silver
Width of body 105 cm, depth 46 cm, length of axle 216 cm
Carter 120

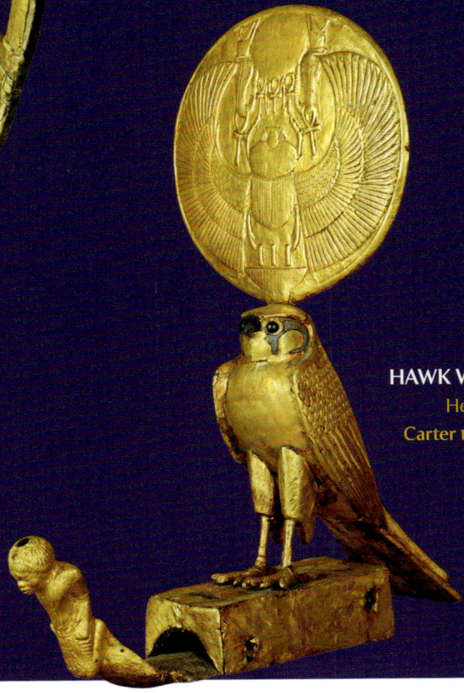

HAWK WITH SUN DISK
Height 40 cm
Carter 122f = Carter 160

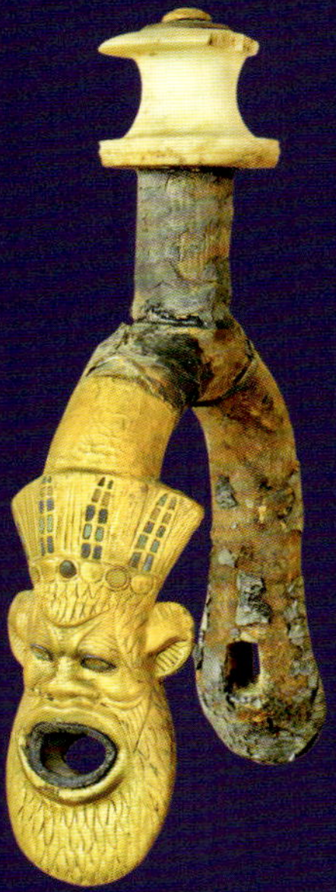

WOODEN SADDLE FROM CURRICLE-LIKE HARNESS
wood, gold, glass
Carter 158

Six complete chariots, several of them specifically for hunting, were found in the tomb, along with fragments and fittings from others. Too wide to fit through the narrow passageway leading into the tomb, they were first dismantled. Once in the tomb they were not reassembled. The parts of four of them were stacked in the Antechamber; two more were in the Treasury. The example here, considered to be a state chariot driven during official functions and ceremonies, is among the most elaborate and finely decorated of the six.

The gilded body of the chariot is decorated with a tight pattern of spirals, a motif adopted from the Aegean or Syria. Three of the king's names are inscribed on the front of the chariot. Figures of captive foreigners decorate the ends of the yoke and the interior of the chariot. On the chariot body, Tutankhamun defeats his enemies as a sphinx.

The fittings for the horses seen here were found loose and belonged to both this and the other state chariot (Carter No. 122). The blinders (also called blinkers), which kept the team from seeing to the side, were appropriately decorated with the sacred eyes of Horus (*wedjats*). The small Bes heads, representing the protective god of joy, belonged to this chariot, but the gilded wooden hawk seen here fits on the center pole of the chariot 122.

Horses and chariots were introduced into Egypt during the Second Intermediate Period from Asia, about two centuries before Tutankhamun's day. The Egyptian version of the chariot was a lightweight vehicle, readily maneuverable and adaptable for hunting, as well as warfare.

THE BURIAL CHAMBER

Compared to the opening of the tomb, the opening of the next room, which lay beyond the north wall of the Antechamber, was a more public event. On the afternoon of 16th February, 1923, Carter, his team, and the Carnarvons were joined by Pierre Lacau (head of the Antiquities Service), other notable Egyptologists, and Egyptian and foreign dignitaries. Forty people crowded into the Antechamber, almost twice as many as Carter had originally wanted. The eager press was consigned to waiting outside.

Rows of chairs had been arranged for the invited guests in the Antechamber, which by this time had been almost completely cleared of its treasures. Wooden boards protected the guardian statues, which remained in the room. Carter's team had installed a platform so that the top of the wall could be opened. As everyone watched, Carter made a small hole in the wall. After about ten minutes of picking, which must have felt like an eternity to him, he broke through. Having widened the opening a little, he directed the glow of a flashlight through. As Carter later wrote:

> *"An astonishing sight its light revealed, for there, within a yard of the doorway, stretching as far as one could see and blocking the entrance to the chamber, stood what to all appearances was a solid wall of gold. For the moment there was no clue as to its meaning, so as quickly as I dared I set to work to widen the hole..."*

"Its meaning" was an enormous shrine, the outermost of a nested set of four, made of gilded wood inlaid with blue faience plaques in a pattern of *Djed* pillars and *Tjet* knots, the emblems of Osiris and Isis, among the most important of Egypt's funerary deities. There was no longer any doubt about the nature of this room. It was the "Sepulchral Chamber," as Carter called it, or, as we know it today, the Burial Chamber.

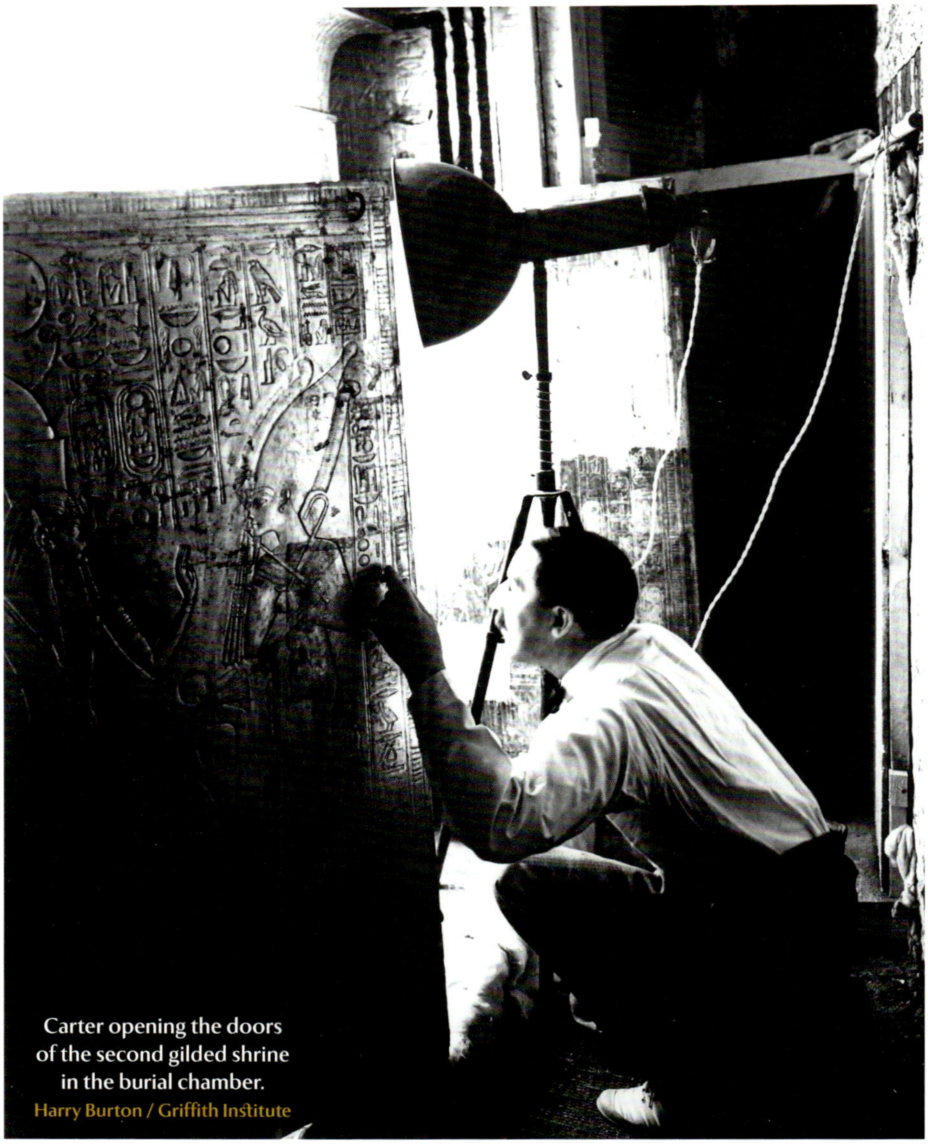

Carter opening the doors of the second gilded shrine in the burial chamber.
Harry Burton / Griffith Institute

Even before the opening, Carter himself had no doubt about this new room. It seems certain to me and many other scholars that Carter, Carnarvon, and Lady Evelyn had gone into the Burial Chamber before, probably at night, although none ever admitted to this publicly. Whatever their reactions might have been on 16th February, the golden wall was no surprise to them. How might they have accomplished this, when witnesses saw Carter pick a hole into the wall?

Robbers had pierced through that wall into the Burial Chamber in antiquity. The necropolis police had plastered over this hole and stamped it with the official seal. In photographs of the Antechamber, taken prior to the official opening of the Burial Chamber, an ancient basket and bundle of reeds lean against the wall between the guardian figures. Behind these humble objects, most likely, was concealed evidence of one of the ancient burglaries. It would have been fairly simple for Carter to have opened the robber's tunnel, then arranged this "still-life" to hide the evidence of the illegal entrance that he and some of his companions had made.

For about two hours, Carter worked with a hammer to enlarge the "official" hole. He handed stones from the wall to his assistant, Arthur Mace, until the opening was large enough to allow him to enter the room beyond. Carnarvon followed. Two-by-two the other visitors would squeeze into the narrow space between the walls and the outer shrine. This structure took the form of the ***sed*** shrine, a pavilion in which the king would, after a certain number of years, celebrate a jubilee. Despite the opulence of the shrine, it had a disappointment waiting in store for them: the seal securing its doors was missing. Had the robbers reached the king's mummy? Carter opened the shrine.

Inside was a linen pall spangled with rosettes draped over a wooden frame, sheltering a second shrine. The pall had disintegrated enough so that the doors of the next shrine were visible – and still bolted shut, its seals intact. The royal mummy had still to be in its original resting place. Everyone now knew this. But it would be more than a year before they would behold the king's face.

For a week after opening the Burial Chamber, Carter's schedule was crowded with visits from the press and a variety of dignitaries, including Queen Élisabeth of Belgium (famed Belgian Egyptologist Jean Capart founded an Egyptological society in honor of her visit). Then the season came to an end, and Carter had to close the tomb. During this time, Carnarvon and Carter had a brief dispute, possibly because of a relationship between the archaeologist and Lady Evelyn. I believe that the Lady Evelyn fell in love with Carter, who did not return the same level of affection. He thought of her as a friend, not a romantic partner. However, Sheikh Ali Abdel Rasoul (whose archaeological adventures will be related in Chapter 7) told me that he saw Lady Evelyn and Carter together in the tomb at night, which could be a sign that he was indeed in love with her. And in any case, because of the disparity between their social stations, Carnarvon could not approve such a match for his daughter. Whatever the truth of the matter was, Lady Evelyn married less than a year after attending the opening of the Burial Chamber.

Tutankhamun's tomb was sealed up again, hidden with rubble and sand until the next excavation season. Carter and his team had their work cut out for them conserving the artifacts they had removed thus far, so that they could be safely transported to the Egyptian Museum in Cairo. To accomplish this, they set up a laboratory in the tomb of Seti II.

Things were not easy for Carter during this period, and Carnarvon's health began to fail. Carnarvon and his daughter headed north to Cairo on 14th March, but only a few days later Carnarvon's condition took a turn for the worse. On 5th April, he died.

Carter left his work in the tomb long enough to bid his benefactor a final farewell, then returned to Luxor to finish the season's work and to move the objects, contained in 89 crates, from the Antechamber to Cairo. To do this Carter had a railroad built from the Valley of the Kings to a spot near the Nile. The crates were then transferred to a barge, which was towed downriver to Cairo. Although arrangements had been made for the artifacts to be moved from the quay at Cairo by rail, the inspector general ordered the crates carried to the museum by porters. Less than one week later, some of the objects were even put on display.

The next season was to begin in October 1923. Earlier, Carter approached Lord Carnarvon's widow about assuming her husband's concession, which she did. Other details were not so easily settled, and Carter spent time arguing with the Antiquities Service and the Ministry of Public Works.

But Carter had more important things to attend to. Objects from the tomb were presenting grave problems for the conservators. And there was the matter of dismantling the shrines in order to reach the sarcophagus and the royal mummy.

On 18th November, workmen and boys were clearing the rubble away from the tomb. The next day, Carter opened the tomb for the season's work, to begin removing artifacts from the Burial Chamber, including the massive shrines. As Arthur Mace recorded in his diary, "Difficulties of removing are going to be enormous."

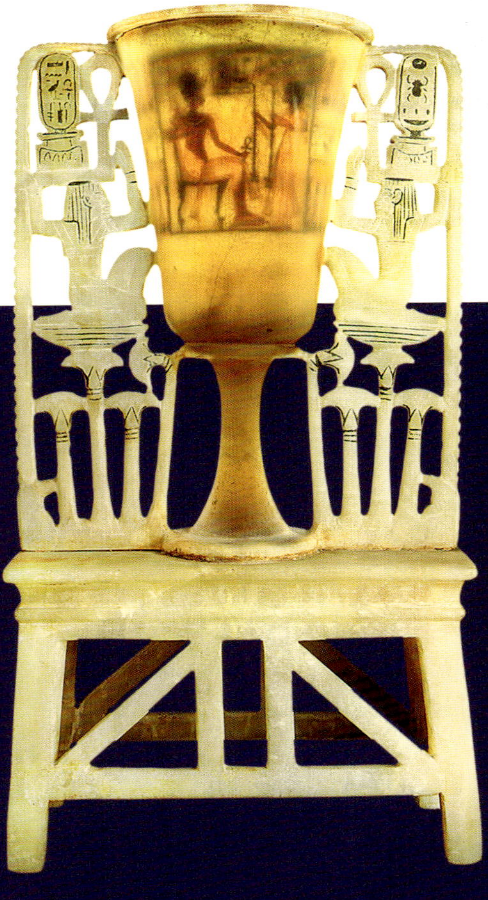

LAMP
Calcite (Egyptian alabaster)
Height 51.4 cm, width 28.8 cm
Carter 173

Objects had been placed between the first and second shrine, including this magnificent lamp. The cup where the oil and wick would be placed has, on either side, an image of the god Heh holding notched palm ribs and kneeling on a basket. When lit, an image of the king wearing the blue crown appears. He sits in a chair with an ***ankh*** in one hand. Ankhesenamun, his queen, approaches, bringing him a pair of notched palm ribs, signifying the years of his reign.

Carter found two trumpets, one of copper or bronze overlaid with gold, and this silver one, wrapped in a bundle of reeds. The king's cartouches appear between the lotus petals that decorate the bell of the instrument. The bell also features a scene in which the gods Amun-Re and Re approach Ptah, god of Memphis. These three deities were closely related and were seen as aspects of a creator god. Ptah was the body, Amun was the hidden name, and Re was the visible aspect. During the reign of Rameses II, less than a century after Tutankhamun, divisions of the army would be named for these gods, and a fourth division would take the name of Seth, the god of chaos.

Trumpets appear in depictions of the Egyptian army, and this trumpet may have been intended for military use. Wear on its surface indicates that it was played. Along with the trumpet was a wooden core designed to fit inside. Painted with a lotus motif, it was probably intended to prevent the metal from being crushed while being transported.

The delicate instrument shattered during an attempt to play it in 1939. It was perfectly restored when British military bandsman James Tappern played both trumpets on a BBC radio broadcast later that year, when the whole world could hear the long-silent trumpets.

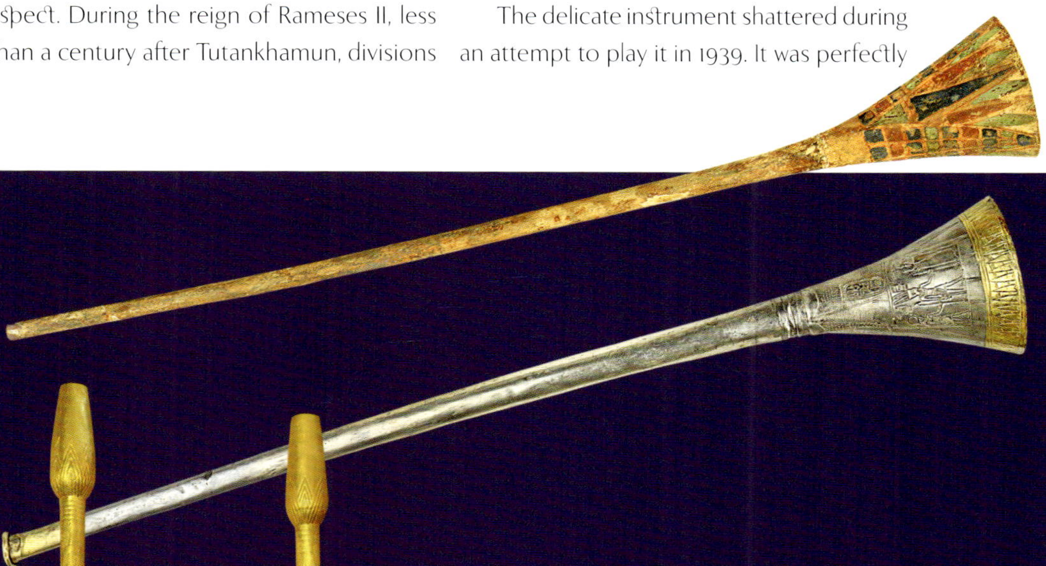

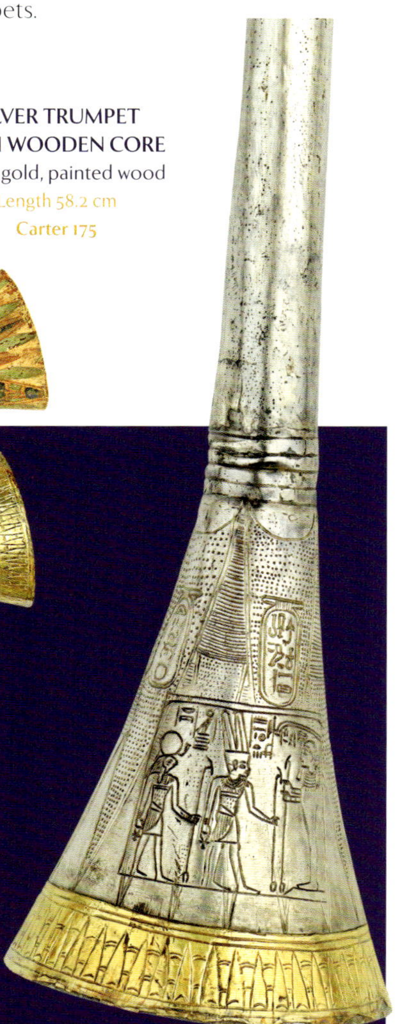

SILVER TRUMPET WITH WOODEN CORE
Silver, gold, painted wood
Length 58.2 cm
Carter 175

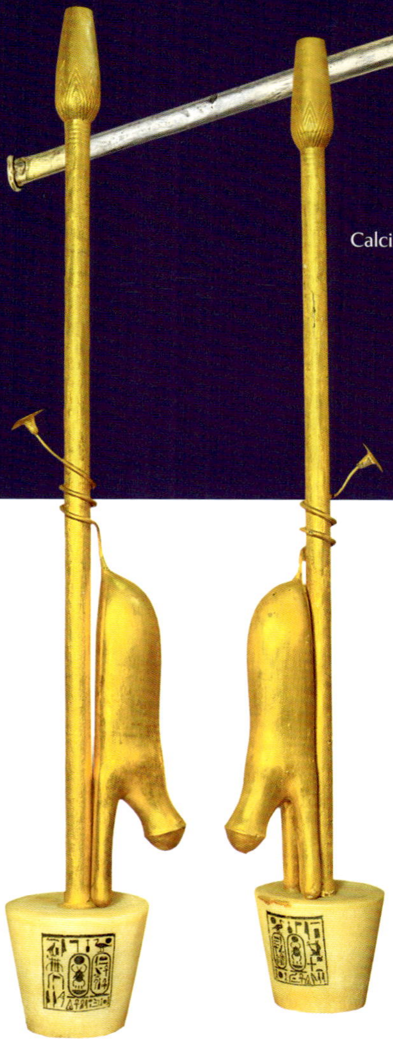

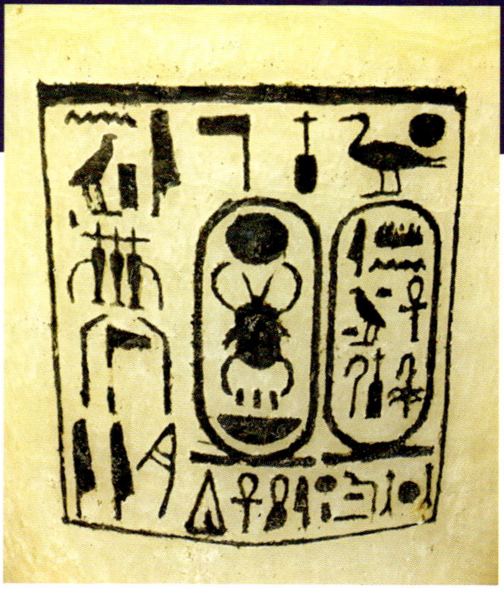

ANUBIS FETISHES
Calcite (Egyptian alabaster), gilded wood, bronze
Height 167 cm
Carter 194 (left and detail)
and Carter 202 (right)

Known as an ***imiut***, "He Who is in the Bandages," each of these curious objects represents a headless animal skin that has been tied by its tail to a pole set into a pot. The tail and the pole each end in a lotus flower. The ***imiut*** was an emblem of Anubis, the jackal god of mummification, who is mentioned in the inscriptions on the pots along with the king's names. The exact significance of this emblem is unknown, but an actual example, made from animal skin, has been found. Carter discovered both of these standing on reed mats, positioned in the corners of the Burial Chamber's western side, a direction the Egyptians identified with the netherworld.

This extraordinary calcite (Egyptian alabaster) jar once held a cosmetic of some type. Carter found residue of animal fats and plant resins inside. The sides are carved in relief and given a painted background, so that the figures of dogs and lions hunting bulls and ibex in the desert stand out. The style is lively, and the artists have even taken the liberty of showing one dog's head from above, as it bites the belly of its prey.

Columns stand on either side. These are in the form of lotus plants, each topped by the head of Bes, a protective household deity.

On the lid reclines a lion, which has the king's throne name inscribed on one shoulder. With its lolling tongue (carved in ivory and stained pink) and crossed paws, the powerful creature appears entirely relaxed, despite the action occurring below, which represents order, in the form of the lion (symbolizing the king) overcoming chaos to preserve the natural order of the world. This is also symbolized by the heads of four foreign enemies that serve as the jar's feet.

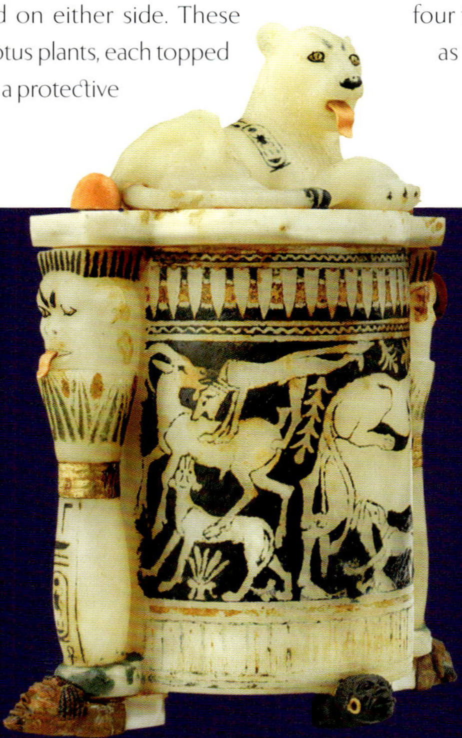

COSMETIC JAR WITH RECUMBENT LION
Calcite (Egyptian alabaster), ivory, gold, copper
Height 26.7 cm, width 22.0 cm
Carter 211

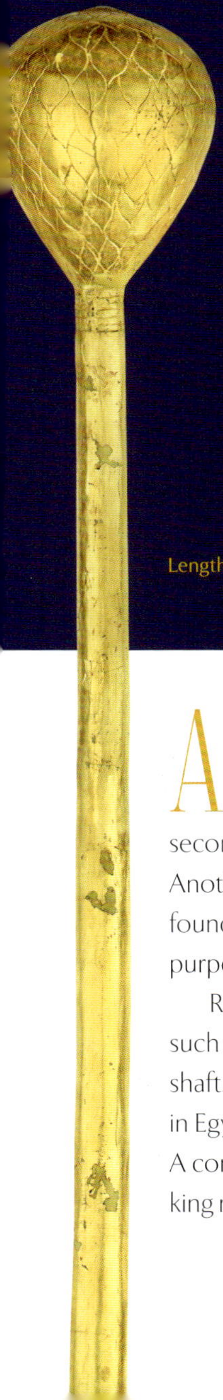

CEREMONIAL MACE
Gilded wood
Length 81.6 cm, diameter of head 12.2 cm, diameter of shaft 3.5 cm
Carter 233

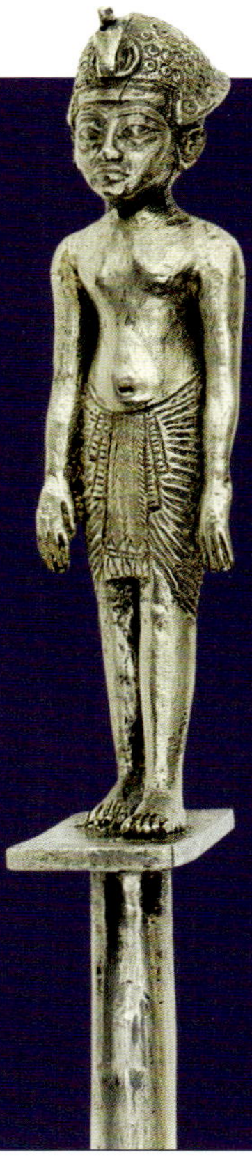

STAFF WITH A FIGURE OF THE KING
Silver
Length 131 cm
Carter 235b

A group of sticks, staffs (see Carter No. 235b), and this mace was found south of the doors into the second shrine (Carter No. 237). Another mace just like this one was found north of the doors. Their ritual purpose is not known.

Real maces had heads of hard stone, such as granite, fastened to a wooden shaft. These weapons began to appear in Egyptian art in the Predynastic Period. A common motif in Egyptian art was the king raising a weapon, often a mace, over his head to smite a prisoner (or group of prisoners) held helpless in his grasp.

This, however, was not a weapon for war. Made of wood and gilded, it was far too light for actual use. During the Opening of the Mouth ceremonial, a mace was one of the objects presented to the mummy. The guardian figures (Carter Nos. 22 and 29) from the Antechamber hold maces, presumably to defeat netherworldly forces that might oppose the king or threaten the tomb.

This staff, one of a pair, was found with the ceremonial mace (Carter No. 233). The figure at the top, cast in silver, represents the king making a gesture of worship. Its counterpart is cast in gold. These might represent lunar (silver) and solar (gold) imagery, perhaps in connection with ceremonies for the king's coronation or his burial.

The shaft is a hollow metal tube of silver. When Carter visited the display of objects from the tomb arranged in the Egyptian Museum in Cairo in October 1925, he found it broken:

I was horrified to find that the silver stick (fellow to the gold stick), now exhibited flat, in one of the glass show cases, was broken in two. This, I was told, was done by one of the European officials when showing it to M. Capart of the Brussels Museum. It seems a shame after all the trouble in preserving those precious objects and safely transporting them to the Museum, that they should be allowed to be handled by persons that do not know how to handle antiquities.

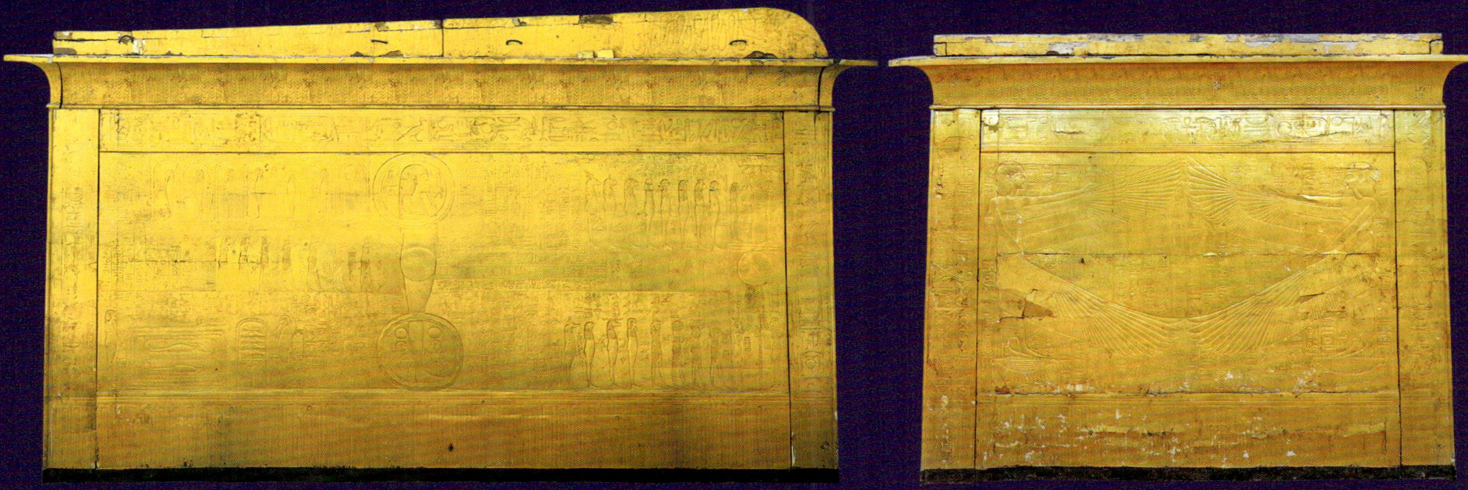

THE SECOND SHRINE
Wood, gessoed and gilded
Height 1.99 m
Carter 237

THE SECOND SHRINE

The daunting task of removing the shrines from the Burial Chamber occupied Carter's mind. These, and not his bureaucratic struggles, were his task at hand for the 1923–1924 field season. Although he had to visit Cairo to try to settle disagreements with the Antiquities Service, during this time he had almost no visitors. (Visitors were a major source of contention between Carter and the Antiquities Service.) Work went on, and, with the help of a small nimble boy who could fit into the cramped space, Carter's team succeeded in dismantling the roof from the first shrine. This allowed them to remove the linen pall with its gilded rosettes and the frame that had supported it, covering the second shrine. On 3rd January, 1924, the doors to the second shrine could be opened.

The second gilded shrine is in the form of a "great house" (*per wer*), an architectural form associated with Upper Egypt since the Predynastic Period. Goddesses introduce Tutankhamun to the gods. On one door, Isis presents the king to Osiris; on the other, Maat (truth and cosmic order) brings him before Re-Horakhty, the sun god. Here both funerary and solar imagery combine. Within the shrine, the sky goddess Nut stands with

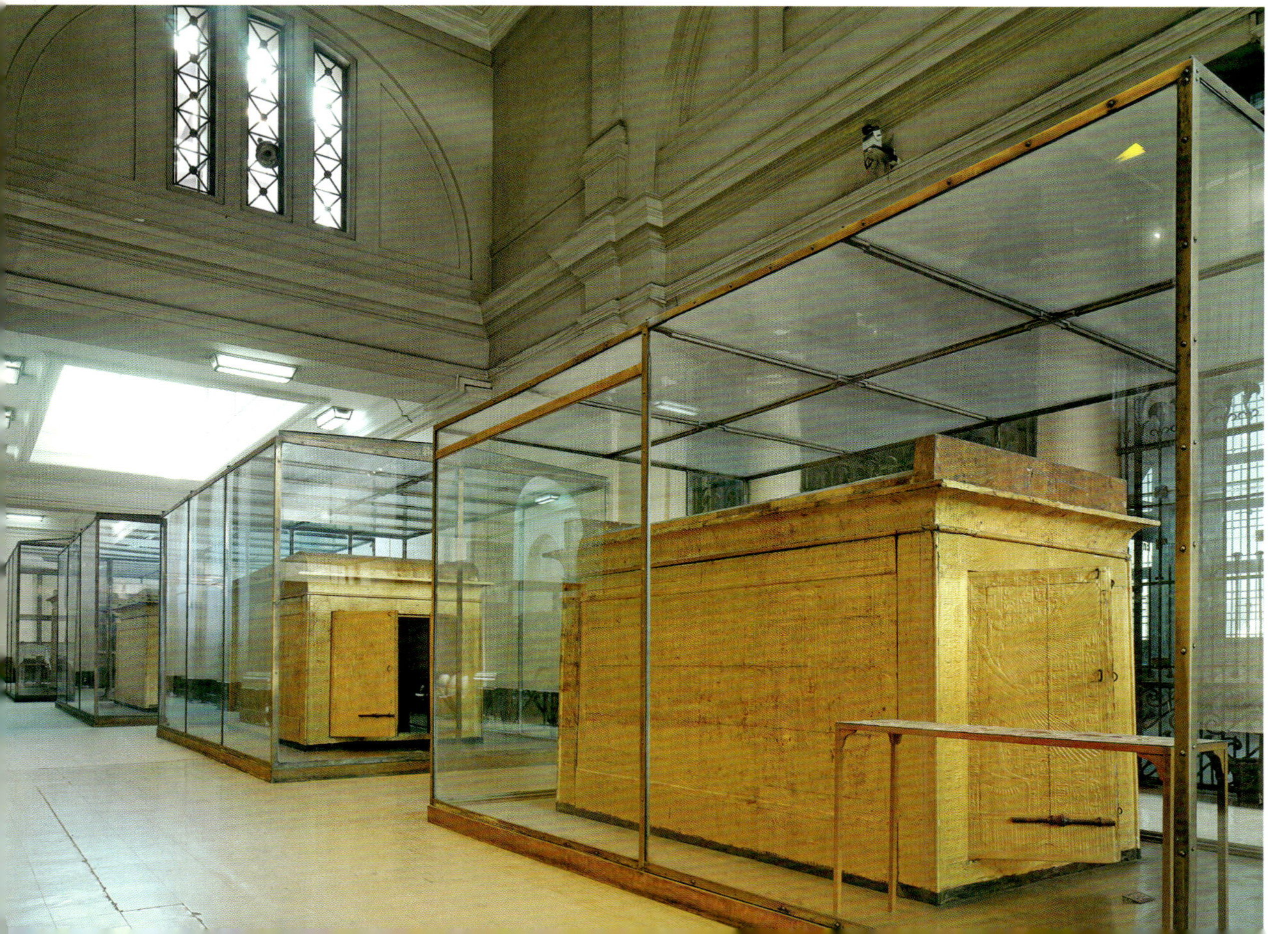

THE GILDED SHRINES OF TUTANKHAMUN
Egyptian Museum in Cairo

her wings outstretched. Deities of the netherworld occupy other panels, which are covered with funerary texts from the ***Book of the Dead*** and the Pyramid Texts.

Carter noticed that Tutankhamun's names were not original to the shrine. It was evident to him that the king's name had been recarved over an earlier name containing the word "Aten." This shrine had likely been used for another burial during the Amarna Period.

Within the second shrine was the third, which looked much like the second and was decorated with texts from the ***Amduat***, as well as more texts from the ***Book of the Dead***. He opened this at 3:00 in the afternoon of 3rd January, while officials of the Antiquities Service looked on. This revealed the fourth, innermost shrine, in the form of the ancient "Palace of the North." It was bolted but not sealed. Within this last structure was the sarcophagus.

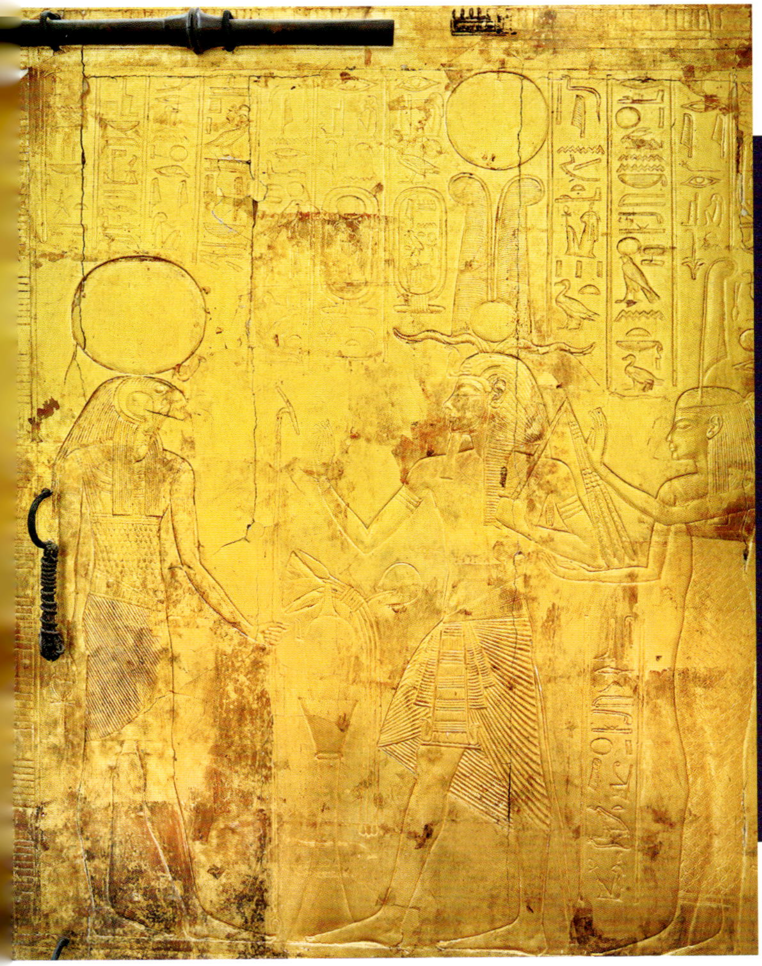

MAAT PRESENTS TUTANKHAMUN TO RE-HORAKHTY
Second shrine
Carter 237

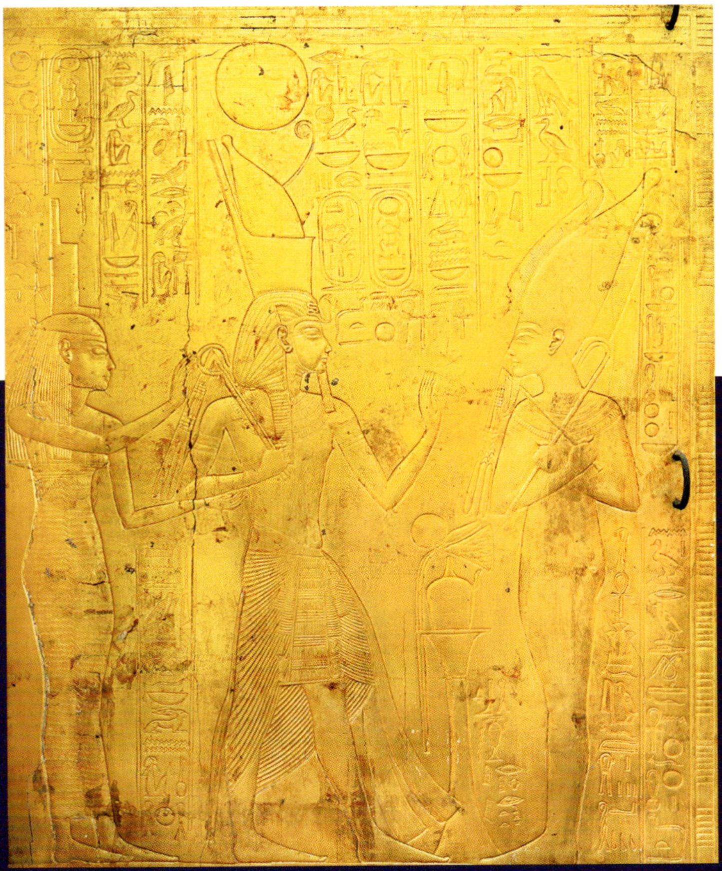

ISIS PRESENTS TUTANKHAMUN TO OSIRIS
Second shrine
Carter 237

Taking great care with the gilded wood, which was already showing signs of deterioration, Carter's team dismantled the shrines. They discovered that the Egyptian artisans had assembled them carelessly and pounded elements into place when they did not fit. As the shrines had survived this negligence, they also survived dismantling. Over the course of two seasons, Alfred Lucas, the conservator, treated them with paraffin wax so that they would be strong enough to endure the trip to Cairo. They are now on display in the Egyptian Museum but deteriorating even further because of the conditions of their display and their original conservation, which was the best that could be done in the 1920s. The climate fluctuates too much, there is too much pollution in the air, and they receive direct sunlight, all of which is very bad for such ancient, fragile objects. It is hoped that a major conservation project will restore this and the other shrines in preparation for their move, with all the other objects from the tomb, to the Grand Egyptian Museum, which is planned to open in 2015.

FAN

These fans, made to be carried by attendants to keep the king comfortable, were found lying between the third and fourth shrine. Besides being symbolic of breath, and therefore of life, they of course had very practical purposes in such a hot climate as Egypt's. For these reasons, "fan-bearer of the king" was an important office.

The cartouche fan contains the throne and birth names of the king under the hieroglyphic sign called *pet*, meaning "sky." Beneath each name is the sign for gold, and above each is the solar disk. The vultures on either side represent the protective goddesses of Upper and Lower Egypt, wearing the white and red crown, respectively.

The other fan depicts two episodes from an ostrich hunt. On one side, the king drives his chariot after two birds, which try without success to flee from his arrows and dogs. On the other side, the king returns from the hunt in the company of his retainers, who carry his prey while the king has feathers tucked under his arm. For the hunt, the king wears a corselet (Carter No. 54k), a pleated kilt that falls to his knees, an archer's wrist-guard, and a Nubian wig, which was popular for men and women at the time (see Carter No. 91). Inscriptions call him "the good god, Nebkheperure, given life like Re forever," and "Lord of might."

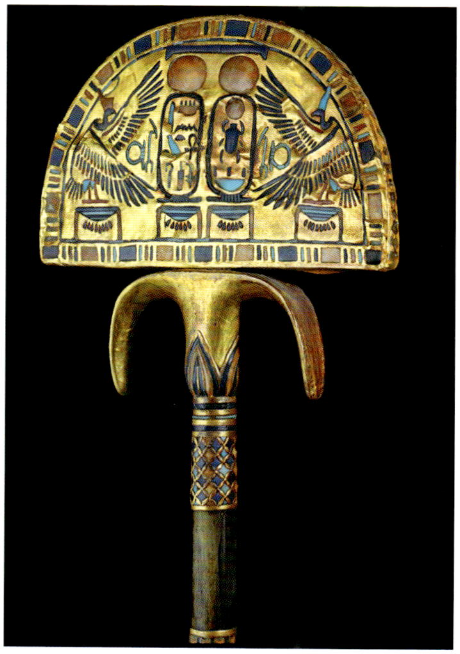

The feathers of the catch depicted on the fan were actually mounted to it, according to the text on the stock, which also says that the hunt took place in the desert east of Heliopolis (near modern Cairo). By the time Carter found the object, the feathers had all but completely deteriorated.

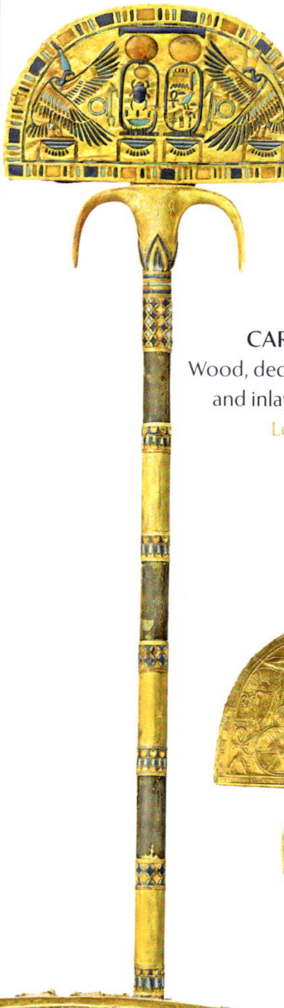

CARTOUCHE FAN
Wood, decorated with sheet gold and inlays of glass and calcit
Length 124.7 cm
Carter 245

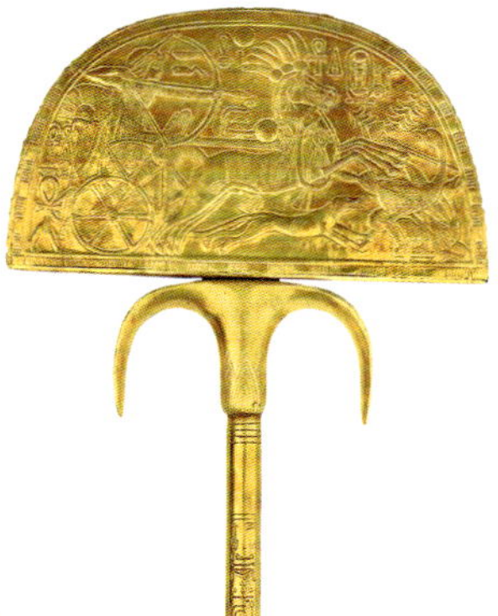

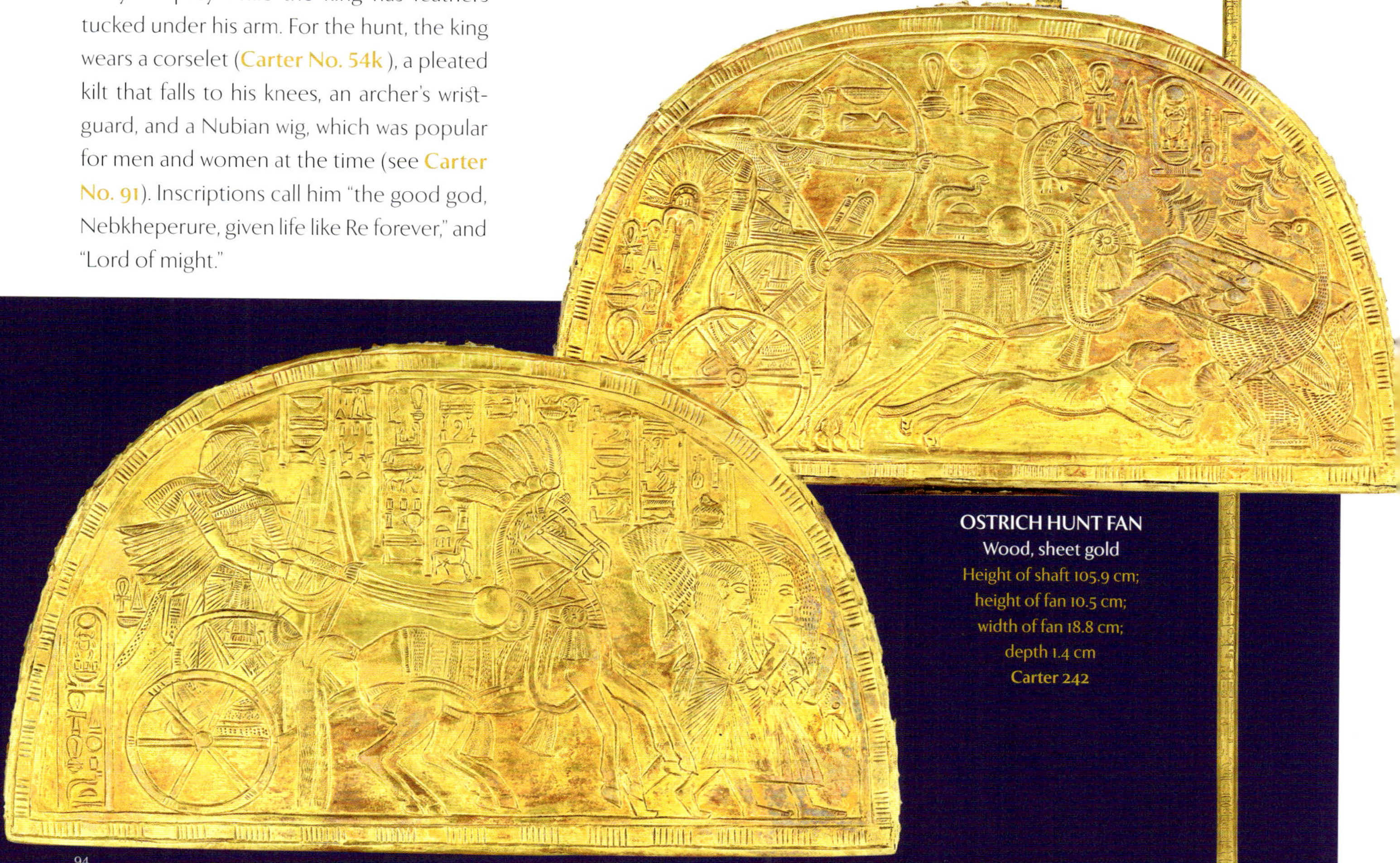

OSTRICH HUNT FAN
Wood, sheet gold
Height of shaft 105.9 cm;
height of fan 10.5 cm;
width of fan 18.8 cm;
depth 1.4 cm
Carter 242

CARTOUCHE

Although Carter recorded that he found this golden cosmetic container, and its "bad-smelling" contents, at the "Bottom of Sarcophagus," it perhaps came from between the outermost and second shrine. It was made in the form of double cartouches – a total of four, back-to-back – with cryptographic writings of "Nebkheperure," the king's throne name.

On one side, Tutankhamun appears as a royal child, meant to signify the newborn sun, which is usually shown as the scarab god Khepri. The object he sits on is given the form of the ***heb*** (meaning "festival") bowl rather than the ordinary ***neb*** basket (meaning "all" and also used for "lord"). Above his head is the sun disk, ***re***. On the reverse, the king appears as an older youth, wearing the blue crown which was associated with being the heir apparent. The face of the figure on the left has been inset with black glass, the color indicating rebirth and fertility.

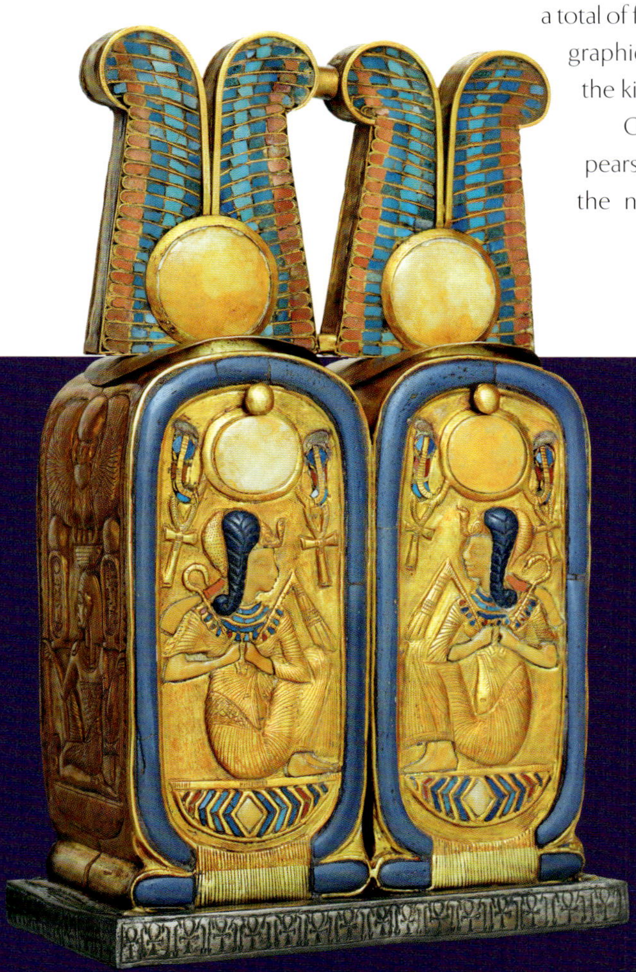

CARTOUCHE COSMETIC BOX
Gold, carnelian, colored glass, silver
Height 16 cm, width 8.8 cm, depth 4.3 cm
Carter 240bis

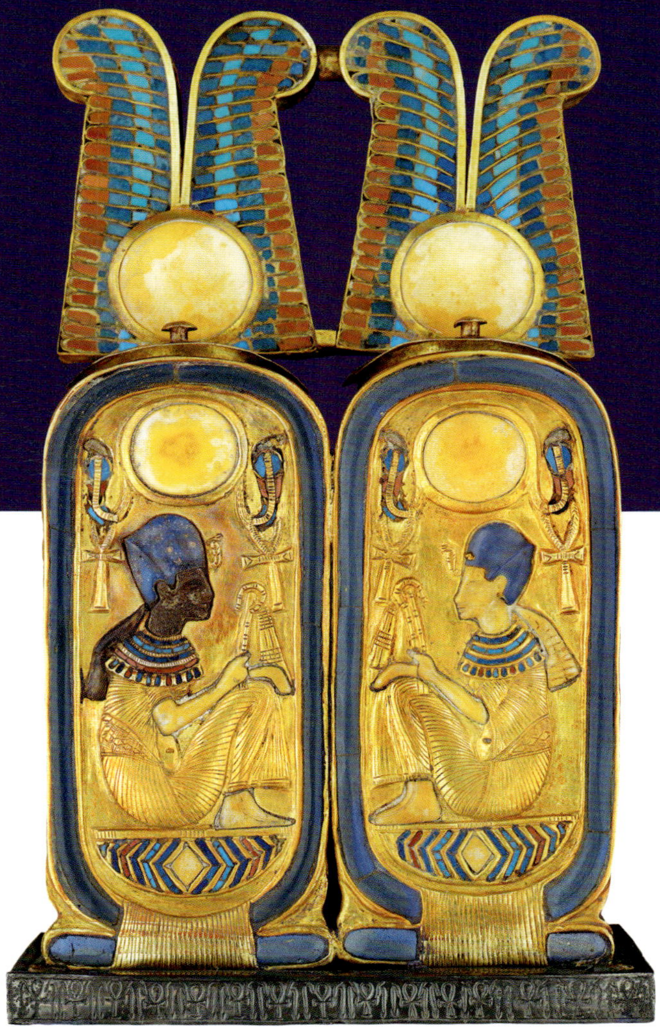

On the short sides of the container, Heh, the god of eternity who appears so often on objects from the tomb, crouches on a ***heb*** basket with his usual emblems of the ***ankh***, notched palm ribs, tadpoles, and ***shen*** rings. The king's name is here, written in its usual form with a scarab beetle.

The bottom of the container, which is made of silver, has been decorated with a marsh scene with flying ducks.

TUTANKHAMUN'S FUNERAL
Burial chamber
East wall

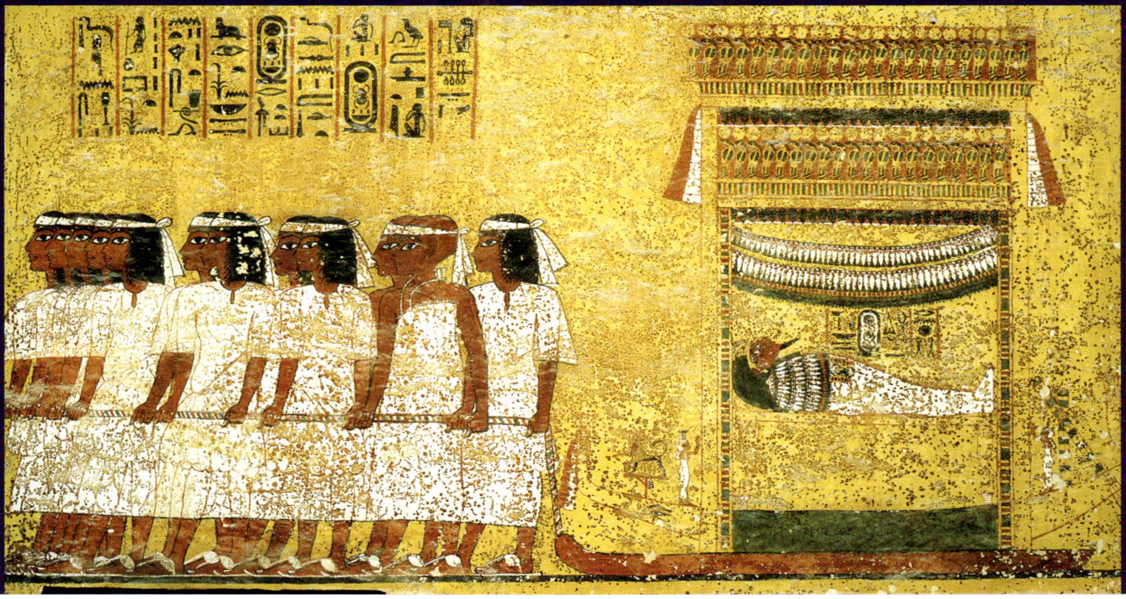

THE DECORATION OF THE BURIAL CHAMBER

Most of the painted scenes on the walls of the Burial Chamber survive today, but one fell victim to Carter's excavation team. Breaching the wall from the Antechamber had damaged part of the decoration. Later, when time came to remove the shrine, the south wall had to be completely removed, but steps were taken to save the paintings and move them to the Egyptian Museum in Cairo.

The ancient workmen had covered the walls in a thick layer of mortar to receive the paint in this room, the only one in the tomb to be decorated. The painters who decorated the chamber drew most of the figures based on a grid of 20 squares. This was a convention held over from the Amarna Period art. (Before and after, Egyptian artists used an 18-square grid.) This resulted in figures that were short-legged, and they were also noticeably soft-looking – another lingering Amarna influence – on a background painted yellow to resemble not only old papyrus, but also gold, the color of divine flesh.

The scenes illustrate the king's passage into the afterlife. The first scene appears on the eastern wall, showing an event that would have taken place between the royal mummification workshop and the tomb in the Valley of the Kings. Here, a dozen noblemen drag a sledge that carries a shrine in the form of a boat. Within the shrine lies the royal mummy,

THE DECEASED KING IS WELL RECEIVED IN THE AFTERLIFE
Burial chamber
North wall

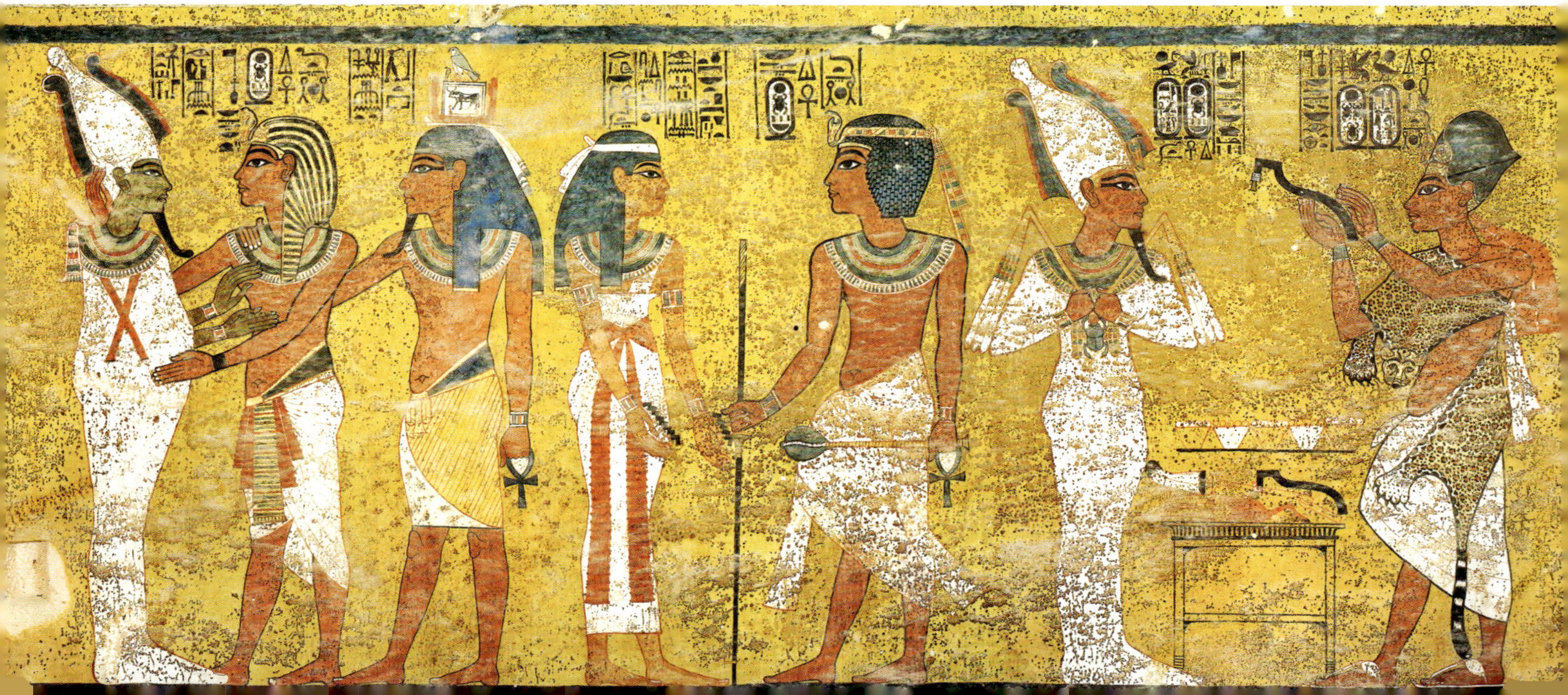

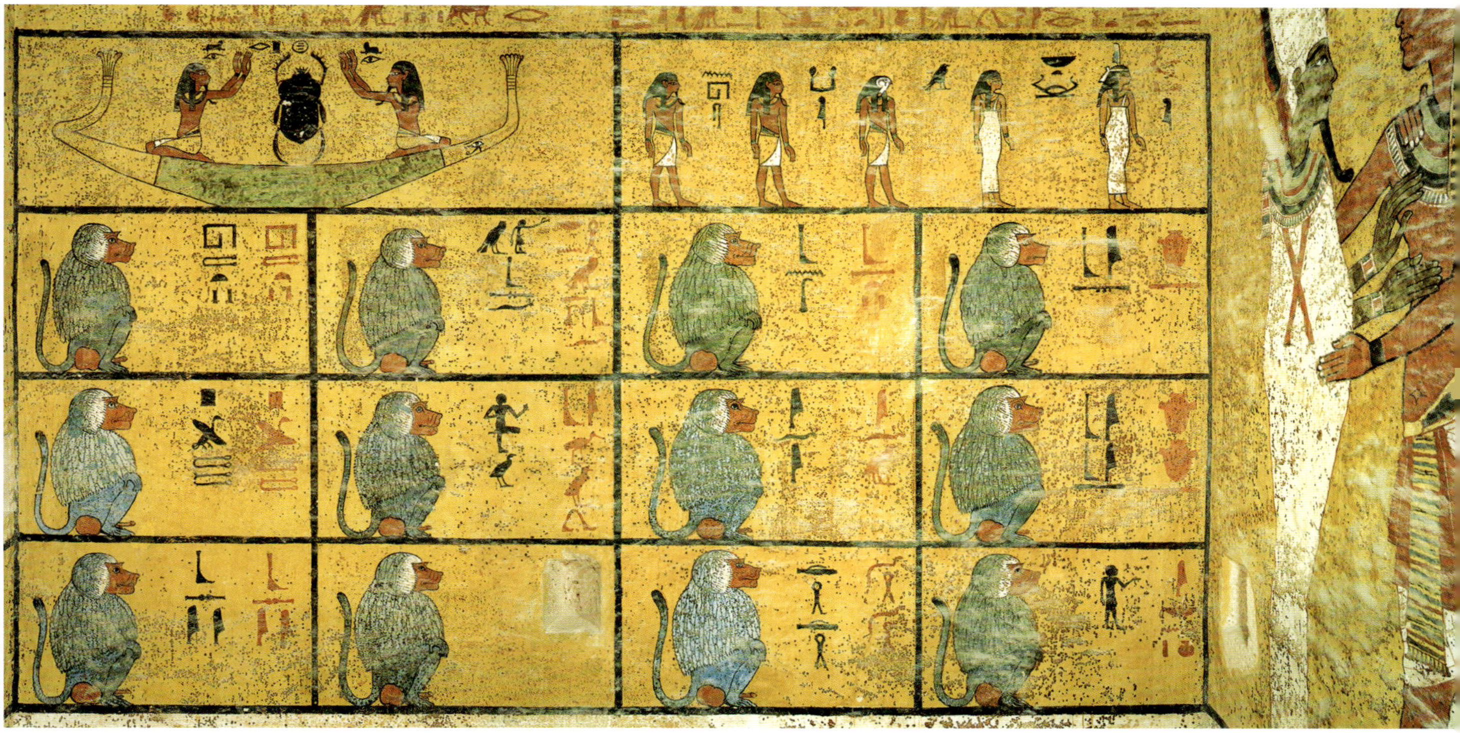

THE BOAT OF THE SUN GOD
Passing in the netherworld through the twelve hours of the night represented as seated baboons.
West wall

bound for the tomb. The dead king is welcomed "in peace to the West," that is, the land of the dead.

The sequence of the scenes proceeds from right to left, so the three vignettes on the north wall come next. In the first of these, Ay, formerly Tutankhamun's vizier and now his successor, wears the blue crown and the leopard skin of a ***sem*** priest. He performs the very ancient ritual known as the Opening of the Mouth on the dead king's mummy, here represented as Tutankhamun in the form of the god Osiris. Ay holds a carpenter's adze, one of several implements touched to parts of the mummy, coffin, or statue in order to allow the deceased to eat, speak, see, hear, breathe, and otherwise function in the afterlife. The next figure is Nut, the sky goddess, who presents in her hands libations of pure water in a gesture known as the ***ny-ny***. She is greeting Tutankhamun, who is now holding a staff, mace, and ***ankh***. Lastly in this scene, the king, shadowed by a personification of his life force (***ka***), embraces Osiris, lord of the West.

On the west wall, the third scene illustrates the first of twelve hours of night, as described in the ***Amduat***. At the upper left, the artists depicted Khepri, embodiment of the sun at dawn, as a scarab aboard the solar barque. Two divine figures, each identified as an "Osiris," honor the god with raised arms. Three gods and two goddesses of the netherworld walk before the barque. The remainder of the wall is occupied by a grid of twelve rectangles, each occupied by a baboon. These represent the twelve hours of night, through which the sun had to travel and also through which the king had to pass in order to reach his eternal life.

The damaged remains of the south wall show Tutankhamun receiving life from Hathor, while Anubis places his hand on the king's shoulder. Behind Anubis, Isis makes the ***ny-ny*** gesture, and behind her squat three more gods of the netherworld. The figures on this wall show different proportions than the rest in the room. These were drawn closer to the traditional, non-Amarna 18-square grid.

HATHOR GIVES AN *ANKH* (LIFE) TO TUTANKHAMUN IN THE PRESENCE OF ANUBIS
Burial chamber
South wall

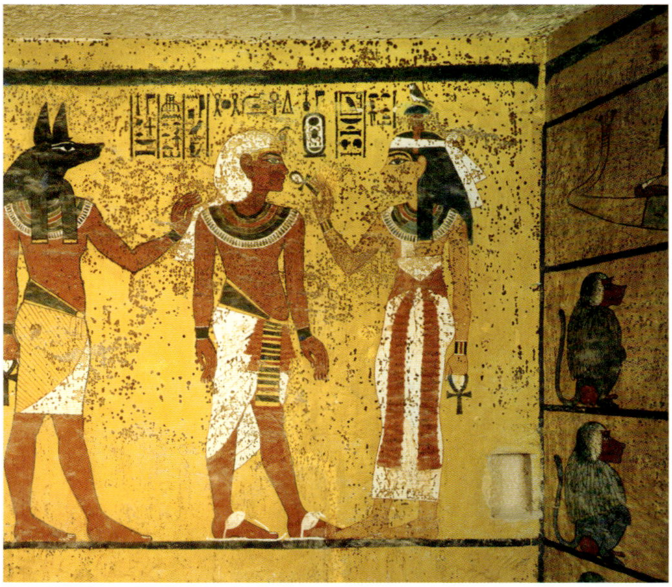

THE COFFINS

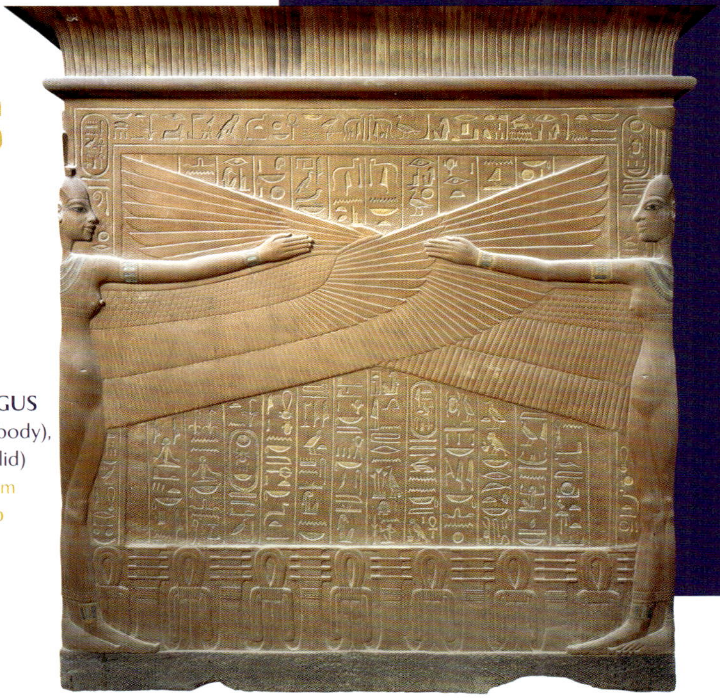

SARCOPHAGUS
Red quartzite (body), red granite (lid)
Length 2.74 m
Carter 240

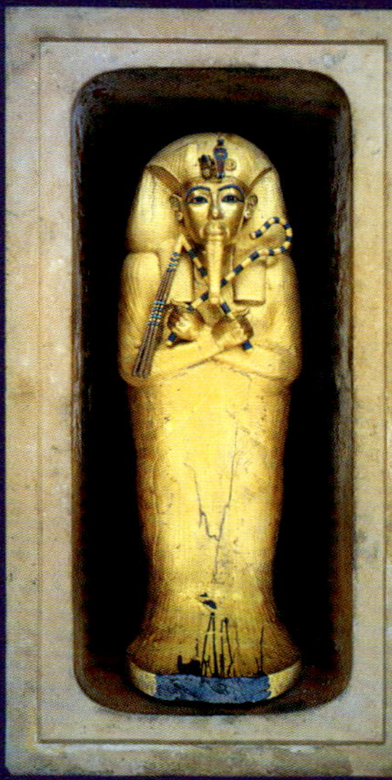

OUTERMOST COFFIN
Gilded wood, sheet gold, colored glass, semiprecious stones
Length 2.23 m
Carter 253

When Carter and his team finally finished dismantling shrines, on 3rd February, 1924, they found the king's magnificent sarcophagus, "intact, with the lid still firmly fixed in its place, just as the pious hands had left it." The body of the sarcophagus was a work of art in its own right, crafted from a single block of red quartzite, the lid was made of red granite. Carter described it as "makeshift," and it was clearly flawed. In antiquity the lid had cracked – perhaps it had been dropped? – and it was repaired with gypsum plaster.

But that could not detract from the beauty of the sarcophagus itself. At each corner a guardian goddess had been carved in high relief. The winged arms of Isis, Nephthys, Neith, and Selket stretch out along the sides to embrace the sarcophagus and, by extension, the mummy within. Texts on sides are spells spoken by the gods, also to ensure the safety of the king's body. At the westernmost end of both long sides, an eye of Horus, or ***wedjat***, allowed the king to look out, but these, too, were protective signs.

Despite persistent arguments about the matter of visitors and how to handle publicity for the excavation, the Antiquities Service and Carter agreed to a date for the opening of the sarcophagus: 12th February, 1924. Carter even invited the Minister of Public Works, Morcos Bey Hanna, who was responsible for the Antiquities Service. When he learned that the opening would reveal a nest of coffins rather than the king's mummy, Morcos declined to attend and sent a delegate instead.

Others were considerably more enthusiastic about the prospect of viewing the coffins. A crowd of dignitaries gathered on the appointed day, eager to be among the first to discover what lay beneath that cracked lid. An elaborate array of pulleys lifted the lid, revealing a shrouded form.... Not the shroud of a mummy but linen draping an anthropoid coffin that rested on a gilded, lion-headed bier.

Drawing back the linen brought to light a magnificent visage: Tutankhamun, in the crossed-arm pose of the mummified Osiris, carved in wood covered with a thick layer of sheet gold. Holding the usual crook and flail in hand, the king wears an unusual headdress, resembling the ***khat*** (which had lunar/nocturnal associations), and, beneath that, a ceremonial wig. At the king's brow were the two protective goddesses of Lower and Upper Egypt: the uraeus, cast in bronze, and a vulture of gilded wood with an ebony beak, both inlaid with colored glass, obsidian, and faience. Around these figures mourners had left a garland of olive leaves and cornflowers. Inlay of calcite (Egyptian alabaster) and obsidian form the eyes of the king, while above them arch brows of dark blue glass. From his chin protrudes a divine braided beard, gessoed and gilded. A feathered pattern, known as ***rishi*** and first used during the Middle Kingdom, decorates the body of the coffin. On the sides, the sister goddesses Isis and Nephthys spread their winged arms to embrace the king. Artists depicted Isis again on the foot of the coffin, where she kneels on the hieroglyphic symbol for "gold."

Even the practical construction details of this coffin were of precious metals. Each side of the coffin lid had a pair of silver handles so that it could be lowered onto the shell. Ten tenons of solid silver joined the two halves. Each tenon bears the king's name and describes him as the "beloved of" a divinity. Silver pins with gold heads fastened the tenons in place.

However well crafted and beautiful the coffin was, it had a serious flaw that was not discovered until the funerary party brought it into the burial chamber: it was too big for the sarcophagus. As a result, they had to chip parts of the foot away. Carter found the pieces of gilded wood within the sarcophagus, where they had been left.

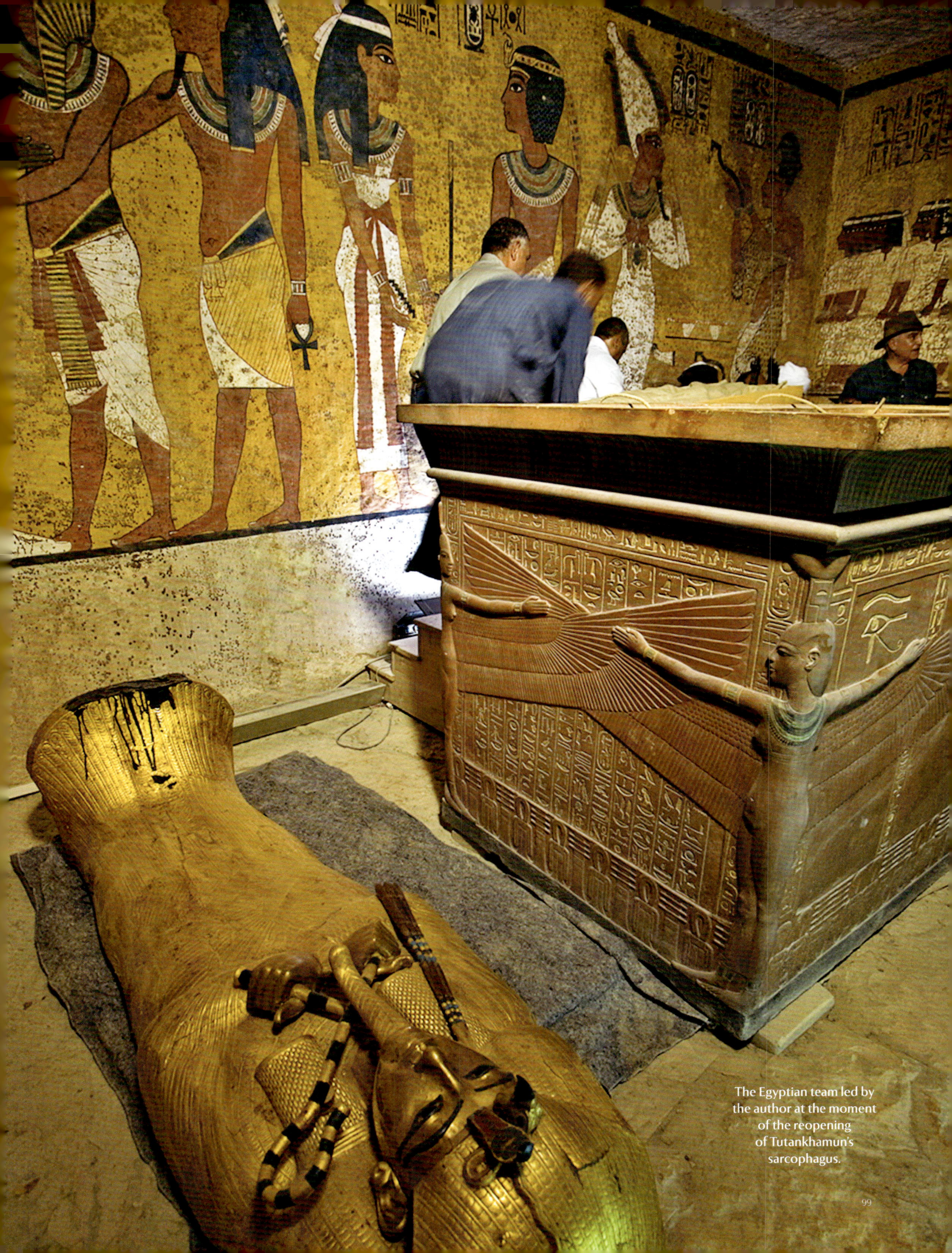

The Egyptian team led by the author at the moment of the reopening of Tutankhamun's sarcophagus.

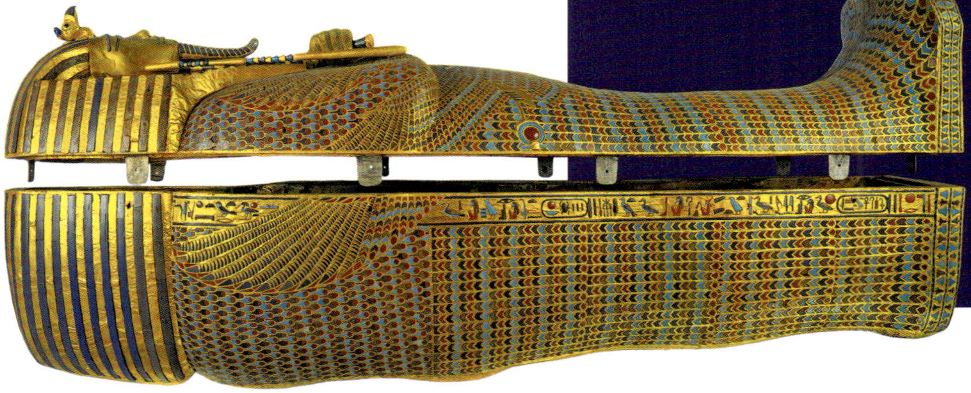

MIDDLE COFFIN
Gilded wood, glass, semiprecious stones
Length 2.04 m
Carter 254

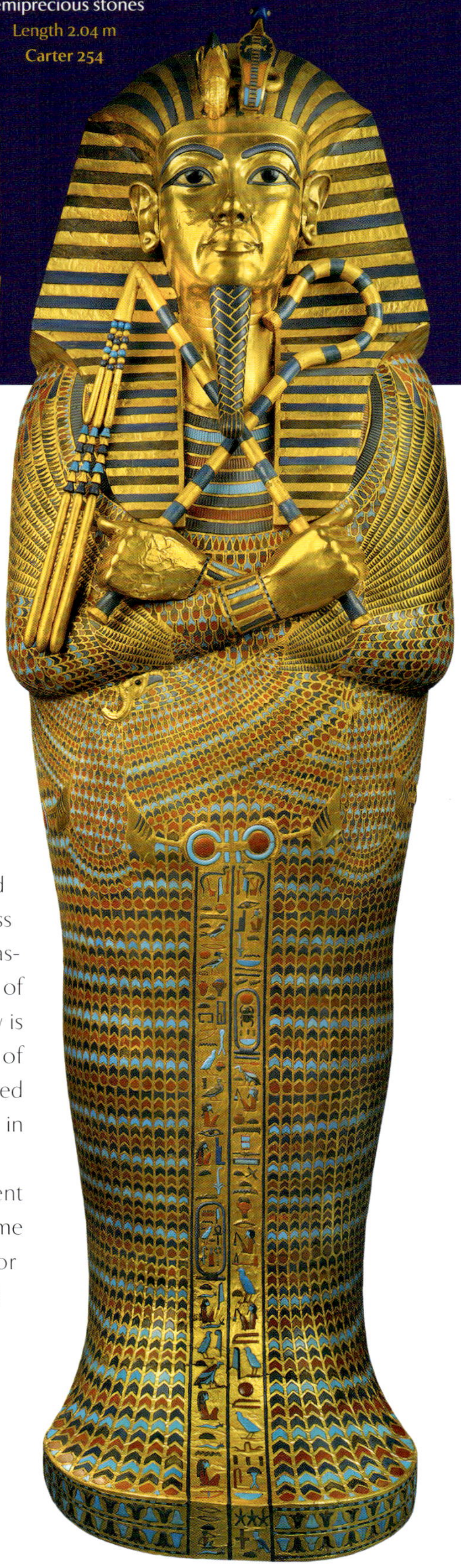

Because of continued bureaucratic troubles, more than a year would pass between the day Carter's team opened the sarcophagus and the day they opened the outermost coffin in October 1925.

To raise the lid from the first coffin, it was necessary to saw the silver pins that fastened the tenons. Only then was the system of pulleys able to raise the lid.

The next coffin was covered by "gossamer" linen, as Carter described it. Through it Carter could see damage wrought by humidity. A garland of flowers and berries lay on the chest, while one of flowers and olive leaves was positioned on the vulture and uraeus of the coffin's headdress.

The team took the lid to the conservation lab. This gave them barely enough room to remove the outer coffin and all its contents by means of the pulleys and slings. The weight of the coffin surprised them. They were, however, able to lift it just high enough to clear the edge of the sarcophagus, in order to slide wooden planks underneath it for support.

Once relieved of its shroud of linen, the wooden middle coffin was found to be, as Carter wrote, "superior to that of the first coffin, in so much that it is more delicate and purer in line and conveys almost greater feeling." Its wood was covered with gold foil inlayed with colored glass and faience. The design was the feathered *rishi* pattern again. This coffin was guarded by the vulture- goddess Nekhbet and the cobra-goddess Wadjet. The king's eyes and eyebrows are inlaid stone and glass. Stripes of dark blue glass inlay the *nemes* headdress, which was associated with the sun. Again, the beak of the vulture that guards the king's brow is of ebony; the cobra head is made of faience. Once again, the king is portrayed with the royal crook and flail, inlaid in faience and glass.

The face on this coffin is different from that of the first and the third. Some have suggested that it was made for someone other than Tutankhamun and was usurped at the king's untimely death. The candidate usually put forward as the original owner is Smenkhkare, Tutankhamun's predecessor.

The middle coffin fit tightly within the first. It had no handles to ease the task of removal. Carter recorded his feelings about this challenge on 20th October 1925:

"Without some experience of handling heavy and yet fragile antiquities under very difficult circumstances, few can realize that nerve racking undertaking and responsibility. The raising of a lid of a coffin or lifting the coffin itself seems a comparatively simple job; but when one realizes that it is deep down in the interior of a sarcophagus where it fits quite closely, that it is in a very fragile condition, that it is immensely heavy, that the overhead room in the chamber is very limited, and that one does not even know whether its wood is sufficiently well preserved to bear its own weight, the reader will perhaps begin to realize what an anxious work it really is.

After consultation with one's colleagues and careful consideration, a plan of action is formed, you begin to carry it out – probably the preparation of which has taken several days, special appliances are devised, and as far as it is humanly possible you have taken every precaution. Everything goes well until suddenly, in the middle of the process, you hear a crack – little pieces of surface ornament fall clink clink on the floor of the sarcophagus or chamber – the only space available is now crowded with your men, and in a moment you have to discover what is happening – what is the trouble, and what immediate action is required to prevent a catastrophe. The reader will perhaps realize that strain upon the nerves.

Again, the interest of seeing some fresh and beautiful object exposed as a lid is being raised will often distract your workmen, for a moment they forget their duty and irreparable damage may be done.

Such is more than often an archaeologist's lot, and afterwards he is asked what were his sensations when so and so was first discovered!"

I personally can attest to the great stress one feels when being confronted with the responsibility for the safety of such a priceless artifact. Carter's team proved themselves up to the task. They raised the middle coffin from the first by first partly pulling out the pins that fastened the lid to the shell. These would serve as the "handles." They attached wires to these pins, then threaded other wires through metal eyelets screwed into the shell of the outermost coffin. All the wires were attached to a scaffold. The coffins were, it must be remembered, still placed on the wooden planks, which held them over the sarcophagus. Carter had these removed, and the outer coffin was lowered back down into the sarcophagus. It is still there to this day.

Now a wooden tray was slid beneath the middle coffin for support, so that the process of removing its fragile lid could begin. Using, once again, metal eyelets (carefully placed so as to cause as little damage as possible to the decoration), the team raised its lid. They found a third anthropoid coffin beneath another pall, this one of a reddish linen with a collar of flowers and gold beads sewn onto it. It had been positioned so as not to cover the face of this coffin.

Here, before them, was the solution to the mysterious weight of the nest of coffins. Removal of the garland and pall revealed that this third, innermost coffin was solid gold. Foreign rulers wrote to Egypt, claiming that gold was like dust there, and here seemed proof of this. But the Egyptians had, during the funeral ceremonies, coated it with a dark, resinous material that Carter had to clean off before the true majesty of the object could be appreciated. Carter wrote that "both technically and artistically," the coffin was "a unique example of the metalworker's art."

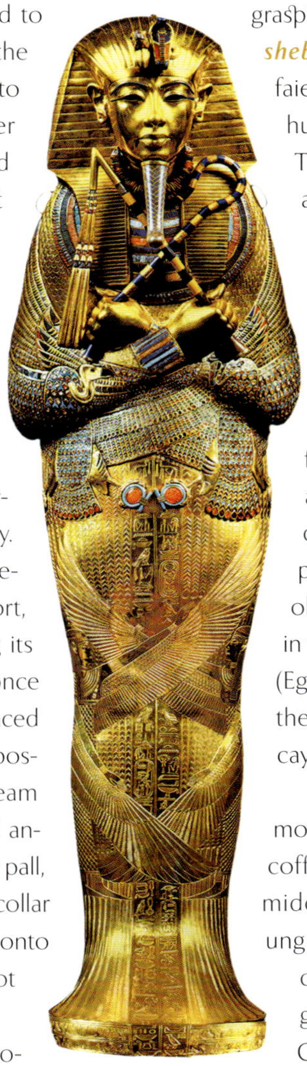

INNERMOST COFFIN
Gold, glass, semiprecious stones
Length 1.87 m
Carter 255

The beaten gold that makes up the coffin ranges in thickness from 2.5 to 3 mm. Details were skillfully chased into its surface. Again Tutankhamun appears as Osiris, wearing the solar ***nemes*** headdress with cobra and vulture at his forehead and grasping the crook and flail. Two ***shebyu*** collars of gold and faience, symbols of divinity, hung around the king's neck. The ***rishi*** pattern appears again, as do Nekhbet and Wadjet, who protect the king's chest. Isis and Nephthys appear over his legs. Decoration at various locations (especially the upper part of the body, face, and headdress) were added in sheet gold, with colored glass and semiprecious stone inlays. The obsidian pupils stand alone in the eye sockets; the calcite (Egyptian alabaster) used for the whites of the eyes has decayed away.

Carter had not yet removed the golden innermost coffin from the gilded-wood middle coffin. Hardened unguents poured during the ceremony had in effect glued the two together. Carter moved this assembly into the Antechamber to give the team more room to work on the problem. They decided to raise the lid of the innermost coffin before trying to separate the two. Using long screwdrivers as levers, they removed gold pins that fixed in place the gold tenons that held the lid to its shell. They removed the lid on 28th October.

This, at last, revealed the king's mummy, and the golden mask that has come to represent not only the king himself, but the wealth and splendor of all of ancient Egypt.

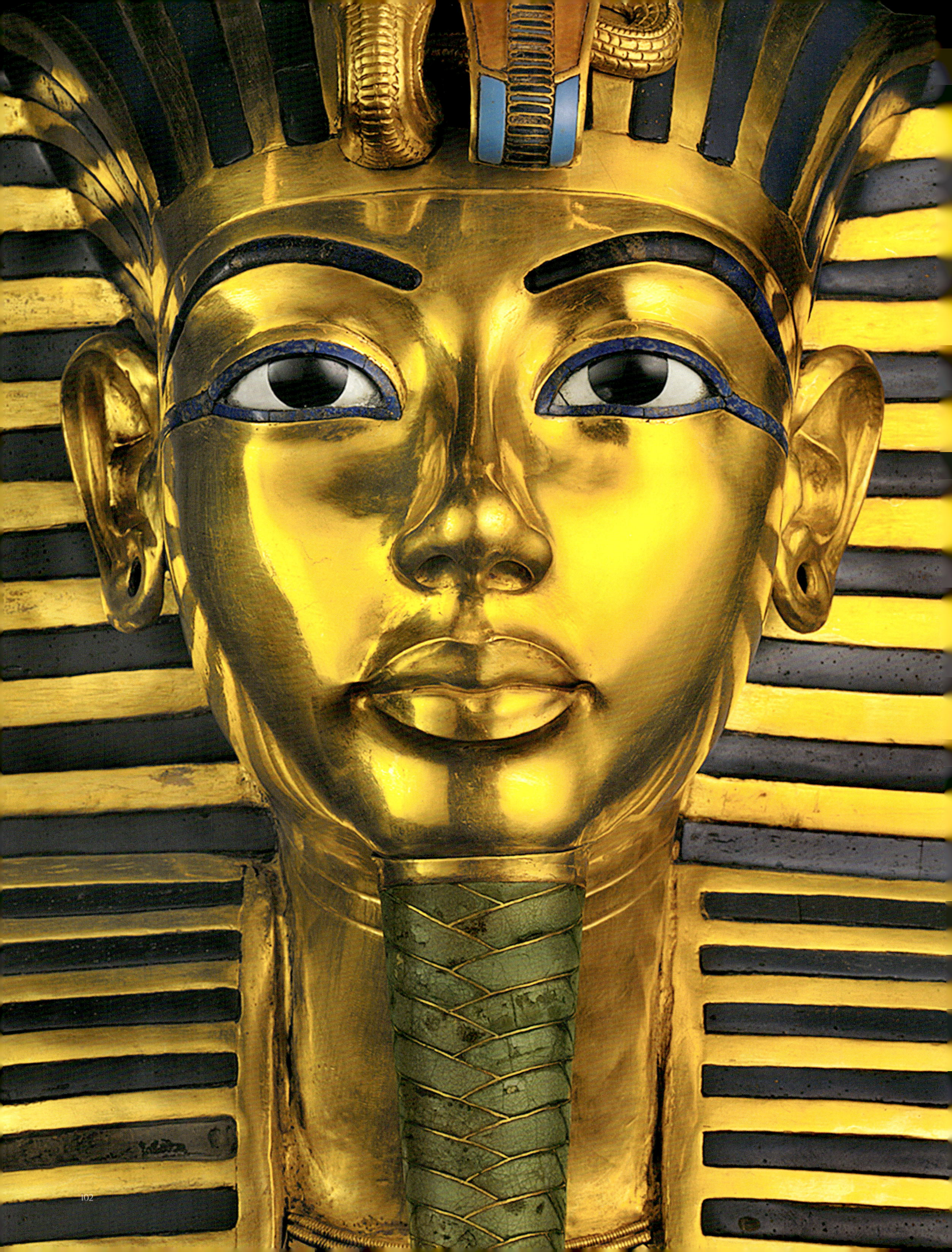

THE GOLDEN MASK

The face on the mask is an idealized portrait of the young king executed in precious materials with unsurpassed craftsmanship. It is one of the most beautiful of objects, and I myself go to see the mask every time I visit the museum. All of my television interviews held within the museum are filmed in front of it. It served as a place in which Tutankhamun's soul could dwell if some ill fate befell the body, and thus was an essential item of the royal burial equipment.

But the king's head was quite stuck inside this marvelous object, on account of the resins used to preserve the mummy. To remedy this situation, Carter had to resort to heated knives to melt and cut through the resin. The process of freeing the mask removed the mummy's head as well.

I can imagine being in Carter's place, seeing this exquisite face for the first time, knowing that within it is the real face of the king. What a dilemma.... Should I remove the mask and do damage to the royal mummy? Or do I leave the two joined together, forever, and exhibit the mummy with the mask in place? My choice is the same as Carter's was: take the mask off, even at the price of damaging the mummy.

The Egyptians thought that the flesh of the gods was made of gold, so fittingly the artisans used this metal to create this masterpiece. They hammered together two thick gold sheets, then gave it the features of the

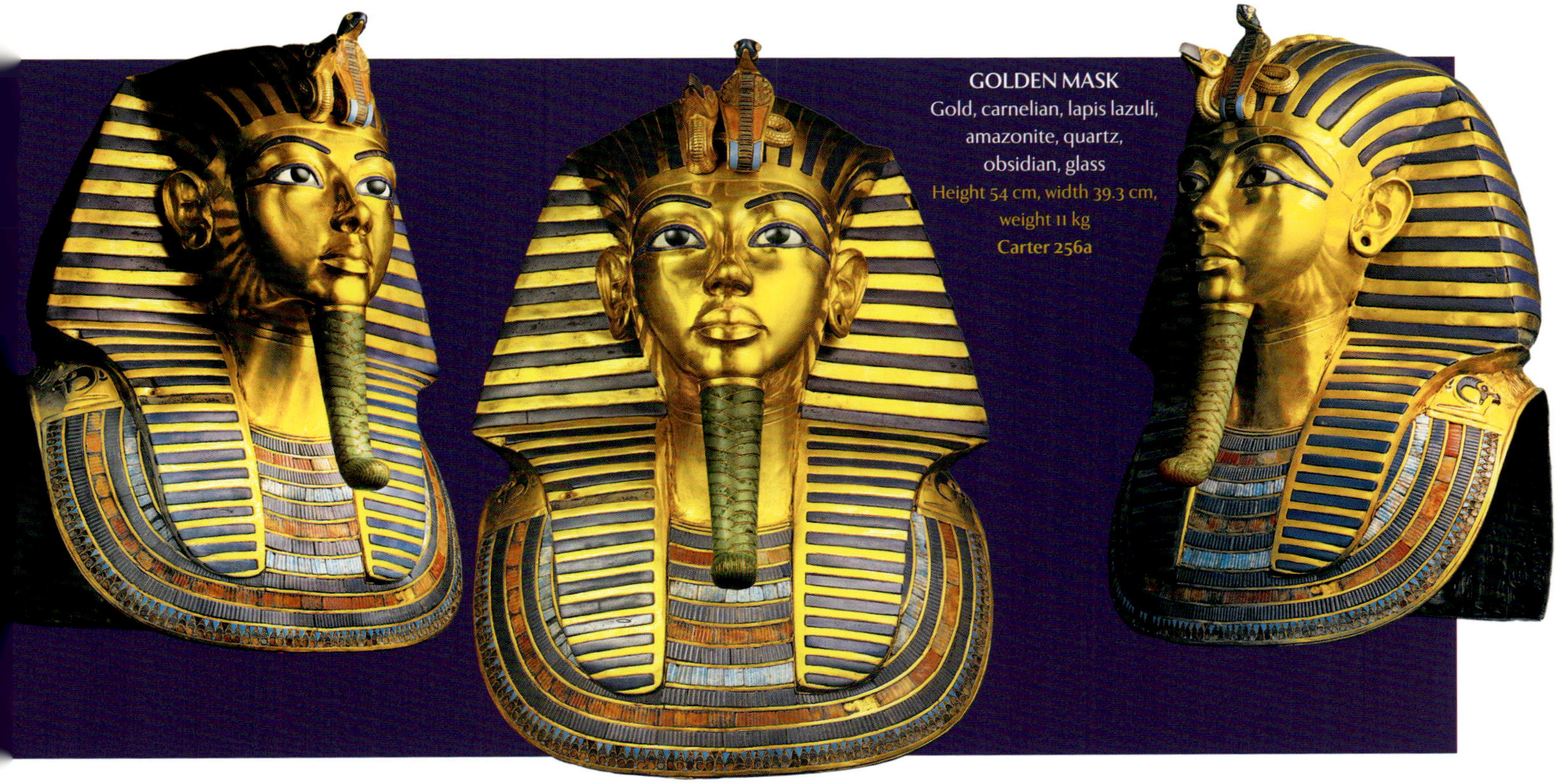

GOLDEN MASK
Gold, carnelian, lapis lazuli, amazonite, quartz, obsidian, glass
Height 54 cm, width 39.3 cm, weight 11 kg
Carter 256a

king. Recent X-ray examination of the mask has revealed that the artisans added thin layers of gold-silver-copper alloy to the gold body of the mask to increase its brilliance.

The eyes were of quartz, inlaid with obsidian for pupils, and given a bit of red paint at the inner and outer corners. Lapis lazuli forms the inlays used for the cosmetic lines of the eye and the curving eyebrows. When Carter found the mask, gold foil covered the large holes in the earlobes, but today the piercings are uncovered. The front of the neck is characterized by two horizontal lines. These, and the full lips and almond-shaped eyes, indicate that the artists who made it learned their craft during the reign of Akhenaten.

The headdress they portrayed is the ***nemes*** headcloth, with stripes and other details of colored stone and glass. The protective vulture and uraeus are solid gold with inlays of lapis lazuli, carnelian, glass, and faience. The king's beard, a symbol of divinity, is a golden framework with blue glass inlay.

An elaborate broad collar covers the chest with 12 rows of beads of lapis lazuli, carnelian, amazonite, and glass, capped at the ends by falcon heads, symbolic of the god Horus. Such collars were worn on festive and ritual occasions and were also presented to divinities. On the shoulders and back of the mask, a protective magical text mentions parts of the body and the mask, connecting them to various deities. In this way the mask protects not only the king's head, but also the entire body.

THE TREASURY

Eventually the politics and personal tragedies associated with the early years of the excavation passed, allowing Carter's "scientific" work to continue fairly smoothly. The nearby tomb of Rameses XI (KV 4) was pressed into service as a storeroom for supplies and "minor objects" (a term that covered mostly small objects other than jewelry). The tomb of Seti II (KV 15) served as a laboratory and photographic studio. The mysterious KV 55 functioned as photographer Harry Burton's darkroom.

On the last day of 1925, Carter transported the solid-gold innermost coffin and mask to the Egyptian Museum in Cairo. Once he returned to the tomb, he spent the rest of the season working on the artifacts found among the mummy wrappings. He returned to England in late May.

Five months later, in late October 1926, he returned for yet another season of work. He had a new room to focus on, known initially as the "store room," but later dubbed the Treasury. The Treasury was entered through the north end of the east wall of the Burial Chamber. Positioned as if protecting the contents of the room was a larger-than-life-size figure of the jackal-god Anubis, reclining atop a gilded shrine.

There was much for the Lord of the Mummy Wrappings to guard. At the far end of the Treasury, against its east wall, was a canopic shrine containing the lungs, liver, stomach, and intestines of the king. Other shrines positioned against the Treasury walls contained gilded statues of the king and a variety of gods, along with boxes and chests filled with all manners of objects, including jewelry. The ancient tomb robbers had gotten this far and Anubis had not been enough to deter them from opening boxes and stealing some of the jewelry before being interrupted.

Carter's removal of objects from the Treasury took more than the entire 1926–1927 season. Work had to resume in the fall of 1927.

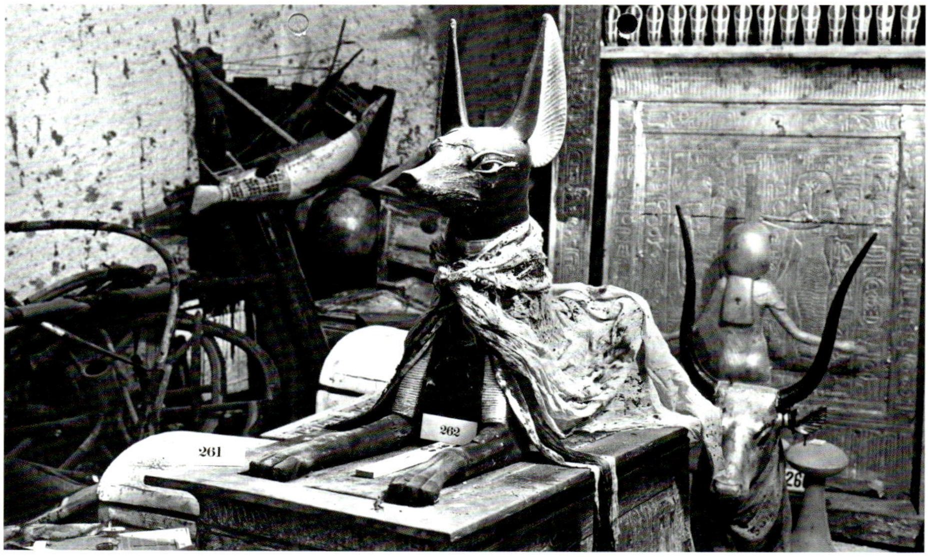

Tutankhamun's treasures as found intact inside the Treasury.
Harry Burton / Griffith Institute

A linen shawl covered the magnificent jackal that stared out of the Treasury from atop a gilded shrine. An inscription in black ink dated the shawl to Year 7 of Akhenaten's reign. Around the canine's neck was a floral collar.

Anubis, divine embalmer and guardian of the dead, was carved of wood, covered with gesso, and painted black. Gilding highlights the inner surfaces of his ears, the collar and scarf. He has been given silver claws and eyes inlaid with calcite (Egyptian alabaster) and obsidian.

Known from the earliest periods of Egyptian history, Anubis played many roles as god of the dead. Priests wearing jackal masks oversaw the embalming. He was a psychopomp (soul guide), and he attended the scales where the deceased's heart would be weighed against the feather representing *maat* (truth and universal order) in the court of Osiris.

The structure on which the jackal reclines is in the form of one side of a pylon, the massive gateway that formed the entrance to ancient Egyptian temples. It sits on a sledge equipped with four carrying poles.

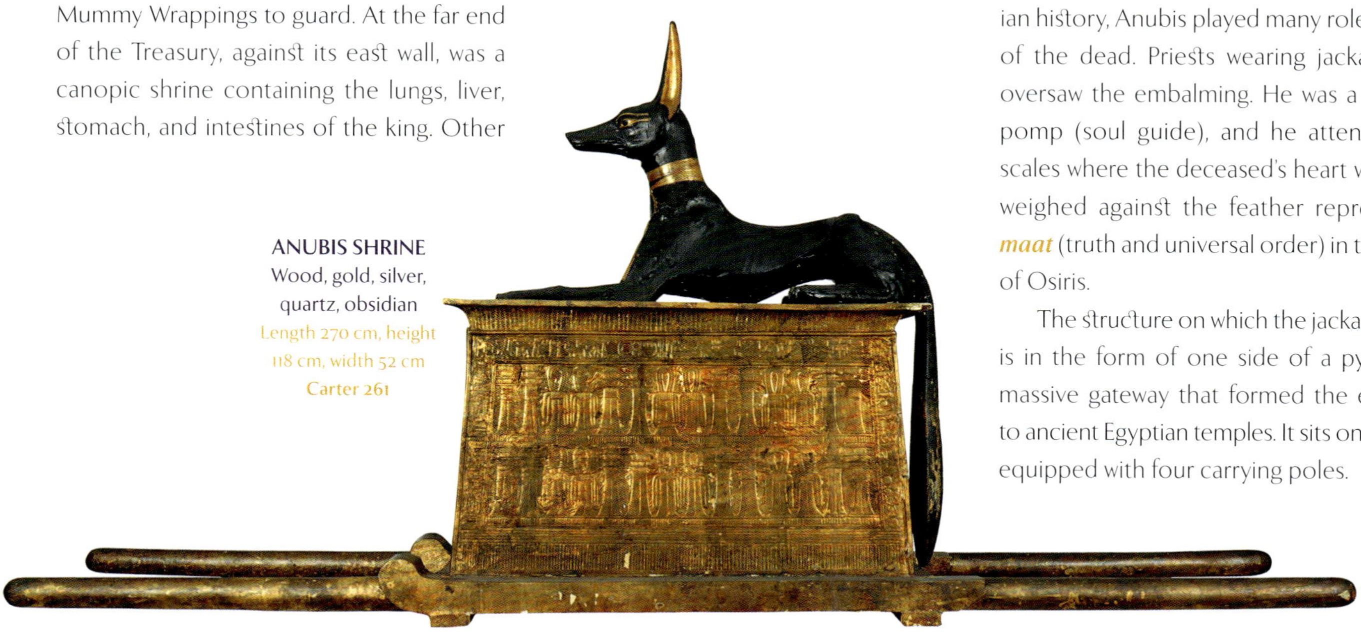

ANUBIS SHRINE
Wood, gold, silver, quartz, obsidian
Length 270 cm, height 118 cm, width 52 cm
Carter 261

INLAID PECTORALS

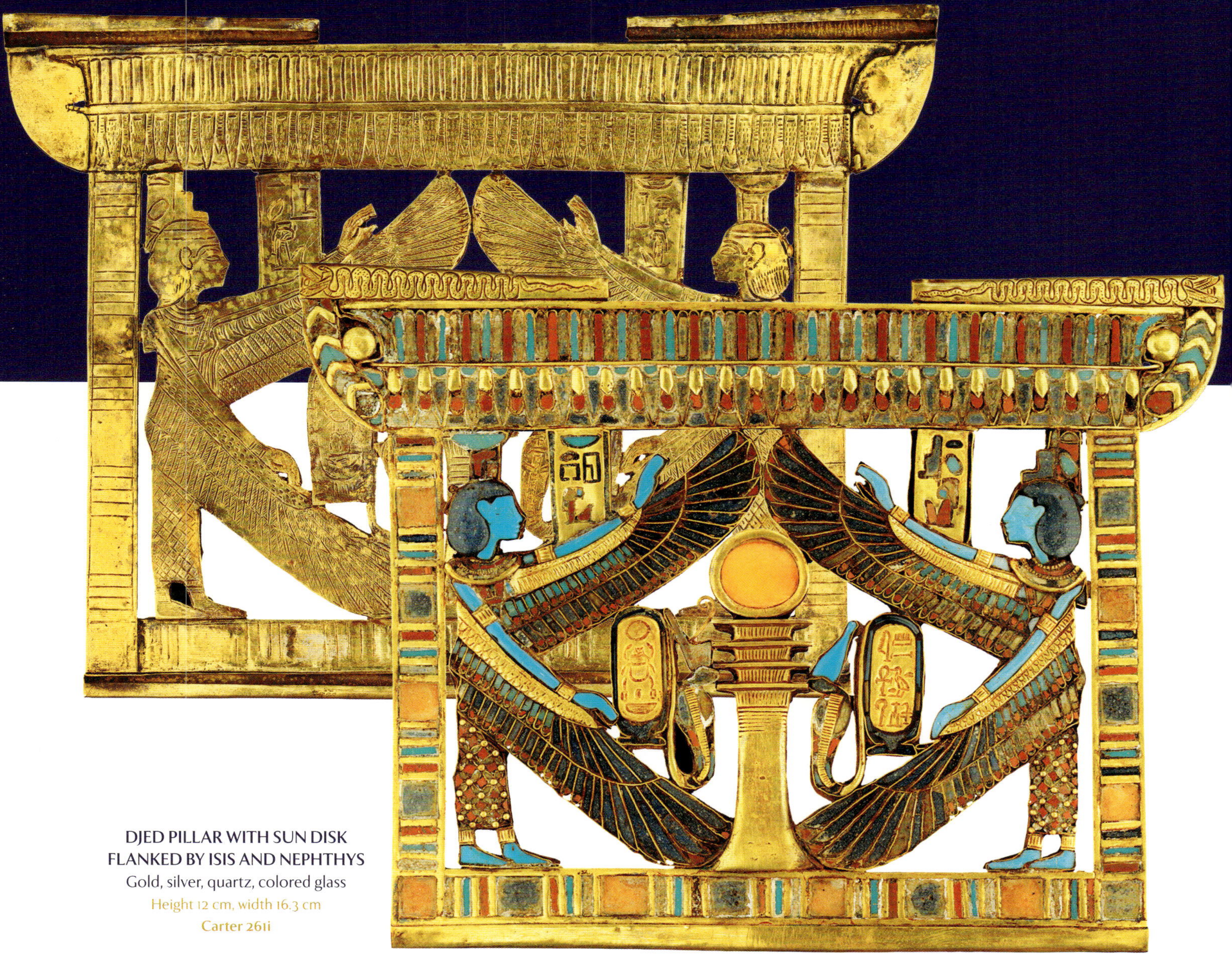

DJED PILLAR WITH SUN DISK FLANKED BY ISIS AND NEPHTHYS
Gold, silver, quartz, colored glass
Height 12 cm, width 16.3 cm
Carter 261i

The Anubis shrine had been violated by robbers in antiquity, but objects were still found within it, including a number of wonderful pectorals, among them the four seen here. The king might have worn them while performing temple rituals or other ceremonial occasions. Each takes the shape of a pylon-shaped shrine, perhaps indicating use within a temple. However, the symbolism tends to the funerary, which could signify that they were intended for use in the tomb. A *djed* pillar, a symbol of Osiris, topped by a solar disk forms the center of the first pectoral. Identified by hieroglyphic signs on their heads and above their wings, Osiris's divine sisters, Isis (on the right) and Nephthys (on the left) stretch out their arms to protect it. Between the wings of these goddesses are Tutankhamun's cartouches, each guarded by a cobra.

The next pectoral features the mummiform figure of Osiris, or perhaps Tutankhamun as Osiris, guarded by a winged cobra wearing the red crown of Lower Egypt and a vulture with the Upper Egyptian white crown. The third here shows the sky goddess Nut with her wings outstretched. Like Isis and Nephthys in the first pectoral, her skin is inlaid in turquoise, a color associated with the day sky and rebirth. The text around her body records a spell spoken by the goddess. Carter recorded that the top of this pectoral originally bore Akhenaten's names, although this is a matter of dispute.

The final pectoral here is the most important, with its large scarab of green feldspar, beside which kneels Isis and Nephthys. Found in the cartouche-shaped box (**Carter No. 269**), this is the king's heart scarab. Usually such scarabs were included in the mummy bandages near the chest. The back of the pectoral records a "heart spell" from the ***Book of the Dead.*** A winged sun disk, symbol of Horus the Behedite, hovers above the scene, which also includes Tutankhamun's names and epithets.

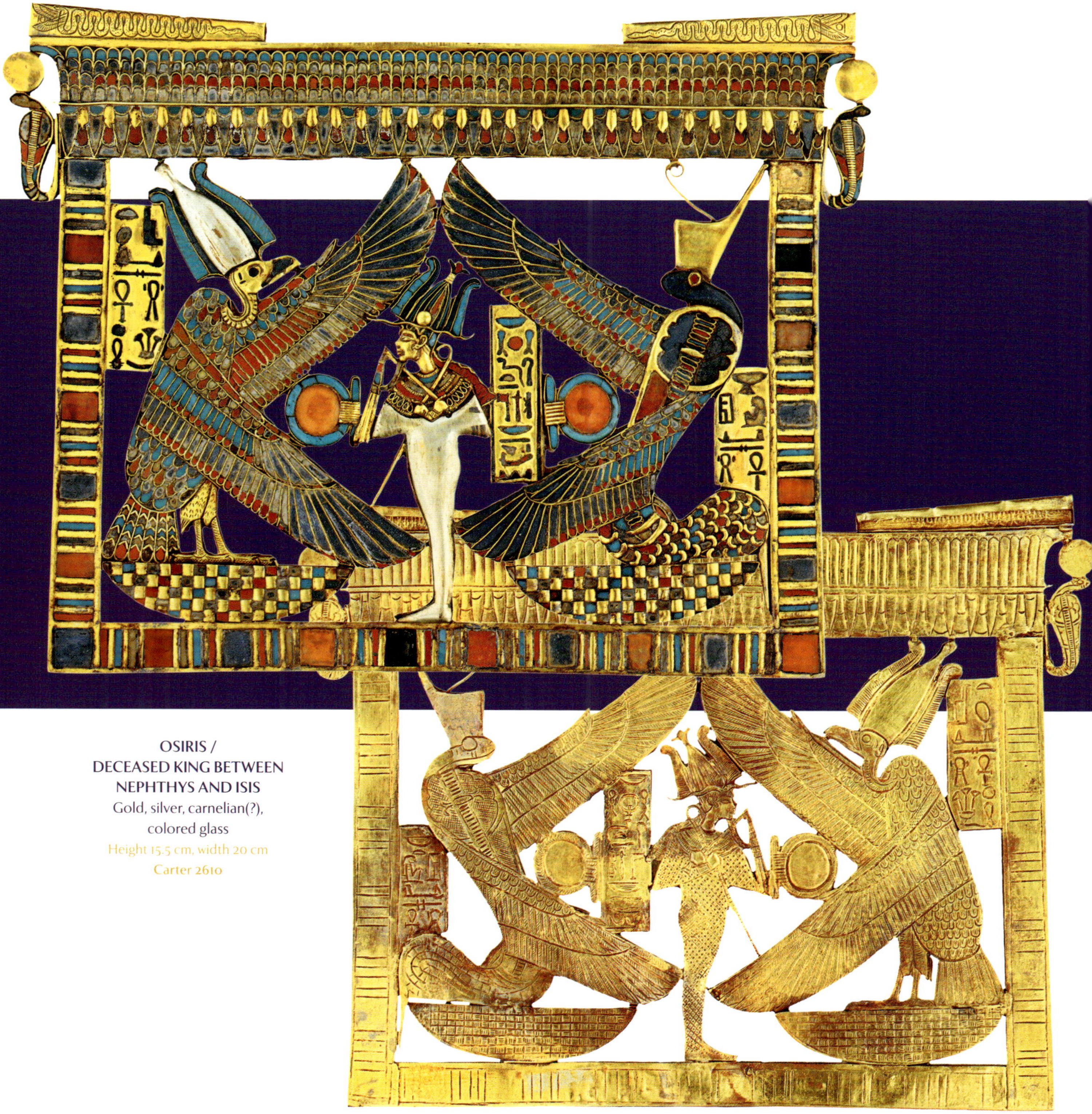

OSIRIS / DECEASED KING BETWEEN NEPHTHYS AND ISIS
Gold, silver, carnelian(?), colored glass
Height 15.5 cm, width 20 cm
Carter 261o

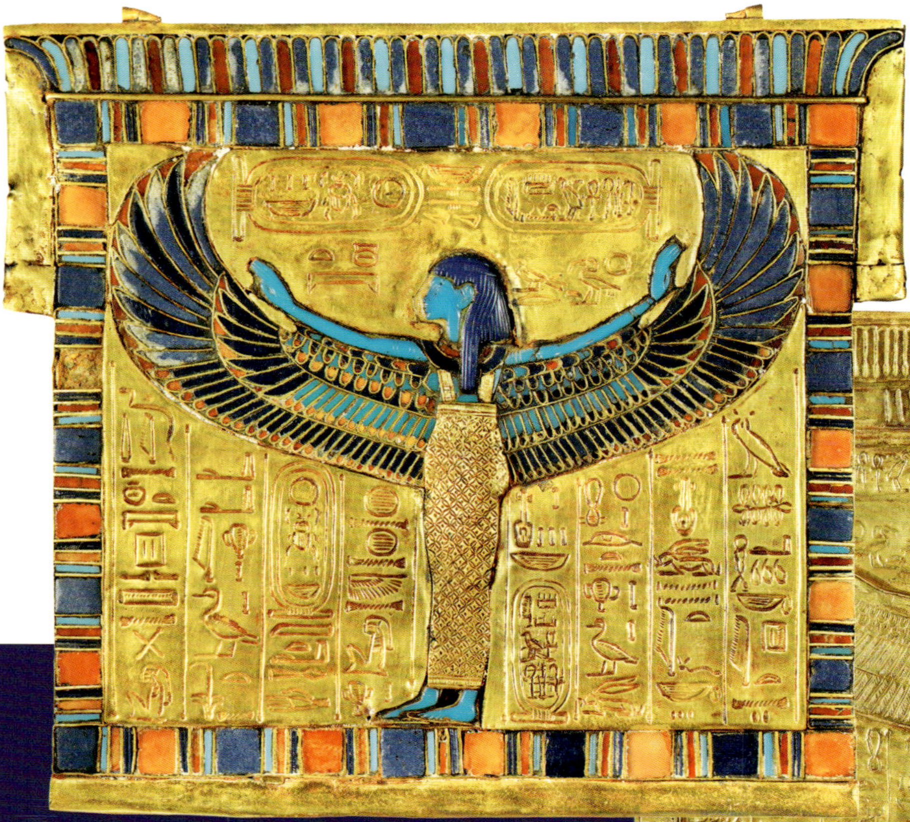

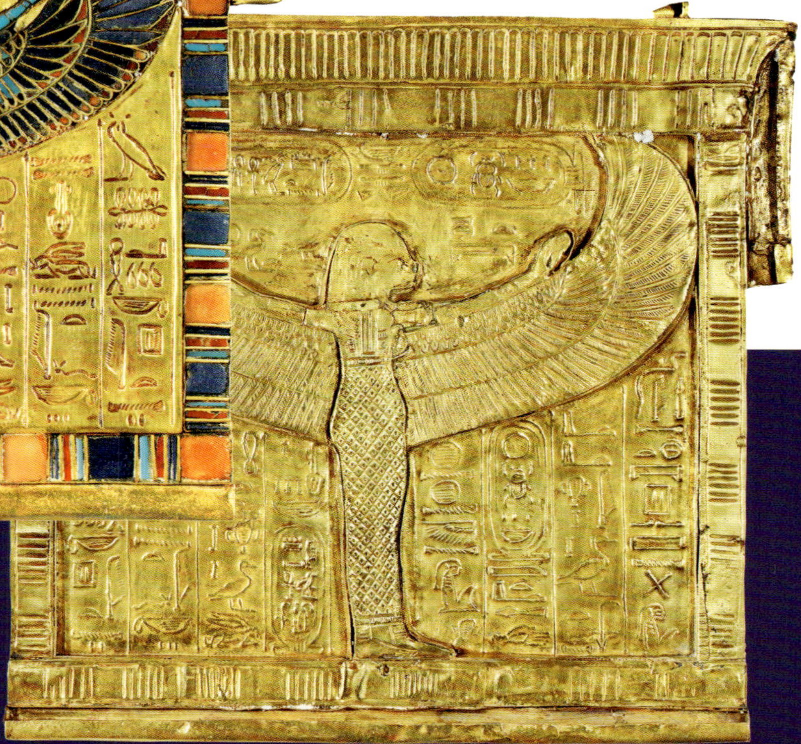

WINGED NUT
Gold, silver, carnelian(?), colored glass
Height 12.6 cm, width 14.3 cm
Carter 261p(1)

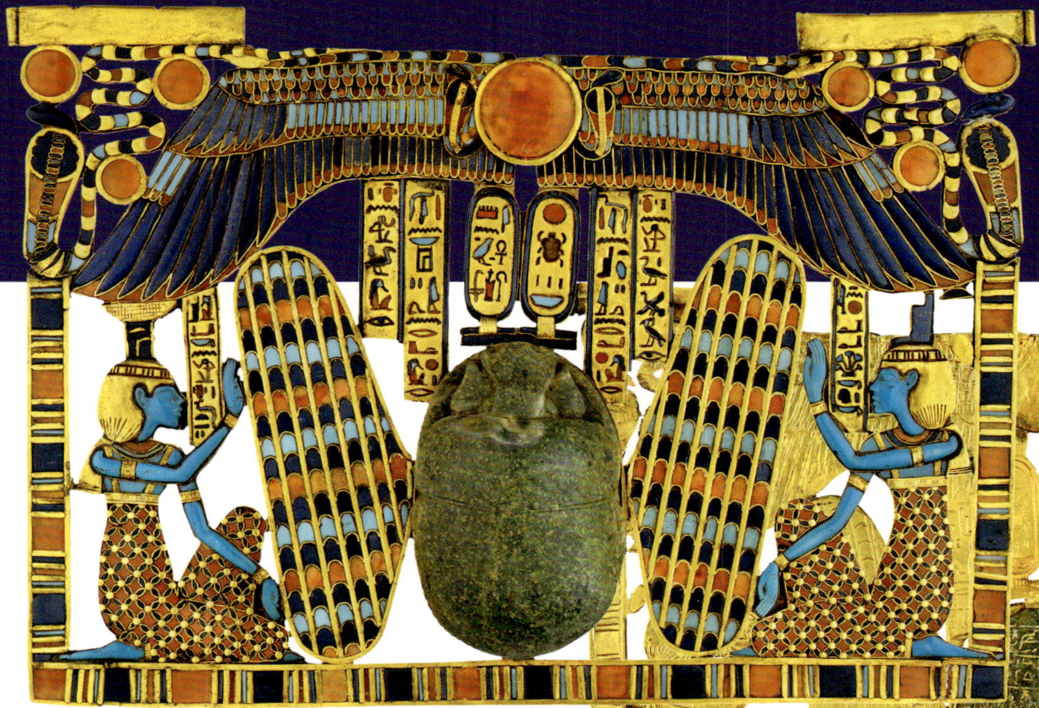

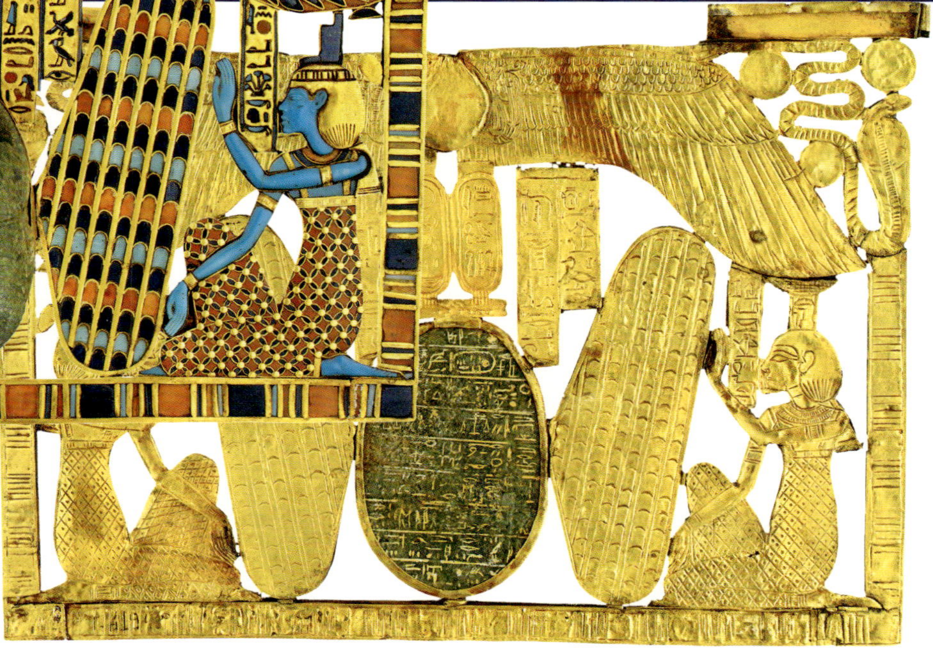

PECTORAL WITH HEART SCARAB
Gold, rock crystal, carnelian, feldspar, glass
Height 16.5 cm; width 24.4 cm
Carter 261m (pectoral) and
Carter 269a(4) (heart scarab)

CANOPIC CHEST AND CANOPY

A gessoed-and-gilded shrine and its matching canopy stood mounted to a sledge, set against the eastern wall of the Treasury, its door facing westward toward the land of the dead. The four posts of the canopy carry the names, titles, and epithets of the king. Spells engraved on the roof of the canopy record spells spoken by the goddesses Nut, Isis, and Nephthys.

The shrine is in the form of the *per wer*, a cult structure of great antiquity, associated with Upper Egypt. It is decorated with images of the goddesses and gods tasked with protecting the viscera of the king, removed during mummification. Each divine pair is traditionally associated with a cardinal direction and a particular organ. On the west are Isis and Imsety, who guard the liver; on the south, Nephthys and Hapy, guardians of the lungs; on the north, Neith and Duamutef, guardians of the stomach, along with the earth god Geb; and on the east, Selket and Qebehsenuef, who guard the intestines, accompanied by the creator god Atum and Ptah-Sokar-Osiris, a composite funerary deity. Spells spoken by these figures surround them. Additional spells, uttered by Nut, Imsety, and Hapy, are found on the top of the shrine, along with other religious formulae.

Exquisite three-dimensional gilded figures of the four canopic goddesses were positioned on the sledge, one on each side of the shrine, identifiable by the hieroglyphic symbol on her headdress: Isis on the west, Nephthys on the east; Neith on the north; and Selket on the south. This last figure and Nephthys were for some reason switched, being positioned on the wrong sides of the shrine.

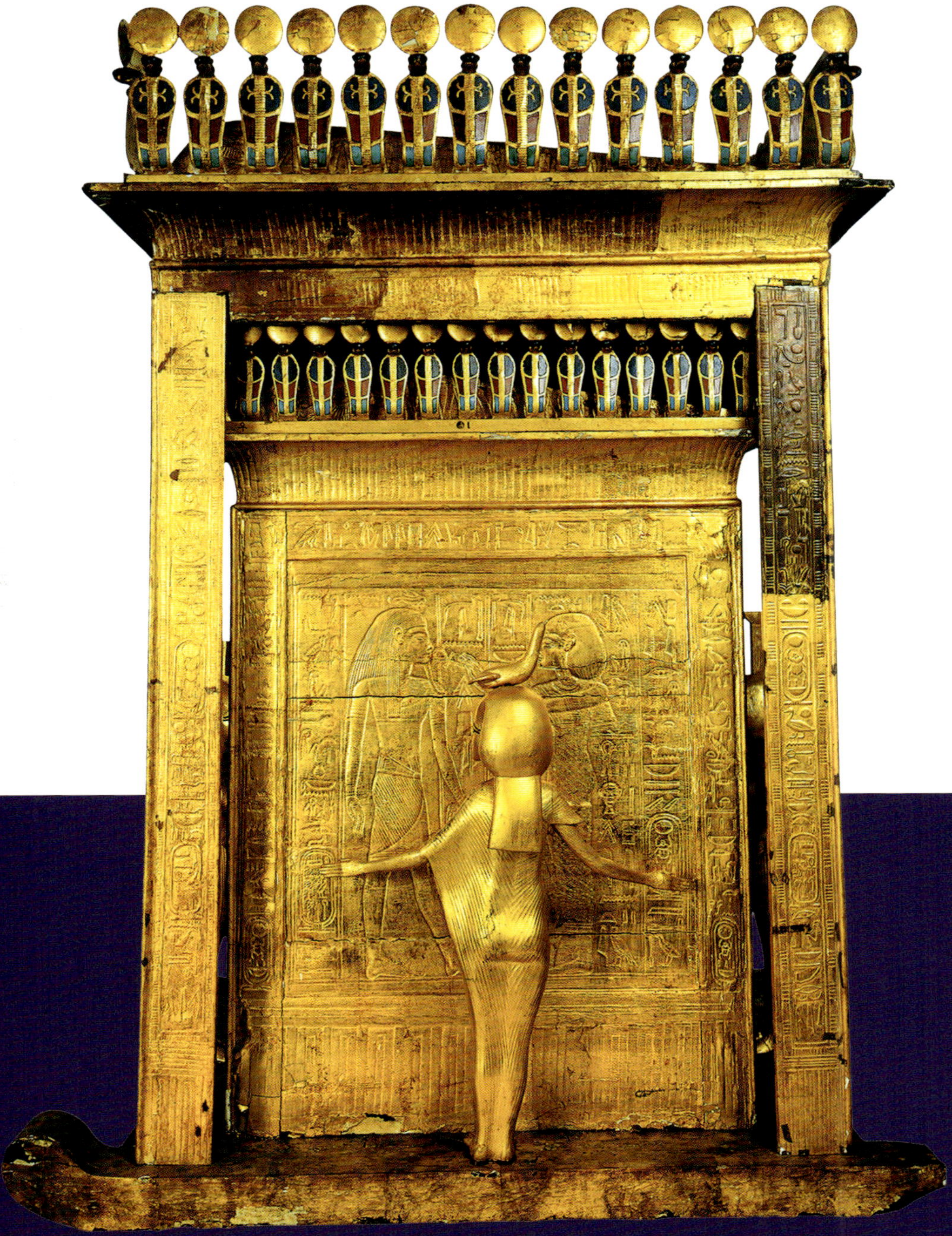

CANOPIC CHEST AND CANOPY
Wood, gessoed and gilded,
with inlays of pottery and glass;
interior of shrine coated in black resin

CANOPY
Height 2 m
Carter 266

SHRINE
Height 136 cm, width 90 cm
Carter 266a

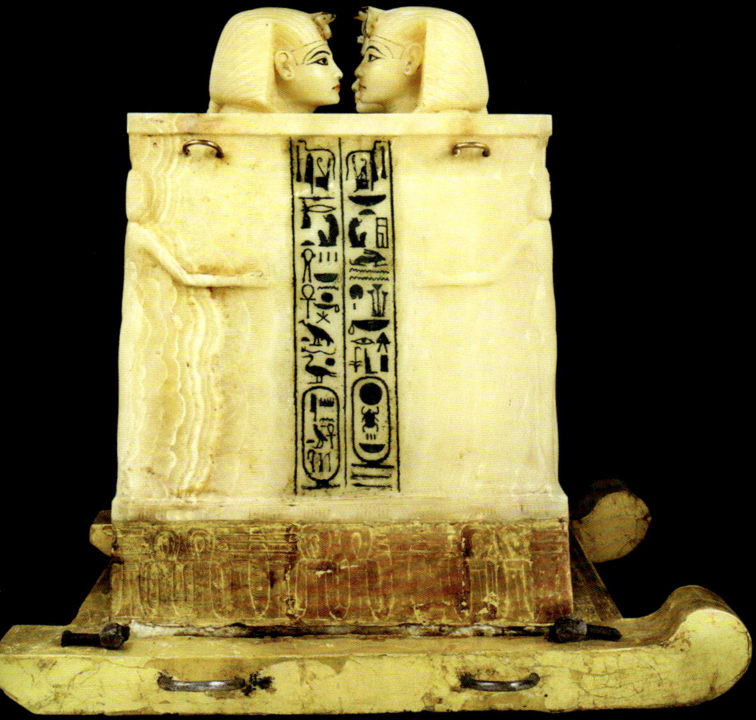
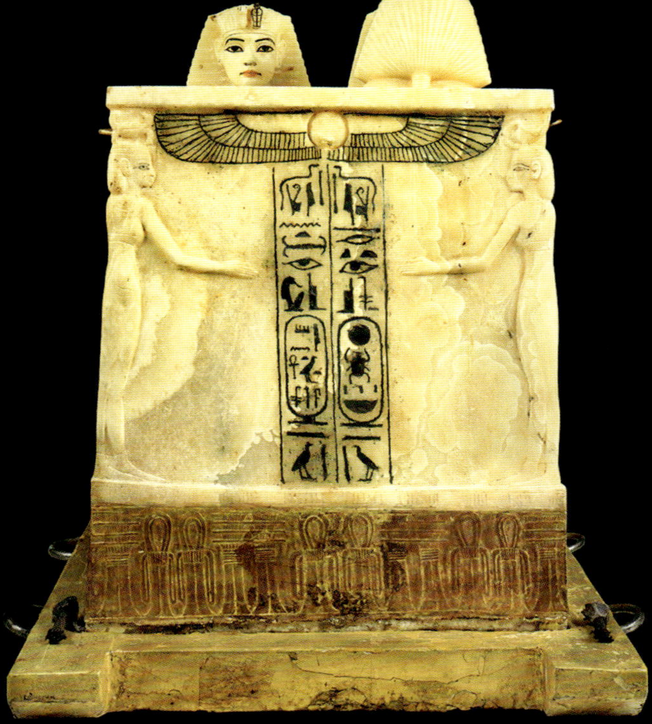
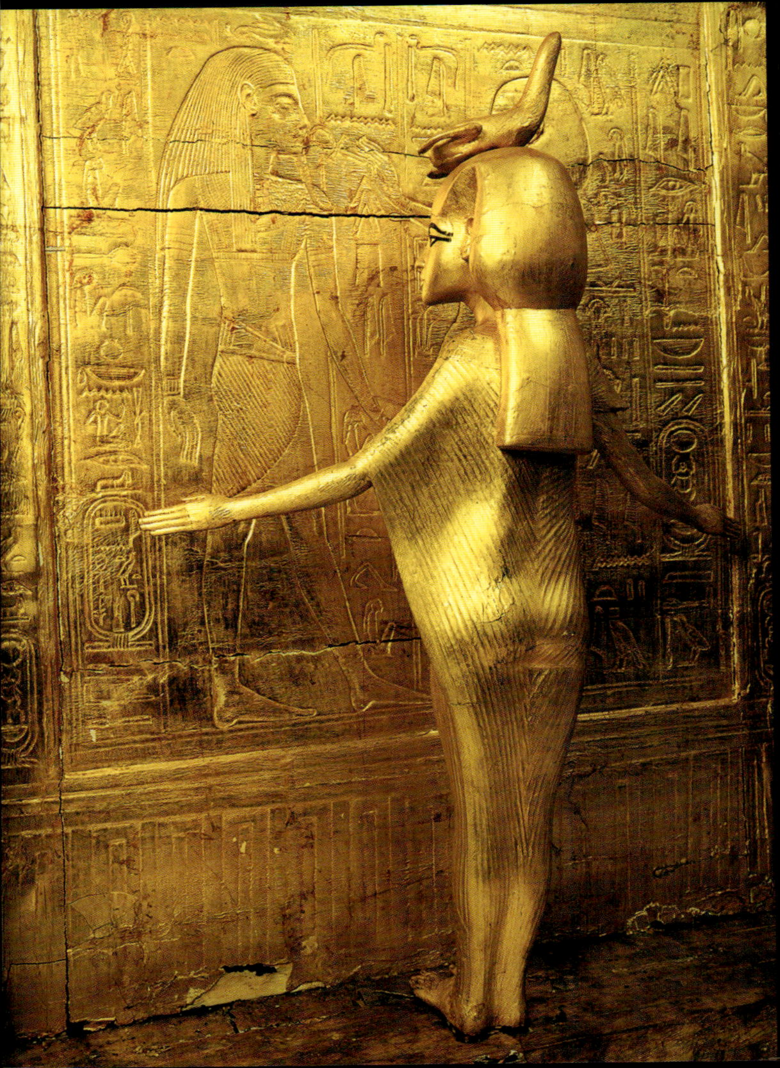
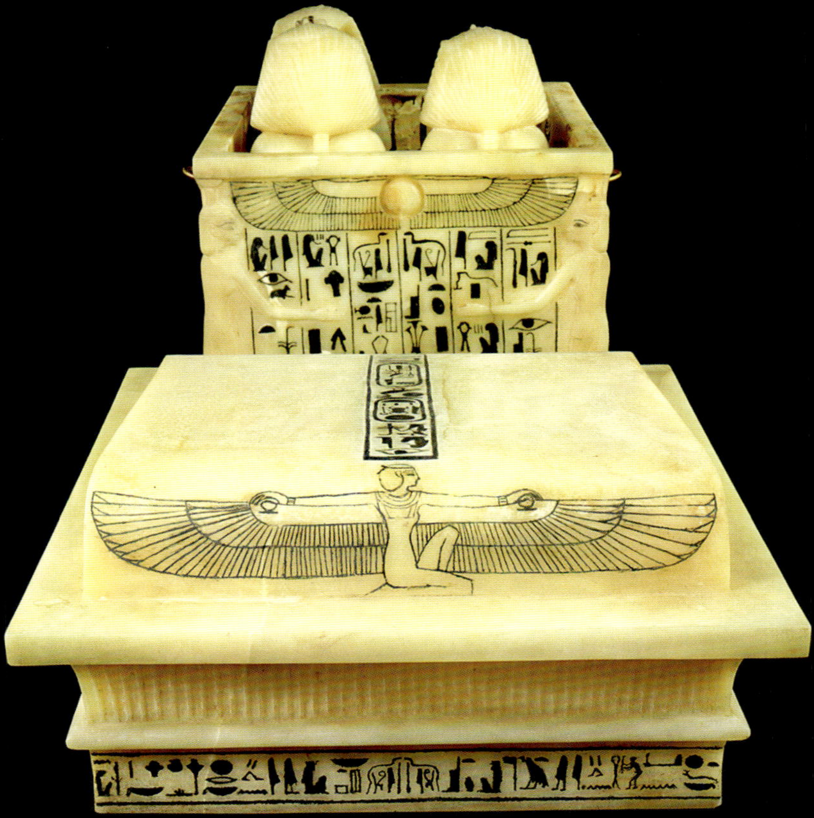

THE HUMAN-HEADED STOPPERS

The canopic shrine had no floor. Within was a smaller sledge with runners covered in silver foil, and on this stood a box carved from a block of fine calcite (Egyptian alabaster). This box was draped by a folded linen sheet. Again the four protective canopic goddesses appear, carved on the corners of the box.

Usually such a canopic box would have four compartments, and in each would be a canopic jar. The box is indeed divided into four compartments, but instead of jars there are only stoppers that cover each division. The stoppers are virtually identical, each in the form of a human head, specifically the king wearing the ***nemes*** headdress. Within the compartments were the king's four canopic coffinettes.

The faces differ from other images of Tutankhamun, so this object, like several others in the tomb, might have been made for his predecessor, Ankh(et)kheperure. How such items came to be among Tutankhamun's funerary goods remains unknown. They might have been in storage, unused, or perhaps they were, for some reason, removed from their original tomb and usurped for the boy-king.

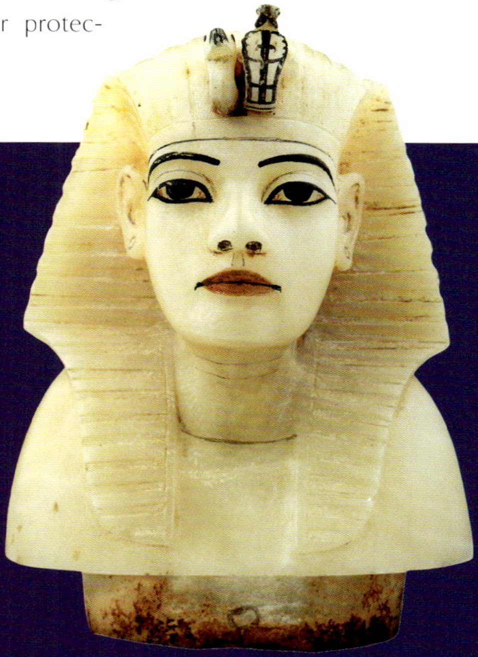

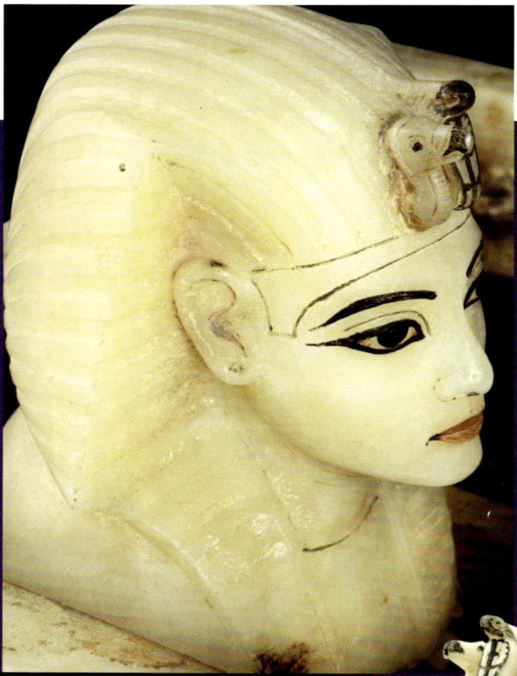

HUMAN-HEADED STOPPERS
Painted calcite (Egyptian alabaster)
Height 24 cm
Carter 266c-f

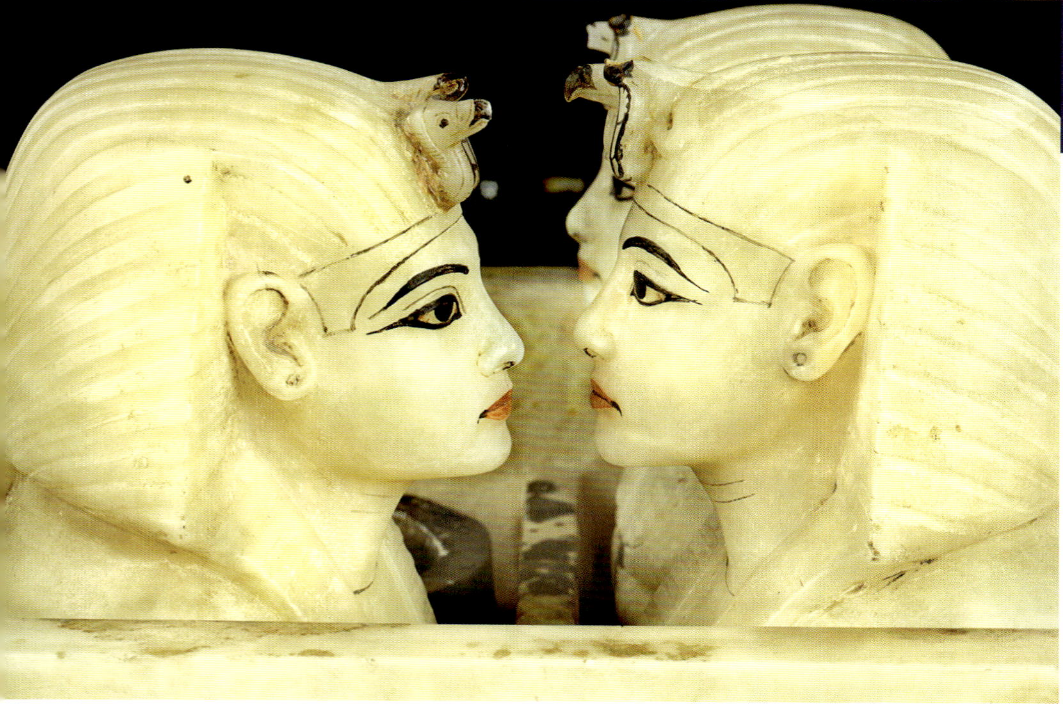

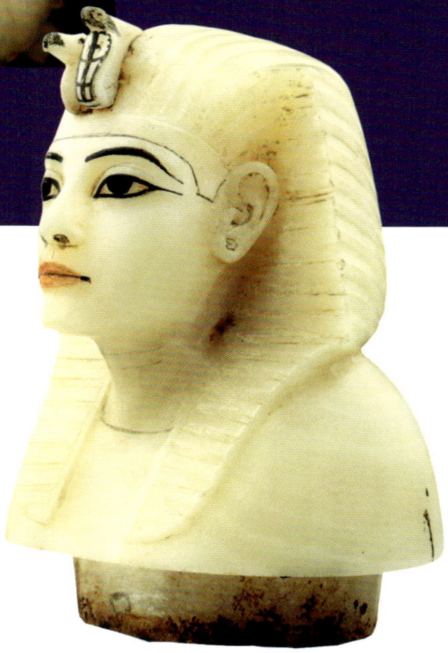

CANOPIC COFFINETTES

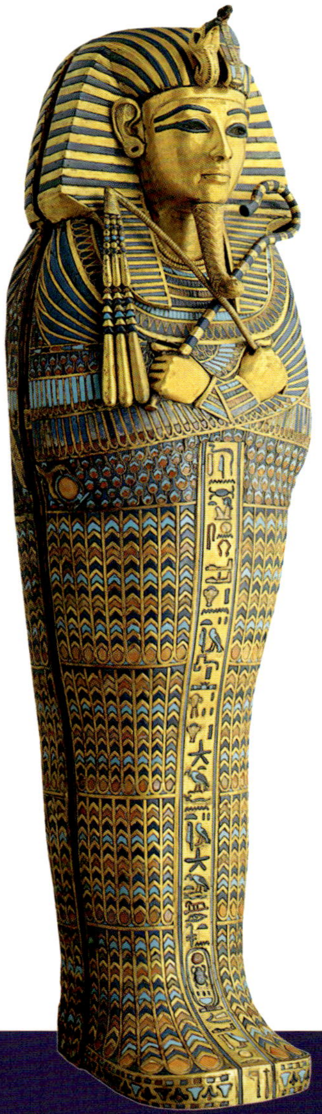

Regardless of whom the canopic chest was created for, it was Tutankhamun's embalmed and wrapped viscera found within it, in four coffinettes.

These exquisite works of art replicate the royal coffin in miniature. They share the feathery *rishi* pattern. Wings of the protective goddesses Wadjet and Nekhbet, in the form of birds grasping *shen* rings ("eternity"), seem to embrace the king's body. Spells spoken by the canopic goddesses to protect the king's organs and the four Sons of Horus, who guarded them, are recorded down the center of each little coffin lid. The sky goddess Nut, standing on the hieroglyph for "sky" (*pet*), stretches across the interior of each lid. She spreads her wings to protect the king on his journey to the afterlife.

Like the faces of the stoppers, the faces of the coffinettes are not quite those of Tutankhamun. It has been discovered that Tutankhamun's cartouches on these coffins are not part of the original inscriptions. Traces can be detected of "Ankhkheperure."

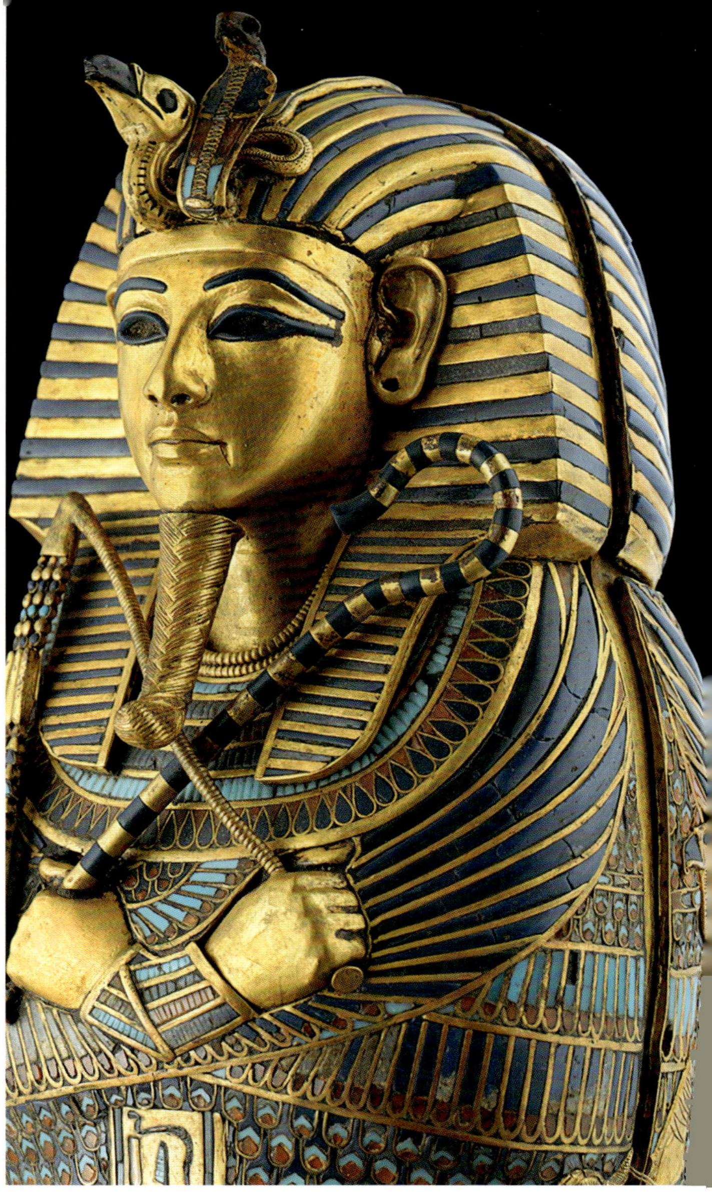

CANOPIC COFFINETTES
Gold, lapis lazuli, colored glass
Lengths c. 39 cm, widths c. 11 cm
Carter 266g

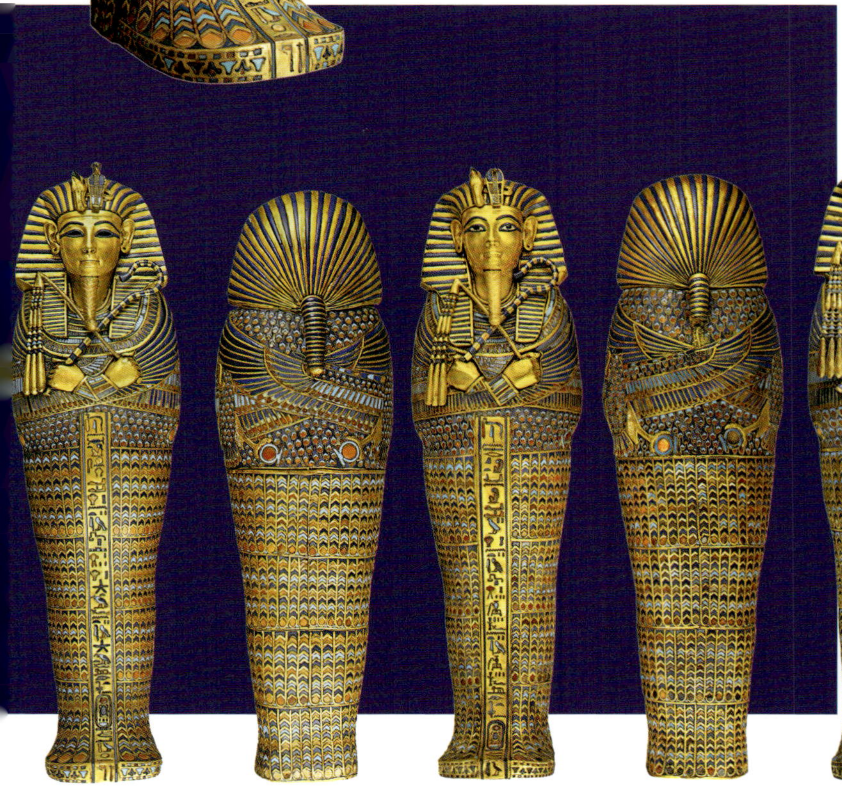

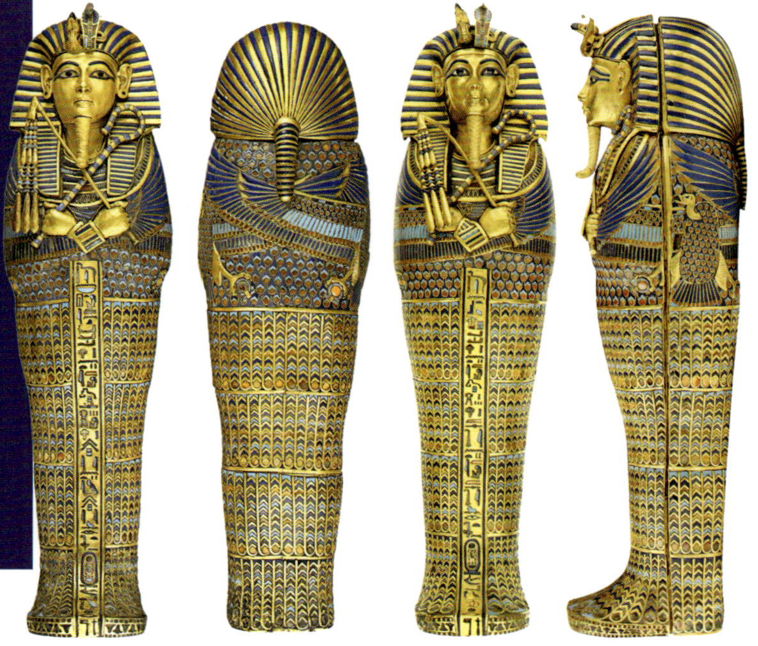

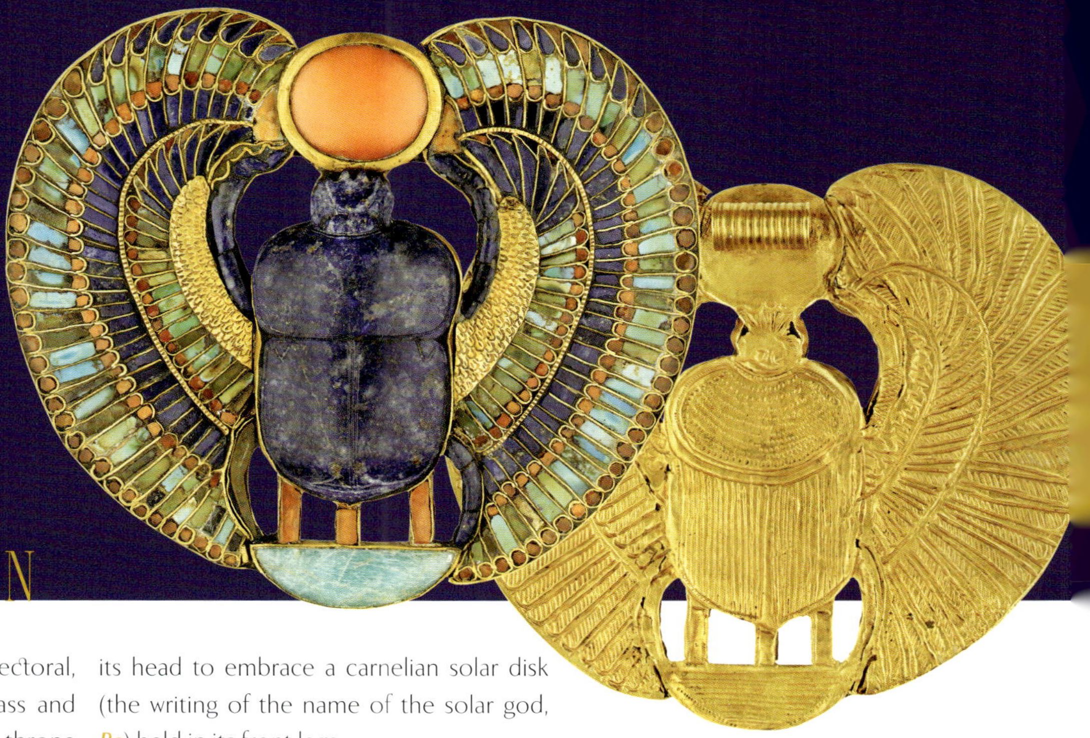

NAME PENDANT
OF
TUTANKHAMUN
Gold, semiprecious stones
Height 9 cm, width 10.5 cm
Carter 267a

NAME PENDANT OF TUTANKHAMUN

The symbols on this elegant pectoral, made of gold with colored glass and stone inlay, form Tutankhamun's throne name, Nebkheperure. To read this rebus, one begins at the bottom, with the turquoise basket or ***neb***, the writing of the word for "all." Above the basket is a scarab made of lapis lazuli; the scarab was called ***kheper***, a word meaning "form" or "manifestation." Three upright lines beneath the scarab create the plural form, ***kheperu***. The scarab's curved wings, which are inlaid with carnelian, lapis lazuli, and turquoise, sweep gracefully over its head to embrace a carnelian solar disk (the writing of the name of the solar god, ***Re***) held in its front legs.

Besides spelling out the king's name, the pectoral embodies one of the many Egyptian images of rebirth. Scarab beetles push balls of dung across the ground, which the Egyptians re-imagined as a divine beetle pushing the solar disk over the eastern horizon at dawn. They had surely seen beetles hatch from dung. This natural scene, of life issuing from filth, inspired or deepened the scarab's connection with resurrection.

Carter found this pendant in one of the boxes between the Anubis shrine and the canopic shrine. The seal of the box (**Carter No. 267**) had been broken and its contents disturbed, though Carter was able to tell that the box had originally held jewelry wrapped in linen. An inscription, translated by the great British Egyptologist Sir Alan Gardiner, reads, "Jewels (?) of gold of the procession made in the bed-chamber of Nebkheperure."

CORONATION PECTORAL

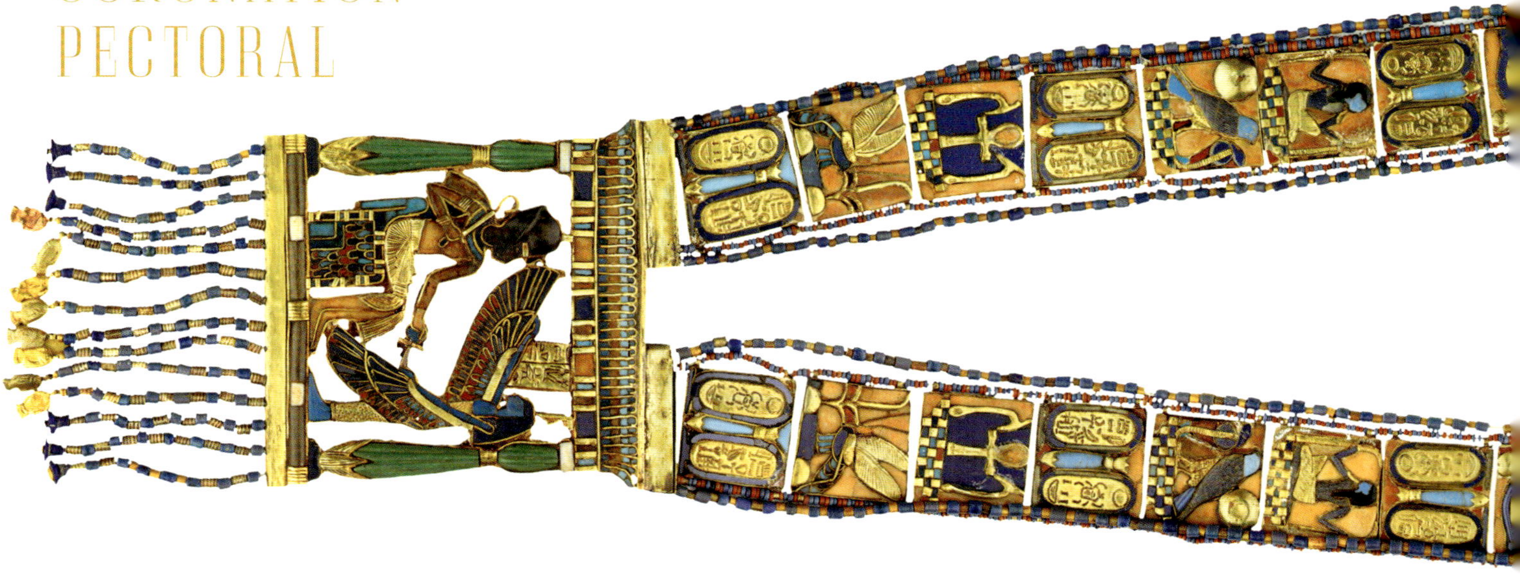

Another piece of jewelry from Box 267 is this elaborate pectoral. It originally had bands and a counterweight, but these were found in the large cartouche-shaped box (**Carter No. 269**). Somehow, during the ancient robbery or its aftermath, the pieces became separated.

The central figure of the scene depicted by this intricately wrought pectoral is the king, wearing a golden knee-length corselet, broad collar, and the blue crown, sometimes called the "war helmet." His hands hold the crook and flail. Although his body is depicted in reddish-brown, the color traditional for men, his face is black. Use of this color associates the king's image with the resurrection and fertility. The king faces Ptah, chief god of Memphis and patron of artisans. Ptah says to the king, "I give to you life, dominion, and all health." Behind Ptah, depicted on a smaller scale, the god of eternity (Heh) holds notched palm ribs symbolizing "millions of years." Above Heh is a basket in which sits a cobra with a solar disk on its head. This is a cryptographic writing of "Nebkheperure," Tutankhamun's throne name.

On the other side of the scene, behind the king, is Ptah's consort, the lioness-headed Sekhmet, goddess of war, disease, and health. Her body is clad in a sheath dress. A broad collar drapes over her chest and a long, dark blue wig with a carnelian solar disk crowns her head. Called here "mistress of the sky," she reaches out to touch the young king's shoulder and says, "I am giving to you years of kingship for eternity." Behind Sekhmet is the king's ***ka***, or life-force, which wears on its head a ***serekh***, a sign used to hold the king's Horus name.

The counterweight shows the king receiving an ***ankh*** from Maat, goddess of truth.

This pectoral seems to relate to the coronation ceremony and the ***sed*** festival, which a king celebrated after 30 years on the throne. Intended to rejuvenate the king, the ***sed*** festival was repeated more frequently after the first.

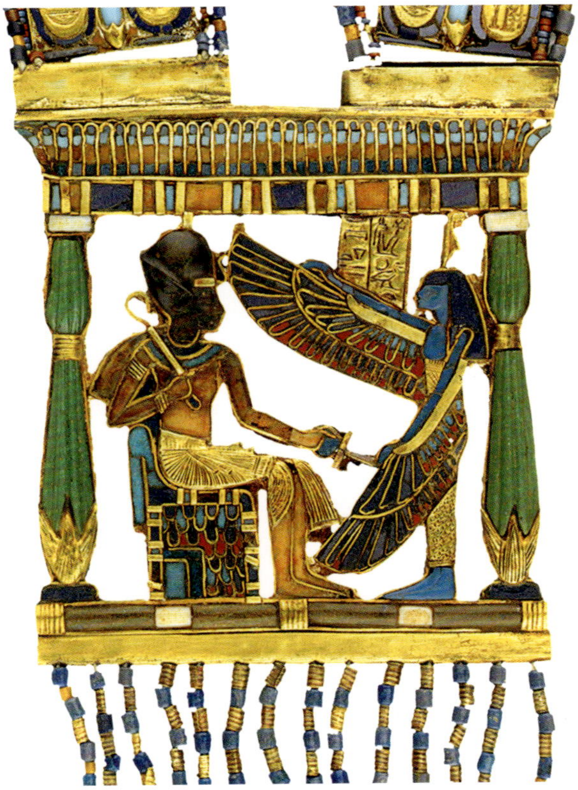

CORONATION PECTORAL, BANDS, AND COUNTERWEIGHT
Gold, silver, glass, semiprecious stones
Pectoral: height 11.5 cm, width 14.1 cm
Carter 267q (pectoral), Carter 269i (bands), Carter 269j (counterweight)

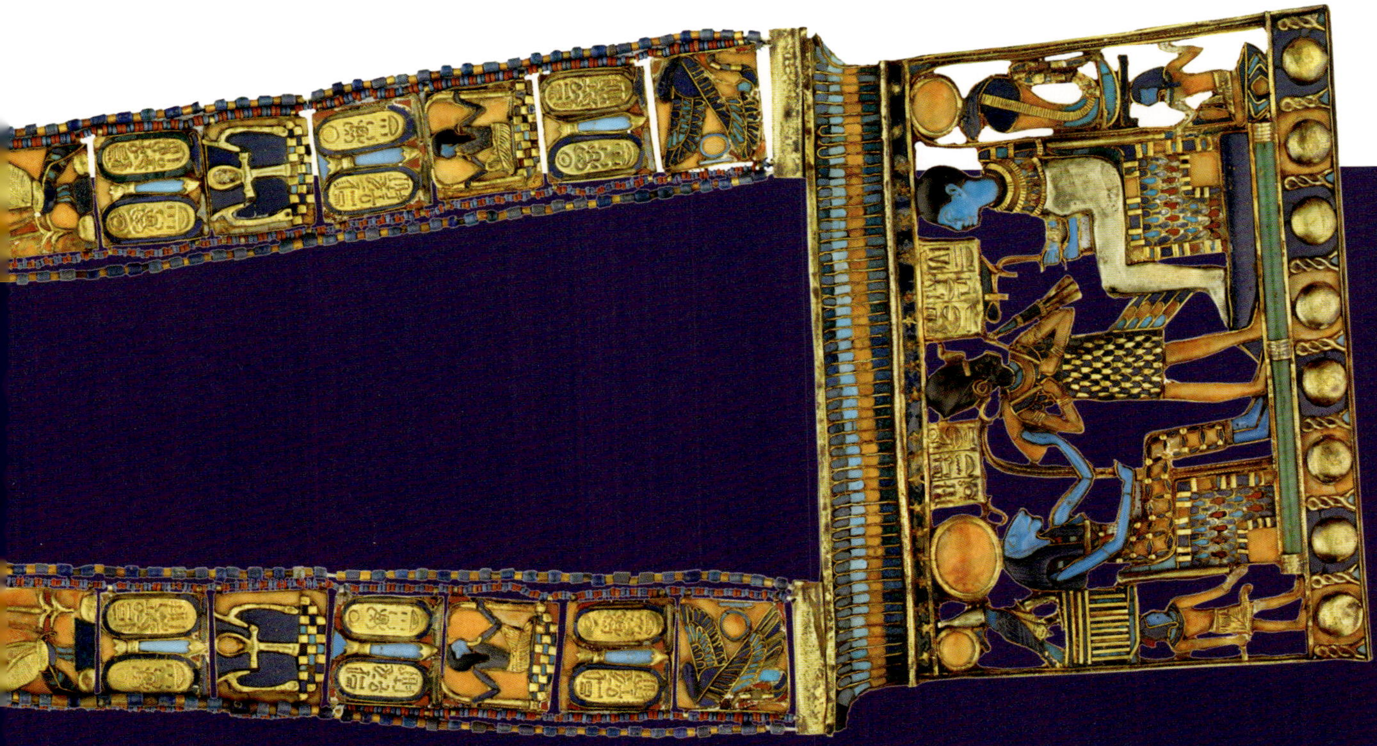

NECKLACES

These four jewels, which vary in quality, came from the same box (Carter No. 267) as the name and coronation pectorals (Carter Nos. 267a and 267q). The king may have worn some of these in life, but others may have been made specifically for the tomb. All have lunar or solar symbolism.

On the first necklace, a papyrus boat is shown between a band of water and the star-studded sign for "sky," which is held aloft by two *was* scepters, which symbolize "dominion." Aboard the boat, two baboons raise their arms in adoration toward a lapis lazuli scarab beetle. The beetle holds the hieroglyphic sign for "eternity" while it pushes a carnelian solar disk along with its front legs. Baboons were associated with Thoth, a lunar deity, but they also were closely associated with the

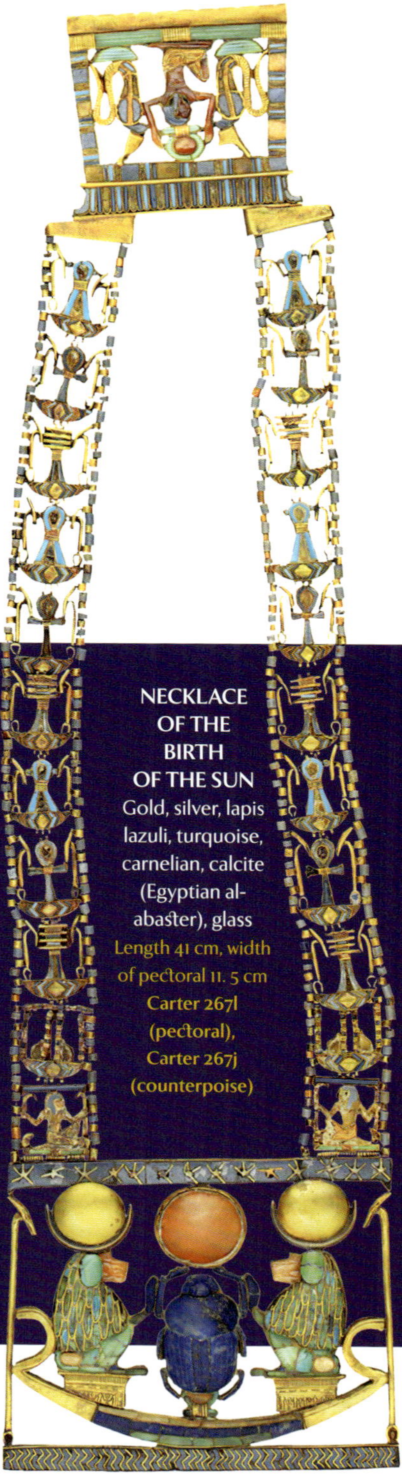

NECKLACE OF THE BIRTH OF THE SUN
Gold, silver, lapis lazuli, turquoise, carnelian, calcite (Egyptian alabaster), glass
Length 41 cm, width of pectoral 11.5 cm
Carter 267l (pectoral), Carter 267j (counterpoise)

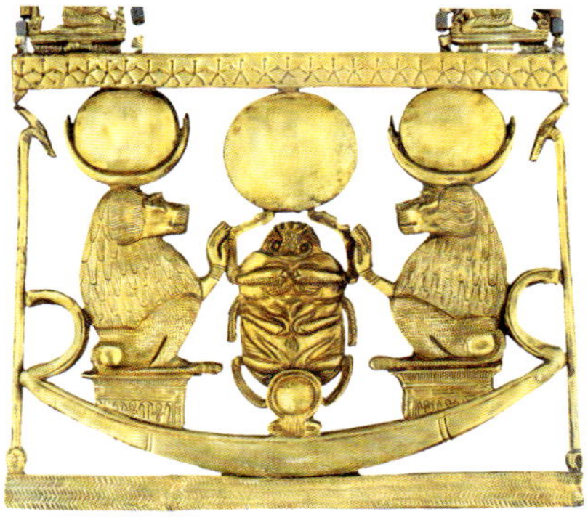

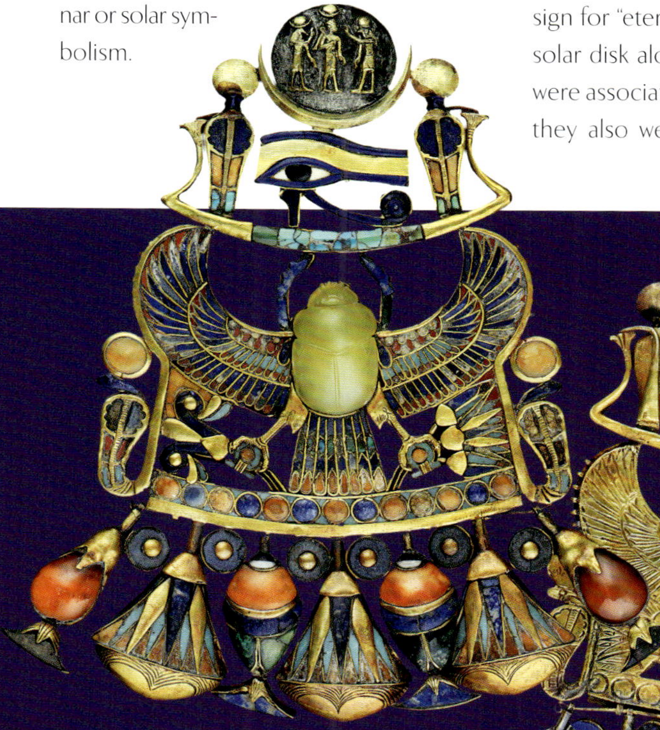

PENDANT WITH CHALCEDONY SCARAB
Gold, chalcedony, carnelian, lapis lazuli, calcite (Egyptian alabaster), obsidian, colored glass
Height 14.9 cm, width 14.5 cm
Carter 267d

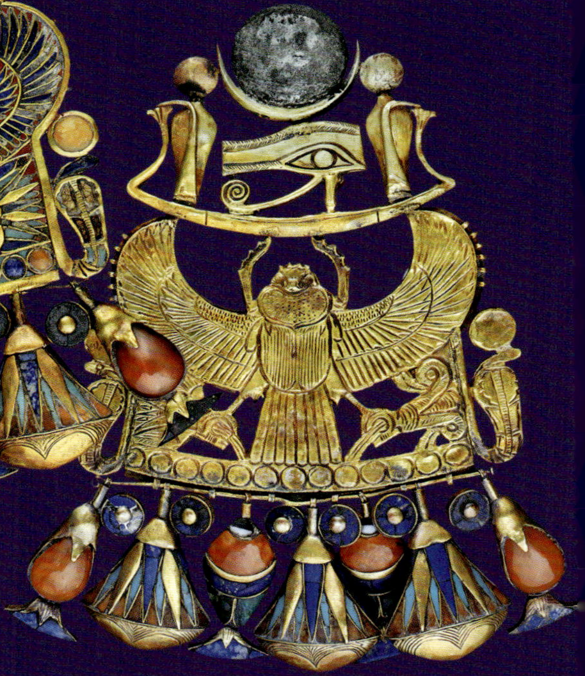

sun. The baboons' habit of making noises at dawn perhaps inspired the Egyptian belief that these animals were worshiping the sun. On the counterpoise, artists depicted the god of eternity, Heh, and cobras wearing the white and red crowns.

Another scarab, this time of green chalcedony, is the centerpiece of the next pendant. Given the legs and talons of a vulture, it grasps the *shen* ring of eternity and the heraldic plants of Upper and Lower Egypt. Instead of a solar disk, it pushes a lunar barque, which has a lunar *wedjat* (the left eye of the sky god), a lunar crescent in gold and a lunar disk in silver. Three figures of gold have been added to the disk. Tutankhamun, wearing a lunar symbol, stands facing the solar god Re-Horakhty. Thoth, shown as an ibis, stands behind the king.

The next pendant consists of a spelling of Tutankhamun's throne name, Nebkheperure, with lunar motifs. The lunar disk and crescent has replaced the solar disk in the front legs of the beetle. The traditional guardians of the sun, uraei, flank the winged scarab.

The sun appears in the next pendant, which has a lapis lazuli scarab. The bands of the pendant, with their repeated scarabs, spell out the king's name, Nebkheperure.

The last piece here is a counterpoise. The god of eternity, Heh, kneels in the center, lifting the lunar eye above his head. Behind Heh as if supporting one of his arms is the knot of Isis," the *tjet*. Solar uraei guard either side of the composition. Beside each cobra is a symbol often associated with Heh, a notched palm rib that rises from the back of a tadpole and *shen* ring. These symbols, taken together, symbolize an eternal reign.

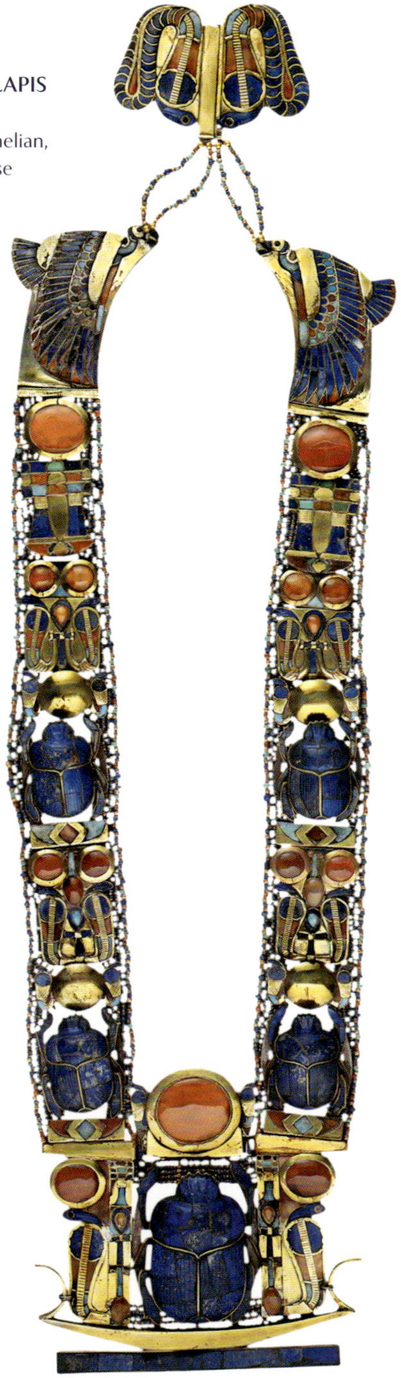

NECKLACE WITH LAPIS SCARABS
Gold, lapis lazuli, carnelian, feldspar, turquoise
Length 50 cm
Carter 267g

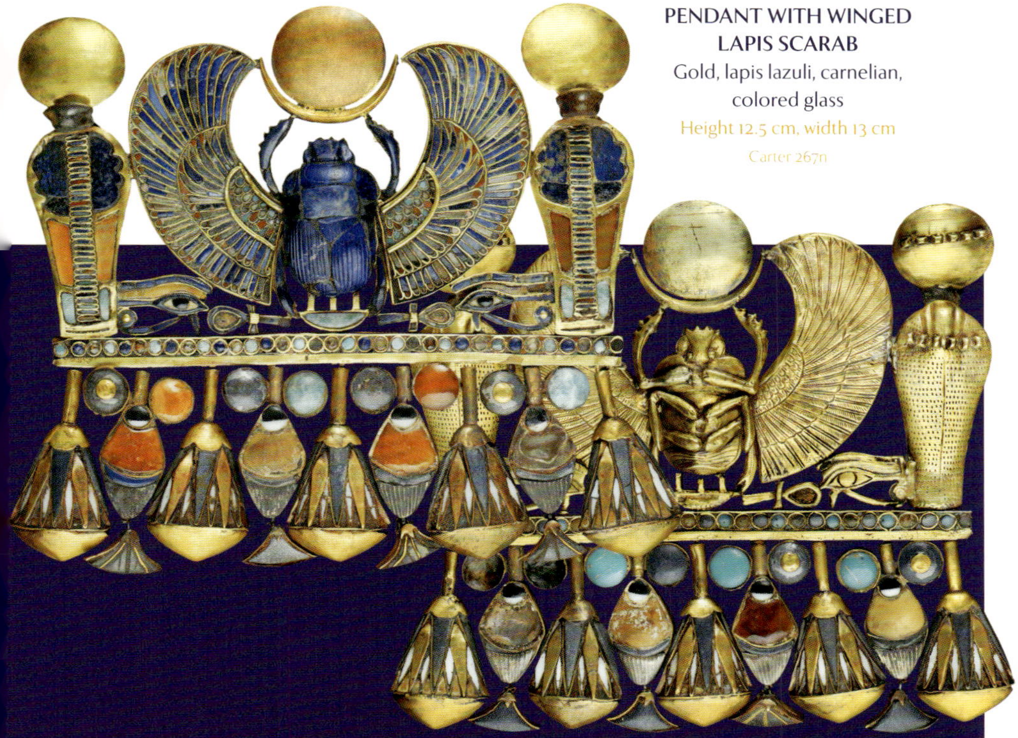

PENDANT WITH WINGED LAPIS SCARAB
Gold, lapis lazuli, carnelian, colored glass
Height 12.5 cm, width 13 cm
Carter 267n

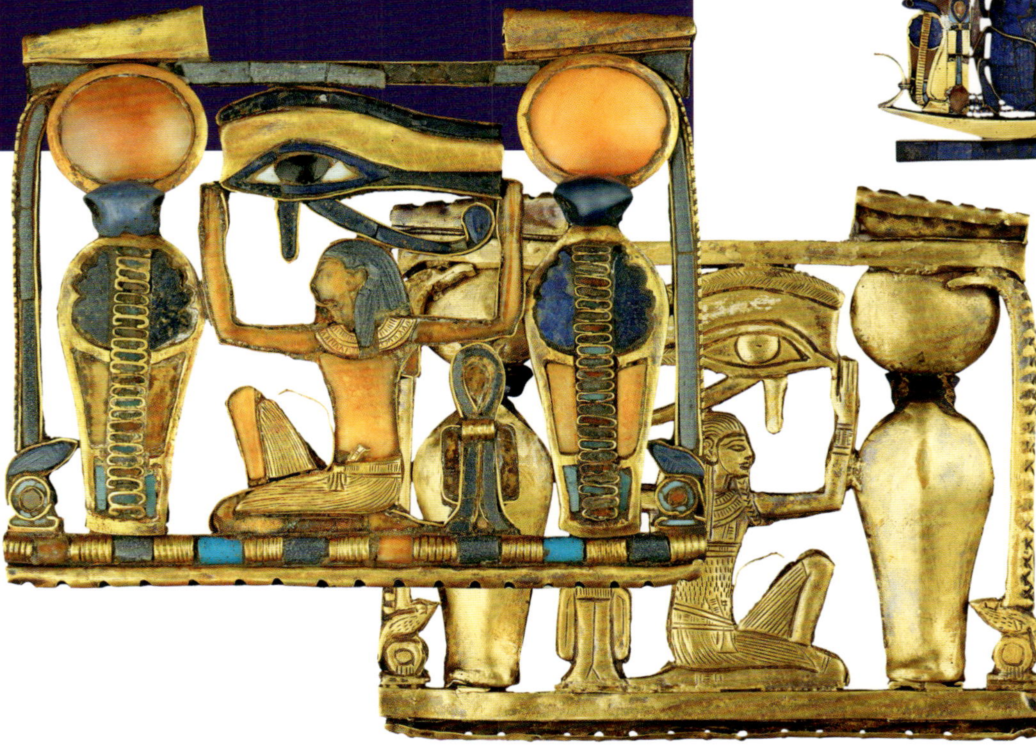

HEH COUNTERPOISE
Gold, carnelian, calcite (Egyptian alabaster), colored glass
Height 6.9 cm, width 8.2 cm
Carter 267e

BOX WITH DELICATE CONTENTS

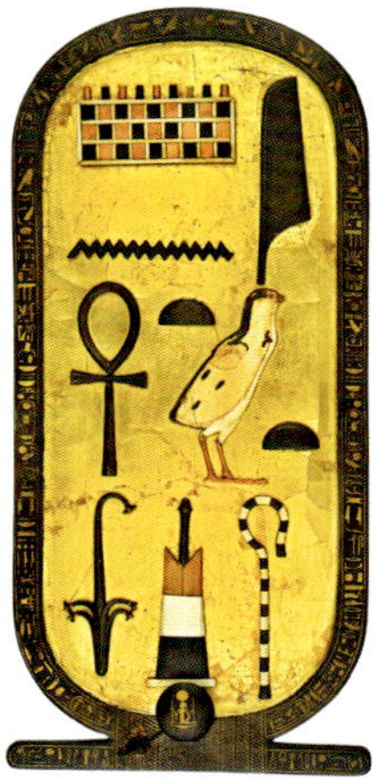

This wooden box takes the form of a cartouche. The top was covered with gesso, gilded, and inlaid with hieroglyphs of ivory and ebony to spell out the king's birth name and a title: "Tutankhamun, Lord of Thebes." Each hieroglyph is carefully rendered with inlay and sometimes with details in paint. The game board (***men/mun***) has its squares and also the game pieces. The quail chick which indicates the ***u*** in ***tut*** has been carefully given spots, and the crook (***heqa***, meaning "Ruler") is shown with alternating black and white bands. The encircling rope of the cartouche is carved with more of the king's names and epithets. Other names appear elsewhere on the box. The knobs feature the god of eternity, Heh.

This box, which contained two of the king's crooks and flails, jewelry, and some clothing, probably stored items used during his coronation ceremony or some other rituals related to his kingship.

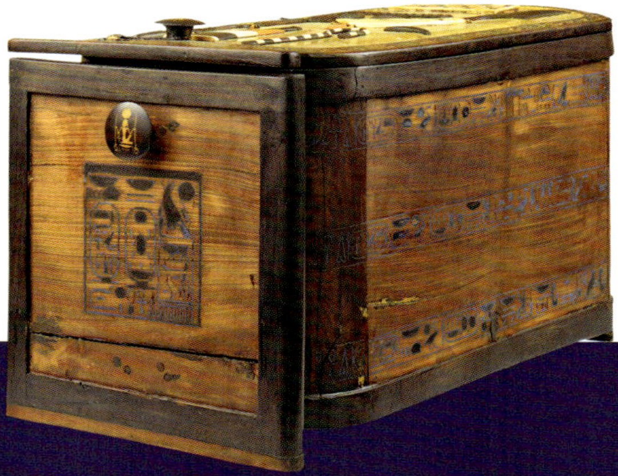

BOX IN THE SHAPE OF A CARTOUCHE
Wood, ebony, ivory
Length 64 cm, width 30.7 cm, height 33.2 cm
Carter 269

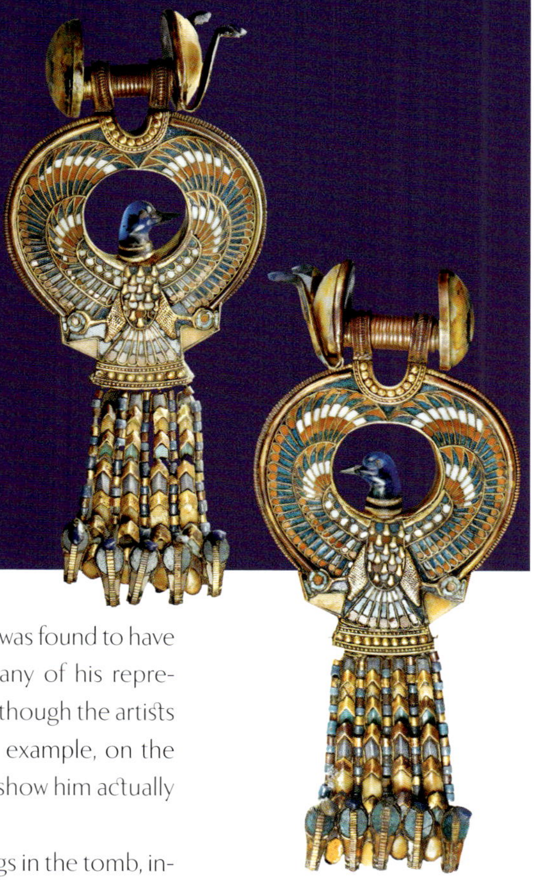

DUCK-HEAD EARRINGS
Gold, quartz, calcite (Egyptian alabaster), colored glass, colored faience
Length 10.9 cm, width 5.2 cm
Carter 269a(1)

Tutankhamun's mummy was found to have pierced ears, as do many of his representations. However, although the artists gave him pierced ears (for example, on the golden mask), they do not show him actually wearing earrings.

But Carter found earrings in the tomb, including this fanciful pair. The bird shown here is given the traditional pose of a falcon, with its wings outstretched, its feet grasping ***shen*** rings, but the head is that of a duck. The earrings have evidence of having been worn, perhaps by the king when he was a child.

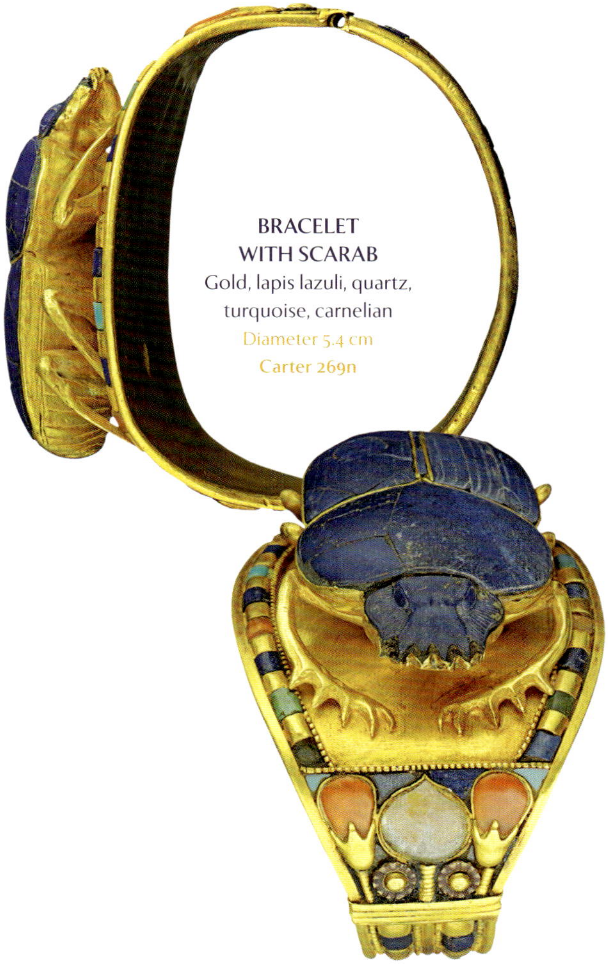

BRACELET WITH SCARAB
Gold, lapis lazuli, quartz, turquoise, carnelian
Diameter 5.4 cm
Carter 269n

A scarab of gold and lapis lazuli tops this bracelet, which was small enough for Tutankhamun to have worn as a child. On either end of the scarab there are inlays of mandrake fruits, which have sexual associations, and poppies.

CROOKS AND FLAILS

The crook and flail, symbolic of south and north, respectively, are two of the most ancient and recognizable symbols of kingly power. The crook, or ***heqa***, is an abbreviated form of a shepherd's crook. The flail, or ***nekhekh***, was originally a fly-whisk. The only examples known from the New Kingdom were found in Tutankhamun's tomb. Four of the six are shown here. (The other pair was found grasped in the golden hands that accompanied the golden mask on the mummy.) Two of those shown here are of a size suitable for a child.

Without doubt Tutankhamun used them when he first became king at the age of nine. The smaller crook gives the original form of his birth-name: Tutankhaten.

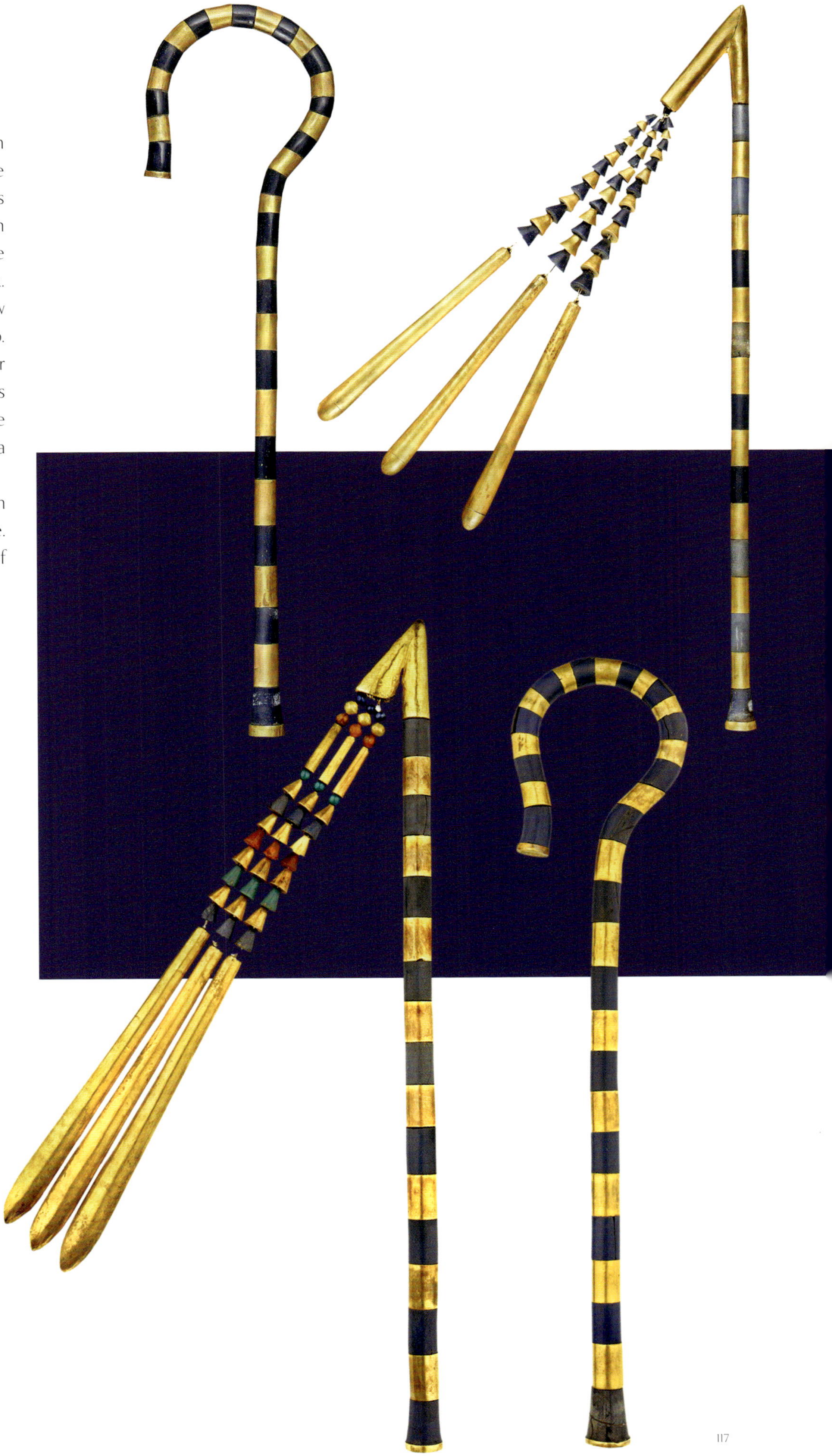

CROOKS AND FLAILS
Gold, base metal, wood, carnelian, blue glass

SMALL CROOK
Length 33.5 cm
Carter 44u

SMALL FLAIL
Length 33.5 cm
Carter 269f

LARGE FLAIL
Length 43 cm
Carter 269e

LARGE CROOK
Length 43.5 cm
Carter 269h

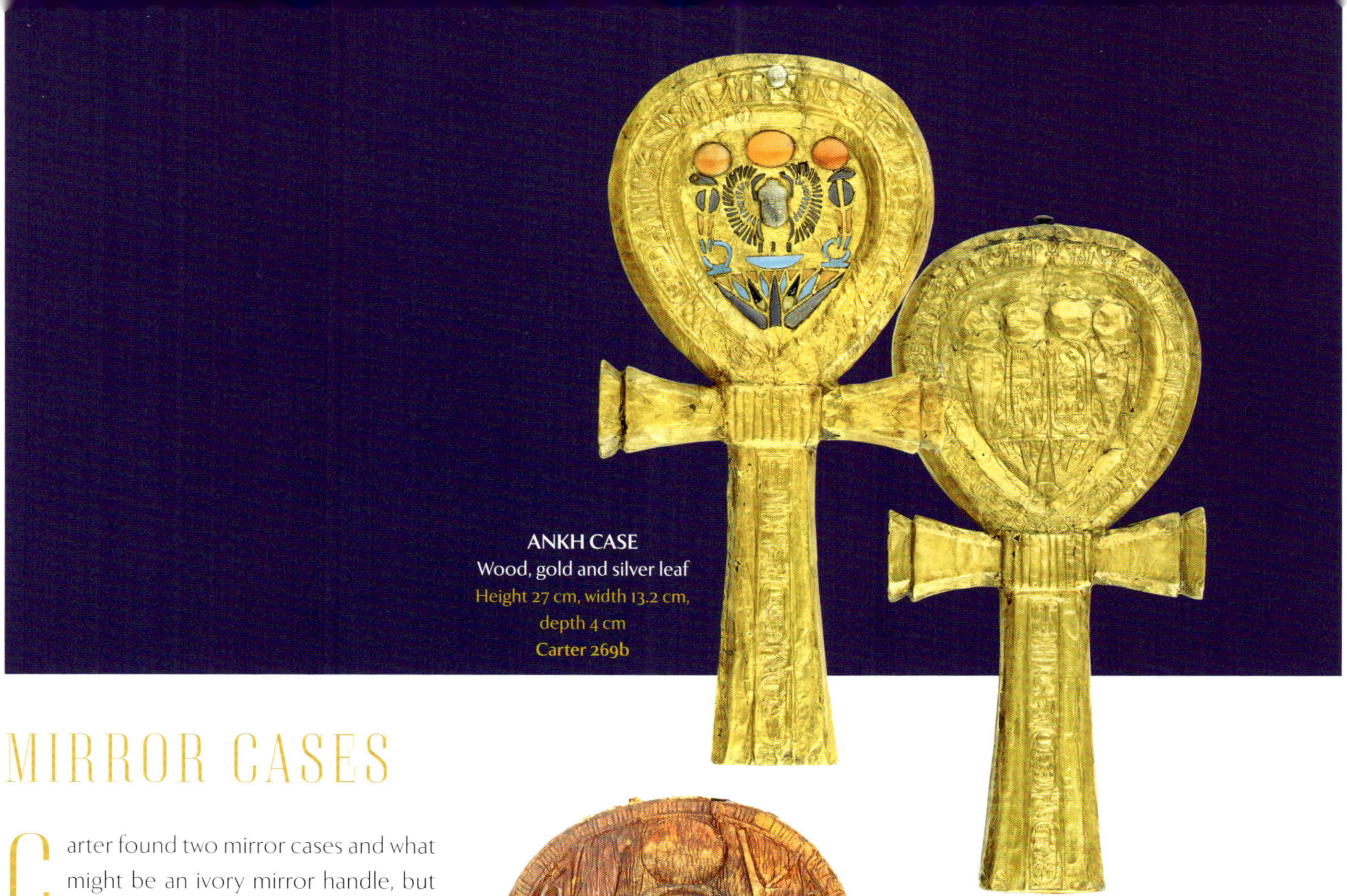

ANKH CASE
Wood, gold and silver leaf
Height 27 cm, width 13.2 cm, depth 4 cm
Carter 269b

MIRROR CASES

Carter found two mirror cases and what might be an ivory mirror handle, but no mirrors, which thieves had probably taken for their precious metals. Mirrors could symbolize either the sun, if made of gold, or the moon, if made of silver, and were associated with goddesses such as Hathor. In daily life they were used for applying makeup.

One case is shaped like the hieroglyph for life, a typically Egyptian play on words, because the word for "life," ***ankh***, was also the word for "mirror." The loop of the ***ankh*** plays the role of a cartouche. In the middle, inlaid in glass and stone, is the king's throne-name. Below the signs of the name is a lotus blossom, so that symbolically the king rises, eternally reborn, from this flower like the god Nefertem (see Carter No. 8).

The second mirror case also contains imagery invoking eternity for the king. Heh, god of eternity, crouches and holds notched palm ribs on the backs of tadpoles and ***shen*** rings. Above the god's head is a shape that resembles the loop of the ***ankh*** sign. In this once again is the king's throne name.

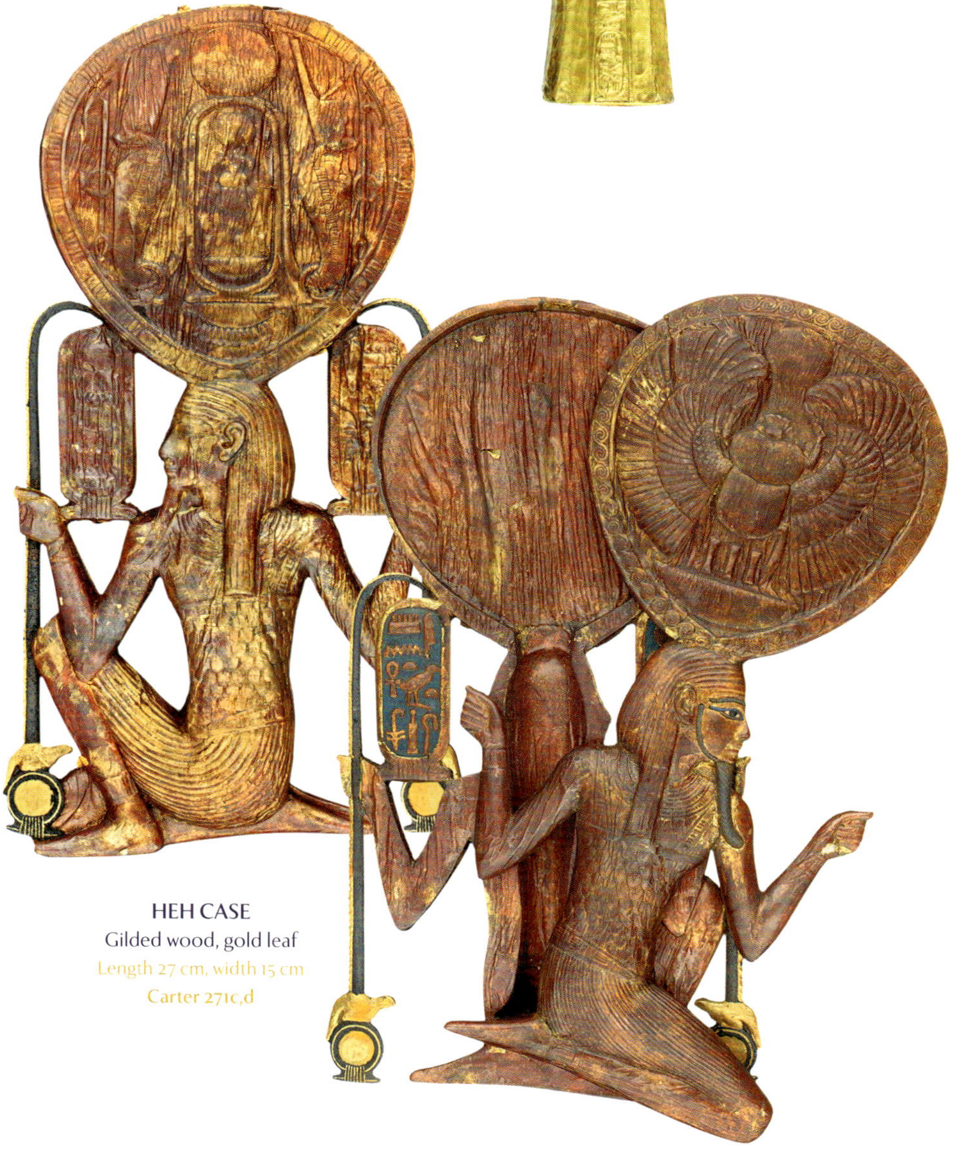

HEH CASE
Gilded wood, gold leaf
Length 27 cm, width 15 cm
Carter 271c,d

The palettes here would have been used to prepare ink of various colors. The first is gilded wood and has an inscription that gives the king's names (including "Tutankhaten") and identifies him as one beloved by Thoth, the god of writing and knowledge. The other palette, of ivory, might have been used for painting scenes. It has wells for not only the usual black and red used by scribes but white, yellow, green, and blue, as well. It was inscribed with the name of Meritaten, Tutankhamun's half-sister. Carter found it between the paws of the Anubis figure. The third palette, found in the Annexe, is only a model, intended for use in the netherworld. The ink was brushed onto the surface of papyrus or wood (or even a bit of broken pottery or stone) with a reed pen. This elaborate case, in the shape of a column, would have held the king's pens. Another tool in a scribe's kit would have been a burnisher, a piece of wood with a padded top for smoothing papyrus. Shaped like a scepter, Tutankhamun's burnisher is made of ivory.

SCRIBAL KIT

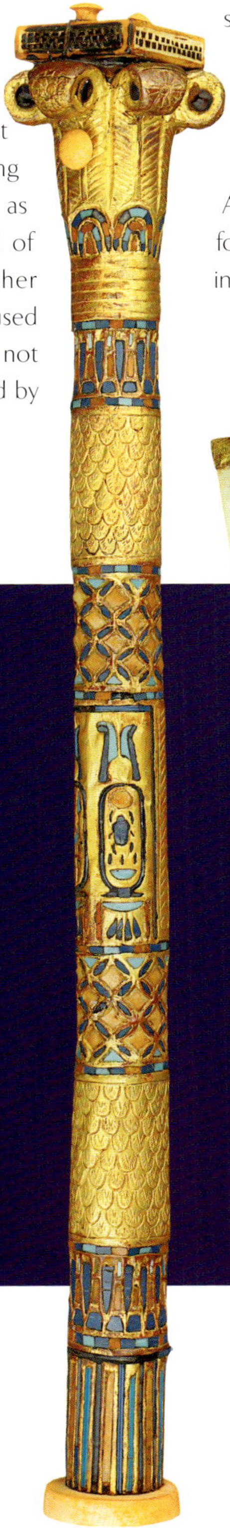

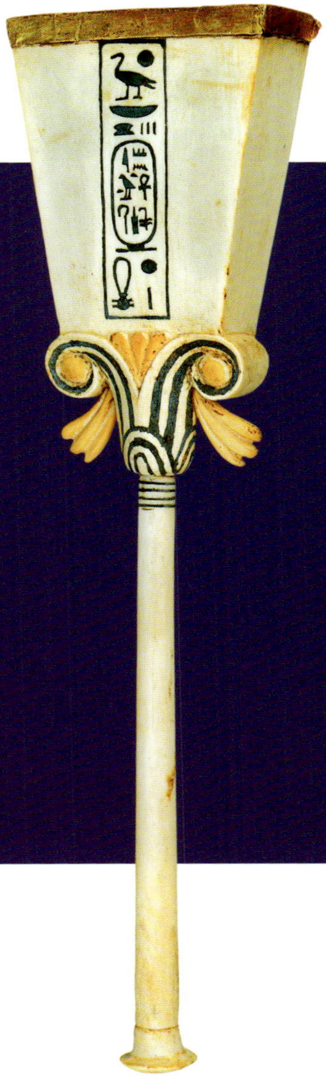

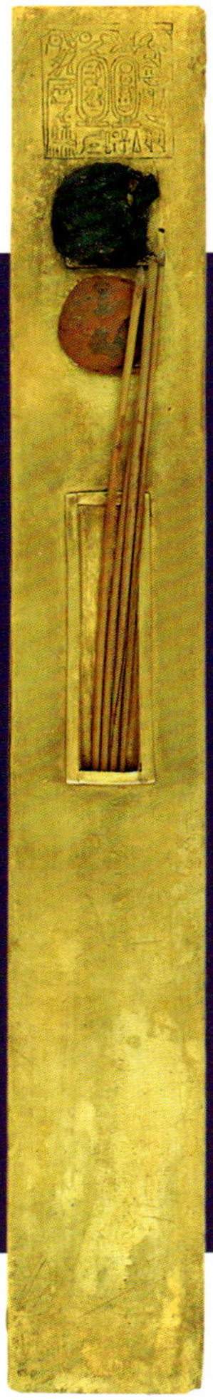

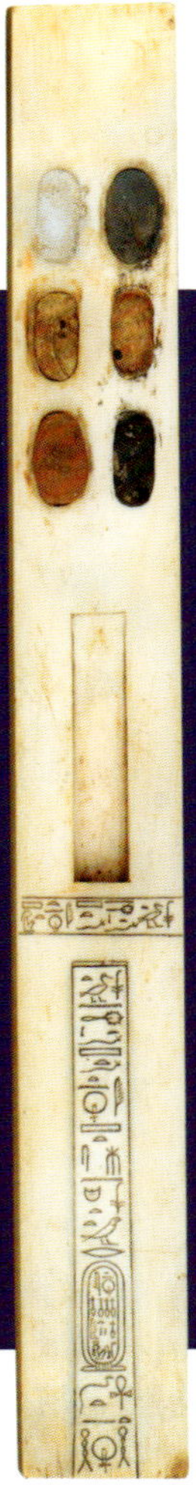

BRUSH HOLDER
Gilded wood, obsidian, carnelian, glass
Length 30 cm
Carter 271e(1)

PAPYRUS BURNISHER
Ivory, gold, linen
Length 16.5 cm, width 4.4 cm
Carter 271g

SCRIBAL PALETTE
Gilded wood
Length 30.3 cm, width 4.3 cm
Carter 271e2

IVORY PALETTE OF MERITATEN
Ivory
Length 21.9 cm, width 2.5 cm
Carter 262

PALETTE
Slate with wooden ends, gesso-gilt
Length 25.5 cm, width 4.5 cm
Carter 620(92)

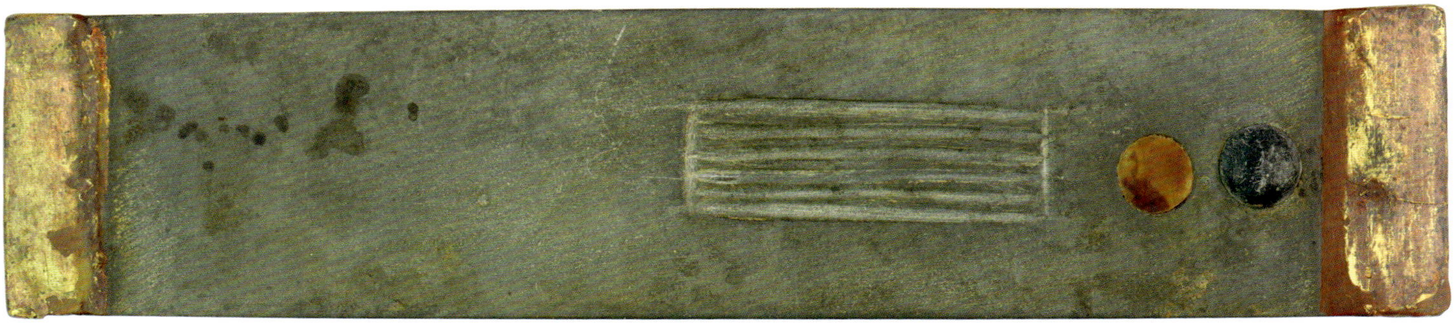

RITUAL FIGURES

The funeral party had dragged a number of small sledges, each with a little wooden shrine coated with resin, to the tomb. These were then arranged along the south and east walls of the Treasury. Behind its sealed double doors, each shrine contained a figure, either of the king or of a netherworldly divinity, wrapped in a linen shawl.

The two figures here represent the king with features influenced by the artistic conventions of the Amarna Period: small waist, soft belly, and pronounced breasts. The face is not Tutankhamun's. They could have been made for Akhenaten or his immediate successor Ankh(et)kheperure, or perhaps some other king. Even without the resemblance, however, they went into the tomb to represent Tutankhamun, as indicated by an inscription that calls him the "good god, Nebkheperure, true of voice." "True of voice" was an epithet given to the dead.

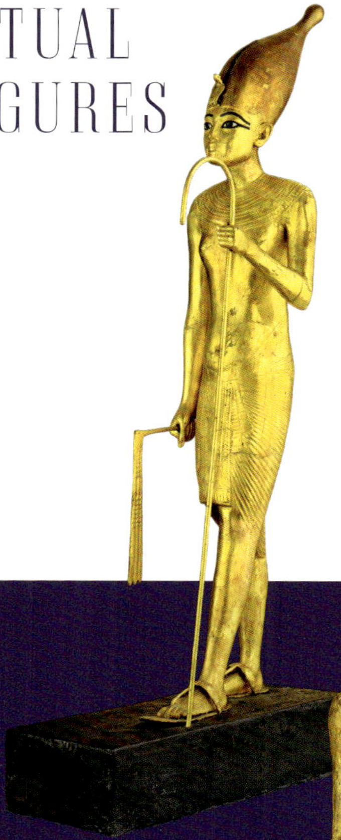

TUTANKHAMUN AS THE KING OF UPPER EGYPT
Gilded wood, bronze
Height 62 cm, width 13.5 cm
Carter 296b

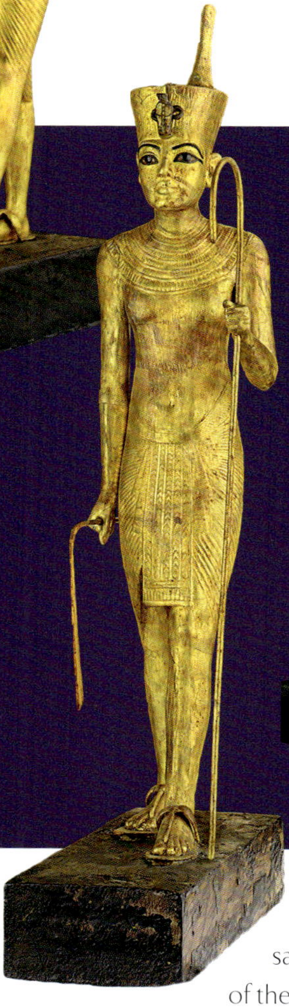

TUTANKHAMUN AS THE KING OF LOWER EGYPT
Gilded wood, bronze
Height 63 cm, width 13 cm
Carter 275b

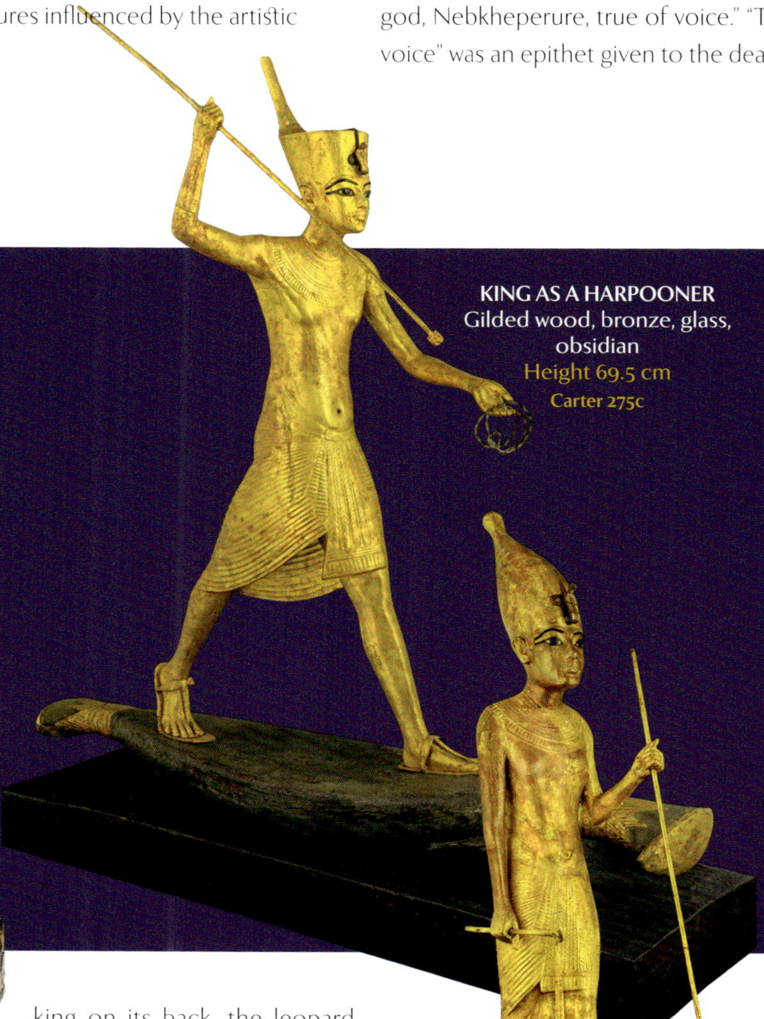

KING AS A HARPOONER
Gilded wood, bronze, glass, obsidian
Height 69.5 cm
Carter 275c

The king appears aboard a papyrus skiff, ready to harpoon prey that is not shown. He is acting as Horus, a god associated with kingly power and lawful order, who battles the forces of chaos, often symbolized by wild animals. Horus's unseen foe here is his uncle, the god Seth, who is to be imagined in the form of a hippopotamus.

Figures were often painted black to associate them with the netherworld. This was the case with the leopard here, which is also associated with the night sky. By carrying the king on its back, the leopard safeguards him through the dangers of the afterlife, so that he can be reborn each morning. It has been suggested, because of the prominent breasts, that the figure did not originally represent Tutankhamun. It might have been made for a female ruler, possibly Nefertiti.

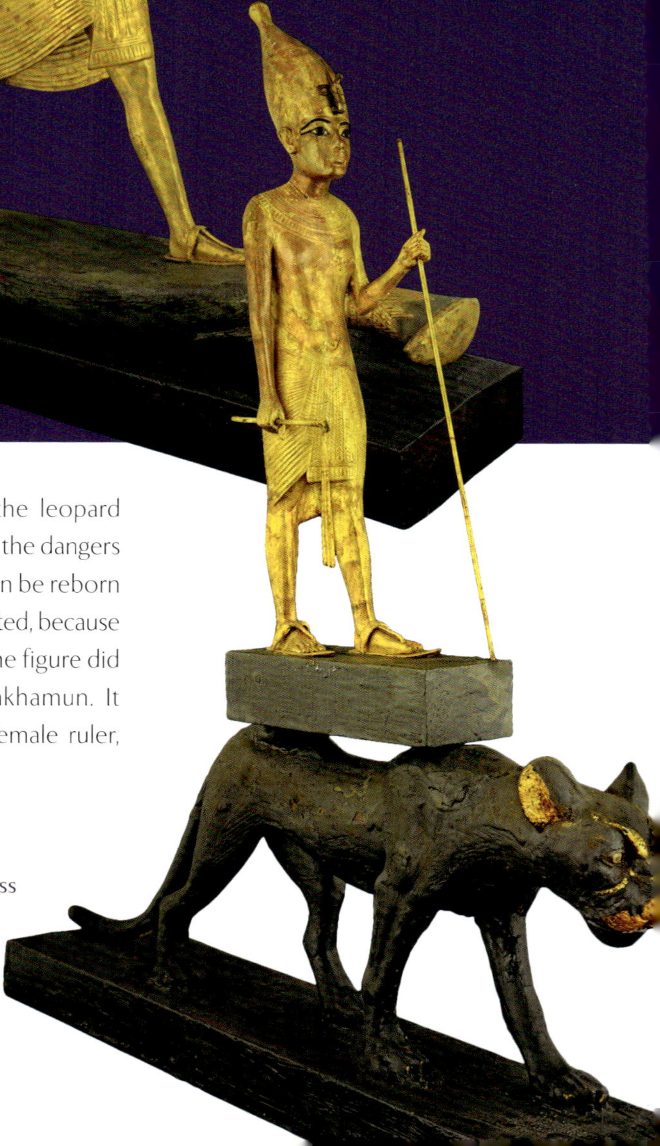

KING ON A LEOPARD
Gilded wood, bronze, glass
Height 85.6 cm
Carter 289a

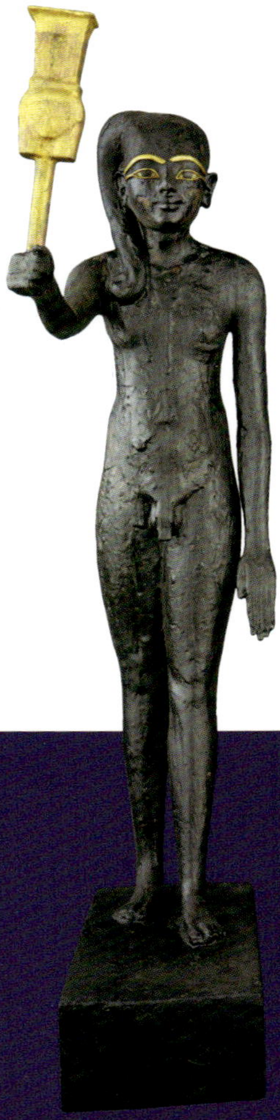

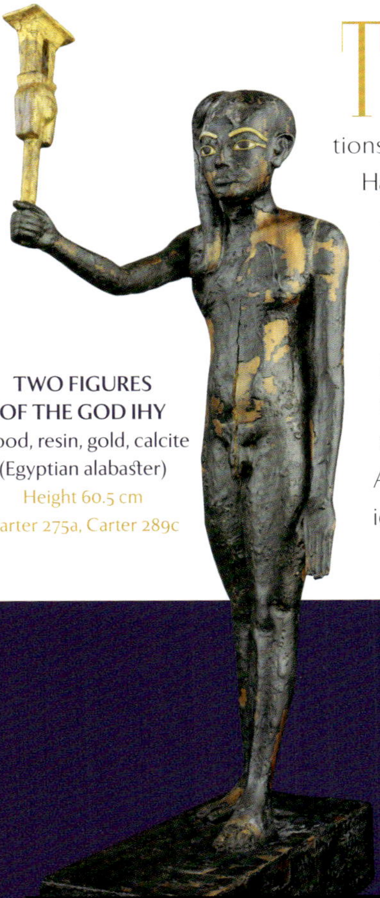

TWO FIGURES OF THE GOD IHY
Wood, resin, gold, calcite (Egyptian alabaster)
Height 60.5 cm
Carter 275a, Carter 289c

The two figures of the young boys, naked and with the side-lock of youth, are representations of Ihy, son of the goddess Hathor. Ihy always appears holding a sistrum, an instrument closely associated with his mother (Carter No. 76).

The god Menkaret, shown here carrying the king in the form of a mummy wearing the red crown, is an obscure deity. An inscription on the pedestal identifies the king as "the good god, Nebkheperure, true of voice, beloved of Menkaret."

The regal figure of a seated woman with the head of a lioness represents Sekhmet, whose name means "the Powerful One." She was at once the destructive goddess of war and disease and the goddess of healing, a guardian of the king. In the Egyptian pantheon, she was the wife of the creator god Ptah, and mother of Nefertem, god of perfume (Carter No. 8). She wears an archaic, tight-fitting dress covered with a beaded net and has on her head the solar disk, symbol of her father Re.

SEKHMET
(detail)
Gilded wood, glass
Height 55.2 cm
Carter 300a

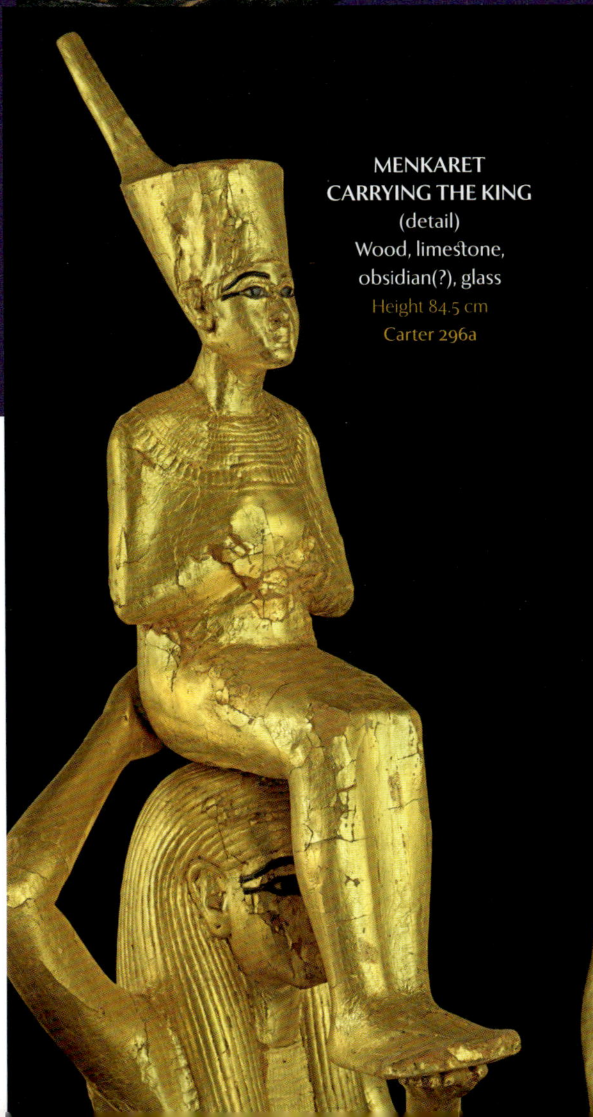

MENKARET CARRYING THE KING
(detail)
Wood, limestone, obsidian(?), glass
Height 84.5 cm
Carter 296a

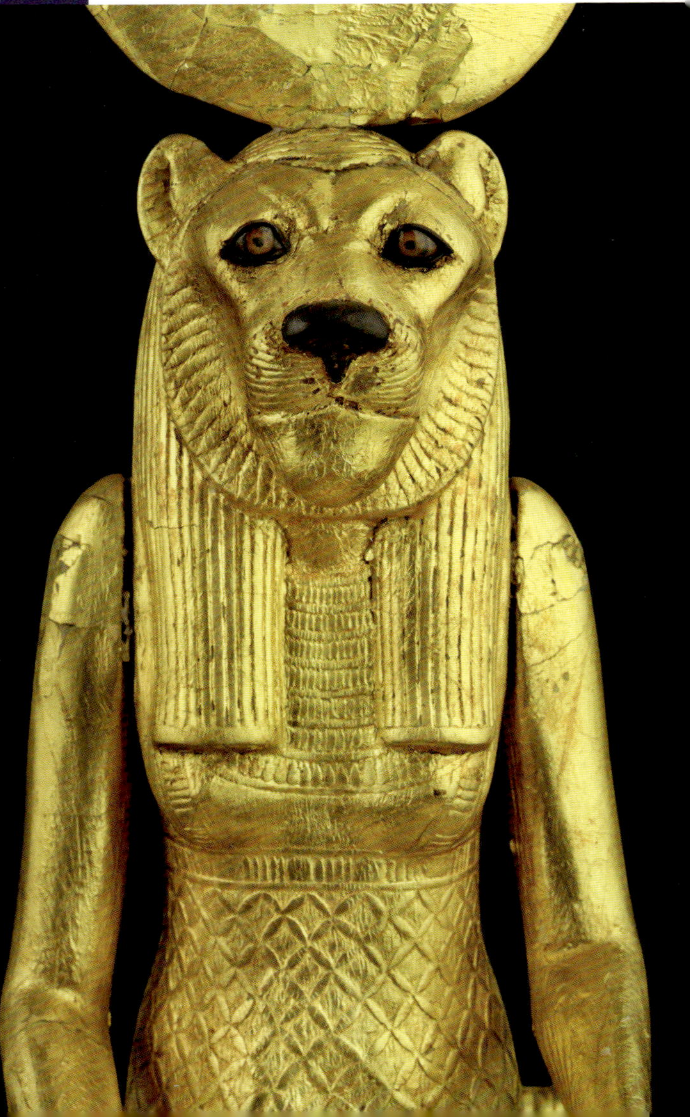

ANTHROPOMORPHIC DEITIES

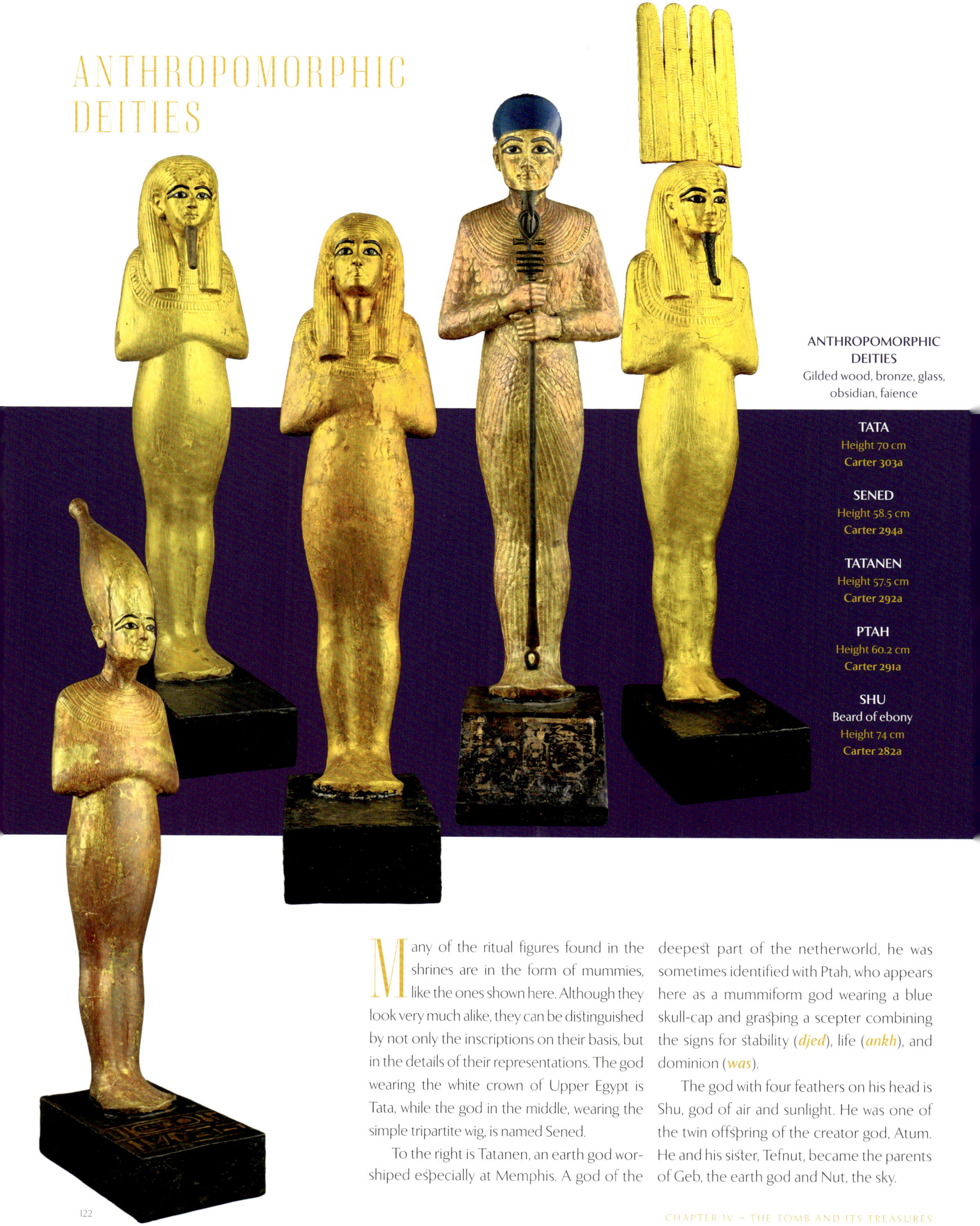

ANTHROPOMORPHIC DEITIES
Gilded wood, bronze, glass, obsidian, faience

TATA
Height 70 cm
Carter 303a

SENED
Height 58.5 cm
Carter 294a

TATANEN
Height 57.5 cm
Carter 292a

PTAH
Height 60.2 cm
Carter 291a

SHU
Beard of ebony
Height 74 cm
Carter 282a

Many of the ritual figures found in the shrines are in the form of mummies, like the ones shown here. Although they look very much alike, they can be distinguished by not only the inscriptions on their basis, but in the details of their representations. The god wearing the white crown of Upper Egypt is Tata, while the god in the middle, wearing the simple tripartite wig, is named Sened.

To the right is Tatanen, an earth god worshiped especially at Memphis. A god of the deepest part of the netherworld, he was sometimes identified with Ptah, who appears here as a mummiform god wearing a blue skull-cap and grasping a scepter combining the signs for stability (***djed***), life (***ankh***), and dominion (***was***).

The god with four feathers on his head is Shu, god of air and sunlight. He was one of the twin offspring of the creator god, Atum. He and his sister, Tefnut, became the parents of Geb, the earth god and Nut, the sky.

An inscription identifies this falcon-headed god as Herwer, "Horus the Elder," the great sky god, whose right eye was the sun and whose left eye was the moon. He was distinguished from Harsaiset, "Horus, son of Isis," who was the offspring of Osiris and Isis.

The other two figures are both Duamutef, one of the four Sons of Horus, who guarded the mummified organs of the deceased. Duamutef, who could appear as a human-headed or jackal-headed mummy, protected the stomach.

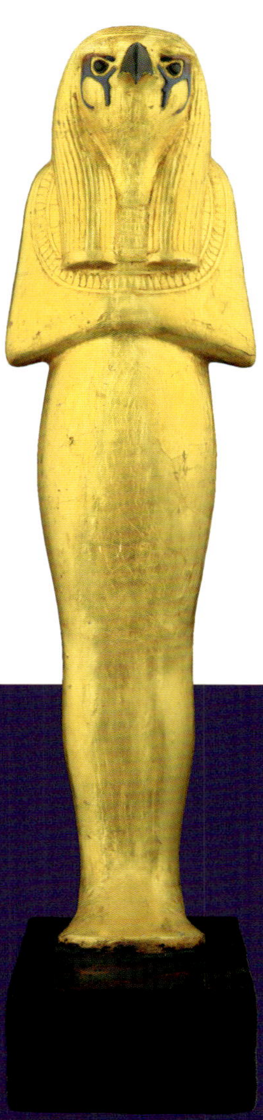

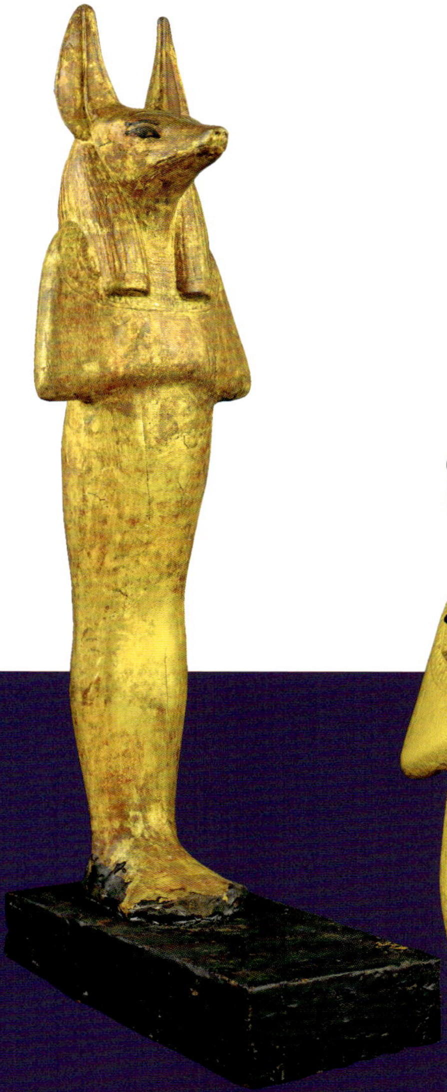

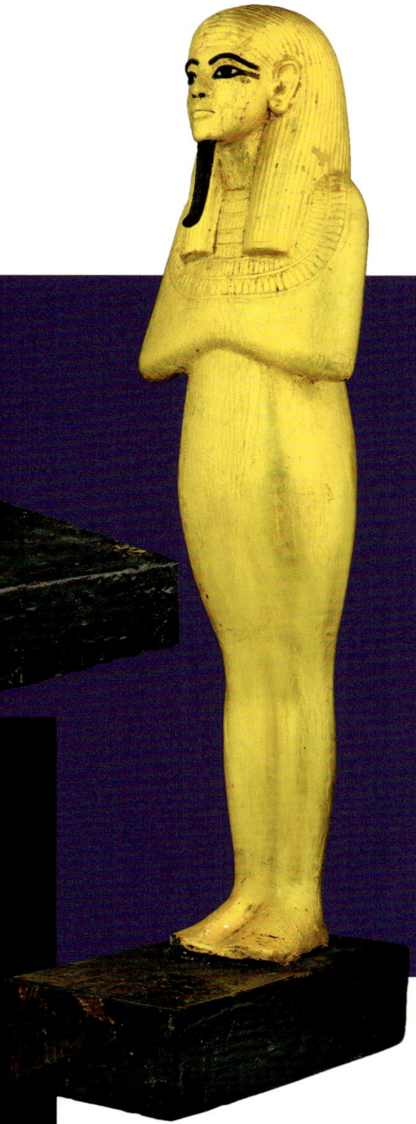

RITUAL FIGURES
Gilded wood, glass

HERWER (HORUS THE GREAT)
Height 56.8 cm
Carter 293a

JACKAL-HEADED DUAMUTEF
Height 58 cm
Carter 304b

HUMAN-HEADED DUAMUTEF
Height 58 cm
Carter 302a

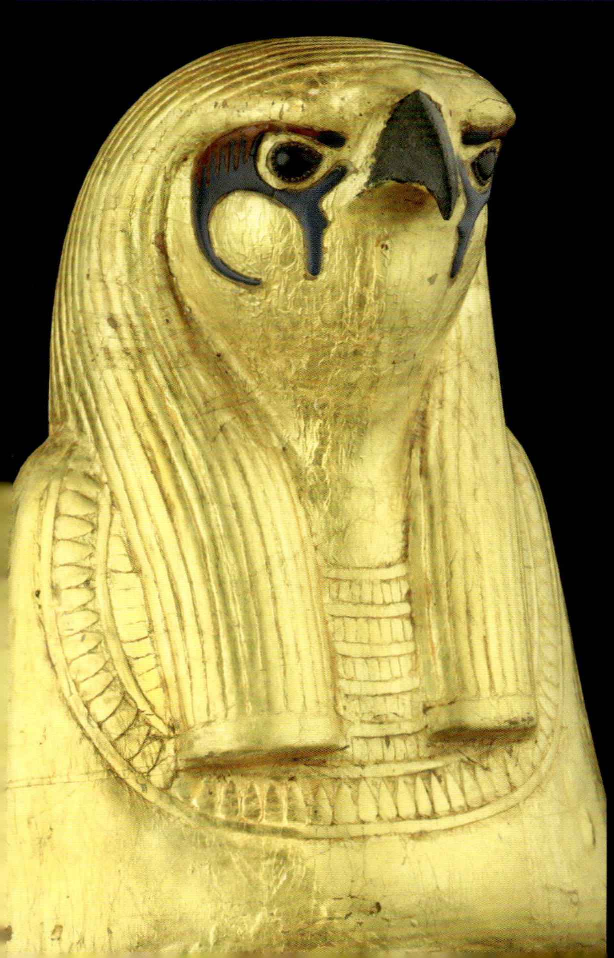

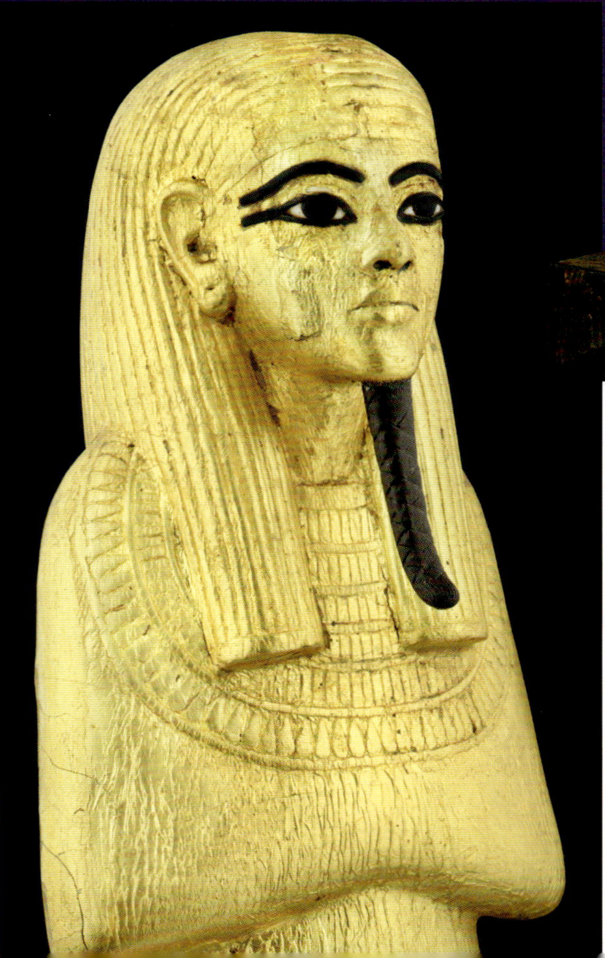

ZOOMORPHIC DEITIES AND OSIRIS

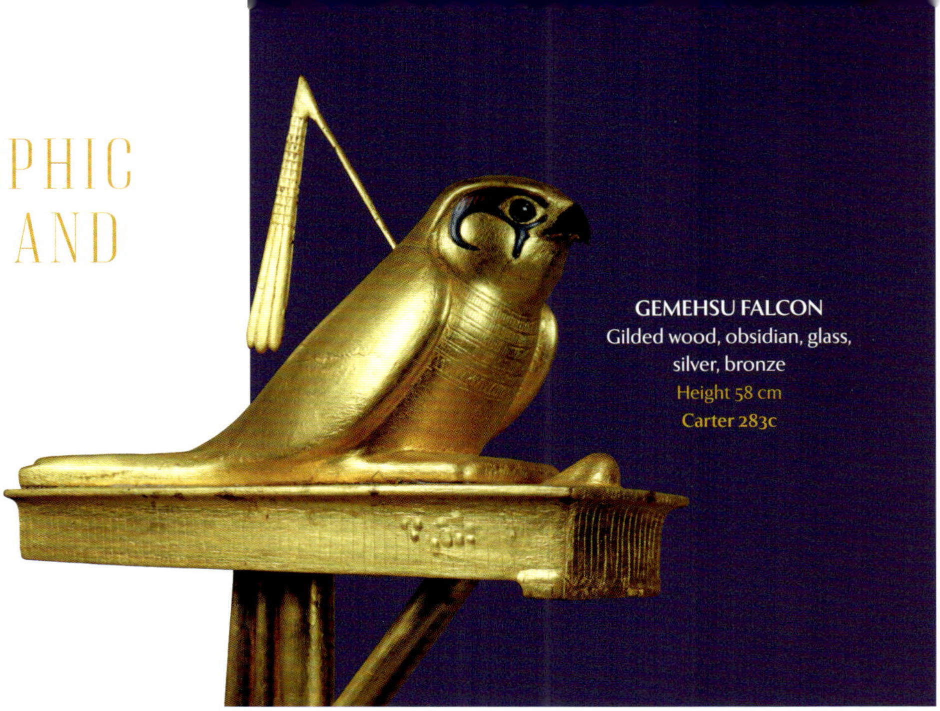

GEMEHSU FALCON
Gilded wood, obsidian, glass, silver, bronze
Height 58 cm
Carter 283c

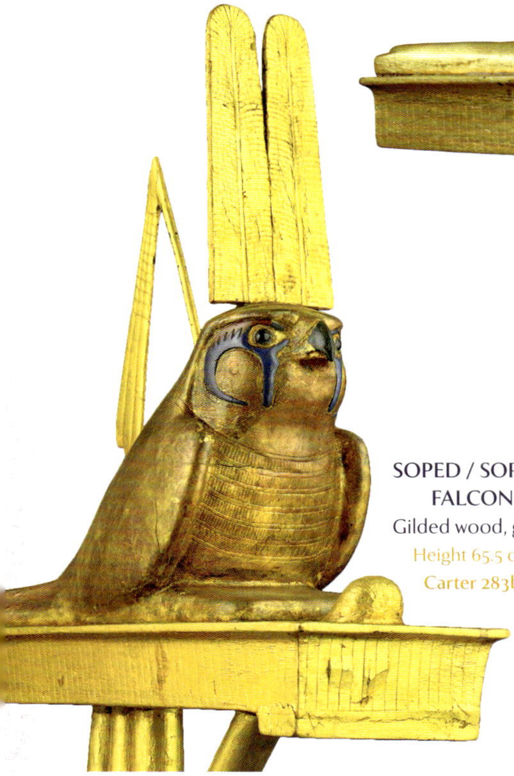

SOPED / SOPDU FALCON
Gilded wood, glass
Height 65.5 cm
Carter 283b

The Egyptians worshiped many falcon gods. The most widely known were Horus and Re and variations on them, such as Re-Horakhty. Towns often had their own gods as well, and local forms of Horus were common. The falcon with the double plumes on its head is identified as Soped or Sopdu, "Lord of the Eastern Desert," who was the personification of Sirius, brightest star in the night sky.

An inscription identifies the second falcon god as Gemehsu. Like Sopdu, it has the flail of kingship rising from its back.

Not all of the ritual objects in the Treasury were made from precious materials. Found in a plain wooden box and wrapped in linen like a mummy, this curious figure was carved from a plank of wood. It shows the silhouette of Osiris, god of the dead, as a mummified man wearing the tall white crown of Upper Egypt flanked by two ostrich plumes. The shape includes his protruding elbows and the ends of the crook and flail of kingship that he holds crossed at his chest. The plank was hollowed out, lined with linen, and filled with what is probably Nile mud. Barley seed sown in this mud had germinated. The growth of living plants from the divine corpse symbolized rebirth, the fertility of the fields, and abundance. Osiris's skin was usually depicted as green, like the sprouts, or black, like the mud that gave rise to them.

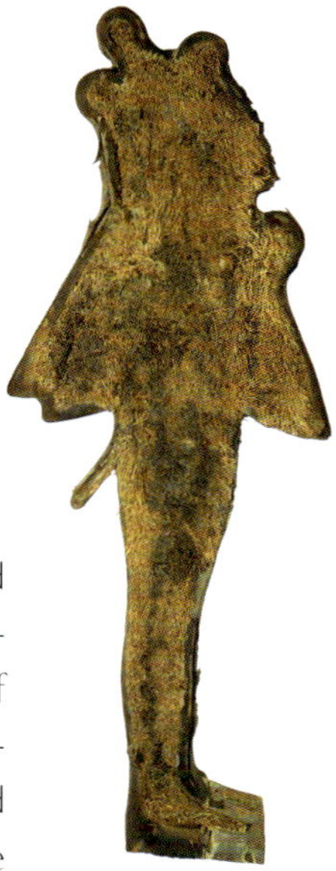

GERMINATING OSIRIS FIGURE
Box of wood; figure of wood, soil, linen
Figure: length 1.9 m, width 75 cm
Carter 288 (box), Carter 288a (figure)

NEST OF COFFINS

The first of these tiny anthropoid coffins identifies the owner as Tutankhamun. It is painted black, a color of rebirth and fertility, and has gold bands with inscriptions, including one in which the king asks the sky goddess Nut to protect him. Below the figure's crossed arms, the vulture goddess Nekhbet stretches her wings out to guard the mummy.

Within this coffin was a smaller one, made of gilded wood, with the prayer to Nut inscribed again. On this coffin, the king wears a ***nemes*** headdress. These first two coffins were glued together and their bottoms remain stuck even today because the black resin painted on the first coffin hardened after the two coffins were nested.

An even tinier anthropoid coffin was within the second. This one, made of wood, contained two items. The first was the wonderfully detailed figure of solid gold seen here. It represents a king, probably Tutankhamun, but Carter thought it was Amenhotep III, even though Amenhotep III never appears with pierced ears such as this little figure has. A tiny necklace of glass beads encircles the king's neck. The figure is a pendant, complete with its gold chain.

The other item found in the innermost coffin was a bundle of linen. Within this linen was the tiniest of the coffins. Around the legs of the coffin had been tied a band of linen with inscriptions naming Amenhotep III's Great Royal Wife, Tiye. As we know now, Tiye and Amenhotep III were Tutankhamun's grandparents. This may be why, inside this final coffin, someone had placed a lock of hair, perhaps from Tiye's own head.

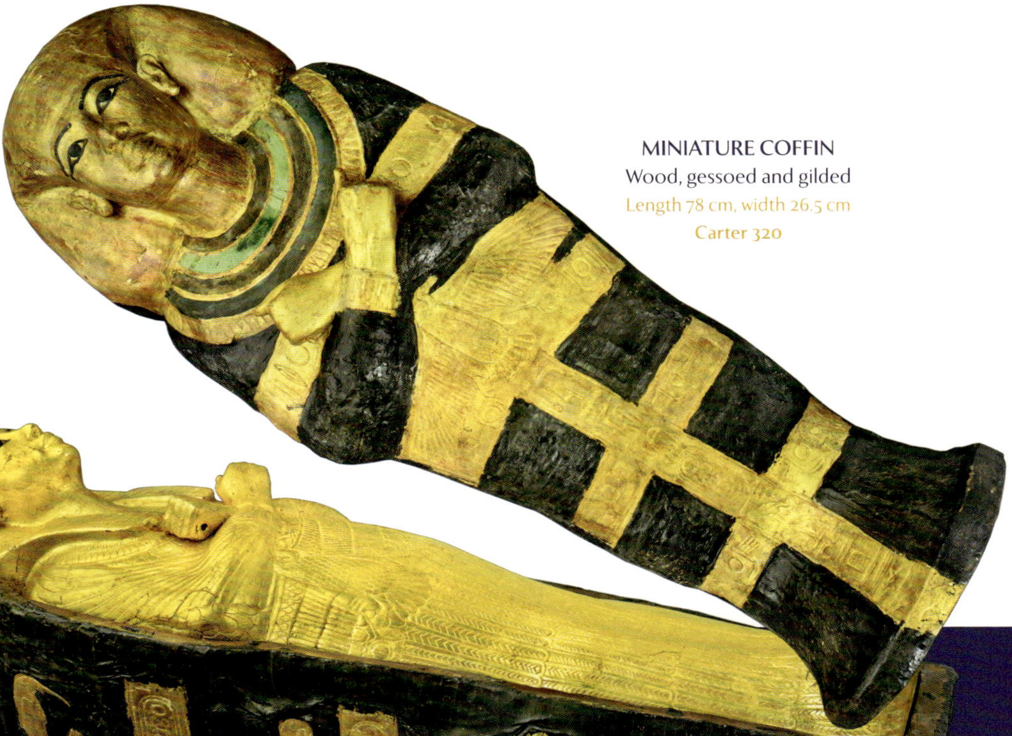

MINIATURE COFFIN
Wood, gessoed and gilded
Length 78 cm, width 26.5 cm
Carter 320

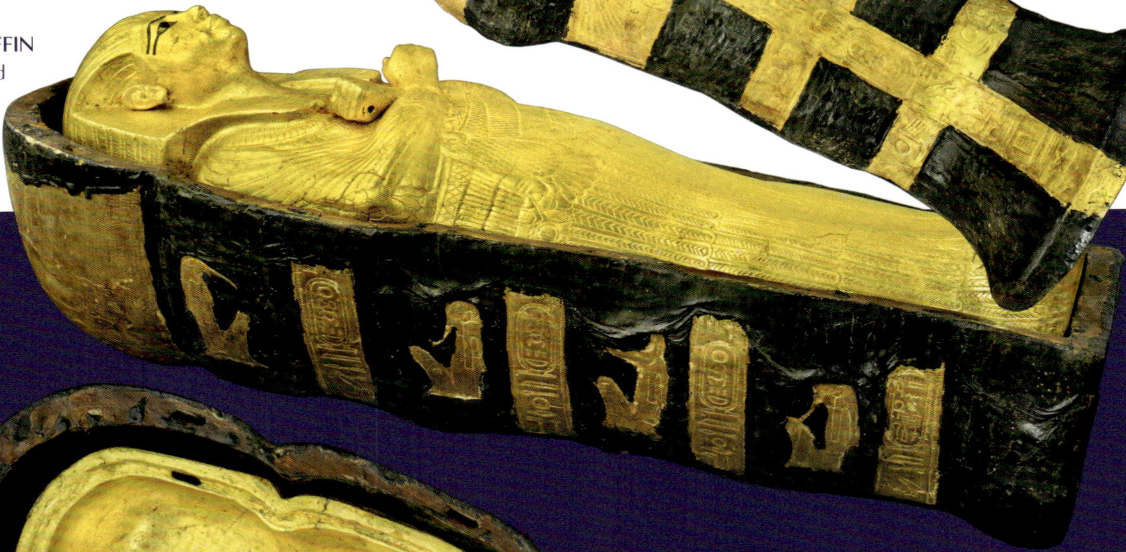

SECOND MINIATURE COFFIN
Wood, gessoed and gilded
Length 74 cm
Carter 320a

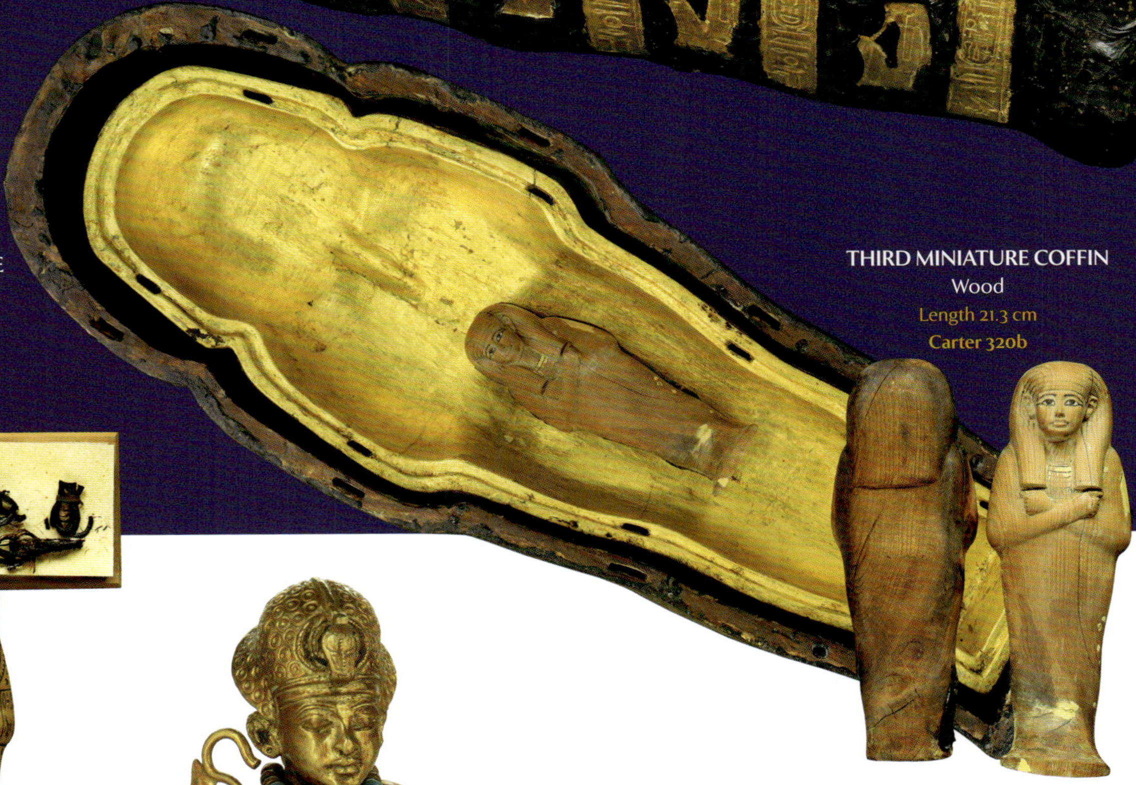

THIRD MINIATURE COFFIN
Wood
Length 21.3 cm
Carter 320b

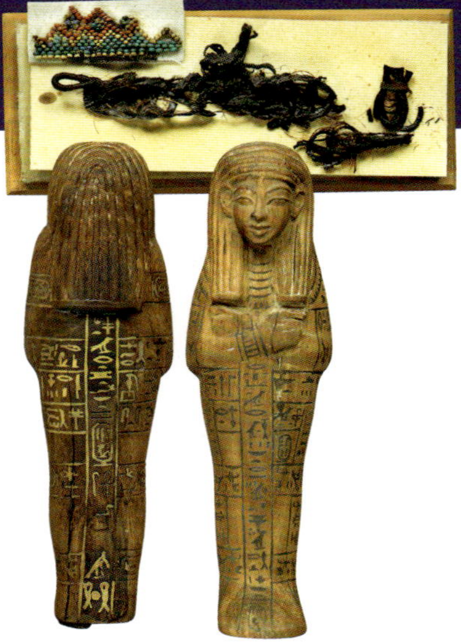

FOURTH MINIATURE COFFIN
Wood
Length 13.2 cm
Carter 320d

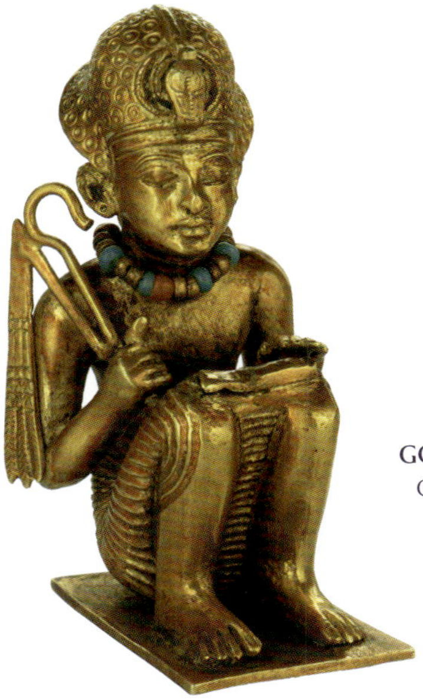

GOLD FIGURE OF THE KING
Gold, glass and linen (chain)
Height of figur 5.4 cm,
length of chain 54 cm
Carter 320c

PLAIN WOODEN BOX WITH FETUSES

Carter's handlist called this a "plain wooden box." There is nothing especially remarkable about this box. There are even others like it from the tomb, but number 317 contained two of its most unexpected treasures.

Inside Carter found two sets of nested anthropoid coffins, wrapped with linen bandages and stamped with the necropolis seal. Inside one set of coffins was a prematurely delivered fetus, perhaps of five months gestation. Inside the other was a somewhat older fetus, carried maybe to full term. Both were girls, but neither had a name. Each was labeled only as "the Osiris." These were almost certainly the stillborn daughters of Tutankhamun and Ankhesenamun, included in their father's tomb so that they, too, could have eternal life.

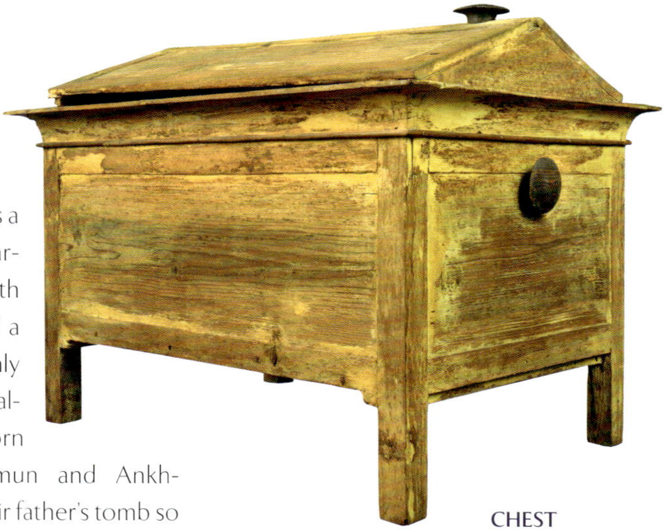

CHEST
Wood, interior coated in black resin
Height 50 cm
Carter 317

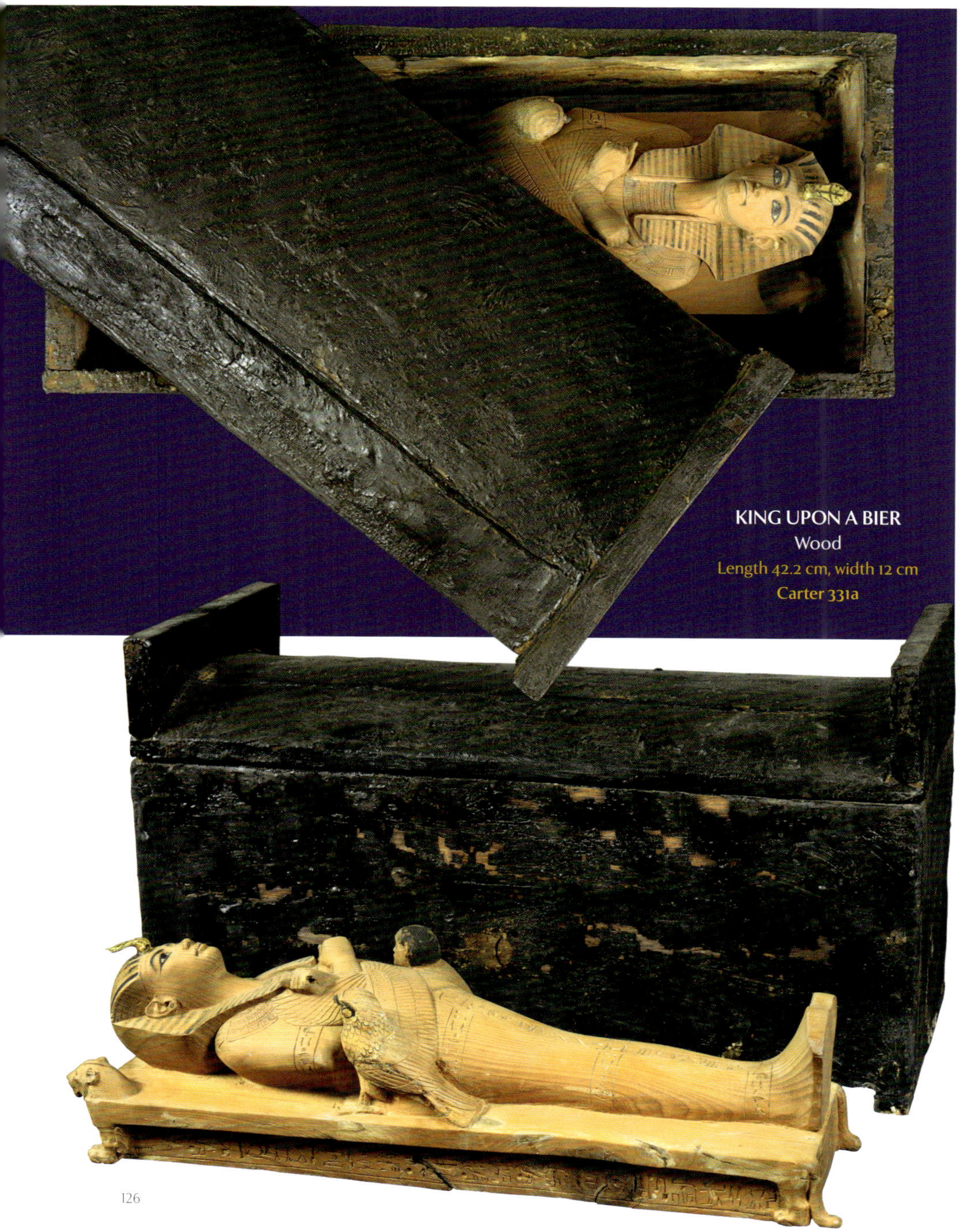

KING UPON A BIER
Wood
Length 42.2 cm, width 12 cm
Carter 331a

KING UPON A BIER

This figure of Tutankhamun as a mummy, laid on a bier, is one of the few objects from the tomb known to have been a gift from one of the king's subjects. An inscription identifies the donor as Maya, overseer of the treasury and overseer of works in the royal necropolis, who also contributed a ***shabti*** to the burial.

The king is accompanied by two birds on the leonine bier. On the king's right is a falcon, probably to be identified as Horus, the son of Osiris. The bird on the left has a human head and represents the king's ***ba***, a sort of soul that would venture outside the tomb. The figure was found, along with agricultural implements, in a coffin box covered with black varnish. Inclusion of the tools indicates that this might have functioned as some kind of servant figure, like the ***shabtis***.

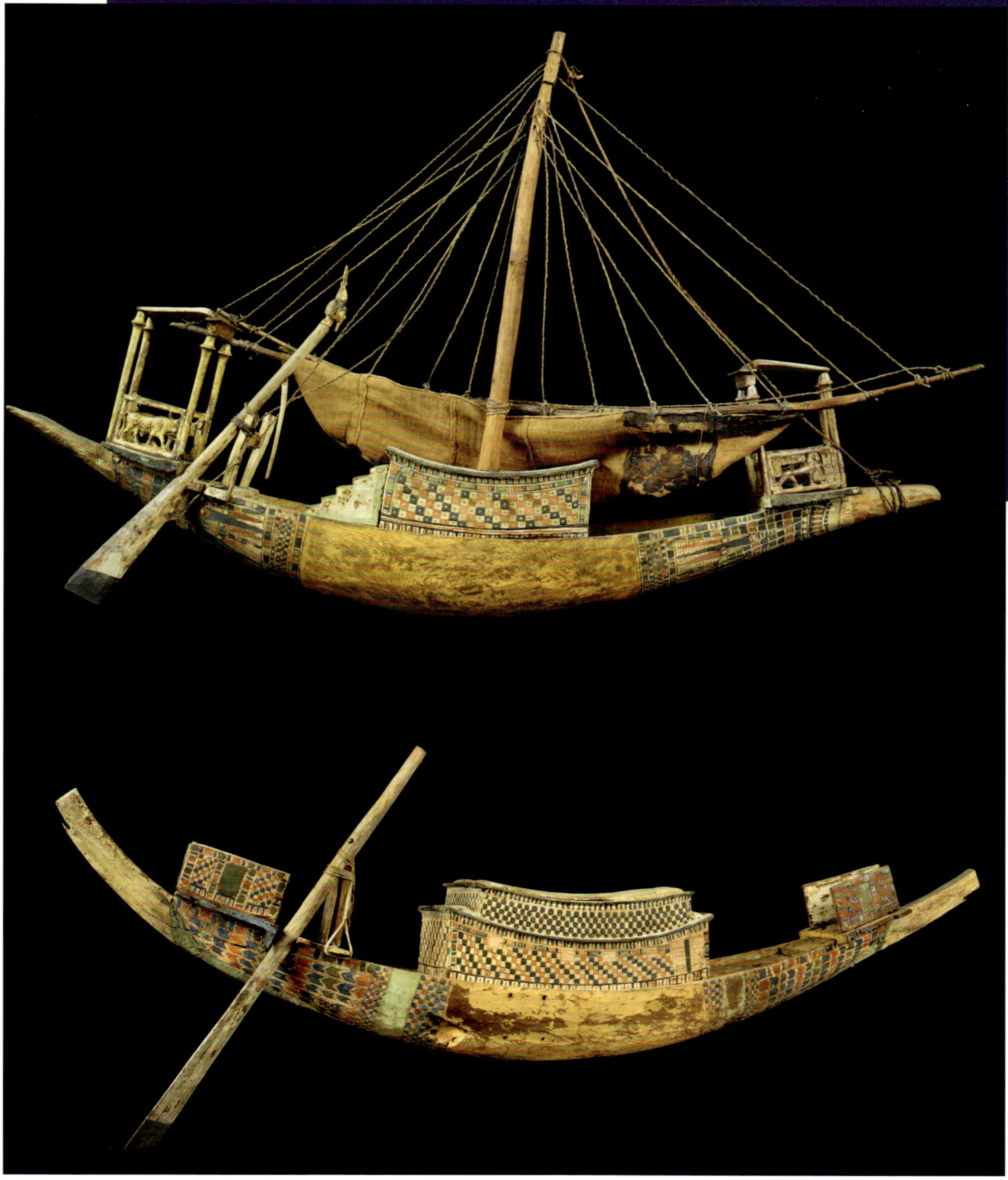

MODEL BOATS
Wood, linen
Length 116
Carter 336

Wood
Length 110 cm
Carter 273

MODEL BOATS

The Egyptians began including boat imagery in their burials during the Predynastic Period. Actual boats were sometimes included in royal tomb complexes, but by the New Kingdom, even kings used models. Tutankhamun had 35 in all, 18 found in the Treasury, while the rest were in the Annexe.

The sailing boat is one of the most elaborate of Tutankhamun's models. The tall mast rises from the middle of the passenger cabin. The sail, made of linen, would have been stretched between the yard (at the head of the sail) and boom (at the foot). Images of the king's head tops each of the two rudders, indicating that this is a royal vessel. The forecastle has decoration of the king as a sphinx, while the sterncastle shows him as a bull.

The second boat is similar, but lacks the sail, and one of its rudders has fallen off. It might have been a barge, towed by another vessel, or perhaps it is meant to be imagined propelled by rowers. New Kingdom models seldom include any crew or oars.

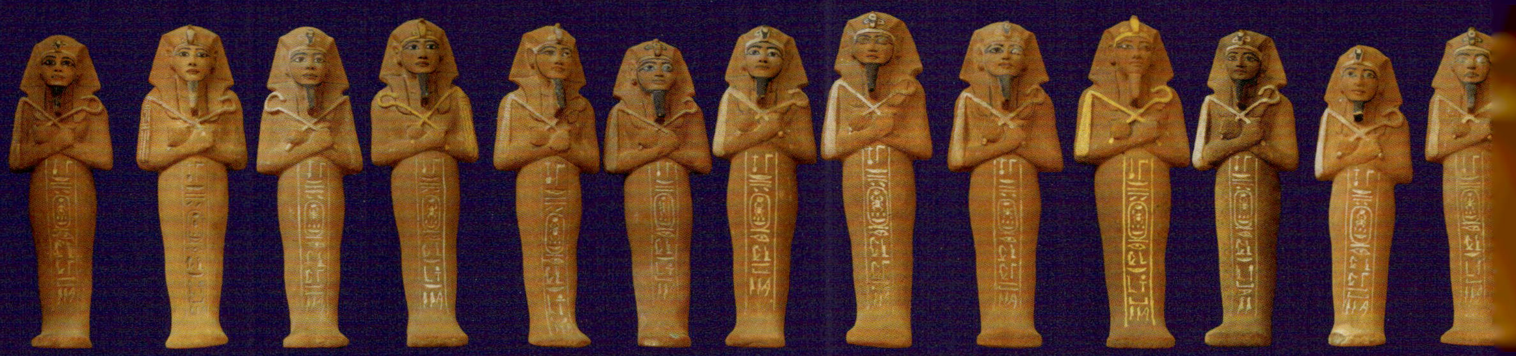

SERIES OF *SHABTI* IN *NEMES* HEADCLOTH

SHABTIS

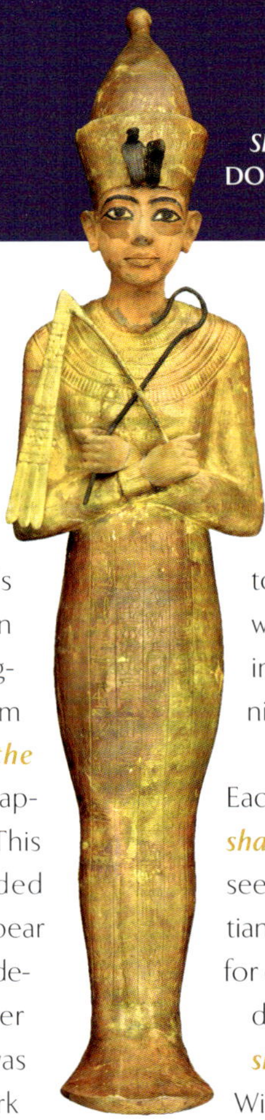

SHABTI WITH DOUBLE CROWN
Carter 330f

For the Egyptians, the afterlife included needs that had to be provided for, not only from their living descendents in the form of offerings, but also by labor performed by the deceased. Particularly agricultural activities were imagined to persist, so that the dead would be supplied eternally with food and drink.

In the Old Kingdom, statues and other images of servants performing these tasks filled this role, but by the New Kingdom, the deceased was expected to plow, hoe, and harvest.

Miniature images of mummies made of wax began to appear in burials of the First Intermediate Period. Late in the Middle Kingdom, spell 6 from the *Book of the Dead* began to appear on them. This spell commanded the *shabti* to appear on behalf of the deceased whenever the deceased was called up for work in the fields.

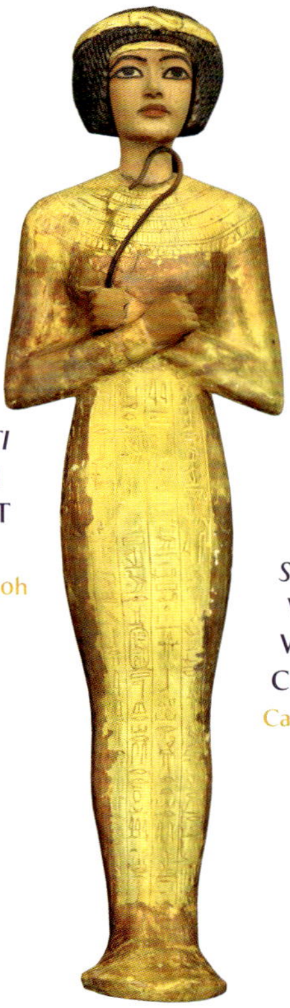

SHABTI WITH SHORT WIG
Carter 330h

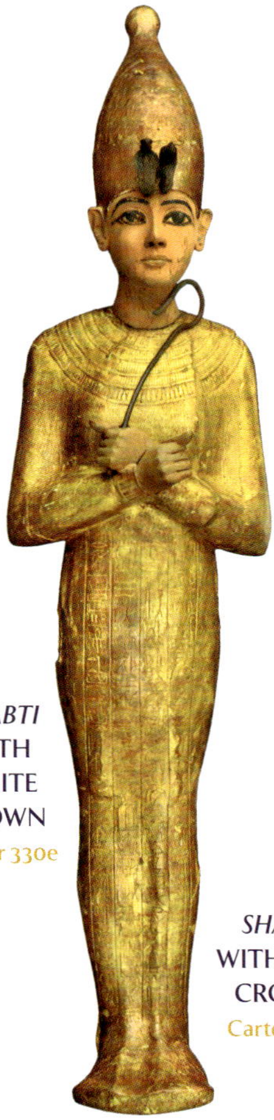

SHABTI WITH WHITE CROWN
Carter 330e

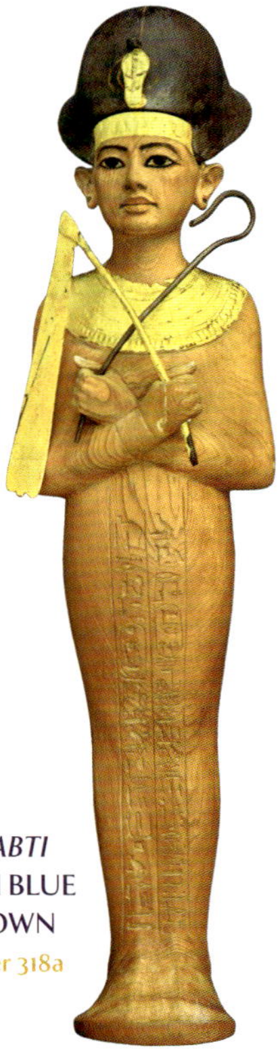

SHABTI WITH BLUE CROWN
Carter 318a

Until the New Kingdom, a burial would ordinarily contain no more than a couple of *shabtis*. Thereafter, a burial might contain literally hundreds of them. All kinds of materials were used, ranging from pottery and wood to faience and stone and even glass. During the reign of Tuthmose IV, craftsman added a new detail: the little mummies now grasped agricultural tools. There were mummies bearing hoes, mattocks, sacks, and baskets. There were also overseer *shabtis* bearing flails or other objects to signify their office.

Tutankhamun had 413 *shabtis*. Each day of the year had its own *shabti*. There were also 36 overseers, one for each of the Egyptian 10-day weeks, plus an overseer for each 30-day month. One hundred and seventy-six of the *shabtis* came from the Treasury. With the exception of one found in the Antechamber, all came from the Annexe.

The king's collection included a wide variety in terms of material, craftsmanship, and even size. The smallest were about 10 cm, and the largest were taller than 60 cm. Materials included wood, granite, limestone, quartzite, calcite (Egyptian alabaster), and faience. The wooden *shabtis* were the finest and largest. Six of them were gifts from two of his officials: Maya, the chief treasurer, and the general Nakhtmin, who was perhaps the son of Ay.

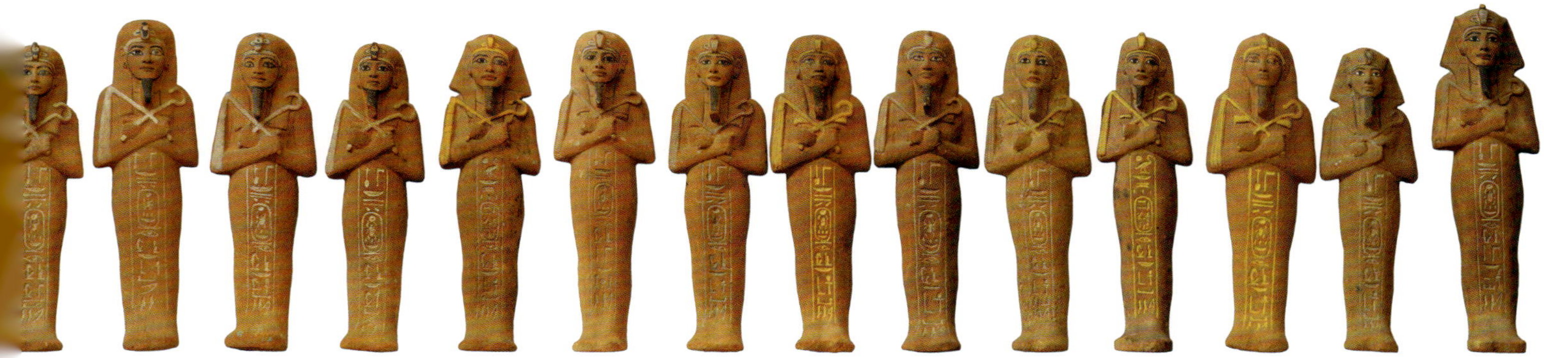

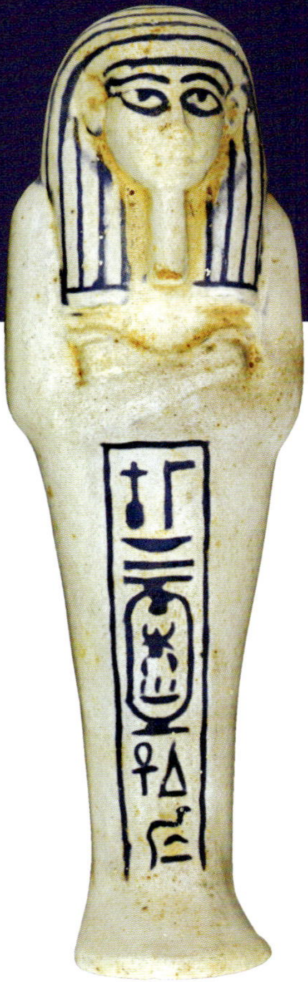

SHABTI
WITH
TRIPARTITE WIG
Carter 519f

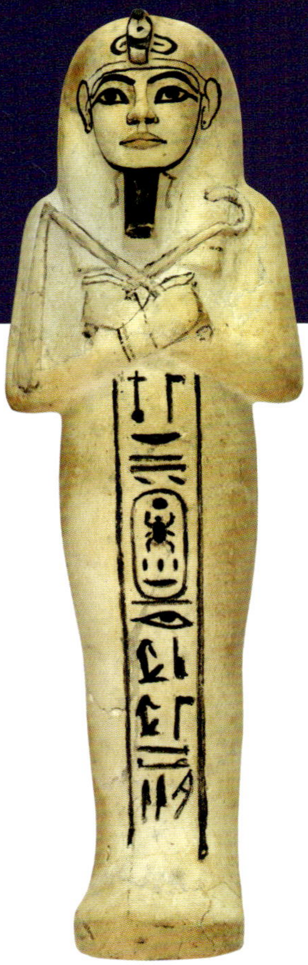

SHABTI
WITH
LONG WIG
Carter 330m

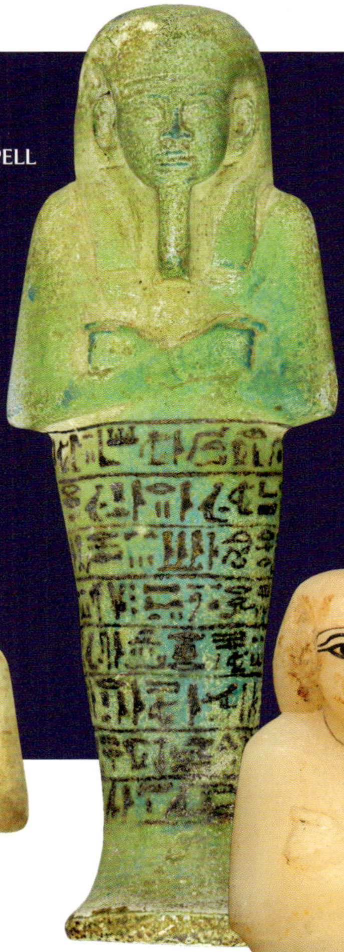

SHABTI
WITH
LONG WIG
WITH SHABTI SPELL
Carter 496d(3)

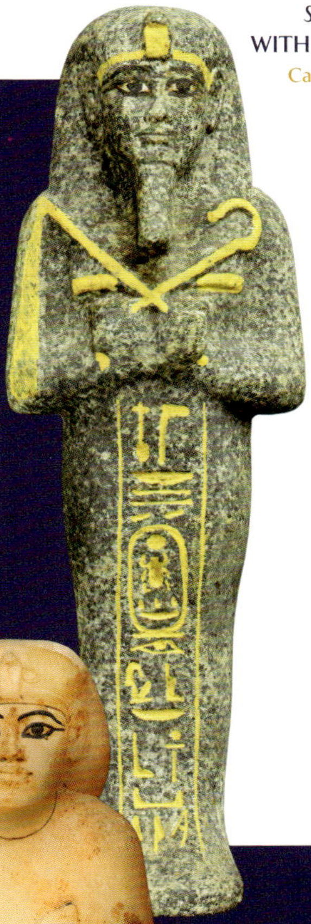

SHABTI
WITH LONG WIG
Carter 322h

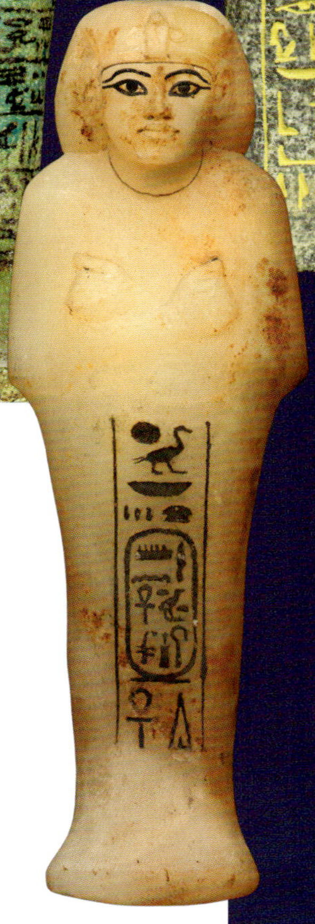

SHABTI
WITH KHAT
HEADDRESS
Carter 328n

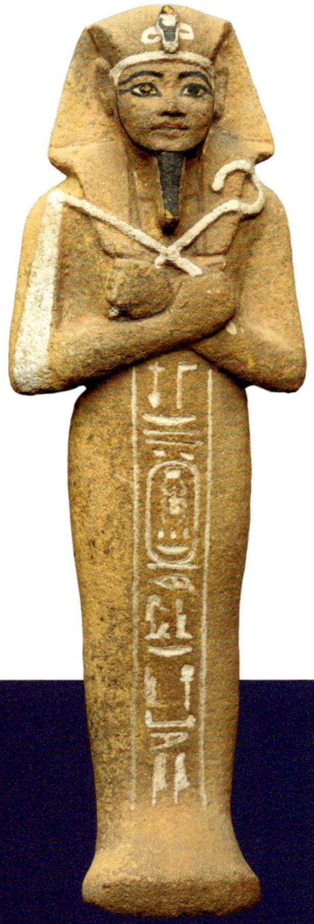

SHABTI
WITH *NEMES*
HEADCLOTH
Carter 514a

THE ANNEXE

In October 1927, nearly five years after first entering the tomb, Carter's team officially began work on the final chamber. A small doorway led from the south end of the north wall of the Antechamber. Beyond was a room stuffed with artifacts: boxes, vessels, furniture, a jumble of antiquities nearly 2 m deep. "The state of this inner room," Carter wrote, "simply defies description."

The tangle of artifacts was so complicated – the pile so precarious – that the only way to tackle the job was from above. The team began their work suspended by ropes until they had cleared enough that they could stand on the Annexe floor, which was more than a meter lower than that of the Antechamber. Surprisingly, it took Carter less than a month to remove the more than 2,000 artifacts that had been deposited in the room. Carter remarked that, unlike in the Antechamber, here no attempt at order had been made.

Originally, the archaeologists determined, the Annexe had been intended to serve as a storeroom for provisions for the afterlife – food, wine, oils, and unguents – but it became a cache for whatever did not fit into the other rooms. The robbers' thievery and the careless returns by the necropolis officials were responsible for the state in which Carter found it.

Tutankhamun's funerary furniture as found in the Annexe.
Harry Burton / Griffith Institute

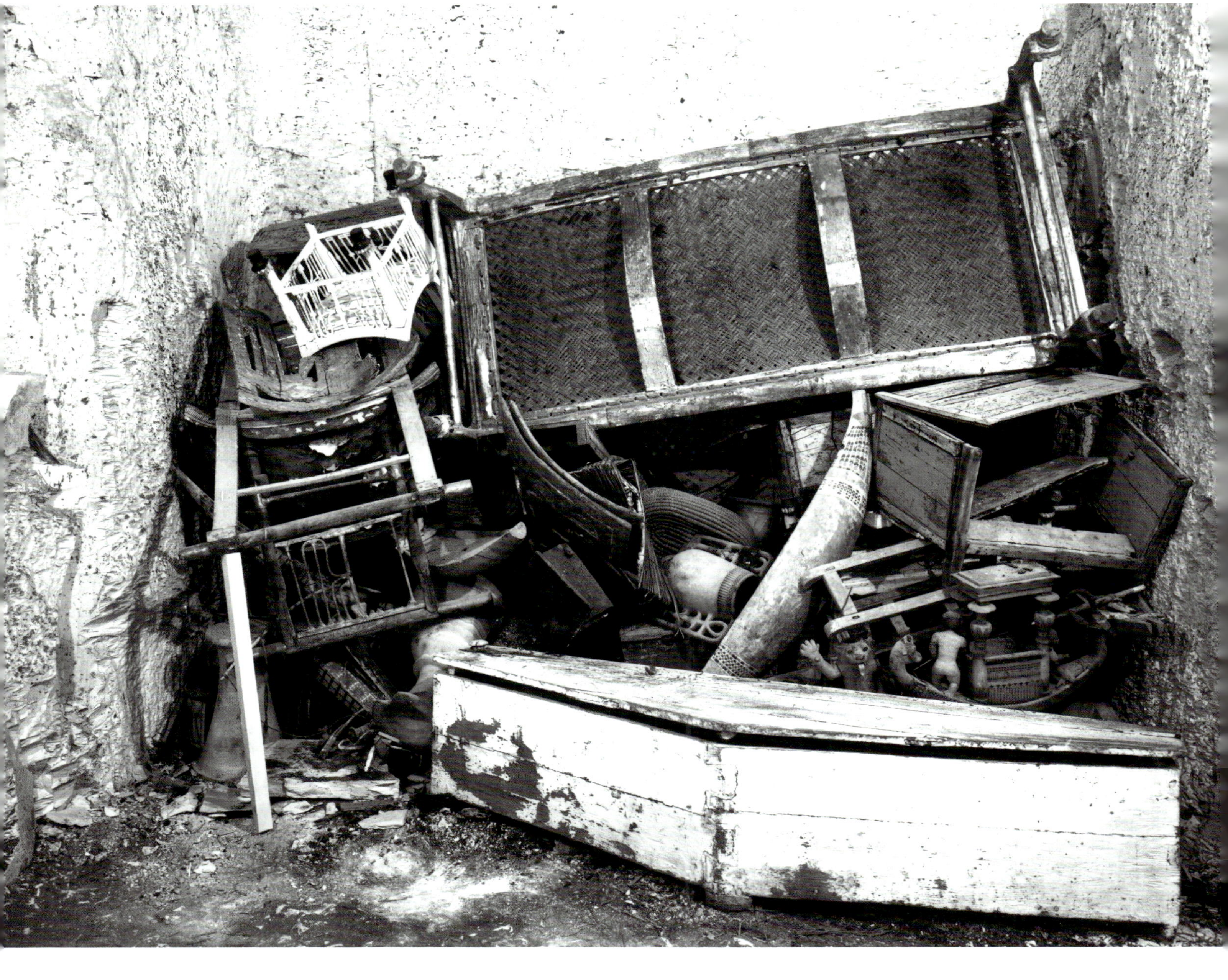

FURNITURE

This small chair was made for the king as a child. The legs are in the form of a lion's, and between are decoration in the form of a complex hieroglyph, with the intertwined heraldic plants of Upper and Lower Egypt around the lungs and windpipe of an animal. This is known as ***sema-tawy***: "Union of the Two Lands," referring to Upper and Lower Egypt, which the king ruled as a united land.

Horus stretches his wings across the back of the chair. He grasps ***shen*** signs, and below his wings are the hieroglyphic symbols for life and dominion. Below, too, is the sign for gold, indicating that he is the "Golden Horus." One of the royal names was called the "Golden Horus" name, and the king was the god's living incarnation on earth. Above Horus's wings are Tutankhamun's cartouches.

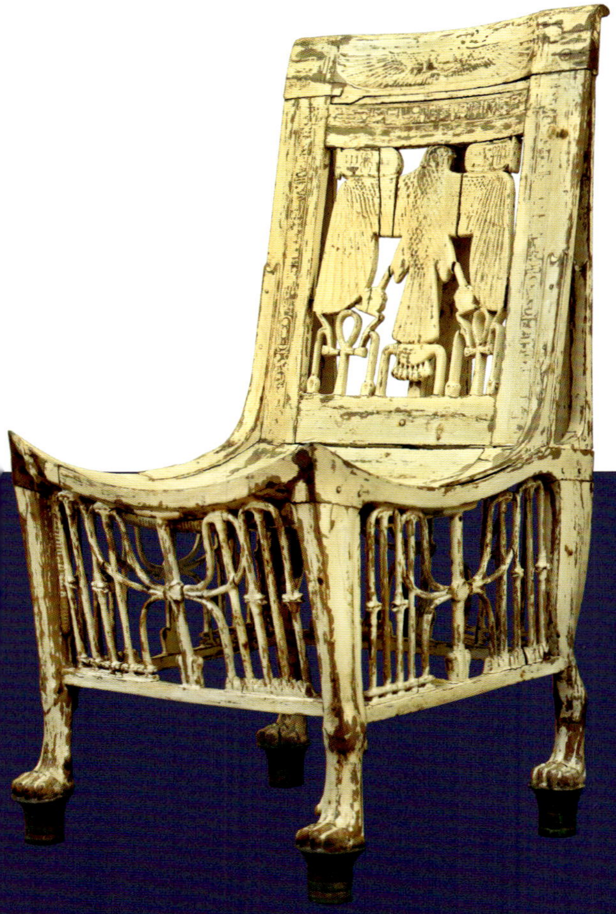

SMALL WOODEN CHAIR
Wood colored white
Height 75 cm
Carter 349

CHEST WITH LONG LEGS AND DECORATIVE FRETWORK
Painted wood, partially gessoed and gilded, colored paste
Height 70 cm, width 43.7 cm, depth 40 cm
Carter 403

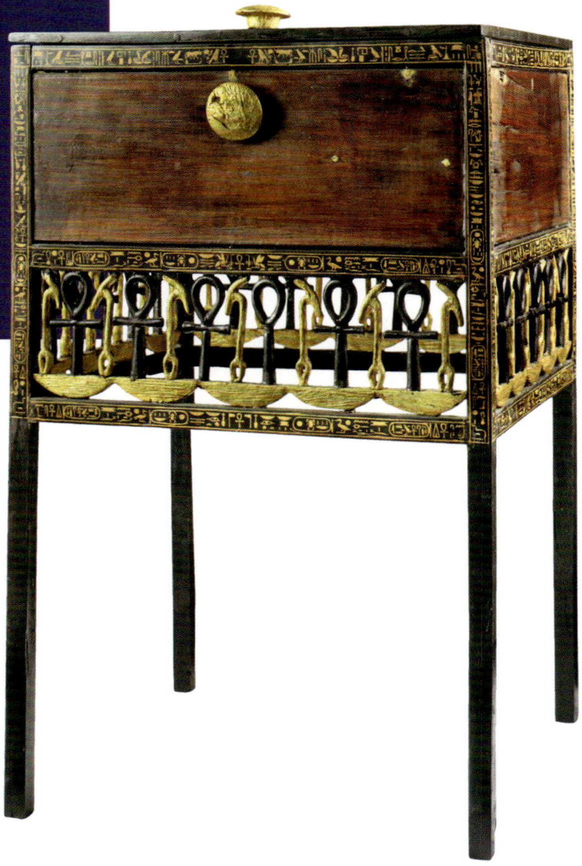

The simplicity and elegance of this chest are particularly appealing. It is made of wood painted reddish in color to imitate cedar wood from Lebanon, with black to imitate African ebony. ***Ankhs*** and ***was*** scepters, signs of life and dominion, sit atop baskets, the sign for "all" (***neb***), to ornament the space between the body of the chest and the stretchers.

Inscriptions along the side panels and the top give some of the king's many names and epithets.

Thieves had broken open the seals and taken anything valuable that it held. When Carter found it, it contained only four headrests (see **Carter Nos. 403a, 403c** and **403d**) and a fragment of sequined clothing.

SHIELDS

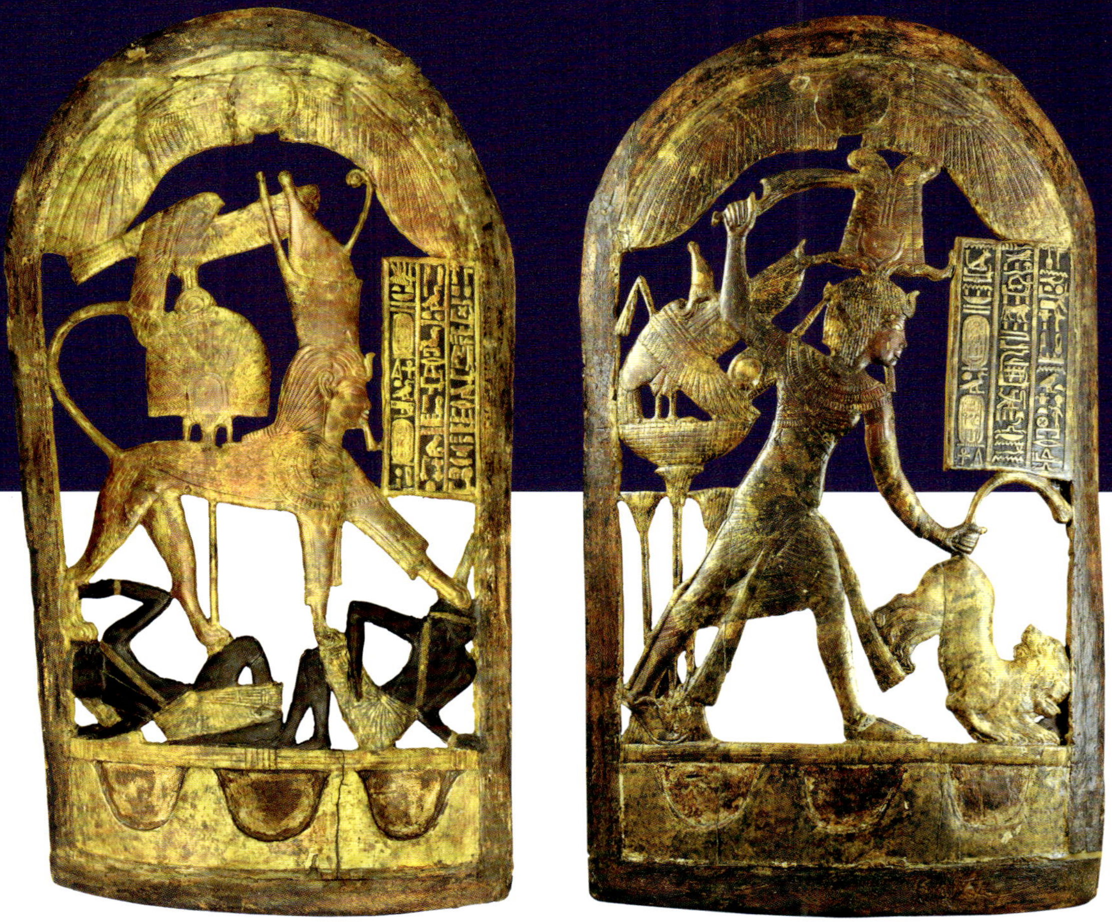

TWO OPENWORK SHIELDS
Gilded wood, hide
Height 89 cm (379a),
Height 88 cm (379b)
Carter 379a (king as sphinx),
Carter 379b
(king smiting lions)

Eight shields were included among the tomb's treasures. The four made of solid wood covered with animal skins might have been made for use in sport or combat. The others, like those here, are too intricately carved to be more than ceremonial.

On one shield, Tutankhamun appears as a sphinx trampling two Nubians beneath his paws. The falcon nearby could be Montu, the falcon-headed war god of Thebes. An inscription identifies the king with this deity. The bottom of the shield is carved into four hills, a hieroglyphic sign representing "foreign lands".

The other shield, in which Tutankhamun is about to slay the pair of lions he grasps by the tail, also identified the king with Montu. Although the king can be portrayed as a lion, lions were also creatures of the desert, wild animals that had to be subdued in order to perpetuate the rightful order of the world.

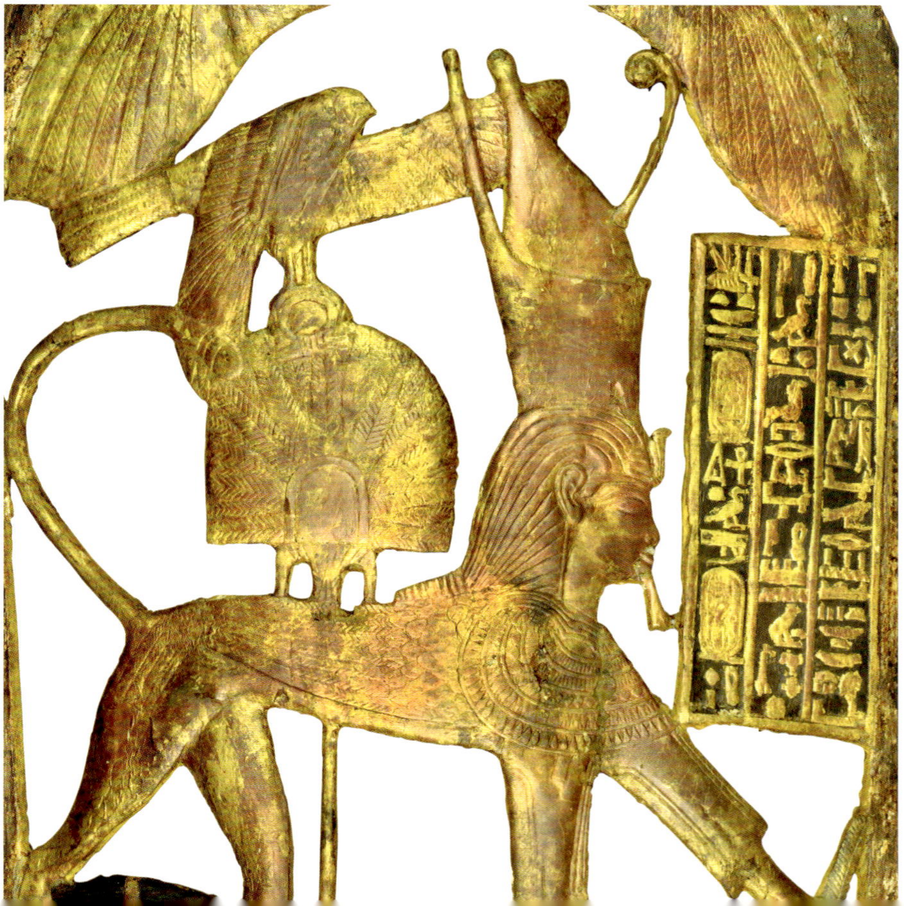

HEADRESTS

An ancient Egyptian would have slept on their side with their head cradled in the curved portion of a headrest such as these. Ordinary headrests, for everyday use, would have been made of wood rather than the more costly materials seen here, and a linen cushion would have been added to make it more comfortable. Headrests also had a symbolic function, as the dead slept.

The symbolism is evident in some of the examples here. The ivory one shown above right is in the form of the god of air, Shu, who holds aloft the sleeper's head instead of the sky. The lions beside him symbolize the hills of the horizon, above which the sun rose each morning.

The folding headrest, also of ivory, shows Bes, one of the most popular Egyptian gods. He protected the vulnerable, such as women, children, and sleepers.

The dark and light blue headrests are made of glass and have the king's name. The deep blue one, in imitation of lapis lazuli, was not recorded in Carter's notes. He seems to have given it to King Fouad as a gift.

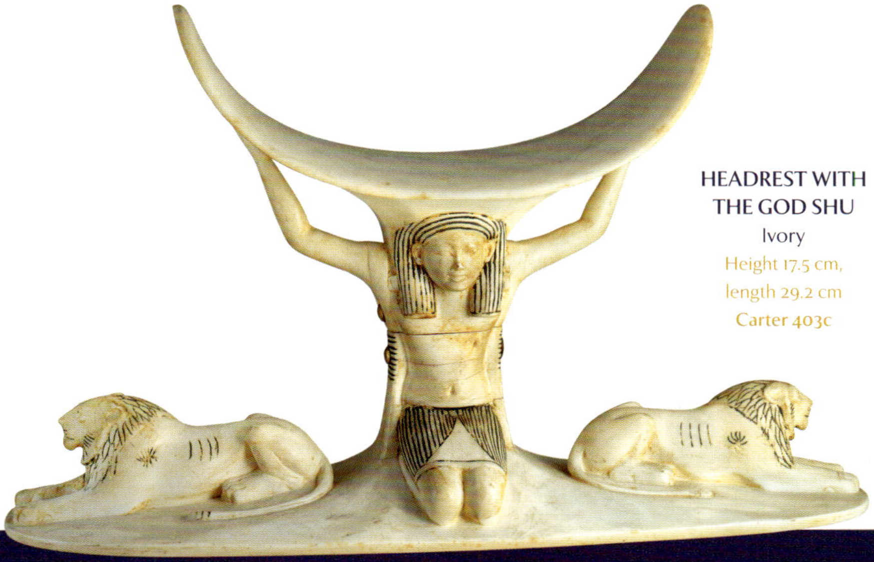

HEADREST WITH THE GOD SHU
Ivory
Height 17.5 cm, length 29.2 cm
Carter 403c

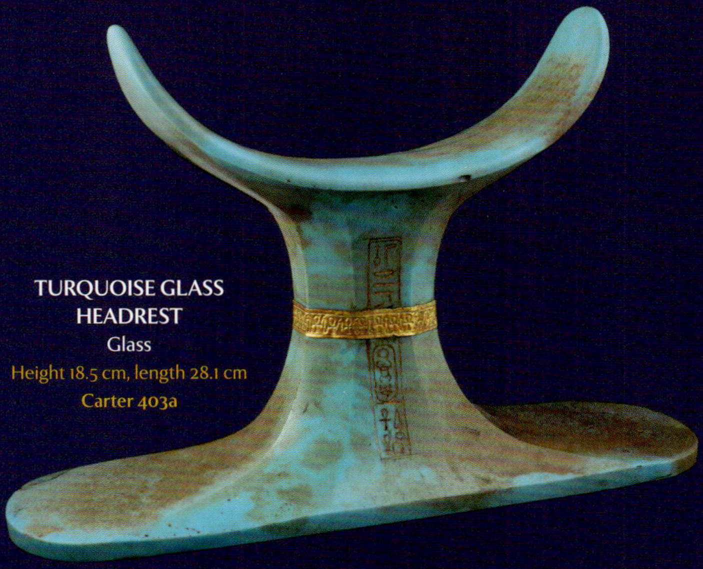

TURQUOISE GLASS HEADREST
Glass
Height 18.5 cm, length 28.1 cm
Carter 403a

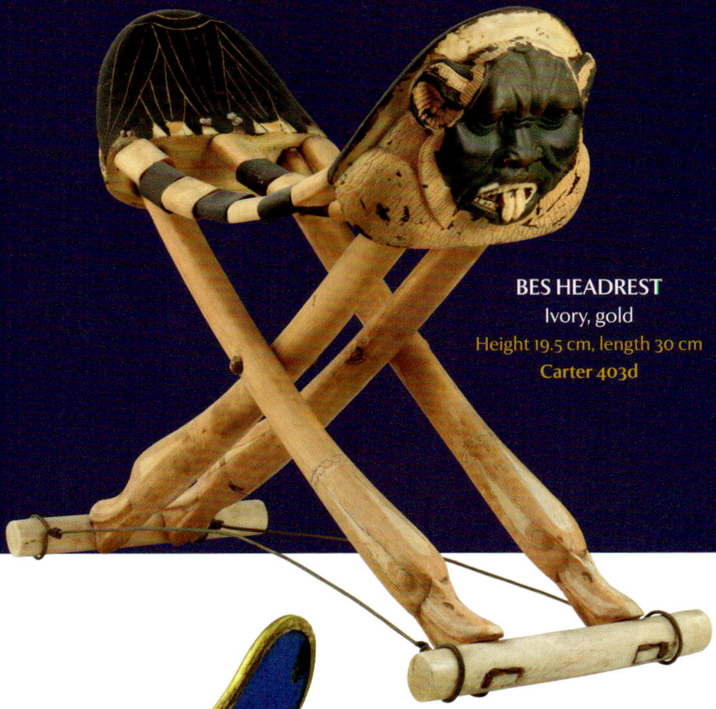

BES HEADREST
Ivory, gold
Height 19.5 cm, length 30 cm
Carter 403d

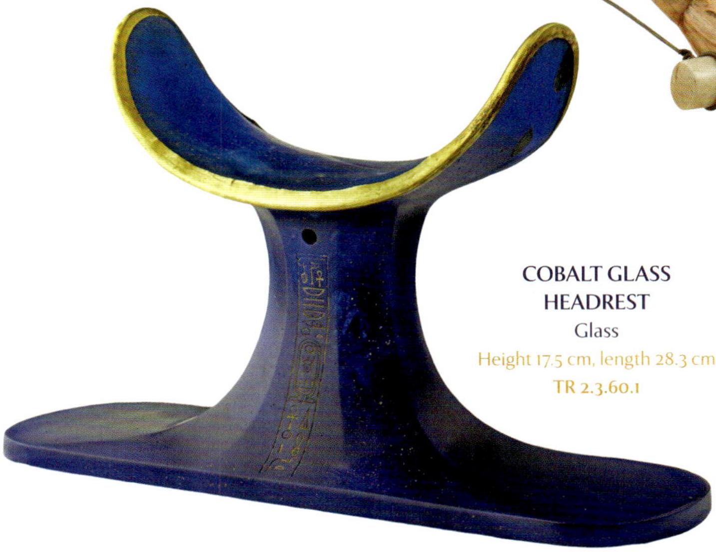

COBALT GLASS HEADREST
Glass
Height 17.5 cm, length 28.3 cm
TR 2.3.60.1

GAMES

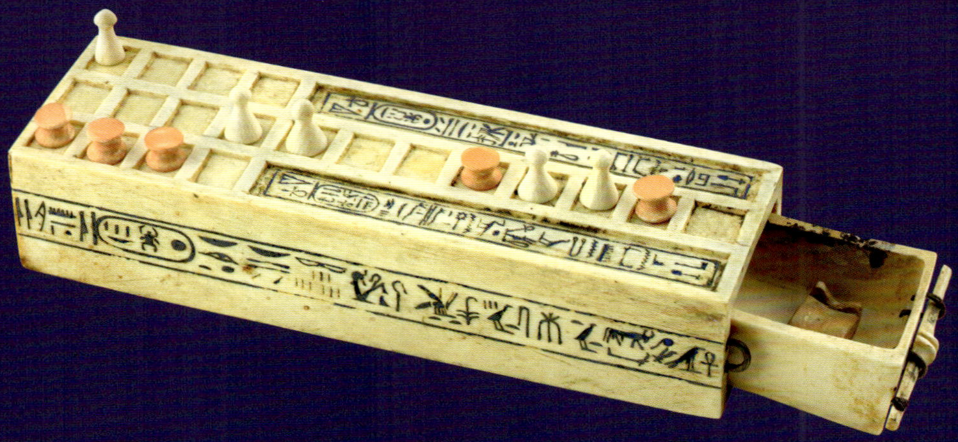

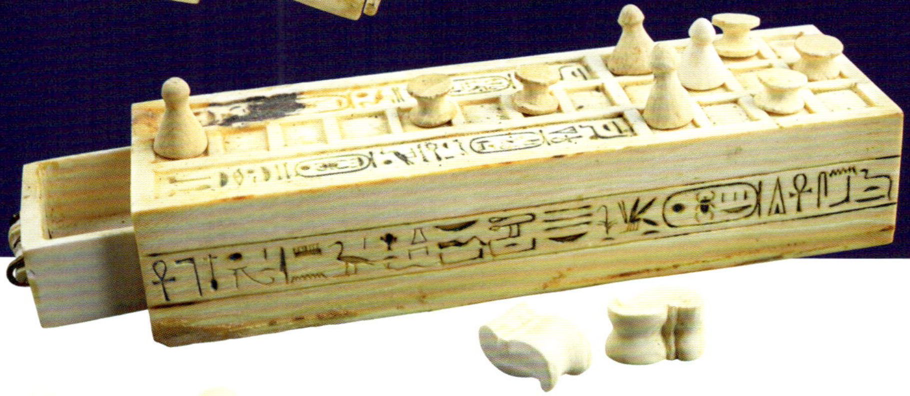

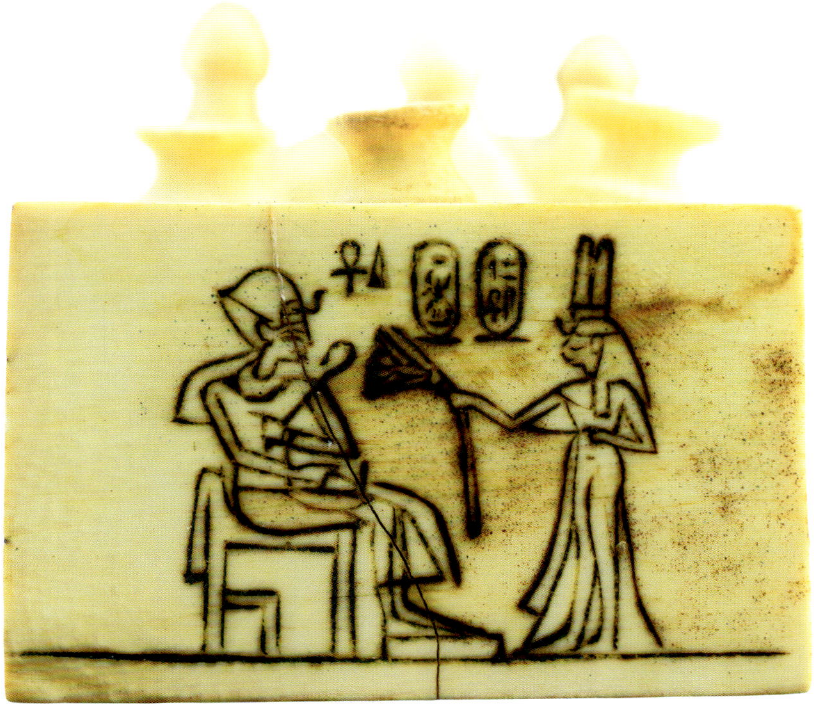

SMALL GAME BOARDS
Ivory
Length 13.5 cm, width 4.2 cm, height 2.8 cm
Carter 585r
Length 13.5 cm, width 4.1 cm, height 2.7 cm
Carter 393

Tutankhamun was given several game boards for his use in the afterlife. Each of the two here was carved from a single piece of ivory. The number and type of their divisions indicates that they were made for playing a game called twenty squares, on one side, and ***senet***, which has 30 squares, on the other. The squares are marked for good luck and bad luck, to help or hinder the players. Each board has a drawer for holding pieces of the game, including the pieces that were moved along the board and the knucklebones thrown to determine a player's moves. Several of these pieces were found in **No. 585r**. Others, belonging to **No. 393**, lay scattered in the Annexe and in the Antechamber. Parcheesi is a modern game that is similar in principle to the games played in ancient times.

Paintings and reliefs in tombs and funerary papyri show the games being played. Sometimes the deceased has an invisible opponent. Successfully maneuvering one's pieces on the board was like successfully navigating the dangers of the netherworld.

These boards were made for Tutankhamun, and contain his names. **No. 585r** also has an image of the king and queen on its drawer.

Tutankhamun was provided with ample stores of perfumed unguents for the afterlife (perhaps 350 liters in all), but thieves had stolen most of these valuable substances. They left behind their containers, which, although beautiful, would have been too readily identifiable to be sold or traded.

The bell-shaped vessel is carved and painted with buds, petals, and geometric patterns. The inscription gives the names and epithets of Tutankhamun and Ankhesenamun, and a wish for everlasting life.

The second vase is more elaborate and takes a form known as a ***situla***. This consists of a thinly carved vase set into a thicker, outer one which has been carved to reveal the inner. The lower portion of the outer vase imitates the sepals of a flower. The upper half shows two pairs of winged uraei whose wings stretch out to the king's cartouche. Between one pair of cobras is an ***ankh*** ("life"), and between the others is a ***nefer*** sign ("beauty"). Another portion of the design is a large writing of the king's throne name.

Both of these vessels retained some of their original contents.

VASES AND VESSELS

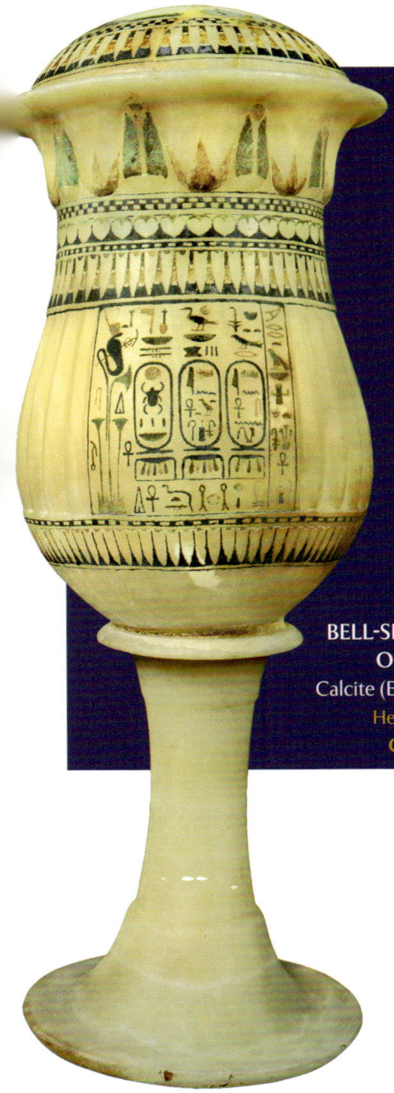

BELL-SHAPED VESSEL ON A STEM
Calcite (Egyptian alabaster)
Height 58.5 cm
Carter 520

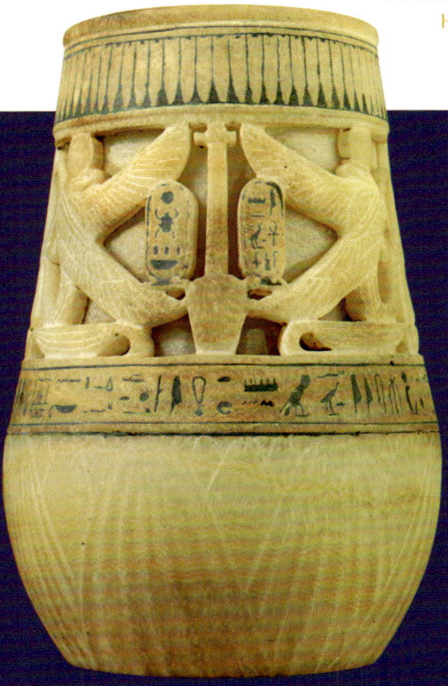

UNGUENT VASE
Calcite (Egyptian alabaster)
Height 25.8 cm
Carter 420

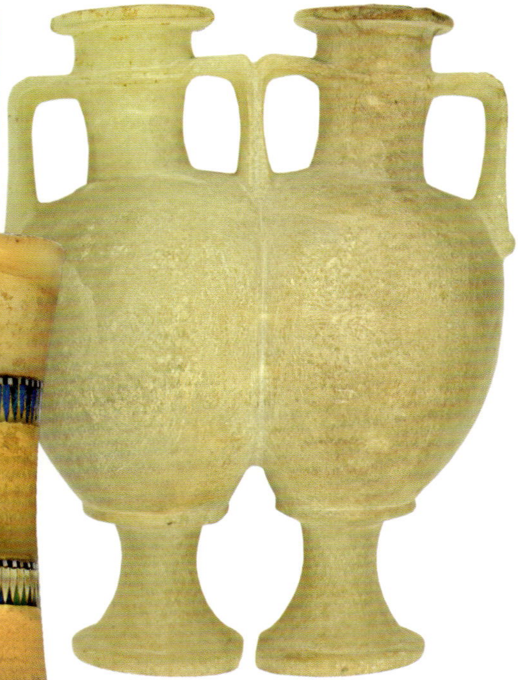

DOUBLE AMPHORA
Calcite (Egyptian alabaster)
Height 28.8 cm
Carter 417

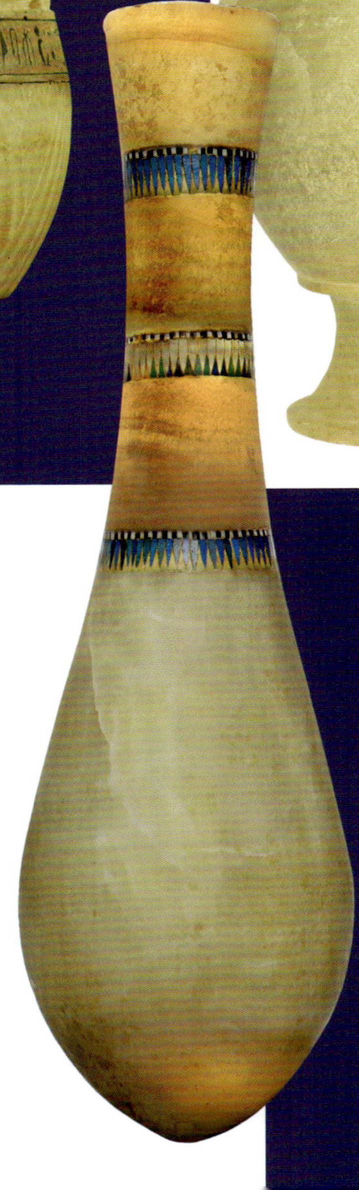

LONG-NECKED VASE
Calcite (Egyptian alabaster), faience
Height 62 cm
Carter 344

The tall, thin vase has inlay of faience and calcite (Egyptian alabaster), imitating necklaces or garlands of lotus petals below a geometric black-and-white band. The double vase is of a general sort known since the Predynastic Period. However, the use of amphoras (a foreign pottery shape) in the design indicates that this is a New Kingdom variation on the motif.

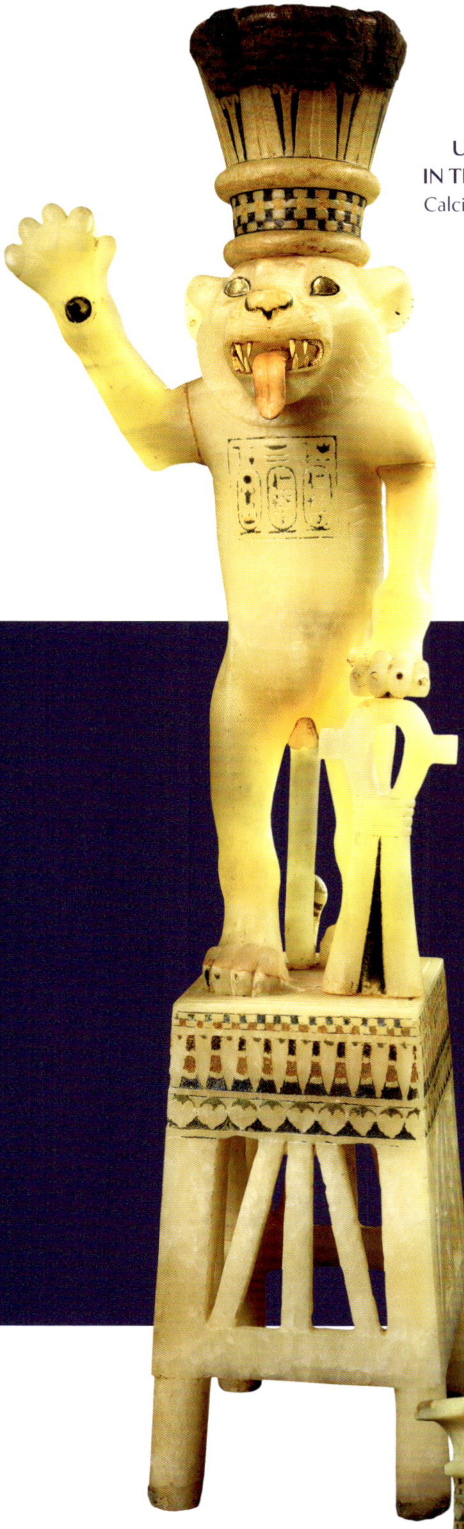

UNGUENT VESSEL IN THE FORM OF A LION
Calcite (Egyptian alabaster), paint, ivory
Height 60 cm
Carter 579

This hollow calcite (Egyptian alabaster) lion looks today to be more charming than fierce. Standing on his hind legs, the lion lays one front paw on a *sa* sign ("protection"). The other paw is, as Carter described it, "clawing the air in noble rage." A tongue made of ivory stained red hangs from the beast's open mouth. The names of Tutankhamun and Ankhesenamun appear on the chest.

The lion's floral crown had been dislodged, probably during one of the robberies when the unguent inside was drained away.

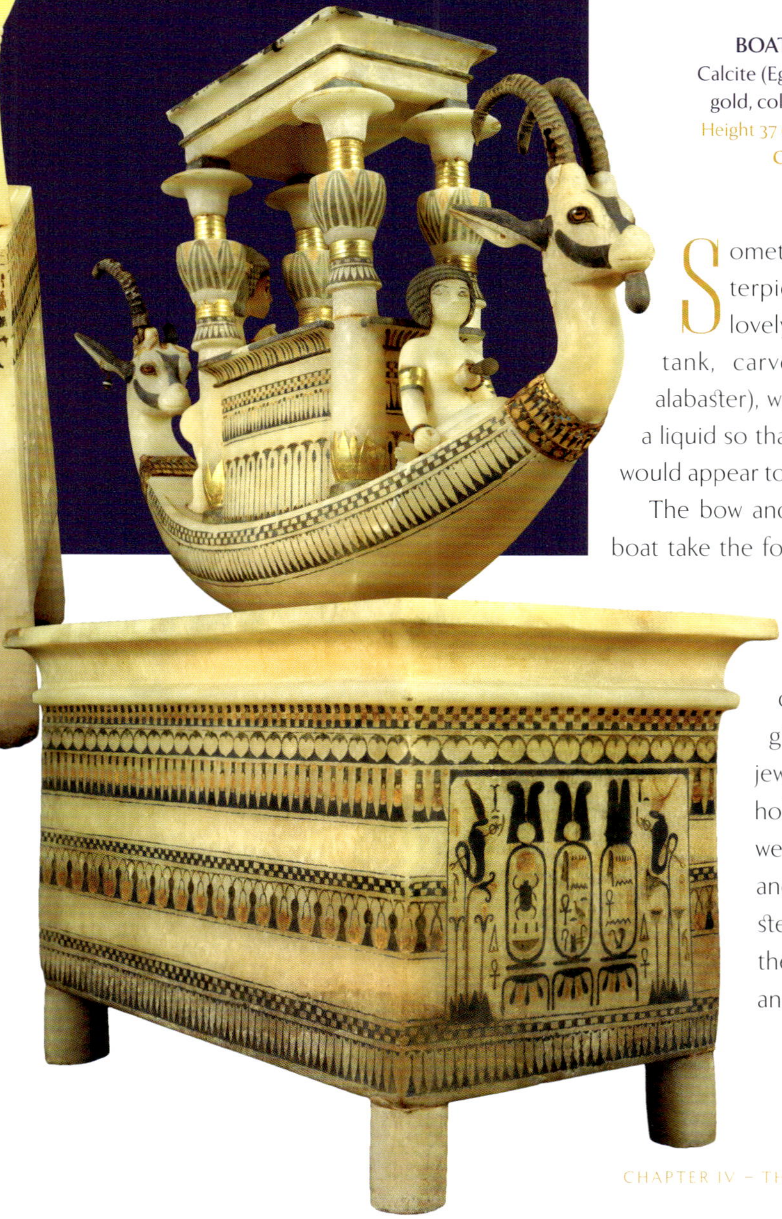

BOAT IN A TANK
Calcite (Egyptian alabaster), gold, colored glass, ivory
Height 37 cm, length 58.3 cm
Carter 578

Sometimes referred to as a "centerpiece," the purpose of this lovely object is unknown. The tank, carved of calcite (Egyptian alabaster), was probably meant to hold a liquid so that the boat that occupies it would appear to be floating.

The bow and stern decorations of the boat take the form of ibex heads with real horns. The shrine carried by the boat has columns that support a roof that covers four screen walls. A girl, naked except for some jewelry, sits before the shrine, holding a lotus. Figures like this were associated with fertility and, therefore, rebirth. At the stern, a woman, a dwarf, poles the boat along. The gods Bes and Ptah appeared as dwarfs.

These amulets represent ***khepesh*** swords, a scimitar-like weapon introduced from Syria during the New Kingdom. One full-sized ***khepesh***, and a child-sized one, were also found in the Annexe. These probably reflect the training that the young king would have been given with the expectation that he would someday have to lead his army into battle.

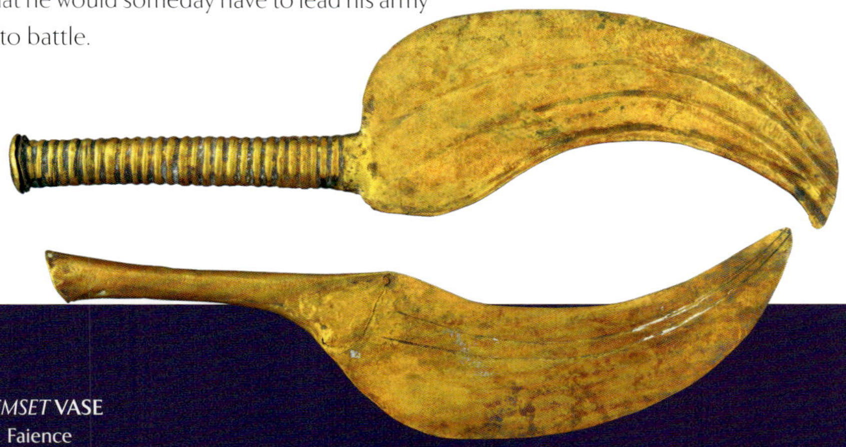

SCIMITAR (*KHEPESH*) AMULETS
Gold
Length 9 cm
Carter 620 (60)
Length 8.2 cm
Carter 620 (61)

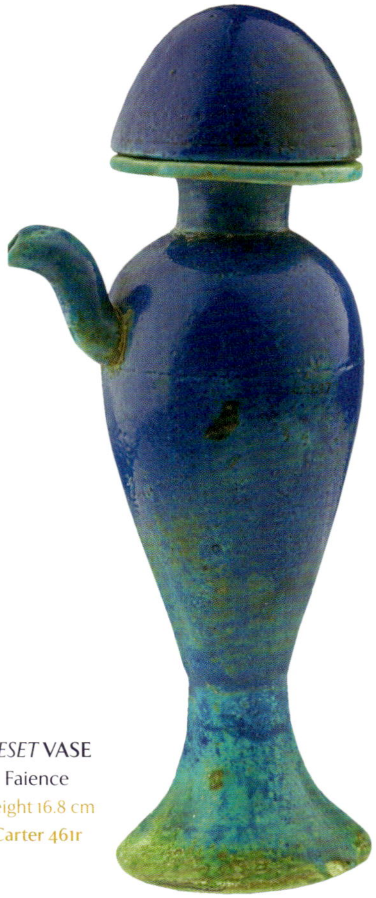

***HESET* VASE**
Faience
Height 16.8 cm
Carter 461r

The shape of the ***heset*** vase, like the dark blue faience one seen here, is used for the hieroglyph meaning "praise." One of the most popular of ritual vase forms, it was used in many ceremonies, including the Opening of the Mouth.

The bluish-green faience ***nemset*** vase is another common Egyptian form, but this one has an unusual feature. The spout takes the form of a feather, perhaps to invoke ***maat***, cosmic order, symbolized by an ostrich plume. Liquid poured from the vase would acquire special properties for ritual purposes.

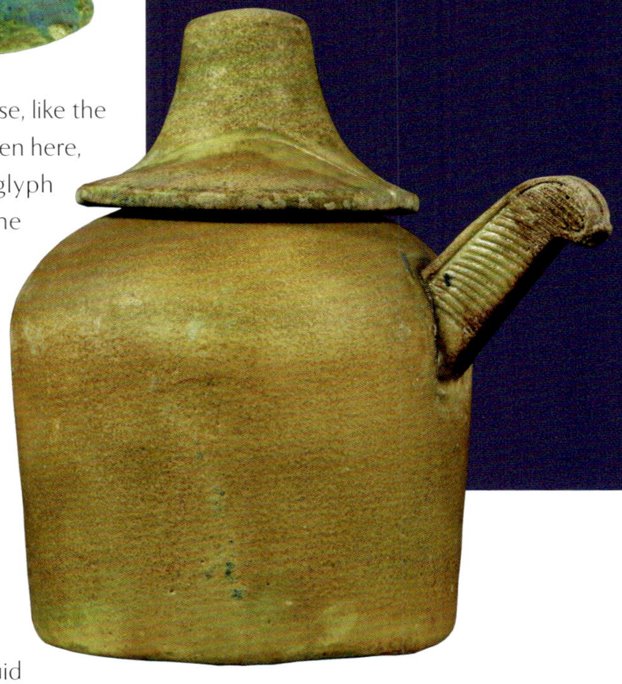

***NEMSET* VASE**
Faience
Height 14 cm
Carter 461b

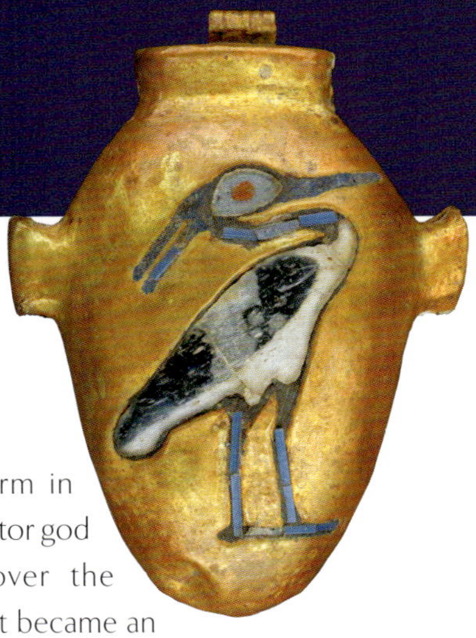

HEART AMULET INLAID WITH A HERON
Gold inlaid with glass
Height 5.8 cm
Carter 620 (67)

Found on the Annexe floor, this hollow gold pendant is inlaid with a heron in various colors of glass. The Egyptians called this kind of bird a ***benu***, a precursor of the phoenix. The Egyptian name comes from the word ***weben***, which means "to rise" and also connects the bird with the ***benben***, the mound of earth that arose from the watery chaos during the act of creation. Considered to be the form in which the creator god Atum flew over the watery abyss, it became an aspect of the soul of the sun god Re.

The back of the amulet has an inscription with Tutankhamun's throne name. Thus associated with the ***benu*** bird, the king might be eternally re-created.

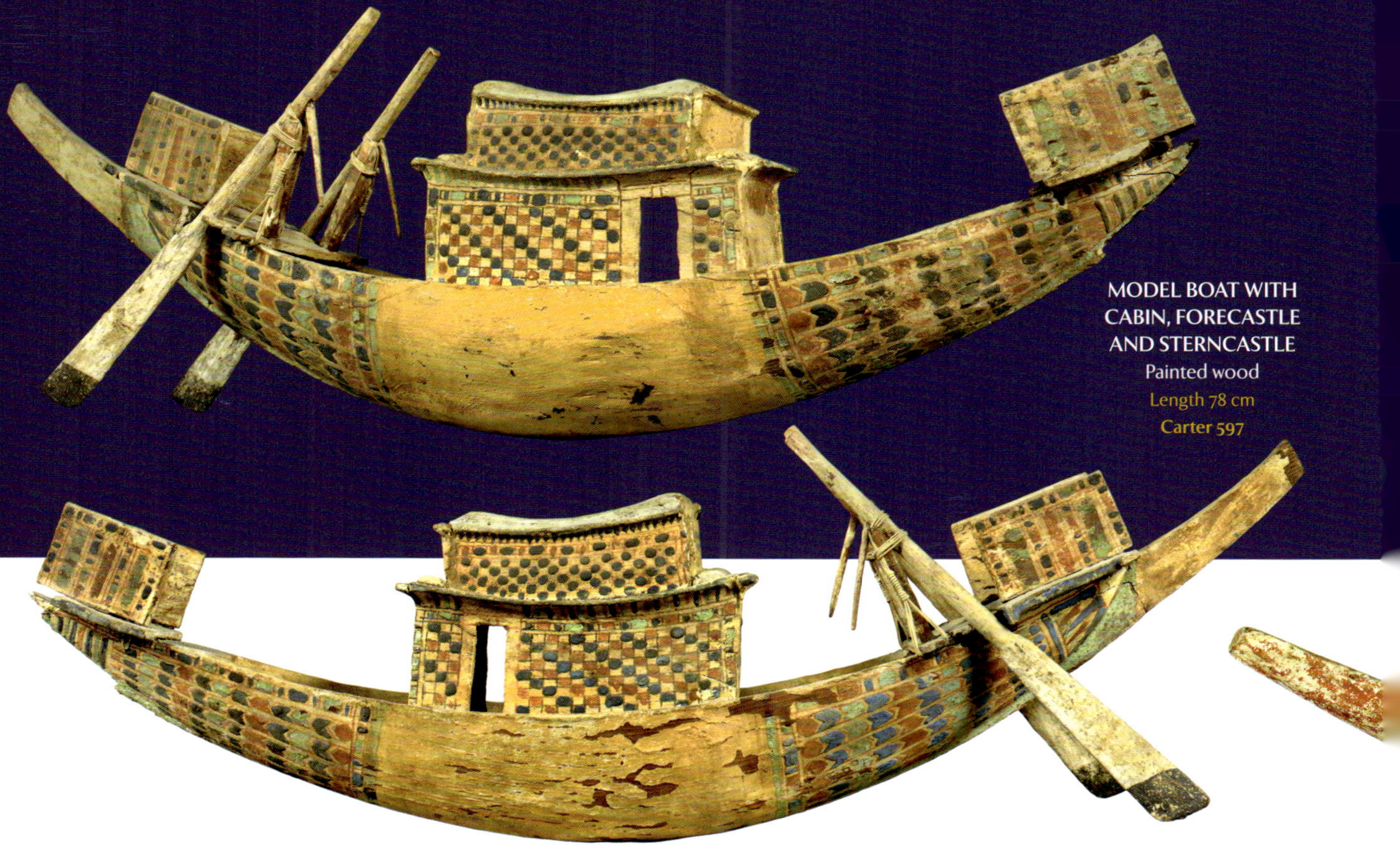

MODEL BOAT WITH CABIN, FORECASTLE AND STERNCASTLE
Painted wood
Length 78 cm
Carter 597

MODEL BOATS

These are some of the 17 model boats found in the Annexe. One, No. 597, has a large cabin with a double roof. At one time, there were columns with lily capitals forward of the cabin, and columns with papyrus buds abaft, to represent Lower and Upper Egypt.

Like many other Egyptian boats of this period, it had a rudder at port and starboard (left and right). Geometric and floral patterns ornament the cabin, hull, and kiosks.

The other two boats are generally similar, if simpler, but their steering gear consists of a single rudder mounted at the stern.

The last watercraft represented is a raft made of bundles of papyrus stalks. This was probably the earliest type of boat used on the Nile. It inspired the form of many divine boats, including the solar barque, and skiffs appear in depictions of ritual hunting and fishing in the marshes, in which the king defeated the forces of chaos in the form of birds, fish, or hippopotamuses (see **Carter No. 275c**). Like the desert, swamps were dangerous places on the fringes of the ordered universe. Papyrus boats were also used to navigate netherworldly waters.

These models served the same purpose, and some would allow the king to sail the sky in the solar barque as well.

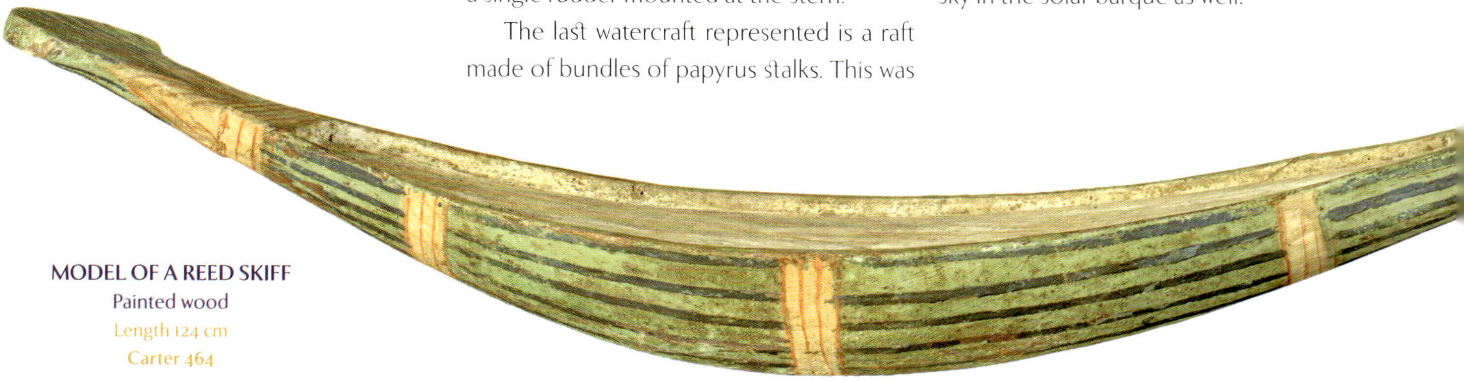

MODEL OF A REED SKIFF
Painted wood
Length 124 cm
Carter 464

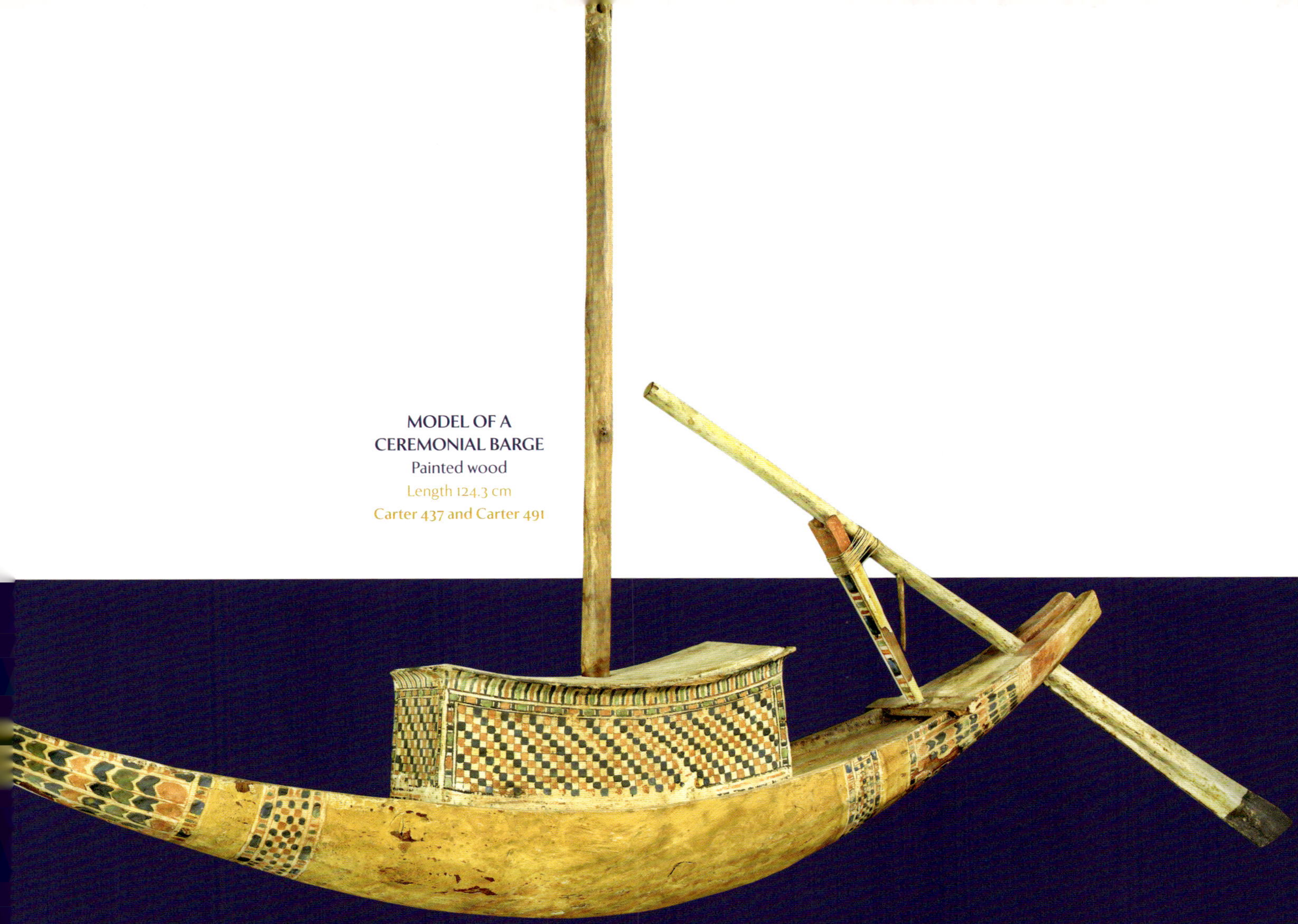

MODEL OF A CEREMONIAL BARGE
Painted wood
Length 124.3 cm
Carter 437 and Carter 491

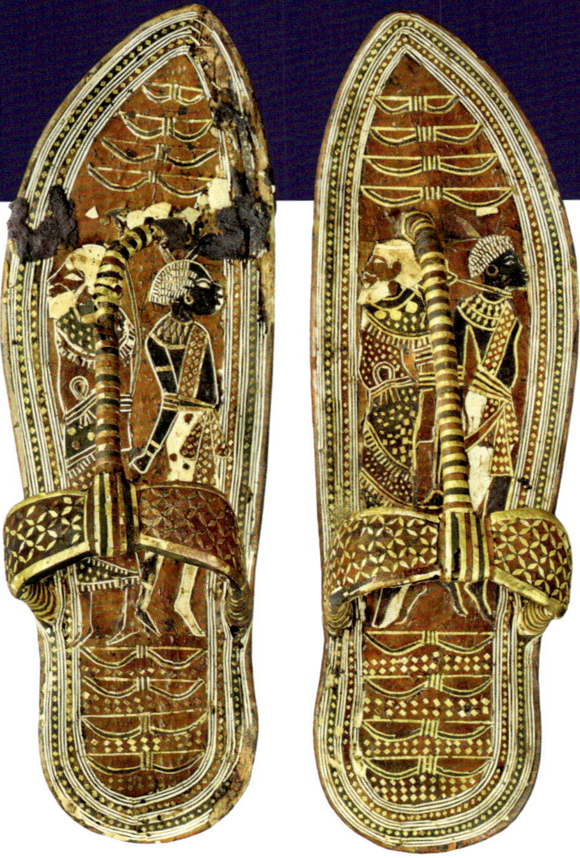

SANDALS WITH ENEMY FIGURES
Wood, bark, leather, gold
Length 28 cm
Carter 397

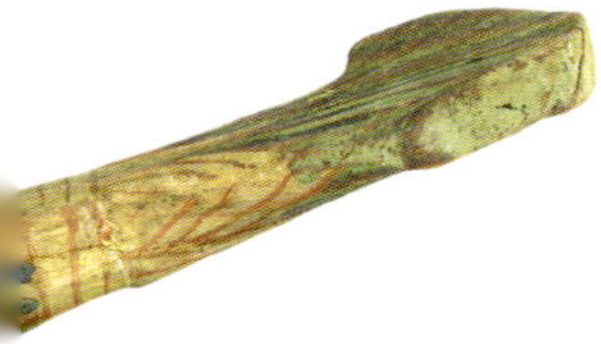

Many kinds of footwear were found in the tomb. Some were ceremonial, meant for the mummy. Others were simple papyrus sandals. This pair is made of wood with elaborate marquetry inlay of leather, gold, and bark. The upper face of each sole is decorated with the image of a Nubian and Asiatic prisoner, with their arms pinned behind their backs and a rope around their necks. Four archer's bows above and four below them signify them as the "Nine Bows," Egypt's traditional enemies.

By wearing these sandals, Tutankhamun would crush the images, and symbolically defeat his foes, but they show no sign of wear.

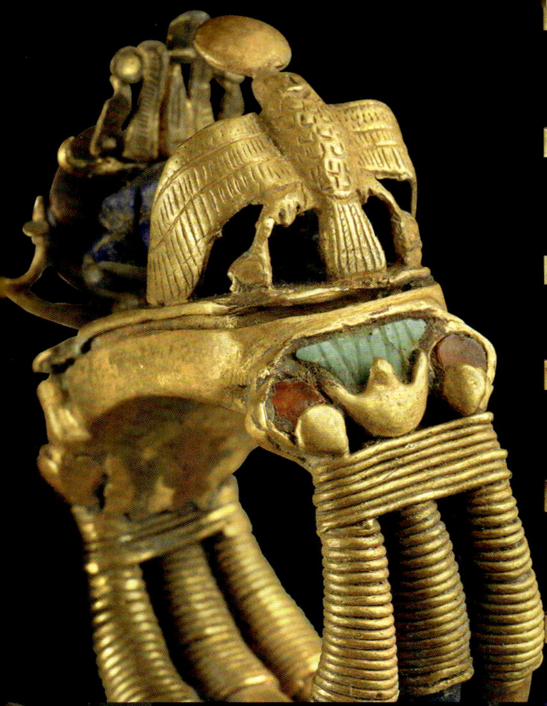
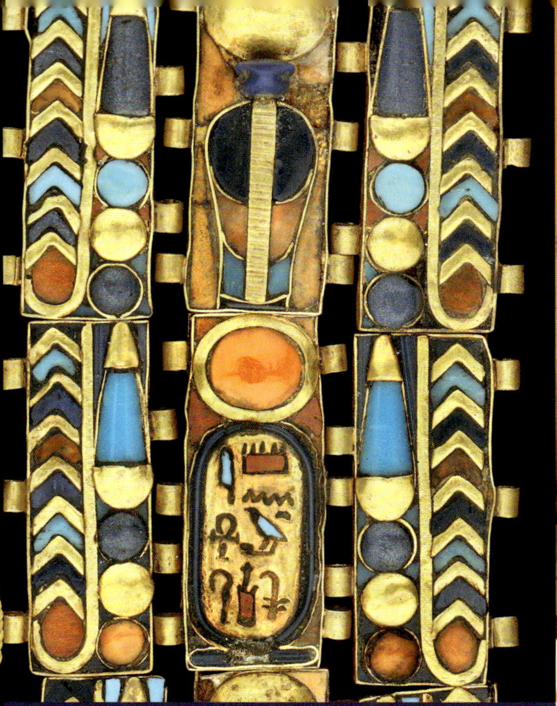
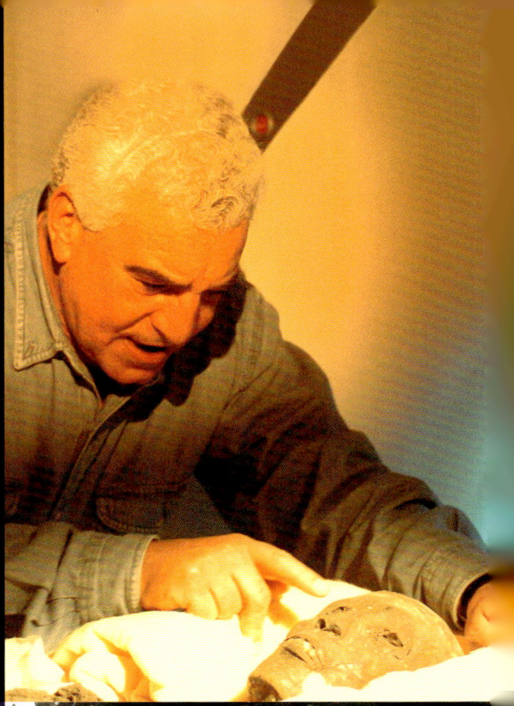
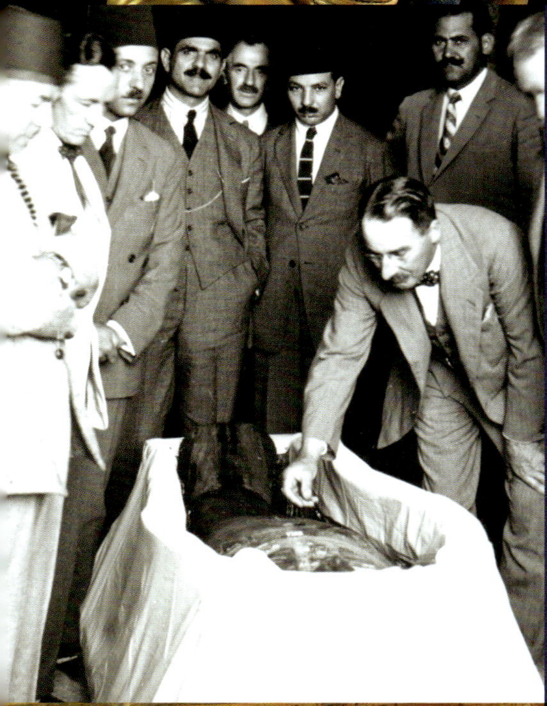

CHAPTER V

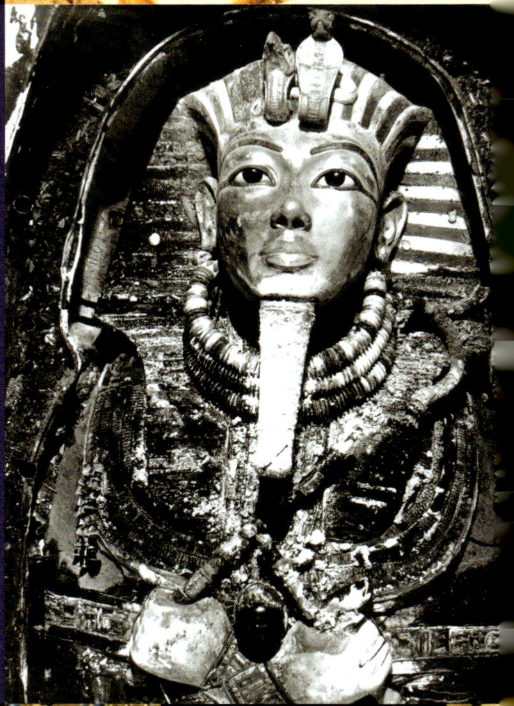
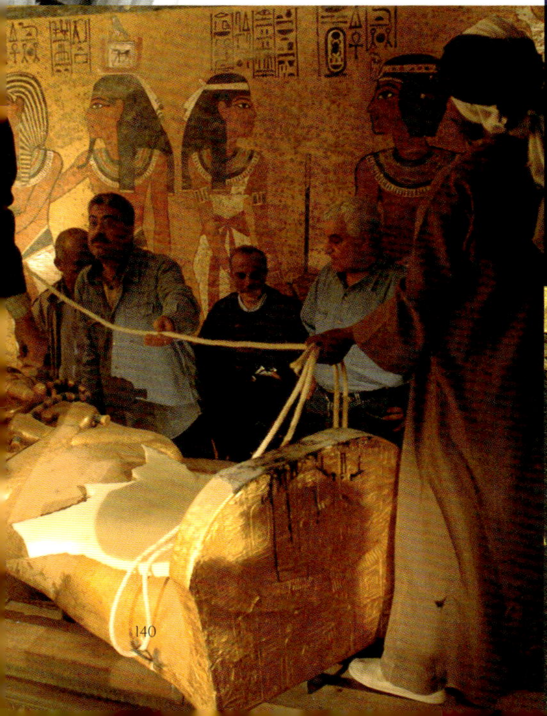
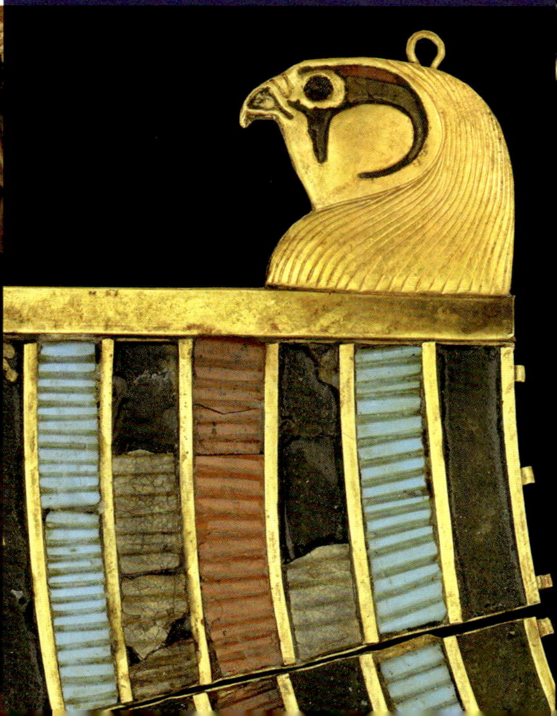
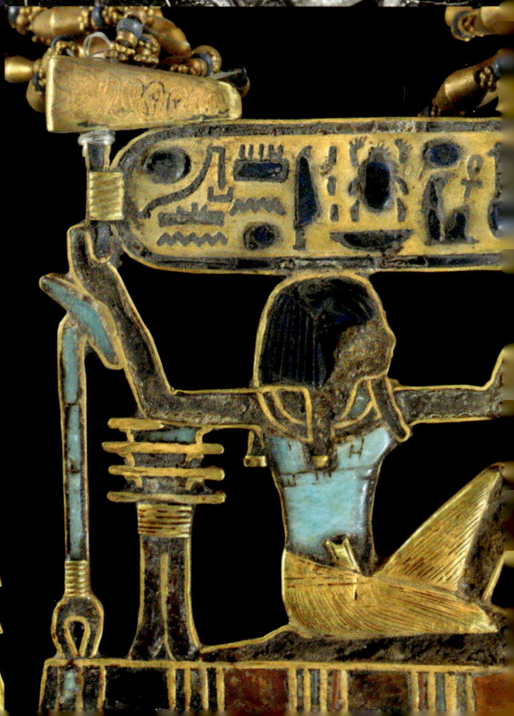

TUTANKH-AMUN'S MUMMY

HOWARD CARTER AND THE MUMMY

Carter's team had lifted the lid of the sarcophagus, revealing the nest of coffins, which had also been opened, one by one. Now, on 10th November, 1925, it was time to remove the lid of the third coffin, which proved to be the innermost – and made of solid gold. They had already found evidence that warned them not to expect Tutankhamun's mummy to be pristinely preserved. Humidity had damaged the linen shroud covering the third coffin. But not even the solid gold coffin could have prepared them to find the stunning gold mask that encased the king's head. This object, magnificent though it was, presented a considerable problem. During the burial, unguents had been poured over the king's body. Because these had hardened, the mummy was in effect glued to not only the mask, but also to the coffin. The second and third coffins were also stuck together. Carter's first attempted solution was to remove the coffins from the tomb and place them outside, where the sun might warm the unguents enough to soften them.

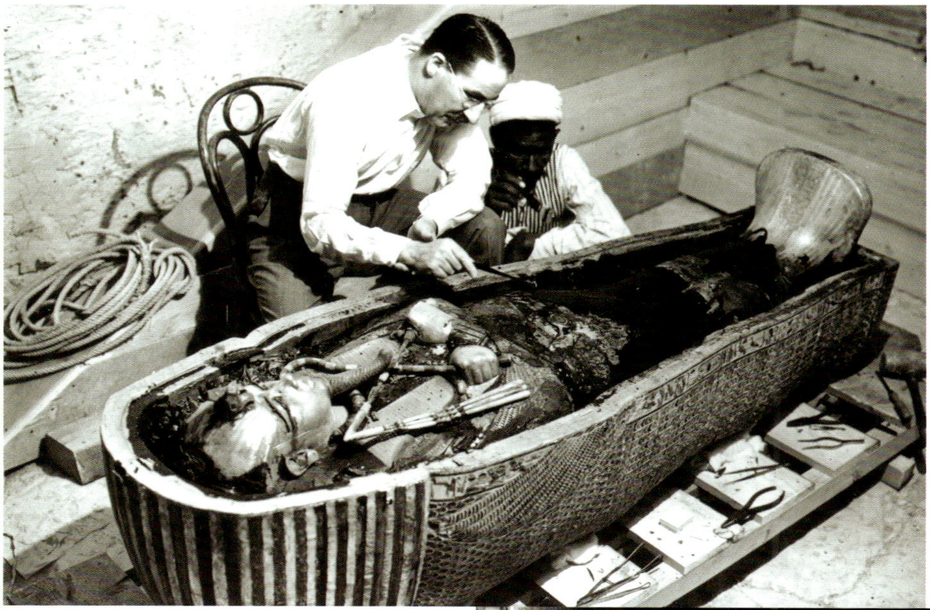

Carter patiently removing the hardened resin and unguents from the innnermost gold coffin.
Harry Burton / Griffith Institute

When this failed to work even after the temperature reached 65 degrees Celsius (149 degrees Fahrenheit), artificial heat was applied. Protecting the surfaces with zinc plates and wet towels, Carter's team used paraffin wax lamps to heat the contents to 500 degrees Celsius (932 degrees Fahrenheit). Eventually, this allowed them to separate the coffins.

Inspection of the mummy began on the next day in the tomb of Seti II (KV 15). In addition to officials from the Antiquities Service and other notable attendees, two experts were on hand: anthropologist Douglas Derry and Professor Salah Bey Hamdi of the Faculty of Medicine in Alexandria. To make it possible for Derry to cut through the linen shroud that was stuck to the mummy, liquid paraffin wax was poured over it. The outer wrappings came away in large pieces, and what lay beneath was in even worse condition. Alfred Lucas, the chemist, suggested that some manner of spontaneous combustion had been responsible for reducing the linen to something like soot. Over the course of four days, Carter and Pierre Lacau, head of the Antiquities Service, carefully removed the bandages, revealing 150 amulets and other jewelry that the embalmers had inserted during the wrapping. The placement of these objects, which were perhaps those most essential for the king's transition to and existence in the afterlife, was carefully recorded.

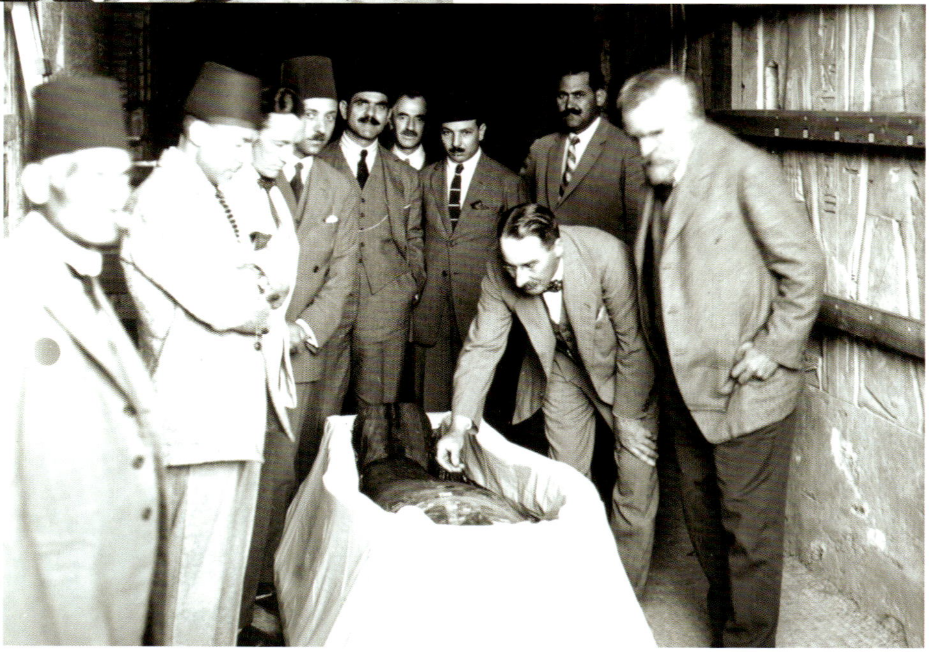

Carter showing his visitors from the Egyptian government the innermost gold coffin.
Harry Burton/Griffith Institute

THE JEWELRY OF THE MUMMY

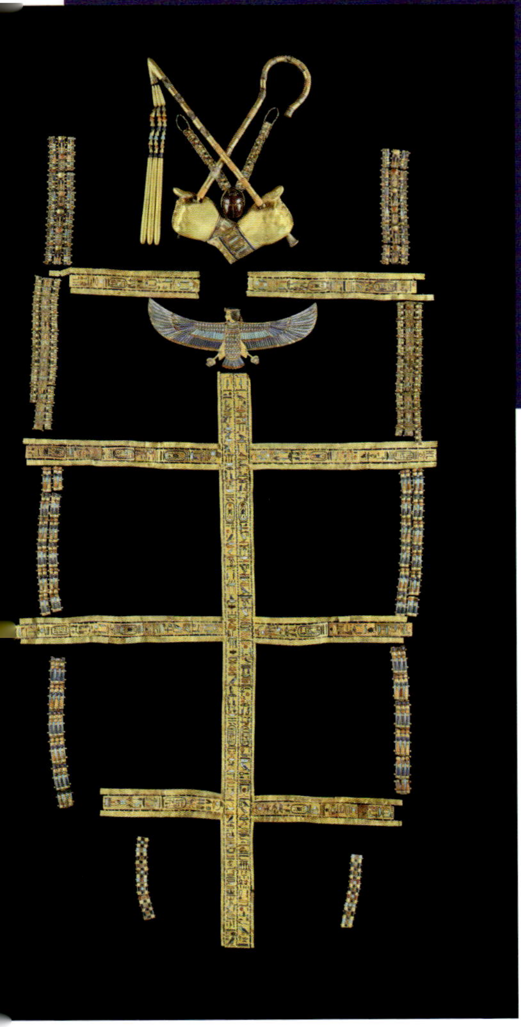

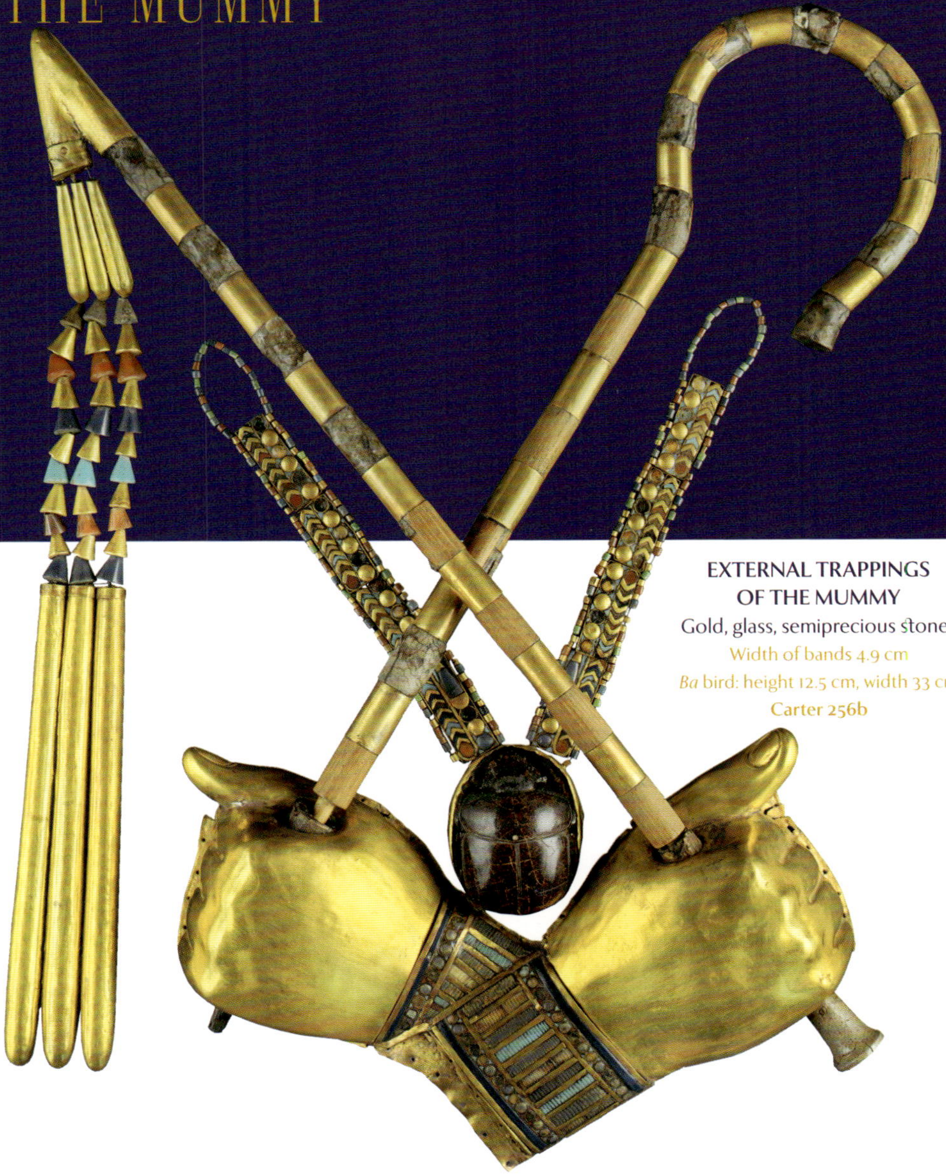

EXTERNAL TRAPPINGS OF THE MUMMY
Gold, glass, semiprecious stones
Width of bands 4.9 cm
Ba bird: height 12.5 cm, width 33 cm
Carter 256b

The mask alone was not enough to provide for the king's protection in the afterlife. Embalmers had sewn additional, beautiful objects onto the outer linen bandages, each with its own special purpose.

There were eight golden mummy bands, imitating in precious metal bands of linen that, on a non-royal mummy, would have held the final layer of bandages in place. Hieroglyphs of colored glass inlay give the names of the king and protective spells spoken by a variety of gods, including the four Sons of Horus (guardians of the organs removed during mummification), Anubis (god of embalming), and Nut (the sky goddess).

The texts on the bands, Carter noticed, were not always in the order they should have been. He also discovered that the cartouches on the bands had been cut out and replaced with plain gold, but that the artisans had missed one of the cartouches. This did not give one of Tutankhamun's names, but instead the name "Ankhkheperure," his predecessor. These bands seemed to have been appropriated from Ankhkheperure's burial equipment for Tutankhamun's use.

Also sewn onto the mummy wrappings was a pair of hands of burnished gold. Wearing wristlets made of colored glass and carnelian, these hands grasp the crook and flail, which are made from silver cores covered with bands of glass and gold. Glass, gold, and carnelian make up the beads of the flail.

The last element of the outer trappings was a bird with an exquisitely rendered human face, representing the ***ba***, or "soul," which could go forth from the tomb. The Egyptians believed that to achieve everlasting life, the ***ba*** had to be reunited with the body and with the ***ka***, or life-force. The gold pectoral has glass inlay to imitate carnelian, turquoise, and lapis lazuli. The bird's claws grasp ***shen*** signs, symbolic of eternity.

COLLARS

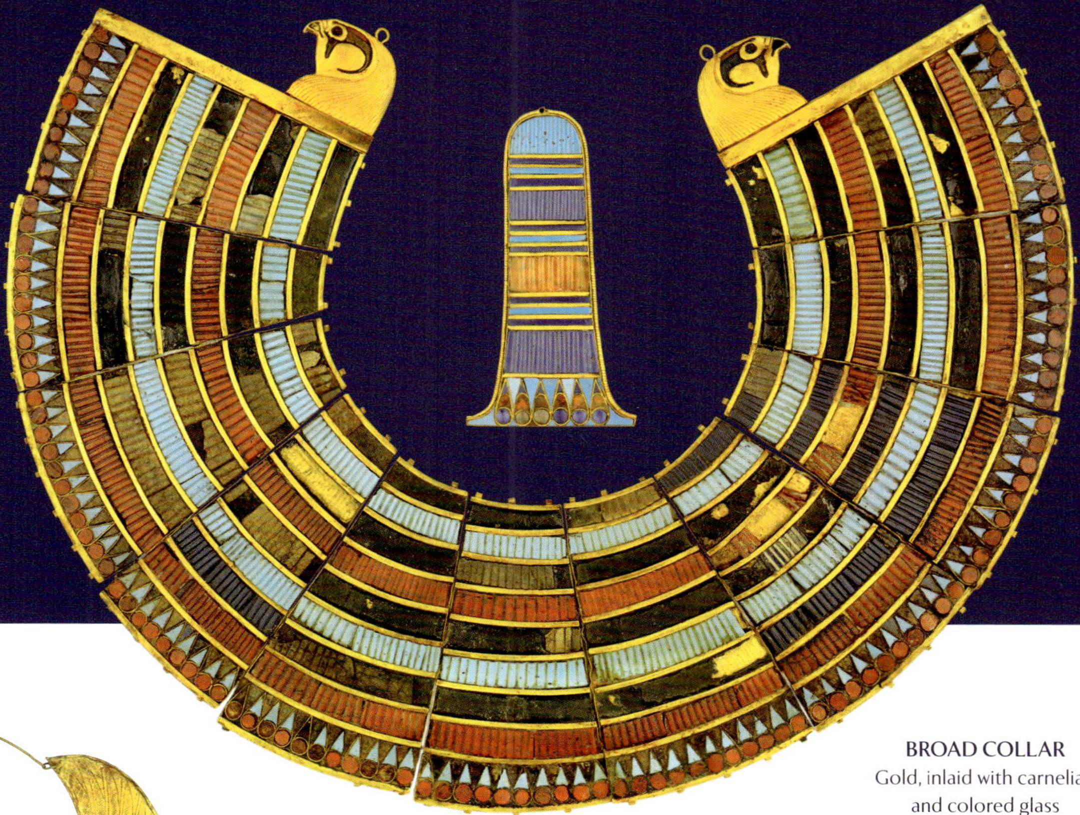

BROAD COLLAR
Gold, inlaid with carnelian and colored glass
Width 35.5 cm
Carter 256aa(1)

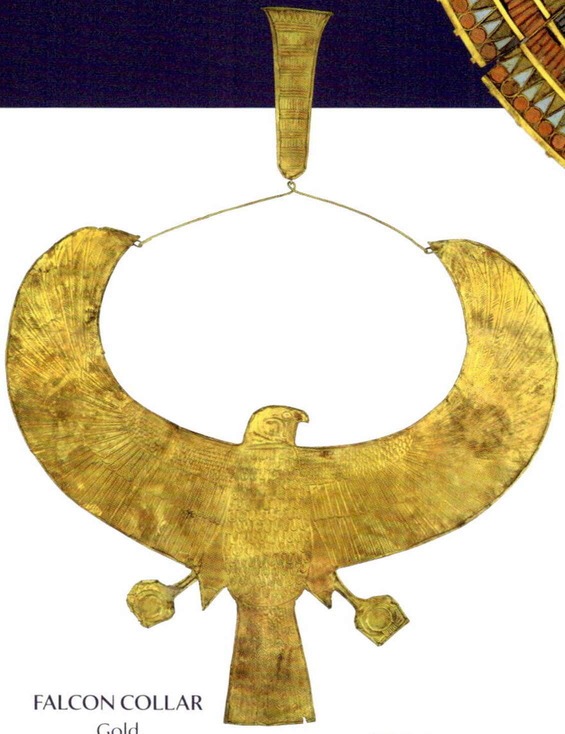

FALCON COLLAR
Gold
Width 30 cm
Carter 256t

The embalmers placed several flexible collars among the bandages of Tutankhamun's mummy. These pieces of jewelry, known as ***wesekh*** ("broad") collars, appear being worn by both sexes, and by humans and divinities, throughout the pharaonic period. Probably modeled after garlands of real floral elements, they were worn mostly for ritual or other official occasions.

This particular collar was not found on the king's chest as one might expect. It had been crushed and folded across the king's lower thighs and knees. It is made of 11 separate plaques held together by threads strung through loops. A gold falcon head, inlaid with glass, forms each end of the collar. From tiny loops soldered to these falcon heads, a gold wire held an inlaid counterpoise in the form of a lotus blossom.

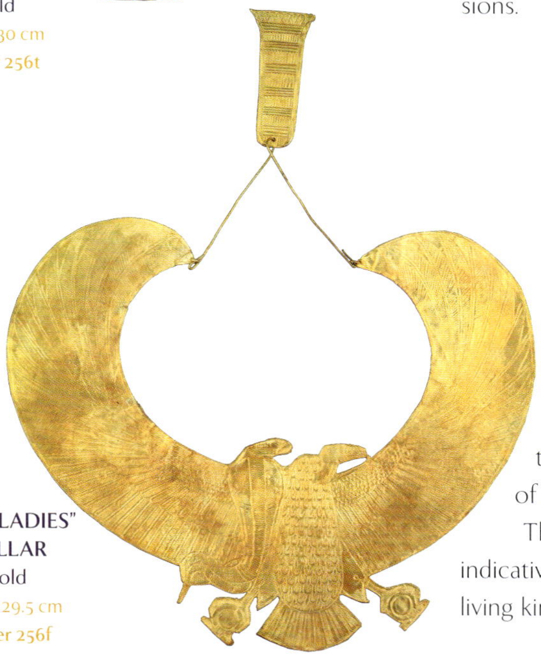

"TWO LADIES" COLLAR
Gold
Width 29.5 cm
Carter 256f

The two collars here, made of thin sheet gold, represent many similar pieces given to the mummy. Detailed chasing decorates the front surfaces. Gold wires were threaded through tiny holes in the wingtips, allowing each piece to have a counterpoise in the shape of elongated lotus blossoms.

The falcon head on the first collar is indicative of the god Horus, with whom the living king especially was identified. One of the oldest of Egypt's many gods, Horus was a deity of both sky and sun. He was identified as either the son of Osiris or of Re.

The second collar unites the cobra of Wadjet with the vulture of her Upper Egyptian counterpart, Nekhbet. These goddesses, known jointly as the "Two Ladies," symbolized the king's rule over a united Egypt, which the Egyptians referred to as the Two Lands, namely the Delta and Nile Valley. The 18th Dynasty originated at Thebes, in Upper Egypt, making Nekhbet a favorite of its kings.

RINGS

One of these rings was found, with four others, wrapped against the mummy's right hand. The other, essentially identical, ring was found in the Antechamber, wrapped in a shawl with yet other rings and placed into Box 44. The triple shanks of these rings are made of resin covered in gold foil. Gold wire has been wound around the end of each shank, which was then bound together with more gold wire.

The bezels are in the form of a cartouche, atop which are dark blue glass scarabs with elaborate gold headdresses. One end of each bezel has a barque with solar and lunar disks; at the other end is a falcon surmounted by a sun disk, likely meant to represent the god Re-Horakhty. The ring from the mummy's hand has inlay of feldspar and red and blue glass and has an inscription beneath the bezel: "the good god, Lord of the Two Lands, Nebkheperure, beloved of Thoth." Thoth, god of wisdom and writing, was associated with the moon.

The king likely wore both of these rings during his short lifetime.

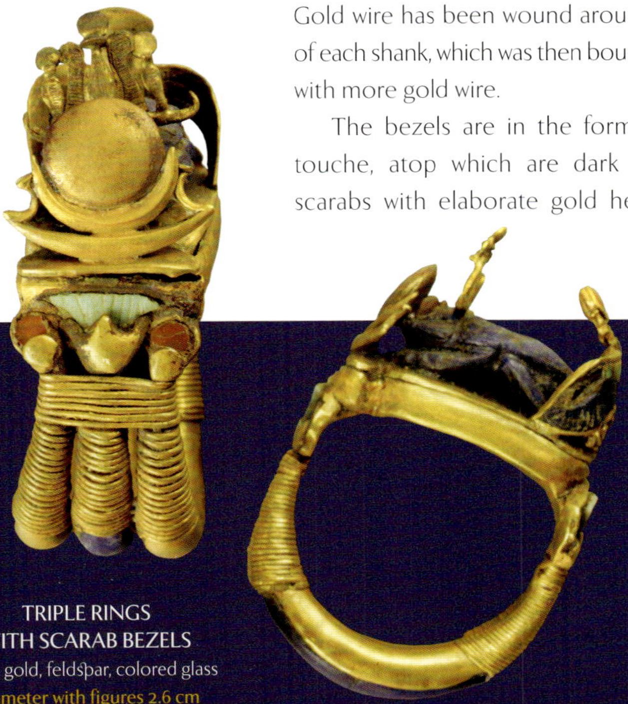

TRIPLE RINGS WITH SCARAB BEZELS
Resin, gold, feldspar, colored glass
Diameter with figures 2.6 cm
Carter 256ff5 (left), Carter 44i (right)

BRACELET

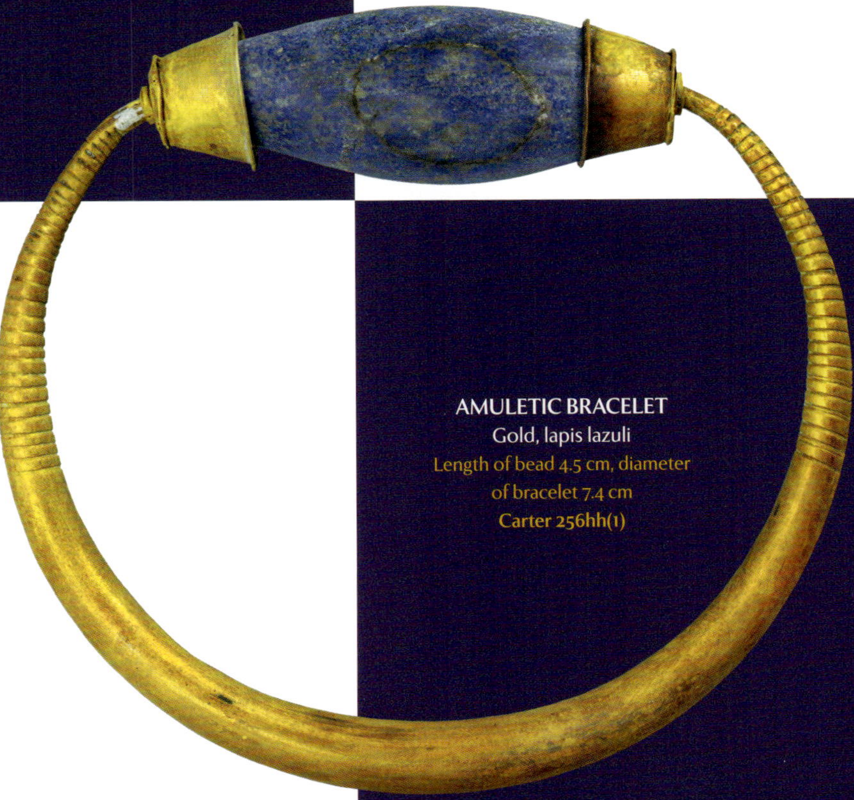

This is one of three gold bracelets found on the chest of the mummy. The barrel-shaped bead mounted on the bracelet is lapis lazuli. The Egyptians particularly prized the deep blue color of lapis lazuli, which was imported from the north, probably ultimately deriving from Afghanistan, where the stone is mined even today. In antiquity one of the Indus Valley civilizations controlled the region. The stone would have made its way through trade routes that passed through Mesopotamia and the Levant.

AMULETIC BRACELET
Gold, lapis lazuli
Length of bead 4.5 cm, diameter of bracelet 7.4 cm
Carter 256hh(1)

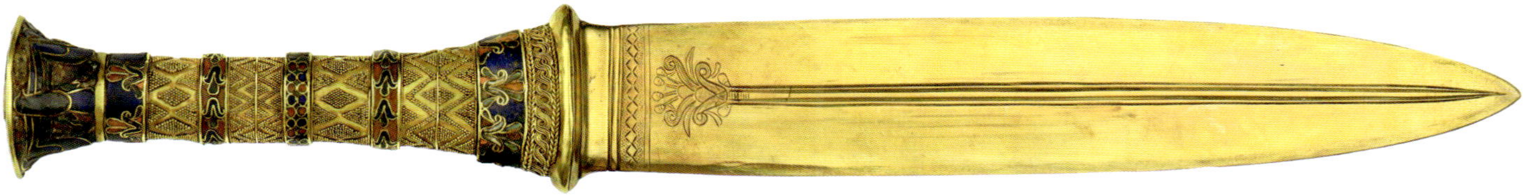

CEREMONIAL DAGGERS AND SHEATHS

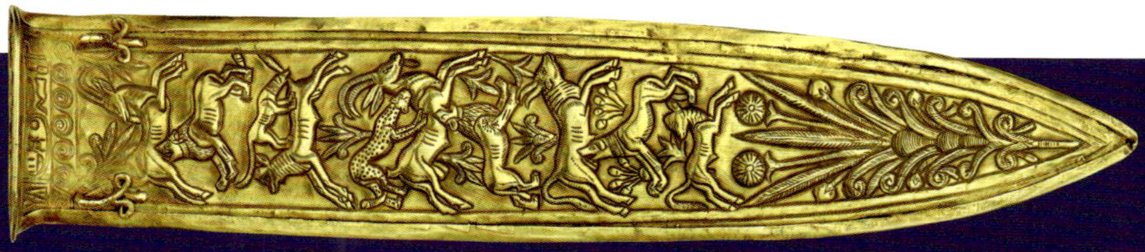

CEREMONIAL DAGGERS AND SHEATHS
Iron, gold, glass, semiprecious stones, rock crystal
Gold dagger: length 31.8 cm, sheath: length 20.6 cm
Iron dagger: length 34.2 cm, sheath: length 22.2 cm
Carter 256dd (gold), Carter 256k (iron)

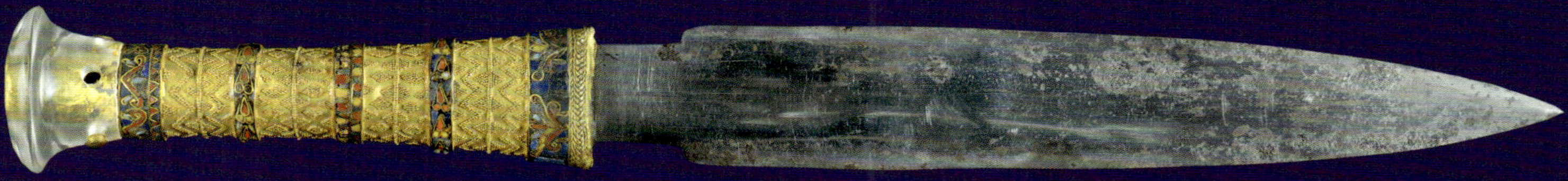

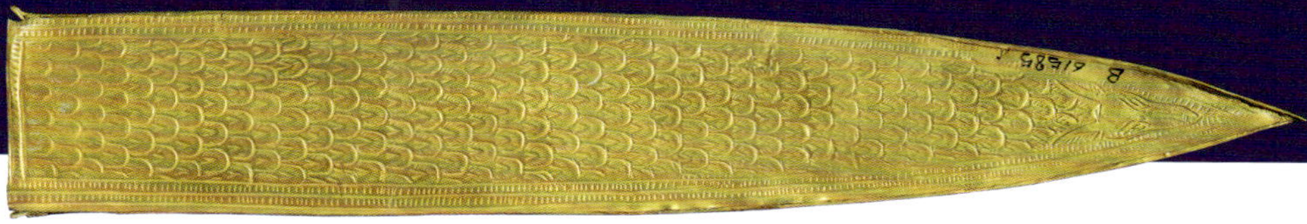

Unlike some of his ancestors, such as Thutmose III, "the Napoleon of ancient Egypt," or some of his later successors, such as Rameses the Great, Tutankhamun does not have the reputation of a warrior king. Nonetheless, his burial equipment included many weapons – slings, clubs, throwsticks, boomerangs, bows, arrows, knives, and swords. Some of these were made small, obviously for a child, so it seems that the boy-king began his training in the arts of war and hunting early. It is even possible that he led the army into battle, despite being only about 19 at the time of his death.

These weapons might have been for use in the netherworld, as well. Embalmers included two daggers among his mummy wrappings. A knife with a gold blade – too soft to have been used in life – had been slipped beneath the golden girdle hung around his hips. A knife with an iron blade lay at his right thigh. These might have been gifts from foreign kings. The decorative motifs have foreign influences. Whether made in Egypt or abroad, both are spectacular examples of the jeweler's art.

The solid gold dagger is stylish and its craftsmen clearly had an outstanding sense of beauty I particularly admire. An Aegean influence is clearly evident in the running spiral at the base of the hilt. The top of the pommel has been given the king's cartouches surrounded by a ring of stylized lilies. The gold blade, intended for show and ceremony rather than for stabbing, bears on each side an engraved floral and diamond pattern. Its sheath is elaborately decorated on one side with a pattern of scales, a band of lilies, and the head of a canine. A hunting scene with more foreign influences, decorates the other. An inscription on the top of the sheath also gives the king's throne name and titles: "the good god, lord of might, Nebkheperure, given life."

The second dagger seems more utilitarian, with its iron blade, but iron was rare. Made of meteoritic iron, this is one of only a very few objects made of this metal known from Egypt during this period. Like the gold dagger, its hilt is ornamented with cloisonné-work and granulation. The pommel is made of rock crystal. Again, the sheath is gold, with palmette and rope patterns on the front, while the back has a feather pattern and jackal's head. The gift of an iron dagger is mentioned in a letter from the king of Mitanni to Amenhotep III, found at Amarna. One must wonder if this could be the same weapon.

NECKLACE

Much of the jewelry included in the mummy's wrappings was probably made particularly for that very purpose. However, Carter noticed that this pendant, and two others found near it on the king's chest, show signs of wear.

The body of the falcon was formed as an openwork cage of gold that encloses a green stone, which could be a kind of chalcedony. The gold head has its details, such as the eyes and facial markings, chased into the surface. Carnelian is used as an inlay for the solar disk atop the falcon's head. The head of the bird is most unusual, being presented in a frontal rather than profile view. Cloisons of gold with inlays of lapis lazuli and carnelian create the impression of feathers of its outspread wings. The tail is given a coordinating design in the form of chevrons.

The pendant hangs from an intricate gold chain that ends in linen thread. From the thread is a counterpoise, the weight of which balances the pendant so that it will hang properly when worn. The counterpoise is made of two carnelian beads and a carnelian heart, partly enclosed in gold. The heart is inlaid on each side with the king's throne name guarded by uraei of dark blue, light blue, and red glass.

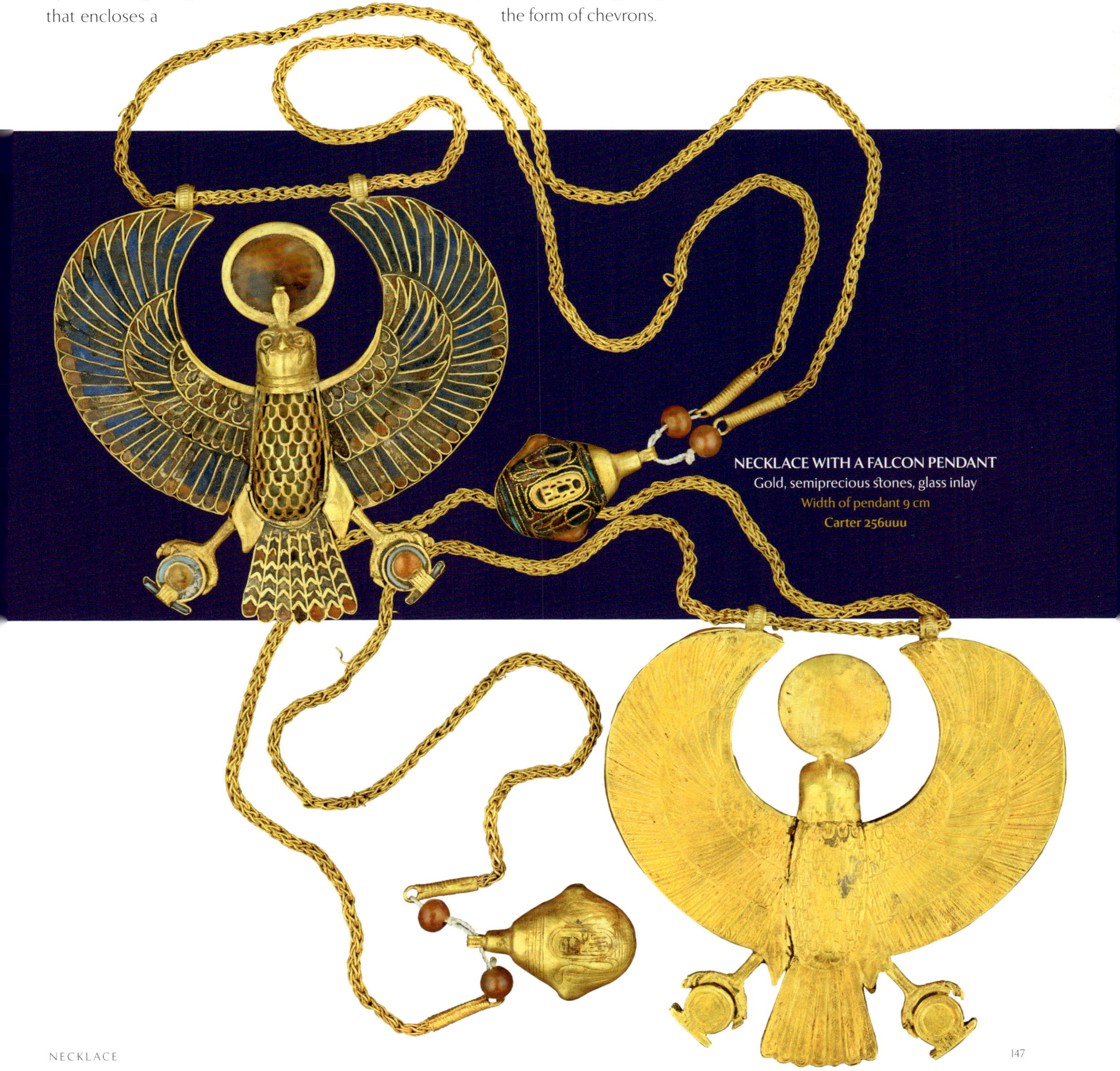

NECKLACE WITH A FALCON PENDANT
Gold, semiprecious stones, glass inlay
Width of pendant 9 cm
Carter 256uuu

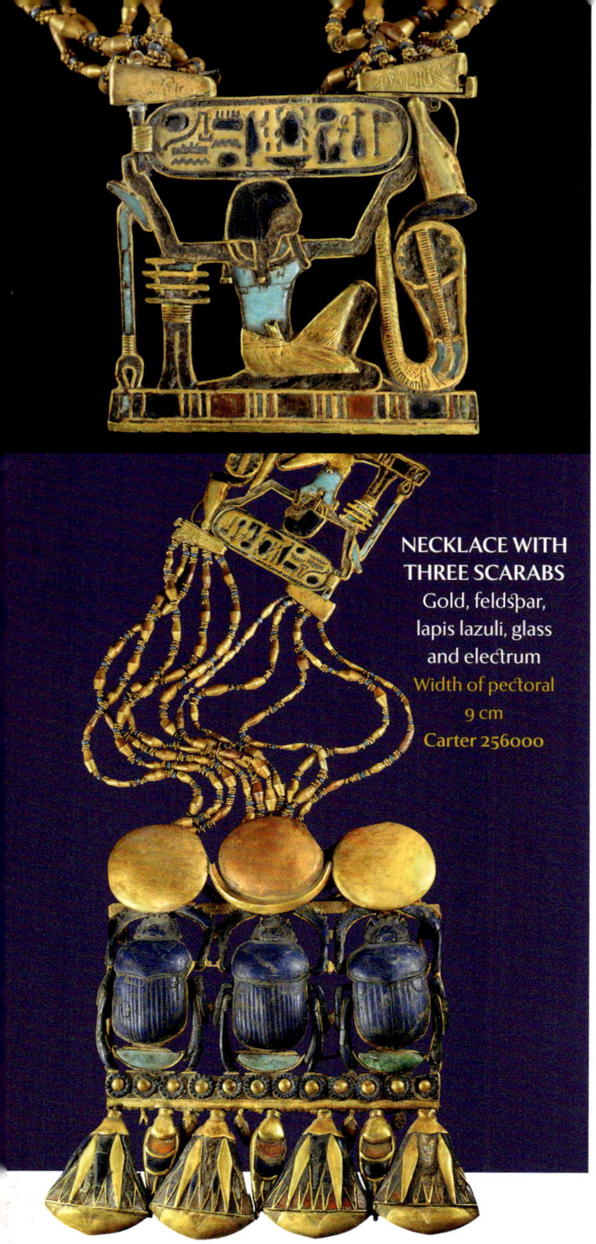

NECKLACE WITH THREE SCARABS
Gold, feldspar, lapis lazuli, glass and electrum
Width of pectoral 9 cm
Carter 256000

Found draped around the king's neck, this necklace suspended its pectoral at the center of his chest. It consists of three scarab beetles of lapis lazuli atop three ***neb*** baskets inlaid with green feldspar. The two outer scarabs support solar disks of gold on their forelegs, while the middle scarab supports the lunar disk and crescent of electrum, an alloy of gold and silver. Together these can be read as the king's throne name, Nebkheperure: the ***neb*** baskets, the scarabs representing the god Kheper, and the solar disks for Re. (Ordinarily, the king's throne name was written with a single beetle, three strokes indicating the plural, and the solar disk.) The baskets sit on a bar ornamented with rosettes, while below hang lotus flowers and buds inlaid with colored glass.

Ten strings of gold beads attach the counterpoise, which was found at the nape of the king's neck. A kneeling god raises a cartouche that reads, "the good god, Nebkheperure, chosen by Amun-Re." Before him is a uraeus wearing the white crown of the south; before him is a ***djed*** pillar and a ***was*** scepter, which signify stability and dominion, respectively. The kneeling god could be Heh, the god of eternity, but it could also be Shu, the air god, who also appears in this pose to hold up the sky.

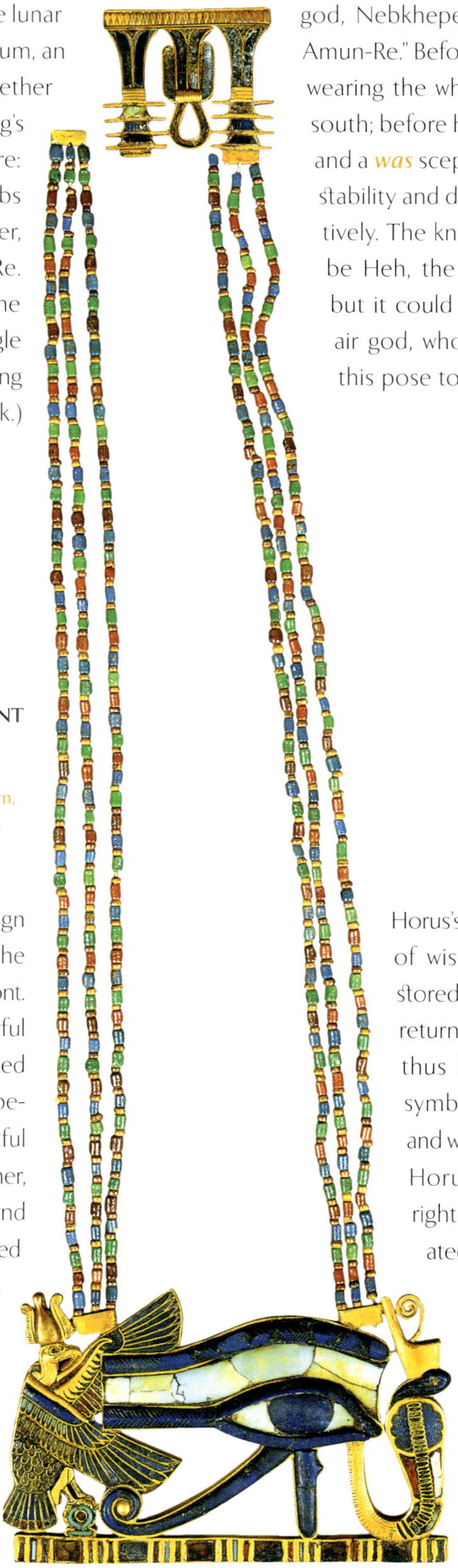

NECKLACE WITH *WEDJAT* EYE PENDANT
Gold, colored glass, semiprecious stone
Width of pectoral 9.5 cm, length of chain 33 cm
Carter 256vvv

Carter found this necklace hanging around the king's neck, between the 12th and 13th layers of wrappings. It features a gold pendant in the form of a ***wedjat***, the eye of Horus, with calcite (Egyptian alabaster) and lapis lazuli inlays. The protective goddesses so often seen in association with the king – Wadjet and Nekhbet – guard the eye. Before the ***wedjat*** is Wadjet, a hooded cobra or uraeus, wearing the red crown of Lower Egypt, while behind sits Nekhbet, with the tall white crown of Upper Egypt, flanked by ostrich feathers, on her vulture head. Nekhbet has the ***shen***, the hieroglyphic sign for eternity, in her claws. Both goddesses are inlaid with colored glass and lapis lazuli; some of the inlay is missing from the uraeus. Below is a bar with colored glass inlays. The design chased onto the back of the pieces matches that of the front.

The ***wedjat*** was a powerful protective symbol associated with the mythical combat between Osiris's son and rightful heir, Horus, and Osiris's brother, Seth, who murdered Osiris and usurped the throne. Conceived and born after his father's death, Horus challenged his uncle when he was old enough to avenge his father's murder and reclaim the throne. One battle resulted in Seth tearing out Horus's left eye. The god of wisdom, Thoth, restored it to health and returned it to Horus. It thus became a lunar symbol, which wanes and waxes each month. Horus's undamaged right eye was associated with the sun.

This pectoral represents the right eye, and thus served to connect the king with the sun.

AMULETS

The Egyptians used many kinds of amulets, both as cult objects and in decorative jewelry. They took the forms of gods, hieroglyphs, animals, objects, whatever the Egyptians associated with protection or power. The importance of amulets to the Egyptians is evident in the numerous examples of amulets and amuletic jewelry included among the wrappings of Tutankhamun's mummy. The examples here are three of a group of eight found in the inner bandages, hung around the king's neck by linen threads. Each is made of thin sheet gold with details chased into the surface.

The first depicts a pair of uraei, intended to represent Wadjet and Nekhbet, patron goddesses of Lower and Upper Egypt, respectively. Nekhbet usually appears as a vulture, but she sometimes is given the form of a cobra.

The second shows a uraeus with the head of a woman. The Egyptians worshipped several cobra goddesses, but only two are commonly depicted as hybrids of human and serpent. One of these is Meretseger, "She Who Loves Silence," who protected the Theban necropolis. The other is Weret-hekau, "Great One of Magic," a goddess associated with Isis. She appears on other objects from the tomb, so this may be her here, as well.

The third amulet takes the form of a vulture, as did four others in the group. They could represent Nekhbet again, but she was not the only vulture goddess. The mother goddess Mut, who was associated with the Egyptian queen, often appeared as a vulture.

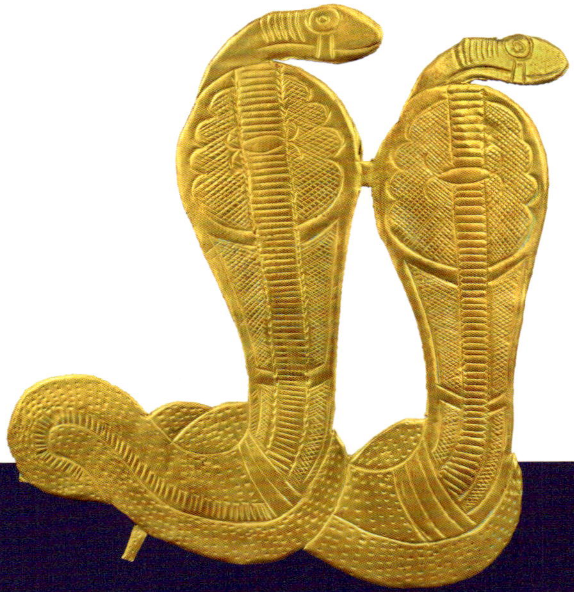

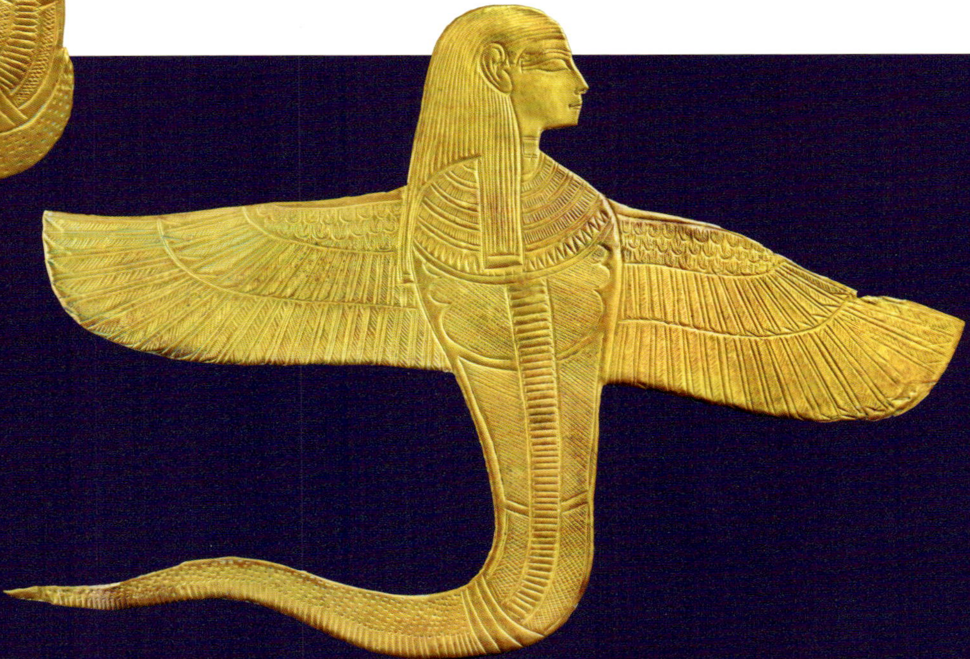

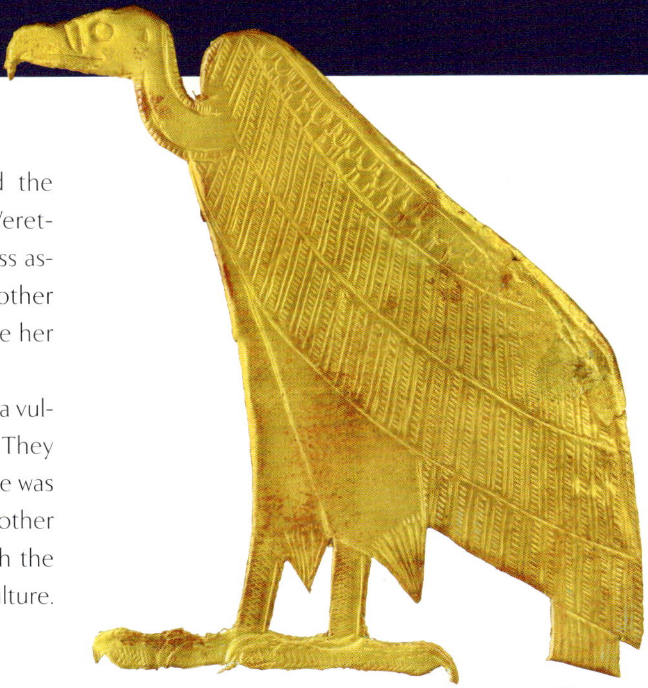

AMULETS
Double Uraeus
Gold
Height 7 cm
Carter 256,4,g

HUMAN-HEADED URAEUS
Gold
Width 13.7 cm
Carter 256,4,f

VULTURE
Gold
Height 6.6 cm
Carter 256,4,h

The papyrus, as a symbol, served many purposes. It represented Lower Egypt, with the extensive wetlands of the Delta. It was also symbolic of life and youth. The color of the plant was often imitated with green feldspar; amulets in the form of the flowering papyrus stalk were commonly made of this stone. The Egyptians called such amulets *wadj* ("green"), and, as prescribed by spells in the *Book of the Dead*, placed them at the mummy's throat during the wrapping. Tutankhamun's embalmers took care to situate these amulets in the right place, which was not the case with every amulet they included in the king's wrappings.

Illustrated next to the papyrus amulets is a hollow gold pendant inscribed "the good god, Nebkheperure, given life." It was found in the Annexe.

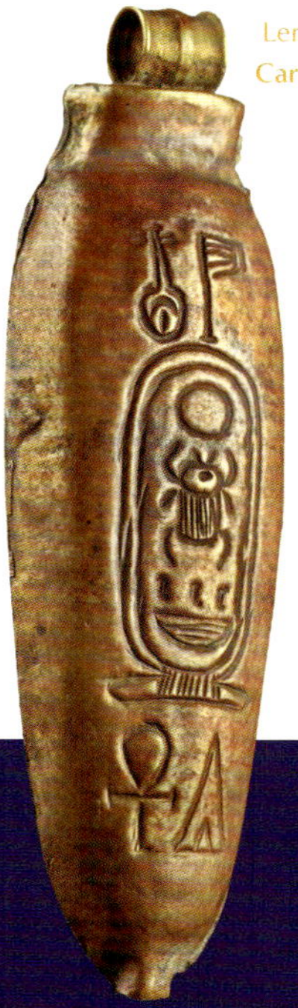

PENDANT
Gold
Length 5.8 cm
Carter 620(69)

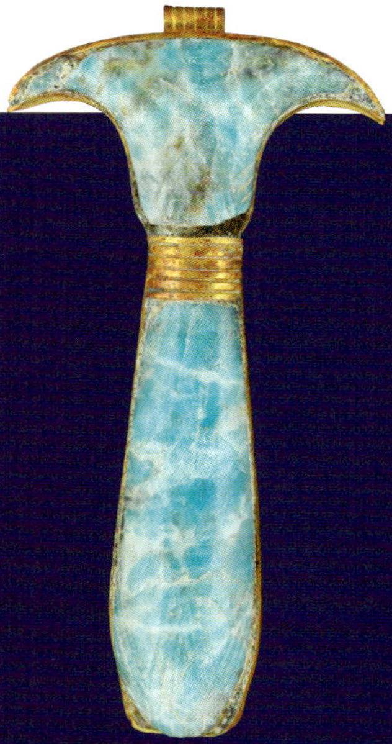

PAPYRUS AMULET
Gold and green feldspar
Length 5.5 cm
Carter 256,4,b

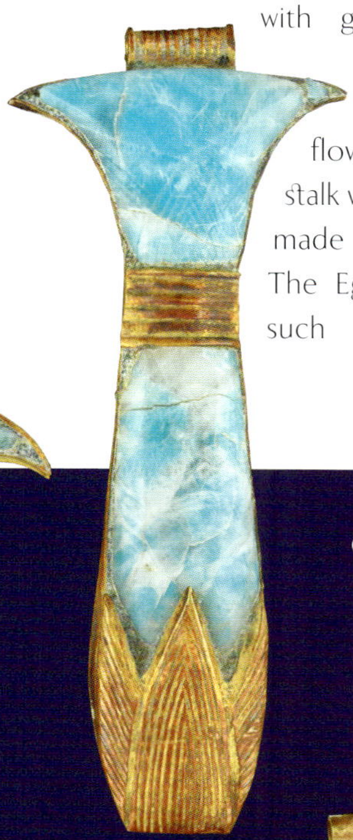

PAPYRUS AMULET
Gold and green feldspar
Length 6.3 cm
Carter 256ggg

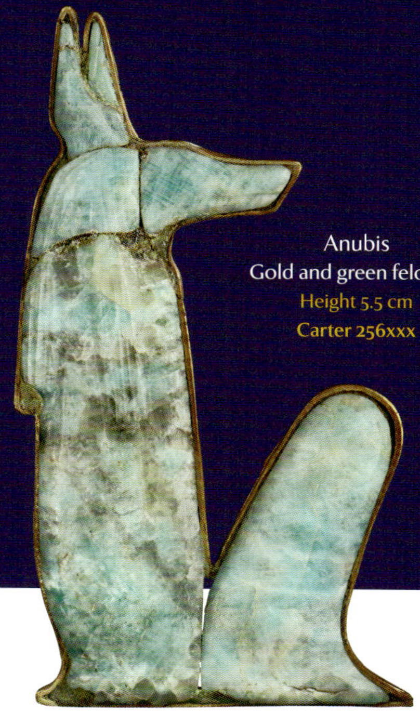

Anubis
Gold and green feldspar
Height 5.5 cm
Carter 256xxx

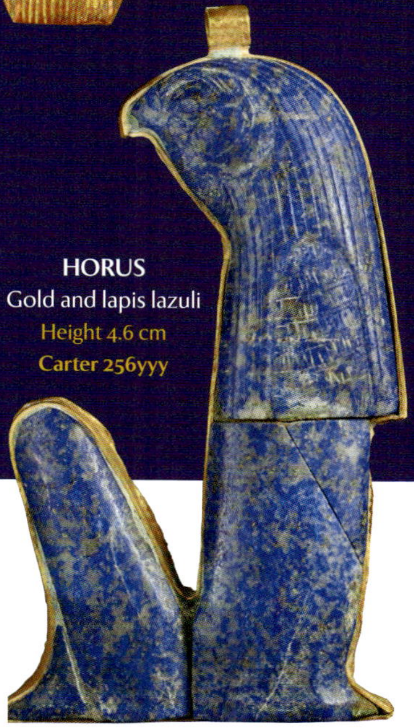

HORUS
Gold and lapis lazuli
Height 4.6 cm
Carter 256yyy

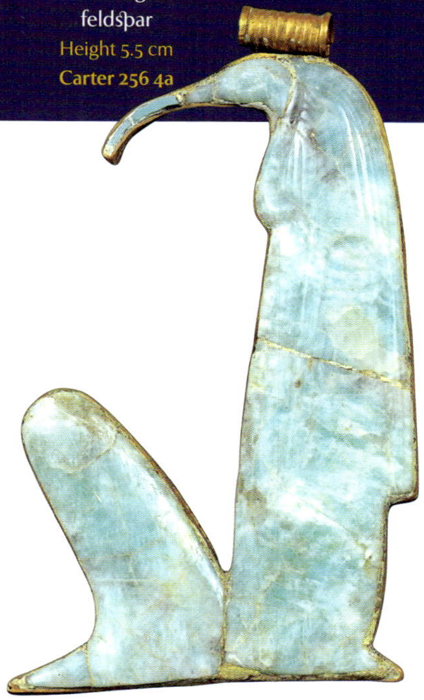

THOTH
Gold and green feldspar
Height 5.5 cm
Carter 256 4a

Gold wire held these amulets around the king's neck, to protect his throat. The gold amulet inlaid with green feldspar represents the Thoth, god of knowledge and the moon, as an ibis-headed man. The falcon-headed amulet with inlay of lapis-lazuli is an image of Horus, son of Isis and Osiris and special protector of the living king. The third amulet shows the jackal-headed god of embalming, Anubis. It, too, has inlay of green feldspar.

The Egyptians very deliberately selected what material to use for a particular amulet. Color and other properties would enhance the effectiveness of its magic. The green feldspar had associations with the life-giving waters of the Nile and new growth. The dark blue lapis lazuli of Horus is reminiscent of the night sky.

Although the ***djed*** pillar was one of the most popular amulets in ancient Egypt, it is not entirely certain what it was meant to represent. Some scholars suggest it is a human backbone, a sacred tree, or perhaps a column wrapped with sheaves of grain. There is no doubt, however, that it was a symbol of Osiris, god of the underworld and resurrection, and indicated "stability" and "endurance." Considered an essential amulet to include among the mummy wrappings, it is often seen on a variety of funerary equipment and can be found as a decorative motif on furniture as well. The lower halves of many coffins have a large ***djed*** pillar running along the middle, where the spine of the mummy would be laid to rest.

Carter found these particular ***djed*** amulets at Tutankhamun's neck, suspended from wires of beaten gold.

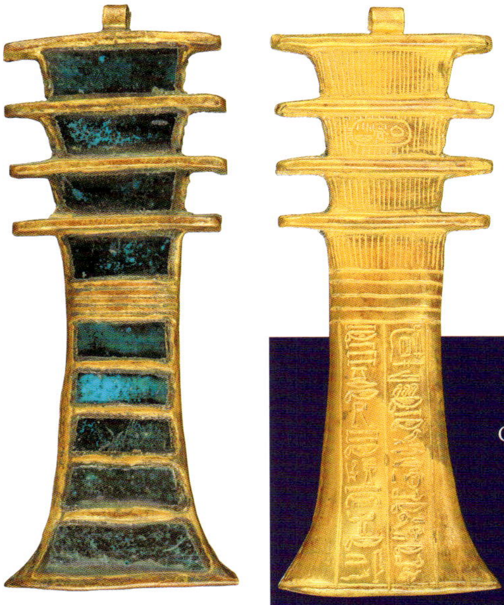

DJED AMULETS

Gold with faience inla
Length 8.8 cm
Carter 256hhh

Gold
Length 9 cm
Carter 256kk

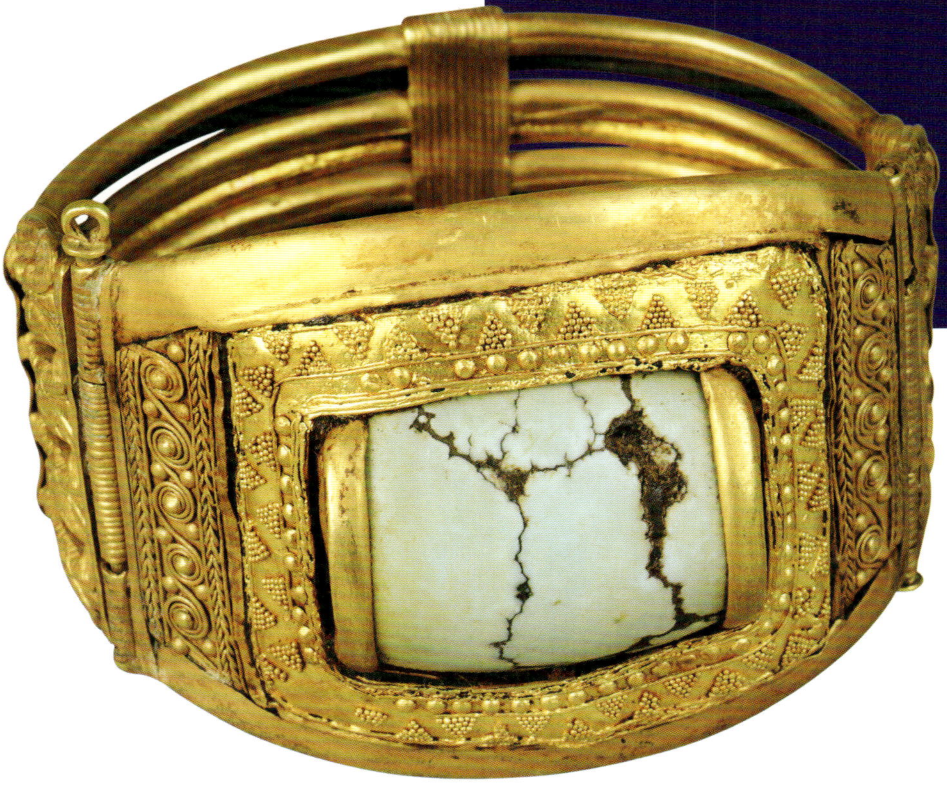

BRACELET
Gold, electrum, and turquoise
Diameter 5.5 cm
Carter 256ww

This exquisite, heavy gold bracelet, a favorite of mine among the objects from the tomb, is set with a piece of turquoise mined in the deserts of the Sinai. Having a color resembling the sky, turquoise was highly prized throughout Egyptian history, and these mines were exploited from the earliest periods until the end of the pharaonic period. It was particularly associated with the goddess Hathor, who was sometimes called "the Mistress of Turquoise."

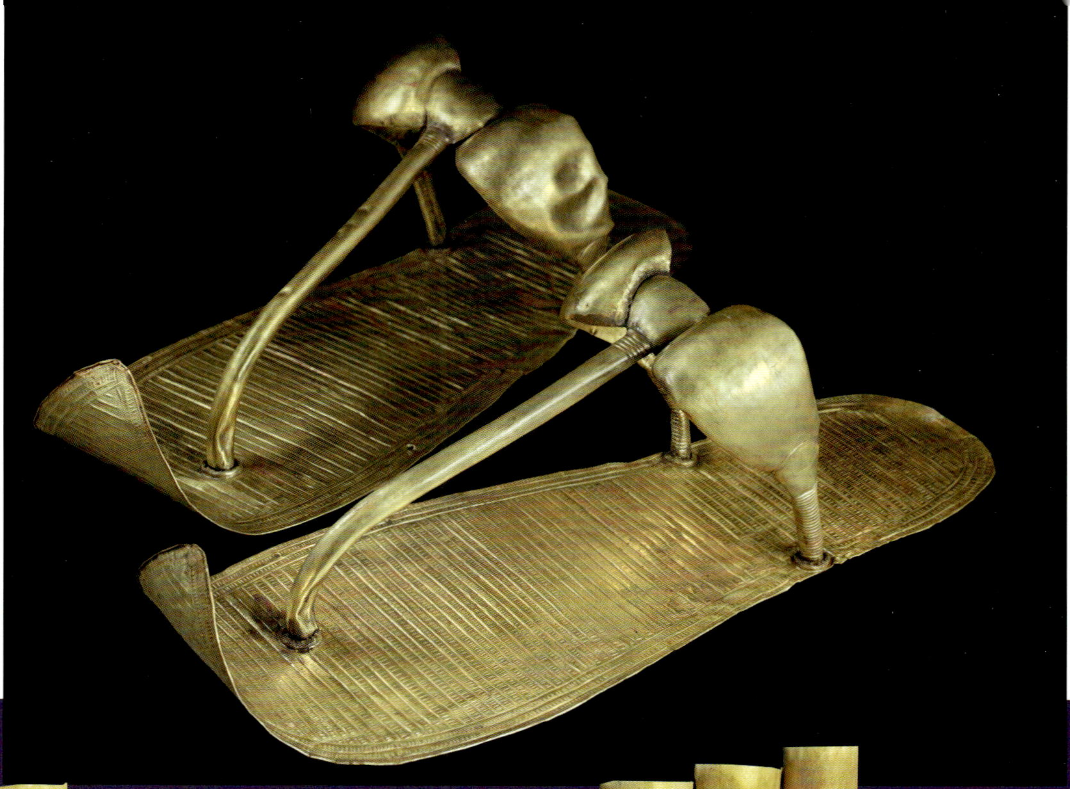

SANDALS, TOE STALLS, AND FINGER STALLS OF THE MUMMY
Gold
Length of sandals 29.5 cm;
toe and finger stalls sizes vary
Carter 256ll

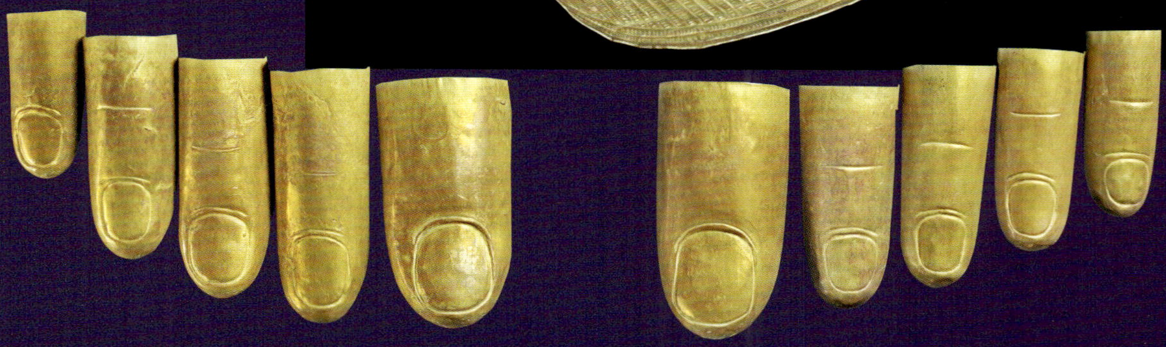

GOLDEN PROTECTION

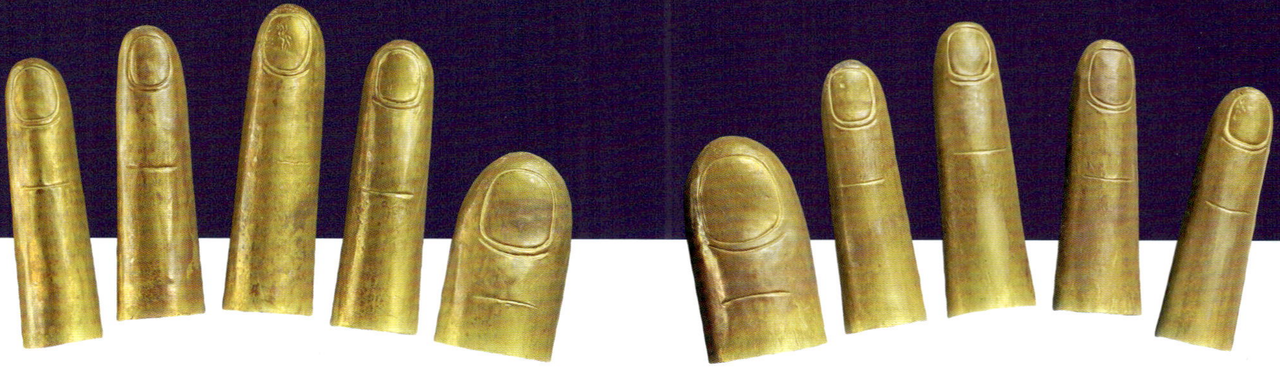

Made of gold, symbolic of the flesh of the gods, stalls (covers) were found on each of the king's mummified fingers and toes, and gold sandals covered his feet. Each toe and finger had been individually wrapped with linen of high quality before the appropriate stall was slid on to cover it. The surface of the stalls have details such as nails and knuckles.

The sandals, also entirely of gold, were created strictly for use on the king's mummy. They were given decoration imitating rushwork, and the straps that run over the instep resemble cording. Aside from the material from which they are made, they appear to be of the usual type that appears in art, with a thong passing between the big and second toe. As found, the tips were upturned to cover the king's middle toes, a shape also seen in the artistic record, for example, on the figures that guarded the Burial Chamber (**Carter Nos. 22 and 29**; see Chapter 4).

The tomb also yielded many pairs of sandals, usually of rush or papyrus, but some of leather. Being appointed to the position of royal sandal-bearer was a high honor. This office existed at least as far back as the Early Dynastic Period; a sandal-bearer appears on the Narmer Palette.

The flexible uraeus (as well as a golden vulture) was once sewn onto a linen headdress that had covered Tutankhamun's head, bound in place by a gold band. Only a small portion of the headdress survived, so it is not known if it was of the ***khat*** or ***nemes*** type. The uraeus is crafted of twelve gold body segments edged with small gold beads strung together by thread. The hood, made of gold and inlaid with carnelian and dark blue glass, was fastened to the jointed body by gold wire that passed through little eyelets. The head is blue glass and has been given obsidian eyes.

The diadem was likely worn over a wig. It was found, however, atop the beaded skull-cap covering the mummy's shaved head, and there is no doubt that this gold object was made very particularly for the young king.

The uraeus and vulture of the diadem were found at the king's thighs, among the wrappings, perhaps so that they would not be damaged.

Clearly they would not have fit in their intended position with the golden mask in place. Their association with the fillet is made clear by the sockets which fit onto fastenings on the headdress; the long body and tail of the cobra ran across the top of Tutankhamun's head and helped the diadem keep its proper shape.

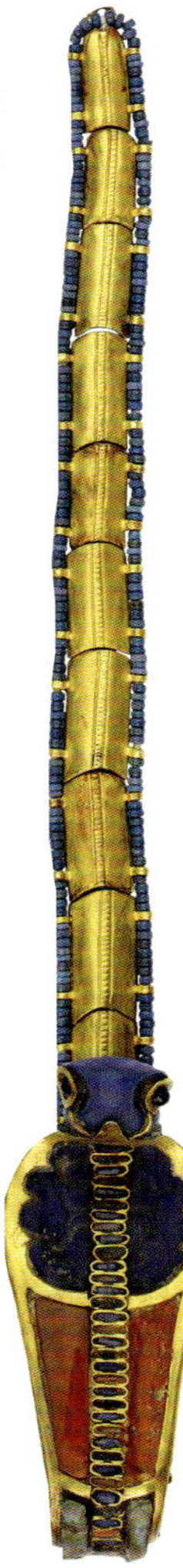

FLEXIBLE URAEUS
Gold, glass, faience, and obsidian
Length 19cm
Carter 256,4,q

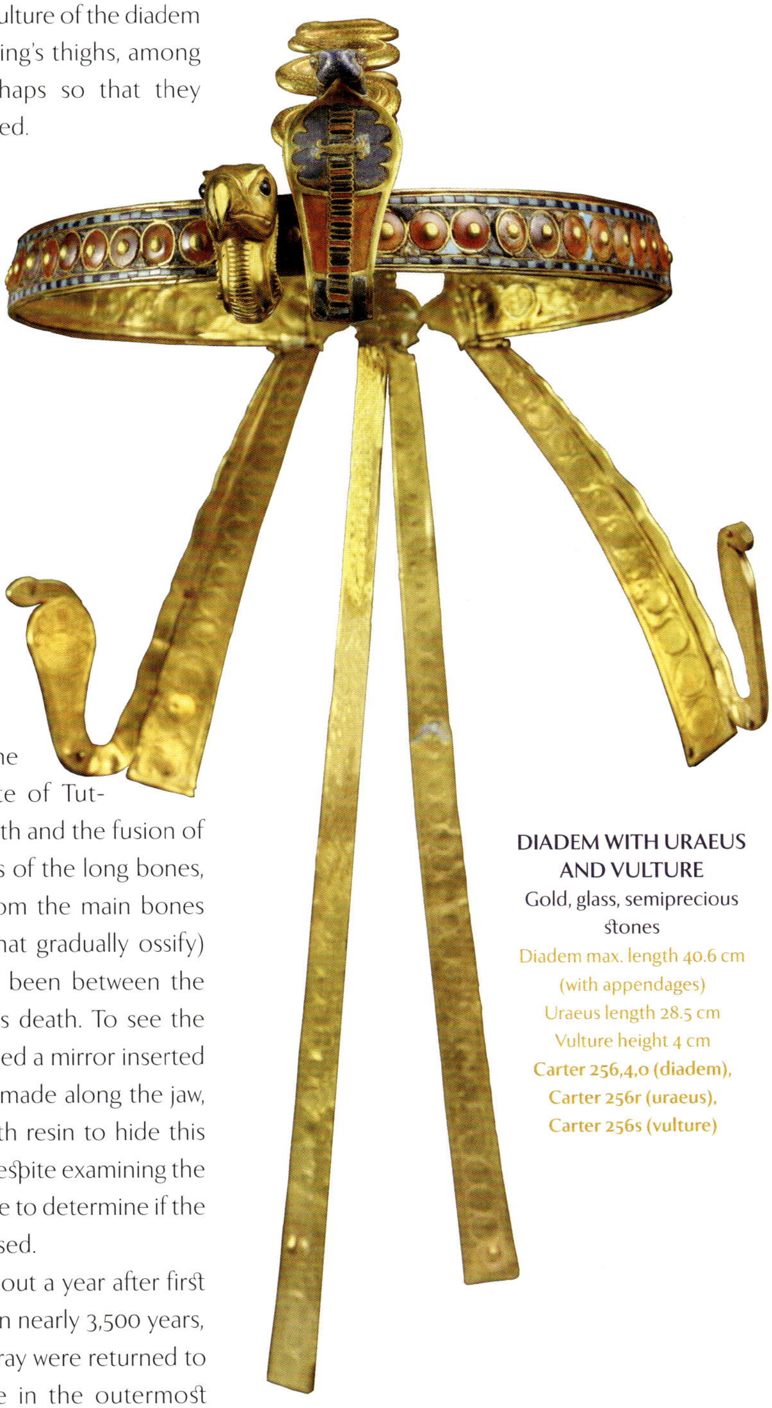

DIADEM WITH URAEUS AND VULTURE
Gold, glass, semiprecious stones
Diadem max. length 40.6 cm (with appendages)
Uraeus length 28.5 cm
Vulture height 4 cm
Carter 256,4,o (diadem), Carter 256r (uraeus), Carter 256s (vulture)

With all of the wrappings and the amuletic jewelry removed, time had come to remove the mummy itself, **Carter No. 256**, from its coffin. This task had to be done in pieces, something Carter neglected to mention in his published description of the event. They decapitated the king at the neck and used hot knives to soften the resin adhering the mask to the skull. The pelvis was separated from the trunk, the limbs were removed, and other damages were inflicted on the royal corpse.

They reassembled the body on a tray of sand, going so far as to use resin to join hands and feet to arms and legs, to make it appear to be intact.

Now Derry and Saleh could do their work. Their examination concluded that Tutankhamun had stood about 5'6" (170 cm) when he was alive. It also noted the shape of the skull was much like that of the mummy found in KV 55, which we now know to be Akhenaten, Tutankhamun's probable father, as we will see in the next chapter. The state of Tutankhamun's wisdom teeth and the fusion of the epiphyses (the ends of the long bones, which are separated from the main bones by layers of cartilage that gradually ossify) suggested that he had been between the ages of 18 and 22 at his death. To see the teeth, Derry possibly used a mirror inserted through an incision he made along the jaw, which he then filled with resin to hide this post mortem wound. Despite examining the penis, Derry was not able to determine if the king had been circumcised.

In October 1926, about a year after first seeing the light of day in nearly 3,500 years, the king and the sand tray were returned to his sarcophagus, to lie in the outermost coffin protected beneath a plate-glass lid.

X-RAYS OF THE MUMMY

In 1968 another examination took place, this time by a team led by Professor R. G. Harrison, an anatomist at the University of Liverpool, who intended to X-ray the body. A sweet smell greeted them when they removed the lid of the coffin. Only now was the dismemberment discovered, and also that Carter had done a poor job rewrapping the mummy. Harrison's team also realized that Tutankhamun was missing one of his thumbs, as well as his penis.

Harrison confirmed some of Derry's observations, including the king's age at death, though he believed it was at the younger end of the 18-to-22 range. He confirmed the similarities between the skulls of Tutankhamun and the KV 55 mummy. These mummies were about the same height and similarly proportioned. Clearly, there was a family resemblance.

X-rays of Tutankhamun's skull revealed opaque material that was probably residue from the mummification process, a fragment of bone inside the skull, and a thickened or "fuzzy" area on the back of the skull. Some people have pointed to this as evidence that the king received a fatal blow to the head. But the fact that the bone is loose in the skull would indicate that whatever event placed it there occurred ***after*** mummification. Otherwise it would have become caught in the embalming material introduced into the skull.

X-rays also revealed scoliosis in the king's spine. Perhaps he was frail, as had been suggested in the past.

The king was returned to his tomb again. He remained at peace until 1978, when James E. Harris, a professor of orthodontics at the University of Michigan, came to Egypt to take additional X-rays of the king's head. Although Harris's team did not publish their findings, they did state that they believed that the king was between the ages of 23 and 27. This opinion, which the team offered without explaining their reasoning, is rejected by most Egyptologists because of archaeological and physiological evidence. Photographs that were taken during Harris's study showed that the king's body had suffered even more damage.

The king's blood was also analyzed through a sample of bone. This demonstrated that his ABO blood type (which is the blood group typing most familiar to people) is A2, and his MN blood type is M/N. These results matched those of the mummy from KV 55. Testing of other royal mummies revealed that Amenhotep III was A2M, while his in-laws, Yuya and Tjuya, were A2N. This meant that the KV 55 body could be Tutankhamun's father, but, at the time, it also left open the possibility that Amenhotep III could be his father, and Queen Tiye, the daughter of Yuya and Tjuya, might be his mother.

The Mystery of the Mummy's Head

This photo, taken by Harry Burton, shows that Carter and Lucas left the head of the mummy covered with linen, turquoise beads and a diadem. This seems to show that although Carter damaged the body of the king when he removed the bandages and the objects wrapped with them, he did not damage the head. What, then, happened to the head to make it appear as it does today? The only possible explanation is that Harrison and Zaki Iskander, director of the Cairo Museum, who had worked with him, were responsible. They used chemicals to treat this part of the body, and this caused the disappearance of the linen, the beads and the diadem.

Tutankhamun's head.
Harry Burton / Griffith Institute

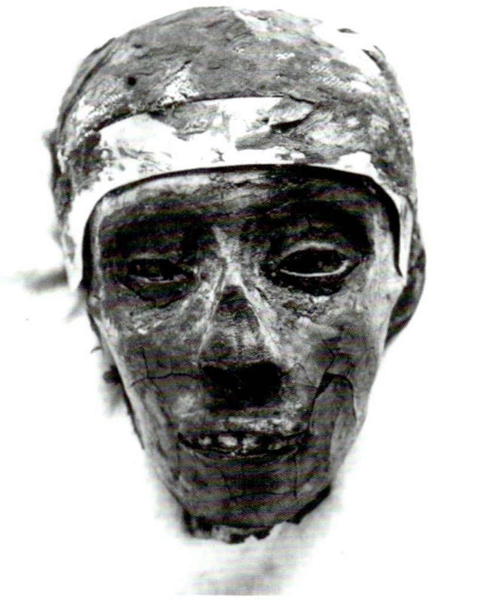

CT SCAN OF THE MUMMY

As Secretary General of the Supreme Council of Antiquities (SCA), I started the Egyptian Mummy Project, which was given the task of inventorying and analyzing all the mummies in Egypt, whether they were royal or private persons. In 2005, the National Geographic Society and Siemens, Ltd., donated to the SCA a CT scanning machine, with a trailer and funding for five years.

A CT scan would reveal new information that X-rays and inspection by human eyes had missed, and we hoped that this would lead to answers to many questions that other studies had raised and perhaps end speculation about the boy-king's murder. It might even open new questions, but that is the nature of science. Like X-rays, CT scans are not invasive, but, unlike X-rays, they produce a three-dimensional image in which different types of soft tissue and bone can be differentiated. It would not be necessary to repeatedly move the body, as is the case with X-rays. The scanner would pass along the mummy, taking hundreds and even thousands of images, each a single "slice" through the body at multiple angles. These are all then compiled together to create a three-dimen-

The author with his team carefully lifting the wooden box containing the mummy of Tutankhamun from the stone sarcophagus.

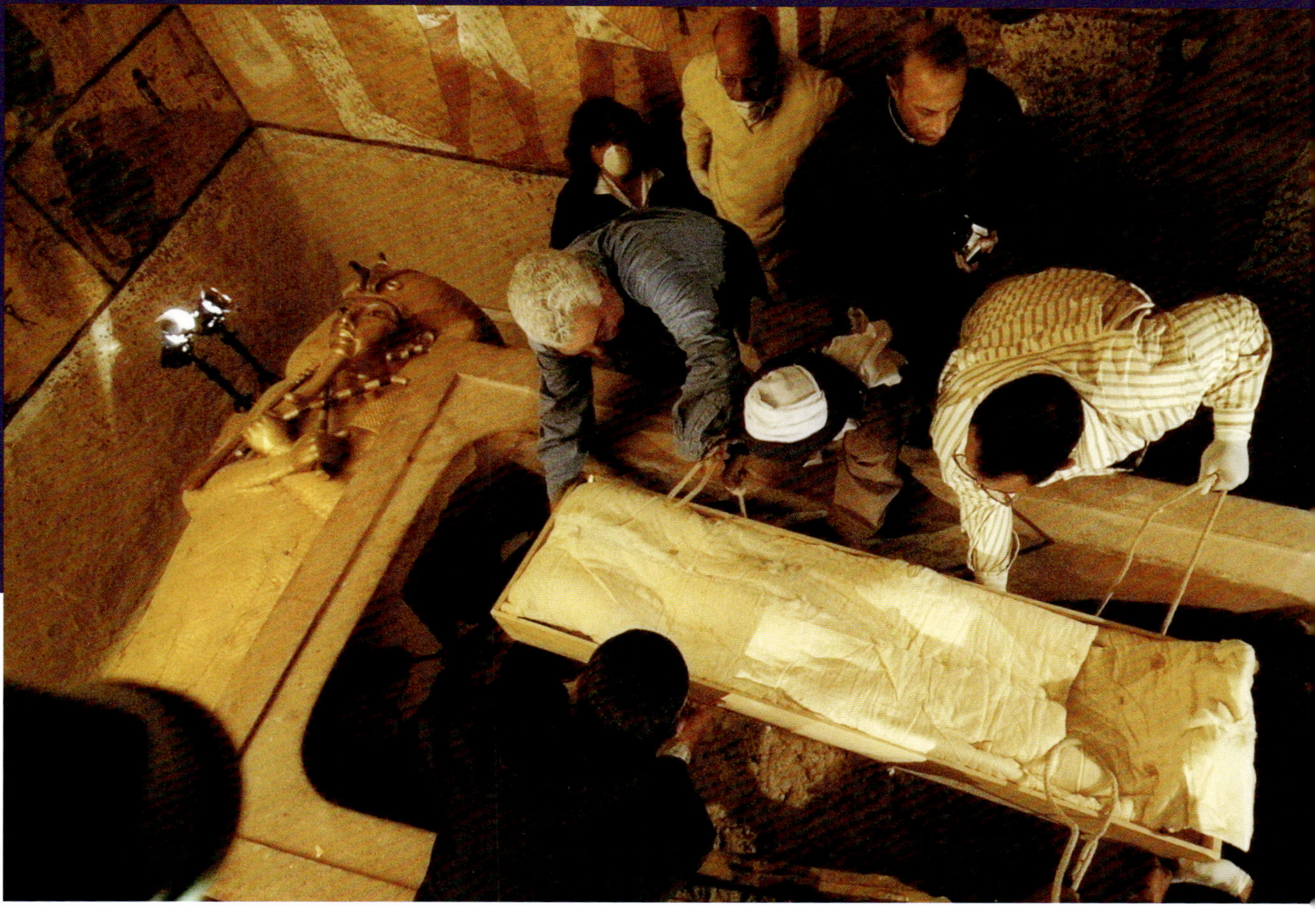

sional image. Information about such things as life expectancy, diseases, injuries, and other health issues of the ancient Egyptians can be derived from studies of such scans.

After the machine arrived in Cairo, we set the trailer up to work in the courtyard west of the Egyptian Museum. The machine had to be calibrated first, and then it began its first scans. We started with non-royal mummies, but in January 2005 the trailer was driven south to Luxor. The mummy of Tutankhamun was too delicate to bring to the scanner, so the scanner would go to the king.

I arrived in Luxor on 4th January, 2005, the day before the scan was to take place. My team included Dr Hani Abdel Rahman, who would operate the machine; Sabri Abdel Aziz, head of pharaonic monuments; Ahmed Soeib, head of conservation; Abdel Hamied Kotb, SCA architect; and a local team from Luxor. All the members of the team were Egyptian – this was the first investigation performed only by Egyptians.

By the time we arrived at the Valley of the Kings, the tourists were already departing. We went into the tomb at 5:30 in the afternoon to make the mummy ready for its move. When we removed the glass that covered the stone sarcophagus, we found that the gilding of the outermost coffin was cracking. This was not a great surprise, considering that the coffin had been sitting in the Burial Chamber without benefit of conservation or climate control for the past 80 years. It took us half an hour to remove the lid.

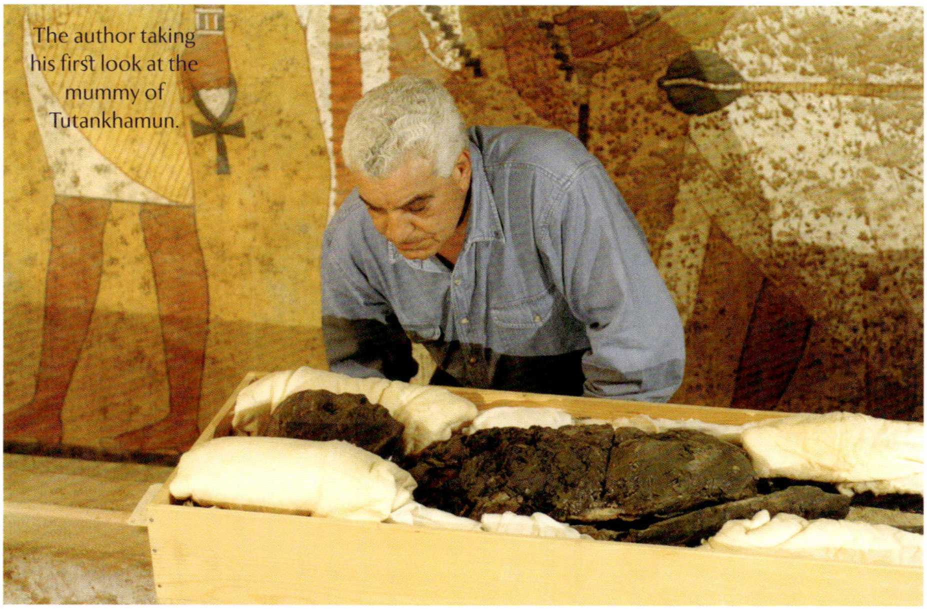

The author taking his first look at the mummy of Tutankhamun.

There inside, covered by a cotton blanket and linen, was the king, still lying on his bed of sand.

With great care I removed the cover from his head, so that I could see his face. I could not help but think that I had anticipated that he would have looked younger. Carter had left a card on his chest, containing the names of people who had participated in past examinations.

The team lifted the sand tray from the coffin to take it to the trailer for scanning the next day. The body was in pieces, of which only the face, hands, legs, and feet were still preserved. It reminded me of an ancient monument lying in ruins in the sand.

The analysis was performed in January and February by a team of Egyptian scientists. Four were radiologists: Dr Mervat Shafik, Dr Essam el-Sheikh, Dr Ashraf Selim, who are professors, and Dr Sherief Abdel Fatah, a lecturer. Dr Fawzi Gaballa is professor of anatomy, and Dr Aly Gamal Edlin is a professor of forensic medicine. We also sought the opinions of three foreign consultants: Dr Edward Egarter, a forensic pathologist from the Archaeological Museum of South Tyrol, Italy, Dr Paul Gostner, a radiologist with the General Hospital of Bolzano, Italy, and Dr Frank J. Rühli, who is an anatomist and paleopathologist from the University of Zurich. There was little debate among the team members about the results.

Some of the analyses of the CT scan confirmed certain results of the older examinations. Using modern developmental markers, the team used the partial eruption of the mummy's wisdom teeth and the state of the epiphyses to determine that the king was 19 at his death. His bones indicated that he was in generally good health, of moderate height, 1.7 m, and had a slight build. There was no sign of chronic disease or childhood malnutrition, indicating that he had been well cared for in his youth. An impacted wisdom tooth probably gave him some pain because it resulted in the thinning of his sinus cavity, but it has no sign of infection, and otherwise his teeth are in good condition. He has large front incisors, slightly misaligned lower teeth, and an overbite, a trait found in his ancestors, other kings in the Thutmoside line. It was also discovered that he had a small cleft in his hard palette (the roof of the mouth), but this was minor and did not result in a harelip or any other deformity of his face.

The CT scan made very evident that he had a very elongated skull, which earlier researchers had noted. Because his cranial sutures had not prematurely fused, the team ruled out that any pathology lay behind this curious shape, which is common in art of the Amarna Period. It is probably just a normal variation in the shape of a human skull.

One diagnosis that the CT scan did not find was scoliosis. Harrison had noticed a bend in the king's spine, but the scan found no deformed vertebrae or rotation. The team concluded that this deformity probably resulted from how the body was positioned during the mummification process.

There was also no evidence of a blow to the head. The loose pieces of bone could not have resulted from an injury received while the king was alive. One fragment proved to be from the topmost vertebra, while the other was from the large opening at the base of the skull, the foramen magnum. Most of the team believed that there is evidence that that area of the skull was used as a second route (after the nose) to put embalming material into the skull. The mummy of King Ahmose has an opening or hole like this on the back of the skull, as well. Pools of solidified matter at the top of the cranial cavity had been introduced into the skull through the nose, but a different kind of material had gathered near the back of the cranial cavity and in the neck, and this had likely been introduced from the foramen magnum. The bone fragments might have been the fault of the embalmers, but it is also possible that Carter's team broke these bones.

Earlier X-rays had revealed an unexpected oddity about the mummy: some of the king's frontal ribs and his sternum are missing.

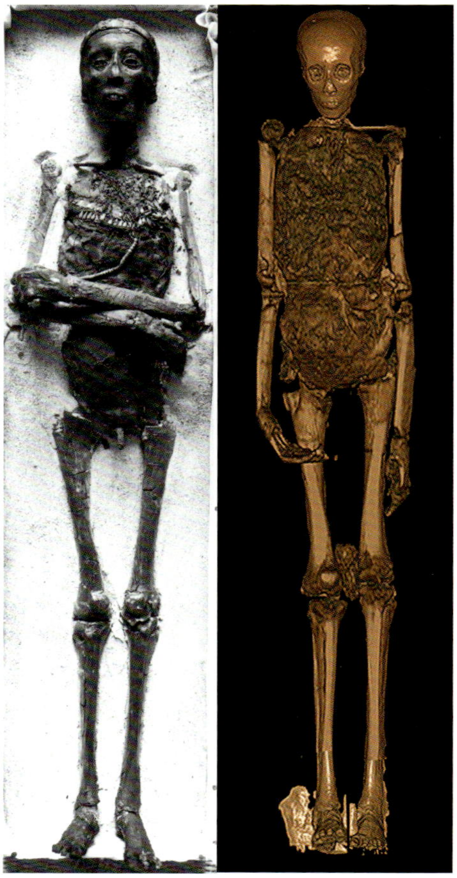

Harry Burton's archive photo of Tutankhamun's mummy and the 3D image made by the Egyptian team of the Mummy Project.

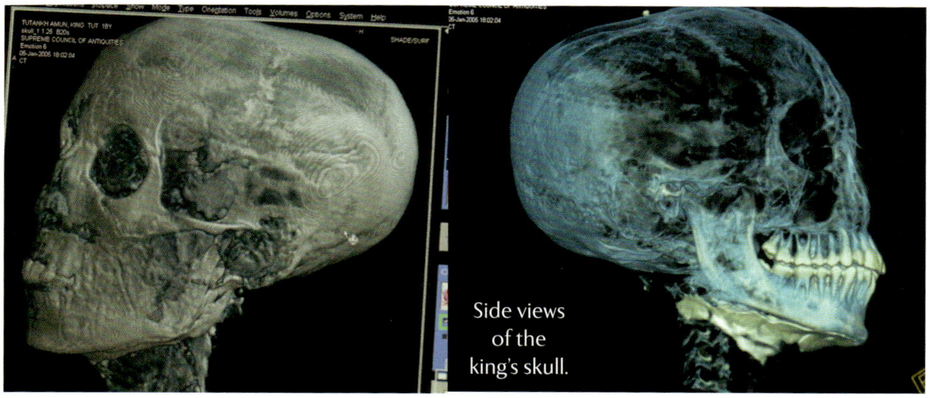

Side views of the king's skull.

People wondered if this was a birth defect. Other ideas were that the king had been in a chariot accident, maybe kicked by a horse, which resulted in the young king's chest being fatally crushed. Perhaps embalmers had removed the ribs for some reason. Derry and Saleh made no mention of this portion of the anatomy being missing, which they surely would have if it had been so at the time of their examination. The photograph on the left shows that a pectoral and a string of beads once covered this area, and Carter's notes say that these were left in place, covered with wax. These items are missing now. Therefore it has been suggested that the ribs were removed sometime 1926 and 1967 in order to steal this jewelry.

Furthermore, examinations revealed no evidence that the king might have received any massive injury to his chest. If he had, there would have been trauma to other parts of the body that are not missing, such as the spine. Instead, radiologists could see that the ends of the ribs had been cut by a sharp instrument. This was not damage the king's body had received during life. It is likely that the damage to the chest was due to its unwrapping in 1925, when Carter's team had used chisels to free the mummy from the solidified resin that had adhered it to the inner sarcophagus and to the golden mask. The CT scan revealed that parts of the ribs (along with clavicles, fingers, toes, and possibly also the penis) are buried within the sand in the wooden box, into which Carter's team had placed the mummy.

Although all of the damage to the head and chest I have just described was post-mortem, the scan did reveal a possible injury that the king received not long before his death. His lower left femur, at the level of the epiphyseal plate, had been fractured. Other fractures of his limbs had likely been caused by Carter's team, but Derry had noted the femur's fracture, which, unlike others, had ragged edges, not sharp ones. Two thin layers of embalming fluid had seeped into this. While the femur might have fractured during embalming, it seems more likely that this happened while the king was alive, no more than a few days before his death. There is no sign that this fracture, which is of a type seen in young men of Tutankhamun's age, had begun to heal extensively. Derry had noted that the king's left kneecap was loose, which could indicate further damage to this limb.

The radiologists stated that the fracture on the left leg resulted from an accident just a few hours before Tutankhamun died, but this accident alone could not have caused the king's death. However, an open wound received during the accident could have become infected. (I should note that part of the team disagrees with this interpretation. They believe that the fracture occurred after death, and that the embalming fluid seeped into the fracture during Carter's examination. This kind of disagreement is the nature of scientific evidence, but I and many other members of the team believe that the injury occurred during life.)

The apparent condition of the king's mummy has led some to say that it was not properly prepared. But the scanner revealed that the embalmers had employed at least five different kinds of embalming fluid, which had been introduced into the body multiple times. They had done their best to prepare their king for the afterlife.

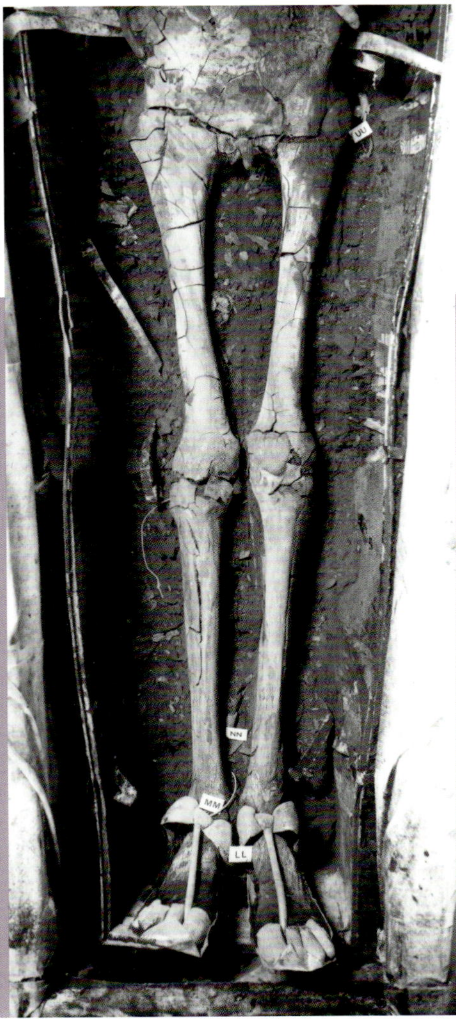

The lower part of Tutankhamun's mummy before taking off the king's sandals and toe-stalls.

The King's Diet

The king had been well fed in life, but what did he take with him to the netherworld? His provisions included 26 jars of wine, labeled with the vintage year, the vineyard, and even the name of the head vintner. Curiously, there was no beer, although beer was a staple drink in ancient Egypt. One jar, made of calcite (Egyptian alabaster), seemed to contain the remains of fruit juice. Fruit was included in the tomb as well. The king had dried grapes, jujubes, sycomore figs, and fruits of persea, grewia, and cocculus, along with almonds and watermelon seeds. Other raw food included a bunch of garlic, legumes and pulses (including lentils, peas, and chickpeas), and safflower seeds (which perhaps were for making oil). Prepared food included a mixture of lentils and fenugreek, and, of course, breads of various kinds. His spices and condiments were juniper berries, sesame, fenugreek, coriander, black cumin, and two jars of honey. For protein, he had beef, as well as meat from goat or sheep. These included ribs, joints, and a beef tongue. He had poultry, as well: ducks and geese.

DNA AND OTHER MODERN TESTS

In 2008–2009, I led a team of Egyptian and German researchers that performed DNA and other forms of analysis on royal mummies, including Tutankhamun's. We hoped to determine his family relationships, as we will explore in the next chapter, but we also wanted to know what ailments these tests might detect.

In contrast to the 2005 CT scan, this new examination revealed that Tutankhamun's spine was slightly curved, giving him a mild case of a condition known as kyphoscoliosis. It also discovered troubles with his feet. His right foot has merely a low arch, but his left foot is genuinely deformed, a clubfoot. This was caused by a bone disorder that was still active at the time the king died. It was something he had suffered from for some while before his death.

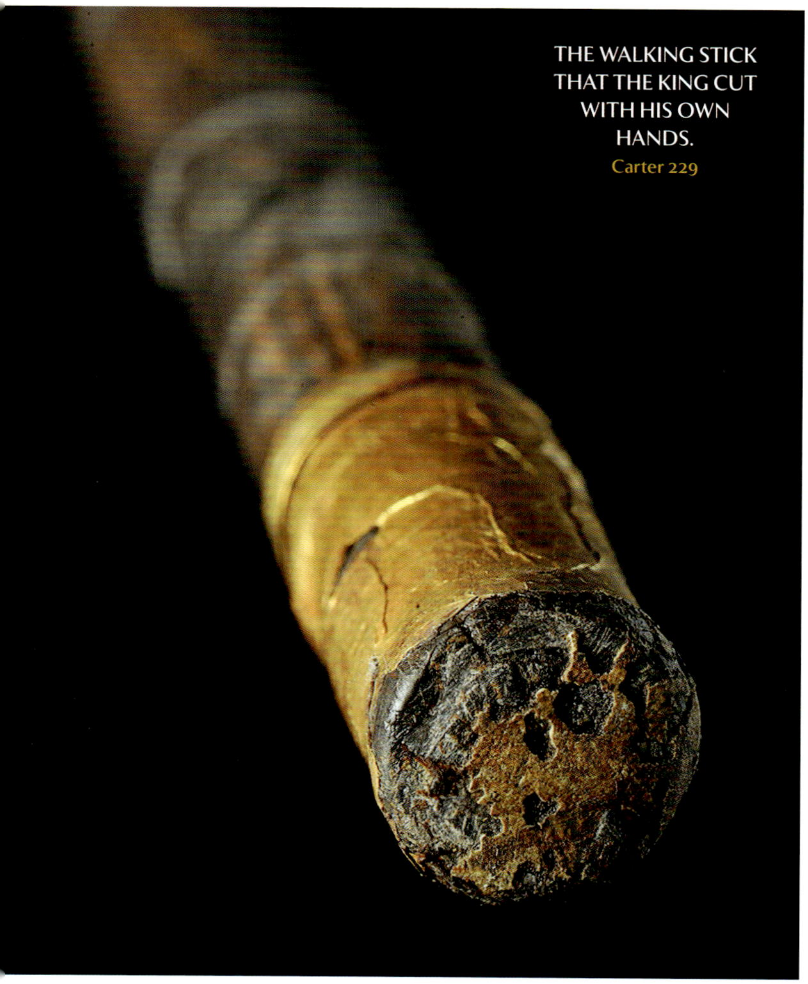

THE WALKING STICK THAT THE KING CUT WITH HIS OWN HANDS.
Carter 229

Scenes that show the king leaning on a stick or shooting an arrow while seated, such as appear on the small golden shrine (Carter No. 108 in Chapter 4), together with the 130 sticks found in the tomb – even one was cut by the king himself – may indicate that the king had problems with his health. However, one should not use artistic representations of the king seated or leaning on a walking stick as evidence of his weak foot. As Ray Johnson of the University of Chicago has said in a discussion about this point, representations of private men of high rank, as well as kings, using walking sticks appear at least as far back as the Old Kingdom. Such images indicate authority, symbolized by the staves in their hands, rather than any physical weakness. In fact, they indicate quite the opposite of frailty. The staff is the ultimate symbol of authority, and to be seated is a privilege, conveying the earthly power of the individual. Thus the presence of so many staves and walking sticks among the objects from Tutankhamun's tomb could simply reflect and reinforce the king's exalted status. However, imagery of a king seated while shooting with a bow is unique to Tutankhamun. I thus believe that, although the sticks indicate the king's high rank, Tutankhamun's disability is reflected in art and in the contents of the tomb. We were also looking for signs of infectious diseases, such as bubonic plague, tuberculosis, leprosy, or malaria, among the royal mummies. Tutankhamun and his grandparents, Yuya and Tjuya, proved to have the malaria parasite. In fact, they all had malaria tropica, the most severe form of the disease. Although the marshes of Egypt provide the right environment for the mosquitoes that harbor the malaria parasite, medical papyri from ancient Egypt do not mention the cycle of fevers and chills that often come with the disease, although the Papyrus Ebers describes an ailment with chills, fever, and enlargement of the spleen. This could be malaria. Insect pests are mentioned in ancient documents, and the Greek historian Herodotus, who lived in the 5th century BC, recorded that nets were used in Lower Egypt to protect sleepers from mosquitoes. The gilded wooden frame that was discovered in the tomb of Queen Hetepheres of the 4th Dynasty may have supported such a net. These attempts to avoid pests have suggested to some scholars that malaria was present in Egypt during the pharaonic period.

It is not known how, or even if, Egyptian physicians treated malaria. We know that his grandparents had the disease but do not know if they died of it in their old age. They may have developed an immunity, as some people do. Some of the botanical material found in Tutankhamun's tomb – seeds, leaves, and fruit – might have been used to treat the ailment. Some people today recommend that a person infected with malaria should avoid alcohol, which would explain the lack of beer in the tomb but not the presence of wine. Meat is to be avoided, according to some, and the king was well provided with that. But fruit may be good during the fevered stage, and the king did have a great deal of fruit. However, we know little about how a royal tomb would ordinarily be provisioned. Perhaps everything that he had was standard.

Could malaria have caused his death? What did kill the young king?

How Tutankhamun Died

We know that he was not murdered. The mummy shows no sign of trauma to the head or to the chest from any blow that the king received during life.

But we also know that the king received different kinds of "blows" against his health. As will be shown in the next chapter, his mother and father were brother and sister, so the king's genetic makeup was weakened by inbreeding. He had a number of disorders related to his feet. The accident, perhaps a fall from a chariot, that gave him the leg fracture could have resulted in an embolism or maybe a wound that became infected. He also suffered from malaria. The continual inflammation from his other disorders may have suppressed his immune system, making the wound or the malaria infection fatal. None of these things alone might have killed him, but delivered together, his weak constitution could not survive them all.

I propose the following theory regarding the young king's death: as shown by the CT scan conducted in 2005, he had suffered an accident a few hours before he died. This might have happened, for example, while he was out hunting wild animals from his chariot in the desert near Memphis. Another young man might have recovered from the type of injuries he received. However, with his disabilities, Tutankhamun succumbed to his wounds, which resulted in his untimely death.

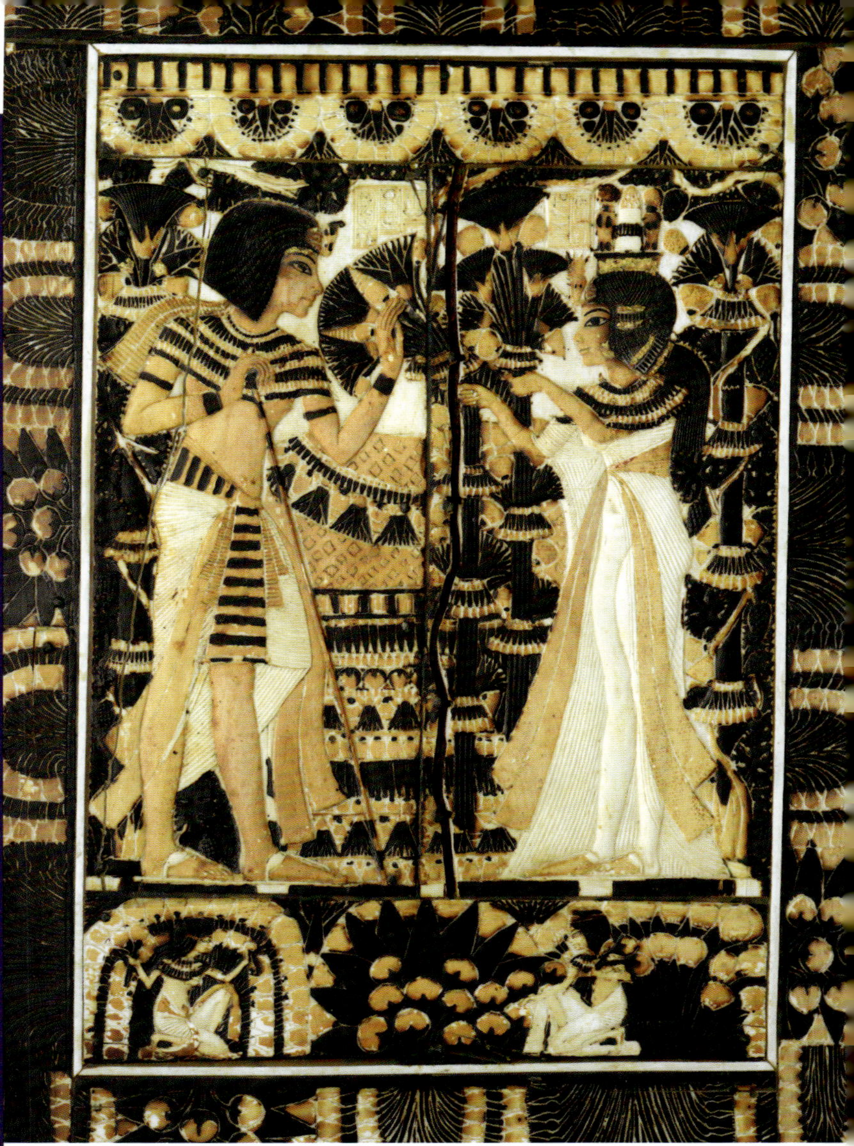

Tutankhamun leaning on a stick, receiving bundles of papyrus and flowers from his queen.

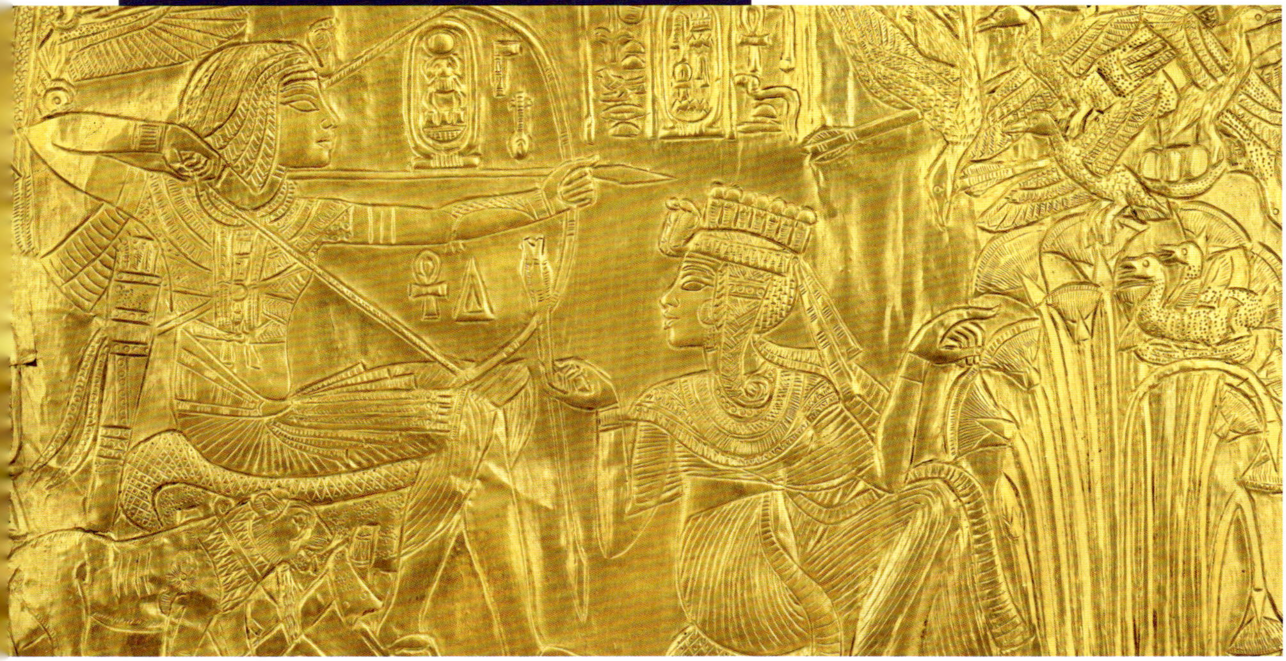

Tutankhamun firing arrows while sitting, hunting birds in the marshes. Scene depicted on the small golden shrine. Carter 108

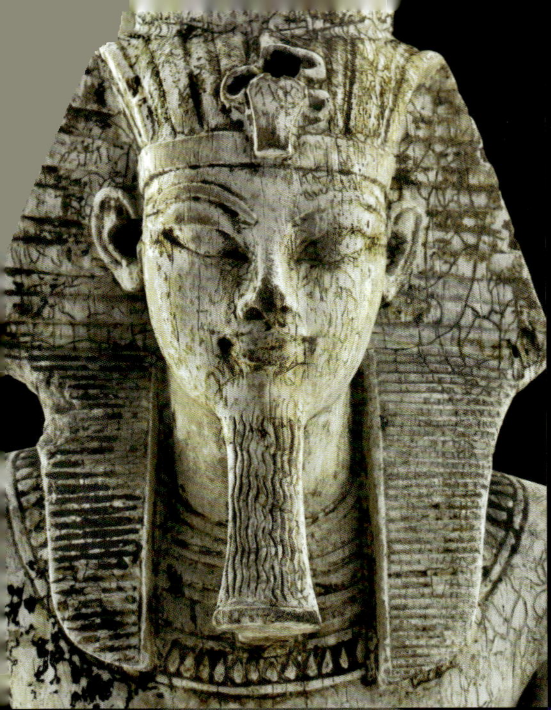
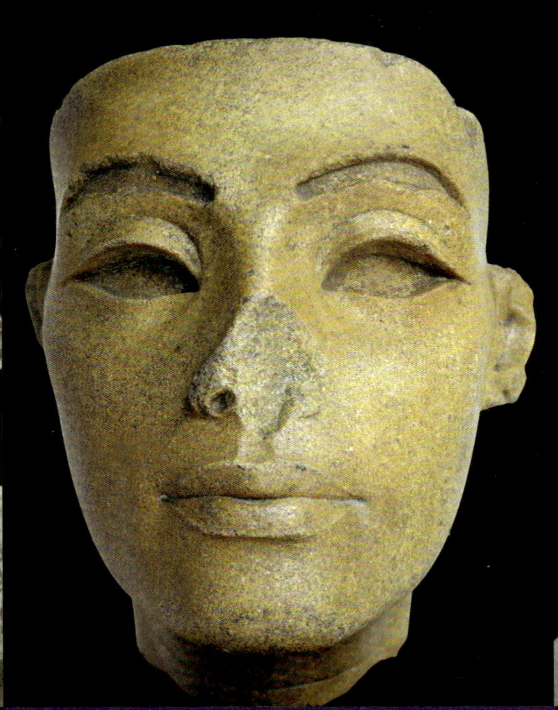
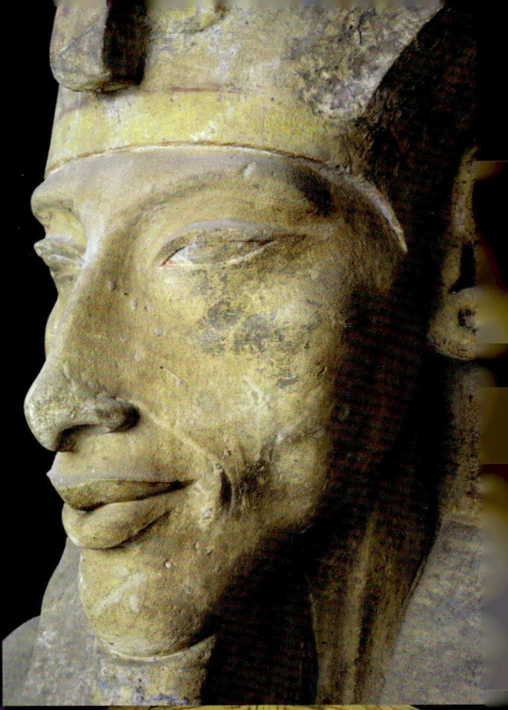
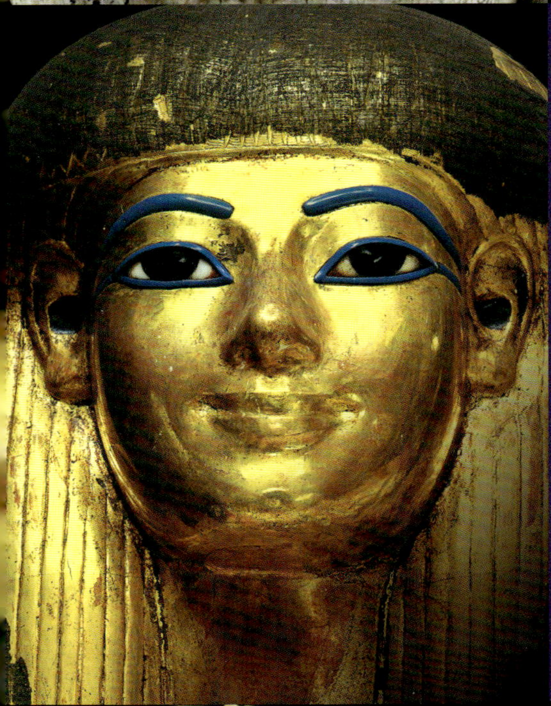

CHAPTER VI

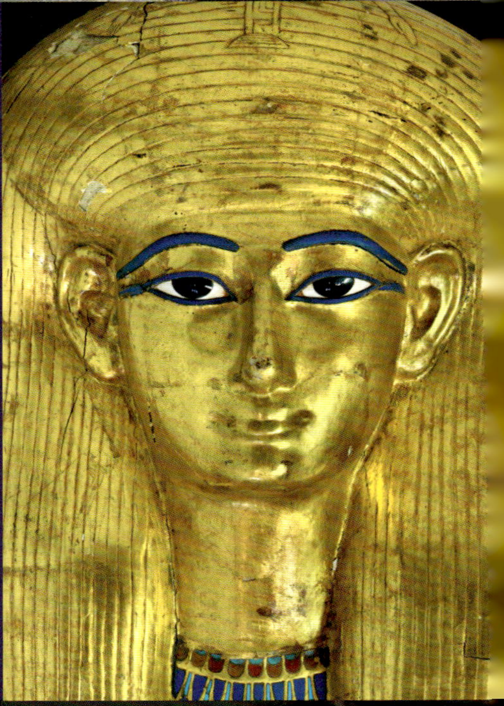
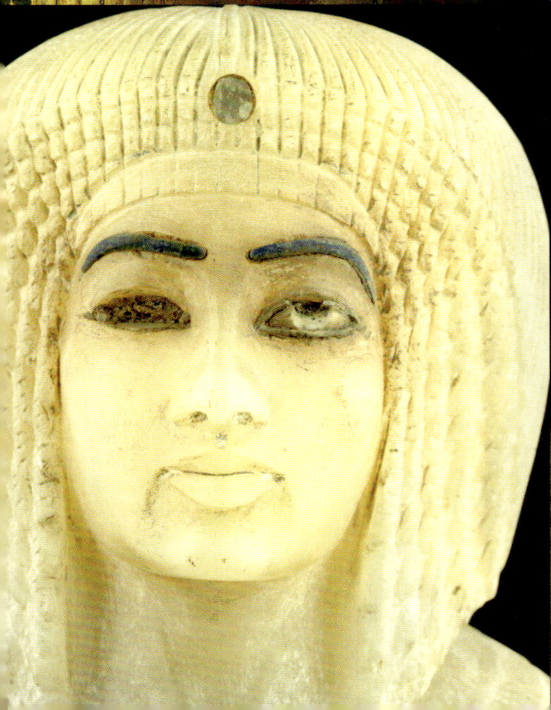
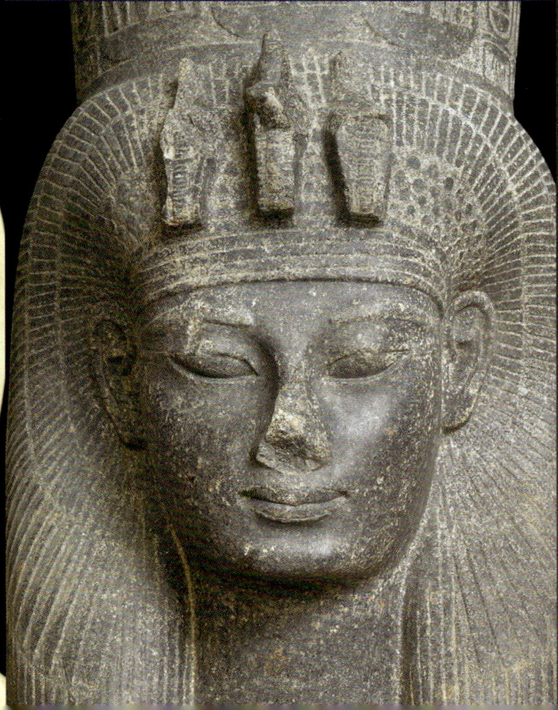
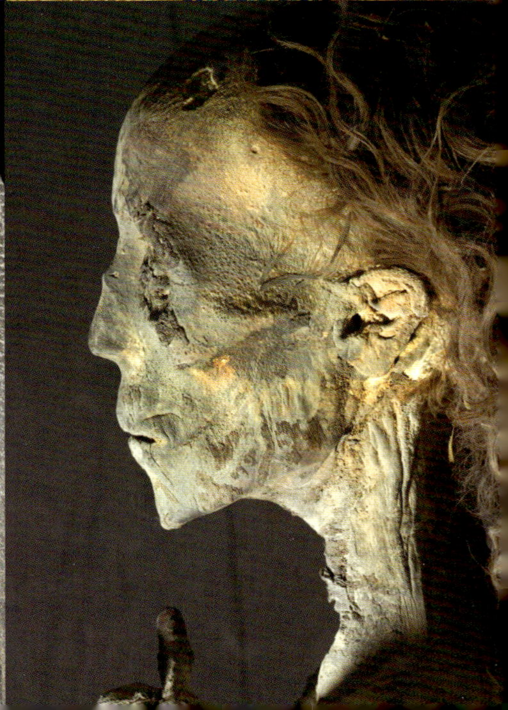

THE DISCOVERY OF THE FAMILY OF TUTANKH-AMUN

THE FAMILY OF THE BOY-KING

Many mysteries have surrounded the family of Tutankhamun. Until not long ago, even the identity of his father was unknown, and the archaeological evidence for some of the familial relationships between individuals who were presumably closely related to him was unclear. There are a number of unidentified mummies thought to belong to members of the royal family of the late 18th Dynasty, but who they were and what relationships existed among them needed to be established.

Unraveling the mysteries of the Amarna and Post-Amarna periods has always generated lively debate among scholars. How we resolved many of these questions – and found new ones – is a story that involves evidence from texts, from artifacts, and from the mummies themselves. First, let me summarize what was, until recently, known, not known, and uncertain about the family of Tutankhamun, starting with Amenhotep III, because these are questions that I hoped to resolve with the King Tutankhamun Family Project.

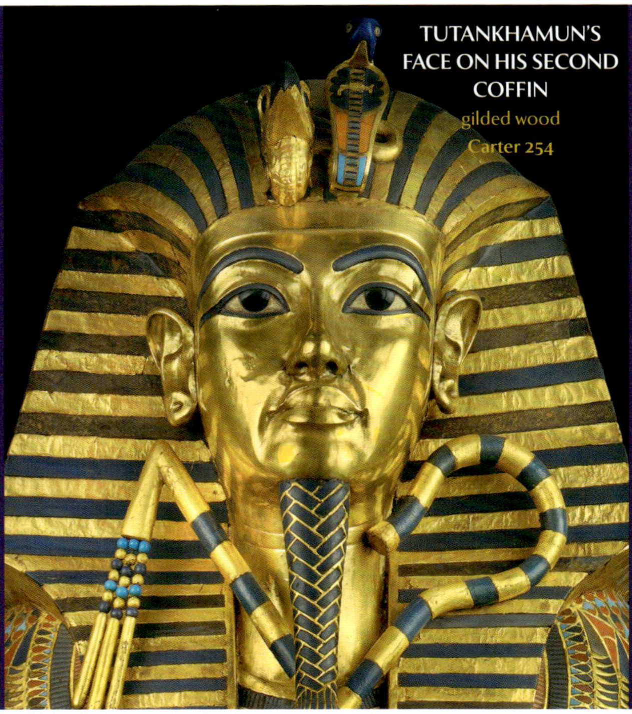

TUTANKHAMUN'S FACE ON HIS SECOND COFFIN
gilded wood
Carter 254

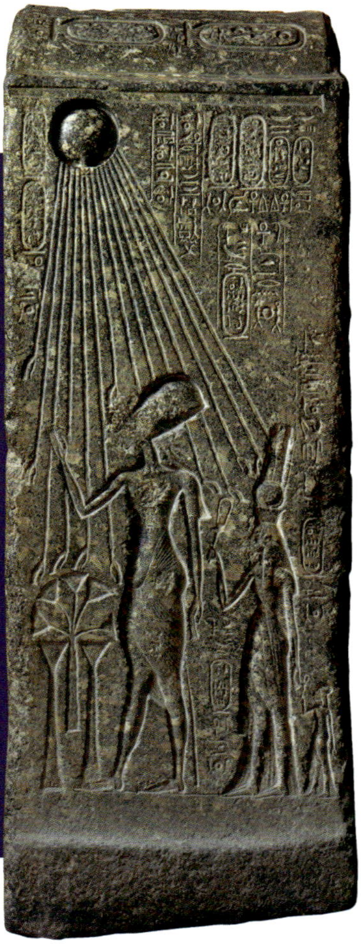

The royal family of Amarna worshipping the Aten.
Granite
Egyptian Museum in Cairo

Amenhotep III ruled for 39 years. During this time his chief wife was Queen Tiye, the daughter of two commoners, Yuya and Tjuya. Tiye gave Amenhotep III at least eight daughters. Their son, Amenhotep IV, succeeded their father on the throne, possibly after a period of time as his father's coregent. The length of this coregency is much disputed, with a length as great as 12 years having been suggested.

Akhenaten's chief wife was a woman named Nefertiti, who was never called "daughter of the king," so we know she was not of royal birth. Another important wife was another non-royal woman named Kiya. Within a few years of his accession, Amenhotep IV changed his name to Akhenaten and founded the new city of Akhetaten, to which he relocated the royal court. His reign saw the elevation of the solar disk, the Aten, to the status of Egypt's chief god. Akhenaten and his principal queen, Nefertiti, served as the high priests of the new cult, as well as deified members of a new holy family, which included six daughters, including Ankhesenpaaten, who was their third-born. Princes do not appear in the art of this period, although the royal tomb may contain a scene depicting a royal son as a baby in the arms of his mother or wet nurse. The strange proportions given to the human figure, especially the king's, during the Amarna Period has given rise to suspicions that a physical abnormality, perhaps caused by Marfan syndrome, had inspired them. Akhenaten died after a reign of 17 years.

Ankh(et)kheperure (also known as Neferneferuaten) seems to have been a female king whose reign overlapped entirely (or almost entirely) with that of Akhenaten. Ankh(et)kheperure was followed by Djeser-Kheperure Smenkhkare, who seems to have been a male king who ruled for less than a year, also perhaps partly or entirely as a coregent of Akhenaten. Already during the reign of these two ephemeral successors of Akhenaten, the return to the orthodox religion appears to have begun.

Smenkhkare's successor was first known as Tutankhaten or Tutankhuaten. A block from Amarna reused at Hermopolis (modern Ashmunein) refers to "the king's son, of his body, his beloved, Tutankhuaten." This block,

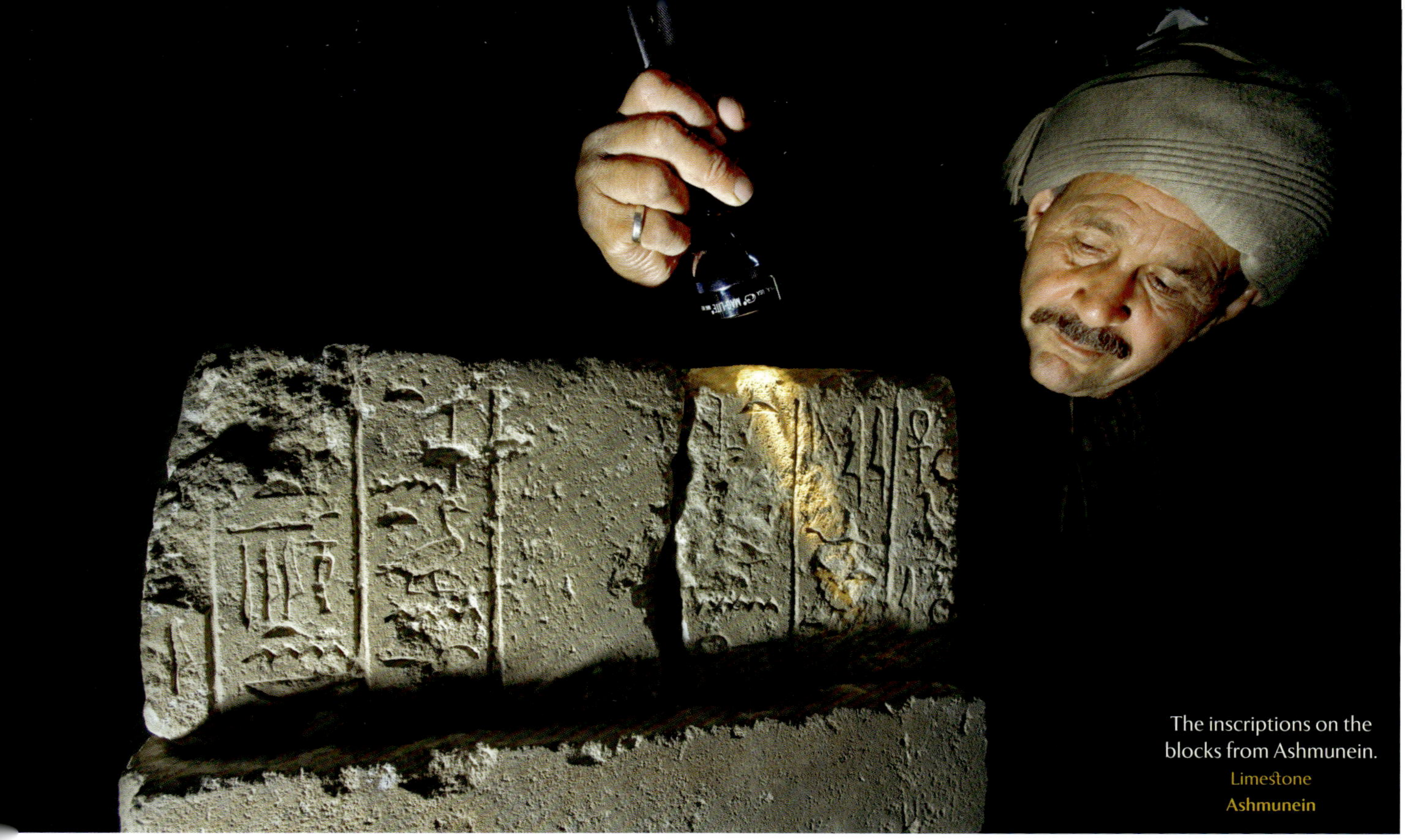

The inscriptions on the blocks from Ashmunein.
Limestone
Ashmunein

which also seems to name Ankhesenpaaten as the daughter of a king, confirms that Tutankhaten was a direct descendant, quite probably the son, of a king. Possibly even before becoming king, Tutankhaten was married to Ankhesenpaaten.

Shortly after ascending the throne, the king changed his name to Tutankhamun, his queen likewise changed her name to Ankhesenamun, the court abandoned Akhetaten for Memphis, and the orthodox religion was restored. Tutankhamun died at about the age of 19 after a reign of nine years, and, having no living children, was succeeded by the elderly Ay.

The identity of Tutankhamun's father has long been the subject of speculation. A number of scholars suggested Amenhotep III. Additions that Tutankhamun made to Amenhotep III's temples at Luxor and Soleb suggest a close connection between these two kings. Tutankhamun describes himself as "renewing the monument of his father." However, these inscriptions do not necessarily mean that Amenhotep III was literally his father. The relationship of "father" and "son" can refer to grandfather and grandson, great-grandfather and great-grandson, or even a man and his son-in-law. Because we know that Tutankhamun was around 19 when he died after a reign of about nine years, he must have been born between years 7 and 11 of Akhenaten's reign. (The exact year depends on how many years elapsed between Akhenaten's death and Tutankhamun's accession. Because we do not fully understand the reigns of Ankh(et)kheperure and Smenkhkare, this remains unknown at present.) Therefore, it is possible for Tutankhamun to have been the literal son of Amenhotep III only if there was a long coregency between Amenhotep III and Akhenaten.

Akhenaten was another favored candidate for Tutankhamun's father. An inscription on an astronomical instrument in the collection of the Oriental Institute of the University of Chicago could be interpreted as referring to Tutankhamun as "the great-grandson of Thutmose IV," who was Amenhotep III's father. If this interpretation is correct, this identification would place Tutankhamun a generation younger than Akhenaten, but this is highly speculative.

Archaeological evidence has suggested that the mummy found in KV 55 belonged to Akhenaten and that there was a connection between this mummy and Tutankhamun. Douglas Derry, the anatomist working with Howard Carter, noticed the physical resemblance between the mummies found in KV 62 and KV 55. Egyptologist Nicholas Reeves proposes that the coffin, jars, and the mummy belong to Akhenaten, based on the fact that the "magic bricks" found at the corners of the tomb were inscribed for him. These

The so-called astronomical instrument bears the royal names of Thutmose IV and Tutankhamun.
Wood
Oriental Institute of the University of Chicago

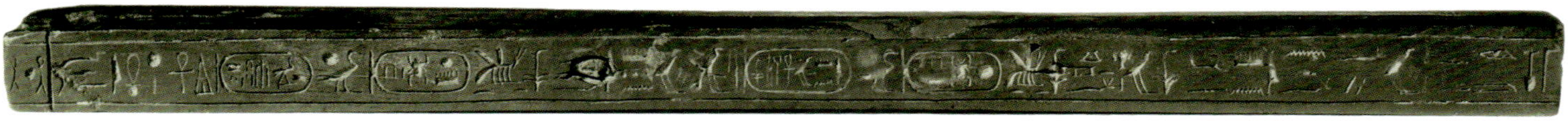

objects, and seals with Tutankhamun's name, may indicate that the young king moved Akhenaten from the Royal Tomb at Amarna to KV 55. The close proximity of KV 55 to KV 62, Tutankhamun's own tomb, further connects the two kings, although this connection does not indicate with any certainty that Tutankhamun was the son of Akhenaten. He could simply have been performing his duties as a member of the extended family.

In Room Alpha of the Royal Tomb at Amarna, there is a scene showing a deceased woman. Another scene adjacent to this shows a female figure holding a baby under a fan, a symbol of royalty. The woman with the baby has just left the chamber of the deceased woman. It has been proposed that this child is Tutankhamun, although this is by no means certain and has been disputed. The suggestion that Smenkhkare might be Tutankhamun's father seems to be based on the identification of the KV 55 mummy as Smenkhkhare's. However, there was always the chance that this mummy could be Akhenaten, although this was often doubted because the mummy appeared to be that of a man in his twenties, far too young to have been a king who ruled for 17 years. If these three men might be his father, who has been proposed as Tutankhamun's mother?

Tiye was the Great Royal Wife of Amenhotep III. Her parents were Yuya and Tjuya, whose mummies are known with certainty, as they were discovered ***in situ*** in their largely intact tomb, KV 46. Tiye's mummy was long unidentified, although the mummy known as the Elder Lady found in KV 35 had been suggested as hers. A lock of hair found within a small coffin inscribed with the name of Tiye in Tutankhamun's tomb matched that of the Elder Lady. A number of scholars suggested that Kiya, an important but secondary wife of Akhenaten, could be Tutankhamun's mother. Some think that Kiya was a Mitannian princess also known as

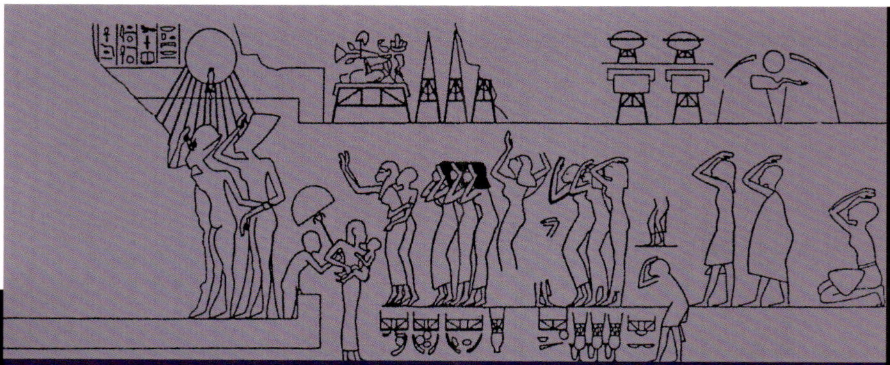

The funerary scene depicted in Room Alpha.
Royal tomb at Amarna

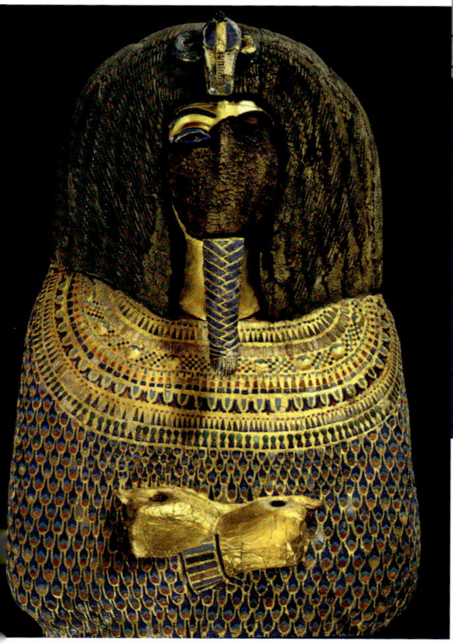

The lid of Akhenaten's coffin from KV 55.
Wood, gold leaf, glass paste
Egyptian Museum in Cairo

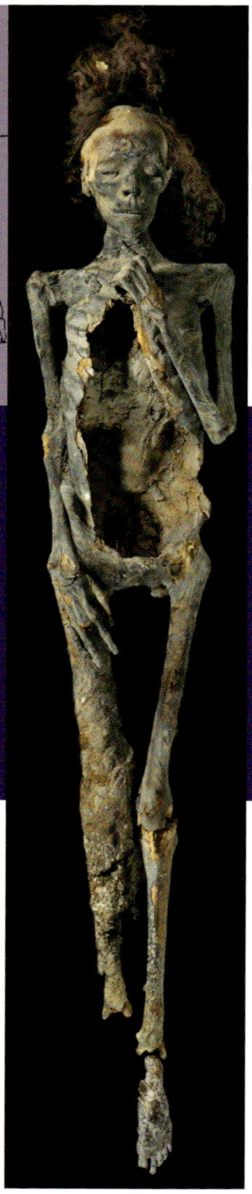

The mummy of the Elder Lady from tomb KV 35.
Luxor, Valley of the Kings
(Now in the Egyptian Museum in Cairo)

Tadukhepa, who was married not only to Akhenaten, but also to his father, Amenhotep III. Few have favored Nefertiti's candidacy as the mother. One of Akhenaten's daughters – either Meketaten or Meritaten – has been proposed, as has Baketaten, youngest daughter of Amenhotep III and Tiye. Another of Akhenaten's sisters, such as Sitamun, has been thought possible, with Amenhotep III as the father. Other sisters whose names we know are Iset C, Hennuttaneb, and Nebetiah. In the Theban tomb (TT 192) of Kheruef, who was Queen Tiye's steward, Amenhotep III is shown with eight unnamed daughters, so there are at least three more, for whom we have no names.

Regarding Tutankhamun's wife, we know she was Ankhesenamun, daughter of Akhenaten and Nefertiti. It has been suggested that the two mummified fetuses found in Tutankhamun's tombs were the still-born female children of Tutankhamun and his wife – or of one of his wives. We also know that the wife of one of Tutankhamun's officials had the title "chief of the harem of Tutankhamun."

These are the questions and possible answers that excavation, ancient art, and texts had given us. To explore further, we turned to medical science.

THE PROBLEM OF ANCIENT DNA

Could modern science unravel any of this mystery? I used to believe not. Mummies had never before yielded enough useful DNA, and there was always the risk of contamination from modern researchers and even from the ancient embalmers. It did not seem worth the risk of damaging these priceless remains. Damage had happened before. When Abdel Halim Nour El Din was Secretary General of the Supreme Council of Antiquities, and Mohamed Saleh was director of the Egyptian Museum, samples were taken from mummies. The sampling procedure, done with the help of Brigham Young University in Utah, left the mummies with holes that could be seen. Not until there could be a project that met my rigorous requirements would I trust the results of DNA tests. It would be otherwise too easy to make mistakes.

The project would have to have two laboratories, each with its own team. These teams would be separate, so that one did not know the results of the other. These labs would have to be specifically devoted to the analysis of ancient DNA from mummies. And they had to be Egyptian, so that we could oversee them properly.

DNA NOW AND THE CT SCAN

Eventually several top geneticists convinced me that the field had advanced far enough that testing the mummies could give useful results. With the financial aid of the Discovery Channel, which we allowed to film the project, we set up two state-of-the-art labs, which would be away from each other, to sequence the DNA. One was prepared in the basement of the Egyptian Museum in Cairo, while the second was located at the Faculty of Medicine at Cairo University.

Yahia Gad, MD and Somaia Ismail, MD, both of the National Research Center, Cairo, led the teams. Other members of the team were Rabab Khairat, MSc, of the Ancient DNA Laboratory, Egyptian Museum and the Institute of Human Genetics, Division of Molecular Genetics, University of Tubingen, Germany; Dina Fathallah, MSc, of the Ancient DNA Laboratory; Naglaa Hasan, MSc, of the National Research Center and the Ancient DNA Laboratory; Amal Ahmed, BPharm, of the National Research Center and the Ancient DNA Laboratory; Hisham Elleithy; Markus Ball, MSc, of the Institute of Human Genetics, Division of Molecular Genetics, University of Tubingen; Fawzi Gaballah, PhD, Sally Wasef, MSc, and Mohamed Fateen, MD, of Learning Resource Center, Kasr Al Ainy Faculty of Medicine, Cairo University; Hany Amer, PhD, of the National Research Center; Paul Gostner, MD, of the Department of Radiodiagnostics, Central Hospital Bolzano, Bolzano, Italy; Ashraf Selim, MD, Department of Radiology, Kasr Al Ainy Faculty of Medicine; Albert Zink, PhD, Institute for Mummies and the Iceman,

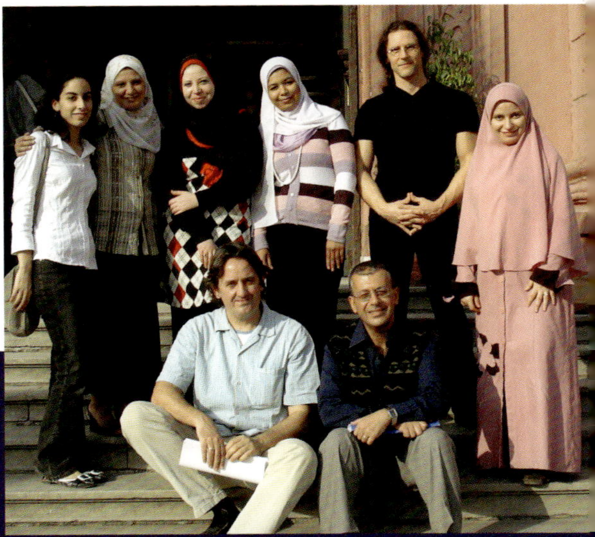

The Egyptian team of the DNA lab, together with the foreign team in front of the Egyptian Museum in Cairo.
Sitting in front f.l.t.r.: Albert Zink and Yehia Gad.
Standing in the back f.l.t.r.: Dina Fathallah, Somaia Ismail, Rabab Khairat, Naglaa Hasan Abu Mandil, Carsten Pusch, Amal Ahmed.

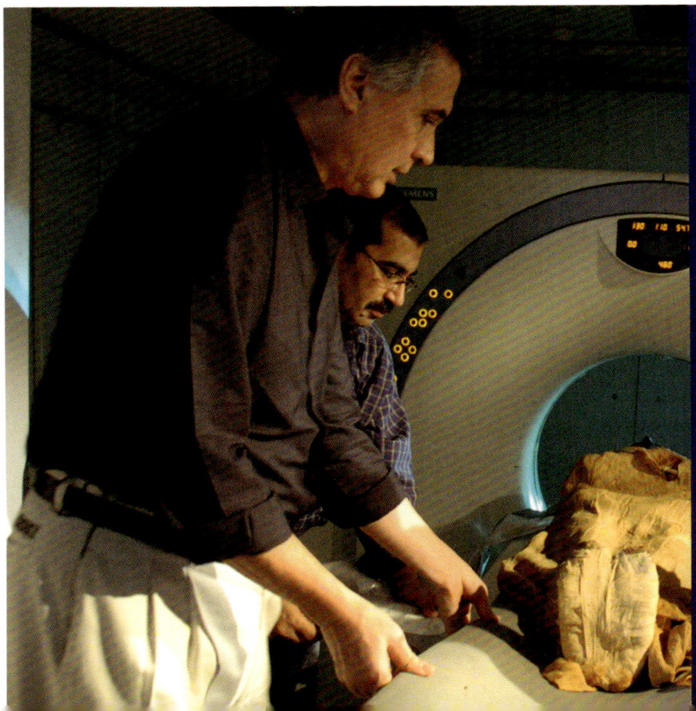

Ashraf Selim and Hany Abdel Rahman scanning the mummies.

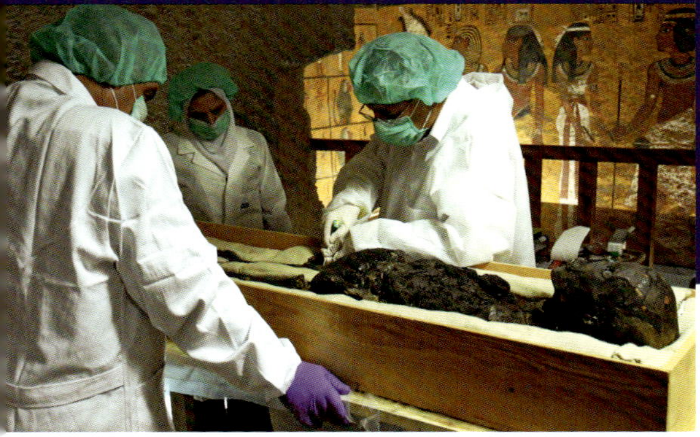

The Egyptian team taking DNA samples from Tutankhamun's mummy.

EURAC, Bolzano, Italy; and Carsten M. Pusch, PhD Institute of Human Genetics, Division of Molecular Genetics, University of Tübingen. To avoid contamination with modern DNA – and to avoid possible contamination from the DNA of the ancient embalmers – a bone biopsy needle would draw samples from deep within the bone, at several locations, for each mummy. Once obtained, the samples would have to be purified so that only the DNA remained. This means using solvents to remove the unguents and other substances used for the mummification. How to accomplish this would vary among the mummies, according to what kind of contaminants the researchers encountered. This would be difficult. The teams would be looking at three kinds of DNA. Each could tell us something different about the mummies. A cell has DNA in two places. Most genetic material (which in humans is perhaps roughly 25,000 genes) is found in an organelle called the nucleus; this is called nuclear DNA. There are two kinds of nuclear DNA we would be looking for. One is the DNA sequences from the Y chromosome. This chromosome is passed only from father to son, and is not found in females. The other kind of nuclear DNA is autosomal. It is found on the 22 pairs of human chromosomes that do not code for sex. Half of this DNA is received from the mother, half from the father. But there are also 37 other genes found in other organelle called mitochondria. Mitochondria are responsible for generating a cell's energy. The DNA found here, called mitochondrial DNA (or mtDNA), provides instructions for the creation of certain enzymes the cell needs to function and also for the creation of molecules vital to the production of amino acids, which in turn become proteins. Both human egg and sperm have mitochondrial DNA, but the sperm's mitochondria does not survive the fertilization process. This leaves the embryo with only its mother's mtDNA. Because a mother passes her mtDNA directly to her offspring of either sex, this would allow us to trace the maternal lines of Tutankhamun's family.

Although most human DNA is the same, there are detectable differences among individuals. Certain areas on the nuclear DNA molecules, called polymorphic regions, can vary. One type of these polymorphic markers is called a short tandem repeat, or STR. Even if only a little genetic material is present, it is possible to analyze STRs because these short sequences of DNA can be "amplified" – that is, techniques of molecular biology can multiply the molecular strands so that they can be more readily analyzed. When two people are closely related, their STRs will correspond to a greater degree.

Once we had our DNA samples, we would be able to compare them. A machine called a DNA sequencer, which used fragment length analysis software, would identify and read the DNA. We would repeat each analysis up to 30 times in order to be sure of the results, which would be considered valid only if they were replicated 80% of the time.

We were also going to scan the mummies with the CT scanner, including Tutankhamun's, as described in Chapter 5.

THE MUMMIES

If we look at the mummies we had to test who would be related to Tutankhamun's, we can see that we had Yuya and Tjuya, Amenhotep III, and Tutankhamun. But we were missing the following mummies from Tutankhamun's family:

1. Queen Tiye, wife of Amenhotep III
2. Tutankhamun's mother
3. Tutankhamun's father
4. Tutankhamun's wife, Ankhesenamun
5. Queen Nefertiti

We also had mummies that could be related to the family of Tutankhamun whose identifications had never been confirmed. Two female mummies found hidden by late New Kingdom priests in a side chamber of the tomb of Amenhotep II (KV 35), known as the Elder Lady (KV35EL) and the Younger Lady (KV35YL), were candidates for some of Tutankhamun's female relatives. There were also two female mummies from a small tomb known as KV 21. This tomb was probably of 18th Dynasty date, and both mummies hold their left hand against their chest. This is generally thought to be a pose given to queens. Perhaps these could be Nefertiti, or Ankhesenamun, or someone else entirely? And, of course, we had the two fetuses from Tutankhamun's tomb. And who was the mummy from KV 55, which earlier studies had shown resembled the young king? Could it be Smenkhkare, maybe, or Akhenaten? Any or all of these mummies might present us with the missing pieces of the Amarna puzzle.

THE RESULTS

Tests on the Y chromosomes among the male mummies would be able to determine a precise relationship among them – if there was any relationship at all. I was skeptical that this would work, but was delighted by the results. With just a 0.01% chance for doubt, the team established that the mummy of Amenhotep III was the father of the KV 55 mummy and that the KV 55 mummy was the father of Tutankhamun. The tests were done to a standard that would have satisfied an FBI paternity test.

Now we had to determine who the KV 55 mummy was. Many believe it to be Akhenaten, whose epithets can be found on a coffin found in that tomb, but others believed the mummy was Smenkhkare. Earlier forensic analysis had determined that the body was that of a man who was at most 25 years old. This was far too young for Akhenaten, who reigned for 17 years and who had two daughters before he was crowned.

Perhaps if we could determine who had given birth to the KV 55 mummy, that would help. We knew that Akhenaten's mother was Queen Tiye, who was long suspected of being the Elder Lady, more formally known as mummy KV35EL. We also knew that this mummy's lovely hair matched the lock of hair found in Tutankhamun's tomb, labeled as belonging to Tiye. If we compared the Elder Lady's DNA to that of the mummies of Yuya and Tjuya, Queen Tiye's parents, that would confirm her identity. And indeed that is exactly what the DNA tests showed: KV35EL shared half of the tested genetic markers with the mummy of Tjuya and the other half with the mummy of Yuya. Radiological examination showed that the queen had died at about the age of 50, and that her parents had each died in their 50s.

Now, what would the tests reveal about the relationship between Tiye and the KV 55 mummy? They showed that Tiye was the mother of that mummy.

There was still the problem of age. A man of 25 years was much too young to be Akhenaten. We performed new CT scans, which revealed degeneration of the spine related to age and osteoarthritis in the knees and legs. This mummy was a much older man than previously thought, between the ages of 35 and 45. That meant almost certainly that this offspring of Amenhotep III and Tiye was Akhenaten. There remains a shadow of doubt, however, because so little is known about Smenkhkare, not even how old he was.

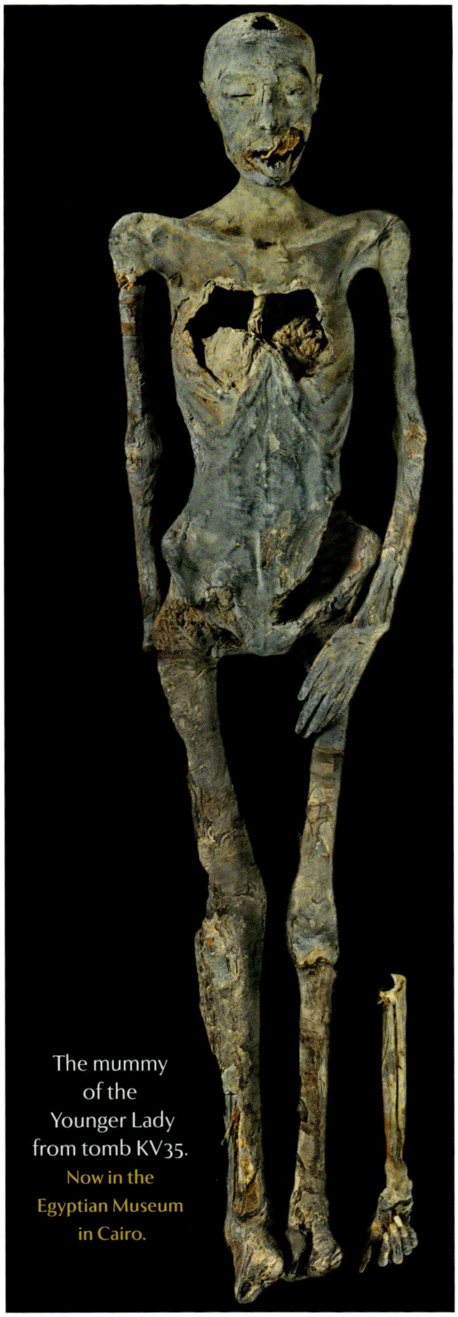

The mummy of the Younger Lady from tomb KV35. Now in the Egyptian Museum in Cairo.

Scans of the mummy did shed light on another aspect of the family. It has often been thought that an abnormality caused by a genetically inherited disease, such as Marfan syndrome, was the reason for the strangely elongated and feminine appearance of the king in the art of the Amarna Period. The scan revealed no abnormality. Instead, the reason for the artistic convention must be sought in Akhenaten's ideas about the Aten and his attempt to show himself as having both male and female qualities, just like the Aten, the god that was both father and mother of all creation.

So now we had to look for Tutankhamun's mother. We were surprised to find our answer so easily. Results of the autosomal DNA tests showed that his mother was the Younger Lady, KV35YL, whose mummy was found with Tiye's, hidden in KV 35. And the tests revealed one more surprise. She was the daughter of Amenhotep III and Tiye. Akhenaten and his full-blooded sister had had a child together: Tutankhamun. (Results of the mtDNA tests will be published later, but it can be said now that they support the results of the other tests of the relationships among the mummies tested for the King Tutankhamun Family Project.)

There is no evidence that either Nefertiti or Kiya was a daughter of Amenhotep III and Tiye. Akhenaten had at least five full sisters whose names we know: Sitamun, Iset C, Henuttaneb, Nebetiah, and Beketaten. Is this mummy one of them? We will probably never know. Incest was not rare in the royal families of Egypt, but in this case, at least, it proved to be fatal. No doubt Tutankhamun's physical weaknesses, which led to his death, were due to this inbreeding.

THE TWO FETUSES

These adult mummies were not the only ones that we had to test. Carter had found two mummified fetuses in Tutankhamun's tomb. Their tiny coffins gave them no names, referring to each only as "the Osiris," a title given to the dead. They are known today by the numbers Carter assigned to them: 317a and 317b.

They are not the only mummified fetuses ever found. Sometime between 1903 and 1906, the Italian Egyptologist Ernesto Schiaparelli found one in the tomb of a son of Rameses III, a man named Amonherkhepeshef, in the Valley of the Queens (QV 55). This stillborn child might have been a child of Rameses III, but we do not know. More recently, a skeleton of a late-term fetus or newborn was found in a shaft below the tomb that Horemheb built at Memphis. It is thought that his queen, Mutnodjmet, might have been buried there, so she may have been the mother. In a Roman Era cemetery at Dakhleh Oasis, 82 fetal and perinatal skeletons were found. These had been buried alongside adults and older children. The only other mummified fetuses known so far come from

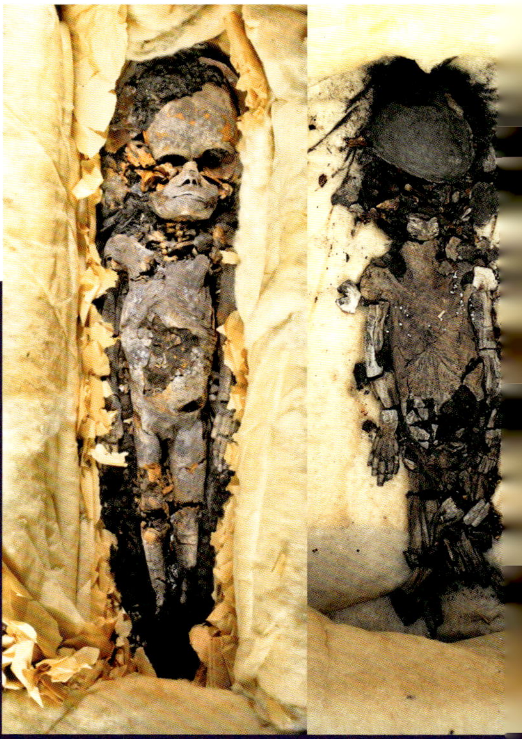

Recent photo of the two fetuses shows the deterioration since the time of the discovery.
Kasr el Aini Hospital in Cairo

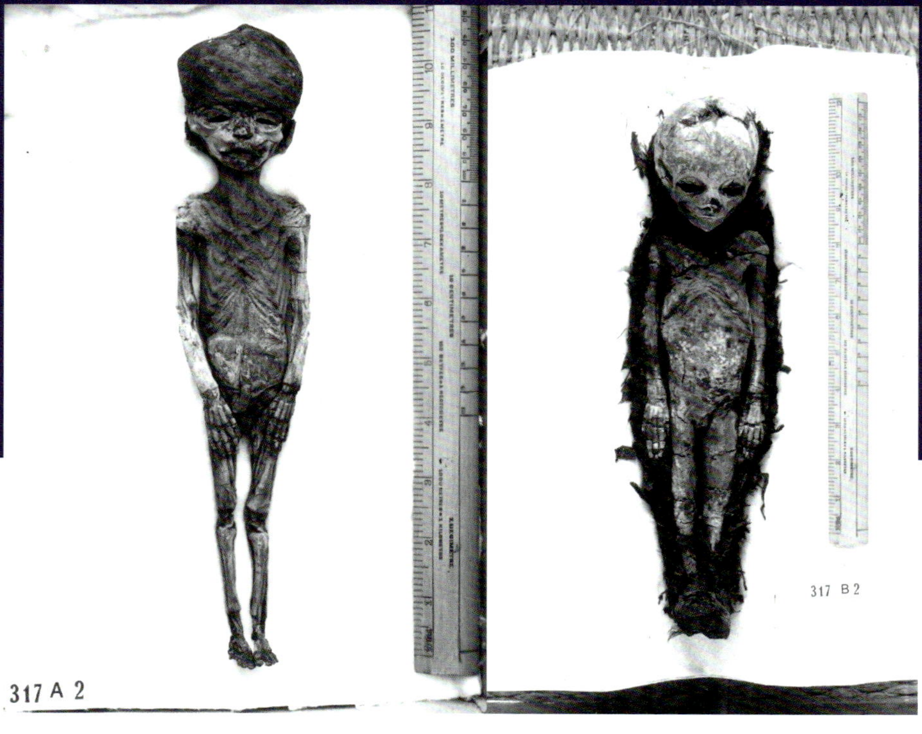

The two mummified fetuses 317a/317b.
Harry Burton / Griffith Institute

the Chinchorro culture of northern Chile, which existed from 5000 to about 500 BC.

Mummy 317a was the smaller of the two from Tutankhamun's tomb. Although Carter unwrapped it in 1925, it was not until 1932 that Douglas Derry, the anatomist from Cairo University on his team, examined 317a and 317b, which he estimated were between five and seven months gestation. Both were female, he reported. He found 317a to be wonderfully preserved, even with part of the umbilical cord still attached. It was a little more than 25.75 cm long. The embalmers had apparently made no incisions to remove the organs, so perhaps it was naturally mummified, with its arms laid in front of its thighs. In 1932, Mummy 317b was not as well preserved. About 36.1 cm long, this fetus still had downy hair on its head, even eyebrows and eyelashes. Its arms were laid straight by its sides. This mummy had a tiny (1.8 cm) embalming incision, and packs of linen seemed to have been inserted into its skull through its nose. After Derry had examined them, 317a and 317b were kept at the Faculty of Medicine at Cairo University.

When James Harris and his team X-rayed Tutankhamun's mummy in 1978, they also examined 317b. They concluded that the fetus was at least 35 weeks gestation and might have been full term at death. It had, Harris thought, many genetic anomalies: Sprengel's deformity (one shoulder blade higher than the other), spinal dysraphism (a class of disorders of the spine, including spina bifida), and scoliosis (abnormal curvature of the spine). But when this mummy's X-rays were reexamined by other experts in 2008, it was concluded that the fetus had been only 30 weeks gestation. What, we wondered, would CT scans show?

To examine each mummy, we tailored the scanner and the computer analysis of the image to take into account these tiny, badly preserved mummies. It took 495 images of 317a and 701 of 317b. With great care, 3D images of the fetuses were created, taking into account not only the soft tissues and tiny bones, but also the linen and embalming materials.

Our conclusions found that 317a was a little longer than Derry had measured, 29.9 cm rather than 25.75 cm. The length of the fetus's humeral bone led us to determine the age to be 24.6 weeks gestation. The mummy was in such poor condition that the scans did not allow us to confirm Derry's conclusion that the fetus was female. The scans also could not detect skeletal deformities, nor was there any indication of what had caused the fetus's death. The scans also suggested that this mummy had been artificially mummified. There were elaborate structures within the body cavity that are probably the visceral packs, and there seemed to be embalming material present within the skull. But the mummy was so poorly preserved that we could not identify embalming incisions or damage to the skull caused by the embalmers, if they had removed the brain.

For mummy 317b, which is somewhat better preserved, we found the embalming incision, which was just a little bigger (1.8 cm) than Derry had reported, and we again found structures in the body cavity that are almost certainly visceral packs. The embalmers had also taken care to fill out the mummy's legs to give them the right shape, although they did so in such a way to give it a larger left thigh than right. However, in order to truly ascertain what kind of mummification was used on either mummy, chemical analysis will need to be performed. This mummy was evidently female and measured about 45 cm long. Based on the state of development of the bones and teeth, we assessed its age to be 9 months (36.78 weeks). It had no sign of most of the deformities of the bones Harris had reported, only a mild form of scoliosis. The other abnormalities were instead due to many injuries to bone and soft tissue that the body had received after death. Once again, the scans found nothing to indicate why the fetus had died.

We also carried out DNA studies to see if these would prove what was long believed, that these were the premature or stillborn daughters of Tutankhamun. Because of the poor condition of these mummies, we could not obtain the kind of quality DNA that we did from the others. In fact for Mummy 317a, the risk of contamination was so great, and the deterioration of the mummy was so bad, that we received inconclusive results. Even so, results showed that Mummy 317b has a greater than 99.9% probability of being the stillborn child of Tutankhamun. There is little doubt, however, that Tutankhamun is also the father of 317a.

SEARCHING FOR NEFERTITI

Of all the queens of ancient Egypt, none is as famous as Nefertiti, the beautiful 18th Dynasty queen who ruled alongside her husband, Akhenaten. Her fame and influence lives on long after her death. In May 2013, at the Festival of Legendary Ladies held in Morocco, Nefertiti was ranked alongside Om Kalthoum, Marilyn Monroe, and Coco Chanel, as a woman who had possessed beauty, power, knowledge, glory, and stardom – women whose fame made history and whose reputations have never died. Ironically, in ancient times Nefertiti virtually disappeared during the last years of her husband's reign, with just a single inscription, dated to Year 16, known after Year 12. There is no mention of what became of her or what happened to her mummy. It is one of ancient Egypt's greatest mysteries.

In 2003, Joanne Fletcher, a British Egyptologist with the University of York, made a documentary for the Discovery Channel, claiming that the Younger Lady was none other than Nefertiti. Many people – I among them – rejected her theory. We were right. The DNA tests showed that the Younger Lady from KV 35 was not only Tutankhamun's mother, but also Akhenaten's sister. As I have said, we have no evidence suggesting that Nefertiti was the daughter of Amenhotep III and Tiye.

So we began to investigate if some other mummy might be Nefertiti or her daughter, Ankhesenamun, who was both Tutankhamun's sister and his wife. If a mummy is Ankhesenamun, DNA should reveal her to be the mother of the fetus mummies, 317a and 317b.

We had noticed that the Egyptians sometimes put mother and daughter together.

For example, we discovered that the priests had hidden the Younger Lady together with her mother, Queen Tiye, in KV 35 to keep them both safe from tomb robbers. This made me think about the two female mummies found in KV 21. Possibly these could be Nefertiti and one of her daughters. They had been found in 1817 by Giovanni Battista Belzoni, the famous Italian explorer, who described them this way:

> *"At one corner of this chamber, we found two mummies on the ground quite naked, without cloth or case. They were females, and their hair pretty long, and well preserved, though it was easily separated from the head by pulling it a little."*

Flooding and other environmental effects had caused the mummies to deteriorate since then. An American archaeologist, Donald Ryan, collected the two mummies and put them in two boxes within the tomb to protect them.

The first mummy, later dubbed KV21A, is made up mostly of the rear side of a torso, with most of the spine intact. Both feet are painfully distorted, the right even more so than the left. No trace of its skull remains. Mark Papworth, an archaeologist who belonged to Ryan's team, suggested that this woman was about 25 years old when she died. She had had a slender build in life and was of medium stature, about 1.62 m tall. The second mummy, called KV21B, is a little taller than the first one and better preserved.

Thinking that it would be important to study them, I had these mummies moved to the Egyptian Museum. It proved to be very difficult to obtain useful DNA from them, and the results were not as good as for the other mummies. Nonetheless, tests did show that KV21A is very likely the mother of the two fetuses found in Tutankhamun's tomb. But is she Ankhesenamun? The DNA tests could not firmly establish her identity as the daughter of Akhenaten. Research needs to continue to confirm these results, and to identify mummy KV21B.

The prestigious *Journal of the American Medical Association* reviewed the results of the King Tutankhamun Family Project rigorously over the course of eight months. When the *JAMA* gave its approval and agreed to publish them, I held a press conference at the Egyptian Museum in Cairo and announced what we had found. The newly identified mummies are now displayed in cases before the Second Mummy Room. Meanwhile, Dr Gad informs me that his team is currently finishing analyzing the rest of the data from the mummies and hopes to submit a new manuscript for publication in the near future. This new analysis includes mtDNA and other genetic data, and will address the issue of DNA decay due to changes after death. It will present more genetically technical details and will focus on the challenging technical aspects of analyzing ancient DNA.

That the peer-reviewed *JAMA* accepted the results of the tests proved to me that we now have important tools with which to explore ancient Egyptian history through mummies. We will need them, because the Valley of the Kings will always have more mysteries for us to unravel.

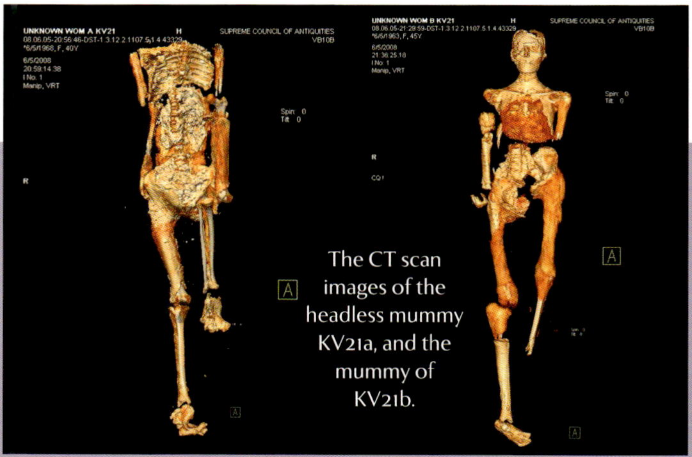

The CT scan images of the headless mummy KV21a, and the mummy of KV21b.

The Search for Nefertiti's Sister

We began to look for the remains of the body of a woman found in the tomb that Horemheb built at Saqqara. After excavation, these bones, which are thought to have belonged to Horemheb's queen, Mutnodjmet, had been placed in a storage magazine. I entered every magazine near the New Kingdom tombs of Memphis without locating them. I even went more than 15 m down into the shaft in Horemheb's tomb, and still I found nothing.

Robert Hari, an Egyptologist at the University of Geneva, among others, has indicated that Mutnodjmet, whose name is also given as Mutbenret, was the sister of Nefertiti. Mutnodjmet had the titles "Sister of the King's Chief Wife" and "Daughter of the King." She was the daughter of Ay, who became king after Tutankhamun. It is certain that she had a connection to Nefertiti and perhaps was her twin sister.

Geoffrey Thorndike Martin, field director of the Amarna Royal Tombs Project, had found the bones in the shaft leading to the burial chamber in Horemheb's tomb. Paleopathologist Eugen Strouhal studied these remains, which included the skull, and determined that Mutnodjmet had died at the age of about 40. She may have died in childbirth because the bones of a fetus or newborn were found with her. If they can ever be tested for their DNA, this queen's remains may yield important clues about Tutankhamun's family.

KING TUTANKHAMUN'S PEDIGREE

(BASED ON DNA ANALYSIS)

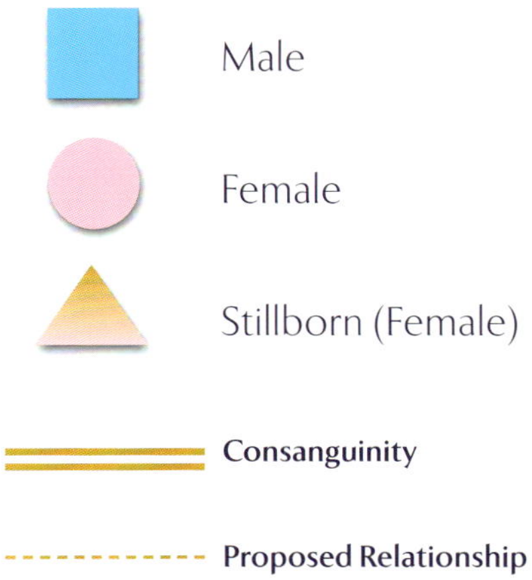

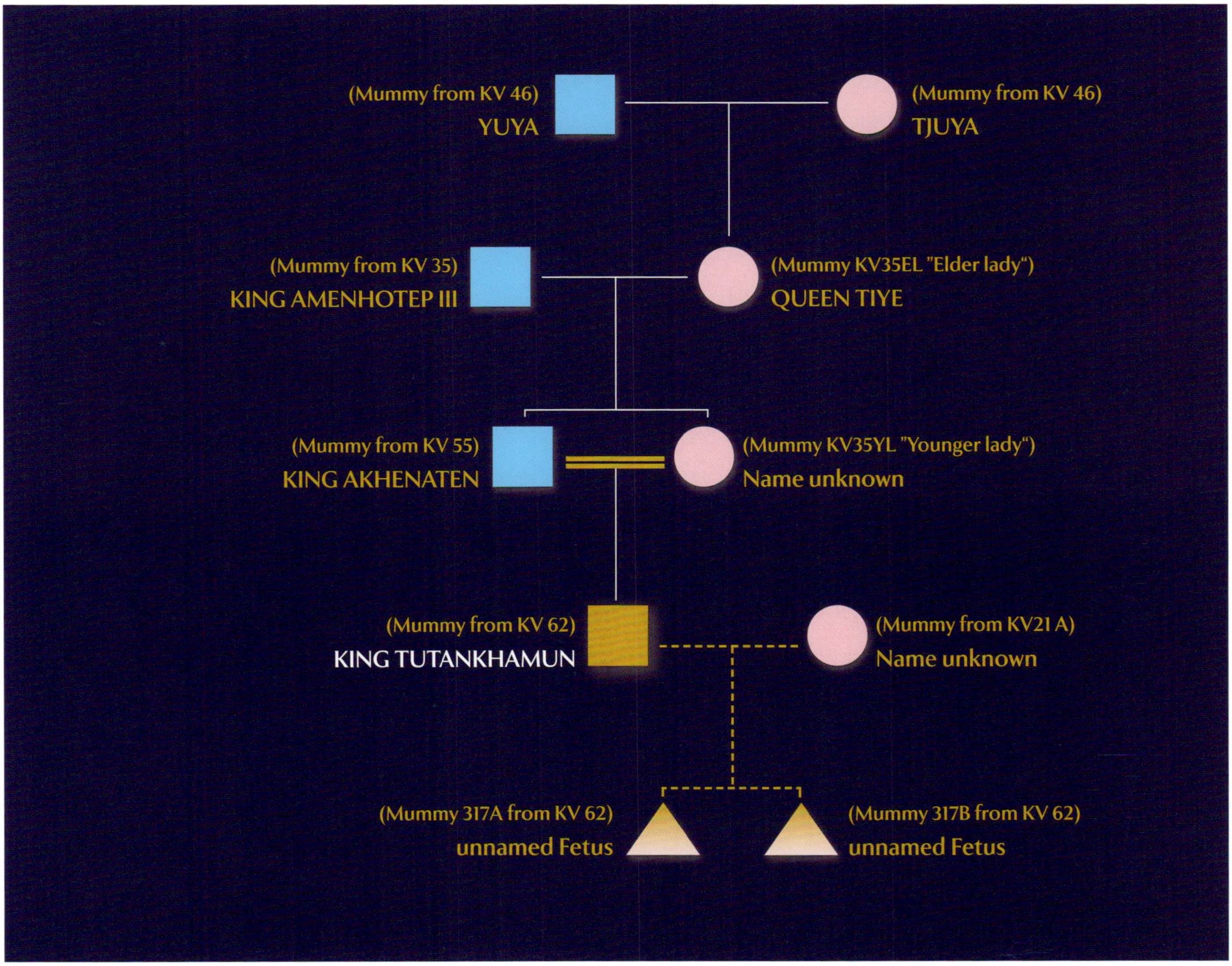

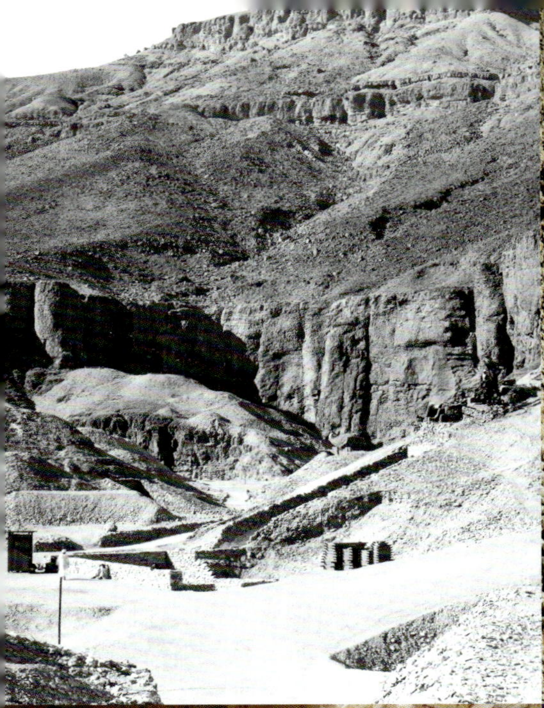

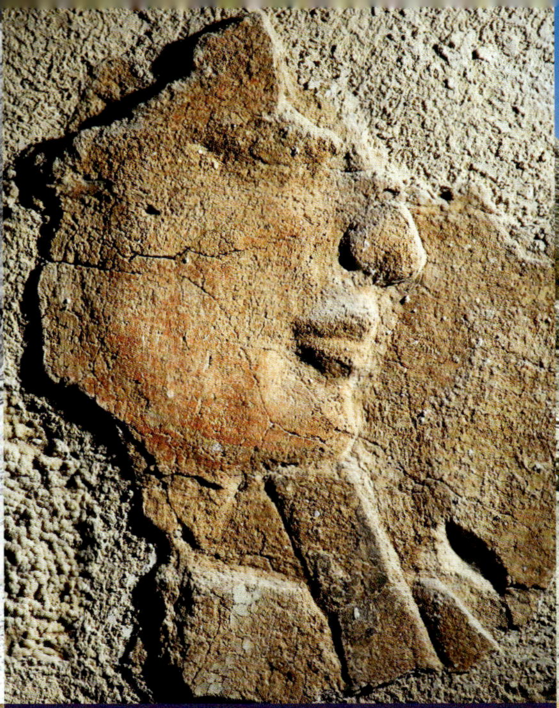

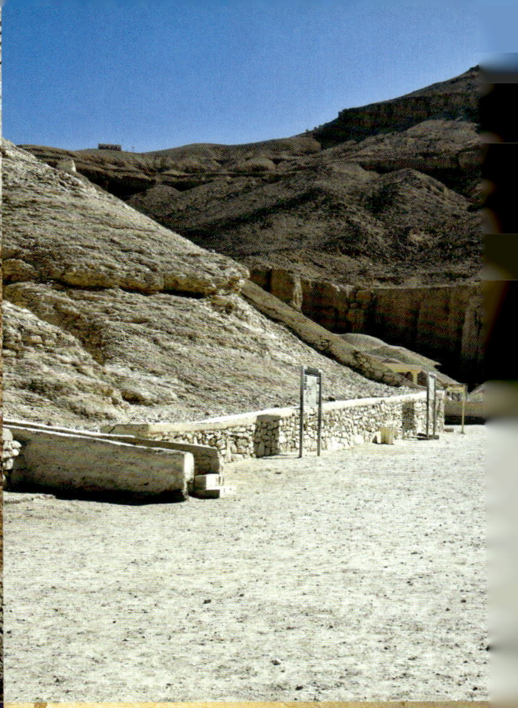

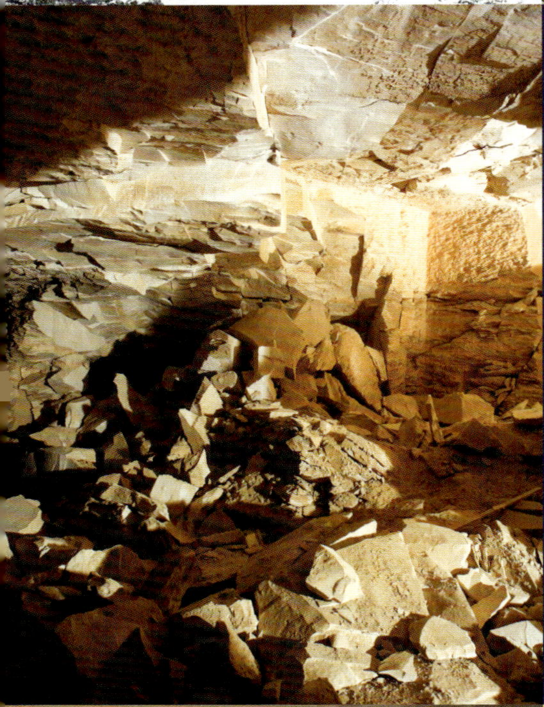

CHAPTER VII

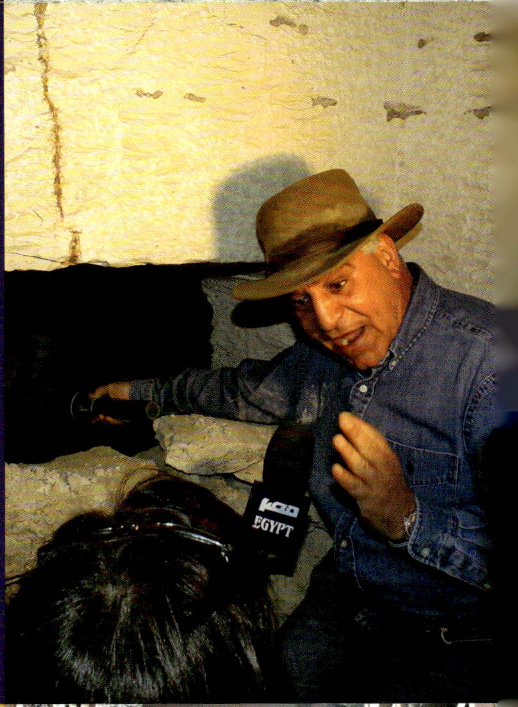

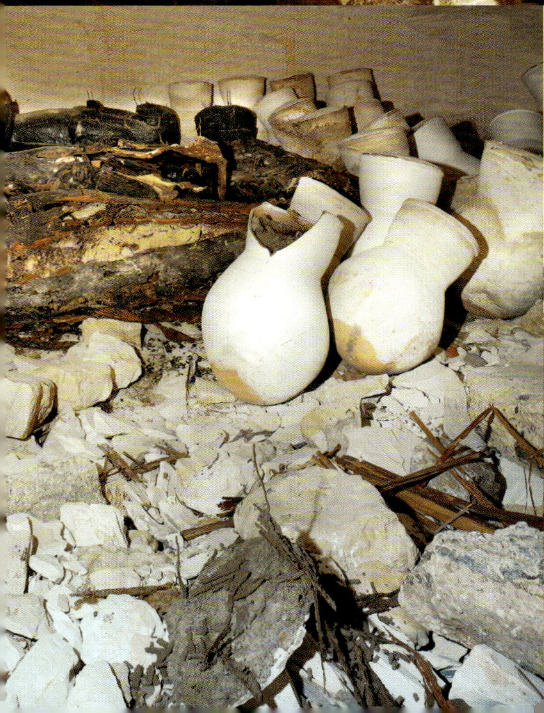

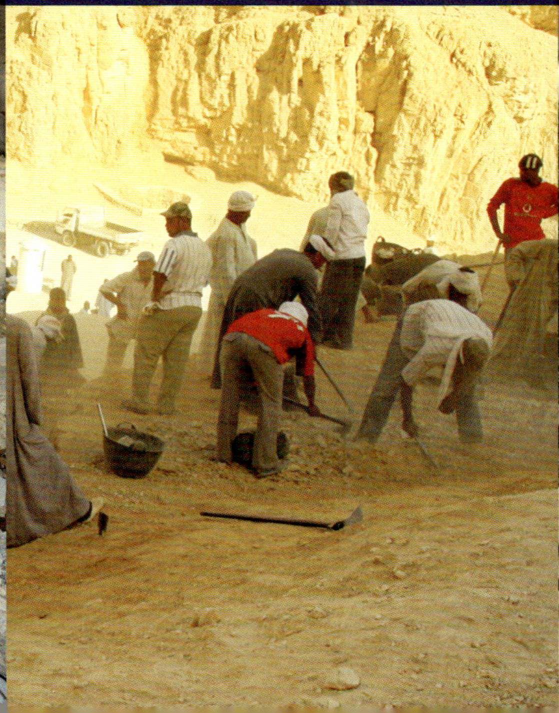

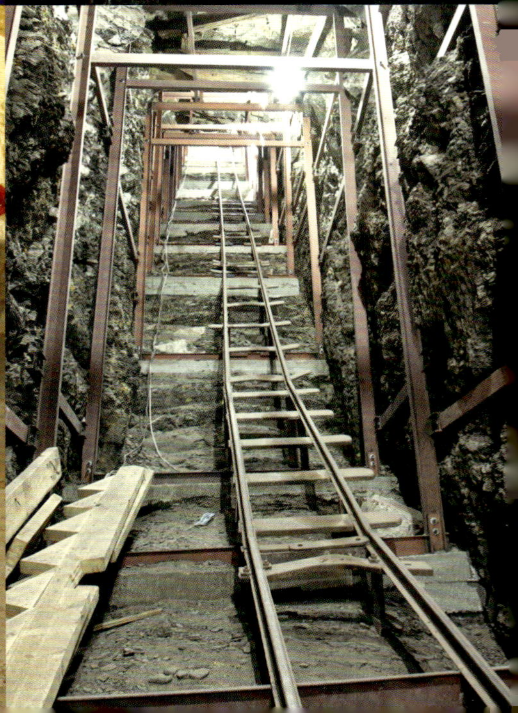

THE VALLEY OF THE KINGS AND FINDS

AFTER THE DISCOVERY OF TUTANKH-AMUN

THE STORY of Howard Carter and his discovery of the tomb of Tutankhamun made a deep impression on me when I was young, as did visiting the Valley of the Kings when I was a youth. Finally, in 1974, I had my first opportunity to work as an inspector in the royal necropolis of Thebes. The year before, foreign archaeological missions had been forbidden from working in Egypt except at Alexandria, Cairo, and Luxor. This meant that many expeditions came to work in Luxor, and each needed its own inspector. I was assigned to a number of projects, including the University of Pennsylvania's expedition at Malqata, where Tutankhamun's grandfather, Amenhotep III, had built a palace.

Of course, I met with other Egyptians who worked with the excavations. I had also met Sheikh Nagdy, who was a second-generation chief guard of the west bank. We would meet at the El Marsam Hotel, owned by the last member of a famous family of tomb robbers, the Abdel Rasouls, who had found a cache of royal mummies at Deir el-Bahri in the 19t century. Sheikh Nagdy was fond of beer, so when I had to ask a favor of him, I bought him not just one bottle but two.

I wanted to go into the Valley of the Kings on the night of the full moon, so I needed him to go with me. He agreed, and we went together, but at the tomb of Tutankhamun we went our separate ways. He sat contentedly there beside the locked gate with his beer, while I went past the tomb of Amenhotep II and began to climb up the mountain alone. The moon was bright overhead, lighting my

Archival photograph of the area of Tutankhamun's tomb in the Valley of the Kings. The entrance to Tutankhamun's tomb (KV 62) lies to the right of the large entrance of Rameses VI's tomb
Harry Burton / Griffith Institute

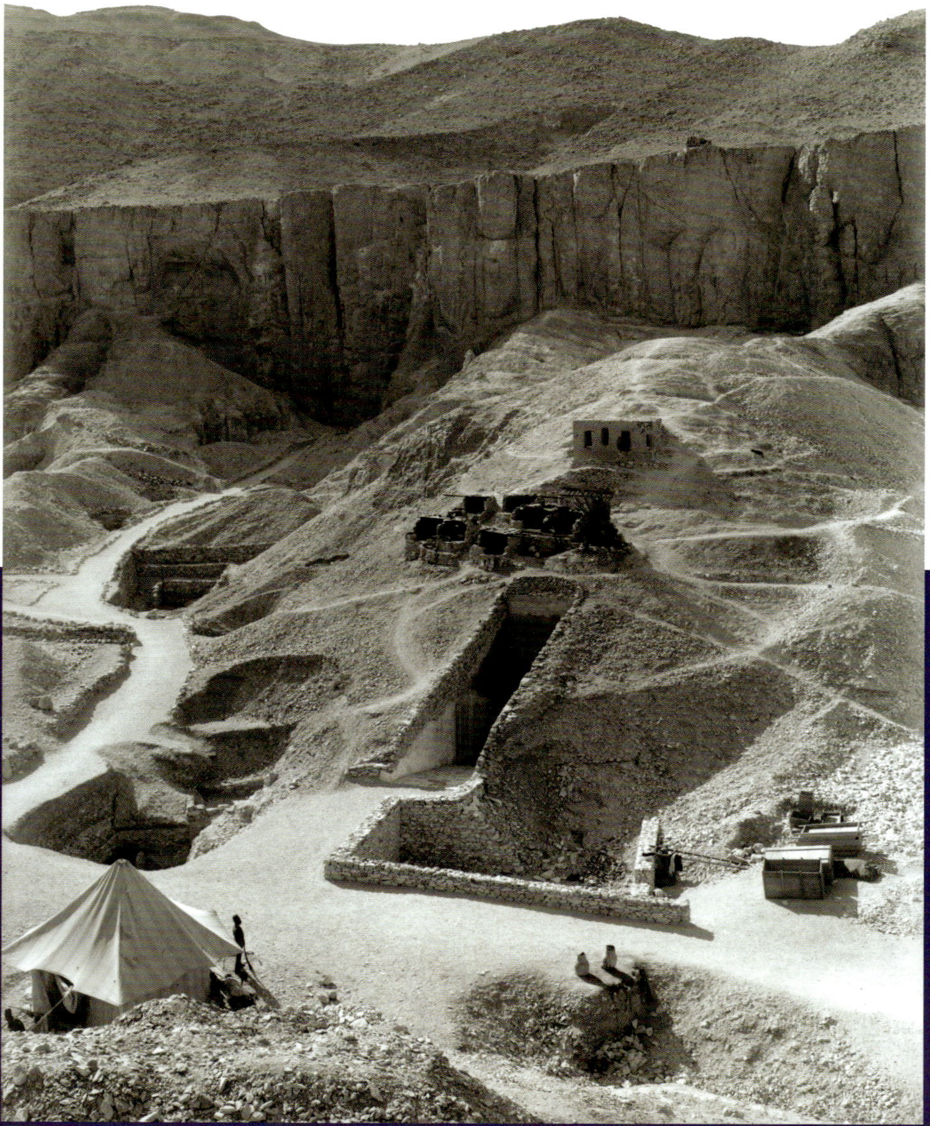

way. It was quiet here, without the tourists. This is why the goddess of the highest peak of the valley was called Meretseger, which means "She Who Loves Silence." There is romance in a place like this, even when one is alone and all is silent. The valley below me, the moon overhead. The Egyptians must have felt very close to their gods here. I passed the night on the mountain.

When I awoke at dawn, the sun was shining down upon the tombs. When you experience a sight like this, you do not have to ask why the Egyptians made the sun, which can be so brutal at noon on a summer day, the center of their religion and considered it to be the source of creation and of rebirth after death.

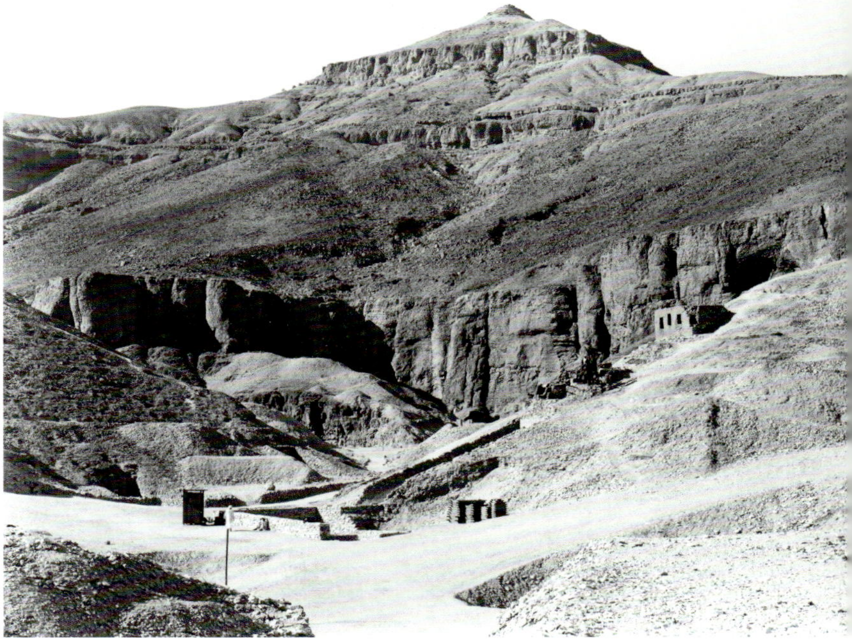

The Valley of the Kings, the last resting place of the kings and queens of the New Kingdom.

After I descended the mountain, I found that I was not the only one who had spent the night in the valley. Sheikh Nagdy was still there, asleep before Tutankhamun's tomb.

It is difficult to be alone in the Valley of the Kings, and I did not have that opportunity again until 2004. By this time, I was no longer just an inspector of antiquities, but the Secretary General of the Supreme Council of Antiquities. This time I climbed to the peak from a different spot, facing the tomb of Seti I. I had things other than "romance" on my mind this time. I was still thinking of Howard Carter and the tomb of Tutankhamun, but I was also thinking critically, as a researcher. Had Carter really found the final treasure hidden in the valley? Most everyone doubted that anything important was left to be found. Of course, Theodore Davis had doubted that too, a hundred years ago! But maybe now this was true. After all, no one had found anything significant since Carter and the tomb of Tutankhamun, more than eighty years before.

At the time, I thought about what no one has ever yet found anywhere, but which might be somewhere in the Valley of the Kings: the tombs of Amenhotep I of the 18th Dynasty and Rameses VIII of the 20th Dynasty. And what about many of the royal women and queens of the Amarna Period, the children of Akhenaten and Nefertiti? Where was the tomb of Ankhesenamun? Of Nefertiti? I also thought about who had found what had been found: foreigners. Not a single tomb had been found by an Egyptian expedition. I decided that I would change that by starting ***Egyptian*** excavations in the Valley of the Kings.

Even today, no one imagines that there are more new tombs to be found. But on the other hand, we know of tombs that have been lost. These tombs were found by early archaeologists, but their locations have been forgotten. There are about 19 of these lost tombs. Among them are KV 21, 27, 28, 31, 33, 41, 48, 53, and 54. Among them, too, used to be KV 5.

THE REDISCOVERY OF KV 5

KV 5, which is also known as the tomb of the sons of Rameses II, has had an interesting history even in modern times. Richard Pococke, an English traveler, noticed its entrance in 1738. In 1825, James Burton, a British Egyptologist, penetrated about 25 m into the tomb, sketched a plan of its chambers, and inscribed his name inside. The Prussian Egyptologist Karl Richard Lepsius recorded it on a map of the area in 1850. Howard Carter even began to work in the tomb in 1902, but he found it was not worthwhile to continue the excavation. Eventually an American Egyptologist, Elizabeth Thomas, published it in the 1960s, believing that it was used as the tomb for the children of Rameses II. After this, it was forgotten.

Then, in 1987, the SCA needed to widen the parking lot for the valley. Realizing that hidden tombs could be damaged or destroyed by the new construction, the Theban Mapping Project, under the directorship of Kent Weeks, received permission from the SCA to investigate the area. Within days, they had rediscovered the entrance to KV 5. This was the first rediscovery in the valley since Carter found Tutankhamun's tomb, which lay 70 m from KV 5. It took years of work to realize the scope of what they had found. The announcement made on 18th May, 1995, in New York made it sound as though KV 5 was only newly discovered, and it was announced as the tomb of the sons of Rameses the Great.

The entrance had been cut into the bedrock. Its depth is about 4.46 m and its width 2.84 m, and it is 4.17 m long. Although

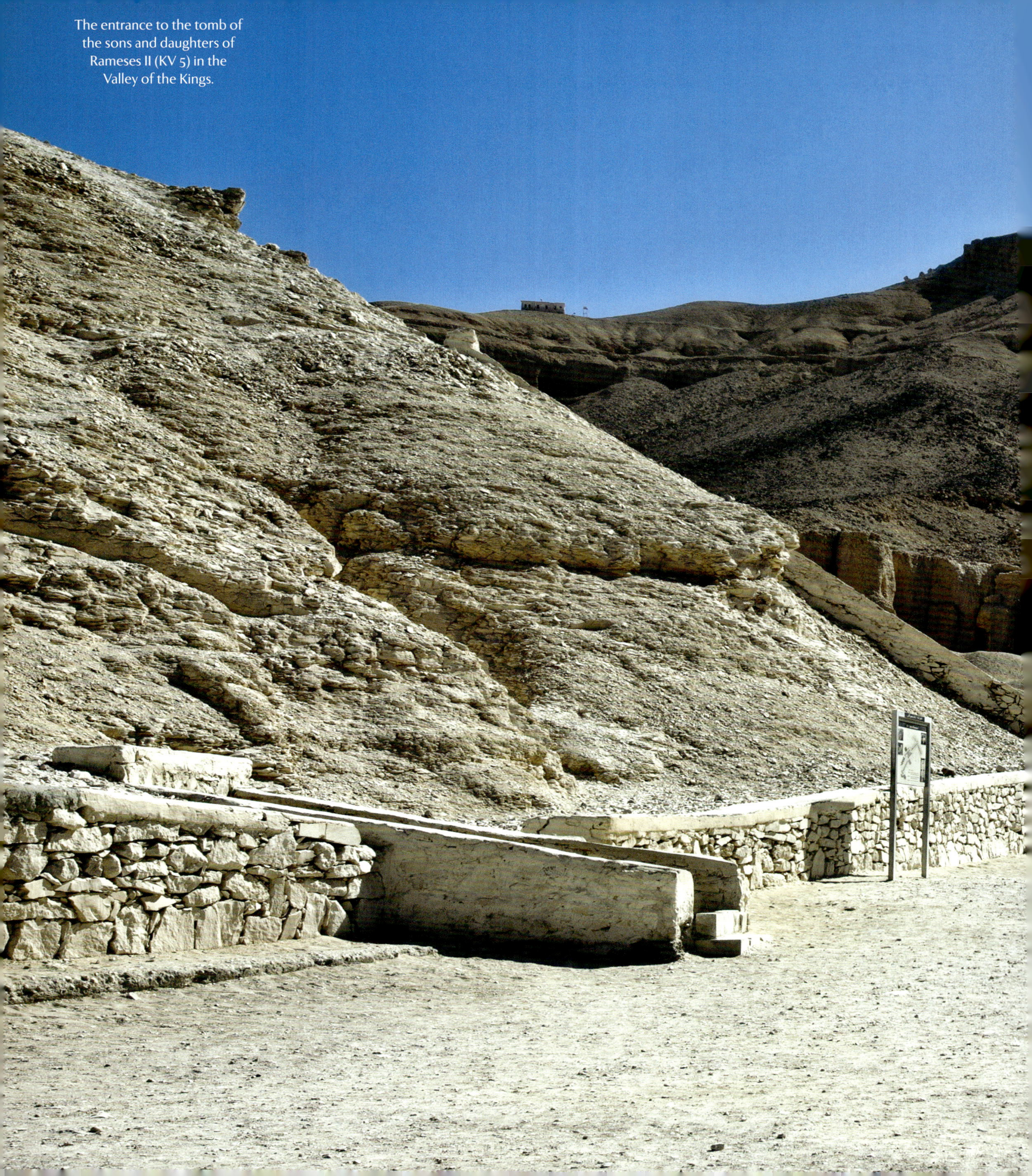

The entrance to the tomb of the sons and daughters of Rameses II (KV 5) in the Valley of the Kings.

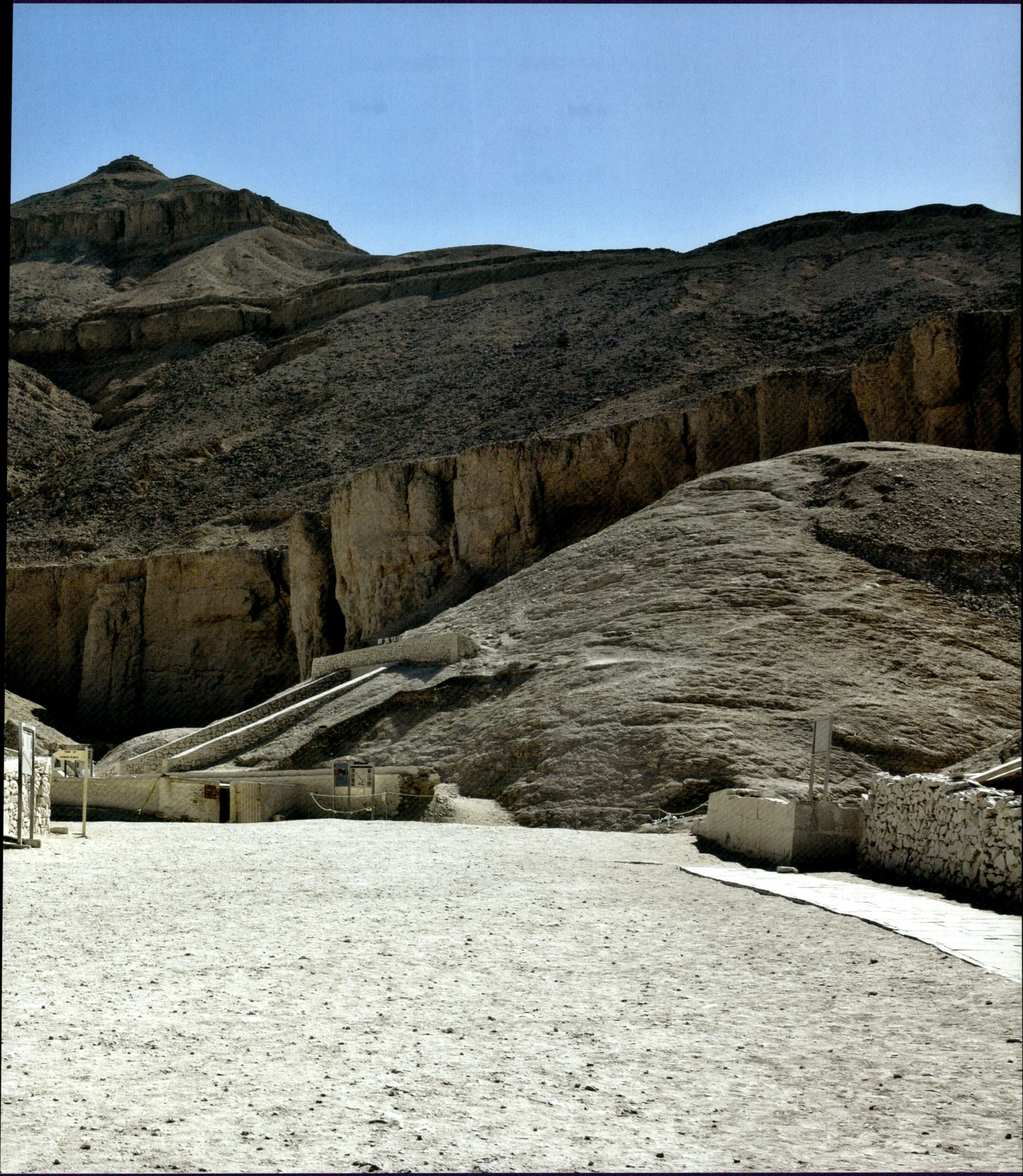

there were once probably 12 steps that led down to the tomb, only six remain. At the entrance, the team discovered the cartouche of Rameses II, something that James Burton had mentioned finding in 1825. Along with another cartouche of this king, the left lintel of the doorway bears a figure of the goddess Maat.

The plan of the tomb is so complicated that I can only call it "labyrinthine." We could tell that a significant part of the tomb dates to the 18th Dynasty, but it was reused in the 19th Dynasty by Rameses II.

It starts with the narrow entrance I have just described, which leads directly to a wider chamber. Then, after passing through a second room, the visitor comes to a hall with 16 pillars. The original tomb consisted of only the first two chambers and part of what is now this hall, which was enlarged by Rameses II, who further added many secondary rooms. Some of these have domed ceilings, an architectural feature found in other Ramesside tombs.

In 1995, excavation revealed a T-shaped extension to the east. This area of the tomb is especially remarkable because of the large number of side chambers that stem from the corridors. Such a plan is unique, never used before or after in the Valley of the Kings. The complicated nature of the tomb was made even clearer when it was discovered that the floor was covered with multiple layers of plaster. Possibly even more tombs awaited discovery beneath this floor, and at the end of 1995 the excavation team indeed found two complete corridors to the west that bend 37 degrees toward the tomb of Rameses II. More than 20 chambers extend off these additional corridors.

The tomb's first chamber, room 1, which is rectangular in shape, was filled with the remains of debris from the flash floods to which the valley is occasionally subjected.

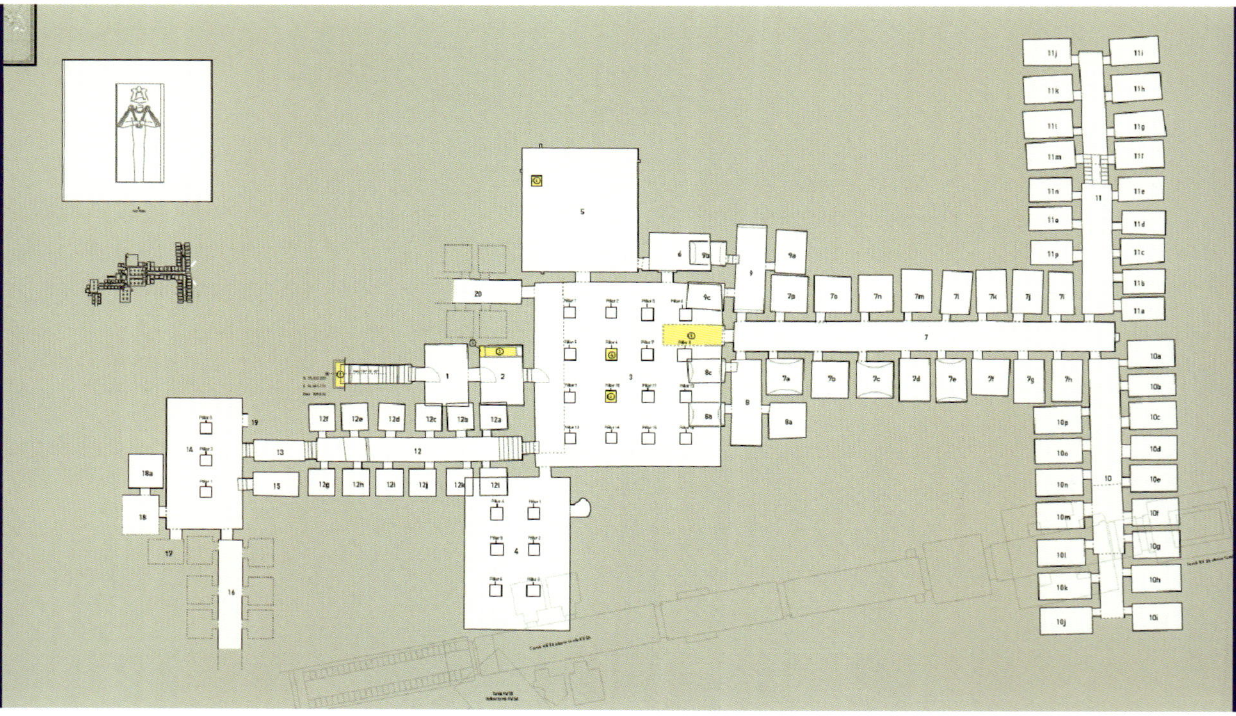

Plan of KV 5

The walls were covered with a thick layer of gypsum because the natural rock surface of the walls was in too poor a condition to receive decoration.

The most important scene in this room occupies the southern half of its western wall. It includes the cartouche of Rameses II surrounded by solar disk and shows Rameses II and, behind him, prince Amonherkhepeshef. The king is giving offerings of two vessels of liquid to the god Sokar, who is seated, and the goddess Hathor, who embraces the god with her left arm and holds an ***ankh*** in her right. Sokar here is hawk-headed, wearing the ***atef*** crown. He grasps an ***ankh*** sign with his right hand. Above the king and the prince are nine columns of hieroglyphs that say that Amonherkhepeshef is the first-born son of the king.

On the south wall, we again find the name of Rameses II inside a cartouche. I will describe the scenes one encounters from east to west.

First, we see one of Rameses II's other sons, named Rameses after his father, and four lines of inscriptions. Here the king and the young Rameses stand before the god Nefertem-Hor-Hekenu. The middle part of this wall is damaged, so we see only parts of Prince Rameses. The eastern part of the southern wall shows Rameses accompanied by his ***ka*** (spiritual double or life-force) and the name of Horus.

The north wall is perhaps the second most important in the tomb. Its inscription is still visible. We see a prince, followed by his ***ka***, and Rameses II offering incense to Ptah, the great god of Memphis. On the eastern part of this wall, the king is followed by a prince who holds a fan.

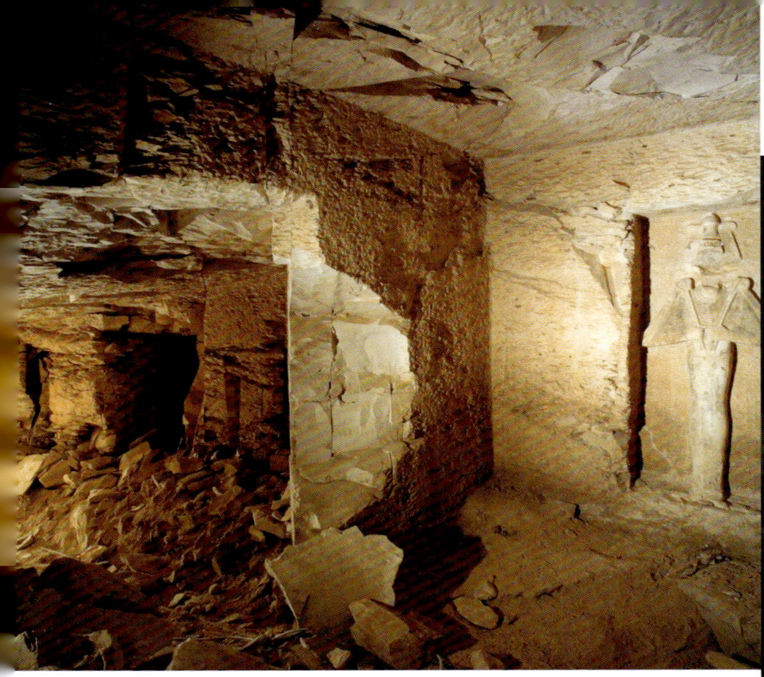

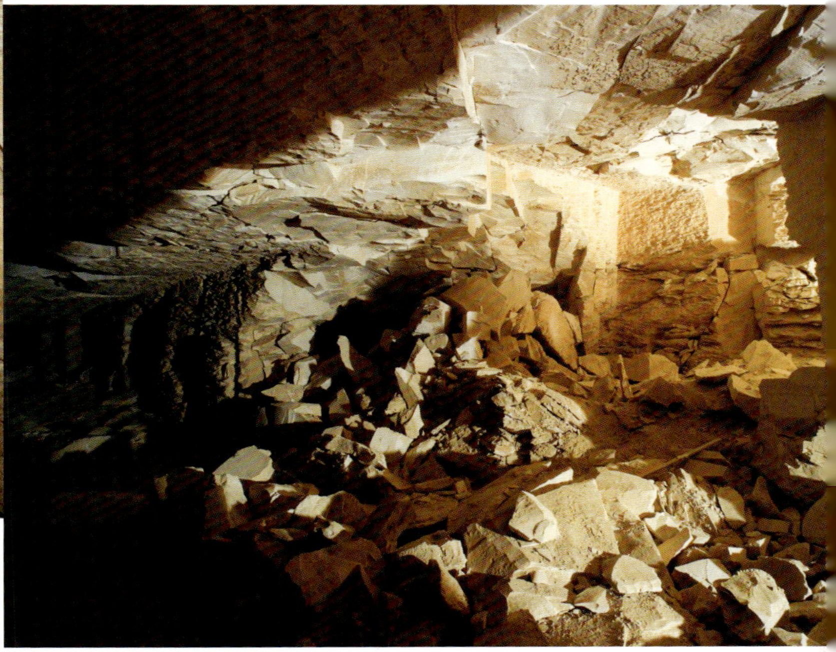

Views of the badly preserved architecture and decoration of KV 5.

Chamber 2, similar to the first, is 3.63 m long and 5.01 m wide, for a total of 18.18 m^2. Six stone blocks cover over a rectangular hole on the north wall. Here the important scenes are again placed on the southern wall, where we see the goddess Hathor in the form of a cow aboard her boat. In front of her is Rameses II, portrayed on a smaller scale. A prince holds a fan and scepter in the company of the king, who is giving an offering of cloth to the goddess. On the north wall, again the king is accompanied by a prince (whose name is not preserved), standing before a god who cannot be identified because of the condition of the wall. Three ***shabtis*** and 15 canopic jars were found in this room. Furthermore, in the floor of this chamber, the skeleton of a man and other skulls were found.

The third room is another important chamber in the tomb. With a length of 15.72 m for the north wall and 15.55 m for the south, and a width from east to west of 15.54 m, for a total of 244.61 m^2, it is the largest chamber anywhere in the Valley of the Kings. Its ceiling is held up by 16 pillars, each with an average width of 90 cm. All the pillars were at one time covered with a layer of plaster, which would have been inscribed with texts and decorated with scenes. Seven entrances to other rooms can be found in this chamber, each measuring about 70 cm by 115 cm.

The west wall of this room contains important scenes representing four seated princes, each wearing a long dress. It is in this room that James Burton inscribed his name in 1825. Objects found here included two ***shabtis***, one inscribed with the name of King Seti I and the other with no inscription, and seven canopic jars.

Rectangular like the others, room 4 is entered from the third. Pieces of decoration from the walls were found in the floor, showing scenes of a priest and a god and an ***ankh***, so perhaps this room was also decorated. Of the next two rooms, 5 and 6, the former is the better preserved, but both remain unexcavated due to the dangers of working there. It is possible to see one pillar and four niches cut into the walls. Room number 6 has two entrances.

Room 8 is again rectangular and can be entered from a door in the south side of the corridor, which is designated number 7. The room contains three entrances to three side rooms. On the west wall is an image of the king who wears two ram horns and the solar disk. Behind him is a god that cannot be identified due to the extent of damage to that portion of the wall.

One enters room 9 by a door on the north side of corridor 7. On the right door jamb are the remains of an image of Anubis and inscriptions. This room has three other entrances, each leading to yet another side room.

Rooms 13 and 14 have no decoration, but a number of small faience objects and fragments, and also glass fragments, were found here. From room 14, one can enter room 15.

Corridor 7 can be entered from room number 3, the pillared hall. The corridor has 20 doors leading to side rooms, including room 9. On the western end of the corridor, excavators found a niche with a statue of the god Osiris, carved of limestone, about 160 cm tall. Although the head has been lost, it is thought that this image represents Rameses II as the god.

Perhaps the most important thing in this corridor is a scene found on the wall between the doorways to rooms 7 and 9. It shows Osiris sitting on his throne while behind him Hathor stands holding the ***ankh*** in her left hand and places her right hand on Osiris's shoulder. Before these divinities we see a hawk-headed god wearing the double crown. The inscriptions indicate that this is Horus, son of Isis, and he presents Rameses II to Osiris and Hathor, who has the title "Lady of

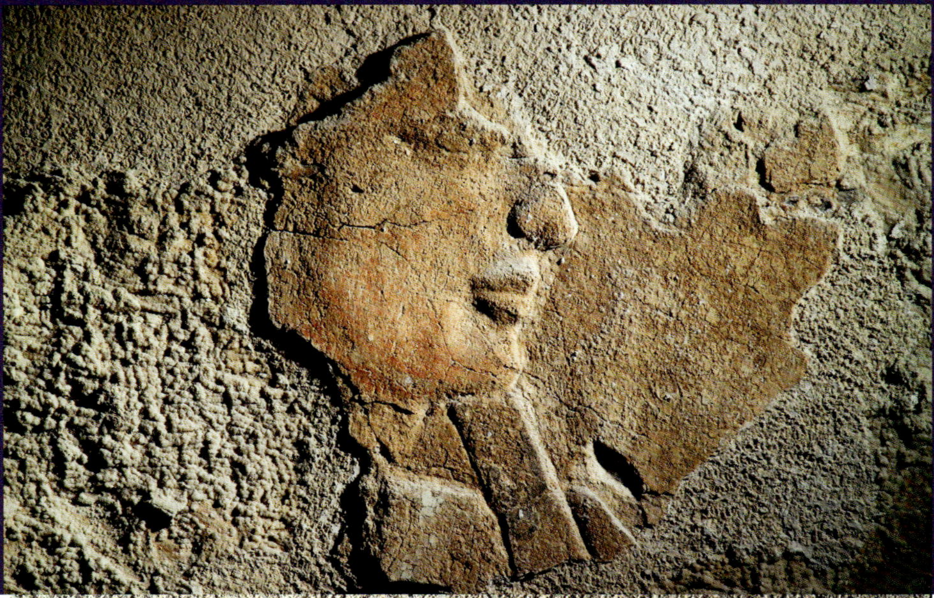

Remains of wall reliefs in KV 5.

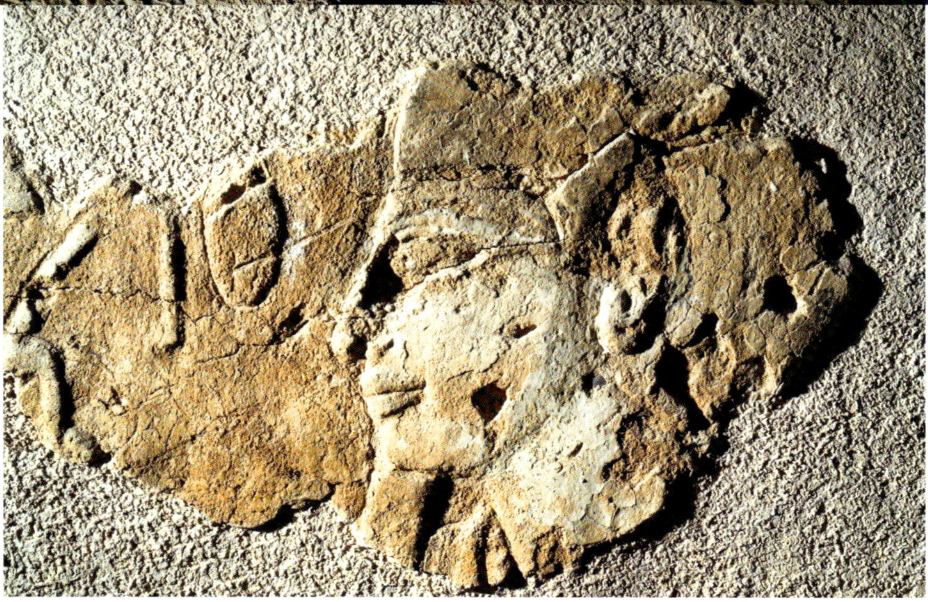

the West," which associates her with the netherworld.

Another image, on the north wall between rooms 7o and 7p, represents a prince (whose name is not preserved) standing behind Rameses II, who gives offerings of cloth and a lotus flower. The other half of this scene features a god in the form of a ram, perhaps Khnum or Anubis in an unusual form, seated on his throne. Behind him is the goddess Hathor. Similar scenes are known from the tombs of Meryetamun (QV 68) and Bent'anta (QV 71), both daughters of Rameses II.

Other corridors, numbered 10, 11 (which are reached through corridor 7), and 12 (which is reached through the 16-pillared hall), also have multiple side chambers. To my knowledge, excavation has revealed more than 150 chambers, giving the tomb a total area of 1,266.47 m^2. The Theban Mapping Project believes that it could be connected by a tunnel or corridor to the tomb of Rameses II (KV 7).

Although this tomb is commonly called the tomb of the sons of Rameses the Great, I do not believe that the evidence from this tomb supports the idea that it was ever used for burial during the 19th Dynasty. I believe that, on the contrary, this is a cenotaph or symbolic tomb built by Rameses II for his family.

The evidence for this is:

1) The statue of Osiris found in the tomb.
2) The niches that have been found are too small to have been used for burial; they are, instead, symbolic.
3) The bones from the tomb have never been fully studied. I think that these would prove to be intrusive burials of later date, perhaps Greek or Roman. It has been suggested that the skeleton, found with its arms crossed on its chest, is Ptolemaic.
4) If the sons of Rameses II were buried in this tomb, we would have found evidence of mummification, but in fact there is no evidence of such burials.
5) No evidence of coffins has been found.

Fragments of canopic jars inscribed for several of Rameses II's sons have been found in the tomb. If these jars were originally interred here, then there would be no question regarding the function of KV 5. However, it remains possible that these fragments are the results of activities by priests in a later period because the points I have mentioned are strong evidence that it functioned as a cenotaph. However, the tomb and its objects need more careful analysis so that we may be certain what purpose it served.

THE DISCOVERY OF AN EMBALMING CACHE IN THE VALLEY OF THE KINGS (KV 63)

The Valley of the Kings still holds new surprises, in addition to rediscovered old ones. In 2005, Otto Schaden of the University of Memphis was working in KV 10, which belonged to King Amenmesse of the 19th Dynasty. At the time, the SCA was working on a project to reroute the damaging floodwaters that sometimes pour into the valley. The area around KV 10 had to be cleared down to the level of the bedrock. Ali al-Asfar, the head of the west bank, lacked the funds to clear the sand, so he asked Schaden to do that.

Schaden did as he was asked, and when he encountered the beginning of a shaft that no one knew existed, he wrote to me and sent photographs. It did not look very impressive at the time. It was just a shaft covered with stones. Because of this, I did not make a public announcement of the find. The shaft had to be excavated first, so we could see what was inside. This was, after all, very close to Tutankhamun's tomb, only about 14.5 m away. Carter had missed finding this shaft. Might it be related to the boy-king's tomb? We had to determine this before letting the world know about the discovery.

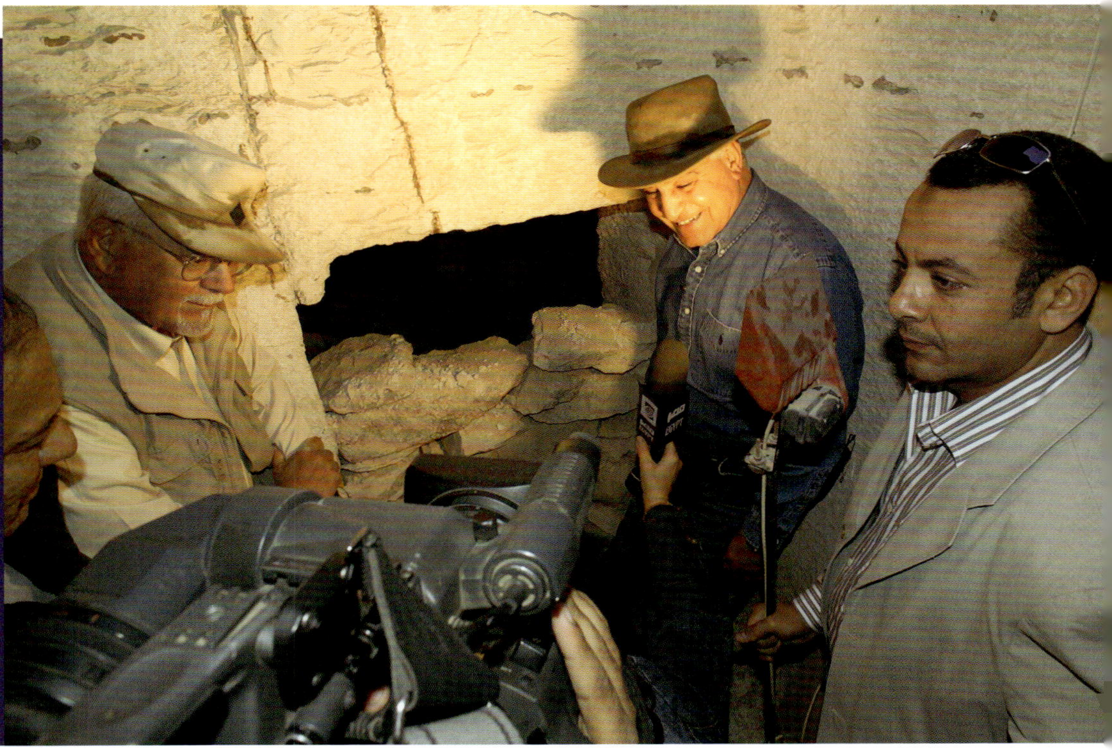

The media around Otto Schaden (left) and Zahi Hawass at the bottom of the shaft of KV 63.

Having been given a permit by the Permanent Committee of the SCA, Schaden began excavation of the shaft in 2006. Every day I received an e-mail from him, documenting what he was doing, until finally he reached a depth of 5.24 m from the surface. That is when I went to see for myself. Even at that point I believed that whatever lay at the bottom of the shaft would not be found intact.

Soon Schaden's team arrived at what might be the entrance to a chamber. They asked me to be present, to hold an official opening. I arrived at Luxor on the morning of February 10, 2006. What a scene I found! There were members of the media, from Egypt and around the world, everywhere. Everyone wanted to know what new treasure had been discovered in the Valley of the Kings.

I was wearing my excavation clothing – even my famous hat – and descended the ladder down the shaft, slowly. When I reached the bottom, I could see that there were no seals on the stone rubble that confronted us, filling a niche or doorway. We began to remove the stones until finally we had a hole about 2 cm high. After they made their hole, Carter and Carnarvon had used a flashlight. Having made our hole, Schaden and I did the same.

Beyond the rubble a chamber opened, one unseen for more than 3,000 years. Soon the whole world would see it.

When we returned from the bottom of the shaft, Schaden and I answered questions from journalists for more than three hours. An hour later, they put our answers out for everyone to know: for the first time since Howard Carter had discovered the tomb of Tutankhamun, a new tomb had been discovered in the Valley of the Kings. At last, as so many people had hoped and wondered, there was a KV 63.

There is no wall decoration in KV 63, which made me suspect that it was a cache to hide mummies. During the Third Intermediate Period, just after the New Kingdom, priests removed mummies from the royal tombs, which were being looted by robbers. They hid them in the hills around Thebes, including within the Valley of the Kings. The most famous of these caches was found at Deir el-Bahri in 1871 by the Abdel Rasoul family, and another (including the mummies of Queen Tiye and the unidentified Younger Lady) was found by the archaeologist Victor Loret in KV 35 in 1898. KV 55 was probably a similar cache created during the reign of Tutankhamun, and the tomb of Horemheb may also have held one.

But that is not, it seems, what KV 63 is. It appears to be a place where embalming materials were stored, perhaps after a royal funeral. A similar cache, KV 54, containing remains of Tutankhamun's mummification and funerary feast, was discovered in 1907.

KV 63 was found to contain 28 large jars, some being pottery, others calcite (Egyptian alabaster). Most of them retain their seals. There are also eight coffins: six for adults, one for a child, and one for an infant. Their condition is very poor. The ancient priests coated them with resin, and termites have eaten most of the wood away. Even so, traces of their beauty remain, particularly the beautiful face of Coffin F. Curiously, they were used for storage – not of mummies but of other objects. In them were calcite (Egyptian alabaster) vessels, miniature pottery vessels, potsherds from vessels small and large, natron used in embalming, linen, bits of wood, pieces of blank papyri, small animal bones, and sealings. One coffin contained long sticks with

KV 63 as found, intact and equipped with large jars, coffins and mummification material.

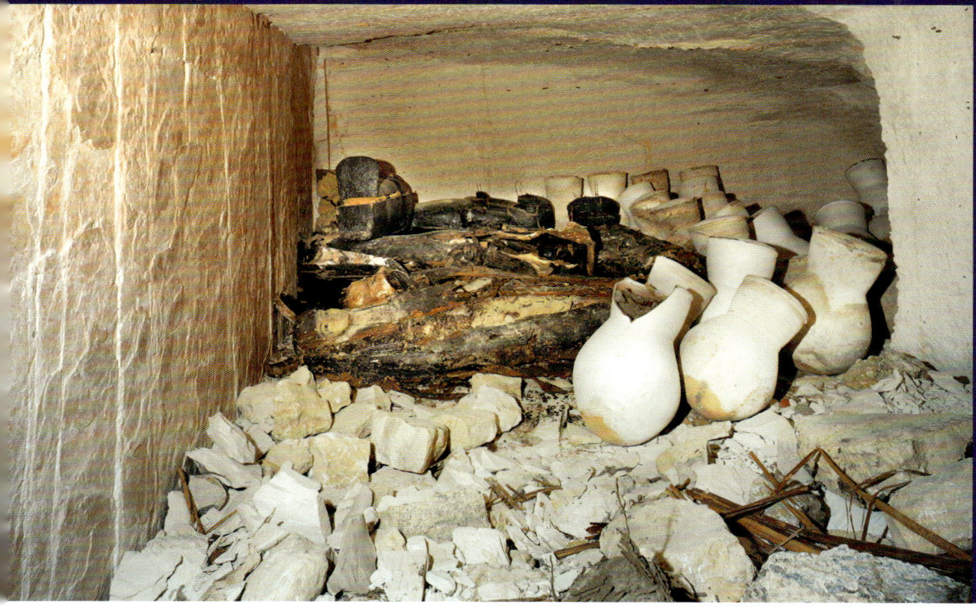

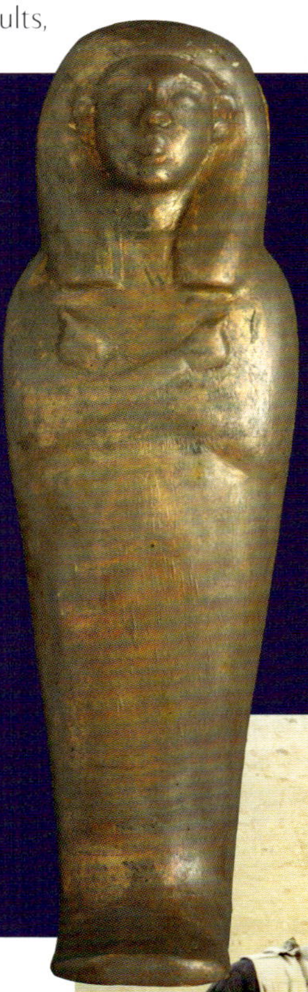

The gilded bronze coffinette found in KV 63.

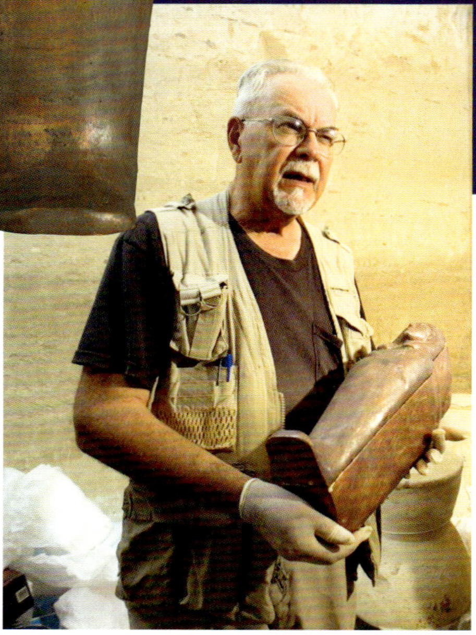

linen stuck to one end, probably for cleaning within mummies, and cloth collars with flowers along the edges. These collars were probably worn by mummies or perhaps by mourners. All these things probably came from a royal mummification workshop that would have been operating near the entrance to the valley.

The child's coffin contained pillows filled with down and bearing inscriptions ("life, prosperity, health," a phrase often appearing after a king's name). There was even a coffinette, about 42 cm long, of gilded bronze. Although exquisite, it had no inscriptions.

The jars were found to contain material much like that in the coffins. There were smaller vessels or pieces of vessels, bandages soaked with resin, natron, bits of rope or twine, "trays" made of clay used during the embalming process, and the impressions of seals. One of the most unusual finds was some pieces of a bed with lions' heads at its ends. These could represent the divine pair Shu (air) and Tefnut (moisture), the first-born offspring of the creator god. This bed had been purposefully broken and seemed to have no legs. But Schaden had shown me some snake-like prongs, which I suggested they try to use as the legs of this bed. They fit.

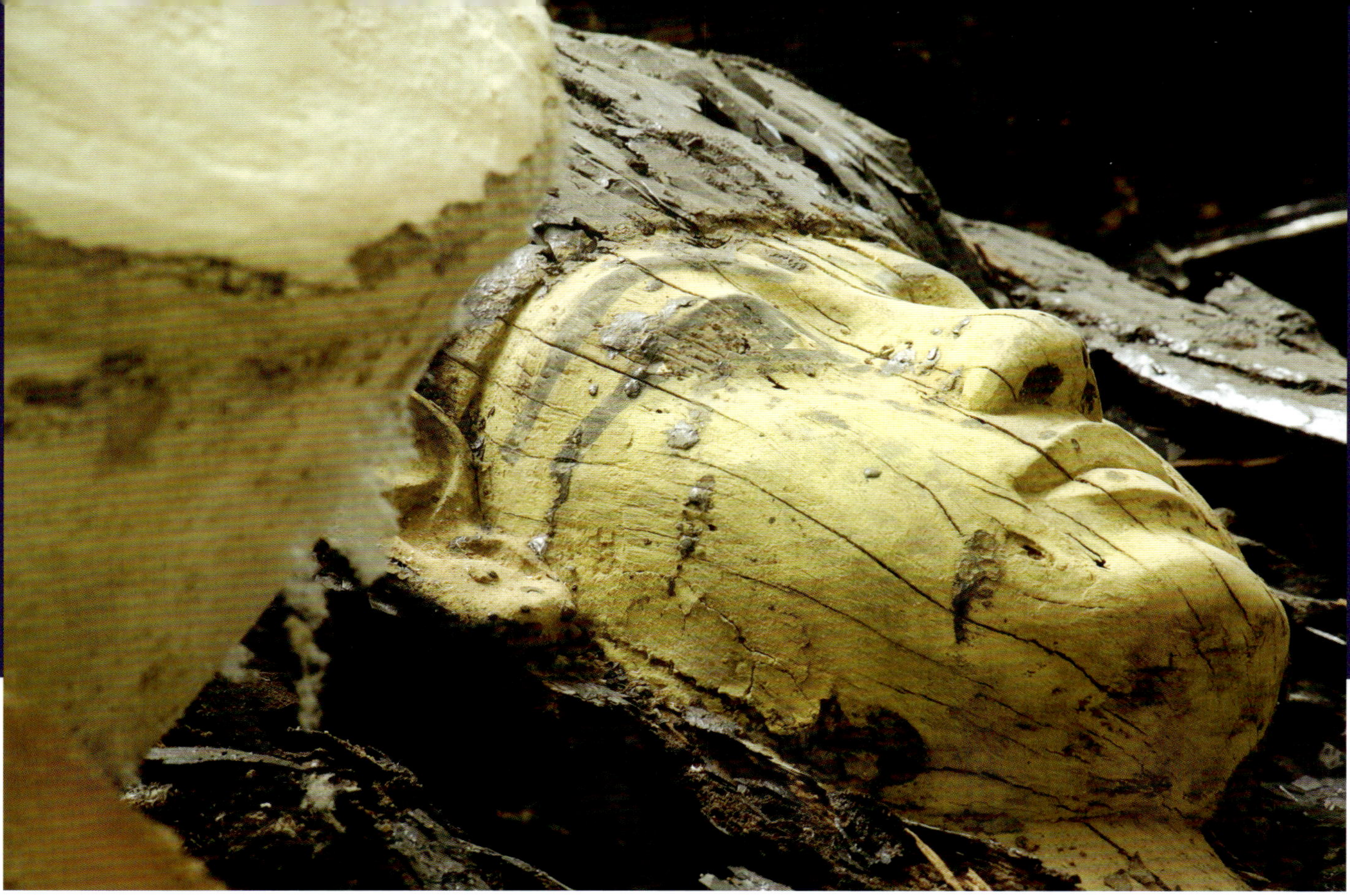

The female face on the lid of one of the wooden coffins from KV 63.

The owners of most of the coffins are unknown because of lack of legible inscriptions, and some were never decorated at all. We know that Coffin A belonged to a woman named Henutwadjbu. Bands on this coffin mention several gods, including Anubis and Isis, and Henutwadjbu is refered to as "the Osiris." Another of the coffins, however, belonging to another woman, the royal nurse Iny, has no trace of these gods. Re is mentioned, however, leading Schaden to propose that this coffin was made during the reign of Akhenaten.

The coffins and jars stylistically date to the late 18th Dynasty. The jars are very much like those found in the cache from Tutankhamun's funerary feast (KV 54) and in the tomb of Yuya and Tjuya (KV 46). The official necropolis seal used in the tomb is also found in Tutankhamun's tomb, and two other seal types match sealings found in the young king's tomb and in KV 55. An inscription on a wine jar, which says "Year 5, wine from Tjaru" (a site in the eastern Delta) is very close to one of Tutankhamun's, which also has a date of Year 5 and has "wine from the estate of the Aten in Tjaru." Perhaps they held the same vintage. Other inscriptions mention the names of the god Amun-Re and the Aten. KV 63 clearly dates from the reign of Tutankhamun.

The lack of decoration makes me believe that this is not a tomb created originally for Nefertiti or Ankhesenamun. When it was first found, I myself thought it might have been a tomb made for Kiya that was later used as an embalming cache. Otto Schaden believes that it was made as an embalming cache. Ray Johnson has pointed out to me that the coffins are mostly female, and that one of them belonged to a nurse from the Amarna Period. Also, there is enough mummification material for only one person. All of this makes him think of Tutankhamun's widowed queen. Why might there be no cartouches of Ay, who married her, among the material? Johnson also points out that there were few inscribed objects from the other embalming cache, KV 54, and he also suggests that Ankhesenamun was in some disgrace from having tried to marry a Hittite prince.

Schaden found only one complete cartouche in association with KV 63, a crude seal impression (no. 2) that clearly says Menkheperre (Thutmose III). Seal no. 41, found in jar 3, has an incomplete cartouche. Schaden believes that this fragmentary name should be restored to be either Nebkheperure (Tutankhamun) or Kheperkheperure (Ay). The close relationship between this shaft, KV 63, and Tutankhamun's tomb, KV 62, suggests that the cartouche was that of the young king. There is also the matter of the bed. As the last thing on which the king's body had been laid, it could not be used again or destroyed, so the priests broke it up and placed it inside one of the jars. Furthermore, one of the faces on the coffins bears a resemblance to Tutankhamun's. Given all of this and the Amarna artifacts, I suggest that KV 63 is the embalming cache of Tutankhamun.

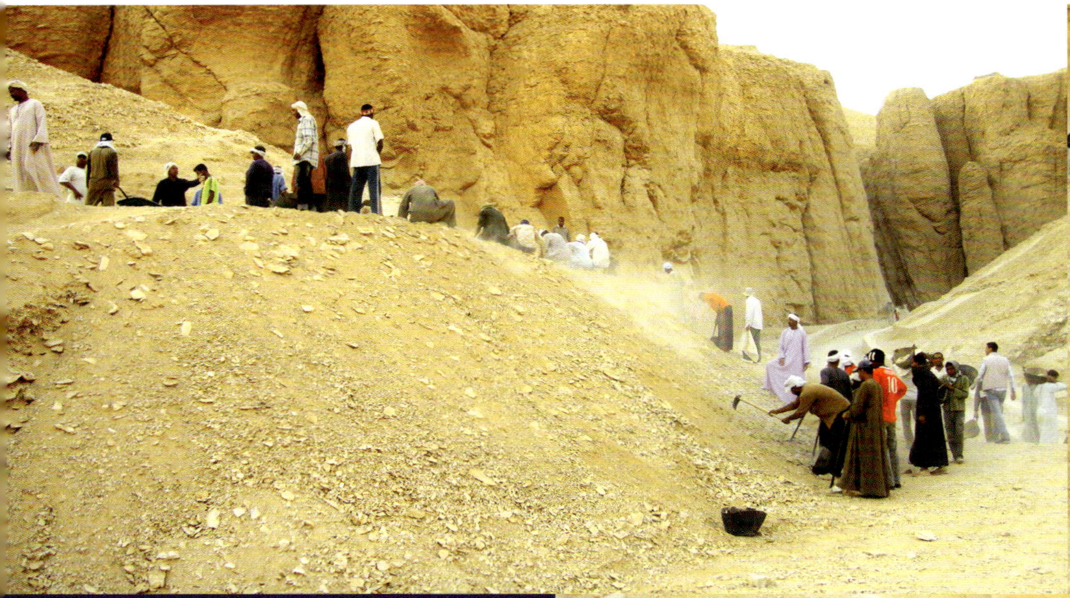

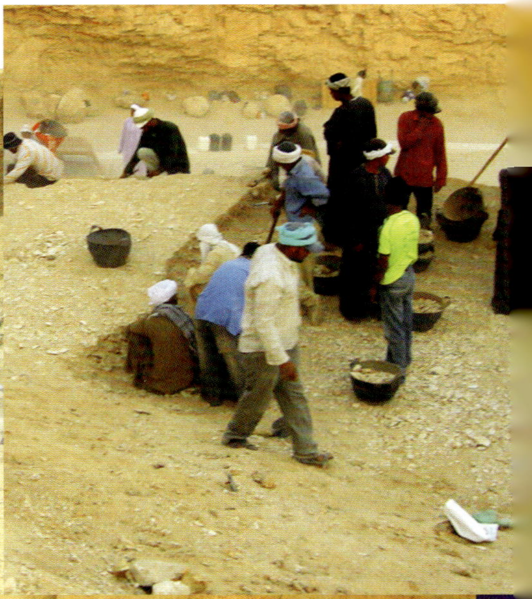

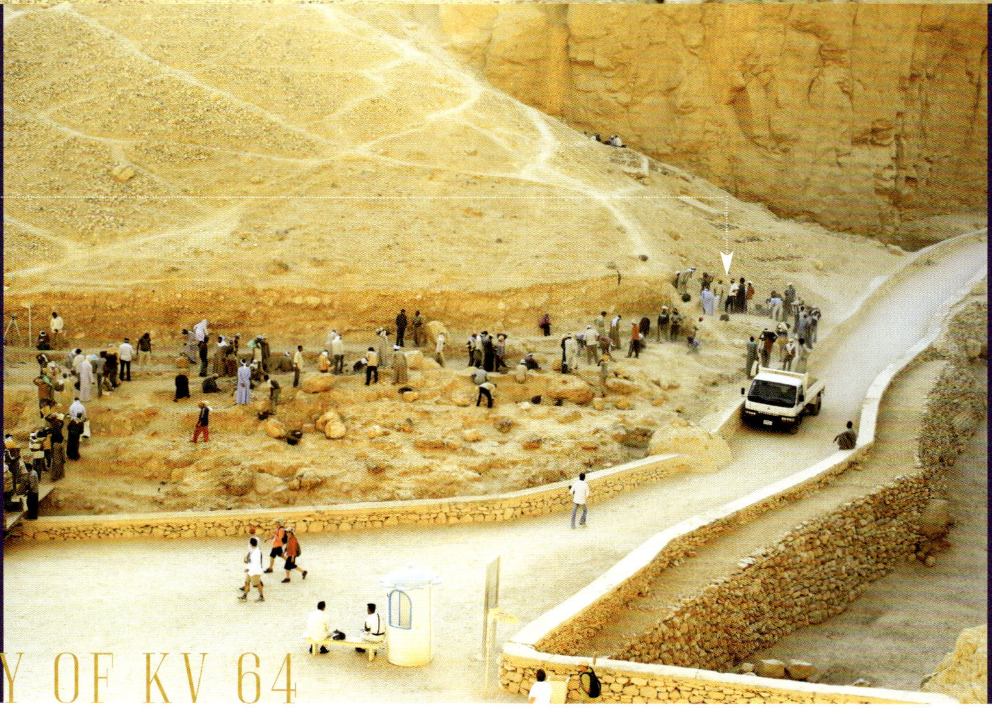

The work of Ahmed El Leithy from the Egyptian Mission at the site of KV 64.

THE DISCOVERY OF KV 64

The discovery of KV 64 was also an accident. A Swiss expedition, from the University of Basel, had received permission from the Permanent Committee of the Supreme Council of Antiquities to clean the shaft of KV 40. The committee later gave them permission to build a wall around its entrance. I received a report from Ahmed El Leithy, who was the field director of the Egyptian expedition working in the Valley of the Kings under my direction. This was during the time when the SCA had become known as the Ministry of State for Antiquities, during the Revolution, and I was Minister. His report and its accompanying photographs told me that the Swiss excavation had gone beyond their concession and into the area assigned to El Leithy to be excavated by the Egyptian expedition. Not only had they gone beyond the area they were supposed to be working in, they had done something else they did not have permission to do: excavate.

El Leithy explained what had happened. His area was between KV 29 and KV 40. His team had worked there from 2009 to 2011 and succeeded in excavating down to the ancient floor of the valley. They were then going to excavate down to the bedrock, but they paused their work because the Swiss expedition had begun to clean the shaft of KV 40. El Leithy decided that they would wait until the Swiss had built their wall, which was supposed to be no more than one meter from the shaft opening. The Swiss had done exactly this before, with other shafts of 18th Dynasty tombs. El Leithy informed the Swiss director that his team would return to excavate the rest of the area. (This is written in a report to me by El Leithy, as well.)

The Swiss worked on 25th January, 2011, which in Egypt is a holiday celebrating the police, and began to excavate in the area of the Egyptian expedition. The Swiss director insisted that they had to excavate 3 m from the shaft, even though 1 meter was clearly specified in their concession. The Swiss team's Egyptian inspector halted their work and reported it to the director of Luxor, who agreed that the Permanent Committee had not given the Swiss any right to excavate. Unfortunately, the Egyptian expedition, although scheduled to resume work on 29th January, had to stop work in their concession because of the political situation in Egypt. By then the Revolution was underway.

A month and a half later, on 12th March, 2011, the Swiss continued their illegal excavation. The director claimed to have written permission from the director of Luxor to do so.

At the time, I was too busy dealing with the situation in Cairo. The Egyptian Museum had been looted, young people were rioting for jobs – I left my own job for a time, and during my period of resignation, the Swiss managed to obtain approval from the SCA to continue the work they had begun without permission.

When KV 63 was announced, the Valley of the Kings was crowded with members of the press. KV 64 has had virtually no publicity at all. This is because the new antiquities authorities unfortunately did not realize the importance of the discovery and therefore did not call for a press conference to announce the discovery. But the University of Basel has done good work in the valley. They were able to identify KV 32 as the tomb of Queen Tiaa, wife of Amenhotep II, and they have undertaken impressive scientific work to preserve the Valley of the Kings.

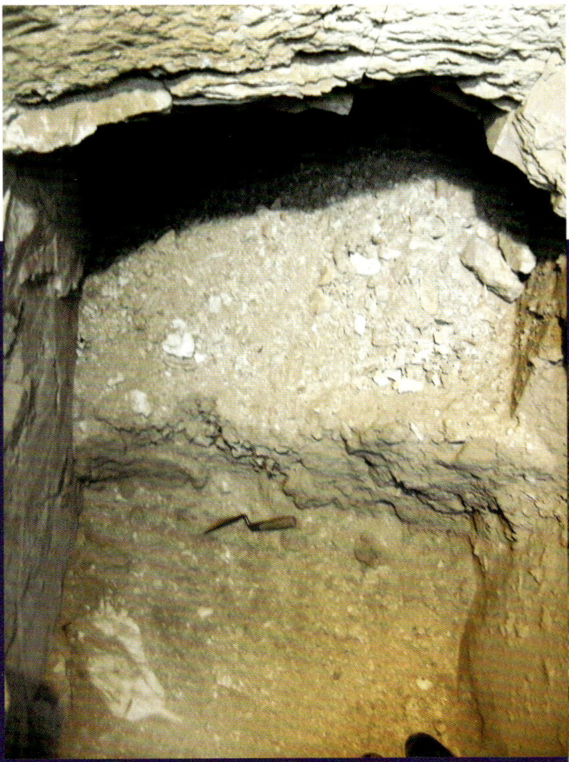

The entrance from the shaft to the burial chamber of KV 64.

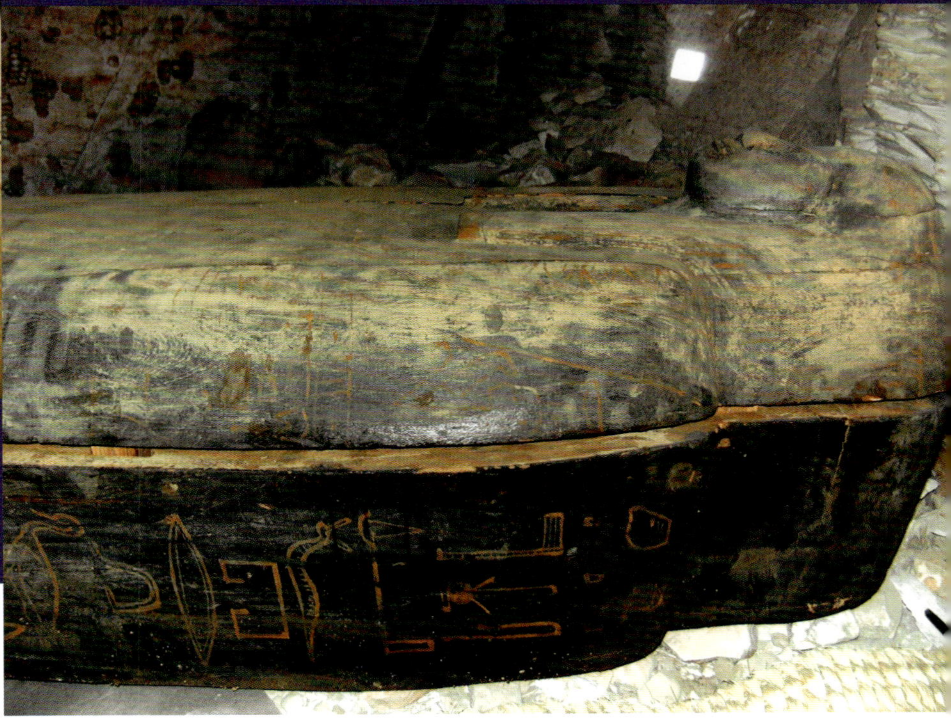

The wooden coffin of Nehemesbastet found in KV 64.

KV 64 is about 3.5 m deep, and they found in the north part of the tomb a wooden coffin, painted black and bearing an inscription in yellow. Near the foot of the coffin, against the wall, was a painted wooden stela. The owner is a woman named Nehemesbastet, daughter of Nakhtefmut. She was a songstress of Amun. The coffin contained a carefully wrapped mummy and is the first intact tomb of a middle-class woman ever found in the valley. It dates to the 21st Dynasty. The beautiful stela shows the Lady Nehemesbastet in a thin white dress before an offering table and a seated falcon-headed god. She addresses a prayer to many gods.

Other finds in the tomb included pottery from the 18th Dynasty. This shows that an earlier burial existed, but no trace remains of the name of the original tomb-owner. The team believes that this tomb originally belonged to a princess of Amenhotep II and was taken over for the singer in the 21st Dynasty.

THE SECRET TUNNEL OF SETI I IS REVEALED

I first learned about the tunnel of Seti I while working with the University of Pennsylvania at Malqata in 1974. Sheikh Ali, who owned the El Marsam Hotel on the west bank, often spoke to me. He was about 70 years old at the time. I remember him as a nice man, tall, with a long moustache. We would sit together and from him I heard many stories, especially about his family, the famous AbdelRasouls. Maybe the best one was one that took place a century before, in 1871, when AhmedAbdel Rasoul was herding his livestock in the Valley of the Kings.

One of Ahmed's goats became unruly, and he had to chase after it. Just as he caught up with the animal on the cliffs at Deir el-Bahri, he came upon a shaft. Of course, he went down inside, and here he found a treasure of antiquities. He could not know that he had found an important cache of royal mummies, including Ahmose I (founder of the 18th Dynasty), Thutmose III, Rameses II, and others. But he did know that he had found treasure. His family began to sell these objects on the antiquities market, and because they had the names of kings, the antiquities eventually caught the attention of the authorities. In their investigation, the authorities questioned one of the members of the family. This resulted in a quarrel among them that led to the revelation of the cache to the Antiquities Department. The mummies were taken from their ancient hiding place to Cairo, where they would be safe in the museum, in 1881.

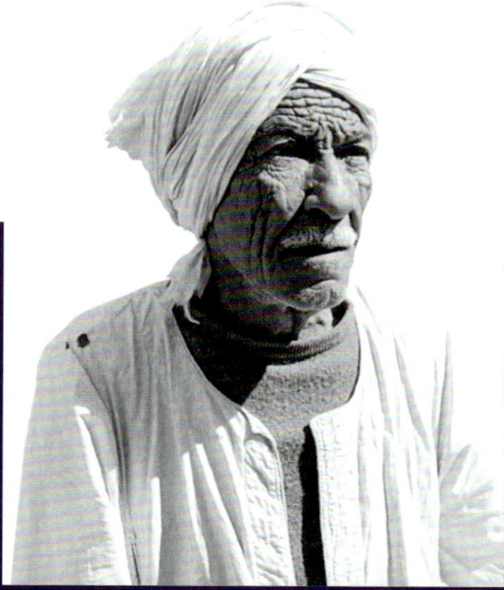

Sheikh Ali Abdel Rasoul in his old age.

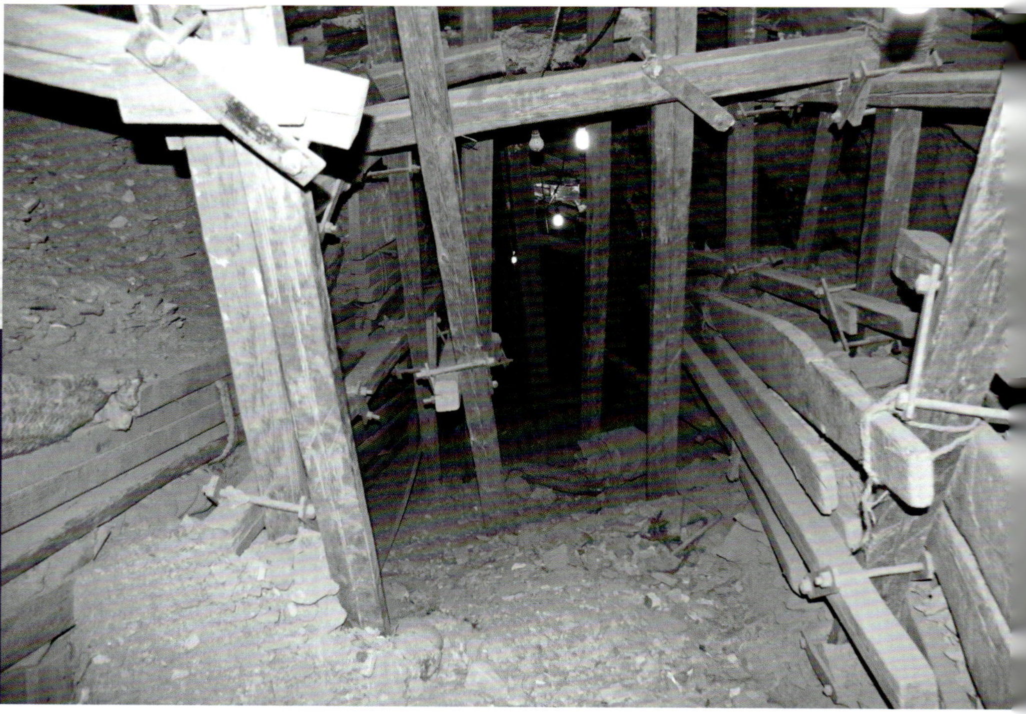

Archival photo of the tunnel inside the tomb of Seti I (KV 17).

Now their descendant owned a hotel in Luxor and met many archaeologists who excavated in the Valley of the Kings. I was one of them, but he saw something different in me.

So once he took me to the tomb of Seti I. This tomb, KV 17, had been first discovered by Giovanni Belzoni, a circus strongman who had become an adventurer and an archaeologist, though his methods were not scientific or even careful. He had found a tunnel at the far end of the burial chamber, which lay 100 m from the entrance. But Belzoni got only a short distance in the tunnel before he gave up. Howard Carter had worked here, too, in 1902 & 1903, while he was chief inspector of Upper Egypt. Although he restored the entrance, the dangers of falling rock held him back.

Sheikh Ali brought me to this tunnel. He believed that at its far end there was another tomb.

Sheikh Ali himself had tried to find it. In 1960, the Antiquities Department even gave him a permit for excavation here, in the tunnel extending from the burial chamber. His team had dug to 136 m, but the conditions of the work were too dangerous. The tunnel might collapse. His men were afraid, and so

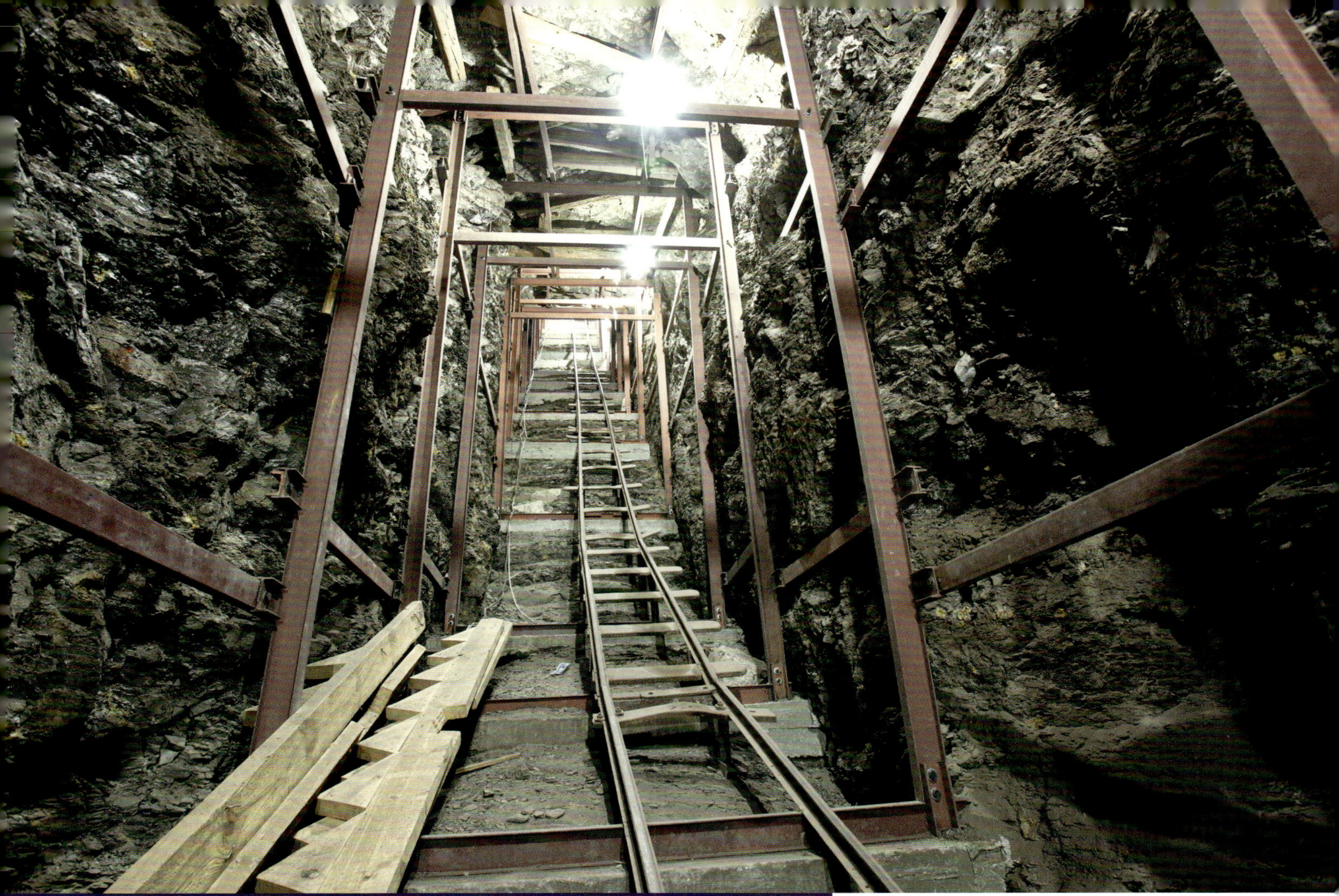

The railway installed inside the tunnel of KV 17 in order to remove the debris and continue the excavation of the 176.5m long tunnel.

was the Antiquities Department, so that put an end to Sheikh Ali's excavation.

He wanted me to continue it someday. He was certain that I was going to become head of the Antiquities Department, and when I did, I had to continue on with his work. He made me promise this. He believed that Seti I's real burial chamber lay at the far end of this tunnel.

The purpose of the tunnel was a subject of debate in the field. Most believed that it was built for a ritual purpose, so that the soul of the king could find his way to the kingdom of Osiris in the netherworld, where he would be resurrected. Some, however, believed, as Sheikh Ali did, that it led to the king's true burial chamber.

Sheikh Ali's belief that I would become head of the Antiquities Department proved true. What about his prediction about what lay at the end of the tunnel? In November 2007, I began a project to find out.

Among my assistants were people I had known and worked with for a long time, people I could trust for their expertise: Tarek El-Awady, who would later serve as the director general of the Egyptian Museum in Cairo; Moustafa Abdel Shakour, archaeologist; Aiman Hamed, who would be the soil mechanic engineer; and two top ***reises*** (supervisors), Gamal El Gasab and Saed Ibrahiem, who would be in charge of the workmen.

We knew that we faced many difficulties. Howard Carter and Sheikh Ali had proven that to us. We studied the geological conditions carefully so that we could protect the workmen and the architecture of the tunnel

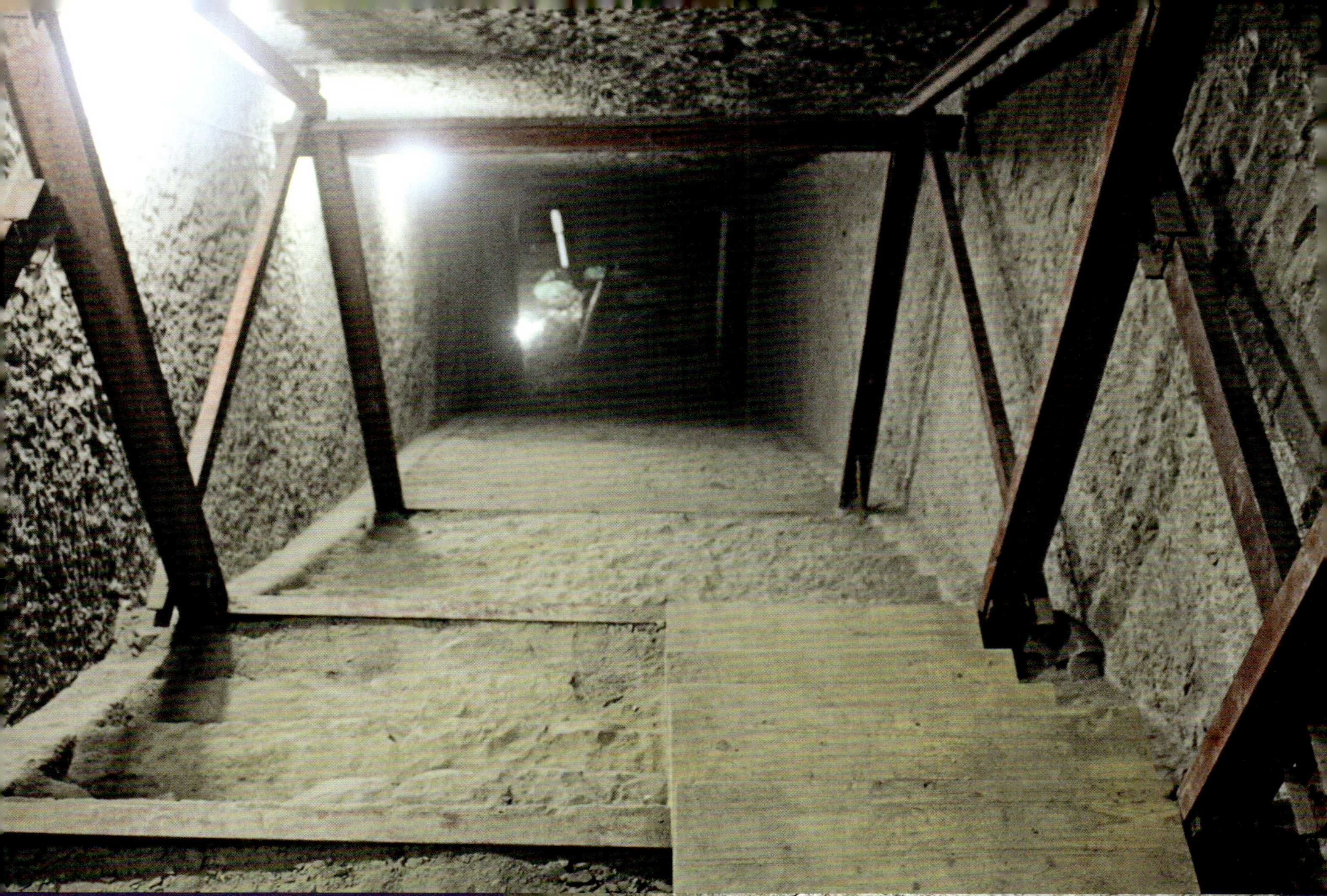

The first stone steps found inside the tunnel after 140 m.

The graffiti found on the last stone gate inside the tunnel.

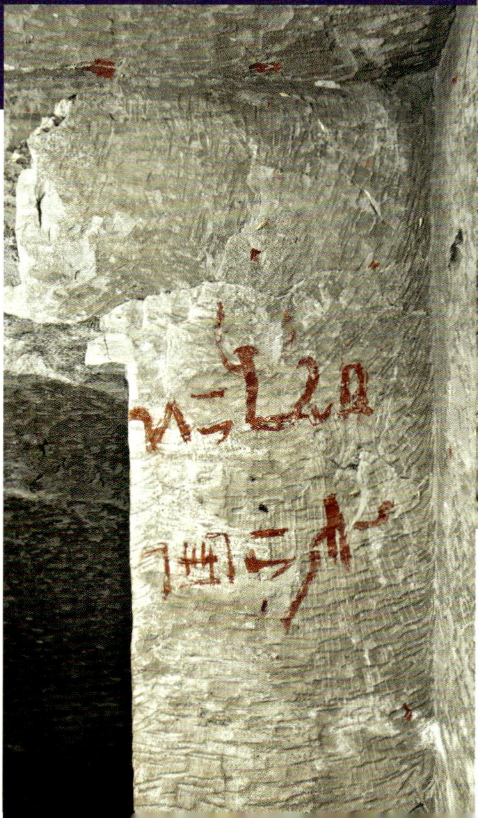

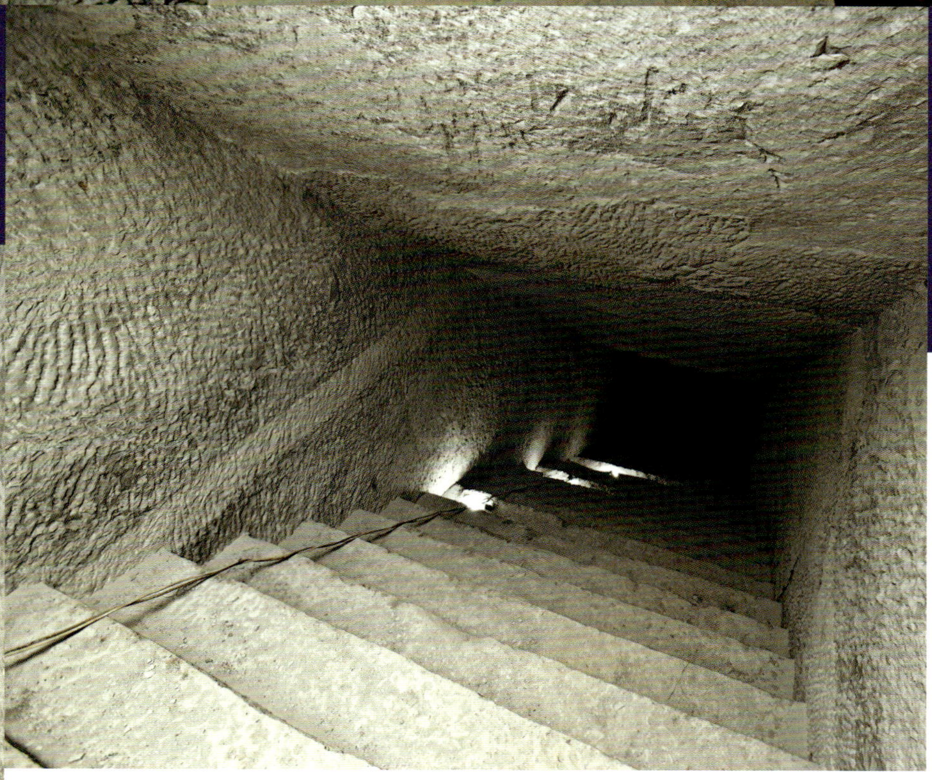

The last passage inside the tunnel.

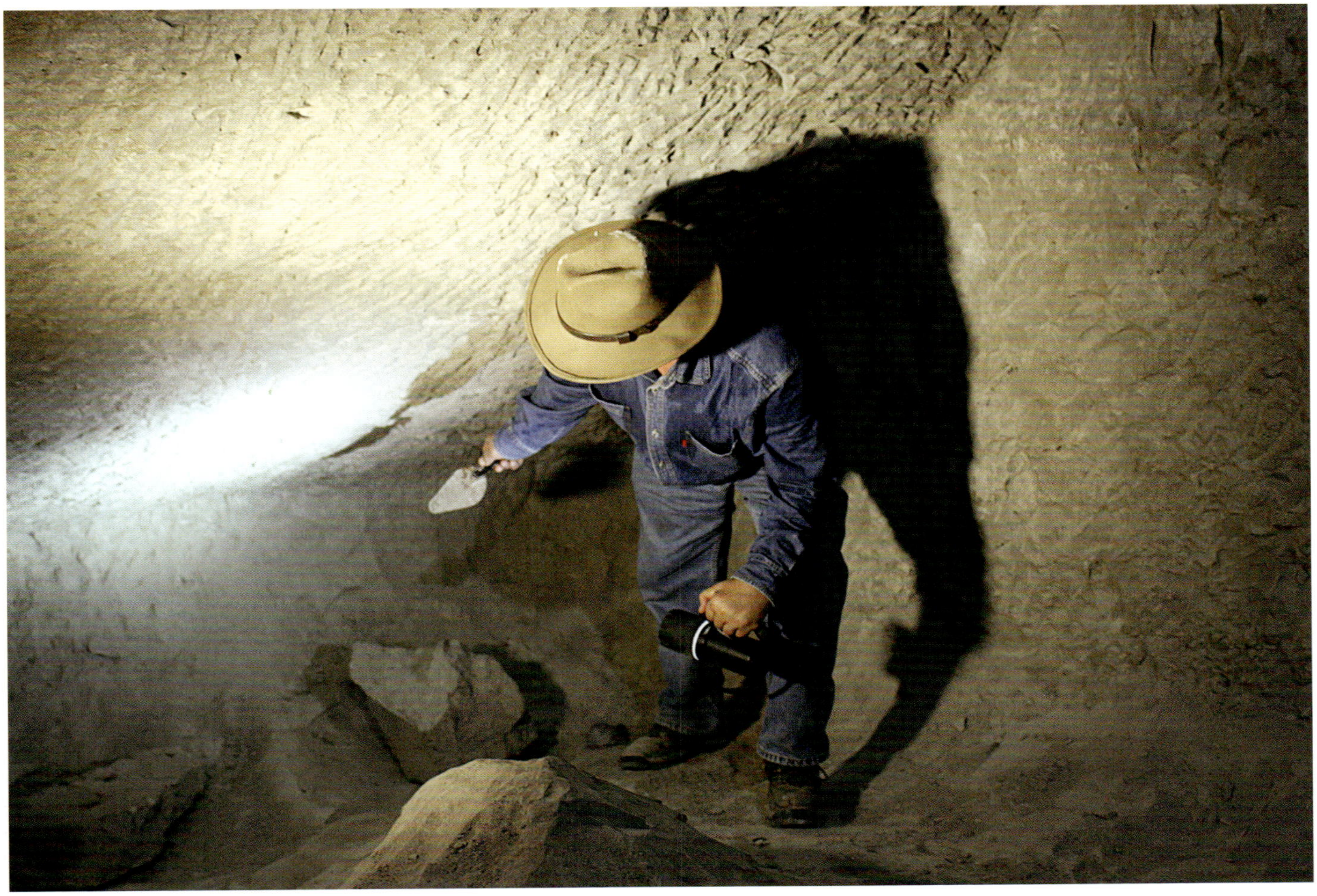

The blind end of the tunnel.

and the rest of the tomb. We created a system of steel beams that served as a framework to support the ceiling. To help clear the rubble we would be excavating from the tomb, we built a small railway.

And so we began to excavate. Upon reaching where Abdel Rassoul's team had last worked, we discovered that they had erred in their digging. Without realizing it, they had left the ancient passageway. We had to excavate the correct path, which is exactly what we did. We were now digging through debris that no one had ever touched before, and began to find interesting things. Besides sherds of pottery, there were two royal ***shabtis***, a boat made of faience, and fragments of stone with the name of Seti I. Then, we found steps cut into the rock. By this time we had lengthened the excavated portion of the tomb to a distance of 140 m from the entrance.

We noticed that the tunnel had a new shape here, compared to what we had dug before. And we found more steps, 54 in all. We seemed to have found the type of stairway that would ordinarily descend into a royal tomb.

We had come to another corridor, this time with smooth walls. Workmen had been in the process of preparing it for decoration, but they had gotten no further than laying gridlines to guide the artists. At the end of this corridor was a gateway on which someone had written in hieratic, "Raise the door jamb and widen the passage." These were instructions for the ancient laborers. But what were they working to build? Tarek El-Awady and I believed that they were extending the tomb – to build another tomb within it.

There was one more stairway, beyond the gate with the graffiti. This one consisted of 37 steps, the last of which was unfinished. They led to a blank wall. We think that this is as far as the workmen had gotten when word arrived that the king, Seti I, had died. At that time they ended their work, 174.5 m from the entrance.

So we had not found a burial chamber. We had not found a golden treasure, which is what Sheikh Ali wanted to find. But I had found something more important – an answer to the question of what lay at the end of the tunnel. Of course, this kind of answer raises even more questions. Seti I reigned for only 12 years. If he had lived longer, and his workmen had worked longer, what might we have found? Maybe an answer lies in KV 7, the tomb of his son, Rameses II, who ruled for 66 years. If Rameses II's tomb were in better condition, perhaps we could see if he, too, had constructed such a tunnel. But to do that will take a major restoration effort in KV 7. It has been victimized by many flash floods that come into the valley. But perhaps someday we will know.

THE SEARCH FOR THE TOMB OF RAMESES VIII

In 2004, I had promised that there would be an Egyptian team excavating in the Valley of the Kings, and when I put together such a team three years later, I set the tomb of Rameses VIII as our goal. Egyptian Egyptologists Afifi Roheim, from the pyramids at Giza, and Ahmed El Leithy, from Minya, would work with me. The target of our excavation was in the area around the tomb of Merenptah, KV 8. We found, to the south, an area of cut rock that looked like it might be the entrance of a tomb. Graffiti in the area suggested this, as well. But though the Egyptians had started their work, they had not finished it. Natural cracks in the cliff that were not known until the ancient workmen began their project caused them to abandon the spot.

We found about 20 more graffiti between Merenptah's tomb and that of his father, Rameses II (KV 7). In one of these, the vizier Userhat wrote, "I built a tomb for my father, Amennakht." Maybe we could find this tomb. Eight months of work ended without the discovery of Amennakht's tomb, or the tomb of Rameses VIII. But we did find another ancient structure, 153 m long, created to direct waters from flash floods downhill to a reservoir. The ancient builders had created it with twists and turns so that the force of the flowing water would decrease. This was not the only structure the Egyptians built to control the flash flood water – there were other channels, plus dams – but this was the largest and most complete found in the Valley of the Kings.

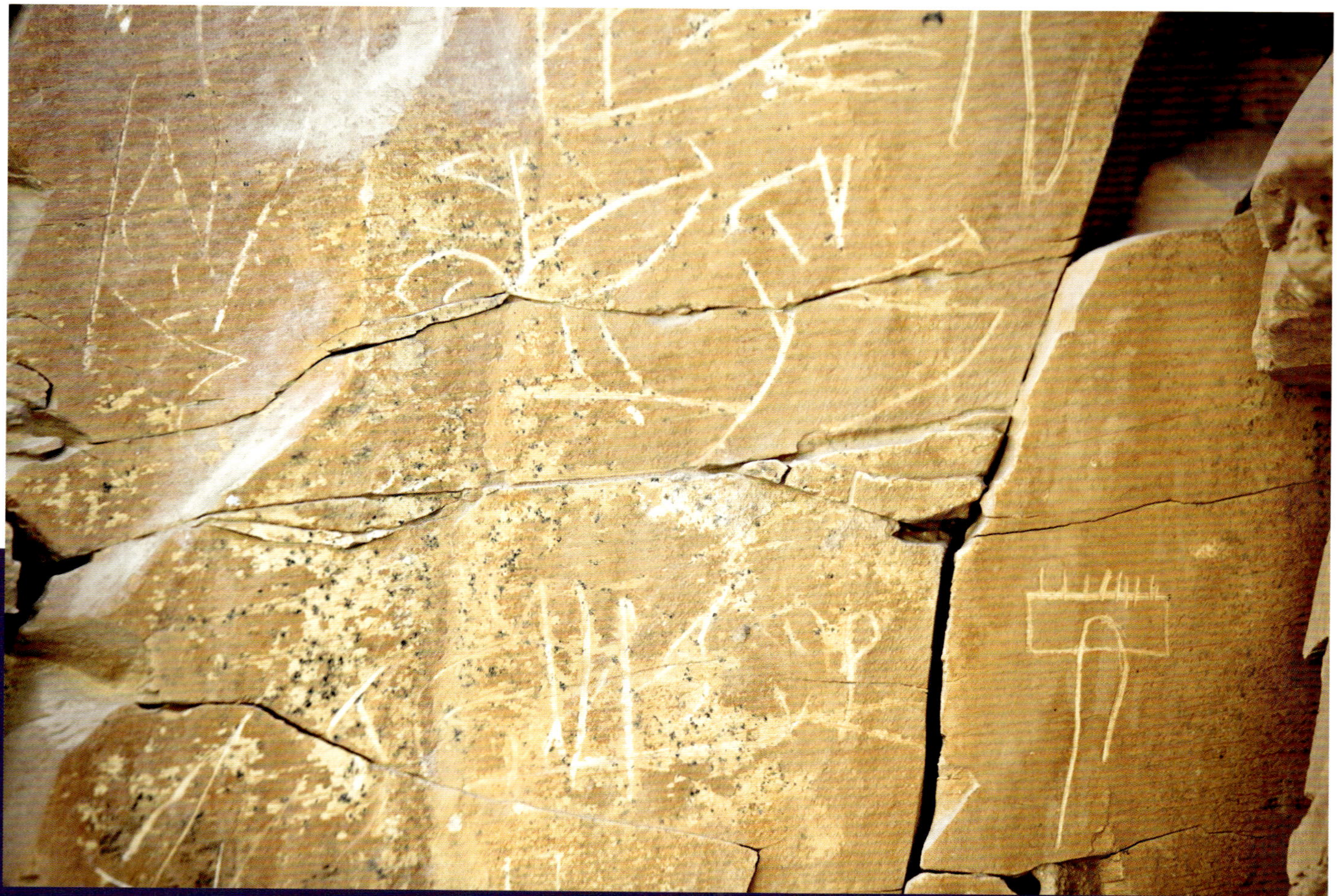

Graffiti left on the rocks of the Valley of the Kings by the ancient tomb builders and visitors.

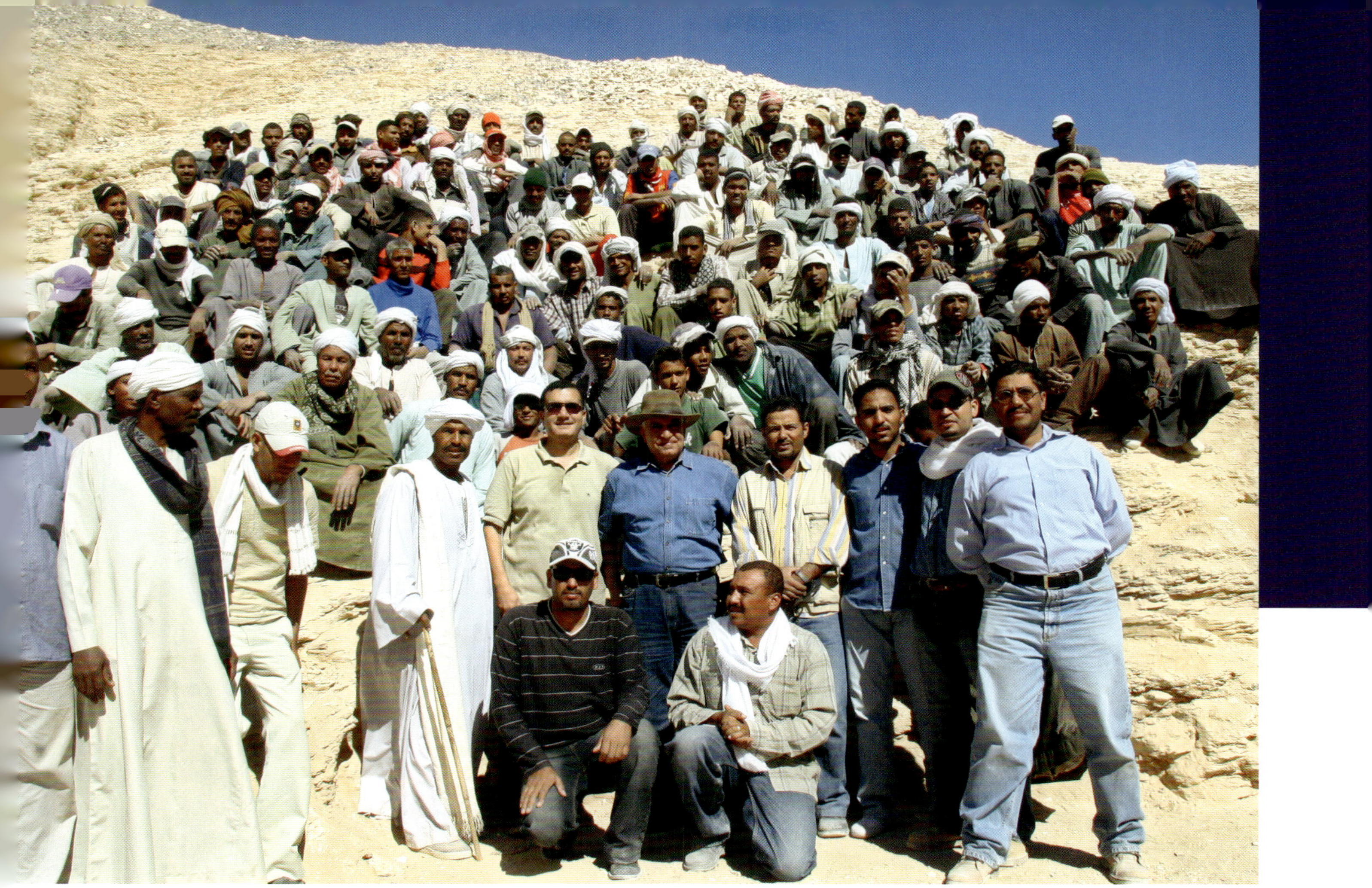

The author and his excavation team at the Valley of the Kings.

EXCAVATION IN FRONT OF THE TOMB OF TUTANKHAMUN

When Howard Carter was searching for the tomb of Tutankhamun, he dug through the huts of workmen who had built tombs for the 19th and 20th Dynasties. These huts had been built on a layer of mud deposited by a very heavy flash flood that had occurred during the late 18th Dynasty. As a result, some tomb entrances, such as Tutankhamun's and KV 63, were hidden. Maybe other tombs would be here as well.

On 31st March, 2006, Nicholas Reeves and Geoffrey Martin of the Amarna Royal Tombs Project held the concession to excavate in the central area of the Valley of the Kings. Six years before, a Japanese team working with the Amarna Royal Tombs Project had undertaken a ground-penetrating radar (GPR) survey. On 3rd August, 2006, Reeves announced that the GPR data had been reanalyzed and that there was an anomaly in the survey data on the eastern side of the central area. This had been an area of speculation for some time. A hydraulic survey published by Stephen Cross, an Egyptologist and geologist, had also detected an anomaly thought by some to be evidence of a tomb about 16 m southeast of the wall that guards the entrance to the tomb of Tutankhamun, and the Canadian Egyptologist Lyla Pinch Brock proposed that one of the lost Theban tombs (KV "C") might be beneath the old rest house built for tourists.

Our Egyptian team undertook to explore this area through excavation, and through the course of the work recorded 5 m of flood deposits above the bedrock of the valley. The team encountered the six workmen's huts that Howard Carter had hastily recorded in his search for Tutankhamun's tomb. Some of the huts shared walls, and each had an entrance that opened in a different direction. These entrances had been

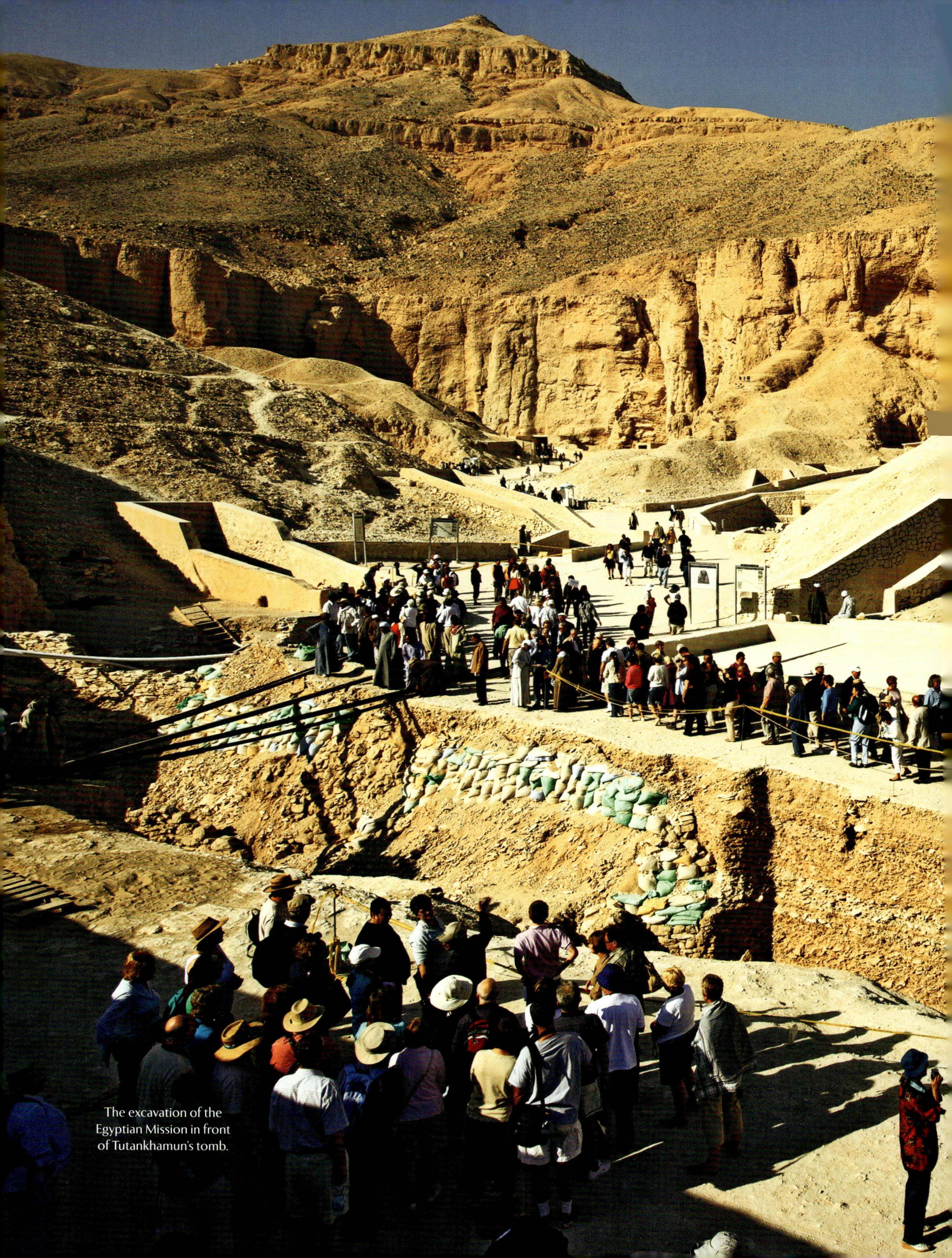

The excavation of the Egyptian Mission in front of Tutankhamun's tomb.

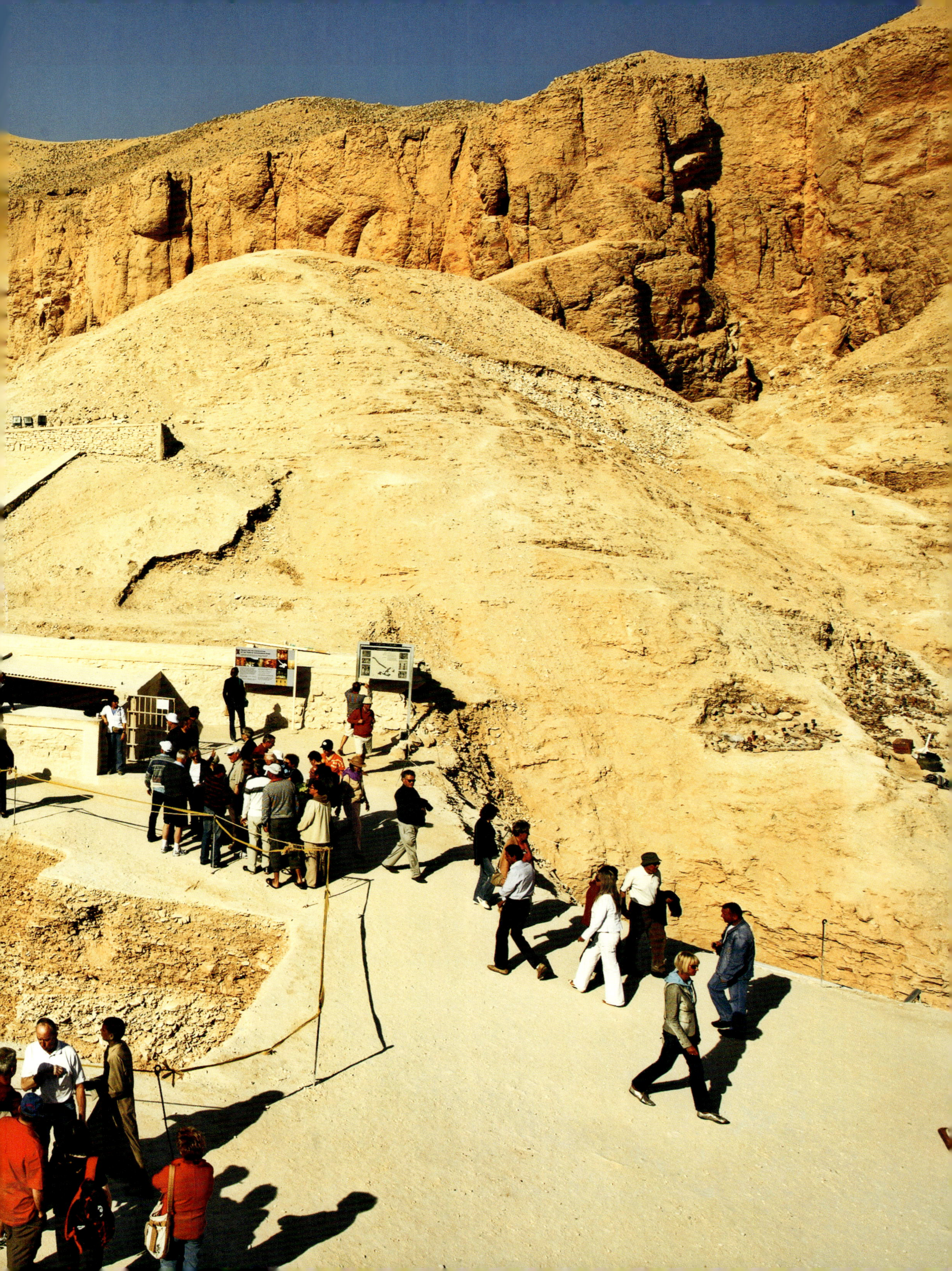

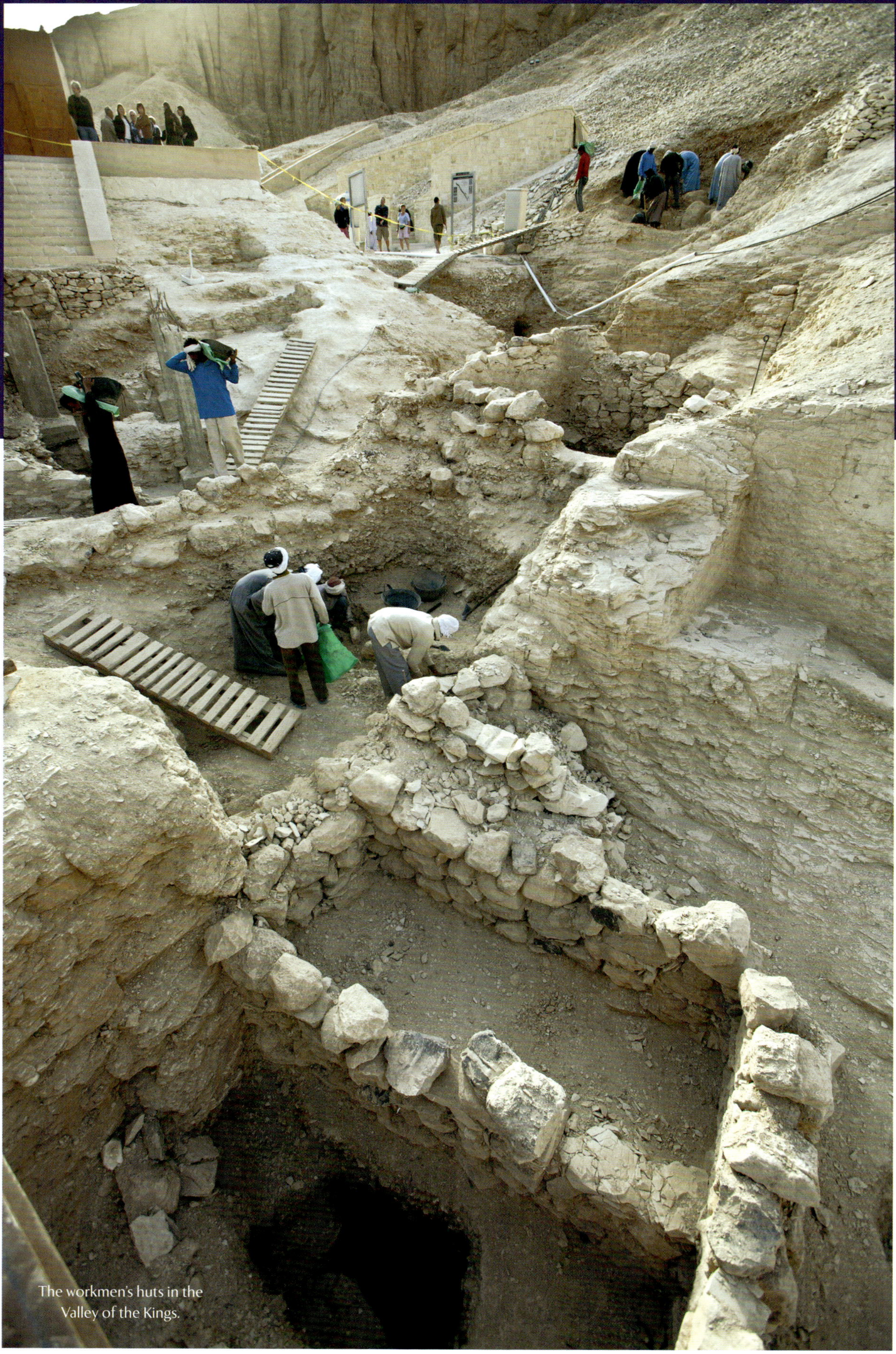

The workmen's huts in the Valley of the Kings.

closed up, something that perhaps Carter had ordered done. One of the huts had been used as a storage room and still contained a reed basket. Before the huts had been built, we discovered, the area had been used for more temporary habitation by the men who had built and decorated the royal tombs nearby.

But we found no tombs. The other eight anomalies proved to be merely a natural fissure in the bedrock. Even KV "C" was not to be found, though we dismantled the tourist rest house and the office of the inspector of antiquities.

Nonetheless, we found a number of artifacts of interest. We found inscribed blocks with fragments of text (such as cartouches of Rameses II, and an inscription mentioning "Year 9" of an unnamed king) and scenes (one of these depicts Anubis on a platform). We found more than 100 ostraca (fragments of pottery or stone) on which workmen had written or drawn. One ostracon showed two goats engaged in sex, while another had a sketch of a woman, perhaps a lonely workman's wife. ***Shabtis***, amulets, late 18th Dynasty pottery, tools, raw materials for making paint, botanical remains, bits of funerary furniture, fragments of glass and other objects turned up in the excavations. Fragments of a sarcophagus and even pieces of painted plaster from tomb walls were also discovered. A limestone platform recessed to hold vessels and a block, also of limestone, with abbreviated signs that refer to the workmen's names were found near the tomb of Merenptah. That was the signature of the workmen to show that they had come to work. We also found evidence of queens here: an image of a queen in a worshiping position, and a block with the incomplete name of an unknown queen.

Even if a project does not find what it sets out after, no archaeological excavation is ever completely unproductive.

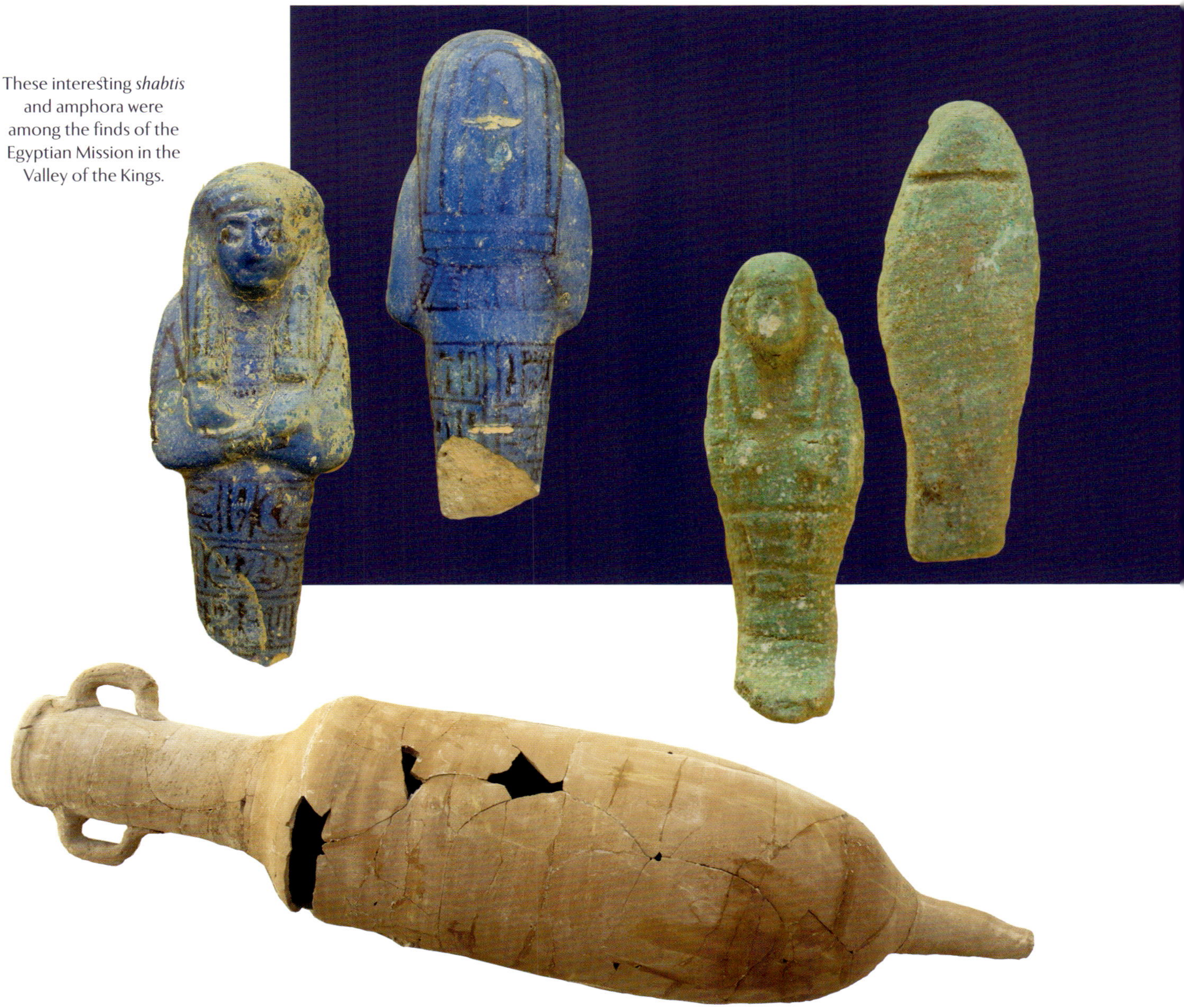

These interesting *shabtis* and amphora were among the finds of the Egyptian Mission in the Valley of the Kings.

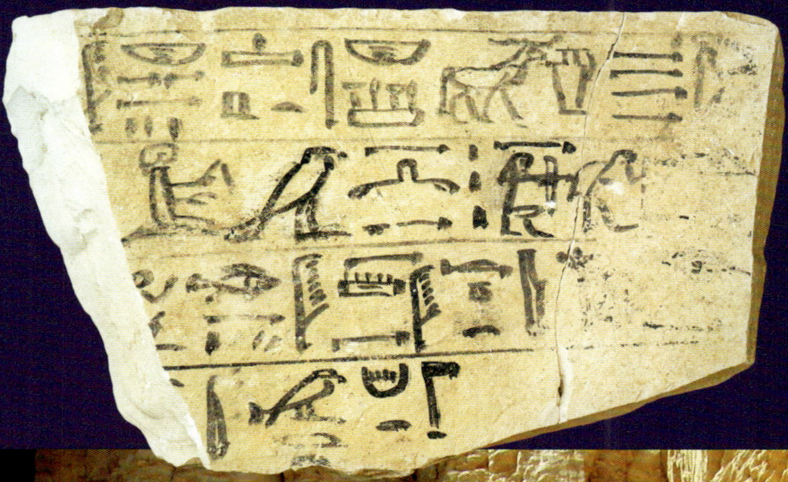

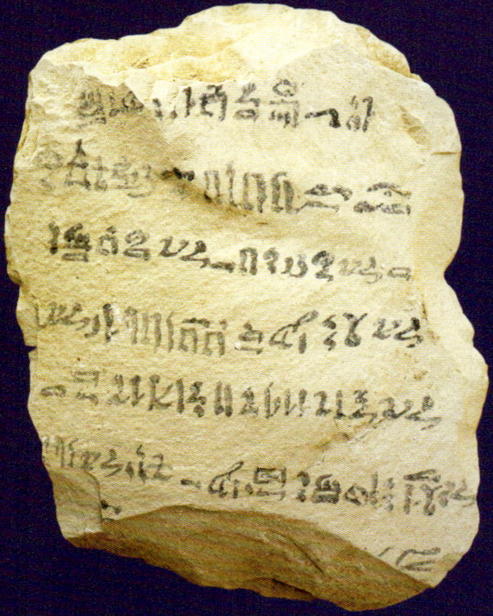

Two of many ostraca found by the Egyptian Mission working in the Valley of the Kings. The one on the left refers to the great god's wife Tiye.

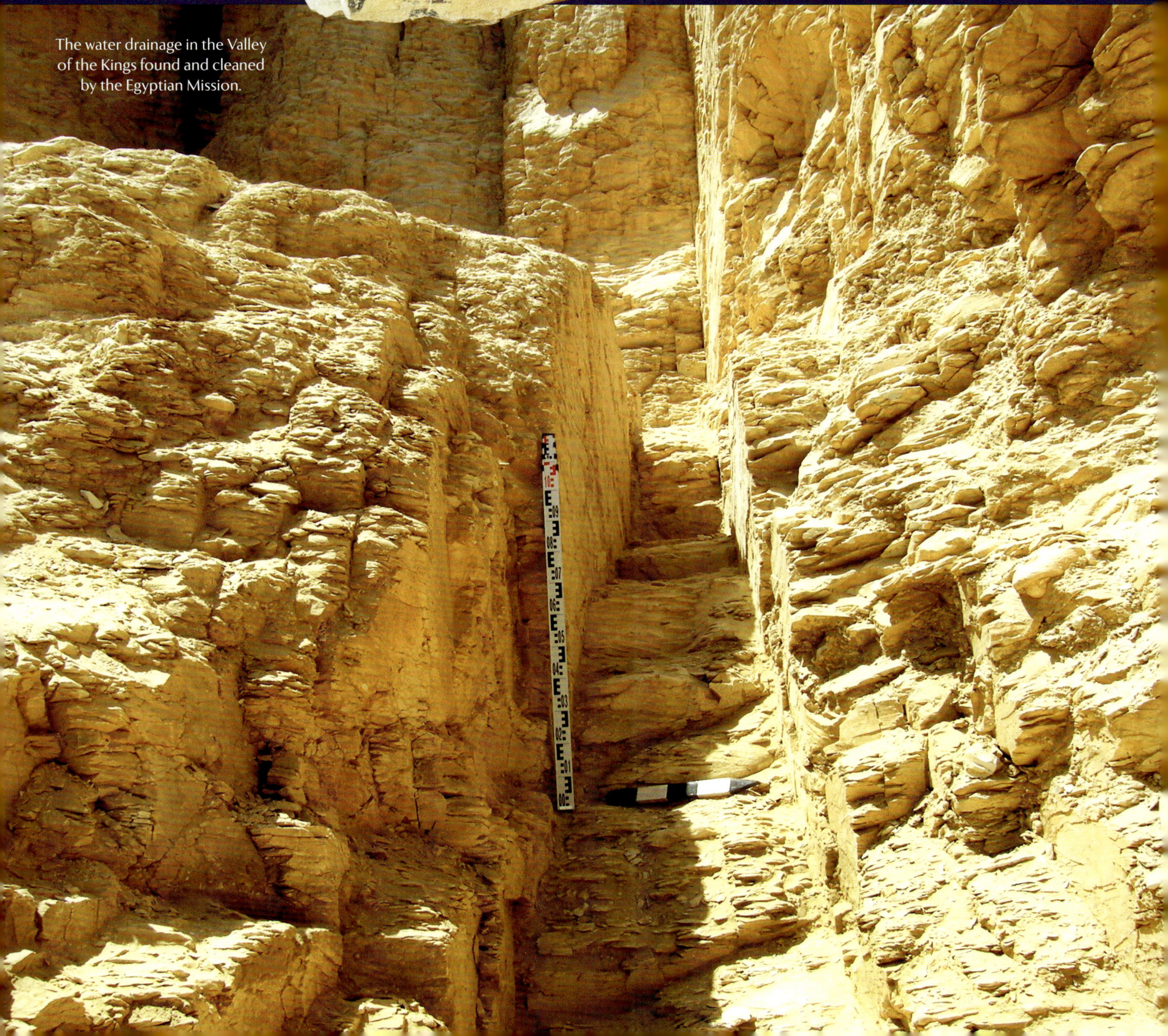

The water drainage in the Valley of the Kings found and cleaned by the Egyptian Mission.

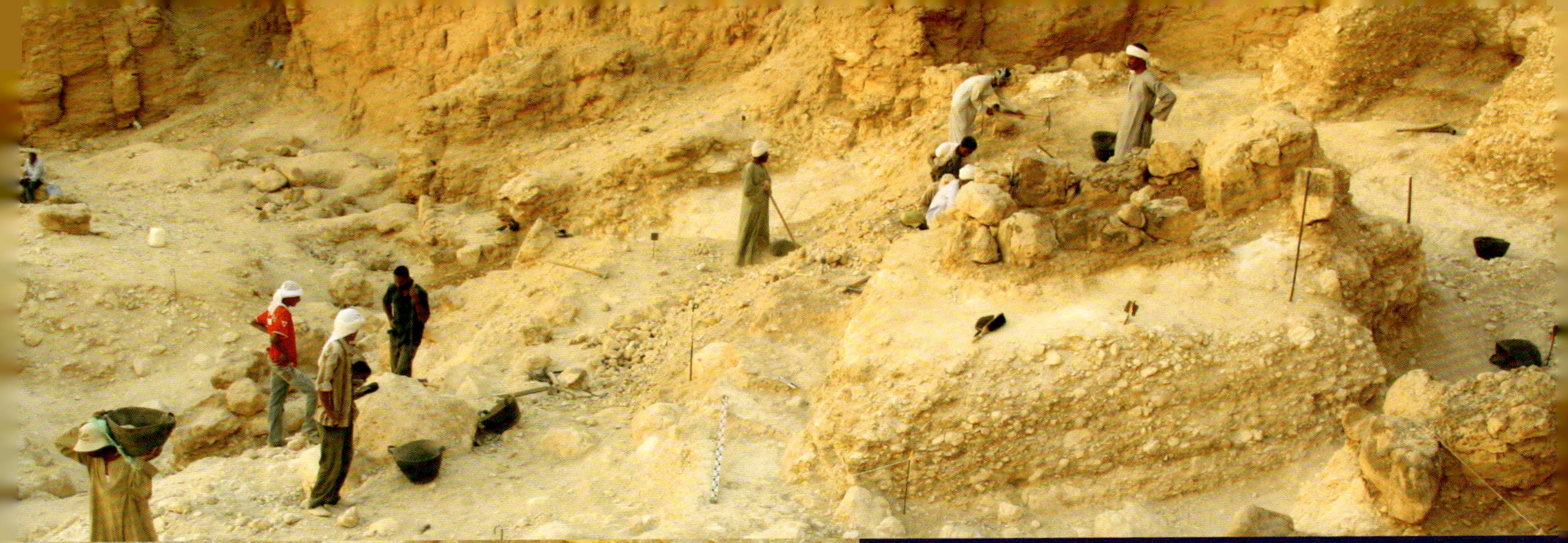

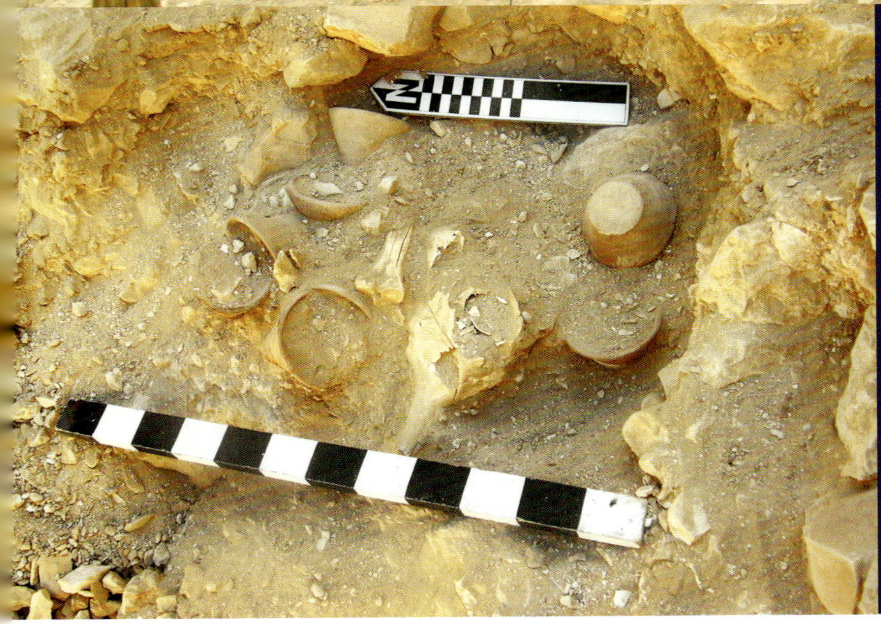

The excavation site of the Egyptian Mission in the Valley of the Monkeys and the intact tomb foundation deposits found at the site.

EXCAVATION IN THE VALLEY OF THE MONKEYS

The wadi to the west of the Valley of the Kings is known as the West Valley or as the Valley of the Monkeys. Four tombs have been found here so far: KV 22 (Amenhotep III), KV 23 (Ay), KV 24 (owner unknown), and KV 25. The owner of KV 25 is unknown, but possibly it was begun on behalf of Akhenaten before he moved the royal court to Amarna. I believe that more tombs remain to be found in the Valley of the Monkeys. Graffiti and a number of worker's huts, constructed on a platform made of stone rubble, certainly indicate that there is something more to be found in this wadi. The tomb of Tutankhamun's wife, Ankhesenamun, may be here too, perhaps near Ay's, KV 23, which might have been begun for Tutankhamun. Ay was not only perhaps Ankhesenamun's grandfather but he was her husband as well, after she was widowed.

When we excavated the workmen's huts, we came upon four foundation deposits, ritual offerings buried before construction of a building or tomb. In the southwest corner of hut number 12 we found 10 pottery cups, a pottery vessel, a model copper ax, and animal bones, surrounded by a half-circle formed of six blocks of stone, three of which were flint. A deposit in the southeast corner of another hut likewise contained pottery and a model ax, while the northeast corner deposit was much like these but with more remains of seeds. Another model ax and the remains of an ax head were found in the northwest deposit.

Carter had found five foundation deposits associated with the tomb of Amenhotep III. Four flanked the tomb entrance and the fifth was found directly before it. Here Carter uncovered more than 150 pottery vessels, model tools, and 99 cartouches made of faience. The cartouches gave not the name of Amenhotep III but of his father, Thutmose IV. We suspect from this evidence that another tomb from the late 18th Dynasty lies here somewhere. Perhaps it will prove to be Ankhesenamun's or Nefertiti's, but only future excavation will tell.

THE REDISCOVERY OF KV 53 BY THE EGYPTIAN EXPEDITION

In 1905–1906, Edward Ayrton, who was sponsored by the American millionaire Theodore Davis, found six tombs in the Valley of the Kings: KV 48, KV 49, KV 50, KV 51, KV 52, and KV 53. KV 50–52 contained animal mummies, and so it has been believed that these tombs were prepared for Amenhotep II's pets. Sand had covered over some of these tombs, including KV 53, and so they were lost. In our search for four of the lost tombs, we found KV 53 first, in the wadi leading to KV 35, the tomb of Amenhotep II. Our new excavations are helping us to correct the plan published online by the Theban Mapping Project, which was based only on Ayrton's information.

The square shaft leads to a rectangular chamber. Ayrton wrote that the tomb had been robbed and the only object of note that he found was an ostracon with the name of a man, Huri, who was "overseer of scribes in the Place of Justice," meaning the royal Theban necropolis. This might indicate that Huri was the tomb owner. Nicholas Reeves writes that a stela for the goddess Meretseger was found here, as well. In the debris covering the floor, we found much more than this: sherds of pottery, bits of linen, and pieces of wood that might have been part of a coffin. And we found four wonderful lids from canopic jars, in the form of human heads, with eyebrows and eyes in black paint and the hieroglyphic sign representing a scorpion carved atop each. A 15.5 cm long piece of metal in the form of a V was apparently made from gold. There was a Canaanite amphora dateable by its shape to between 1400–1300 B.C. We found bones, as well, and three human skulls. One of these people had been a man who was about 45 at the time of his death. Another was a younger man, about 20 years old. The last skull belonged to a woman of about 23. Possibly the 45-year-old was the owner and the younger individuals were his son and daughter, but we do not know for sure. We do know, however, that the tomb itself is from the 18th Dynasty.

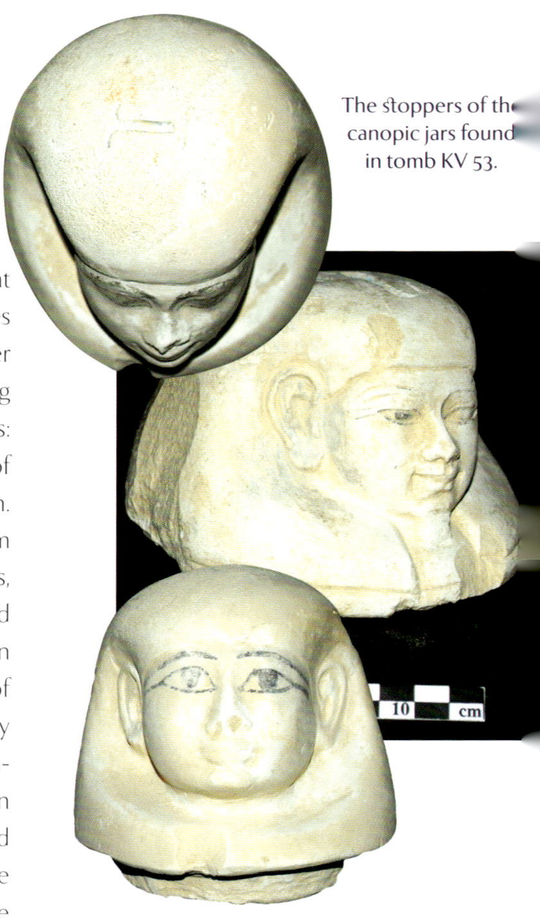

The stoppers of the canopic jars found in tomb KV 53.

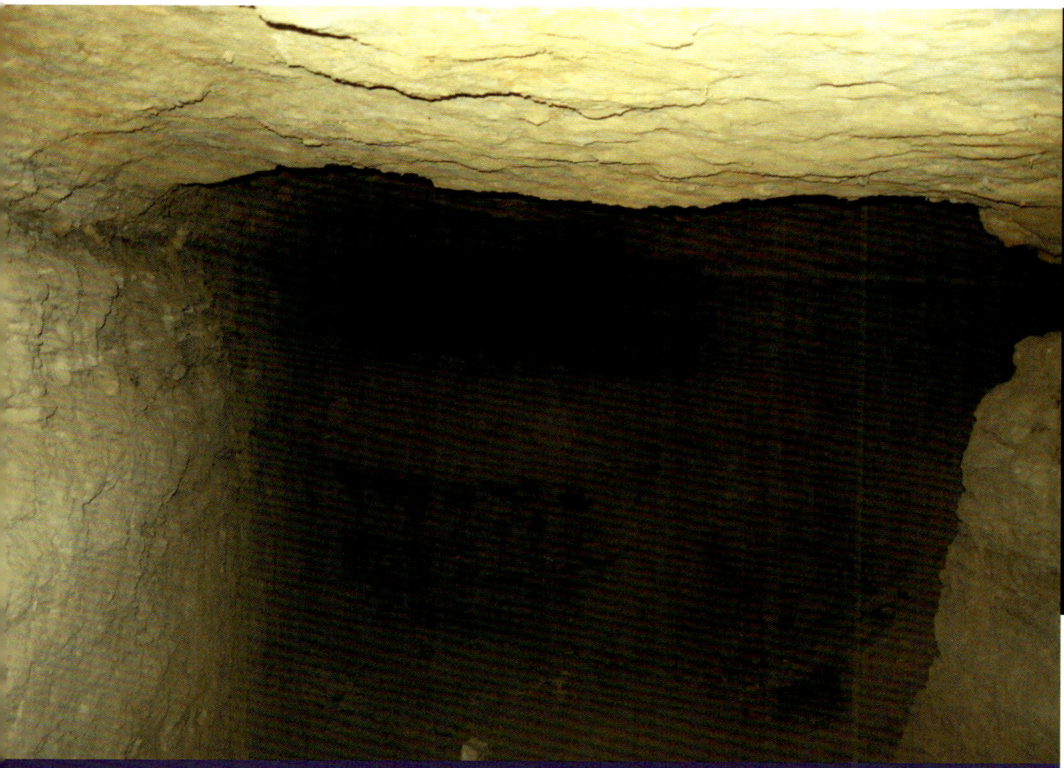

The view into tomb KV 53.

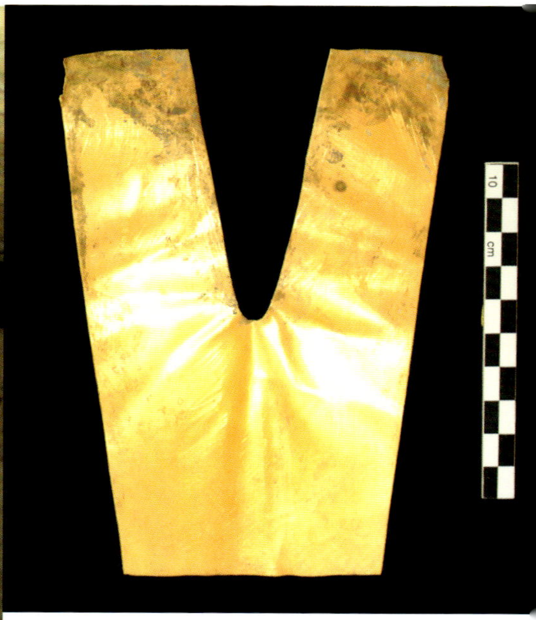

The V-shaped piece of gold from tomb KV 53.

THE REDISCOVERY OF THE MISSING PIECES

of the Colossal Statue of Amenhotep III and Queen Tiye at the Egyptian Museum

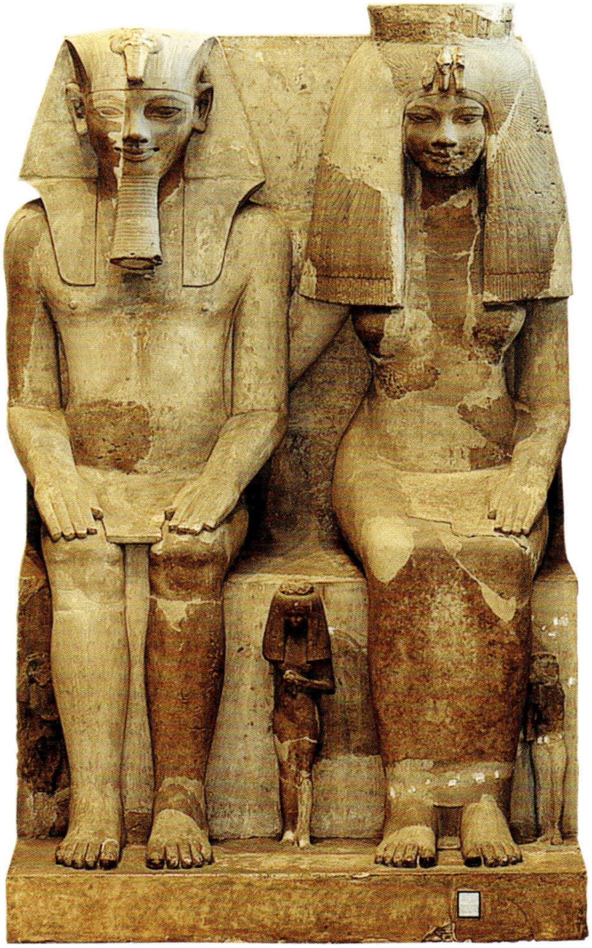

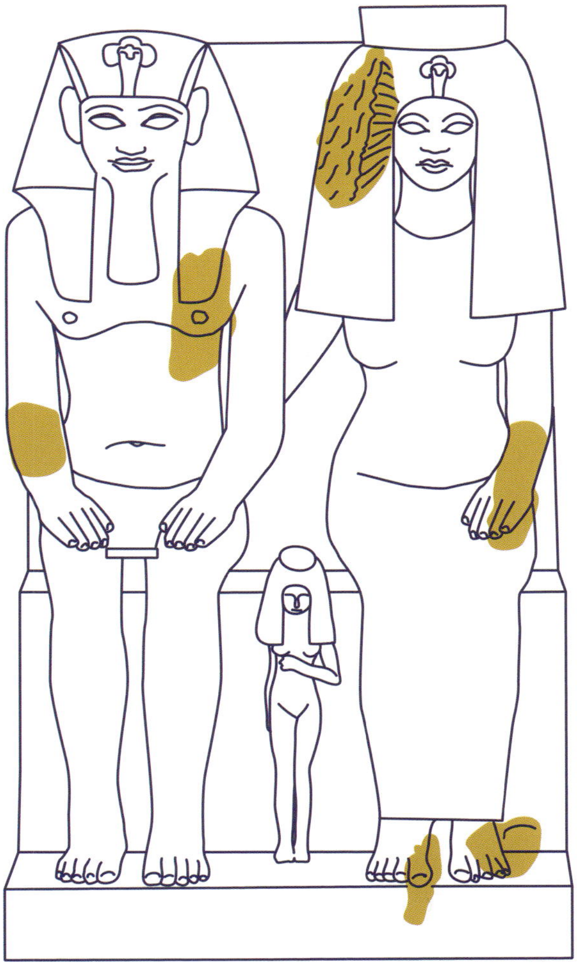

A USAID-funded project, supported by the Ministry of International Cooperation, was begun in 2009 to decrease the level of the water table around the temples on the west bank of Luxor. The team that worked under me included Abdel Ghaffar Wagdy, Mohamed Abdel Badea, El Taieb Mohamed Khodary, and Omar Abou Zeid. In the course of our work at Medinet Habu, site of Rameses III's funerary temple, we found pieces of colossal statuary. We began to search for the statue that these pieces could belong to. It was difficult because they did not feature any inscriptions, and thus could not be easily dated. We realized, however, that colossal figures of the 18th Dynasty belong only to Amenhotep III and have been found either at the king's funerary temple at Kom el-Hitan or here, at Medinet Habu.

We began to wonder if these blocks might be part of the famous seated statue depicting him and the queen that now looks out over the first floor of the Egyptian Museum. This double statue, made of limestone, had been found near the Roman Court at Medinet Habu in 1859 by the French archaeologist, Auguste Mariette. Although discovered at Medinet Habu, it originally stood at a great southern gate at the funerary temple of Amenhotep III at Kom el-Hitan, which is to the east of Medinet Habu. When it was discovered, many parts of the figures were missing and had to be restored by filling in the gaps. This restoration work was performed at the turn of the last century, led by an Italian artist and restorer who clearly showed the distinction between the original pieces of the statue and the restored portions.

Through careful comparison, we were able to confirm that the pieces we had found – including the queen's wig, left arm and leg, part of the king's ***nemes***-headdress, chest, and right leg, as well as portions of the base – matched gaps in the statue in Cairo.

With the newly discovered pieces of the original stone incorporated into the restoration, the statue will be about 70% complete.

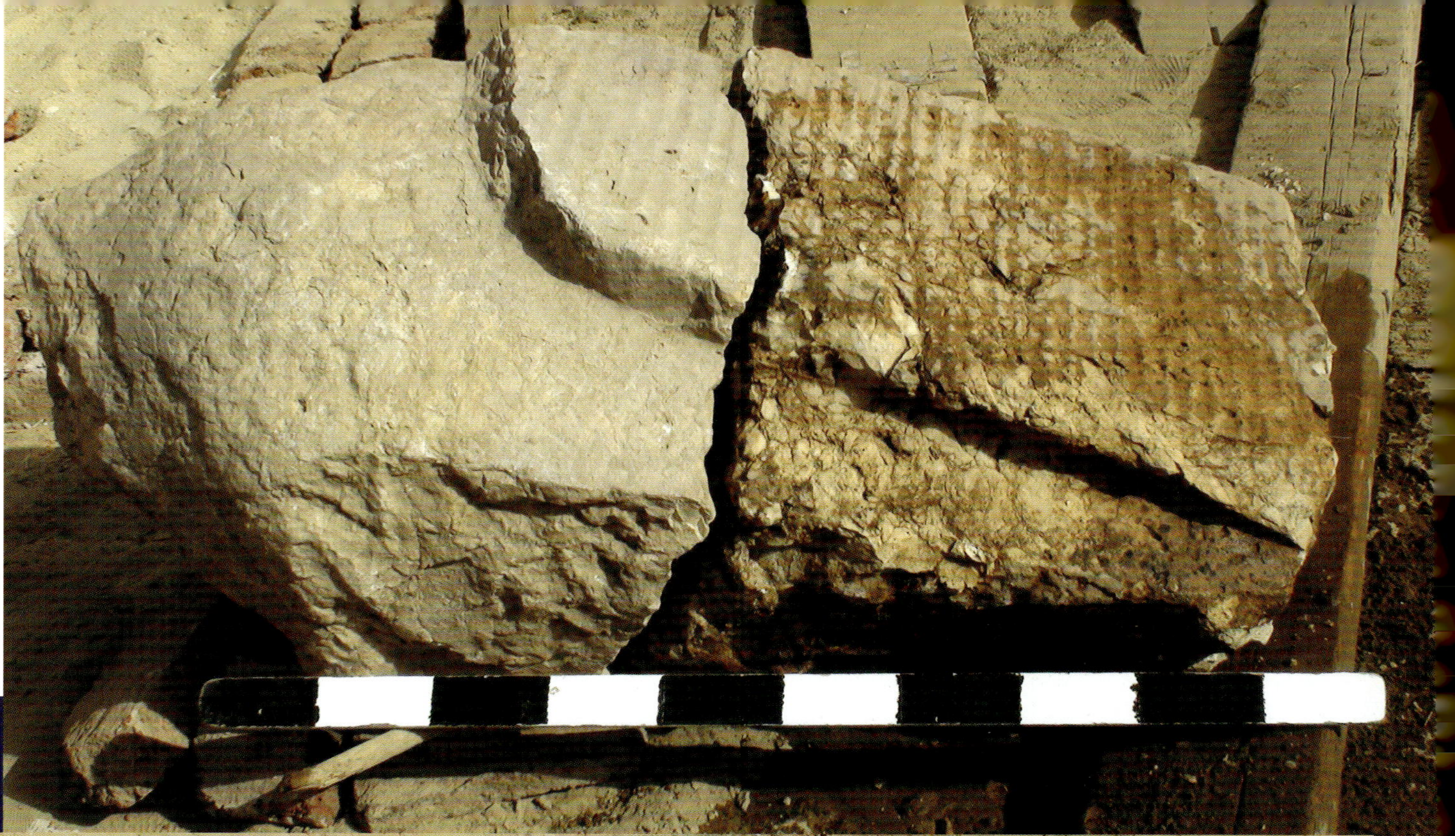

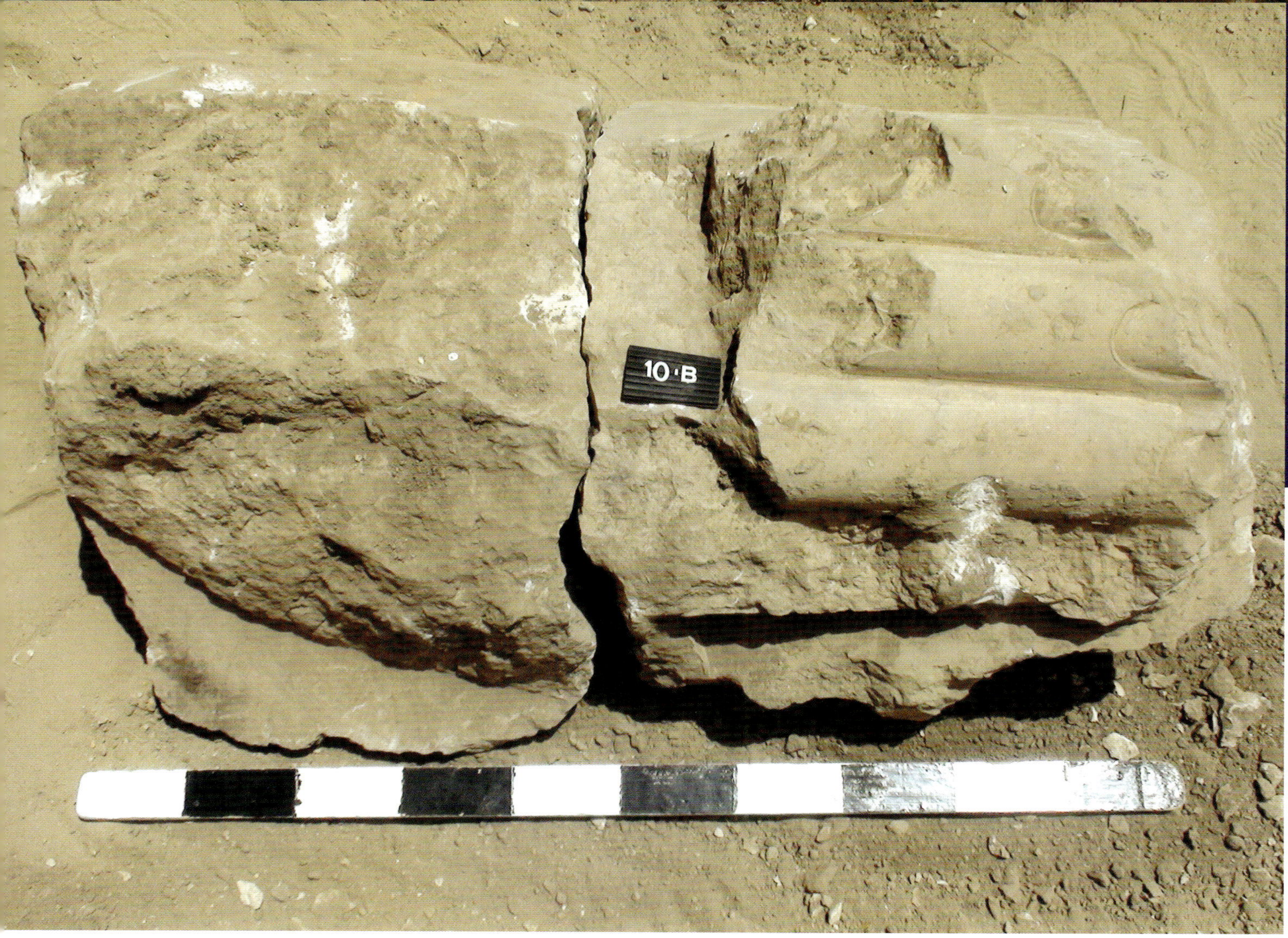
10 B

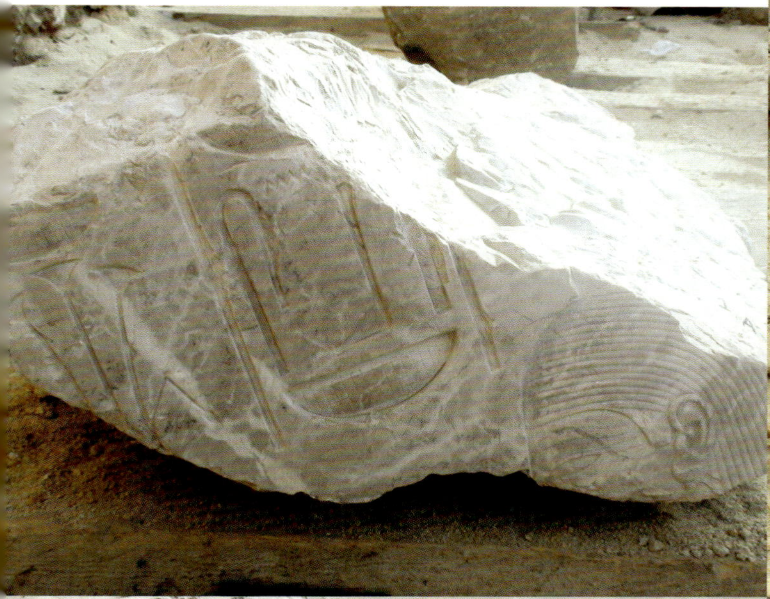

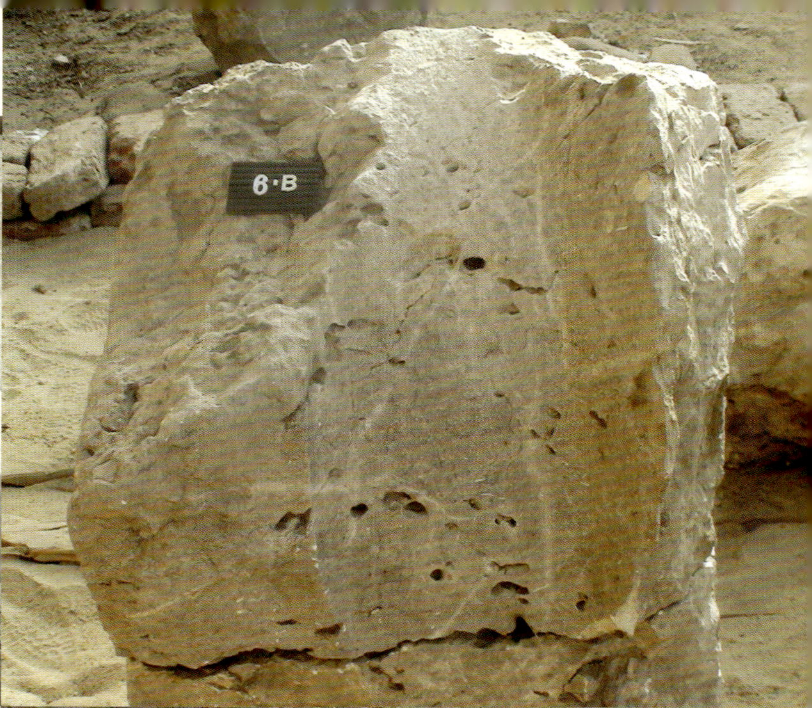
6·B

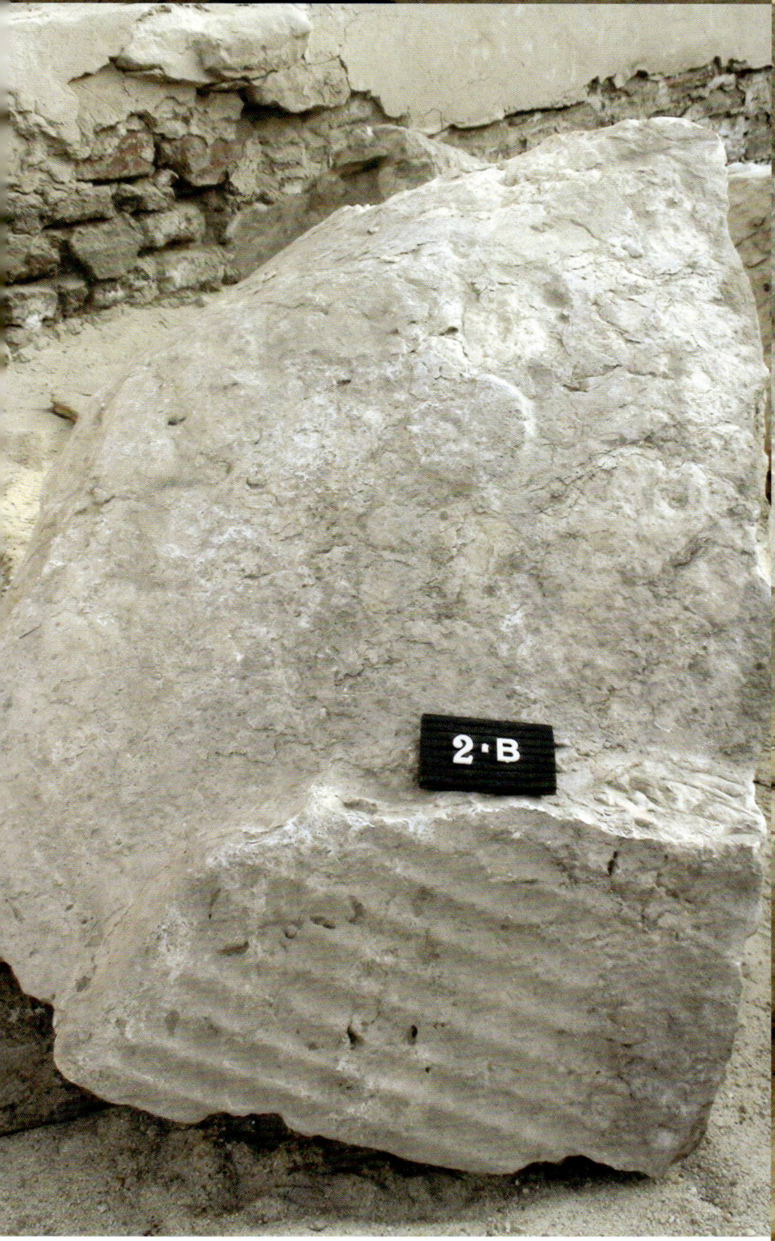
2·B

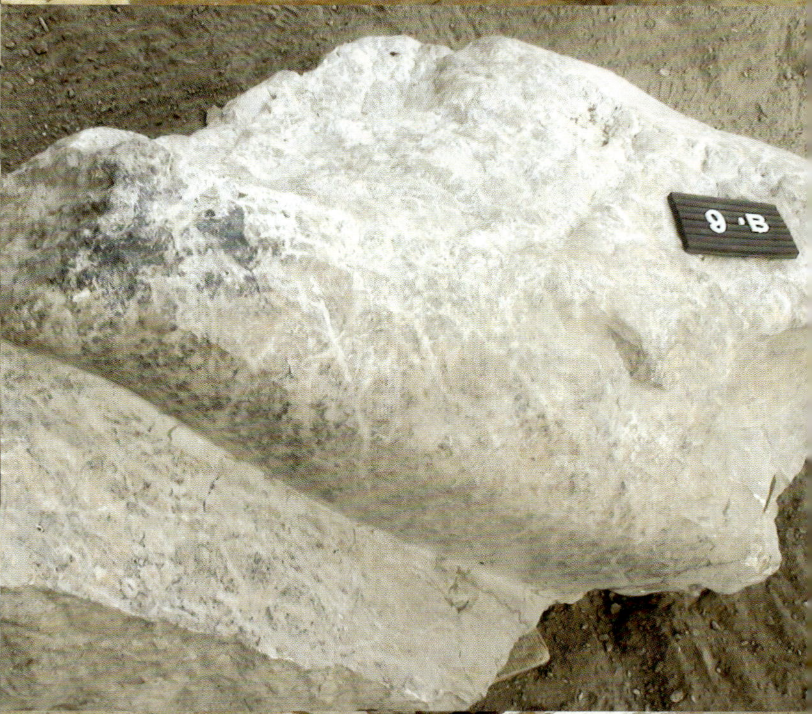
9·B

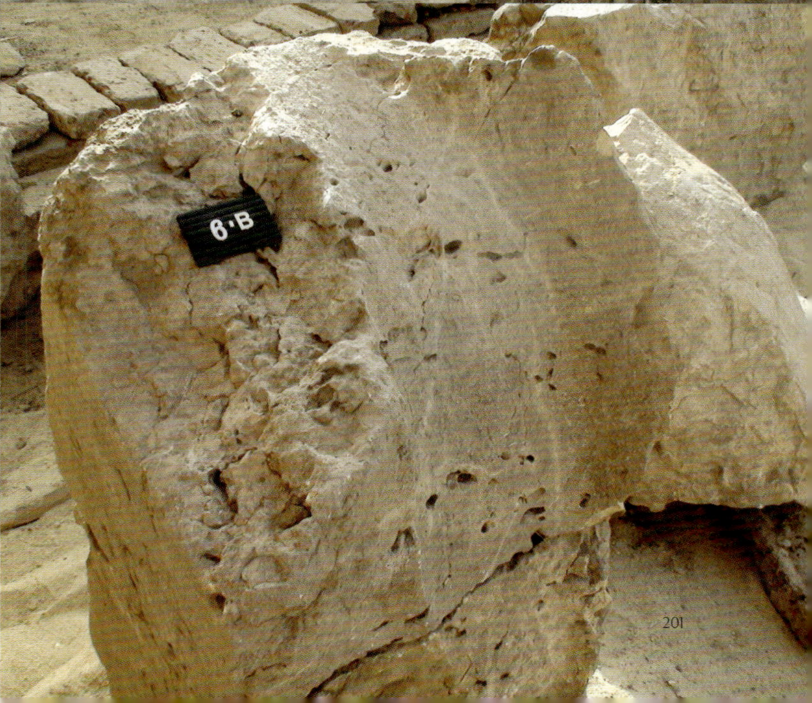
6·B

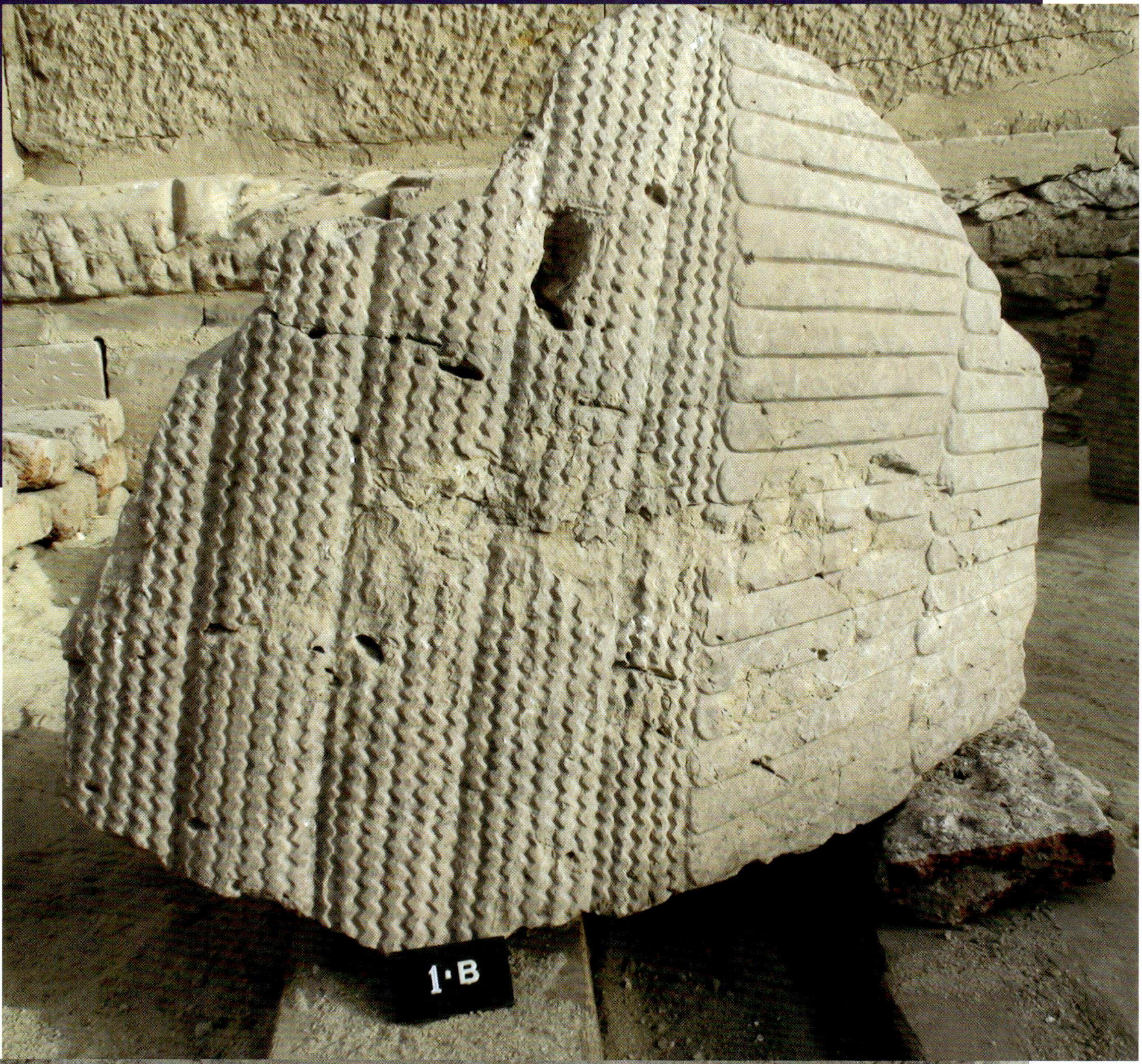
1·B

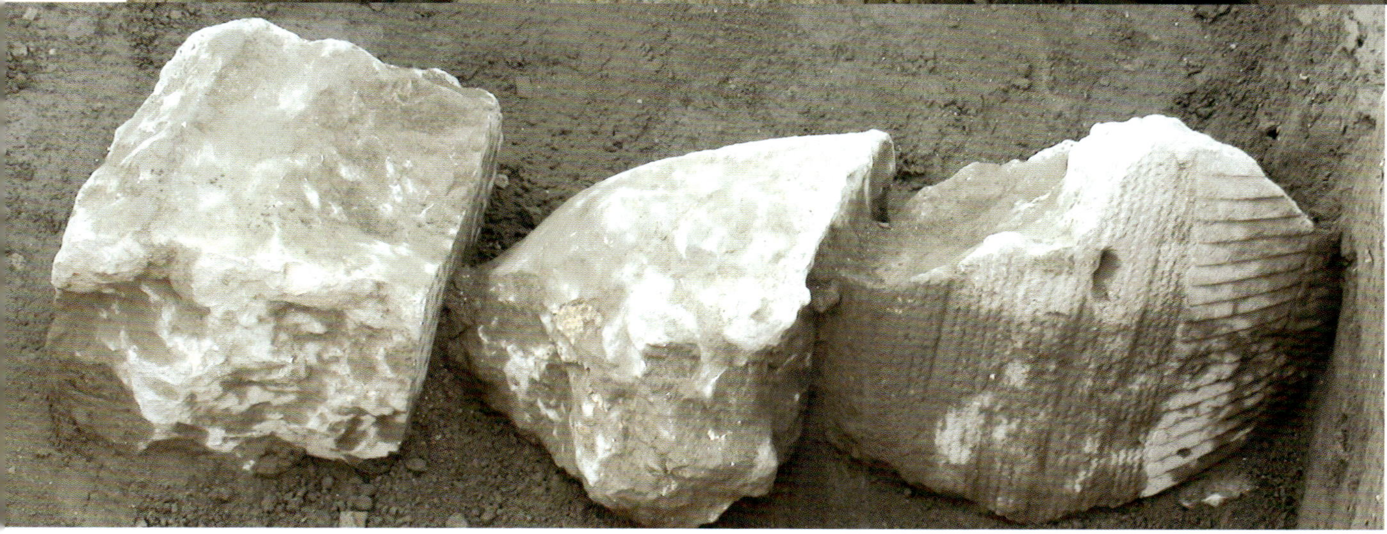

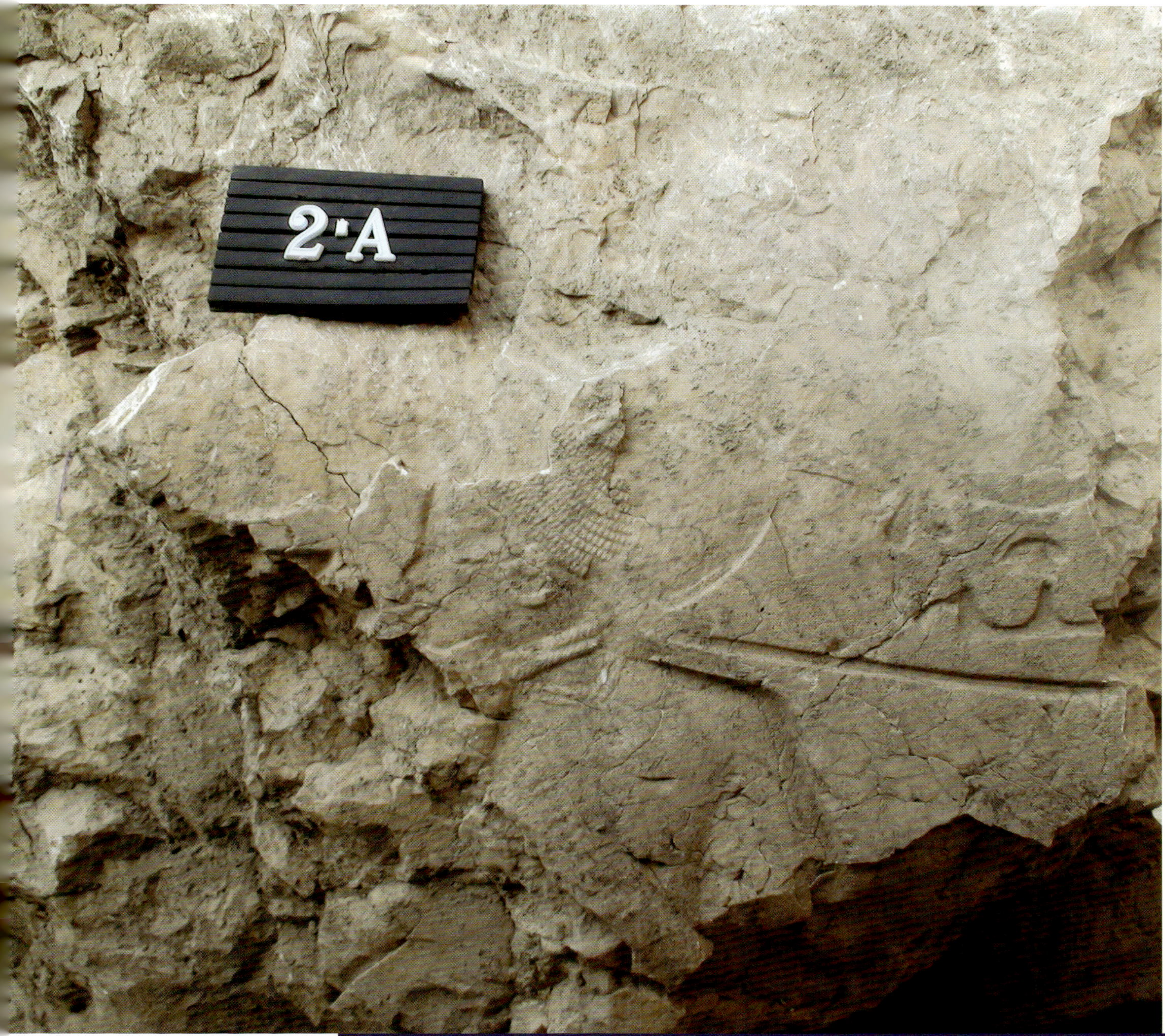

The recently discovered fragments from the colossal statue of Amenhotep III and Tiye.
Now in the Egyptian Museum in Cairo.

THE EXCAVATION OF THE GERMAN EXPEDITION AT AMENHOTEP III'S TEMPLE

Hourig Sourouzian and Rainer Stadelmann of the German Archaeological Institute are working inside the funerary temple of Amenhotep III at Kom el-Hitan, which is the largest temple on the west bank. Its most visible features today are the famous pair of statues known as the Colossi of Memnon. In the great peristyle court of the temple, the German expedition has found approximately 65 statues of the goddess Sekhmet, which could indicate that Tutankhamun's grandfather was ill at the end of his reign. He might have put these statues in his temple for that purpose because although Sekhmet was the goddess of war, she was also the goddess of healing. Besides an image of Amenhotep III as a sphinx, they have also found a headless sphinx of Queen Tiye. Excavation has also revealed a calcite (Egyptian alabaster) statue of a striding hippopotamus (perhaps an image of Seth or some kind of celestial symbol), and a seated statue of the king made of diorite, very similar to a statue that can be seen in the British Museum. Sourouzian and Stadelmann have also been able to restore and re-erect a colossal image of Amenhotep III and Queen Tiye, which now stands at the site.

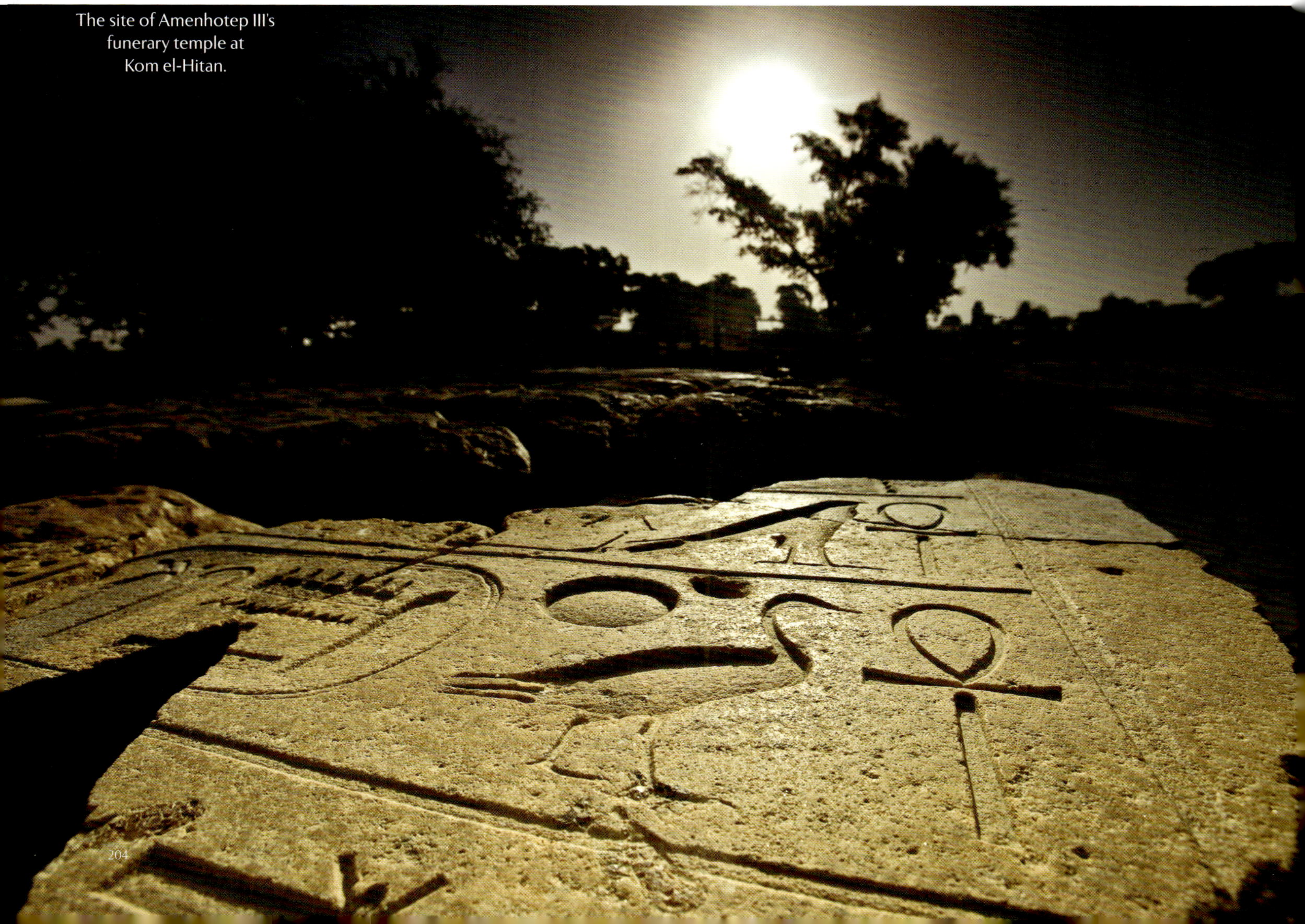

The site of Amenhotep III's funerary temple at Kom el-Hitan.

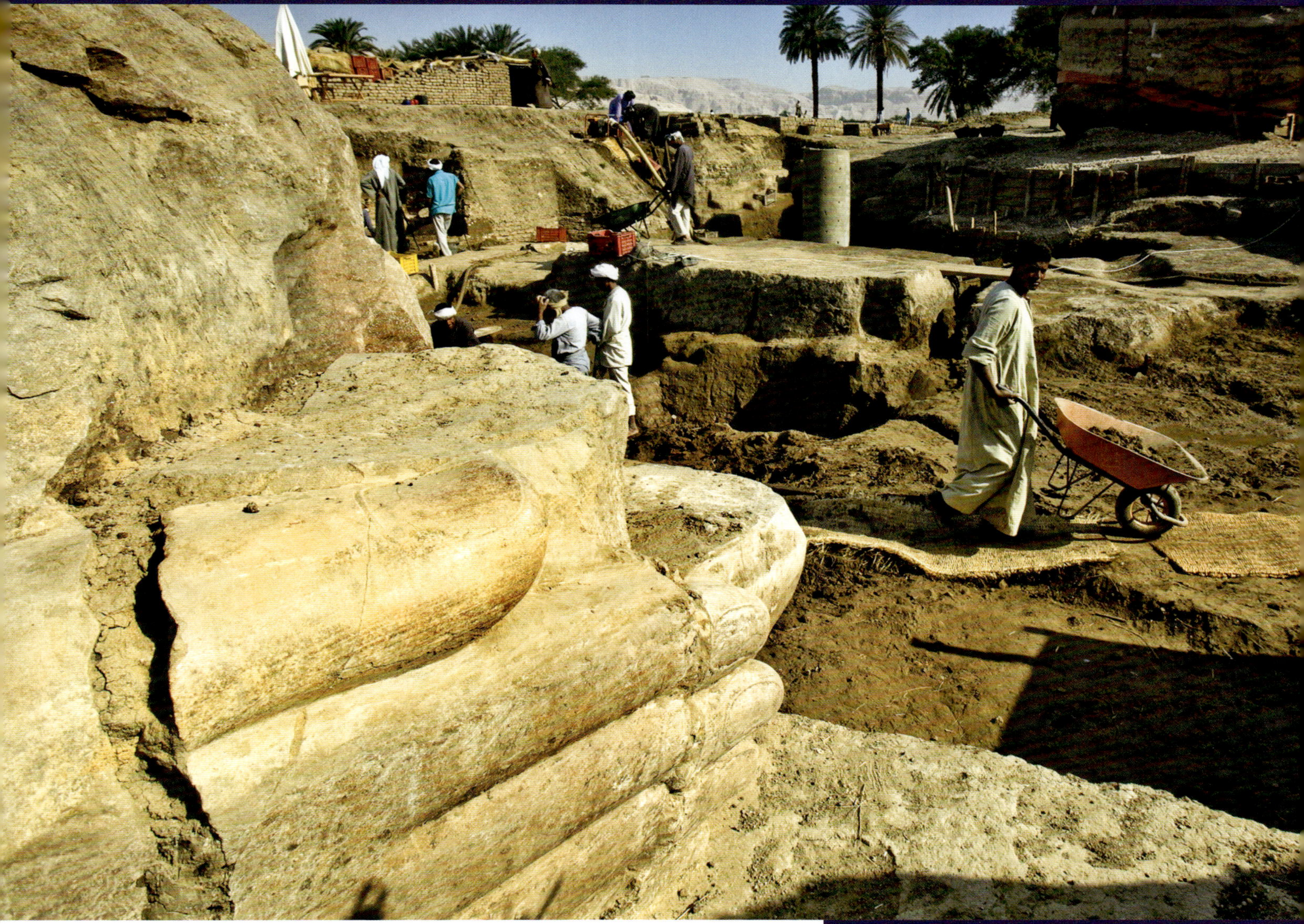

Also among their finds was an enormous head of the king, 2.5 m tall and 78 cm wide, wearing the red crown of Lower Egypt. Found at the west end of the southern portico of the temple, this beautifully preserved fragment perhaps was originally placed between the two columns of the court. In previous seasons, the expedition found a piece of the beard, large pieces of the body, as well as sizeable parts of the back slab. Sourouzian and her team have done excellent work to reconstruct the statue and place it where it once stood. Another quartzite royal head, the eyes of which are missing, has also been found, as have 160 pieces of a large royal stela made of the same type of stone.

I must say that this is some of the most impressive work conducted by a foreign mission in Egypt and shows how we all work together to maintain and preserve these monuments. I admire the conservation work performed under Sourouzian and Stadelmann. Their efforts have protected the northern wing of the third pylon with modern bricks and are conserving the calcite (Egyptian alabaster) blocks of another royal statue in front of the third pylon. They are also doing work on the temple causeway and the south stela. I visited this excavation many times and was impressed by the scientific methods of research and the careful reconstruction of the statues, pottery, and the temple itself. The German expedition has been able to determine the plan of the temple of Amenhotep III and to uncover this great achievement of Tutankhamun's grandfather.

Remains of the colossal statues from the site of Kom el-Hitan.

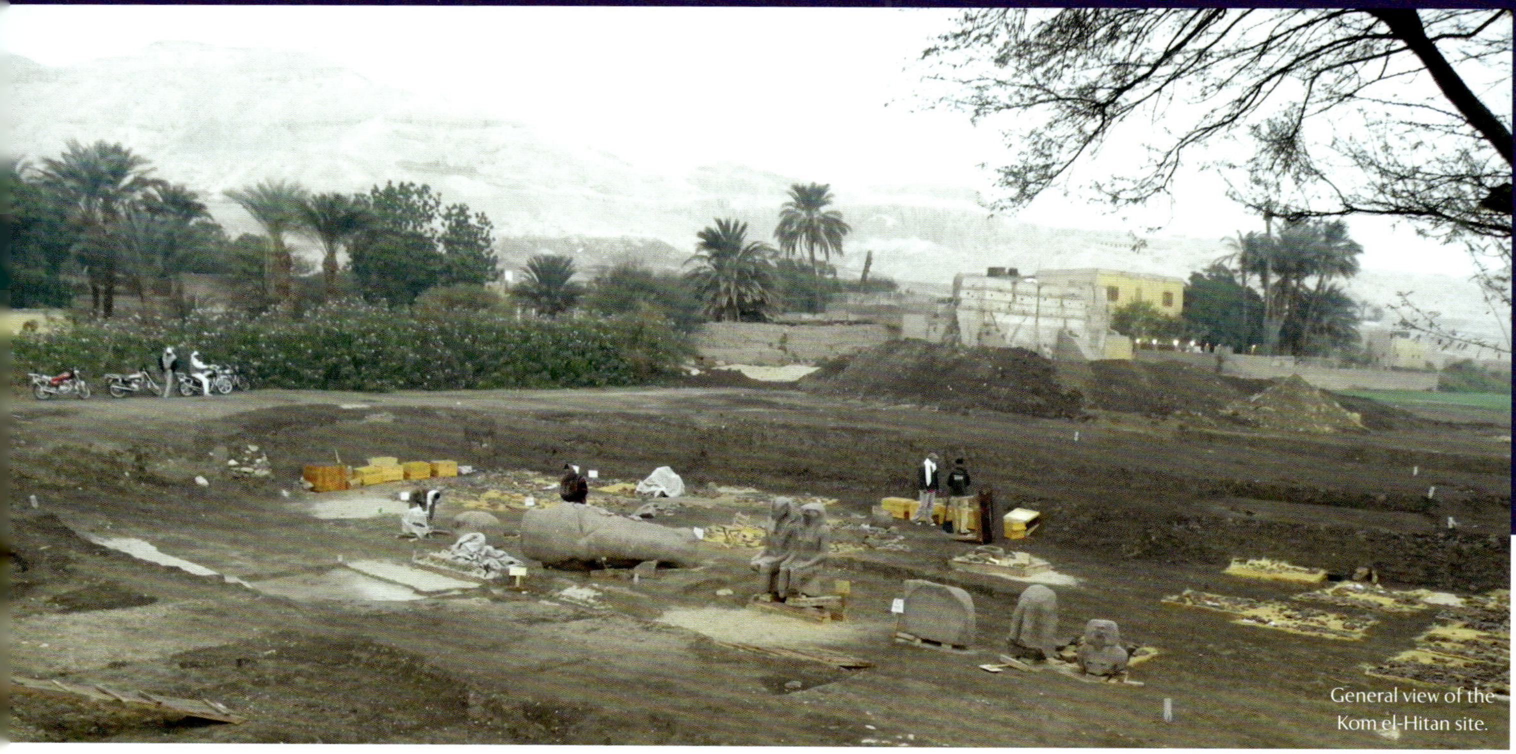

General view of the Kom el-Hitan site.

THE DISCOVERY OF THE CACHE OF STATUES OF AMENHOTEP III BY THE EGYPTIAN EXPEDITION

As part of our attempt to manage the water table on the west bank, we had to excavate sites for the installation of a new sewer system. A team of Egyptian archaeologists, led by Abdel Ghafar Wagdy, El Taieb Mohemed Khodary, Omar Abou Zied, worked under my supervision to accomplish this.

Our excavation of Amenhotep III's vast temple complex at Kom el-Hitan took place in the northwestern area of the temple, in an area about 700 m^2. Here we found statues of the king in the company of a variety of gods, including Amun, Horus, Re-Horakhty, even the scarab god, Khepri. One, made of dark red granite, is a sphinx. They are of all kinds of different stones, ranging from red granite to white calcite (Egyptian alabaster), from black basalt to sandstone.

One particularly spectacular statue, about 3.65 m tall, represents one of the solar baboons that are shown worshiping the sun. We found it lying face down, about 40 cm below the surface of the ground. Part of its head, including the left eye and part of the snout, were missing. The sculptors portrayed the hairy mane of the baboon, and around its neck is a collar made up of signs called ***kheker***, which is the hieroglyph for "ornament." The arms and the left portion of the chest have been lost. Also missing is the stone that occupied the space between the baboon's legs. Here the king might have appeared.

A fragment (c. 63 cm tall) of another smaller statue made of red granite shows Amenhotep III and the hawk-headed Re-Horakhty, sitting together. Re-Horakhty, was a sun god whose cult center was located at Heliopolis in Lower Egypt. The king has his left hand on his knee. The fingers were missing, but we found them and had them restored. The lower half of the statue has also been found. Because of the important role Re-Horakhty, played early in the reign of Akhenaten, it will be displayed in the Akhenaten Museum in Minya, near Amarna.

Another of the statues shows Amenhotep III in the company of the god Horus, son of Isis. The son of Isis was only one of the many forms of Horus worshiped by the Egyptians, and he is identified in this piece by an inscription on the back. Although he appears in this statue as a man with the head of a hawk wearing a tripartite wig, Horus son of Isis often takes the form of a young boy sucking on one finger and wearing the sidelock of youth. Here he wears a broad collar as he sits with his hands resting on his thighs. One hand grasps an ***ankh***. The king, shown as an old man with a big nose and thick lips, sits very close beside him. He wears a ***nemes***-

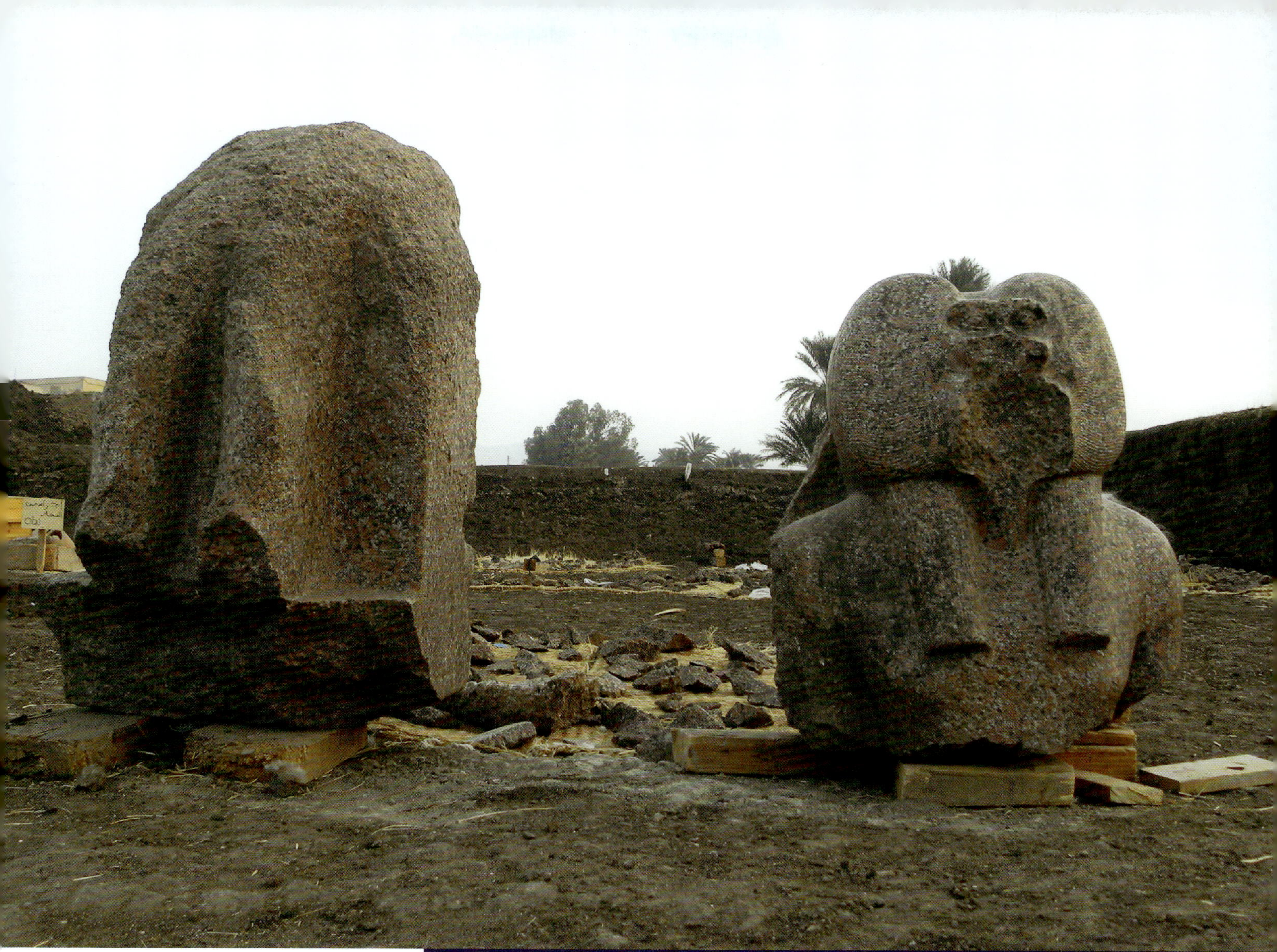

headdress and uraeus. Like the god, he too wears a broad collar. He has features associated with the Amarna Period, but the artists made a mistake in this statue, giving the king a left eye that is noticeably larger than the right.

We also found what we thought at first was a block of red granite, but this proved to be the back of a large statue lying face down. After excavation, we could see that it showed the king of Egypt side-by-side with the king of the gods, Amun, although the head of the god and his characteristic headdress with two tall feathers are missing. The figure of Amenhotep III, which is better preserved than the god's, wears the double crown, the tip of which is broken. The uraeus poised at his brow also has some damage, and most of his false beard is missing. Traces of a broad collar worn by the king survive. We found a fragment of his missing right arm. Here the

The red granite statue of a baboon.
18th Dynasty, time of Amenhotep III

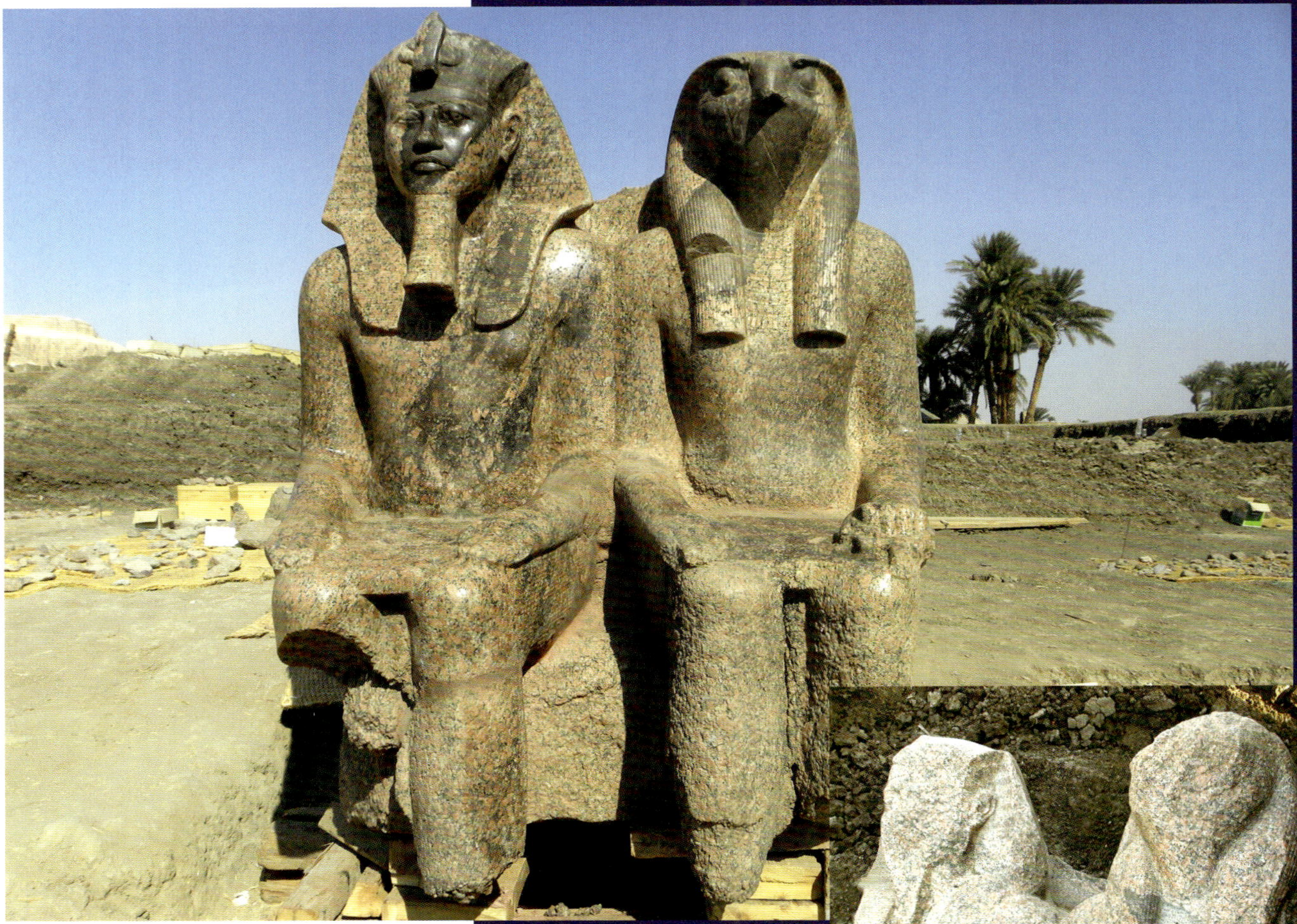

The red granite statue of Amenhotep III and the god Horus, son of Isis.

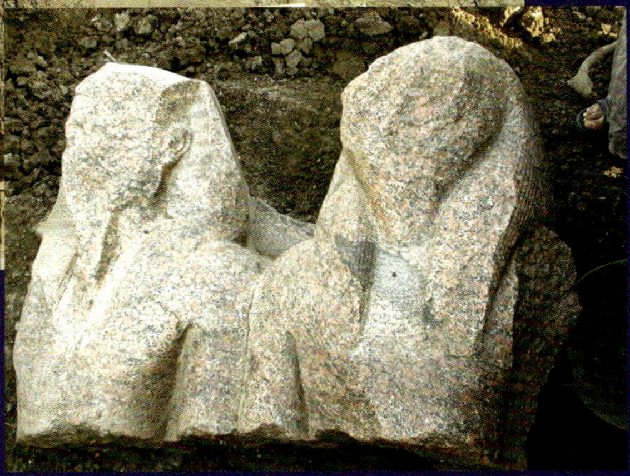

The red granite statue of Amenhotep III and Re-Horakhty.

king is presented as a young man, and he much resembles his grandson, Tutankhamun.

Ray Johnson has observed that all of these images indicate that this area of the temple appears to have been an enormous solar court, with statues of solar deities and colossal images of solar baboons and scarabs. An obelisk may have stood here, as well. Other temples had a solar court in this position, north of the main temple axis.

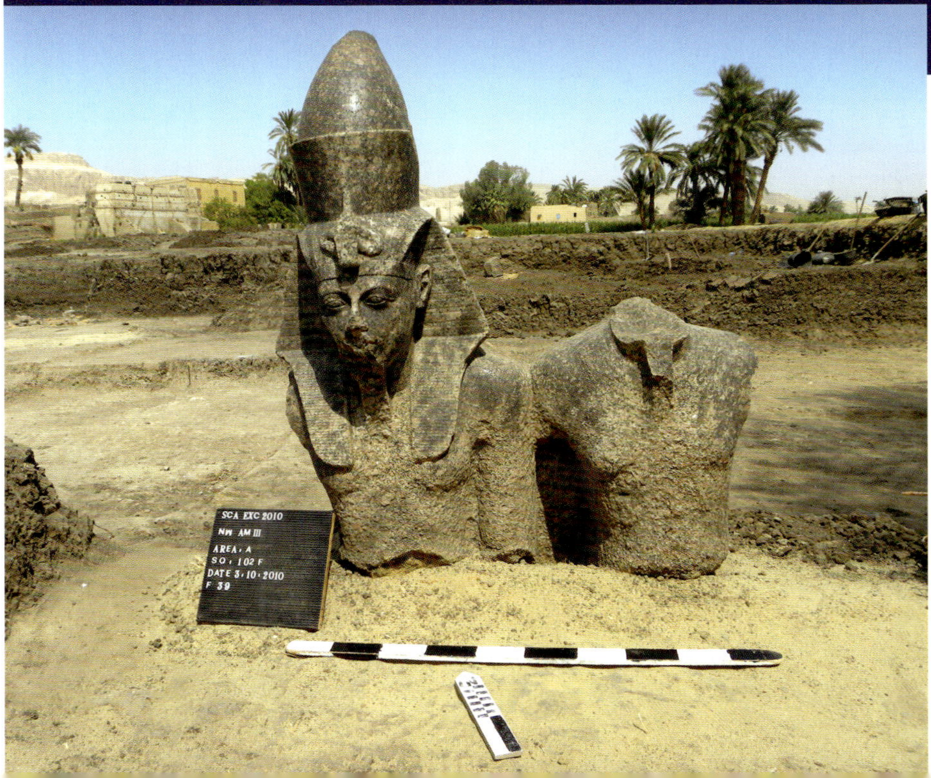

The red granite statue of Amenhotep III and the god Amun.

TUTANKHAMUN'S STATUES STOLEN FROM THE EGYPTIAN MUSEUM

The Egyptian Revolution began on 25th January, 2011 at Tahrir Square, where the Egyptian Museum is located. When I entered the museum six days later, I saw the damage done by looters. They had broken a statue of Tutankhamun standing on the back of a black leopard into many pieces, and they had done the same to a statue of Tutankhamun holding a harpoon. Thanks to the skills of the museum's restoration team, these statues have both been repaired.

This happened on the 28th, when looters entered the museum after the police abandoned Tahrir Square, where the Revolution had begun. Although many people – civilians, not the police – came together to protect the museum, looters had taken advantage of a fire escape at the back of the building, which led up to the roof. On the roof, they broke a skylight and used electrical wire to lower themselves down 10 m to the museum floor. One of the looters fell in his attempt and landed on a display case, injuring his leg and leaving blood on the floor. Fortunately, it was dark within the museum, and the rooms containing the gold and the royal mummies were sealed. But display cases were broken and objects were scattered all about.

A careful inventory revealed that about 54 objects were missing. Only 28 remain missing today. Among those recovered was a beautiful statuette of Akhenaten holding an offering table in his hands. A young man found it near a garbage can in Tahrir Square. One of the missing objects is a figure of Tutankhamun that had been carried by the god Menkaret (**Carter No. 296a;** see Chapter 4). The thief took the entire statue from its display case. We found only the figure of the god.

A few of Tutankhamun's other objects were stolen, but a happy surprise occurred when I returned to my job as Minister of State for Antiquities after a brief resignation. One day, I met with one of the members of the SCA who told me that he had met some young people who wanted to return antiquities that they had. The next day he brought to me a bag. In the bag I found a gilded standing statue of Tutankhamun wearing the red crown and uraeus and the royal kilt. The upper part of one of the young king's fans was returned as well, as was the gilded bronze trumpet, a companion to the silver one (**Carter No. 175**) shown in Chapter 4. Another piece related to Tutankhamun that was returned was a ***shabti*** from the collection of Yuya and Tjuya. Other than the figure of Tutankhamun held by Menkaret, the only object from the tomb that remains missing is a standing figure of the king wearing the crown of Lower Egypt.

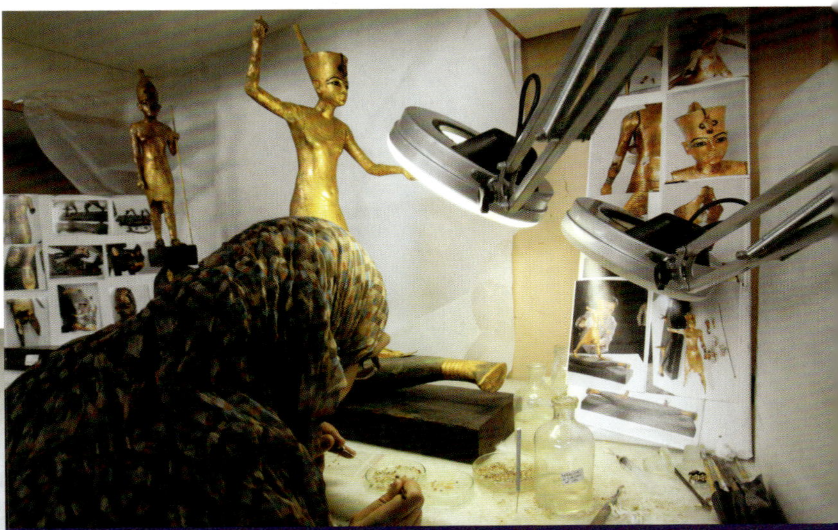

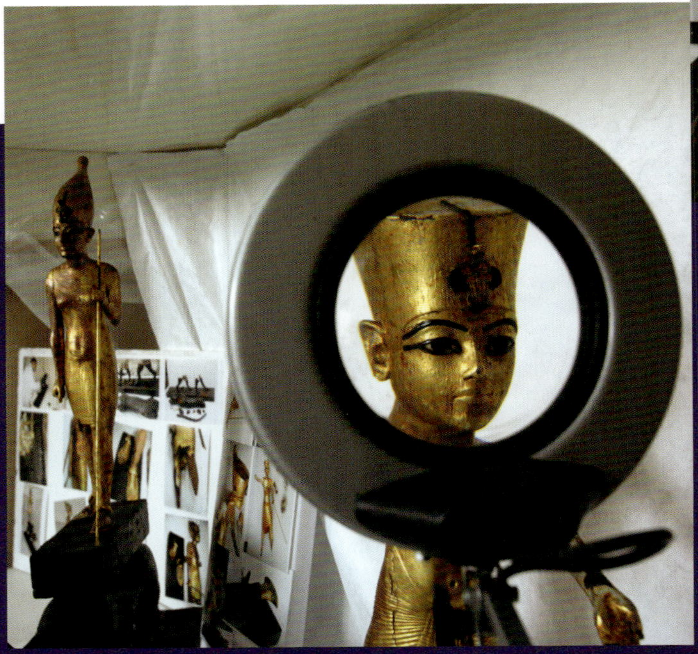

In the conservation laboratory of the Egyptian Museum, the restoration of the recovered statues of Tutankhamun on a boat and on a leopard.

Once the museum had been secured after the looting, I felt relief that at least none of the masterpieces from the Gold Room – such as Tutankhamun's mask – had been taken. When the National Museum of Iraq in Baghdad was looted during the 2003 war, more than 15,000 objects had been stolen. This is why I announced on CNN, "The Cairo Museum is safe and that means Egypt is safe." I added that we would undertake a complete inventory of the museum and announce exactly what was missing at that time. But some irresponsibly quoted only the first part of my statement, neglecting to mention that we were going to inventory the museum before saying more.

I did not want to announce what had been taken until we had performed a complete inventory. It was impossible before that was done to know what had been taken. But we did know that none of the contents of the Gold Room or the museum's other most iconic masterpieces had been stolen. And I did not want to take anything away from the brave people who had linked arms to defend the museum with their bodies after the police had abandoned Tahrir Square and the museum.

PROTECTING THE VALLEY OF THE KINGS

The Valley of the Kings does not only need to be explored, it also needs to be protected. Not much had been done in the past. The World Monument Fund gave money to improve the Valley of the Kings, and that resulted in only displays in front of the tombs, with plans, descriptions, and photographs of some tomb scenes.

I started real efforts in 2002. The west bank was in trouble, and the situation at Deir el-Bahri, site of Hatshepsut's funerary temple, was horrible. I have even called it a "zoo." The first thing we did was build a wall around the area containing the antiquities. This proved extremely helpful, and it helped to guard the monuments during the 2011 Revolution.

With the help of the governor of Luxor, we moved villagers from Qurna, where houses had been built atop tombs, to a different spot. They were compensated for their old property and given a new village with a school, hospital, post office, and traffic facilities, all paid for by the Supreme Council of Antiquities. One of the tombs at Qurna, which had been covered by a house, belongs to Huy and dates to the reign of Tutankhamun. Another built-over tomb was being used by the homeowner to store looted antiquities. Excavation at the old village of Qurna has revealed many new tombs.

We asked the Getty Conservation Institute to plan a management program for the Valley of the Queens. Among the Getty's efforts was a visitor center at the entrance to the Valley of the Kings, a project undertaken with the help of the Japanese government. At this center, which is located safely away from the tombs, visitors can view an introductory film, find educational material, and use other facilities. An electric trolley, called the Taftaf and painted the color of sand so as not to draw attention to itself, brings tourists from this center to the valley. Beyond the antiquities area, tourists can shop the bazaars, enjoy food at a cafeteria, and even make use of telephones and the post office, and there is a parking lot as well. We have restored the rest house used by Howard Carter and made it a museum to display his personal effects. There is even a 3D image of Carter

The rest house of Howard Carter on the west bank of Luxor after being restored and opened to the public.

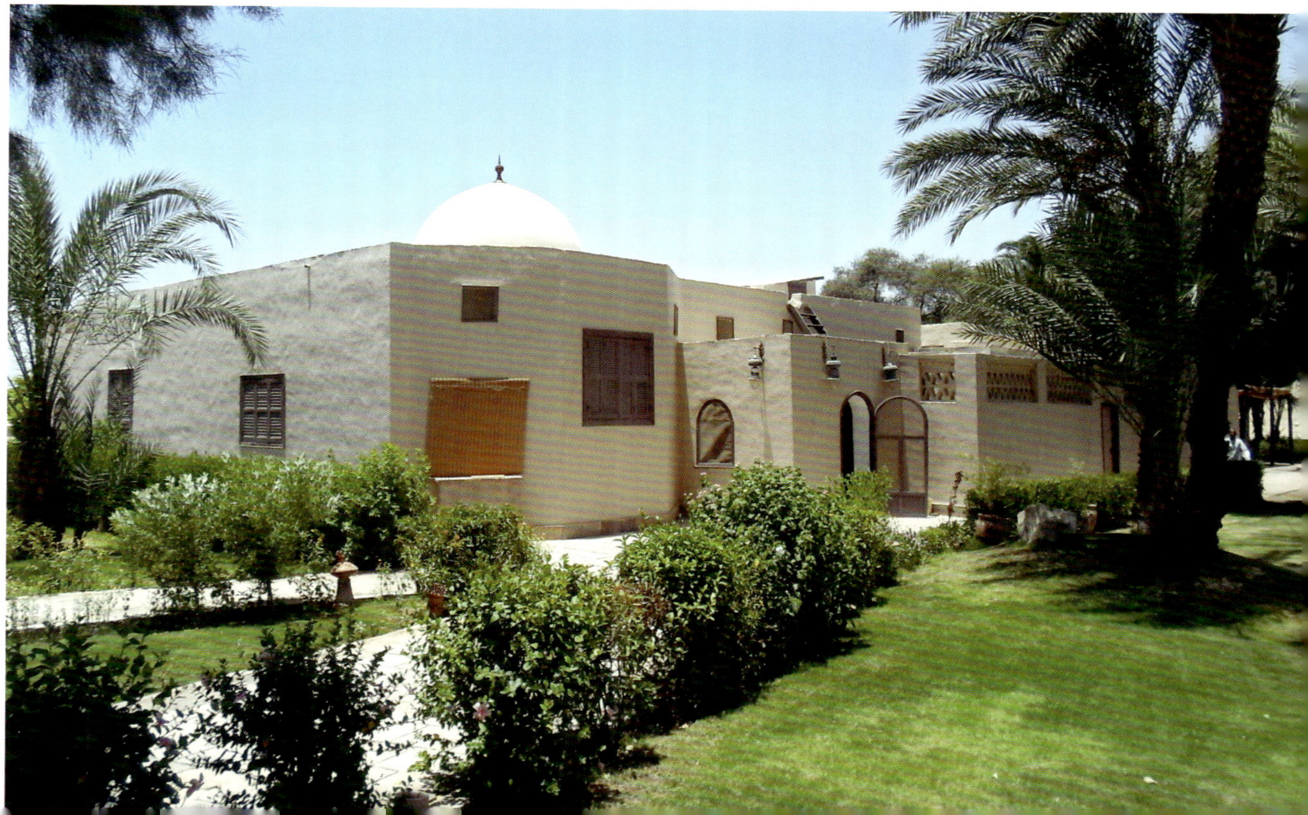

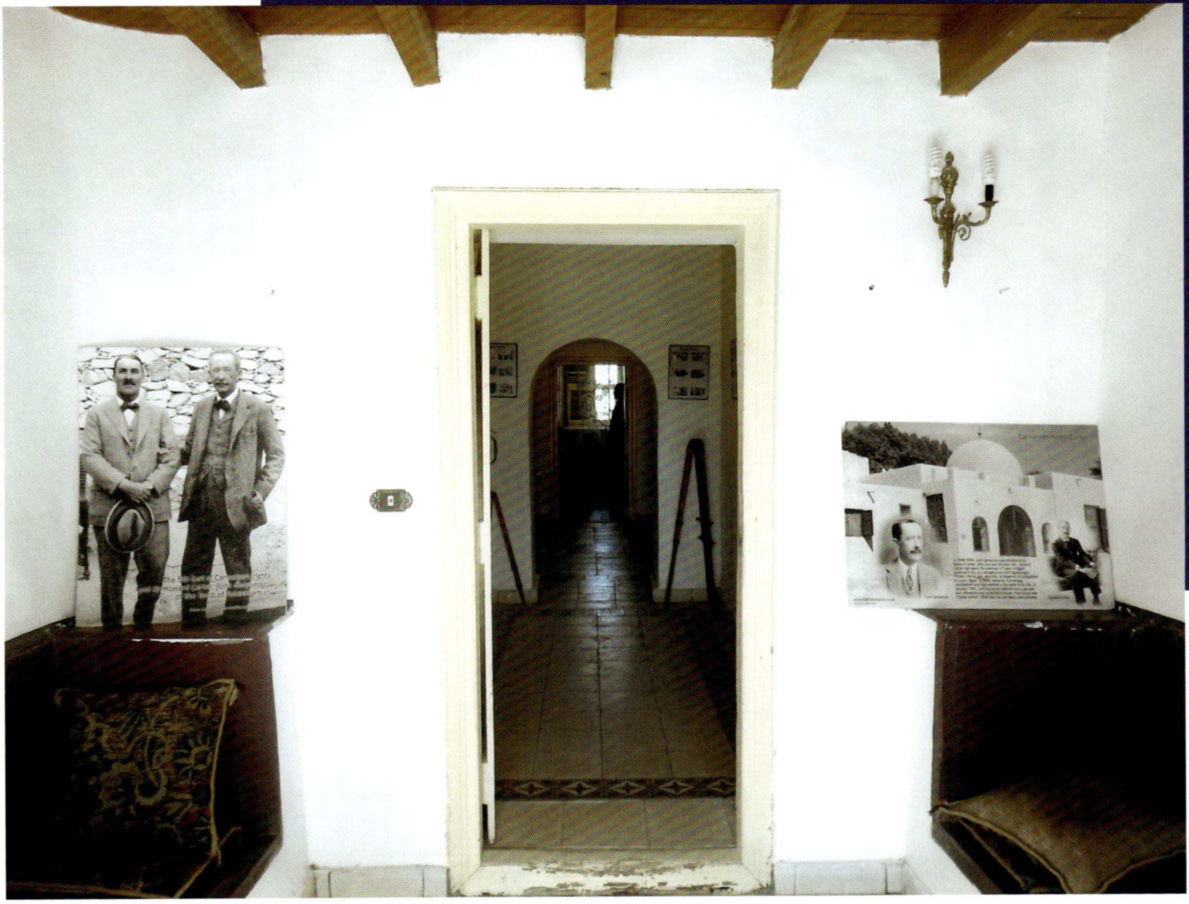

Inside the rest house of Howard Carter.

who greets visitors and delivers a lecture about his work.

But there is still the matter of conserving tombs and other ancient monuments, a problem that is being examined by a professor at Cairo University. USAID has funded projects to address the rising water table that so badly affects the west bank and the floods that damage tombs in the valley. The Getty Conservation Institute has studied black spots that have begun to grow on the walls of Tutankhamun's tomb and has developed a preservation plan for the third coffin that still lies in the sarcophagus in the tomb.

North of Carter's rest house, we planned to construct a replica valley in which copies of the tombs of Tutankhamun, Queen Nefertari, and Seti I would be built. These three tombs have been meticulously scanned with lasers. As the most famous and most beautiful tombs in the valley, they have in the past received large numbers of visitors each day. This takes a toll on the decoration, and if allowed to continue, it will destroy them. Giving the public access to replicas will give tourists the same experience and spare the original tombs from further damage. But this is a plan that will have to be implemented in the future because tourism in Egypt has suffered so greatly that it is impossible to make such an investment now. There will also be a center dedicated to studying and conserving the west bank.

Meanwhile, however, the Valley of the Kings Foundation, based in Switzerland, has finished the replica of Tutankhamun's tomb. In late 2012, based on an agreement signed several years ago, the European Union presented the tomb to Egypt. It will be installed near Carter's rest house, and when this is done we will be able to close Tutankhamun's tomb to the public, as we have closed the tomb of Nefertari to protect its stunning but vulnerable wall paintings. Like Nefertari's tomb, Tutankhamun's will be available to be viewed for a special fee. Funds generated in this way will go to the protection of the valley.

The Valley of the Kings needs much protection. Although it is not their intent, visiting tourists do great damage to the fragile tombs by increasing the amount of moisture in the air within them. They also do not realize that even a simple thing like a photographer's flash can harm the colors that remain on the walls. A systematic plan to open some tombs while closing others, in rotation, to allow for restoration and maintenance must be put into place.

Howard Carter took care of the artifacts he found in Tutankhamun's tomb and when he served as chief inspector of the west bank, and he clearly loved Egypt and the Egyptians. We should remember that and continue to preserve a legacy that belongs not just to Egypt, but to the entire world. The Valley of the Kings has much more for us to discover, but at the same time we must not neglect what has already been discovered in the past.

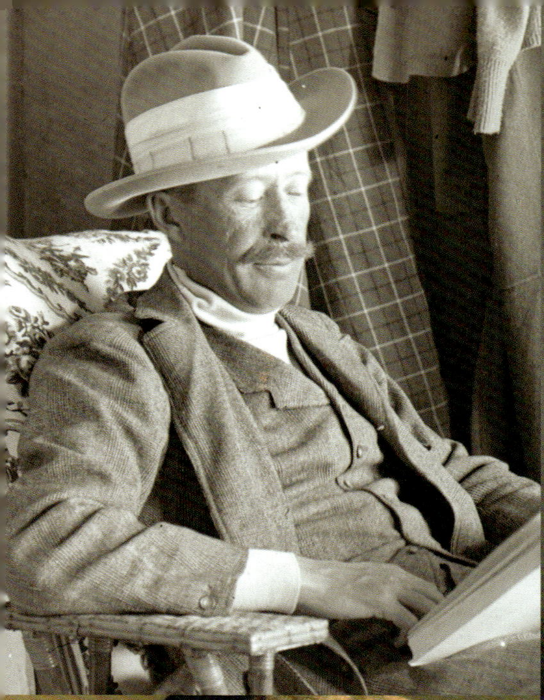

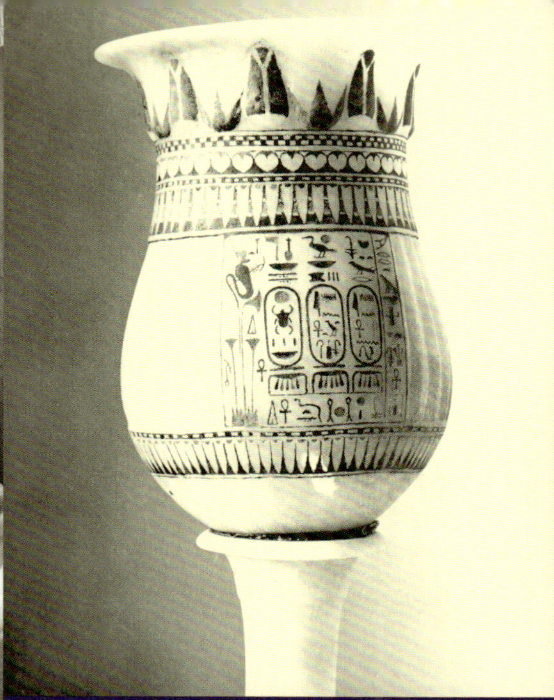

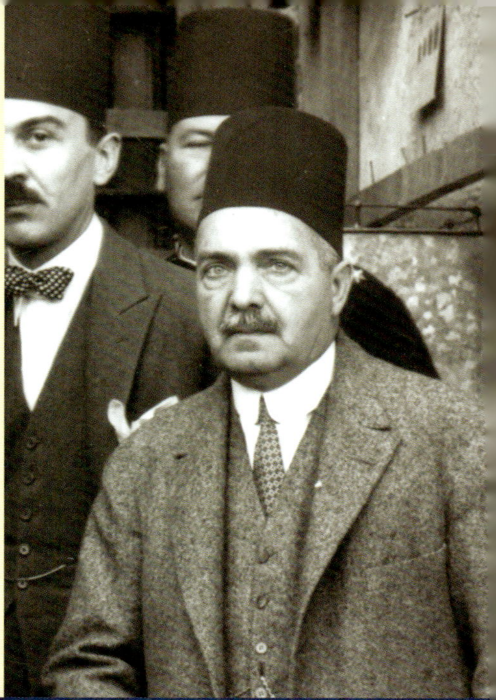

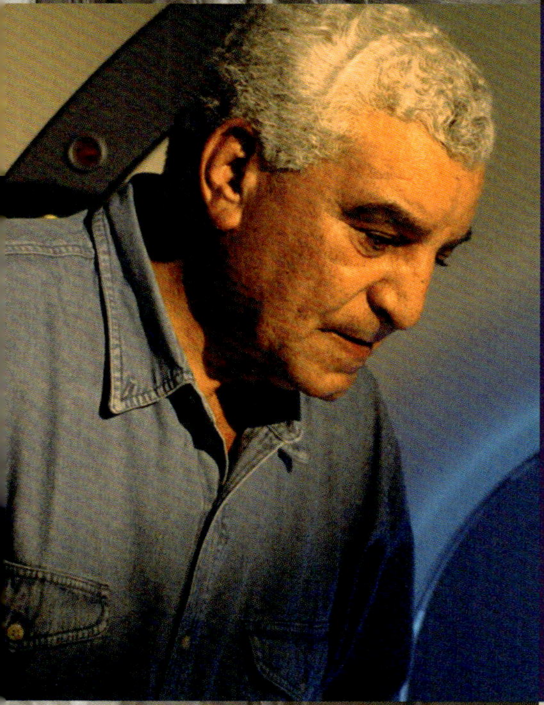

CHAPTER VIII

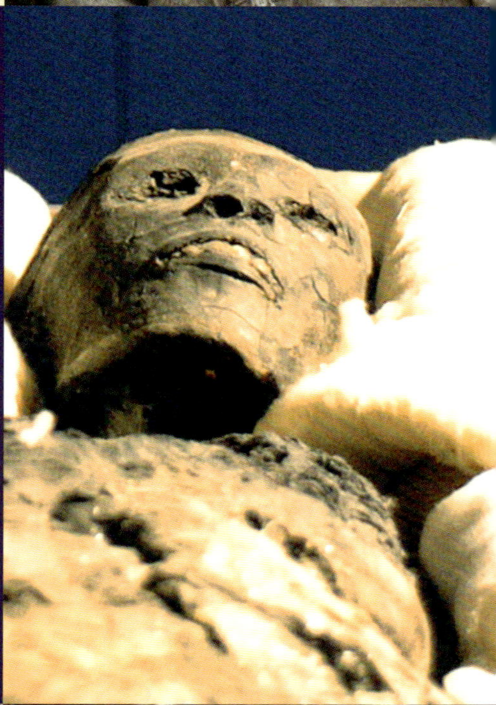

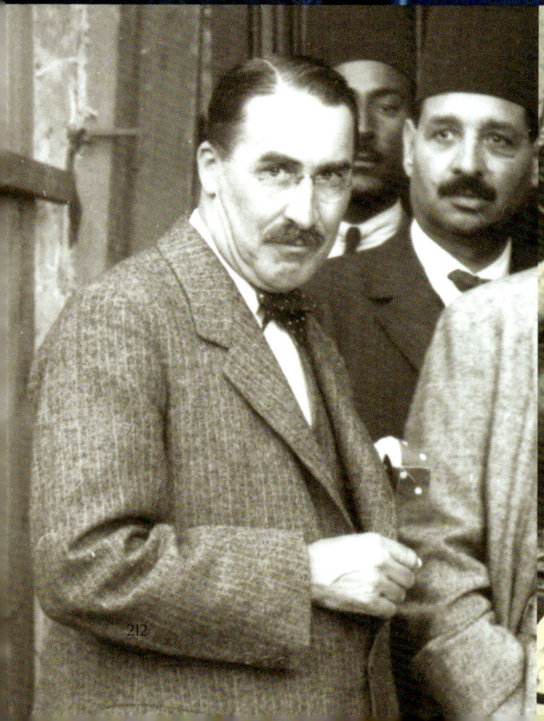

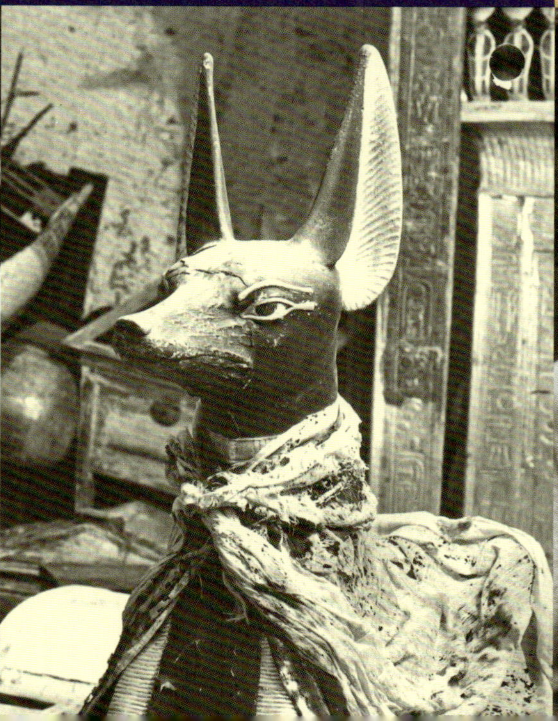

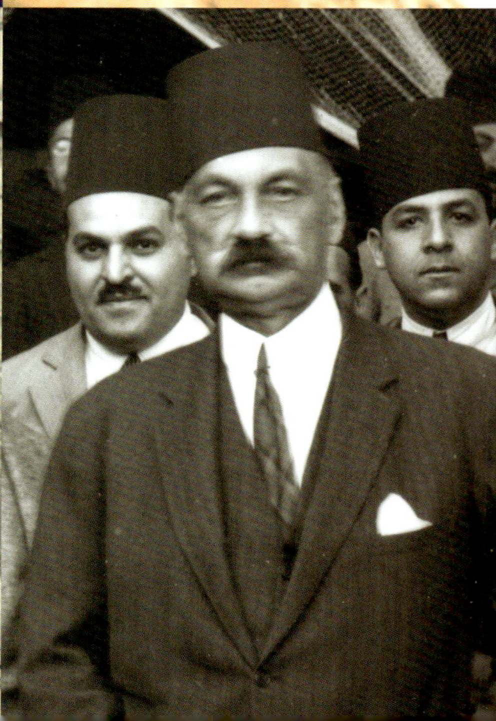

THE CURSE OF TUTANKH-AMUN

The word "curse" became famous all over the world after the discovery of the tomb of Tutankhamun.

We know that Lord Carnarvon died in early April 1923. Weeks before, he had received a mosquito bite, which became infected. The infection led to him coming down with pneumonia, and this ailment caused his death. This happened only five months after Carter's discovery of Tutankhamun's tomb.

Carnarvon's death opened up a flood of many untrue stories about the curse of the pharaohs. Newspapers were inundated with them. Reporters wrote them because they could not uncover any true stories about the tomb, since Carnarvon had signed a contract giving exclusive reporting rights to the London *Times*.

This was not the first time that the world had heard about mummies and their curses. In 1827, an English novelist named Jane Webb Louden wrote a futuristic story called *The Mummy!, Or, a Tale of the Twenty-Second Century* in which the mummy of Cheops is brought back to life like Frankenstein's Monster. Another story, written in 1869 by Louisa May Alcott (who is best known for writing the famous novel *Little Women*), was called "Lost in a Pyramid, or the Mummy's Curse," in which a man brings back a present from a tomb for his beloved fiancée, only to suffer from the curse. The late 19th and early 20th centuries are filled with all kinds of mummy's curses in short stories and novels. However, the curse of Tutankhamun was first found in the newspapers.

News of Carnarvon's death spread around the world. Even before he died, while he lay ill in the Shepheard Hotel in Cairo, a letter by the novelist Marie Corelli spread rumors that a curse was at work. Upon his death, many believed that something far more sinister than a mosquito was responsible.

The stories connected Carnarvon's death with a curse, and newspapers published reports of all kinds of strange happenings. One journalist wrote that while Lord Carnarvon was dying, the lights of Cairo flashed on and off many times and Carnarvon began to speak in a language that no one understood. Lord Porchester, Carnarvon's son, said that his father's favorite dog, named Susie, had howled and keeled over dead at Highclere Castle at the very moment of Carnarvon's death in Cairo.

The press also claimed in print that a mud brick had been discovered in front of the statue of Anubis found in the Treasury (**Carter No. 261**, Chapter 4), and on this brick was the following inscription:

It is I who hinder the sand from choking the secret chamber. I am for the protection of the deceased, and I will kill all those who cross this threshold into the sacred precincts of the Royal King who lives forever.

Some of this is true. Carter found a "magical brick" of unbaked clay on the floor in front of the Anubis shrine. These bricks were features of royal burial chambers from the 18th Dynasty onward. One would be sealed up in each of the four walls of the burial chamber. Each brick carried a figure of Osiris, Anubis (as a jackal), a reed torch, or a ***djed*** pillar and had a slightly different spell from the ***Book of the Dead***. Carter found four bricks in Tutankhamun's burial chamber walls.

Lord Carnavon, resting enjoying peace and quiet on the veranda of Carter's rest house on the west bank of Luxor.
Harry Burton / Griffith archive

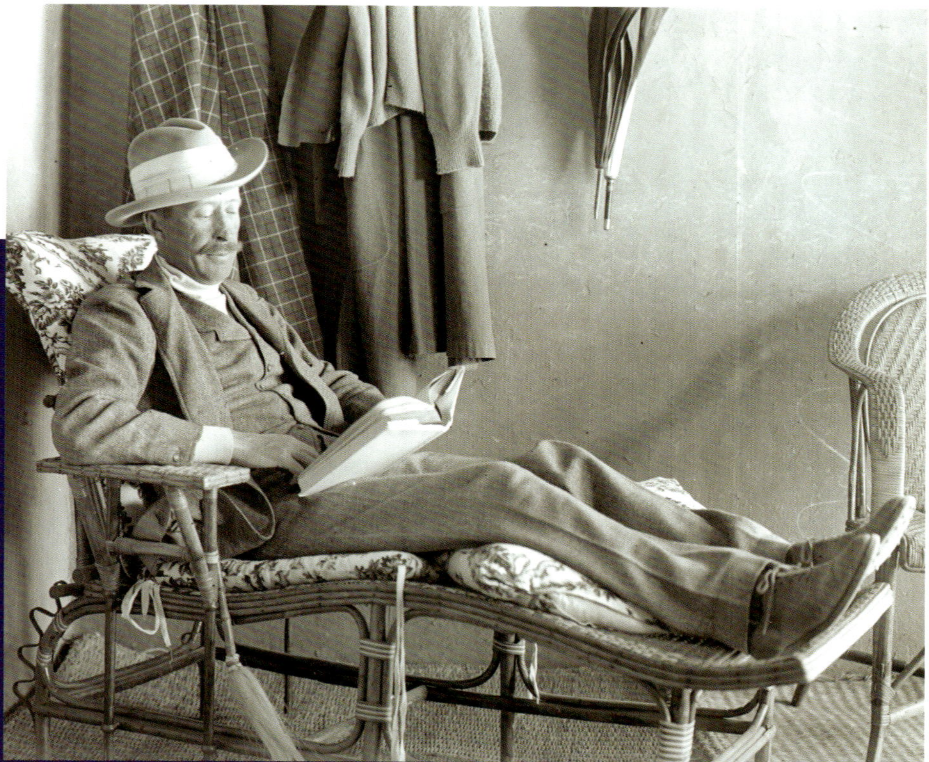

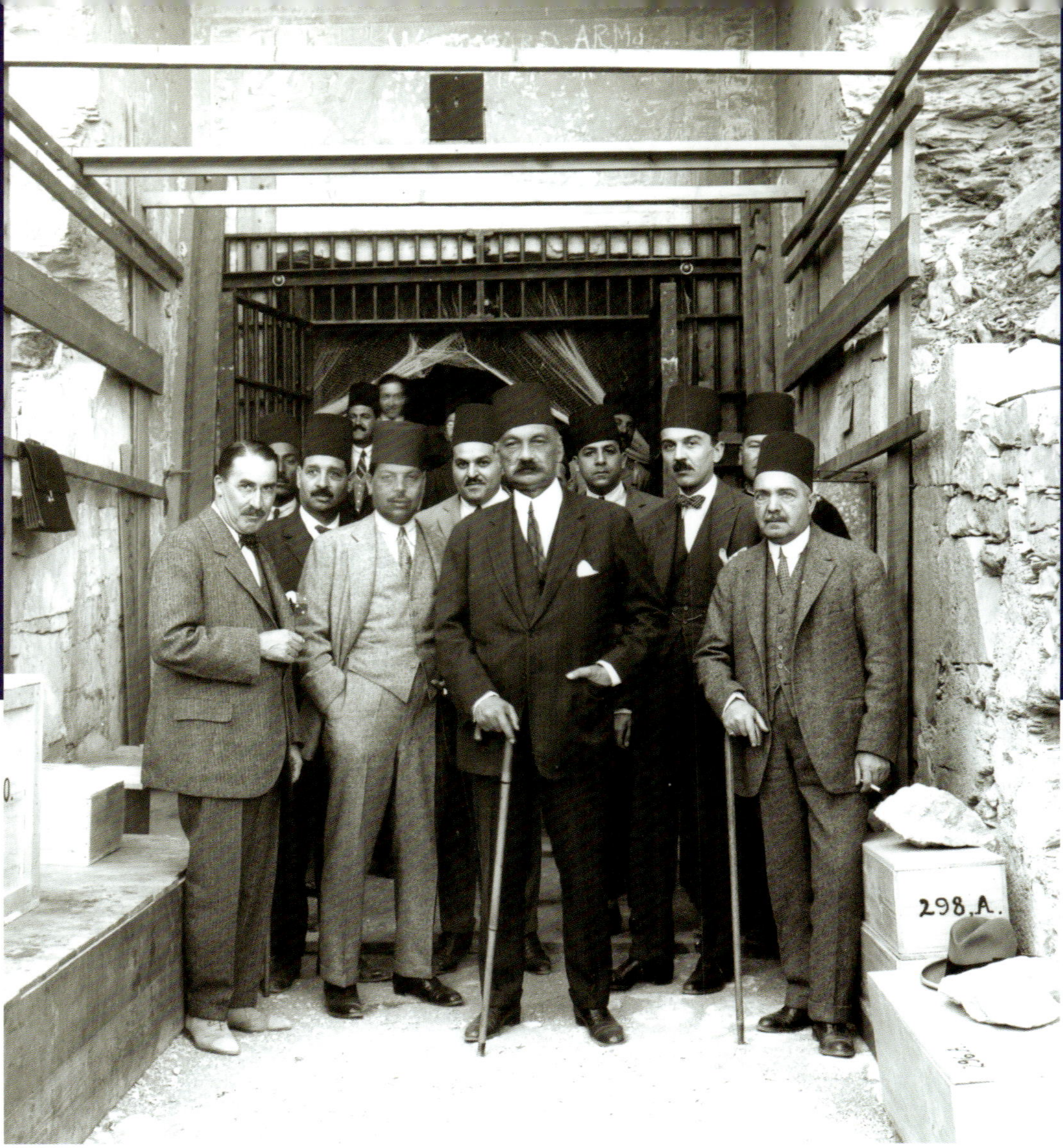

Howard Carter and a group of Egyptian government officials standing outside the tomb of Seti II (Kv 15) during their visit to the tomb of Tutankhamun.
Harry Burton / Griffith Institue

This was a fifth, perhaps placed to guard the Treasury from robbers. The text on this brick reads, according to Carter:

> "It is I who hinder the sand from choking the secret chamber and who repel that one who would repel him with the desert-flame. I have set aflame the desert (?), I have caused the path to be mistaken. I am for the protection of the Osiris [the deceased]."

The brick and its "curse" was not enough for the newspapers. They also published a photograph of the second golden shrine and claimed that an inscription threatened:

> "They who enter this sacred tomb shall swift be visited by wings of death."

According to reporters, Carnarvon was not the only one affected by the curse. Carter asked for a radiologist to come from London, but the man died before he could reach the tomb to examine the mummy. Lord Carnarvon's younger brother, Aubrey Herbert, died suddenly in September 1923. When an Egyptian prince was murdered by his jealous wife in a hotel in London, the press claimed that the soul of an ancient Egyptian princess had escaped from her tomb and possessed the wife, causing her to commit the crime. The curse was at work when the French Egyptologist Georges Aaron Bénédite fell outside the tomb and died. The cold that turned into pneumonia and claimed the life of American railroad magnate Jay Gould, who had also visited the tomb, was likewise the result of the curse.

The press was willing to blame the death of anyone connected to Egypt on the wrath of the pharaohs.

Such stories did not end in the 1920s. They reappeared in the 1970s, when objects from Tutankhamun's tomb were to be exhibited all over the world. Mohammed Mahdy, who was head of the Egyptian Antiquities Service at the time, was hit by a car and killed after signing the contract that permitted Tutankhamun's artifacts to go abroad.

Philipp Vandenberg, a German author, wrote a book titled *The Curse of the Pharaohs*, which is full of stories and claims that a tablet from the tomb of Tutankhamun reads:

> "Death will slay with his wings whoever disturbs the peace of the pharaoh."

Foreigners were not the only ones talking about a curse. The discovery of the tomb was the talk of people in Luxor. The contract that Lord Carnarvon had signed with the *Times* of London on 9th January, 1923, upset everyone. It angered the foreign press – and also the Egyptian press, who could not report on an important excavation taking

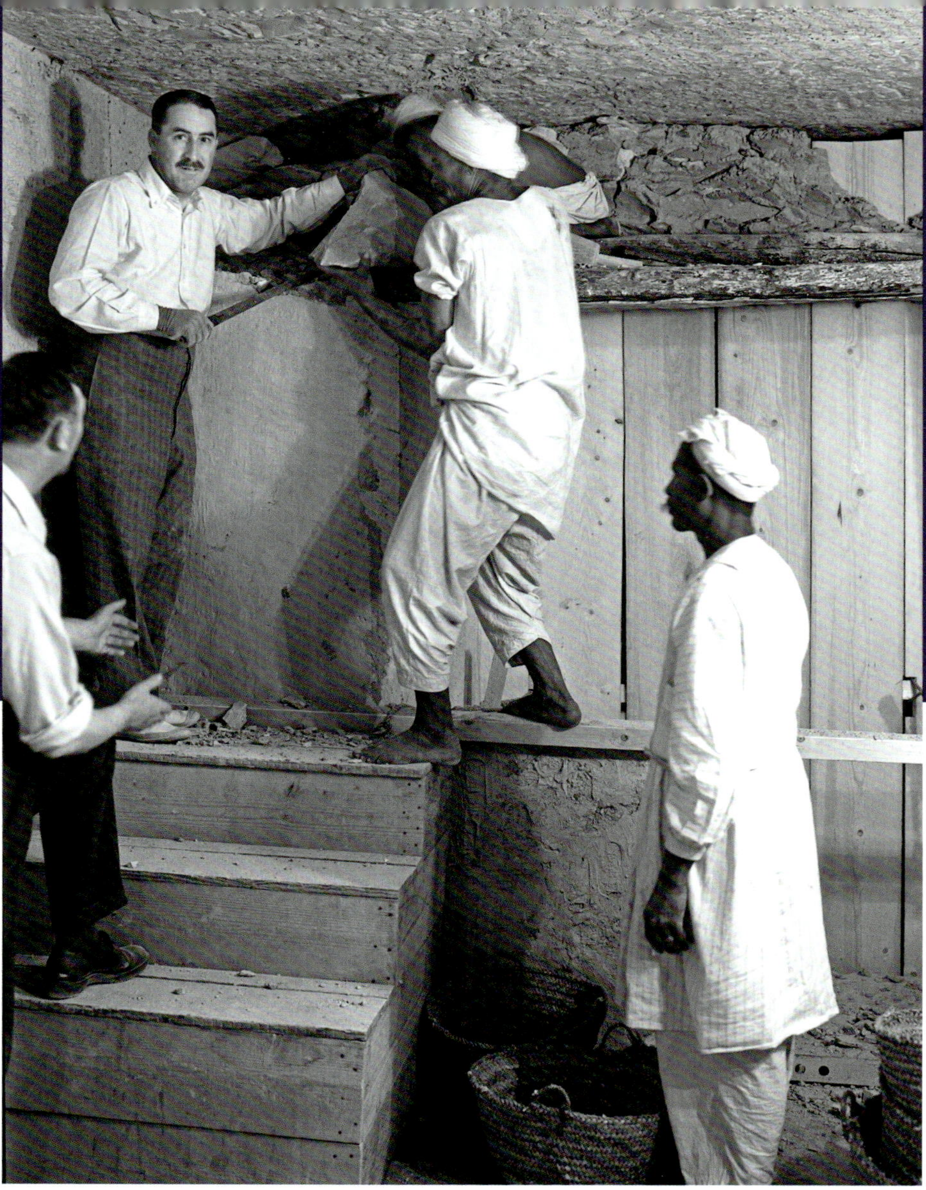

Carter dismantling the blocking wall to get into the burial chamber.
Harry Burton / Griffith Institue

place in their own country. Furthermore, the Egyptians were angry at Carter for his orders that barred them from visiting the tomb.

Morcos Bey Hanna, who as Minister of Public Works was in charge of the Antiquities Service, took steps to dismiss Carter from his work in Egypt. The Egyptians were happy about his decision and marched through the streets to greet the Minister, crying, "Long live Morcos Bey, Minister of Tutankhamun!"

Of course, there were all kinds of human "curses" associated with Carter's excavations. Carnarvon wanted to make a division of the objects and take half of what Carter had discovered in the tomb, but the Egyptian government refused because the tomb was found intact and in such a case the contents of a tomb could not be divided. All objects had to stay in Cairo. Carnarvon's claims that the tomb had been broken into twice and, therefore, was not intact did no good. But Carter was able to return to his work, after offering to apologize. He continued to work with the artifacts from the tomb to conserve them, a task that was completed in 1932. Carter died at the age of 64 in London on 2nd March, 1939. The "curse" did not die with him, however.

In 2005, when I decided to examine the mummy of Tutankhamun with the CT scanner, I discovered that all the media wanted to come with me. I intended to go south to Luxor early in the morning, but when I arrived in Luxor, I went directly to my hotel and told my driver, as well as Mansour Boraik, who was the director of Luxor, and Moustafa Waziri, the head of the west bank, to come pick me up at 5:00 in the afternoon. I wanted to arrive in the valley when all the tourists leave.

After the car picked me up at the hotel, the driver nearly ran over a young boy, but the child was saved at the last moment. Boraik laughed and said, "This is the beginning of the curse!"

On our way to the west bank, I received a call from my sister to tell me that her husband had died. Boraik continued to talk about the curse, but this time he was more serious. When I left the car in the Valley of the Kings, Yasser Shebl, secretary of the Minister of Culture, called me to say that the Minister, Farouk Hosni, had suffered a heart attack and had been taken to the hospital.

Then I discovered that Boraik had left. It seems that these three incidents made him believe in the curse of Tutankhamun.

I gave an interview to a Japanese television crew in front of Tutankhamun's tomb. After I finished the interview, a thunderstorm brought down heavy rain like a flood. The Japanese team, which surely had not anticipated a rainstorm in the desert, ran away, saying, "The curse of King Tut! The curse of King Tut!"

We began the preparation for moving the mummy from the sarcophagus to the CT scanner, which was set up in its trailer. I placed the king's mummy with great care on the tray of the machine. One minute later, the machine stopped operating ...

This was a fine machine made by the foremost manufacturer of such equipment. Would we have to return Tutankhamun to his tomb, having failed to conduct our scan?

For the first time even *I* could believe that there really was a curse of Tut...

Finally, after an hour, the machine – which had needed additional cooling, a problem we solved with simple electric fans – worked again and gave us wonderful results.

But was the curse of Tutankhamun really done with me?

When I sent Tutankhamun's objects on a tour of Europe, the United States, and Japan, the exhibit brought over $120 million to Egypt, and Egypt received free publicity in every city – public relations worth millions of dollars. A jealous journalist who had no knowledge of antiquities whatsoever used the January 2011 Revolution as an opportunity to attack me. He went to the office of the Attorney General and presented a report claiming that I was the one who selected the precious objects of Tutankhamun to travel abroad and also that I used them to promote my clothing line. He went on to claim that all the money that resulted from the Tutankhamun exhibit went to me...

The Attorney General appointed a committee that over the course of a year examined the evidence to see if this jealous man was telling the truth or not. During this case, this journalist published many lies. I had to leave my job as Minister of State for Antiquities... and newspapers claimed that this was a result of the "curse of Tut."

After a year, the committee had determined that all of the objects in this exhibit had been chosen by a committee headed by Mohamed Saleh, a former director of the Egyptian Museum, and that the objects were never used by my clothing line. This line was created as a fundraiser for a hospital for children with cancer, and the committee found that all the money generated by the exhibit was in the account of the SCA.

After all these stories, some might think that I believe in the curse. Before I give you my opinion, let me tell you one more tale. In 2000, I was excavating underground at the Bahariya Oasis. I had a lamp in my left hand and an ax in my right hand to remove the stone rubble from the entrance of the tomb of the governor of Bahariya. When I saw in front of me the face of a statue, I pulled the electric cable and lamp to see it more clearly. Then, my lamp came off the cable and gave me an electrical shock so strong that I was unconscious for almost a full minute. When I came to, I told my assistant, Mahmoud Afifi, who was near me, "If I had died, everyone would believe in the curse!"

So is there an ancient curse that haunts those who disturb the dead?

Although many people say it is true that the pet canary Carter brought from England to Luxor for good luck was swallowed by a cobra, I can tell you that all the stories about the curse of Tutankhamun are either completely made up or have simple, natural explanations. People's cuts can become infected, and these infections can become fatal. Electricity can fail and the lights of entire cities can flicker and go off. Electronic equipment is sensitive to temperature and does not always work well in the desert heat. People do drop dead. Men and women can become jealous and do things to hurt others.

And why would the pharaohs curse us for finding them? The dearest wish of the ancient Egyptian was to have his or her name live forever. Tutankhamun, after languishing in complete obscurity for thousands of years, would likely be grateful rather than angry that his tomb was discovered. He is now the best known and most talked about of all Egyptian kings.

But if you leave a mummy or other organic material inside sealed tombs for a thousand years, a tomb can contain germs – bacterial, viral, or fungal – that cannot be seen. Archaeologists who have entered these tombs can develop infections. In my career, I found the Valley of the Golden Mummies at Bahariya Oasis. When we discovered a tomb, we opened it for a few hours until the bad air disappeared and the fresh air entered. Only then did we begin our work, and we discovered the mummies without encountering any curses.

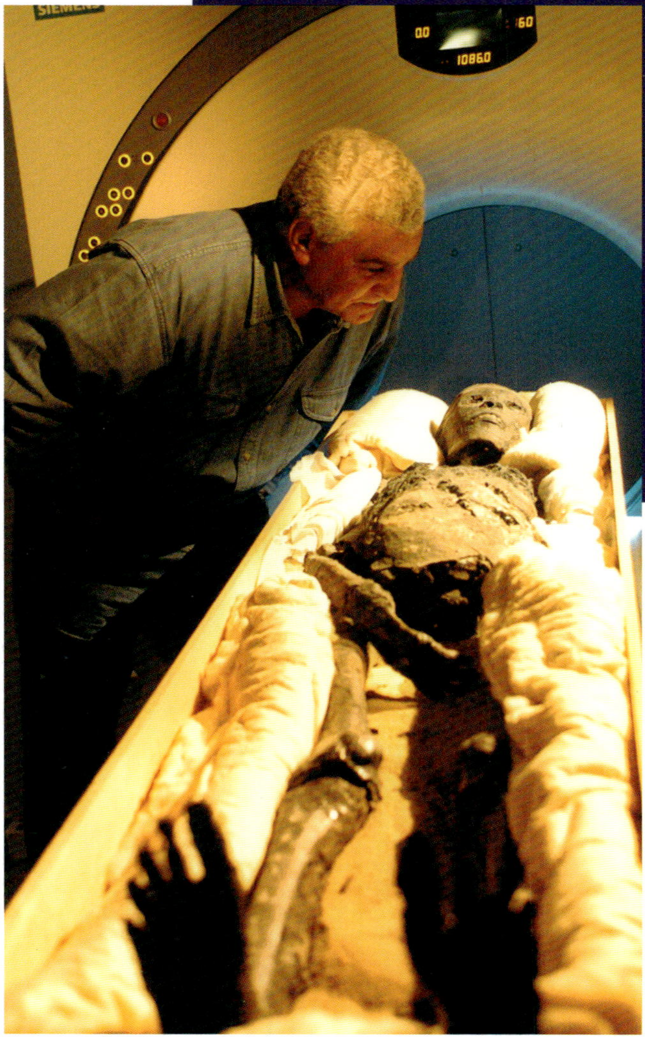

The first CT scan of the mummy revealed new information about the life of the boy-king.

CHAPTER IX

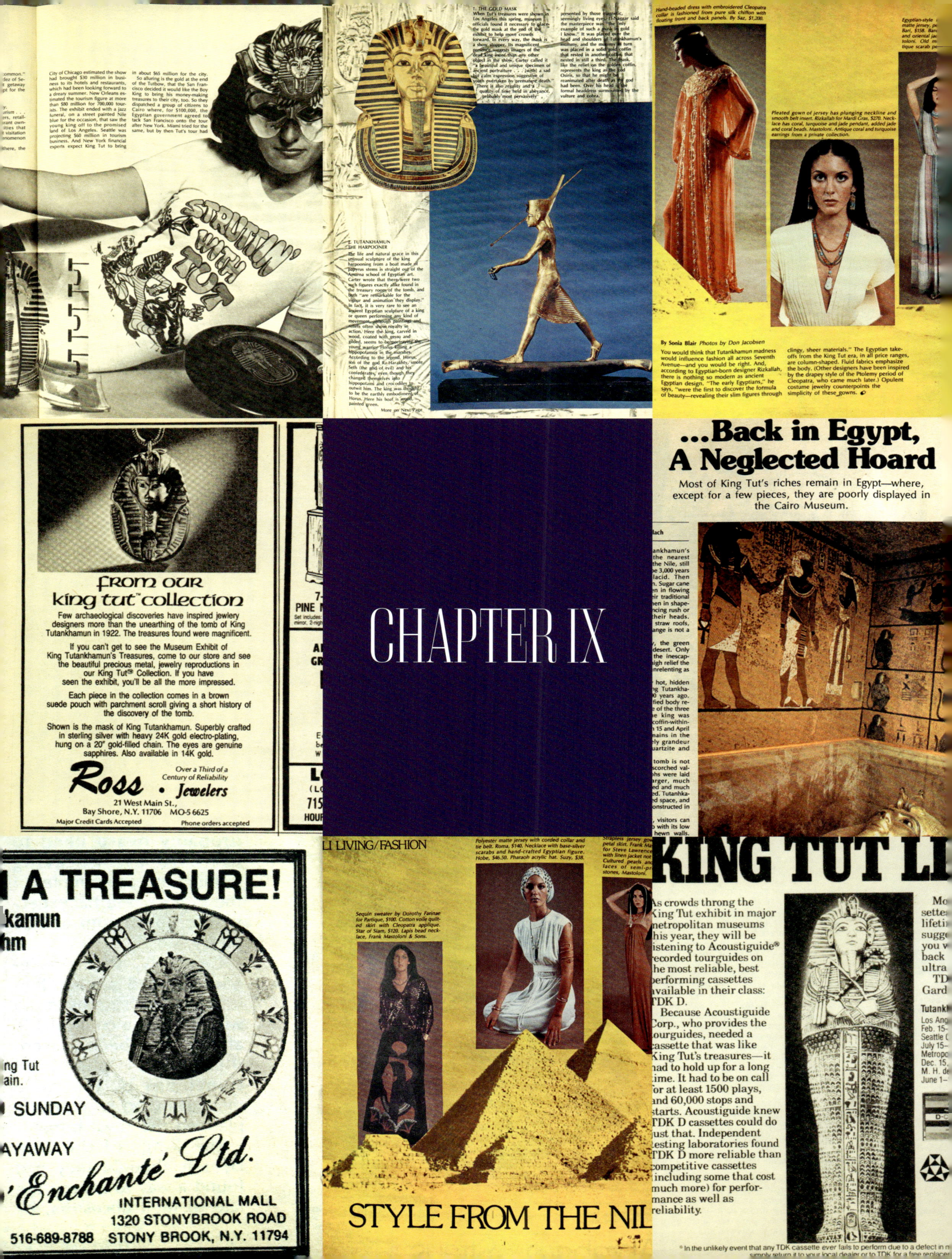
STRUTTIN' WITH TUT
...Back in Egypt, A Neglected Hoard
Most of King Tut's riches remain in Egypt—where, except for a few pieces, they are poorly displayed in the Cairo Museum.
from our king tut collection
Few archaeological discoveries have inspired jewelry designers more than the unearthing of the tomb of King Tutankhamun in 1922. The treasures found were magnificent.
If you can't get to see the Museum Exhibit of King Tutankhamun's Treasures, come to our store and see the beautiful precious metal, jewelry reproductions in our King Tut Collection. If you have seen the exhibit, you'll be all the more impressed.
Each piece in the collection comes in a brown suede pouch with parchment scroll giving a short history of the discovery of the tomb.
Shown is the mask of King Tutankhamun. Superbly crafted in sterling silver with heavy 24K gold electro-plating, hung on a 20" gold-filled chain. The eyes are genuine sapphires. Also available in 14K gold.
Ross Jewelers
Over a Third of a Century of Reliability
21 West Main St., Bay Shore, N.Y. 11706 MO-5 6625
Major Credit Cards Accepted
Phone orders accepted
By Sonia Blair Photos by Don Jacobsen
A TREASURE!
SUNDAY
Enchanté Ltd.
INTERNATIONAL MALL
1320 STONYBROOK ROAD
516-689-8788
STONY BROOK, N.Y. 11794
LIVING/FASHION
As crowds throng the King Tut exhibit in major metropolitan museums this year, they will be listening to Acoustiguide® recorded tourguides on the most reliable, best performing cassettes available in their class: TDK D.
Because Acoustiguide Corp., who provides the tourguides, needed a cassette that was like King Tut's treasures—it had to hold up for a long time. It had to be on call for at least 1500 plays, and 60,000 stops and starts. Acoustiguide knew TDK D cassettes could do just that. Independent testing laboratories found TDK D more reliable than competitive cassettes (including some that cost much more) for performance as well as reliability.

TUTMANIA

After 55 objects from Tutankhamun's tomb arrived in Washington, D.C., and the exhibit opened to visitors on 14th November, 1976, more than 835,924 visitors came to see it. This was just the beginning of the Treasures of Tutankhamun tour in America, which had started in the Soviet Union three years earlier. Tutmania spread throughout the United States.

Amei Wallach, the art critic for *New York Newsday*, wrote a very interesting article on Tutmania that appeared in *Newsday's* magazine, *LI*, on 10th December, 1978, just 10 days before the exhibit opened at the Metropolitan Museum of Art in New York: "The hottest show in town this month won't be on Broadway but in a museum." The Treasures of Tutankhamun exhibit had already visited five other American cities before arriving in New York. America was in the grip of Tut Hysteria, which went by other names, too: Tutmania, Mummy Madness, Tut Glut, Egypt Fever, and even the Pharaoh Faucet (which it seemed nobody could turn off). For her readers, Wallach selected ten "must-see" objects from the exhibit, which she emphasized were listed in no particular order:

1. The golden mask
2. The statue of Tutankhamun as a harpooner
3. The gaming board
4. The Selket figure
5. The vulture collar
6. The sun god on a lotus (Tutankhamun as Nefertem)
7. The ornate chest (with plaques of painted ivory)
8. The miniature effigy of the king lying on a bier
9. The small golden shrine
10. The silver pomegranate vase

Although the exhibit was carefully arranged and educational, and discussed by important art critics like Wallach, a great spirit of fun accompanied it. At the New Orleans Museum of Art, toilets were called "Tutlets" and ladies' rooms became "mummies' rooms." All across America, people in the streets were wearing T-shirts that said things like "I Love My Mummy" and "Struttin' with Tut." Steve Martin and the Toot Uncommons (members of the Nitty Gritty Dirt Band) had a hit record, "King Tut," singing about all the people who lined up to see him.

And a huge number of people did line up to see Tutankhamun. To get a ticket, people often stood in line for two hours or more – sometimes even for twelve hours. Many things happened in these lines. People met each other and later married because of "Tut." Others fought and ended divorcing... In Chicago, the official number of visitors was 1,349,742. In New Orleans, 870,755. (New Orleans sent the exhibit off to its next venue, Los Angeles, with a traditional jazz funeral down a street painted blue like the Nile.) In Los Angeles, 1,250,620. In Seattle, 799,318, and in Washington D.C., 832,853 visitors.

What did the Americans think of what they encountered on display? Most had never seen anything like this before. I open a guest book to pages dating to 2nd and 3rd August, 1978, when the exhibit was in Seattle. In it, the mayor of Seattle, Charles Royer, expressed his gratitude in enormous letters. Then other visitors added their impressions: "breathtaking," "incredible," "gorgeous," "fabulous," "exquisite," "outstanding," even "neato" and "far-out." (This was, after all, the 1970s.) "I am overwhelmed," a doctor from California wrote, and so did others. It was not only the glamorous appearance of the objects that impressed people. One woman wrote, "Great opportunity to relive the past."

Someone from Anchorage, Alaska, neatly printed, "Can I take it home with me?" Someone might have tried to do just that. There is a police report dated to 8th August, 1978, about an incident that occurred five days earlier. A woman from St. Helens, Oregon, reported suspicious activity by a well-groomed white male in his 30s, 6 feet (1.8 m) tall, 170 pounds (77 kg), wearing tan cut-off pants and a shirt with a tan-and-blue print. This man seemed to be trying to push a wire under the Plexiglas case surrounding the golden mask. Police investigation discovered what appeared to be pry marks on and under the Plexiglas. But of course the would-be thief failed to steal the mask. The police never learned who he was, and they even doubt that there was any "serious" attempt to open the case.

Tutankhamun was not just in the museums. "King Tut" was everywhere. Bottles of wine had the king's cartouches on their labels. Restaurant menus offered "Pharaoh's Fish." A restaurant in Washington, D.C., created a special $39 dinner at which people could "dine with the pharaohs." (And of course $39 in the 1970s was much more than $39 today.) Napkins had hieroglyphs. People could eat Tut tacos, read by Tut lamps, and sleep under Tut sheets.

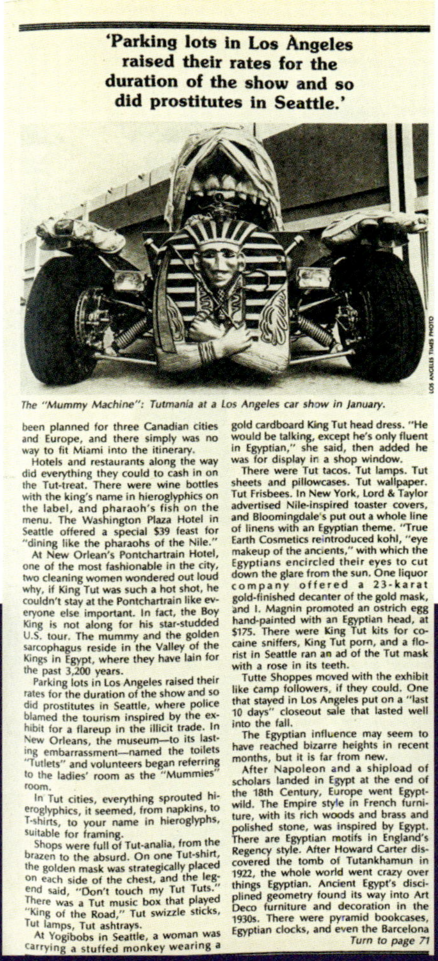

'Parking lots in Los Angeles raised their rates for the duration of the show and so did prostitutes in Seattle.'

LOS ANGELES TIMES PHOTO

The "Mummy Machine": Tutmania at a Los Angeles car show in January.

been planned for three Canadian cities and Europe, and there simply was no way to fit Miami into the itinerary.

Hotels and restaurants along the way did everything they could to cash in on the Tut-treat. There were wine bottles with the king's name in hieroglyphics on the label, and pharaoh's fish on the menu. The Washington Plaza Hotel in Seattle offered a special $39 feast for "dining like the pharaohs of the Nile."

At New Orlean's Pontchartrain Hotel, one of the most fashionable in the city, two cleaning women wondered out loud why, if King Tut was such a hot shot, he couldn't stay at the Pontchartrain like everyone else important. In fact, the Boy King is not along for his star-studded U.S. tour. The mummy and the golden sarcophagus reside in the Valley of the Kings in Egypt, where they have lain for the past 3,200 years.

Parking lots in Los Angeles raised their rates for the duration of the show and so did prostitutes in Seattle, where police blamed the tourism inspired by the exhibit for a flareup in the illicit trade. In New Orleans, the museum—to its lasting embarrassment—named the toilets "Tutlets" and volunteers began referring to the ladies' room as the "Mummies" room.

In Tut cities, everything sprouted hieroglyphics, it seemed, from napkins, to T-shirts, to your name in hieroglyphs, suitable for framing.

Shops were full of Tut-analia, from the brazen to the absurd. On one Tut-shirt, the golden mask was strategically placed on each side of the chest, and the legend said, "Don't touch my Tut Tuts." There was a Tut music box that played "King of the Road," Tut swizzle sticks, Tut lamps, Tut ashtrays.

At Yogibobs in Seattle, a woman was carrying a stuffed monkey wearing a gold cardboard King Tut head dress. "He would be talking, except he's only fluent in Egyptian," she said, then added he was for display in a shop window.

There were Tut tacos. Tut lamps. Tut sheets and pillowcases. Tut wallpaper. Tut Frisbees. In New York, Lord & Taylor advertised Nile-inspired toaster covers, and Bloomingdale's put out a whole line of linens with an Egyptian theme. "True Earth Cosmetics reintroduced kohl, "eye makeup of the ancients," with which the Egyptians encircled their eyes to cut down the glare from the sun. One liquor company offered a 23-karat gold-finished decanter of the gold mask, and I. Magnin promoted an ostrich egg hand-painted with an Egyptian head, at $175. There were King Tut kits for cocaine sniffers, King Tut porn, and a florist in Seattle ran an ad of the Tut mask with a rose in its teeth.

Tutte Shoppes moved with the exhibit like camp followers, if they could. One that stayed in Los Angeles put on a "last 10 days" closeout sale that lasted well into the fall.

The Egyptian influence may seem to have reached bizarre heights in recent months, but it is far from new.

After Napoleon and a shipload of scholars landed in Egypt at the end of the 18th Century, Europe went Egypt-wild. The Empire style in French furniture, with its rich woods and brass and polished stone, was inspired by Egypt. There are Egyptian motifs in England's Regency style. After Howard Carter discovered the tomb of Tutankhamun in 1922, the whole world went crazy over things Egyptian. Ancient Egypt's disciplined geometry found its way into Art Deco furniture and decoration in the 1930s. There were pyramid bookcases, Egyptian clocks, and even the Barcelona

Turn to page 71

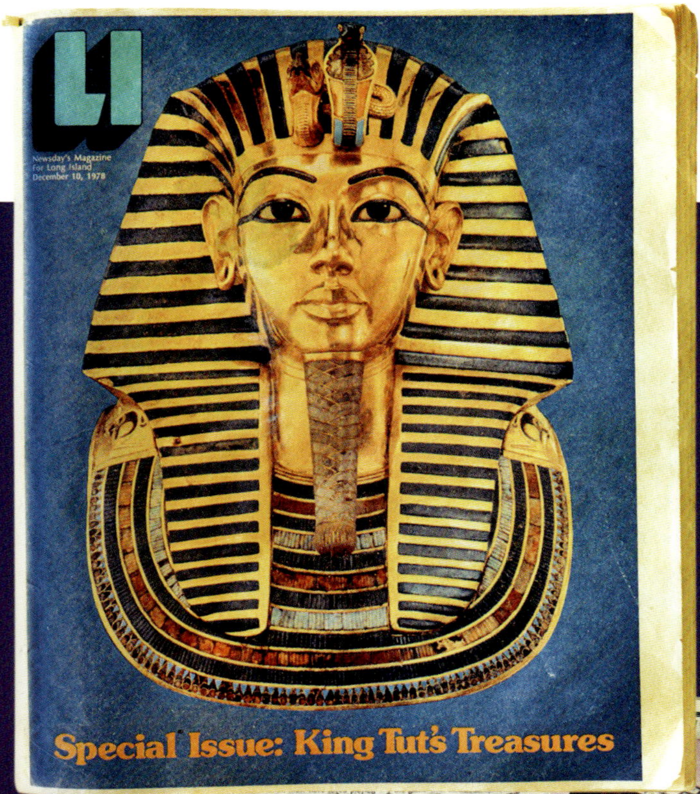

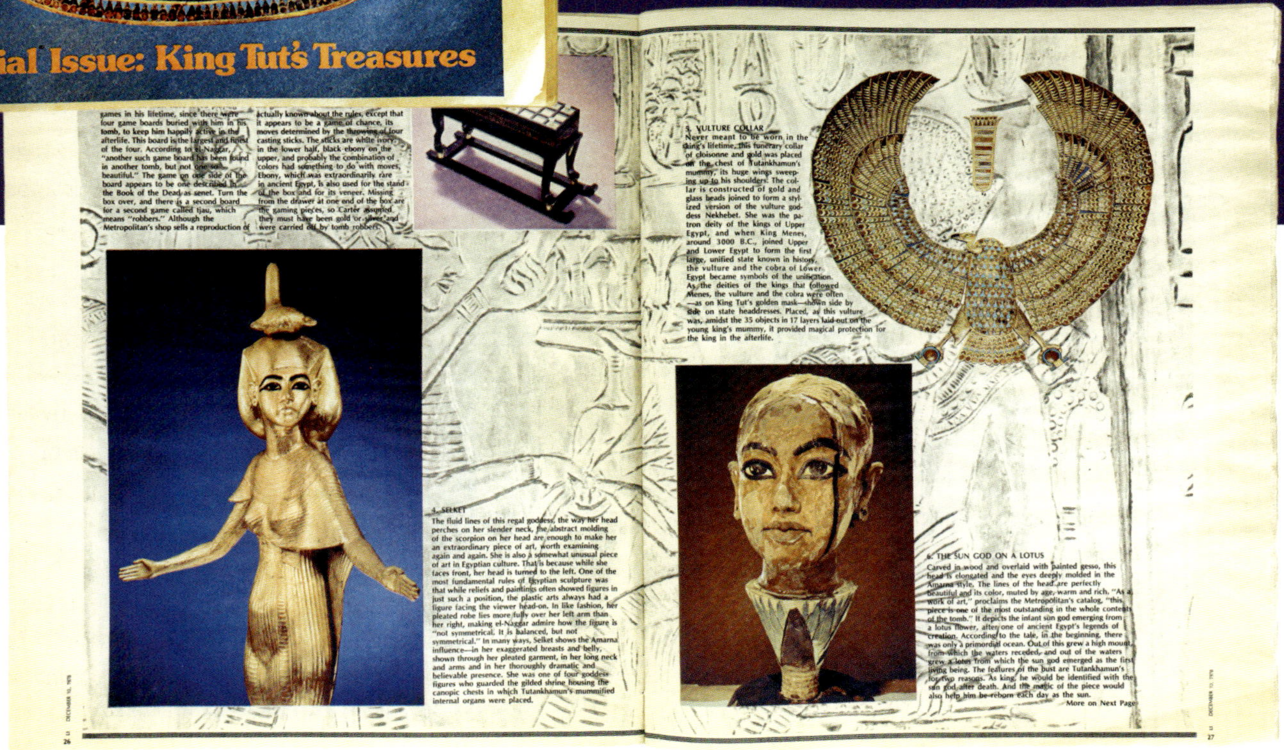

games in his lifetime, since there were four game boards buried with him in his tomb, to keep him happily active in the afterlife. This board is the largest and finest of the four. According to el-Naggar, "another such game board has been found in another tomb, but not one so beautiful." The game on one side of the board appears to be one described in the Book of the Dead as senet. Turn the box over, and there is a second board for a second game called tjau, which means "robbers." Although the Metropolitan's shop sells a reproduction of actually known about the rules, except that it appears to be a game of chance, its moves determined by the throwing of four casting sticks. The sticks are white ivory in the lower half, black ebony on the upper, and probably the combination of colors had something to do with moves. Ebony, which was extraordinarily rare in ancient Egypt, is also used for the stand of the box and for its veneer. Missing from the drawer at one end of the box are the gaming pieces, so Carter assumed they must have been gold or silver and were carried off by tomb robbers.

4. SELKET

The fluid lines of this regal goddess, the way her head perches on her slender neck, the abstract molding of the scorpion on her head are enough to make her an extraordinary piece of art, worth examining again and again. She is also a somewhat unusual piece of art in Egyptian culture. That is because while she faces front, her head is turned to the left. One of the most fundamental rules of Egyptian sculpture was that while reliefs and paintings often showed figures in just such a position, the plastic arts always had a figure facing the viewer head-on. In like fashion, her pleated robe lies more fully over her left arm than her right, making el-Naggar admire how the figure is "not symmetrical. It is balanced, but not symmetrical." In many ways, Selket shows the Amarna influence—in her exaggerated breasts and belly, shown through her pleated garment, in her long neck and arms and in her thoroughly dramatic and believable presence. She was one of four goddess figures who guarded the gilded shrine housing the canopic chests in which Tutankhamun's mummified internal organs were placed.

5. VULTURE COLLAR

Never meant to be worn in the king's lifetime, this funerary collar of cloisonne and gold was placed on the chest of Tutankhamun's mummy, its huge wings sweeping up to his shoulders. The collar is constructed of gold and glass beads joined to form a stylized version of the vulture goddess Nekhebet. She was the patron deity of the kings of Upper Egypt, and when King Menes, around 3000 B.C., joined Upper and Lower Egypt to form the first large, unified state known in history, the vulture and the cobra of Lower Egypt became symbols of the unification. As the deities of the kings that followed Menes, the vulture and the cobra were often —as on King Tut's golden mask—shown side by side on state headdresses. Placed, as this vulture was, amidst the 35 objects in 17 layers laid out on the young king's mummy, it provided magical protection for the king in the afterlife.

6. THE SUN GOD ON A LOTUS

Carved in wood and overlaid with painted gesso, this head is elongated and the eyes deeply molded in the Amarna style. The lines of the head are perfectly beautiful and its color, muted by age, warm and rich. "As a work of art," proclaims the Metropolitan's catalog, "this piece is one of the most outstanding in the whole contents of the tomb." It depicts the infant sun god emerging from a lotus flower, after one of ancient Egypt's legends of creation. According to the tale, in the beginning, there was only a primordial ocean. Out of this grew a high mound, from which the waters receded, and out of the waters grew a lotus from which the sun god emerged as the first living being. The features of the bust are Tutankhamun's for two reasons. As king, he would be identified with the sun god after death. And the magic of the piece would also help him be reborn each day as the sun.

More on Next Page

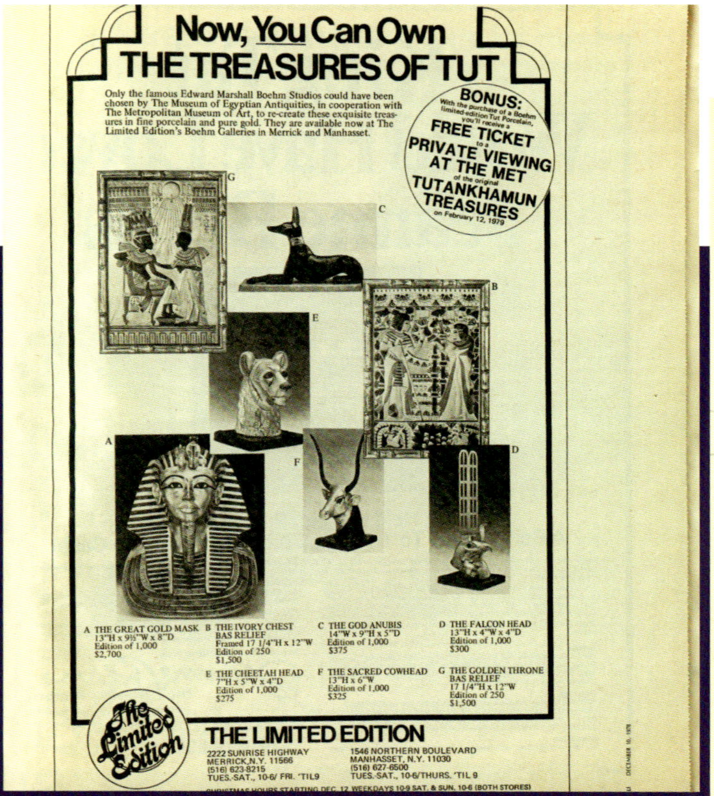

Now, You Can Own THE TREASURES OF TUT

Only the famous Edward Marshall Boehm Studios could have been chosen by The Museum of Egyptian Antiquities, in cooperation with The Metropolitan Museum of Art, to re-create these exquisite treasures in fine porcelain and pure gold. They are available now at The Limited Edition's Boehm Galleries in Merrick and Manhasset.

BONUS: With the purchase of a Boehm limited-edition Tut Porcelain, you'll receive a FREE TICKET to a PRIVATE VIEWING AT THE MET of the original TUTANKHAMUN TREASURES on February 12, 1979

A THE GREAT GOLD MASK 13"H x 9½"W x 8"D Edition of 1,000 $2,700

B THE IVORY CHEST BAS RELIEF Framed 17 1/4"H x 12"W Edition of 250 $1,500

C THE GOD ANUBIS 14"W x 9"H x 5"D Edition of 1,000 $375

D THE FALCON HEAD 13"H x 4"W x 4"D Edition of 1,000 $300

E THE CHEETAH HEAD 7"H x 5"W x 4"D Edition of 1,000 $275

F THE SACRED COWHEAD 13"H x 6"W Edition of 1,000 $325

G THE GOLDEN THRONE BAS RELIEF 17 1/4"H x 12"W Edition of 250 $1,500

The Limited Edition

THE LIMITED EDITION

2222 SUNRISE HIGHWAY
MERRICK, N.Y. 11566
(516) 623-8215
TUES.-SAT., 10-6/ FRI. 'TIL9

1546 NORTHERN BOULEVARD
MANHASSET, N.Y. 11030
(516) 627-6500
TUES.-SAT., 10-6/THURS. 'TIL 9

CHRISTMAS HOURS STARTING DEC. 12 WEEKDAYS 10-9 SAT. & SUN. 10-6 (BOTH STORES)

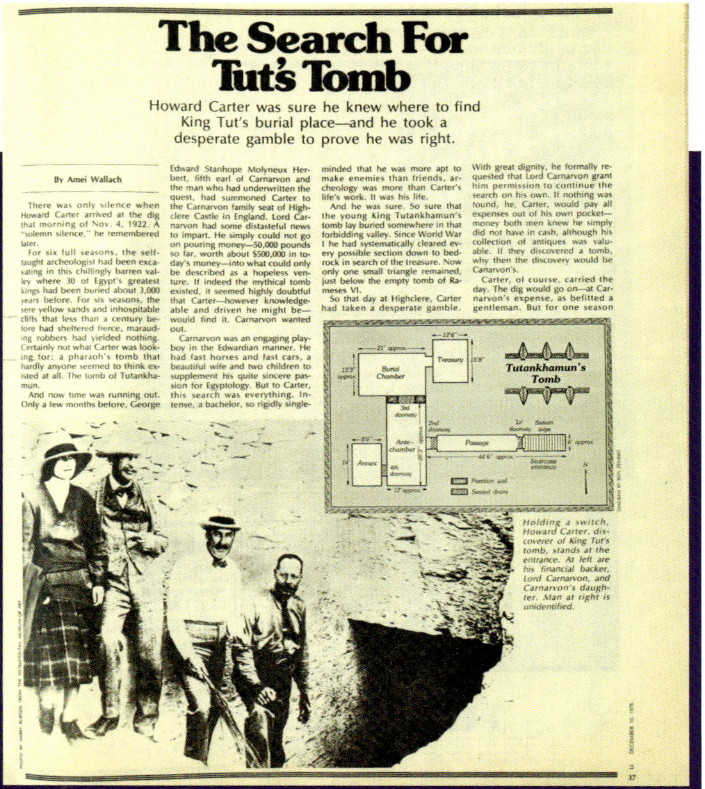

The Search For Tut's Tomb

Howard Carter was sure he knew where to find King Tut's burial place—and he took a desperate gamble to prove he was right.

By Amei Wallach

There was only silence when Howard Carter arrived at the dig that morning of Nov. 4, 1922. A "solemn silence," he remembered later.

For six full seasons, the self-taught archeologist had been excavating in this chillingly barren valley where 30 of Egypt's greatest kings had been buried about 3,000 years before. For six seasons, the sere yellow sands and inhospitable cliffs that less than a century before had sheltered fierce, marauding robbers had yielded nothing. Certainly not what Carter was looking for: a pharaoh's tomb that hardly anyone seemed to think existed at all. The tomb of Tutankhamun.

And now time was running out. Only a few months before, George Edward Stanhope Molyneux Herbert, fifth earl of Carnarvon and the man who had underwritten the quest, had summoned Carter to the Carnarvon family seat of Highclere Castle in England. Lord Carnarvon had some distasteful news to impart. He simply could not go on pouring money—50,000 pounds so far, worth about $500,000 in today's money—into what could only be described as a hopeless venture. If indeed the mythical tomb existed, it seemed highly doubtful that Carter—however knowledgeable and driven he might be—would find it. Carnarvon wanted out.

Carnarvon was an engaging playboy in the Edwardian manner. He had fast horses and fast cars, a beautiful wife and two children to supplement his quite sincere passion for Egyptology. But to Carter, this search was everything. Intense, a bachelor, so rigidly single-minded that he was more apt to make enemies than friends, archeology was more than Carter's life's work. It was his life.

And he was sure. So sure that the young King Tutankhamun's tomb lay buried somewhere in that forbidding valley. Since World War I he had systematically cleared every possible section down to bedrock in search of the treasure. Now only one small triangle remained, just below the empty tomb of Rameses VI.

So that day at Highclere, Carter had taken a desperate gamble. With great dignity, he formally requested that Lord Carnarvon grant him permission to continue the search on his own. If nothing was found, he, Carter, would pay all expenses out of his own pocket—money both men knew he simply did not have in cash, although his collection of antiques was valuable. If they discovered a tomb, why then the discovery would be Canarvon's.

Carter, of course, carried the day. The dig would go on—at Carnarvon's expense, as befitted a gentleman. But for one season

Tutankhamun's Tomb

Holding a switch, Howard Carter, discoverer of King Tut's tomb, stands at the entrance. At left are his financial backer, Lord Carnarvon, and Carnarvon's daughter. Man at right is unidentified.

Of course, all of this involved money. There was no fee for tickets to see the Treasures of Tutankhamun exhibit, although people might have to pay the usual admissions fee to the museum. (Despite this, at some venues people sold their tickets to others for as much as $45. Although free, there was a limited number of tickets.) Instead, Egypt was meant to profit financially, and collect funds to help upgrade the Egyptian Museum in Cairo, from the merchandise sold in the museum shops. Although this is what was announced, all this money, which amounted to $10 million, went to UNESCO. The money from sales through the gift shops paid a percentage of the net, not the gross, which turned out to be not very much. There are other ways that foreign museums benefited. Because of interest generated by Tutankhamun's exhibit, some museums experienced a dramatic increase in membership. For example, the Field Museum in Chicago had 30,000 members before the exhibit. After, that number swelled to 70,000. Being able to host an exhibit like the Treasures of Tutankhamun also increased the prestige of some museums, which allowed them to host other important, large-scale exhibits in the future.

Tutankhamun's economic effects went far beyond the museum doors, too, because hotels, shopping centers, restaurants and other businesses benefited from the presence of the young king's treasures. In Los Angeles, parking fees went up, and in Seattle, prostitutes raised their prices! Overall, the Treasures of Tutankhamun attracted $30 million to the city of Chicago. Other cities did even better: New Orleans, $80 million; Seattle, $60 million; New York, $65 million.

Long before the 1970s exhibit, Tutankhamun had generated business for Americans. Discovery of the tomb inspired Hollywood films such as *The Mummy* with Boris Karloff (1932). Many movies used mummies for comedies or spoofs, including *Abbott and Costello Meet the Mummy* in 1955, and *I Was a Teenage Mummy* in 1962. In Los Angeles, a woman fainted near the golden mask. But when she woke up, she said she had fainted not because she had finally seen in person this icon of the pharaohs. She had fainted because she realized that at the same time Cary Grant was also looking at the mask! Many of the rich and famous, such as Elizabeth Taylor (who had played Cleopatra in 1963), came to see the new celebrity in town.

Tutankhamun gave some people the idea that they had lived past lives in Egypt of the pharaohs. In L.A., a woman in a gold lamé dress and headdress adorned with colorful feathers claimed to be the reincarnation of Tutankhamun's mother! But there was a serious side to "Tutankhamania" as well. In the United States, the exhibit prompted discussions about the race of Tutankhamun and the rest of the ancient Egyptian population.

The curse was part of Tutmania, too. In his book *Tutankhamun: The Untold Story*, published in 1978, Thomas Hoving, who had just retired as director of the Metropolitan Museum of Art, accused Carter of stealing from the tomb. People thought that a turquoise blue faience sphinx that the Metropolitan Museum bought at auction from the Parke-Bernet Galleries in 1972 had come from the boy-king's tomb. While it is true that it came from Howard Carter's estate, Carter's notes indicate that it had been found in the tomb of Amenhotep III. Hoving left his job just before the Tutankhamun exhibit, which he helped to be arranged was shown in New York. In his book, he says that Carter was making eyes at Lord Carnarvon's daughter, Evelyn, and that created conflict between the two men. Hoving even had evidence from letters Evelyn had sent to Carter, but her family refused to give him permission to publish them. Is this a little bit of the curse?

It seems that the curse of Tutankhamun punished Gamal Mokhtar, who left his job as chairman of the Egyptian Antiquities Organization after the exhibit opened in Washington, D.C., in a dramatic fashion. Fouad El Orabi, who was an ex-military officer, took over because he was a friend of Abdel Monem El Sawy, Minister of Culture and Information. Special thanks are due to Mokhtar, who was responsible for changing Egyptian antiquities from being merely local to being truly international.

Tutmania continued on even after the Treasures of Tutankhamun tour ended. In 2005, I was Secretary General of the SCA when it was decided to send another "Tut" exhibit to the United States, Tutankhamun and the Golden Age of the Pharaohs. At the opening in Los Angeles, I went with Omar Sharif. The actor was invited as a guest because he had narrated the exhibit's introductory film. One night, we were invited to have dinner at one of the restaurants in L.A. When the dinner was over, Sharif gave 20 euros to the parking attendant. This man looked at the euros. He did not understand what this foreign money was, so he threw it on the ground. Omar did not like that and tried to hit him. I was able to grab his hand and prevent him from touching the attendant. But once the parking attendant found out that he had nearly been struck by Omar Sharif, he took Sharif to court. Newspapers picked up on the story and one of them even tried to blame this on the curse of Tut.

The city was covered with photographs of Tutankhamun, and everything else became "Tut-ified." On his cable television program, *The Daily Show*, John Stewart imitated me with my accent and wore my hat! The *Los Angeles Times* even published a profile of me. The opening party at the L.A. County Museum of Art was amazing, complete with a red carpet and, of course, many movie stars who came to see the exhibit, just like stars in the 1970s had done.

At the Field Museum of Natural History in Chicago, the Exelon Company sponsored the exhibit. There was a press conference, and many people gave speeches. The organizers spoke and so did the exhibit sponsors. I would speak last and take questions from the press. But the CEO of Exelon, John Rowe, could not attend because President George W. Bush was in Chicago that day and they were having lunch together. So Rowe sent his assistant. At the press conference, the assistant delivered Rowe's greetings to everyone and went on about how John Rowe loved Egypt so much that he even had an Egyptian coffin in his office.

When I gave my speech, I told everyone that Egyptian antiquities cannot be shown within homes and offices. Egyptian antiquities belong in a museum. I could not accept someone who had a pharaonic coffin in his office as a sponsor of the Tutankhamun exhibit. I said Tutankhamun would not like this. Rowe would have to give his coffin to the Field Museum as a gift, I said, if he wanted to continue to be a sponsor for the exhibit.

This stole the front page of all the newspapers, even the *Chicago Tribune*, from President Bush. Rowe did not think that I was serious and refused to do as I asked. The next day, I wrote an official letter to the Field Museum and the exhibit organizers telling them to remove Exelon's name from the exhibit. In the end, Rowe agreed to give the coffin to the museum. And the newspapers said on the front page that two pharaohs had fought, but the real one won.

This became good publicity for the exhibit.

In Philadelphia, the opening party was in December. It was terribly cold and snowy. When we arrived at the Franklin Institute in black tie, we saw a camel in front of the building. I felt bad for the camel. In my speech I remarked about the poor, freezing animal and said that King Tut is unhappy, too – this is why he covered the city with snow.

In New York, the exhibit was shown at Discovery Times Square on Broadway. I call it a "hole" because it is so small. Actually, we decided to put the exhibit in this place because the Metropolitan Museum has a policy of never charging for special exhibitions. This would have led to a repeat of 1978 for us, resulting in Egypt getting no funds for its own museums. By displaying Tutankhamun at Discovery Times Square, Egypt earned about $8 million to help preserve its antiquities.

Atlanta gave the exhibit another amazing reception. I spoke at the Fox Theater, which has a wonderful Egyptian Revival ballroom, before an audience of about 4,500 people who had paid for their tickets. Among them were three girls between the ages of 8 and 9 who had written to me through my fan club, hoping to meet me.

Peter Lacovara, curator of ancient art at the Michael C. Carlos Museum of Emory University, and Mark Lach, senior vice president of Arts and Exhibitions International, announced the names of the three girls and asked them to come to the stage after I had given my speech.

After I had finished speaking, Lach brought the three girls in front of me. They stood about a short distance away. The one in the middle was about 8 years old. Finally, she walked toward me and said, "Hug me!" It seemed that the audience heard her, so I gave her a hug. Then she said, "More," and I gave her an even bigger hug. The 4,500 people gave a standing ovation.

When I asked the girl why she needed a bigger hug, she told me that she hoped to get some of my passion for archaeology, so that she could keep it with her always.

That is the real Tutmania.

CONCLUSION

Despite the many books written about the Golden King – including this one – there will always be new things to learn about him. This is, in fact, why I wrote this book. Until recently, we did not know about Sennedjem, the king's tutor, whose tomb was found at Akhmim. DNA analysis, with the support of archaeological information, has identified members of the king's family. As each new discovery brings more questions, so much more work remains to be done to uncover the truths about Tutankhamun and his family.

The two female fetuses that Carter found in the Treasury await improved DNA testing. Derry's physical examination showed that they were female, and modern science has shown that they could be the children of Tutankhamun, but our study of them cannot be considered complete without the mummy of their presumed mother, Ankhesenamun. So, where is she? The two mummified women found in KV 21, known as KV 21A and KV 21B, could be the key. There is a connection between the two fetuses and KV 21A, but only further examination will determine whether or not KV 21A is Tutankhamun's widowed queen. The Revolution of 25th January 2011, interrupted our work, so perhaps in the near future additional technology will improve upon the results we have obtained so far.

And perhaps we will be able to demonstrate that the headless mummy, KV 21B, is Nefertiti because we know that the ancient Egyptians kept related mummies together when they moved the bodies from their original tombs to safer hiding places. It would be logical for KV 21B to be Ankhesenamun's mother if KV 21A is, indeed, Ankhesenamun, but the DNA team of the Egyptian Mummy Project will have to perform the tests necessary to determine whether or not our logic has given us the correct answer. We also must continue the search for the missing bones of Queen Mutnodjmet, Nefertiti's sister. Scientific analysis of her remains could shed light on the identity of mummy KV 21B.

DNA analysis revealed a very important discovery with a mystery still attached to it, by finding and identifying the mummy of Tutankhamun's mother, the Younger Lady found in KV 35. Even though we know her son and even her parents – Amenhotep III and Tiye – her name remains lost to us. Some people suggest that this is Nefertiti, but as I explained in Chapter 6, this identification is impossible: we know without question or doubt that Nefertiti was not the daughter of Amenhotep III and Tiye. Furthermore, if Nefertiti had been Tutankhamun's mother, we would expect to see images of the little prince at Amarna in his mother's company. On the contrary, Nefertiti is always accompanied only by her daughters. So which of Amenhotep III and Tiye's daughters gave birth to Tutankhamun? A future line of research might reveal her name.

The Valley of the Kings itself is still hiding secrets from us, too. Whether or not we have Ankhesenamun's body, there is the separate question of where her tomb is. This is something else we expect to find in the future. Our excavation in the Valley of the Monkeys, near the tomb of Ay, revealed some clues about that. We believe that Ay married the widow of Tutankhamun, and, if that is so, we expect to find her buried near Ay, who succeeded the young king on the throne. We found four foundation deposits near Ay's tomb, filled with knives and blue pottery dated to the reign of Ankhesenamun's grandfather, Amenhotep III. The Egyptians, before they constructed a temple, created foundation deposits to announce the construction of the building. But the foundation pits associated with tombs were different. Four or five of these were dug and objects placed in them *after* the construction of the tomb. So the Egyptian team that I led will continue to excavate near Ay's tomb in the hope that we will discover Ankhesenamun's tomb in the Valley of the Monkeys. Perhaps, too, future excavation will bring to light the tomb of Queen Tiye and other tombs of the queens of the 18th Dynasty, who were buried in the valley.

More excavation in the valley could also reveal the missing tombs of Thutmose II and Rameses XIII. Archaeologist John Romer also has suggested that the area near the Valley of the Kings known as the Western Valley could contain the tombs of kings of the 21st and 22nd Dynasties.

But the Valley of the Kings needs more than further exploration. It desperately needs conservation. Implementation of a conservation project for the tombs must be completed, with the establishment of a conservation center just south of Howard Carter's rest house. This center would be responsible for the study and preservation of the valley and its treasures.

In cooperation with the Swiss-based Society of Friends of the Royal Tombs of Egypt, we were planning laser scans to record and create exact replicas of the tombs of Tutankhamun and Seti I in the Valley of the Kings and the tomb of Nefertari in the Valley of the Queens.

The Society finished the replica of the tomb of Tutankhamun, which the European Union funded to bring to Egypt. Unfortunately, the place where it is to be installed remains undecided. It was once proposed in a lack of vision by those in charge of antiquities in Egypt for it to be installed in the museum at Sharm el Sheikh, at the southern end of the Sinai Peninsula. The Grand Egyptian Museum has also been considered. But these suggestions show a lack of understanding of the real importance and the goal of the replica. It is crucial that the replica be located not in some distant place like the Red Sea coast or Cairo, but in Luxor, near the original, in the vicinity of Carter's rest house. It is likewise important to continue with the replicas of the tombs of Seti I and Nefertari.

These royal tombs are unique, and they are fragile, prone to damage from the carbon dioxide and moisture introduced by even the most careful of visitors. If tourists continue to visit them in great numbers, in less than a century they will be lost. The only solution that will both preserve the tombs and allow tourists to experience these ancient monuments is to provide a replica valley near Luxor and to open more original tombs in the real valley, to disperse the tourist traffic that is now concentrated on just four or five open tombs. We must devise a rotation system by which some tombs are available to the public for a period of time while others are closed.

Conservation is also needed for the 4,500 objects from the tomb of Tutankhamun that will be moved from the Egyptian Museum at Tahrir Square to the Grand Egyptian Museum at Giza. It is hoped that a team of foreign and Egyptian restorers will start immediately on a plan to conserve the objects before the transfer and that the moving of these priceless artifacts will be undertaken by experts. Once completed, when the treasures are housed in the shadow of the pyramids, the new display will return again to us the magic of the Golden King.

There is only one mystery I believe that we will never solve, and that is how the young king died. We do know that Tutankhamun had an accident shortly before his death. We know that the blocks showing the king hunting, described in Chapter I, were from a palace in the area around Memphis, and we are certain that there was a rest house belonging to him near the Sphinx. The Restoration Stela also tells us that he occupied a palace in this region. This is where the accident may have happened, in the desert of Memphis. But the nature of the accident and the real manner of his death will, I think, remain unanswered questions.

However, I hope this book has shown that science and archaeology can help us find the answers to many other mysteries. More advanced technology will shed new light upon the remaining secrets of Tutankhamun and the Valley of the Kings.

The valley is unique, and I and others hope that those who have responsibility for it will possess the right vision to undertake its proper conservation and preservation. This is necessary for scholars to accomplish their work and for everyone to experience the ancient wonders and mystery of the Valley of the Kings.

APPENDIX 1

List of Objects Found in KV 62
Based on A Handlist to Howard Carter's Catalogue of Objects in Tutankhamun's Tomb

compiled by Helen Murray and Mary Nuttall

The complete list of objects, along with Howard Carter's notecards and Harry Burton's photographs, can be viewed at the Carter Archives of the Griffith Institute website: http://www.griffith.ox.ac.uk/gri/carter/HomePage.html. [In color: Object (or human remains) featured featured in Chapters IV, V, and VI]

Stairway and entrance corridor

1a	Scarab (green glazed steatite)
1b	Fragment of ivory
1c	Clay seals, most of the royal necropolis
1d	Fragments of resin
1e	Fragments of glass
1f	Potsherds with hieratic writing
1g	Fragments of vases (stone)
1h	Fragments of pottery
1i	Animal bones
1j	Pieces of wood, rushes, etc.
1k	Parts of a box with name of Smenkhkare
1l	Parts of a box with name of Tutankhamun
1m	Fragments of ties from boxes
2	Fragments of pottery
3	Mud seals from jars
4	First doorway (blocking, sealing, and seal impressions)
5a	Fragments of vessels and lids from vessels (stone)
5b	Red cups, probably from the foundation deposit (pottery)
5c	Fragments of plaster seals from jars
5d	Fragments of mud boxes from the foundation deposit(?)
5e–f	Splinters of wood (some with gesso and gold)
5g	Fragments of faience
5h	Pieces of feldspar
6	Skins
7	Vases (calcite=Egyptian alabaster)
8	Image of Tutankhamun as Nefertem
9	Vase (pottery)
10	Clay seals
11	Fragment of jar (pottery)
12a	Pendants (faience)
12b	Pieces of gold foil
12c	Inlaid gold plaques from jewelry
12d	Rings and ring fragments (faience)
12e	Fragments of faience (including a game piece)
12f	Floral pendants (faience)
12g	Razors (bronze)
12h	Fragments of resin
12i	Clay seal
12j	Fragments of inlay (ivory, ebony)
12k	Shells from a necklace(?)
12l	Dried fruit
12m	Pieces of worked semi-precious stones
12n	Assortment (fragments of metal work; yoke and basket from *shabti*; bronze arrowhead; gold and bronze staple)
12o	Labels (wood)
12p	Fragments of mineral (feldspar?)
12q	Fragments of glass
12r	Dom-palm nuts
12s	Cup, perhaps from foundation deposit (pottery)
12t	Fragments of lids of vases (stone)
13	Second doorway (blocking, sealing, and seal impressions)

Antechamber

14 Cup (calcite = Egyptian alabaster)
14a Box (wood with ivory, ebony, and red wood veneer)
14b Box in the shape of a cartouche
15, 15a Assortment (pottery, pieces of reeds, etc.)
16 Vase (calcite = Egyptian alabaster)
17 Leaves on wooden frame
18 Bouquet
19a Bouquet
19b(1) Reed circle
19b(2) Lid of rush basket
19b(3) Piece of reed
19b(4) Pieces of papyrus matting
20 Jar (calcite = Egyptian alabaster)
21 Hunting Box; Painted box containing garments, garment fragments, rolls of linen, and other objects (21a – yy) including:
21a, b, f, g, h, i, j Sandals
21c Headrest (gilded)
21d Ceremonial robe
21k, l Shoes
21t Cloak (leopard-skin)
21u Collar (faience)
21x Tapestry – woven garment, 2 pieces
21z Child's glove (linen)
21dd Bead necklace (resin)
21jj Gold sequins
21nn Loincloth
21vv Archer's gauntlet
21ww, xx Board (wood, gesso, paint)
21yy Pendant (gold)
22 Guardian statue wearing *nemes*
22a Covering from guardian statue (linen)
23, 24 Jars, painted (pottery)
25 Vase (faience)
25a Ring (glass)
25b Strip of linen
26 Basket lid
27 Vase fragment (calcite = Egyptian alabaster)
28 Doorway to Burial Chamber, plaster on surface
29 Guardian statue wearing *khat*
30 Footrest (wood)
31, 31a Vases (faience)
32 Chest containing vessels (vases, cups) made mostly of stone or glass and other objects including:
32a – b, d, e Vases (calcite = Egyptian alabaster)
32c Cup
32i Kohl pot (serpentine)
32j, l Vases (glass)
32o Paint slabs, 4
32p, q Knives (limestone)
32s Lumps of resin
32t Balls of incense
32u Dried fruit
32v Gold cap or boss
32w Ostrich feathers (broken)
32x Garlic (?)
33 Stand (?) (wood)
34 Hassock (with beadwork)
35 Lion bed
36a Papyrus reeds
36b, c Jar stopper (calcite = Egyptian alabaster)
36d End of cane
36e Clay sealing
37 Shrine-shaped box on sledge
37a containing standard of the tenth nome of Upper Egypt (Aphroditopolis)
38 Shrine-shaped box on sledge with seal
38a – c (38a) containing standard of the tenth nome of Upper Egypt (Aphroditopolis) (38b), standard being covered with linen (38c)
39 Child's chair (ebony, ivory)
40 Painted box (calcite = Egyptian alabaster) containing:
40a Pomegranate (ivory)
40b Caps, beads, etc. (gold)
40c Clay(?) sealings, 2
41a – d Torch-holders (bronze, wood) (41c)
42 Basket
43 Box (ivory, ebony, red wood) containing many objects mostly of cloth (43a – q), including:
43e, i, j Gauntlet and gloves (linen)
43p Ring (faience)
43q(1) – q(3) beads (faience, resin, white glass)
43q(7) Scrap of limestone from the floor
44 Casket (gilded and inlaid) containing mostly objects of gold and some pieces of cloth (44a – jj), including:
44a Pieces of open-work plate gold with granular designs, 4 (44a(1), 44a(2))
44c, e, f, g, h, j Rings (gold)

44d, i Rings (gold, glass)
44k, l, o, gg Scarabs (stones or gold and glass)
44n, cc, dd Collars and necklaces (faience)
44p, v Model adzes
44q Robe (leopard skin)
44u Small crook
44cc, dd Necklaces (faience)
44ee Armlet (faience, gold)
44ff Glove (linen)
44hh Sphinx (lapis lazuli)

45 Vase on a stand (calcite = Egyptian alabaster)

46 Bundles of cloth and other objects (46a - vv) including:
46a Arrows, 3 (reed)
46b, c Collars (faience)
46d - g, i - l, ss, uu, vv groups of loincloths (linen)
46o - p, cc - ee, hh, nn Gauntlets and gloves
46q Archer's pad (linen)
46w Knuckle - bones, 2 (ivory)
46x Game pieces, 5 (faience)
46y *Tjet* - amulet (glass)
46z *Djed*-amulet (glass)
46aa Mallet (ebony)
46bb Quiver (linen)
46qq, rr Collars (faience)

47 Bedstead (ebony)

48 Walking - sticks and bows, including:
48a - c Walking - sticks with bound Nubian foe (48c)
48d Walking - stick with bound Asiatic and Nubian foes
48e Walking - stick with gilt top
48f - k(2) Compound bows
48l Simple bow
48m - w Staffs and walking sticks
48x Quiver (tapestry woven) with arrow
48y Arrow (reed arrow)

49 Arrow

50 Box containing mostly garments, cloth, and sticks, including:
50a Shirt (yellow linen)
50d, f(1-4), h, n - q Shawls
50l Tiny rolls cloth (linen)
50v - cc, kk - qq, uu - xx Sticks
50dd - 44 Measuring rods
50gg Trumpet
50yy Arrows, 69 (reed)

51 Bouquet

52 Reed pad

53a Collar (glazed)

53b Pads with rings

54 Box of ebony and red painted wood containing a variety of objects:
54a-ddd(4), 54b including: Snake (bronze with gold inlay)
54c Model knife (painted wood)
54d, e Throw - stick (wood, plaster, gilt)
54f Tapestry - woven polychrome garment
54g Libation vase (dark blue faience)
54h Bowl (green faience)
54j Wine strainer
54k Corselet
54l Libation vase (faience)
54n, t, u Drinking cups (faience, glazed)
54w Vase (faience)
54x, z - dd, ii, jj, ll - pp Ewers (faience)
54q Scarab (glass, gold)
54s Cosmetic container in shape of duck or goose (ivory)
54ff Figure of a king (glass)
54qq - rr Wine cups, 6 (faience)
54yy Scarab (gold plate, carnelian, blue glass)
54bbb Vase (faience)
54ddd Ring box (ivory)
54ddd(4) Winged scarab (bronze, gold)

55 Cylindrical jar (calcite = Egyptian alabaster)

56 Box (ebony, red wood)

56a Armlet (stone)

57-61 Ungent vases (calcite = Egyptian alabaster) (58)

62a - vv Boxes of prepared food, 48

63, 63a Rings (faience)

64 Support for bed legs(?) (wood)

65 Arrows and strip of papyrus

66 Stool (wood, papyrus)

67a Low stool (wood)

67b Remains of a sandal

68. Box, painted white (wood) containing

68a - c cloth (68a - b) and a clay sealing (69c)

69 Ewer (faience)

70 Bow

71 End of chariot pole and fruit

72 Nuts, fruit

73 Cow bed

74 Uraeus (wood, inlay, gold)

75-76 Sistra (wood, gold)

77a Simple bow

77b Compound bow

78 Stool (wood)

79 Box, rounded (ebony, red wood) containing mostly textiles, including:
79a - b, f, m Loin-cloths
79e Stick handle (?) (metal, glass, stone?)
79i - p, t, u Bundles of bandages
79q Finger-stall (linen)

79r Gauntlet (linen)
79v Armlet (crystalline limestone)

80 Bed (wood)

81 Stool (wood, ivory)

82 Chair (ebony, papyrus)

83 Stool (ebony, ivory)

84 Stool, painted white (wood)

85a Sandal with beads

85b Upper part of stick

85c Sandal (leather)

85d Label (wood)

85e Part of a chariot harness

85f Fragments of a bowl, 2 (faience)

86 Dish (pottery)

87 Chair, carved (cedar)

88 Footrest (wood)

89a - b Gauntlets (linen)

90 Footrest

91 Throne

91a Hinged piece of portable pavilion 123

92 Footrest (wood), found with numerous small objects (92a - l), including:
92c Sequin from Box 21aa (gold)
92d Uraeus head from throne 91 (faience)
92e Animal horn
92f Feet from small figure(?) (ivory)
92h Armlet (crystalline limestone)

93 Basket

94a Sandal

94b Model hoe (wood)

95a Stick (wood, gold)

95b One stick from portable pavilion 123

95c Piece of chariot harness

96 Jar lids, 2 (limestone)

97 Basket (reed) containing:
97a Dom fruit
97b Pieces of two rings (faience)

98 Staff with handle with granulated goldwork decoration

99 Decayed cloth and bread

99a *Ankh* (faience)

100a Stick (wood, gesso, gold) gold

100b Decorated stick (wood)

100c Adze handle (wood)

100d Inner sole of sandal (leather?)

100e Arrow (reed)

100f - h Textiles

101 Chest (ebony, painted white wood) containing objects (101a - aa), mostly textiles, including:
101a,f, h - j Shawls
101n Captive Nubian perhaps from side of chariot (wood, gold)
101o Head - rest (wood)
101v Scarves, 2
101w Necklace with pectoral (wood) and scarab (stone)
101z(2) Feather pendant from corselet 54k

102 Piece of papyrus

103 Chariot yoke pole

104a - b Sandals

105 Fragment of jar (pottery)

106a Adze (wood with bronze blade)

106b Dish (pottery)

106c Fragments of large jar

106d Fragments of plaster

106e Pieces of wood, 2

107 Saddles from harness of light chariot, 2 (wood)

108 Golden shrine for statuettes

108a Stand for statuette

108b Parts of corselet 54k

108c Necklace and snake-deity pendant (gold)

109 Pole-collar from chariot 120 (gold, inlay)

110 *Shabti*

111 Lid of box 115

112 Hawk decoraton from chariot (wood, gesso, gold)

113 Pieces of pavilion 123, 2

114 Decorative disk from chariot (crystalline limestone)

115 Box, painted yellow (wood)

115a Fragments of dishes (pottery)

116 Torso of Tutankhamun (wood)

117a Basket (reed)

117b Leather from a chariot

117c Fragment of plaster

118 Various fragments from chariot

119 Partitioned tray (reed) containing:
119a Pieces of decoration from chariot (leather, gold)
119b Decorative disk from chariot (quartzite? limestone?)
119c Remains of bag (linen)
119d Dom fruits, 2
119e Remains of bread(?)
119f Seeds

120 Body of decorated chariot, with other elements, fittings, and decoration (120a - h), including:
120a Chariot axle
120b Chariot pole
120c [= 133 - 4] Chariot wheels
120d [= 159] Yoke (wood)
120f [= 157] Hawk decoration (wood, gesso, gilt)

121 Chariot body and pole

122 Decorated body of a chariot, its pieces, ornaments, and tackle related to the horses being 122a - rrr, including:

122b Chariot pole

122c [= 131, 136] Wheels

122f [= 160] Hawk ornament (wood, gesso, gold)

122i - k (i) Pairs of blinkers (*122i)

122l Bes-head ornaments

122t Figures of kneeling captives, 4 (gesso gold)

122u Part of whip (wood, gold)

122v - qqq Embossed sheet gold from the harness

123 Parts of portable pavilion

124 - 127 Vases (calcite = Egyptian alabaster)

129 Basket

130 Vase (calcite = Egyptian alabaster)

131 [= 122c] Chariot wheel

132 Chariot wheel

133 [= 120c |Chariot wheel

134 [= 120c] Chariot wheel

135 Group primarily of sticks, canes, etc. (wood) (a - dd), including:

135h Decorated walking - stick

135s, x Sticks with forked bottom

135z Compound bow

135cc Whip handle (wood)

136 [= 122c] Chariot wheel

137 Ammut bed

138 Snake - head amulets, 3

139-140 Folding stool (ebony, ivory, gold, leather)

141 Basket

142a Bouquet of leaves

142b Parts of a stool

143 - 145 Chariot Wheels

146 Basket

147a Sandal

147b Papyrus pad with rings

147c Arrowheads, 7

147d Model tool(?)

147e Part of grinder (sandstone)

147f Sequin (gold)

148a - c Fly whisks (horse hair)

149 Stool (wood) and extra foot

150 - 152 Pieces from chariot and tack

153 Bow

153a Ring (faience)

154 Dish (pottery)

155 - 167, 169 Parts of chariot and tack (including objects previously listed as parts of 120 and 122) (160)

168 Fly whisk (horse hair)

170 Fragment of dish (faience)

171 Doorway leading to the Annexe

Burial Chamber

172 Parts necklace(s)

173, 174 Lamps (calcite = Egyptian alabaster)

175 Trumpet (silver, gold)

175a Stopper

175b Ox ribs

175c Broken label (wood)

175d Fragment of pot with a black substance

176 Figure of goose covered with black resin (wood)

177 Libation pot (pottery)

178, 178a Baskets

179 Various objects (bones, potsherds, fragment of ivory box, wooden label, 2 clay seals)

180 Wine jar

181 Emblem coated with black resin (wood)

182 - 192 Rudders (wood)

193 Pair of kiosks on pedestal, coated with black resin or varnish (wood)

194 Anubis fetish

195 Wine jar

196 Emblem (wood)

197 Jar (pottery)

198 Persea twigs

198a Troughs from 196, 199, 200, 201 (clay)

199 - 201 Emblem (wood)

202 Anubis fetish

203 Jar (pottery)

204 Staff with inlay

205 Funerary bouquet

206 Wine jar

207 First (outermost) shrine

208 Framework for pall 209

209 Pall

210 Vase (calcite = Egyptian alabaster)

211 Cosmetic jar with recumbent lion (calcite = Egyptian alabaster)

212 Palm rib

213 - 236 Almost entirely staffs, sticks, and bows, including:

- 218, 233 Maces (wood)
- 219, 232 *Was*-staffs
- 224 Stick with gold decoration
- 226, 234 Gilt bow
- 229 Cane with gold caps
- 235a Gold stick with figure
- 235b Silver stick with figure

237, 237a Second shrine and its seal and cord (237a)

238, 238a Third shrine and its seal and cord (238a)

239 Fourth (innermost) shrine

240 Sarcophagus

240bis Cosmetic box (gold, silver inlaid)

241 Bow (wood)

242 Ostrich hunt fan (wood, gold, feathers)

243 Arrows

244 Bow (wood, gold)

245 Long fan (ebony, gold, glass)

246 Long bow (wood)

247 Long bow (wood, gold)

248 Arrows

249 Reeds

250 *Djed* emblem (wood)

251 Rags and wood chips

252, 252a Linen sheets covering coffin

253 First (outermost) coffin (wood, gold)

253a Bier (wood)

254 Second coffin (wood, gold)

254a Garland from chest and abdomen of coffin

254a(1) Wreath from around vulture and uraeus

254b Shroud

255 Third (innermost) coffin (gold)

255a Pectoral garland

255b Shrouds

256 Mummy of Tutankhamun, on which were found the following, most of which are gold:

- 256a Golden Mask
- 256b(1) Hands
- *256b(2) *Ba*-bird
- 256b(3) Mummy bands, 6
- 256b(4) Ornamental side strap
- 256c Y-shaped amulet
- 256d Oval plaque
- 256e, mmm Vulture collars
- 256f, nnn Collars with vulture and cobra
- 256g, lll Cobra collars
- 256h, i, p,t, *aa(1)-(2), gg Hawk collars
- 256j Apron
- 256k, dd Daggers and sheaths
- 256l, ee Girdles of sheet gold
- 256m T-shaped amulet
- 256n Wristlet

256o Collar of beads (faience)
256q Scarab (black resin) and wire(gold)
256r Uraeus insignia of diadem 256,4,o
256s Vulture-head insignia of diadem 256,4,o
256u - w,cc, jjon which were found the following. Circlets
256x, pp - ss, ww - aaaon which were found the following.
Bracelets (the number 256ss is used twice)
256y, bb Beads and beadwork
256z Hawk collar (cloisonné work)
256ff, vv, bbb, ccc Finger rings
256hh(1) Amuletic bracelet with lapis lazuli bead
256hh(2) Amuletic bracelet with *wadjet*-eye
256hh(3) Amuletic bracelet with inscribed carnelian bead
256kk *Djed*-amulet
256ll Sandals, finger stalls, toe stalls
256mm Bangle (gold wire)
256nn Part of tail 256eee (beadwork)
256oo *Wadjet*-eye bracelet
256ss Scarab bracelet
256tt, kkk Amuletic knot
256uu Bracelet with carnelian swallow
256ddd Bracelet with lapis lazuli
256eee Tail
256fff *Tjet*-amulet
256ggg *Wadj*-amulet
256hhh *Djed*-amulet
256iii Double-leaf amulet
256iiibis *Djet*-serpent amulet
256jjj Leaf amulet
256ooo - qqq, uuu, vvv Pectoral with inlay
256rrr *Wadjet*-eye (faience)
256sss String of beads
256ttt Bead collar with hawk-headed clasps
256www Amuletic bracelet
256xxx Anubis amulet
256yyy Horus amulet
256zzz Serpent-headed amulet
256,4,a Thoth amulet
256,4,b Wadj amulet
256,4,c Large bead
256,4,d Chain
256,4,e Pectoral clasps and pendants, 5
256,4,f Human-headed winged uraeus amulet
256,4,g Double uraeus
256,4,h - j, l Vulture amulets
256,4,k Uraeus amulet
256,4,m Bead collar
256,4,n Fillets (fabric) bound with string
256,4,o Diadem
256,4,p Temple band
256,4,p,bis Headdress (linen)
256,4,q Uraeus insignia of headdress
256,4,p,bis 256,4,r Vulture insignia of headdress
256,4,p,bis 256,4,s Temple band
256,4,t Skull - cap (linen)
256, Linen pad
256, 4, v Amuletic head-rest (iron)
257 Niche in Burial Chamber wall with figure of Osiris
258 Niche in Burial Chamber wall with figure of Anubis
259 Niche in Burial Chamber wall with *shabti*-like figure
260 Niche in Burial Chamber wall with *djed* emblem (wood)

Treasury

261 Anubis shrine covered by linen (261a, b), floral collars (261c), and neck scarf (261d) and containing numerous objects (261e(1) - r), including figures, amuletic jewelry, and other objects, including:

261e(2 - 3), f(2 - 3) Foreleg of an ox, wrapped in linen (faience)

261f(1),(5) Small *shabti* figure wrapped in linen (wood)

261f(4) Figure of Horus (faience)

261f(6) *Wadj* - scepter wrapped in linen (faience)

261g(2) Figure of Thoth (faience)

261g(3) Figure of a heron (beeswax)

261h Small cups, 2 (calcite = Egyptian alabaster)

261i *Djed* pectoral

261j Scarab pectoral

261k *Djed* amulet

261m Large pectoral

261n Pectoral in the form of a pylon

261o Pectoral of Osiris

261p(1) Pectoral of Nut

261p(2) Pectoral with Isis and Nephthys

261p(3) Vulture pectoral

261q Fragment of broken clay seal

262 Ivory scribal palette belonging to Meritaten

263 Reed torch on mud brick

264 Head of Hathor

265 Tazze, 3 (calcite = Egyptian alabaster)

266 Canopy on sledge with figures of Isis, Nephthys, Neith and Selket (wood, gold), in which was found:

266a Canopic chest (wood, gold)

266b Canopic box (calcite = Egyptian alabaster) on sledge covered with linen

266c - f Lids of canopic jars (calcite = Egyptian alabaster)

266g Canopic coffinettes (gold)

267 Casket (ivory, ebony) containing mostly jewelry and pieces of jewelry, including:

267a, p Breast ornaments in form of "Nebkheperure"

267d Pendant with scarab (chalcedony)

267e Heh counterpoise

267f Model of a heron (wax)

267g,h Flexible pectoral with chains and counterpoise

267i Breast ornament in form of vulture

267j Counterpoise

267k Open - work breast ornament

267l Necklace of birth of the sun

267m(1) Breast ornament in form of hawk

267n Pendant with winged scarab (lapis)

267o Breast ornament in form of vulture 2/1

267q "Coronation" pectoral, with Tutankhamun, Ptah and Sekhmet

268 Casket

269 Casket in the form of a cartouche containing primarily a box (269a), pieces of jewelry, and scepters, including:

269a Small box containing:

269a(1 - 3, 5, 6) Ear-rings

269a(4) Heart scarab

269b Mirror case in form of *ankh*

269c(1 - 3) Shawls

269d, h Crook

269i - j Bands and counterpoise for pectoral 267q

269e - f Flails 269g Bracelet with large scarab

269k Pectoral ornament with of lunar symbols

269m Bracelet with amethyst scarab

269n Bracelet with scarab

270 Box with vaulted lid (wood), containing a few miscellaneous objects (270a - c)

270a Sandal - like slippers (leather, gold, beads)

270b Lid of box 269a

270c Anklet (schist)

271 Casket containing various objects (271a - h):

271b Scribal palette(ivory)

271c, d Mirror cases

271e(1) Brush holder

271e(2) Scribal palette (wood, gold)

271f Bowl (ivory)

"271g Papyrus burnisher (ivory)

272 Box with vaulted lid (wood) containing

272a Fan (ivory, ostrich feathers)

272b Persea fruit, 3

273 Model boat

274 Strainers, 2

275 Chest in the form of a shrine containing the following figures:

275a Ihy

275b, d Tutankhamun

275c, e Tutankhamun as a harpooner

276 Model boat with rigging

277 Model granary

278 Wood chips

279, 279a Box containing model hand-mill for grinding grain

280, 280a Chest in the form of a shrine containing figure of Imsety

281, 281a Chest in the form of a shrine containing figure of Mamu

282, 282a	Chest in the form of a shrine containing figure of Shu
283	Square chest containing the following figures:
283a	Serpent named Netjer-ankh
283b	Soped falcon
283c	Gemehsu falcon
284 - 287	Model boats
288, 288a	Box containing germinating Osiris figure
289	Chest in the form of a shrine containing the following figures:
	289a - b Tutankhamun on a leopard, 2
	289c Ihy
290, 290a	Chest in the form of a shrine containing figure of Atum
291, 291a	Chest in the form of a shrine containing figure of Ptah
292, 292a	Chest in the form of a shrine containing figure of Tatanen
293, 293a	Chest in the fcrm of a shrine containing figure of Harwer
294, 294a	Chest in the fcrm of a shrine containing figure of Sened
295, 295a	Chest in the form of a shrine containing figure of Isis
296, 296a - b	Chest in the form of a shrine containing figure of Menkaret (296a) supporting figure of Tutankhamun (296b)
297, 297a	Chest in the form of a shrine containing figure of Kheperyu
298, 298a	Chest in the form of a shrine containing figure of Horus of Letopolis
299, 299a	Chest in the form of a shrine containing figure of Geb
300, 300a	Chest in the form of a shrine containing figure of Sekhmet
301, 301a	Chest in the form of a shrine containing figure of Hapi
302, 302a	Chest in the form of a shrine containing figure of Duamutef
303, 303a	Chest in the form of a shrine containing figure of Tata
304, 304a - b	Chest in the form of a shrine containing figures of Qebehsenuf and Duamutef
305, 305a	Chest in the form of a shrine containing figure of Nephthys
306 - 314	Model boats
315	Box
316	Box containing model tools (iron and wood) (316a - p)
317	Box containing:
317a	Nest of two coffins, 317a; inner coffin 317a(1) containing
317a(2)	Mummy of a fetus
317b	Nest of two coffins; inner coffin 317b(1) containing
317b(2)	Mummy of a fetus
318	Kiosk containing *shabtis* (318a - c)
319	Kiosk containing *shabtis* (319a - o) and miniature tools (319p)
320	Miniature coffin containing:
320a	Second miniature coffin
320b	Third miniature coffin
320c	Statuette of Amenophis III (gold)
320d	Fourth (innermost) miniature coffin
320e	Lock of plaited hair
321	Model boat with rigging
322	Kiosk containing *shabtis* (322a - k)
323	Kiosk containing *shabtis* (323a - q)
324	Kiosk containing *shabtis* (324a - t) and miniature tools (324u)
325	Kiosk containing *shabtis* (325a - f) and miniature tools (325g)
326	Kiosk containing *shabtis* (326a - y) and miniature tools (326z)
327	Kiosk containing *shabtis* (327a - nn) and miniature tools (327oo)
328	Kiosk containing *shabtis* (328a - n) and miniature tools (328o)
329	Kiosk containing *shabtis* (329a - l) and miniature tools (329m - n)
330	Box containing shabtis (330a - o), model scepters (330p), and model tools (330q)
331	Box containing:
331a	Figure of Tutankhamun lying on a funeral bier (wood)
331b	Model tools (bronze)
332	Chariot
333	Chariot and whip
334	Model boat
335	Bow-case

Annexe

336 Model boat with rigging
337 Kiosk containing *shabtis* (quartzite) (337a - c) and miniature tools (337d)
338 Basket
339 Amphora (calcite = Egyptian alabaster)
340 Jar (calcite = Egyptian alabaster)
341 - 342 Baskets
343 Vase (calcite = Egyptian alabaster)
344 Vase (calcite, inlay)
345 Game-box (ebony, ivory)
346 - 348 Baskets
349 Small chair (wood)
350 Shield
351 Folding stool
352 Model boat
353 Unguent jar (calcite = Egyptian alabaster)
354 Hassock
355 - 358 Baskets basket (medium size)
360 Unguent vase (calcite = Egyptian alabaster)
361 Hassock
362 Wine jar
363 - 366 Baskets Oval basket
367 Box containing various objects and parts of objects (367a - r), including:
367a Parts of portable pavilion, 2
367b Sandal (grass)
367d Vase (violet faience)
367e Scarf
367f Pair of gloves
367k Box in the form of a cartouche (wood)
367o Boomerang (wood)
367q - r Forelegs of ox, 19 (faience)
368 Basket
370 Bow box containing:
370a - f Clubs (wood)
370h - i Sickle-shaped weapons (wood)
370k - ee Boomerangs and throw-sticks (some ritual)
370ff - ll Bow staffs
370mm Fragments of bow strings
370nn - zz Arrows
371 - 372 Baskets
373 Pair of sandals
374 Aryballos (serpentine)
375 Model boat
376 Lid of box 548
377 Bedstead (wood, stucco, gold)
378 Footrest
379a - b Shields
380 Kiosk containing *shabtis* (380a - g) and miniature tools (380h) (faience)
381 - 382 Baskets
383 Drawer from game box 345 (wood)
384 Basket
385 Amphora (calcite = Egyptian alabaster)
386 Piece of board with hieratic docket, from lid 537 of box 388
387 Small, thin board (writing horn?) (wood)
388 Table - shaped box
389 Fan stock
390 Arrows, 13
391 Basket
392 Wine jar
*393 Game board (ivory)
394 Vase (gold)
395 - 396 Baskets
*397 Pair of sandals with enemy figures
398 Writing horn
399a Unguent vase (violet faience)
399b Flat lozenge-shaped ritual object(faience)
400 - 401 Baskets
402 Handle of adze (bronze, gold)
403 Table-shaped box containing:
403a - d Head-rests (*403a, c, d)
403e Decayed fragment of robe
404 Vase with name of Thutmose III (calcite = Egyptian alabaster)
405 Vase (calcite = Egyptian alabaster)
406 Crater (pottery)
407 Amphora (calcite = Egyptian alabaster)
408 Vase (calcite = Egyptian alabaster)
409 Wine jar
410 Amphora with name of Thutmose III (calcite = Egyptian alabaster)
411 Wine jar
412 Three-legged stool, painted white (wood)
413 Wine jar
414 Footrest
415 Stock of fan
416 Basket
*417 Double amphora (calcite = Egyptian alabaster)

418	Kiosk containing *shabtis* (418a - g) and miniature tools (418h)
419	Baskets
420	Unguent vase (calcite = Egyptian alabaster)
421	Vase (calcite = Egyptian alabaster)
422	Basket
423	Aryballos (calcite = Egyptian alabaster)
424 - 429	Baskets
430	Arrows, 17
431	Wine jar
431b	Hassock
432	Wine-jar seal
433	Basket
434	Wine jar
435	Unguent vase (calcite = Egyptian alabaster)
436	Basket
437	Model boat
438	Poles from portable pavilion, 3
439 - 441	Basket and remains of baskets
442a	Decayed fragments of mat (linen)
442b	Footrest
442c	Ritualistic palette
442d	Remains of mats (reed, linen)
442e	Footrest
443 - 447	Baskets
448 - 449	Vases (calcite = Egyptian alabaster)
450 - 452	Baskets
453, 453b	Box containing fragments of a sandal
454 - 455	Baskets
456a	Pieces of bead-work
456b	Lumps of galena
457	Fragment of broken papyrus covering of a rushwork support
458	*Shabti*
459	Kiosk containing shabtis (calcite = Egyptian alabaster) (459a - g) and 84 tools (459h)
460	Model boat
461	Box containing:
461a - q	*Nemset* - vases (faience) (*461b)
*461r - y	Heset vases (faience)
462 - *464	Model boats
465	Pole from portable pavilion
466	Bedstead (wood, gold)
467	Four-legged stool, painted (wood, gold)
468a - o	Sticks and staffs
469	Pomegranate vase (silver) 2/1
470 - 474	Baskets
475	Vase (calcite, inlay)
476 - 478	Baskets
479 - 480	Bowls (calcite = Egyptian alabaster)
481	Model boat
482	Vase (calcite = Egyptian alabaster)
483	Jug with name of Amenhotep III (calcite = Egyptian alabaster)
484	Basket
485	Bowl (calcite = Egyptian alabaster)
486	Wine jar
487	Box (possibly for cubit measure), containing:
	488a Shield (part of a pair with shield 492)
	488b Shield
489 - 490	Wine jars
491	Model boat
492	Shield (part of a pair with shield 488a)
493	Box
494	Lid of box
495	Basket
496	Kiosk containing *shabtis* (496a - e) and miniature tools (496f)
497	Bedstead
498 - 502	Wine jars and fragment of a wine jar
503	Stopper for jar
504 - 507	Baskets
508 - 509	Wine jars
510	Basket
511	Footrest
512	Kiosk containing *shabtis* (512a - e) and miniature tools (512f)
513	Model boat
514	Kiosk containing *shabtis* (514a - d) and miniature tools (514e)
515	Basket
516	Wine jar
517	Kiosk containing *shabtis* (517a - h) and miniature tools (517i)
518	Baskets
519	Kiosk containing *shabtis* (517a - f) and miniature tools (517g)
520	Bell-shaped vessel on a stem (calcite = Egyptian alabaster)
521	Basket
522	Lid of box
523	Wine jar
524	Vase (calcite = Egyptian alabaster)
525	Triple string of disk-beads (faience)
526 - 528	Baskets
529	Lid of 519
530 - 535	Baskets
536	Fragments of wine jar
537	Lid (of box 388)
538	Basket
539	Wine jar 2/3
540	Lid of casket 551
541	Wine jar
542 - 544	Baskets
545	Shield (wood, hide) (part of a pair with shield 566)
546	Lid of box 550

547 Headdress box containing various small objects:
- 547a Fragment of cap
- 547b Double circlet
- 547c Bracelet
- 547d Head-rest
- 547e Ornament (gold)

548, 548a Box containing head-rest
549 Wine jar
550 Box
551 Ornamental casket (lid is 540)
552 - 555 Baskets
556 Model boat
557 Rushwork
558 - 559b Baskets
560 Wine jar
561 Ritual sickle (wood, gold, electrum, glass, calcite)
562 Basket
563 Wine jar
564 - 565 Baskets
566 Shield (part of a pair with shield 545)
567 Basket
568 Wine jar
569 Basket
570 - 571 Wine jars
572 Part of model boat
573a - f Baskets
574 Lid of box 79
575 Lid of box 594
576 Foot panel of bedstead 497
577 *Sekhem* sceptre
578 Boat in tank (calcite = Egyptian alabaster)
579 Lion - shaped unguent vessel (calcite = Egyptian alabaster)
580 Four - legged stool belonging to game box 345
581 Model boat
582 Group of sticks and other weapons including:
582a Scimitar (bronze)
582b Staff
582c - i Sword-sticks
583 Jar (calcite = Egyptian alabaster)
584 Vase in the form of an ibex (calcite = Egyptian alabaster)
585 Chest (wood) containing many small objects (585a - dd), including:
- 585a - h, q Bracelets (ivory)
- 585i - l Braclets (wood)

585m Bracelet (horn)
585r Game board (ivory)
585u Mandrake fruit, 2, one with name of Thutmose III (blue glass)
585v Pair of knuckle-bones (resin)
585y Slings (for throwing stones), 2 (linen)
585z Archer's gloves (leather) with arm guards (linen)
585aa Fire bow and drill
585cc Archer's wrist guards for hunting
586 Folding bedstead
587 Box containing several small objects:
- 587a Cuirass (leather)
- 587b *Tjet* amulet (faience)
- 587c Pair of sandals
- 587d *Djed* amulet (glass)1/0

588 Single-handled jar with names of Amenhotep III and Tiye (calcite = Egyptian alabaster)
589a - c Baskets
590 Rushwork
591 Basket
592 Footrest (wood)
593 Games box (wood, ivory, gold)
594 Box
595 Stool
596 Bundle of fan, sticks, etc:
- 596a Stock of fan with name of Akhenaten
- 596b - j Sticks
- 596k - t Bow staffs 396u - v Arrows

597 Model boat
598 Part of a model boat
599 - 600 Stocks of fans
601 *Shabti* (wood)
602 Kiosk containing *shabtis* (602a - f) and miniature tools (602g)
603 Vase (calcite = Egyptian alabaster)
604 Vase (calcite = Egyptian alabaster)
605 Kiosk containing *shabtis* (605a - g) and miniature tools (605g)
606a - d Supports for bedstead
607 Group of weapons:
- 607a - 3 Clubs (wood)
- 607f Boomerang (ebony)

608 Kiosk containing *shabtis* (608a - e) and miniature tools (608f)
609 - 610 Model boats
611 Kiosk containing *shabtis* (611a - c) and miniature tools (611d)
612 Model Boat
613 Footrest (wood)
614 Group of vessels (pottery) (614 - ak)
615 Lid of box 547
616 Basket
617 Model boat
618 Basket
619 Group of ornaments (gold), wire (gold), and decayed leather
619a - d Sword - stick guards (probably for 582c - f)

620 "Rubbish" found on the floor:

620(1)	Lid of vase (calcite = Egyptian alabaster)
620(2)	Dish (calcite = Egyptian alabaster)
620(3)	Bowl (?) (calcite = Egyptian alabaster)
620(4 - 6)	Boomerangs (ivory)
620(7 - 10)	Throw - sticks
620(11 - 12)	Snake batons
620(13)	Pair of castanets (ivory) 3/0
620(13)	Ivory ape or monkey 3/0
620(14 - 17)	Amuletic *was* - scepters (faience)
620(18 - 20)	*Tjet* - amulets (faience)
620(21 - 23)	*Djed* - amulets (faience)
620(24)	*Ankh* - amulet (faience)
620(25)	*Tjet* - amulet (wood)
620(26)	*Djed* - amulet (wood)
620(27)	Amuletic(?) mallet (faience)
620(28)	Lozenge - shaped amulet (faience) 1/0
620(29 - 30)	Vases (faience)
620(31 - 32)	*Heset* vases (faience)
620(33)	Small libation vase (faience)
620(34)	Small saucer (faience)
620(35 - 36)	Pair of vases (wood)
620(37)	Aryballos (silver)
620(38, 40 - 42)	Bracelet (faience)
620(39)	Armlet (faience armlet)
620(43 - 45)	Anklets
620(46)	Bracelet (lapis lazuli)
620(47 - 49)	Ear (or hair) rings
620(50)	Metal ornament
620(51)	Dog (bronze)
620(52)	Scimitar (bronze)
620(53)	Razor (bronze)
620(54)	Spatula (bronze spatula)
620(55)	Hones of grit - stone, 4
620(56)	Handle from chisel(?)
620(57)	Modeler's tool (wood)
620(58)	Tool (for leather work?)
620(59)	Tool (wood)
620(60 - 61)	Scimitar (*khepesh*) amulets) (gold)
620(62 - 63)	Flint knives (amuletic?)
620(64)	Sickle (wood)
620(65)	Glass rods
620(66a - g)	Finger-rings with royal names (faience)
620(66h - w)	Finger-rings (faience)
620(67)	Heart amulet inlaid with a heron
620(68 - 78)	Amulets
620(79 - 81)	Pigments in bivalve shells (black, red, white)
620(82)	Lumps of white material (pigment?), 2
620(83)	Lumps of red ochre
620(84)	Bivalve shell
620(85)	Cake of greenish-blue pigment in bivalve shell
620(86)	Orpiment
620(87)	Blue frit
620(88)	Grey (almost black) substance
620(89 - 93, 114)	Scribal Palettes (*620(92))
620(94)	Pair of ear-studs
620(95)	Box in the form of a cartouche (wood)
620(96 - 109)	Labels with hieratic inscriptions (wood)
620(110)	Gaming-sticks, 2 pairs (ivory)
620(111)	Most of a lid of a small ornamental box
620(112)	Loaves of bread or cakes
620(113)	*Shabti*
620(115)	238 miniature tools from *shabtis*
620(116)	Jar-stand with hieratic inscription (calcite = Egyptian alabaster)
620(117)	Loaves or cakes containing fruit, 2
620(118)	Parts of portable pavilion
620(119)	Sandals, 32 pairs
620(120)	Spur
620(121)	Lid of painted box
620(122)	Jar-stand (calcite jar)
620(123)	Double circlet

APPENDIX 2

OBJECTS OF TUTANKHAMUN IN MUSEUMS WORLDWIDE

KV 62 VALLEY OF THE KINGS, THEBAN NECROPOLIS

The outermost coffin, which has been restored by the Getty Conservation Institute, remains in the sarcophagus in KV 62. The king's mummy remains in the tomb, as well.

EGYPTIAN MUSEUM, CAIRO

There are records for 4,500 objects of Tutankhamun in the Egyptian Museum at Tahrir Square in Cairo. All of the objects are displayed in rooms on the upper floor of the museum.

In Room 4 are the middle and innermost coffin that protected the mummy. Also in Room 4 is the golden mask and other jewelry and objects found during the unwrapping of Tutankhamun's mummy.

Other objects are shown in Gallery Nos. 15, 20, 25, 30, 35, 40, and 45. In Gallery Nos. 8, 9, and 10 are the animal couches, the canopic assemblage, and the shrines.

AGRICULTURAL MUSEUM, CAIRO

The Agricultural Museum is located at Dokki. Here, the visitor may see a great deal of botanical material from the tomb.

KASR EL AINI HOSPITAL, CAIRO

The two mummified fetuses found in the tomb were placed by Douglas Derry at this hospital, which belongs to the Faculty of Medicine at Cairo University. The two fetuses are now in poor condition because of lack of proper conservation.

OBJECTS IN STORAGE IN THE EGYPTIAN MUSEUM, CAIRO

- 360 arrows
- 12 bows
- 1 long bow string
- textiles and garments including 2 collars with sequins, 3 gloves, 11 gauntlets, 30 head cloths, 120 loin cloths, 23 scarves, 12 shawls, fragments of various garments, 7 pieces of linen, 2 cloth strip for binding, 36 rolls of bandages, 6 strips of linen, 1 small bag, 1 scrap of rope
- 2 cords-and-tassels, 2 bracers, 24 linen coverings from gilded figures of gods
- 1 part of the great ball of linen, 1 sample of cloth reserved for study, 1 wrapping, 2 rugs, 2 tassels, 22 sandals
- 2 boxes of various objects
- 8 wine jars
- 41 sticks;
- 41 wooden boxes for food offerings
- 23 bowls;
- 1 head-rest
- 1 vase
- 4 jugs
- 1 dish
- 1 bracelet
- 13 beads
- 6 pieces of gilt gesso from the pall support
- 6 pieces of unknown black material from the floor
- 4 pieces of resin
- contents of a basket
- 1 faience fragment
- 1 boomerang
- 1 part of a tenon from a shrine
- 1 fragment possibly from a chariot
- botanical remains including barley, melon seeds, *Ziziphus spina-christi* fruit and seeds, fibre, coriander seeds, persea fruit, date fruit and seeds, dom palm nuts, etc.

OBJECTS IN STORAGE AT THE GRAND EGYPTIAN MUSEUM, CAIRO

These objects were moved from storage in the Egyptian Museum to the storage facilities at the Grand Egyptian Museum:

- 20 arrows with flared ends (one arrow is in the Luxor Museum with register no. 3570, made of wood and reed
- 3 arrows with bullet-shaped top (reed and bronze)
- 5 arrows with tips missing (reed, one arrow is in the Luxor Museum, register no. 3577)
- 7 arrows with almost blunt tips (reed); arrow with pointed bronze point (reed and bronze)
- 2 arrows with bronze heads, traces of feather fletching (reed)
- 2 arrows with spear-shaped tip (reed, wood, bronze; one is in the Luxor Museum with register no. 3608)
- 25 arrows with spear-shaped tip (reed, bronze, wood)
- 26 arrows with pointed tips (reed, wood)
- 38 arrows with bullet-shaped tip (reed and bronze)
- 26 arrows with spear-shaped tips (reed, bronze; two are in the Luxor Museum, register nos. 3701, 3716)
- 7 arrows with head of plain wood and paint (reed, wood)
- 7 arrows with ivory tips (reed, ivory; one is in the Luxor Museum, register no. 3732)
- 7 arrows with string recesses of bone and wood heads (wood, read, bone)
- 2 arrows with bullet-shaped tip and ivory notch for string (reed, bronze);
- 24 arrows with bullet-shaped tips (reed, bronze)
- 7 arrows with pointed wooden heads (reed, wood).

OBJECTS IN THE LUXOR MUSEUM, LUXOR

- Head of Hathor as a cow (gilded wood, cooper, lapis lazuli)
- Model boat (wood)
- Model boat adorned with a royal head with *atef*-crown (wood)
- Pair of sandals (plant fiber)
- Pair of small sandals (plant fiber)
- Arrow with a bronze tip (wood, bronze)
- Arrow without its tip (wood)
- Arrow with a bronze tip (wood, bronze)
- 2 Arrows with bone heads (wood, bone)
- Head of a statue of god Amun wearing a crown, with the features of Tutankh-amun (limestone)
- 5 Oval baskets with lids (palm leaf) Bed with lion legs (wood)
- 3 Naos (shrines) (wood)
- 2 Rectangular boxes with vaulted lid (wood)
- *Shabti* holding a *heqa*-scepter (gilded wood)
- 3 *shabtis* with cartouche of Tutankh-amun (gilded wood)
- Headrest (wood)
- Statue of the god Amun with Tutankh-amun's features (limestone)
- Statue of Tutankhamun as a sphinx (Egyptian marble)
- Sling (fiber) for slingshot
- 2 Bows (gilded wood)
- Long bow with golden tips (wood)
- Long bow (gilded wood)
- Bow with names of Tutankhamun (gold, wood, linen) (Thebes Hall)

OBJECTS IN STORAGE IN THE LUXOR MUSEUM, LUXOR

- Arrow with bronze head (bronze, wood)
- 14 Oval baskets (palm leaf)
- Naos (wood)
- Rectangular box with vaulted lid (wood)

OBJECTS IN STORAGE ON THE WEST BANK OF LUXOR

The following objects were moved to temporary storage quarters on the west bank:

- A number of boxes with the cartouche of Tutankhamun (wood)
- A group of mud seals with inscriptions and seals of Tutankhamun
- A group of pottery vessels of different sizes and shapes
- A group of funerary furnishings of different sizes and shapes (baskets)
- A group of 30 boxes with vaulted lids

The following objects are in storage on the west bank:

- Baskets of fruit (dom-palm and *Zizi-phus spina-christi*)
- Baskets of fruit (dom-palm and *Zizi-phus spina-christi*) with lids
- Wooden box with lid on which is the name Nebkheperure
- Seals of the doorway of the tomb

All of these objects now in storage at the Luxor Museum and on the west bank were brought there by John Romer when he cleaned KV 4 (tomb of Rameses XI) be-tween 1977 and 1979. This tomb had been used for storage by Howard Carter during the excavation of KV 62.

OBJECTS RETURNED BY THE METROPOLITAN MUSEUM OF ART (MMA), NEW YORK

In 2007, I had lunch with Philippe de Montebello, director of the Metropolitan Museum, and David Rockefeller, the American banker, at a hotel. I asked de Montebello to return to Cairo pieces from Tutankhamun's tomb held in the museum's collections, and he told me that it was not in his hands to do so.

I later told this story to Dorothea Arnold, curator of the Egyptian Art Department. I could see that in her heart she wanted to fulfill my request, but she did not have the authority. I am sure that she spoke to Thomas Campbell when he became the MMA's new director. The MMA has always helped to train young Egyptian Egyptologists and has also aided in the recovery of stolen artifacts. Campbell, Arnold, and another Egyptologist with the MMA, Marsha Hill, came to me with a letter. This was their proposal: "We are very pleased to advise that the Metropolitan Museum of Art's Board of Trustees has authorized the Museum to enter into a dialogue with Egypt concerning 19 works in its collection which the Museum has identified as coming from the tomb of Tutankhamun."

Through negotiation, the MMA agreed to show the pieces for six months with the Tutankhamun and the Golden Age of the Pharaohs exhibit at the Discovery Times Square Exposition in New York, and then for another six months at the MMA. Then the objects would come back to Egypt in 2011, in the care of Atef Abou el Dahab, vice head of the Pharaonic Sector of the SCA.

What the MMA has done sets a great example for other museums to follow.

These are the objects formerly in the collection of the Metropolitan Museum of Art in New York that are now in the collection of the Egyptian Museum in Cairo:

1. Finger ring with the prenomen of Tutankhamun
2. Finger ring with the prenomen of Tutankhamun
3. Nail from the second (middle) coffin of Tutankhamun
4. Nail from the third (innermost) coffin of Tutankhamun
5. Fragments of wood from within the innermost shrine of Tutankhamun
6. Hardened, partly resinous dark fluid in a glass beaker
7. Nail from the tomb (gold)
8. Nail (silver with gilded head)
9. Rosette from pall that hung within the outermost shrine in the burial chamber
10. Fragments of pall from within the outermost shrine in the burial chamber
11. Textile fragment
12. Fragment from a linen bag
13. Fragments of matting
14. Fragments from the innermost shrine in the burial chamber
15. Fragments of the sarcophagus(?)
16. Figurine of a puppy
17. Bracelet inlay in the form of a sphinx
18. Broad collar and two dishes of beads
19. Part of a handle of a fan(?)

OBJECTS OUTSIDE OF EGYPT

Objects related to Howard Carter are now held in collections in a variety of American cities, including Brooklyn, Detroit, Saint Louis, and Kansas City and, of course, Highclere Castle in Hampshire, England, home of the Carnavons. Specimens from the tomb were sent to the Royal Botanic Gardens, Kew (botanical specimens) and the Victoria and Albert Museum, London (linen fragments).

Artifacts and other remains from KV 54, the pit containing the remains of Tutankhamun's mummification and funerary feast, are in the Metropolitan Museum of Art, the American Museum of Natural History, and elsewhere.

MONUMENTS CONNECTED WITH KING TUTANKHAMUN

At Giza: remains of a rest house south of the Valley Temple of Khafre.

Two blocks with scenes of Tutankhamun found being used as part of a house foundation. One shows Tutankhamun smiting an enemy and the second shows Tutankhamun seated, shooting an arrow, with Ankhesenamun seated at his feet.

A tomb situated to the west of the Red Monastery (Sohag) with inscriptions clearly dating the tomb to the reign of Tutankhamun.

Saqqara:
- Tomb of Maya, treasurer.
- Tomb of Maia, wet-nurse.
- Tomb of Horemheb, general.

Blocks with the king's name in the Ashmunein storage magazine.

Additions made by Tutankhamun at the Temple of Thutmose III at Medinet el-Ghorab.

Scenes of the Festival of Opet in the Great Colonnade Hall in the Temple of Luxor.

The tomb of Huy (TT 40) on the west bank of Luxor.

Wooden box overlaid with gold leaf found by Émile Amélineau at Om el-Gaab (1895–1899).

Two colossal standing statues in red quartzite inscribed by Ay and usurped by Horemheb (source unknown).

Additional monuments and bibliographic citations may be found by consulting B. Porter and R. L. B. Moss, *Topographical Bibliography of Ancient Egyptian Hieroglyphic Texts, Reliefs, and Paintings, Vol. 2: Theban Temples*, 2nd ed. (Oxford, 1972), 558.

APPENDIX 3

Objects from Tutankhamun's tomb first traveled abroad in 1961 as an introduction to ancient Egypt.
The exhibit was displayed in Washington, DC from 1961–1962, then went on to tour many other cities in the United States, Canada, and elsewhere around the world:

TUTANKHAMUN'S TOURS

Tutankhamun Treasures

UNITED STATES

WASHINGTON, DC
National Gallery of Art
3rd November – 3rd December 1961
247,054 visitors

PHILADELPHIA, PENNSYLVANIA
University Museum
15th December 1961 – 14th January 1962

NEW HAVEN, CONNECTICUT
Peabody Museum of Natural History
1st – 28th February 1962

HOUSTON, TEXAS
Museum of Fine Arts
15th March – 15th April 1962

OMAHA, NEBRASKA
1st – 31st May 1962

CHICAGO, ILLINOIS
Oriental Institute
15th June – 15th July 1962
125,000 visitors

SEATTLE, WASHINGTON
Seattle Art Museum
1st – 31st August 1962

SAN FRANCISCO, CALIFORNIA
California Palace of the Legion of Honor
15th September – 14th October 1962

LOS ANGELES
Los Angeles County Museum of Art
30th October – 30th November 1962
118,403 visitors

CLEVELAND, OHIO
Cleveland Museum of Art
15th December 1962 – 13th January 1963

BOSTON, MASSACHUSETTS
Museum of Fine Arts
1st – 28th February 1963

SAINT LOUIS, MISSOURI
City Art Museum of Saint Louis
15th March – 14th April 1963

BALTIMORE, MARYLAND
Walters Art Gallery
1st – 31st May 1963

DAYTON, OHIO
Dayton Art Institute
15th June – 15th July 1963
30,000 visitors

DETROIT, MICHIGAN
Detroit Institute of Arts
August – September 1963

TOLEDO, OHIO
Toledo Museum of Art
15th September – 15th October 1963

RICHMOND, VIRGINIA
Richmond Museum of Art
November 1963

NEW YORK
Carnegie International Center
19th December 1963 – 15th January 1964

(More than 1,300,000 people saw this tour in the United States.)

CANADA

MONTREAL, QUEBEC
The Montreal Museum of Fine Arts
January 1964 – 23rd February 1964

WINNIPEG, MANITOBA
December 1964 – January 1965

VANCOUVER, BRITISH COLOMBIA
January – February 1965

QUEBEC CITY, QUEBEC
March – April 1965

The Tutankhamun Exhibition

(45 objects)

JAPAN

TOKYO
Tokyo National Museum
21st August – October 1965
1,300,000 visitors

KYOTO
Kyoto National Museum
October – November 1965

FUKUOKA
Fukuoka Prefectural Culture Center
December 1965 – January 1966
586,000 visitors

Tutankhamun and His Time

(45 objects)

FRANCE

PARIS

Petit Palais

2nd February – 4th September 1967

1,240,975 visitors

Treasures of Tutankhamun

(50 objects)

GREAT BRITAIN

LONDON

British Museum

29th March – 1th April 1972

1,694,117 visitors

Treasures of Tutankhamun's Tomb

(50 objects)

UNION OF SOVIET SOCIALIST REPUBLICS

MOSCOW, RUSSIA

Pushkin Museum of Fine Arts

December 1973 – May 1974

LENINGRAD, RUSSIA

Hermitage Museum

July – November 1974

KIEV, UKRAINE

National Art Museum of Ukraine

January – March 1975

How the "Treasures of Tutankhamun" came to the United States in the 1970s is a story unto itself. An important source appears in the 10th December 1978, issue of ***LI***, a weekly magazine published by *Newsday*. Amei Wallach, the well-known art critic, interviewed Thomas Hoving, who had just left his position as director of the Metropolitan Museum of Art (MMA). Gamal Mokhtar, who was a very good friend of mine after he left the Egyptian Antiquities Organization (EAO), was another invaluable source of information.

In the interview, Hoving said that Mokhtar, the chairman of the EAO, was on a trip to the United States in 1974 when he stopped in New York and had lunch at the MMA with Hoving. According to Hoving, during lunch Mokhtar asked him if the American people had any interest in seeing the treasures of Tutankhamun. Hoving said to Wallach, "I lurched across the table and wrestled a ballpoint pen into his fingers and attempted to have him sign the tablecloth. We would fill in the rest of the tablecloth as a contract."

Gamal Mokhtar himself told Ali Radwan, professor of Egyptology at Cairo University, and me a different story. When Mokhtar was visiting the son of his sister in Los Angeles, Hoving asked him to stop in New York on his way back. Hoving was the one who wanted Tutankhamun to come to the United States. He asked Mokhtar, not the other way around. Mokhtar told Hoving that it was difficult to make that kind of decision, because if he did, the Egyptian press would attack him. Mokhtar explained that every time Tutankhamun traveled, it had to do with politics. Each of the recent visits to the Soviet Union, England, and France, had happened for some political reason.

It just so happened that President Richard Nixon was planning to visit Egypt. Mokhtar told Hoving that if Nixon asked President Anwar Sadat for Tutankhamun, then things would be much easier.

It seems that Hoving contacted people in the U.S. State Department to ask Nixon to make this request. Nixon arrived in Cairo, greeted by millions of people. This was the first time an American president had visited Egypt. Nixon asked Sadat for Tutankhamun, and Sadat agreed.

The next year, 1975, the Minister of Culture informed Mokhtar of Sadat's permission, and Mokhtar conveyed the news to Hoving.

Now the American venues had to be chosen. Hoving had the U.S. State Department do this because if he was in charge of who would – and who would not – get the exhibit, his decisions would earn him enemies all across America. But Mokhtar told Hoving that the Metropolitan Museum of Art had to be completely responsible for all the arrangements of the exhibitions, including the contracts, insurance, transportation, everything – including selection of the objects. Especially because he would also have to raise the funding to bring the exhibit to the United States, Hoving was hesitant to agree. But he and the MMA had to agree to these terms. They had to bring Tutankhamun to the United States, and Mokhtar had told him that this was the only way to do it.

So Hoving came to Cairo with two colleagues from the MMA, Richard Morsches, the museum's operations chief, and Christine Lilyquist, curator of the Egyptian Art Department. Together, they chose the objects and also negotiated the contract. This was in 1975. They wanted to take the golden throne, but the curators of the Egyptian Museum warned that the throne, which had stood in its showcase since 1932, was too fragile. Instead they took the cedar throne and also the head of Tutankhamun as Nefertem. Lilyquist had such good relations with one of the curators that she was able to choose the 55 best objects from the collection – including the Golden Mask. If I could send this now as part of an exhibit, it would bring many, many millions of dollars to Egypt.

During the contract talks, Mokhtar often said that the Egyptian people had a complex about America and so he was careful when he negotiated the contract. Then Mokhtar and Hoving went to see Sadat at the rest house at El Kanatir. Hoving in a joking way said to Sadat what Mokhtar had told him. This angered President Sadat, who said in his way that the Egyptian people had no complex after the 1973 war.

In the contract it was stated that Egypt would receive money from ticket sales, but by law some of the museums could not sell tickets. The MMA was one of these and asked instead for a donation. No one could enter for free. The contract also gave Egypt 100% of the net profit from the museum and catalog sales. However, the museums could claim any figure for the net, so instead they negotiated for 50% of the gross sales.

My own investigation has shown that the money from the Tutankhamun exhibit did not go directly to the Egyptian Antiquities Organization. It went to UNESCO. It is in a special account, and as of five years ago there was about $10 million of that money that had not yet been used.

Gamal Mokhtar attended the American opening of the Tutankhamun exhibit at the National Gallery of Art in November 1976. President Sadat then changed the government and, with the curse of Tutankhamun still at work, Mokhtar resigned.

Treasures of Tutankhamun

(55 objects)

UNITED STATES

WASHINGTON, DC

National Gallery of Art
17th November 1976 – 15th March 1977
832,853 visitors

CHICAGO, ILLINOIS

Field Museum of Natural History and the University of Chicago
14th January – 14th August 1977
1,349,742 visitors

NEW ORLEANS, LOUISIANA

New Orleans Museum of Art
16th September 1977 – 15th January 1978
870,755 visitors

LOS ANGELES, CALIFORNIA

Los Angeles County Museum of Art
15th February – 15th July 1978
1,250,620 visitors

SEATTLE, WASHINGTON

Seattle Art Museum
15th July – 15th November 1978
799,318 visitors

NEW YORK, NEW YORK

Metropolitan Museum of Art
15th December 1978 – 15th April 1979
1,300,00 visitors

SAN FRANCISCO, CALIFORNIA

M. H. de Young Memorial Museum
11th June – 30th September 1979

Other cities, including Boston, sent representatives to Cairo to ask to receive the exhibit, but they were denied. However, there were some successes. People associated with the De Young Museum in San Francisco were determined to host Tutankhamun. One was Ian White, director of the museum. The other was the late Walter Newman, who was head of the museum's board of trustees and was married to the daughter of I. Magnin, the famous and wealthy man who owned women's fashion stores in San Francisco. (Sadly, Walter Newman died as I was writing this book.) At the time I was inspector of the Giza Pyramids and lived in a rest house located west of the Great Pyramid. I met them through a friend of mine and was able to introduce them to Fouad El Orabi, who was head of the EAO. It was decided that San Francisco would be the last city in the United States for the exhibit, and it ran there from June to September 1979.

The exhibit then traveled to Toronto, where it stayed from November 1979 to January 1980, before moving on to West Berlin for February to May 1980, and then other German stops:

CANADA

TORONTO, ONTARIO

Art Gallery of Ontario
1st November – 31st December 1979

WEST GERMANY

BERLIN

Ägyptisches Museum und Papyrussammlung
16th February – 26th May 1980

COLOGNE

Kölnisches Stadtmuseum
21st June – 19th October 1980

MUNICH

Haus der Kunst
22nd November 1980 – 1st February 1981

HANNOVER

Kestner-Museum
20th February – 26th April 1981

HAMBURG

Museum für Kunst und Gewerbe
15th May – 19th July 1981

After Hamburg, the Tutankhamun exhibit was banned from further travel.

When the exhibit was transferring from Toronto to Berlin in 1981, the Egyptian curator, Abdel Aziz Sadek, was moving the artifacts from their boxes to the displays. The scorpion on the headdress of the goddess Selket, one of the guardian figures that once surrounded Tutankhamun's canopic shrine, fell to the ground and shattered.

Expert conservators were able to restore the goddess to her original glory, but this accident started a storm in Egypt. The press began to attack the EAO for sending such fragile, priceless objects abroad. In my opinion, it was a big mistake at that moment in time to send the best artifacts around the world. The head of the Supreme Council of Antiquities (SCA) during this time was Shihata Adam. As a result of the accident, the Egyptian Parliament passed a measure that prevented the treasures from leaving the country ever again.

This decision held for more than 20 years, denying an entire generation the opportunity to see the artifacts from Tutankhamun's tomb except in books and on television, unless they were fortunate enough to visit Egypt themselves.

In 2002, Dr Peter Blome, director of the new Antiken Museum in Basel, Switzerland, came to Egypt to ask for a new traveling exhibit featuring the treasures of Tutankhamun. Minister of Culture Farouk Hosni and I went to Parliament to try to convince the government to approve the Basel Museum's request. Months before, terrorists had massacred many tourists at the temple of Hatshepsut at Deir el-Bahri. Some of the tourists were Swiss, and this moved the Egyptian government to send the exhibition to Switzerland as an apology.

I thought that we would not, this time, send masterpieces. Instead other objects from the tomb would be part of an exhibit called "Tutankhamun and the Golden Age of the Pharaohs." At this time, I was Secretary General of the Supreme Council of Antiquities, and I appointed Mohamed Saleh, former director of the Egyptian Museum, and

Mamdouh El Damaty, the present director, and other Egyptologists to choose all of the objects. I never interfered with their decisions and all of the necessary committees gave their approval to the selections.

This new Tutankhamun exhibit ran from 7th April to 3rd October, 2004, and was seen by 620,000 people in Basel. As a result, I was able to bring 5 million euros back to Egypt. I met Dr Wenzel Jacob, the director of the Bundeskunsthalle in Bonn, Germany, and gave him the exhibit for the same amount of money. The exhibit opened there on 4th November 2004 and, by the time it closed on 1st May 2005, it had brought in 866,812 visitors.

I thought that we should show in the United States as well because I knew how popular it would be there and I wanted to raise money for the Grand Egyptian Museum (GEM) that we are building near the pyramids at Giza. When completed, this will be the largest museum in the world and will cost about $800 million. We needed at least $100 million to build just the conservation rooms and storage.

John Norman and Andres Numhauser of Arts and Exhibitions International (AEI) came to see me in Basel to ask to have the exhibit. I told them that I would ask the National Geographic Society for its support because AEI is a private company, which is difficult for the SCA to deal with. Thanks to Terry Garcia of the National Geographic Society, the Society agreed to do this for us and also to handle publicity for each city. AEI brought AEG from Los Angeles to sponsor the exhibit. Tom Miserendino, Norman, Numhauser, and Garcia came to Cairo for negotiations.

The contract that I created with them needs to be properly noted in the history of Egyptian archeology and museology. Through it I was able to bring to Egypt about $120 million. This was a first success for Egypt.

The exhibit toured the following cities:

Tutankhamun and the Golden Age of the Pharaohs

130 objects, 50 from the reign of Tutankhamun (called in Switzerland and Germany "Tutankhamun - The Golden Beyond - Treasures from the Valley of the Kings," with 120 objects, 50 from the reign of Tutankhamun)

SWITZERLAND

BASEL
Basel Museum of Ancient Art and Ludwig Collection
4th July – 3rd October 2004
620,000 visitors

GERMANY

BONN
Art and Exhibition Hall of the Federal Republic of Germany
11th April 2004 – 5th January 2005
866,812 visitors

UNITED STATES

LOS ANGELES, CALIFORNIA
Los Angeles County Museum of Art
13th June 2005 – 20th November 2005
937,613 visitors

FORT LAUDERDALE, FLORIDA
Museum of Art
15th December 2005 – 23rd April 2006
707,534 visitors

CHICAGO, ILLINOIS
The Field Museum of Natural History
26th May 2006 – 1st January 2007
1,044,743 visitors

PHILADELPHIA, PENNSYLVANIA
The Franklin Institute
3rd February 2007 – 30th September 2007
1,370,000 visitors

UNITED KINGDOM

LONDON, ENGLAND
The 02
15th November 2007 – 24th August 2008
1,096,473 visitors

UNITED STATES

DALLAS, TEXAS
Dallas Museum of Art
27th April 2009 – 28th March 2010
664,000 visitors

SAN FRANCISCO, CALIFORNIA
de Young Museum
27th June 2009 – 28th March 2010
773,970 visitors

NEW YORK, NEW YORK
Discovery Times Square Exposition
23rd April 2010 – 11th January 2011

AUSTRALIA

MELBOURNE, VICTORIA, AUSTRALIA
Melbourne Museum
8th April 2011 – 1st November 2011

JAPAN

OSAKA
Tempozan Gallery
17th March – 3rd June 2012

TOKYO
Ueno Royal Museum
4th August 2012 – 20th January 2013

At about the same time as "Tutankhamun and the Golden Age of the Pharaohs," we made arrangements for a second exhibit, "Tutankhamun: The Golden King and the Great Pharaohs." Another committee, led by Wafaa el Sadik, director of the Egyptian Museum, chose artifacts for this exhibit, which toured:

Tutankhamun: The Golden King and the Great Pharaohs

AUSTRIA

VIENNA

Kunsthistorisches Museum/Museum für Völkerkunde

9th March – 28th September 2008

UNITED STATES

ATLANTA, GEORGIA

Atlanta Civic Center

13th November 2008 – 17th May 2009

INDIANAPOLIS, INDIANA

The Indianapolis Children's Museum

25th June – 25th October 2009

CANADA

TORONTO, ONTARIO

Art Gallery of Ontario

24th November 2009 – 2nd May 2010

UNITED STATES

DENVER, COLORADO

Denver Art Museum

29th June 2010 – 9th January 2011

SAINT PAUL, MINNESOTA

Science Museum of Minnesota

18th February – 5th September 2011

HOUSTON, TEXAS

Houston Museum of Fine Arts

13th October 2011 – 15th April 2012

SEATTLE, WASHINGTON:

Pacific Science Center

24th May 2012 – 6th January 2013

The two exhibits are now back in Egypt. I do not think that anyone will be able to make Tutankhamun's treasures travel again. No one has the courage to take the risk, even in service to humanity, to educate the world and, in service to his country, to raise urgently needed funds that would preserve the monuments of Egypt.

APPENDIX 4

ROYAL TOMBS OF KINGS AND QUEENS STILL TO BE DISCOVERED

AHMOSE
(suggested, KV 31)

AMENHOTEP I
(suggested: KV 39, AN B, DB 320?)

THUTMOSE II
(suggested: KV 42, DB 358?)

AMENHOTEP IV/AKHENATEN
(suggested: KV 55, WV 25?)

SMENKHKARE

RAMESES VIII

QUEENS' TOMBS STILL BE DISCOVERED
(according to the reign of the particular king)

AMENHOTEP I
Sitkamose?
(attested on a 19th Dynasty stela)

THUTMOSE I
Ahmose
Mutnefret

THUTMOSE II
Isis

THUTMOSE III
Sitiah
Nebetta (or Nebtu?)

THUTMOSE IV
Nefertiry
Iaret (sister or daughter)

MUTEMWIA
daughter of Mitanni ruler Artatama

AMENHOTEP III
Tiye
(WV 22, TA 26; Amarna? KV 55?)
Gilukhepa
Tadukhipa
Sitamun
(WV 22?)

RAMESES IV
Henutwati
Tawerettenru

RAMESES VI
Nubkhesbed

RAMESES VII

RAMESES VIII

RAMESES IX
Baketwernel (KV 10?)

RAMESES XI
Tentamun(?)

APPENDIX 5

THE OFFICIAL REQUEST FOR THE RETURN OF NEFERTITI'S BUST

The painted limestone bust of Nefertiti, one of the most famous portraits in the world, was found in the workshop of the sculptor Thutmose by a German excavation headed by Ludwig Borchardt on 6th December 1912, and it is now on display at the New-Museum in Berlin, Germany.

Egypt has wanted it returned for a very long time. In 1987, Mohamed Abdel Kader, who was then chairman of the Egyptian Antiquities Organization, met the ambassador of Germany and asked him to return the bust of Nefertiti. The next day, Dr Kader was fired.

In 2003, Dietrich Wildung, the director of the Berlin Museum, allowed two Hungarian artists to create a bronze nude body for Nefertiti and set the bust on the modern sculpture. I put a stop to it and made a statement that if an Egyptian object is in a foreign museum, it is still an Egyptian object. We have the right to protect it.

The next year, I sent a letter asking to borrow the bust for a special three-month exhibit at the opening of the Grand Egyptian Museum, which at the time was scheduled for 2015. My request was rejected.

In January 2011, as Secretary General of the Supreme Council of Antiquities and with the permission of the Ministry of Culture and the Prime Minister of Egypt, I wrote a polite letter to the Prussian Cultural Heritage Foundation requesting its return. In this letter, which can be found at the end of this appendix, I politely explained why the bust belongs in Egypt, not in Germany. My team had assembled a great deal of information about the discovery of the bust of Nefertiti. This is the story that they uncovered.

Egypt has regulated the export of antiquities since 1835. When the bust was unearthed in 1912, it, like all other antiquities, was considered property belonging to the Egyptian government. There was also a law requiring that finds uncovered during a properly licensed excavation had to be divided. The French Egyptologist Gustave Lefébvre was the inspector in charge at the time. On 20th January 1913, Lefébvre drew up the official account of this division, called a protocol, based on information he received from Borchardt. One of the objects, which is clearly the bust of Nefertiti, is described as "painted plaster bust of a princess of the royal family." This is clearly wrong. The bust is painted limestone, not plaster, and the crown clearly indicated that this was the image of a queen, not a princess.

There was at the time a civil law that clearly stated that an agreement between two parties is invalid if it is agreed to because of a mistake or if the document is fraudulent. Which did Borchardt commit, a genuine mistake or a fraud?

There is evidence that Borchardt did not make an innocent error. When he found the bust in December 1912, he recorded it in his field diary with a small, clearly recognizable drawing, which he identified as the "life-sized painted bust of a queen," of "very good workmanship." He also said that describing the object would be useless. A month and a half later, in his diary entry for 20th January 1913, the day of the division, Borchardt does not call it the image of a "princess" made of "painted plaster." He refers to the "painted queen" as one of the objects of "hard stone." His own record of the division, on the next page of his diary, lists it as "painted queen."

Years later, an eyewitness, Hans Gustav Güterbock, a German expert in the Hittites who immigrated to the United States, wrote that he had objected at the time to saying that the bust was made of plaster. However, Borchardt told him that they would later, when the object was in Germany, make the correct identification as limestone and admit that he had made a mistake when he identified the material for the protocol. Güterbock also claimed that Lefébvre saw just a photograph of the bust and made only a cursory examination of the objects listed in the protocol, which were in open boxes in bad light. Güterbock believed that Borchardt had committed deception.

This is the letter I wrote to the Prussian Cultural Heritage Foundation on 2nd January 2011, with the permission from the Prime Minister of Egypt.

Sunday, January 2, 2011

Prof. Dr. h. c. mult. Hermann Parzinger, President
Stiftung Preußisher Kulturbesitz
Von-der-Heydt-Str. 16-18
10785 Berlin
Germany

Dear Prof. Dr. Parzinger:

I am writing on behalf of the Government of Egypt to submit an official request for the restitution of the painted limestone bust of Nefertiti, accessioned in the Neues Museum as Inventory No. AM 21300.

This request is a natural consequence of Egypt's long-standing policy of seeking the restitution of all archaeological and historical artifacts that have been taken illicitly out of the country, especially those items that are considered unique. The painted bust of Nefertiti is universally recognized as a unique and irreplaceable artifact. Both contemporary and subsequent documentation recording the excavation and division of finds of the group of artifacts that included the bust of Nefertiti confirm that the bust was taken out of Egypt in violation of both the letter and the spirit of the Egyptian laws in force at the time.

Since the first full publication of the Nefertiti bust, which did not appear until over a decade after its discovery, Egypt has made a number of attempts to recover this priceless sculpture and bring it home.

The Government and People of Egypt are eager that this unique treasure be returned to the possession of its rightful owners, the Egyptian People. The Government of Egypt is confident that the German authorities will act in accordance with article 13(b) of the UNESCO *Convention on the Means of Prohibiting and Preventing the Illicit Import, Export, and Transfer of Ownership of Cultural Property (1970)*, which calls on all states party to the convention to "ensure that their competent services cooperate in facilitating the earliest possible restitution of illicitly exported cultural property to its rightful owner." In this context it should be pointed out that in 1978 the Director General of UNESCO issued *A Plea for the Return of Irreplaceable Cultural Heritage to those who Created it*, and called upon "those responsible for preserving and restoring works of art to facilitate, by their advice and actions, the return of such works to the countries where they were created."

Egypt recognizes, and deeply appreciates, the care and effort undertaken by the Government of Germany to preserve and display the painted limestone bust of Queen Nefertiti. Inspired by the excellent relations between our two governments, the Government of Egypt is confident that the German authorities will assist in facilitating its return.

I know that I need not underline the importance of this request, and the significance of the restitution of the painted limestone bust of Queen Nefertiti to Egypt. I sincerely hope that I will soon receive from you a positive response, which will be greatly appreciated by the Government and People of Egypt.

Sincerely yours,

Dr Zahi Hawass
Secretary General, Supreme Council of Antiquities

Borchardt knew what he was doing. By listing the material as plaster, he increased the chances that Lefébvre would agree to let the object go because it was of a less valuable material and because there was a group of other important plaster objects that were going to Germany. Also, by identifying the bust as that of a princess and not a queen, he was clearly hoping to diminish its importance.

Even though he did not physically write the protocol, Borchardt was responsible for its accuracy. By signing a document he knew to be inaccurate, he committed fraud, which nullified the agreement to the division.

Borchardt seemed eager to deal with the division – and ownership of the bust – as quickly and quietly as possible. Mention of finds at Amarna in the 15th January 1913 edition of *Aegyptische Nachrichten* angered him deeply and made him worry that it would endanger the division, even though the article did not specifically mention the bust. His worry persisted even after the division had taken place; in a letter dated 5th February 1913, he said that he would feel calm only when he learned that the bust had arrived in Berlin.

He continued to conceal the bust of Nefertiti even after it had arrived in Germany. The piece was neither displayed publicly nor published properly for a decade: in his 1913 publication of the excavations of the season in which it was found, Borchardt mentions the sculpture merely in passing and provides only a small, strategically (and deceptively) cropped image, choosing to highlight other objects instead. Borchardt even objected to its display, which took place only after the bust was fully published in 1923. It is hard to avoid the conclusion that Borchardt wished to keep this magnificent piece of art out of the public eye for as long as possible so that Egypt would not ask for it back.

Borchardt was right to worry. Once fully aware of the existence and uniqueness of the bust, the Egyptian Antiquities Authority requested its return and entered into the first of a series of negotiations to achieve this goal. Primary documentation for the earliest attempts is scant, but it is clear from all reports that the Egyptian authorities very much wanted the bust returned and seem to have prohibited excavation by the Deutsche Orient-Gesellschaft (German Oriental Society) and the Berlin Museum for a time in an attempt to force the issue. In 1929 an agreement was reached for an exchange: in return for the Nefertiti bust, Germany would receive two very fine statues and an important copy of the *Book of the Dead*. However, apparently due to the political situation in Germany, the agreement was never implemented, although by then there was support for the repatriation of the bust by the sponsor of Borchardt's Amarna excavations, James Simon, and the head of the Egyptian Museum in Berlin, Heinrich Schäfer, as well as by Güterbock. There seems to have been the opinion – recorded in the diary of German journalist Ernst Feder – that Borchardt had deceived Lefébvre and that the situation needed to be corrected.

According to an article published in *La Bourse Égyptienne* on 13th December 1933 (quoting an article from *Le Libre Belgique* of 28th November 1933), the German minister in Cairo had sought an audience with King Fouad that October to inform him that the German government had decided to offer the bust to Egypt to commemorate the anniversary of his coronation. However, in November, the German minister had a second audience in which he informed the king that this had been an error and that no offer was forthcoming. Egypt tried again by memorandum in 1946 to the Allied Control Council, which was in control of cultural artifacts in Germany in the wake of World War II, and again by letter on February 21st, 1947, to the United States Secretary of State. However, the Allied Council, lacking the authority to authorize Nefertiti's return, recommended on 8th March 1947, that a future appeal should be directed to the re-established German government.

How did the Germans receive my letter? They replied by saying that the letter needed to be sent by the Minister of Culture, not by me, the Secretary General of the Supreme Council of Antiquities. But on 25th January 2011, the Egyptian Revolution began. I became a minister but had many other problems within the borders of Egypt to contend with. I had no time to think about Nefertiti or to write yet another letter to the Germans.

The Nefertiti bust has been out of Egypt for a hundred years now. I do not think that anyone is capable of doing anything about it now.

The case is closed, but if I return to the SCA again, I will reopen it. I, and many others in the archaeological community, hold out hope that someday justice will be done and Nefertiti, an important part of Egypt's cultural heritage, will return home.

SOURCES OF QUOTATIONS

(see bibliography for full citations)

CHAPTER I

"You fill every land..." M. LICHTHEIM, *Ancient Egyptian Literature 2*, p. 96.

"My husband has died..." H. G. Güterbock, "The Deeds of Suppiluliumas as Told by his Son, Mursili II," p. 94.

CHAPTER II

"A funeral procession is made for you..." M. LICHTHEIM, *Ancient Egyptian Literature 1*, p. 229

CHAPTER III

"the thieves in the time of the vizier Khaemwaset" A. MCDOWELL, *Jurisdiction in the Workmen's Community of Deir el-Medina*, p. 192.

"Hardly had I arrived..." H. CARTER and A. MACE, *The Tomb of Tut.ankh.Amen 1*, p. 87.

"At last have made wonderful discovery..." HOWARD CARTER's diary 5th November 1922. *Tutankhamun: Anatomy of an Excavation. Howard Carter's diaries and journals.* Griffith Institute website: http://www.griffith.ox.ac.uk/gri/4sea1not.html

"insult" H. CARTER, *The Tomb of Tutankhamen: Statement with Documents*, p. 52.

"Owing to impossible restrictions and discourtesies..." H. CARTER, *The Tomb of Tutankhamen: Statement with Documents*, p. 51.

CHAPTER IV

"Helter skelter in rubbish..." HOWARD CARTER's card No. 1ae. *Tutankhamun: Anatomy of an Excavation. Howard Carter's diaries and journals.* Griffith Institute website: http://www.griffith.ox.ac.uk/gri/carter/001e-c001ae.html

"As we cleared the passage..." HOWARD CARTER's diary 25th November 1922. *Tutankhamun: Anatomy of an Excavation. Howard Carter's diaries and journals.* Griffith Institute website: http://www.griffith.ox.ac.uk/gri/4sea1not.html

"Lord Carnarvon said to me 'Can you see anything'..." HOWARD CARTER's diary 26th November 1922. *Tutankhamun: Anatomy of an Excavation. Howard Carter's diaries and journals.* Griffith Institute website: http://www.griffith.ox.ac.uk/gri/4sea1not.html

"Egyptian notables of Luxor" HOWARD CARTER's diary 30th November 1922. *Tutankhamun: Anatomy of an Excavation. Howard Carter's diaries and journals.* Griffith Institute website: http://www.griffith.ox.ac.uk/gri/4sea1not.html

"I have no hesitation in claiming for it..." H. CARTER and A. MACE, *The Tomb of Tut.ankh.Amen 1*, p. 117.

"An astonishing sight its light revealed..." H. Carter and A. Mace, *The Tomb of Tut.ankh.Amen 1*, p. 247

"Difficulties of removing are going to be enormous." ARTHUR C. MACE's diary 30th November 1923. *Tutankhamun: Anatomy of an Excavation. Howard Carter's diaries and journals.* Griffith Institute website: http://www.griffith.ox.ac.uk/gri/4macedia2.html

"I was horrified to find that the silver stick..." HOWARD CARTER's diary 3rd October 1925. *Tutankhamun: Anatomy of an Excavation. Howard Carter's diaries and journals.* Griffith Institute website: http://www.griffith.ox.ac.uk/gri/4sea4not.html

"bad-smelling" HOWARD CARTER's card No. 240 bis-2. *Tutankhamun: Anatomy of an Excavation. Howard Carter's diaries and journals.* Griffith Institute website: http://www.griffith.ox.ac.uk/gri/carter/240bis-c240bis-2.html

"Bottom of Sarcophagus" HOWARD CARTER's card No. 240bis-1. *Tutankhamun: Anatomy of an Excavation. Howard Carter's diaries and journals.* Griffith Institute website: http://www.griffith.ox.ac.uk/gri/carter/240bis-c240bis-1.html

"intact, with the lid still firmly..." H. CARTER, *The Tomb of Tut.ankh.Amen 2*, p. 45.

"makeshift" HOWARD CARTER's diary 3rd February 1924. *Tutankhamun: Anatomy of an Excavation. Howard Carter's diaries and journals.* Griffith Institute website: http://www.griffith.ox.ac.uk/gri/4sea2not.html

"gossamer" HOWARD CARTER's diary 13th October 1925. *Tutankhamun: Anatomy of an Excavation. Howard Carter's diaries and journals.* Griffith Institute website: http://www.griffith.ox.ac.uk/gri/4sea4not.html

"superior to that of the first coffin...." HOWARD CARTER's diary 18th October 1925. *Tutankhamun: Anatomy of an Excavation. Howard Carter's diaries and journals.* Griffith Institute website: http://www.griffith.ox.ac.uk/gri/4sea4not.html

"Without some experience of handling heavy..." HOWARD CARTER's diary 20th October 1925. *Tutankhamun: Anatomy of an Excavation. Howard Carter's diaries and journals.* Griffith Institute website: http://www.griffith.ox.ac.uk/gri/4sea4not.html

"both technically and artistically," "a unique example of the metal-worker's art." HOWARD CARTER's card No. 255-01. *Tutankhamun: Anatomy of an Excavation. Howard Carter's diaries and journals.* Griffith Institute website: http://www.griffith.ox.ac.uk/gri/carter/255-c255-01.html

"Jewels (?) of gold of the procession..." HOWARD CARTER's card No. 267–5. *Tutankhamun: Anatomy of an Excavation. Howard Carter's diaries and journals.* Griffith Institute website: http://www.griffith.ox.ac.uk/gri/carter/267-c267-5.html

"The state of this inner room..." H. Carter and A. Mace, *The Tomb of Tut.ankh.Amen 1*, p. 104.

"clawing the air in noble rage." H. CARTER, *The Tomb of Tut.ankh.Amen 3*, p. 146.

CHAPTER VI

"At one corner of this chamber, we found two mummies..." G. B. BELZONI, *Narrative of the Operations and Recent Discoveries Within the Pyramids, Temples, Tombs and Excavations in Egypt and Nubia 1*, p. 228.

CHAPTER VII

"I will kill all those..." T. HOVING, *Tutankhamun: The Untold Story*, p. 227.

"It is I who hinder the sand..." H. CARTER, *The Tomb of Tut.ankh.Amen 3*, p. 40-41.

"They who enter this sacred tomb..." T. HOVING, *Tutankhamun: The Untold Story*, p. 227.

"Death will slay with his wings..." P. VANDENBERG, *The Curse of the Pharaohs*, p. 20.

CHAPTER IX

"The hottest show in town..." AMEI WALLACH in *LI: Newsday's Magazine for Long Island*, 10th December 1978.

APPENDIX 3

"I lurched across the table..." THOMAS HOVING quoted by AMEI WALLACH in *LI: Newsday's Magazine for Long Island*, 10th December 1978, p. 41.

BIBLIOGRAPHY

A

ALDRED, C. *Akhenaten and Nefertiti*. London, 1973.

ALDRED, C. *Jewels of the Pharaohs: Egyptian Jewellery of the Dynastic Period*. New York, 1971.

ALLEN, S. I. "Tutankhamun's Embalming Cache Reconsidered." In *Egyptology at the Dawn of the Twenty–First Century: Proceedings of the Eighth International Congress of Egyptology*, edited by Z. Hawass, vol. 1, 23–29. Cairo, 2003.

ALLEN, T. G. "Discoveries at the Tomb of Tutankhamon." *Current History* 20 (1924): 363–373.

ALTENMÜLLER, H. "Papyrusdickicht ünd Wüste. Überlegungen zu zwei Statuenensembles des Tutanchamun." *Mitteilunen des Deutschen Archäologischen Instituts Abteilung Kairo* 47 (1991): 11–19.

ANTHES, R. *Tutankhamun Treasures*. Exhibition catalogue. Washington, 1961.

ANTHES, R., *Tutankhamun Treasures/Tresors de Toutankhamon*. Exhibition catalogue. Montreal, 1961.

ARNOLD, DO. *The Royal Women of Amarna*. New York, 1996.

ASSAAD, H. and D. KOLOS. *The Name of the Dead: Hieroglyphic Inscriptions of the Treasures of Tutankhamun Translated*. Mississauga, 1979.

B

BAIKE, J. *The Amarna Age: A Study of the Crisis of the Ancient World*. London, 1926.

BAKER, H. S. *Furniture in the Ancient World: Origins and Evolution 3100–475 B.C.* London, 1966.

BEINLICH, H. "Das Totenbuch bei Tutanchamun." *Göttinger Miszellen* 102 (1988): 7–18.

BEINLICH, H. and M. SALEH. *Corpus der Hieroglyphischen Inschriftenaus dem Grab des Tutanchamun*. Oxford, 1989.

BELL, L. "An Armchair Excavation of KV 55." *Journal of the American Research Center in Egypt* 27 (1990): 97–127.

BELZONI, G. B. *Narrative of the Operations and Recent Discoveries Within the Pyramids, Temples, Tombs and Excavations in Egypt and Nubia*. London, 1820.

BENNET, J. "The Restoration Inscription of Tutankhamun." *Journal of Egyptian Archaeology* 25 (1939): 8–15.

BIMSON, M. "Glass in the Tutankhamun Treasure." In *6e Congrès de l'Association internationale pour l'histoire de verre, Cologne, 1–7 juillet 1973, Annales*, 291–294. Liège, 1974.

BORCHARDT, L. *Statuen und Statuetten von Königen und Privatleuten im Museum von Kairo: 1–294*, 3 vols. Berlin, 1930.

BOSSE–GIFFITHS, K. "The Great Enchantress in the Little Golden Shrine of Tutankhamun." *Journal of Egyptian Archaeology* 59 (1973): 100–108.

BOURRIAU, J. "A Private Sela of the Reign of Tutankhamun in the Fitzwilliam Museum." In *Pyramid Studies and Other Essays Presented to I. E. S. Edwards*, edited by J. Baines et al., 110–113. London, 1988.

BRACKMAN, A. C. *The Search for the Gold of Tutankhamun*. New York, 1976.

BREASTED, C. "Over the Threshold of Tutankhamun's Tomb." *Asia* 23 (1923): 437–441, 465, 468.

BREASTED, C. *Pioneer to the Past: The Story of James Henry Breasted*. London, 1948.

BREASTED, J. H. *Some Experiences in the Tomb of Tutankhamun*. Chicago, 1923.

BRIER, B. *The Murder of Tutankhamen*. London, 1998.

BRYAN, B. "Portrait Sculpture of Thutmose IV." *Journal of the American Research Center in Egypt* 24 (1987): 3–20.

BRYAN, B. *The Reign of Thutmose IV*. Baltimore, 1991.

BUDGE, E. A. W. *Tutankhamen, Amenism, Atenism and Egyptian Monotheism*. London, 1923.

C

CAPART, J. *The Tomb of Tutankhamen*. Translated by Warren R. Dawson. London, 1923.

Carnarvon, THE EARL OF, and H. CARTER. *Five Years' Explorations at Thebes: A Record of Work Done, 1907–1911*. Oxford, 1912.

CARTER, H. *The Tomb of Tutankhamen: Statement with Documents, also the Events which Occurred in Egypt in the Winter of 1923–24, Leading to the Ultimate Break with the Egyptian Government*. London, 1924.

CARTER, H. and A. C. Mace. *The Tomb of Tut.ankh.Amen*, 3 vols. London, 1923–1933.

CERNY, J. *Hieratic Inscriptions from the Tomb of Tutankhamun*. Oxford, 1965.

CHASSINAT, É. "Tomb inviolé de la XVIIIe Dynastie découvert aux environs de Médinet el–Gorab dans le Fayoûm." *Bulletin de l'Institut Français d'Archéologie Orientale* 1 (1901): 225–234.

CHERF, W. J. "Some Forked Staves in the Tutankhamun Collection." *Zeitschrift für ägyptische Sprache und Altertumskunde* 115 (1988): 107–110.

CHEVRIER, H. "Rapport sur les travaux de Karnak (Mars–Mai 1926)." *Annales du Service des Antiquités de l'Égypte* 26 (1926): 119–130.

COGHLAN, H. H. "Copper Artefacts from Tutankhamun's Tomb." *Journal of the Historical Metallurgy Society* 9.2 (1975): 64–67.

CONE, P. (ed.). *The Discovery of Tutankhamun's Tomb*. New York, 1976.

CONNOLLY, R. C. The X-Ray Plates of Tutankhamen: A Reassessment of Their Meaning and Significance." In *Pharmacy and Medicine in Ancient Egypt: Proceedings of the Conferences held in Cairo (2007) and Manchester (2008)*, edited by Jenefer Cockitt and Rosalie David, 46–50. Oxford, 2010.

CONNOLLY, R. C., R. G. HARRISON, and S. AHMED. "Serological Evidence for the Parentage of Tutankhamun and Smenkhkare." *Journal of Egyptian Archaeology* 62 (1976): 184–186.

COONEY, J. D. *Amarna Reliefs from Heliopolis in American Collections*. Brooklyn, 1965.

COONEY, J. D. "Three Ivories of the Late XVIII Dynasty." *Brooklyn Museum Bulletin* 10.1 (1948): 1–16

COTTRELL, L. *The Secrets of Tutankhamun*. London, 1978.

CROWFOOT, G. M. and N. DE G. DAVIES. "The Tunic of Tutankhamun." *Journal of Egyptian Archaeology* 27 (1941): 113–130.

D

DARESSY, G. *Fouilles de la vallée des rois*. Cairo, 1902.

DARESSY, G. "Rapport sur la trouvaille de Hat–iAy." *Annales du Service des Antiquités de l'Égypte* 2 (1902): 1–13.

DARNELL, J. C. and ABD EL–HAKIM HADDAD. *A Stela of the Reign of Tutankhamun from the Region of Kurkur Oasis. – Studien zur Altäyptischen Kultur* 31 (2003): 73–91.

DARNELL, J. C. and C. MANASSA. *Tutankhamun's Armies: Battle and Conquest during Ancient Egypt's Late Eighteenth Dynasty*. Hoboken, 2007.

DAVIES, N. M. and A. H. GARDINER. *The Tomb of Huy, Viceroy of Nubia in the Reign of Tutankhamun*. London 1926.

DAVIES, N. M. and A. H. GARDINER. *Tutankhamun's Painted Box*. Oxford, 1962.

DAVIS, T. M. et al. *The Tomb of Harmhabi and Touatânkhamanou*. London, 1907.

DAVIS, T. M. et al. *The Tomb of Iouiya and Touiyou*. London, 1907

DAVIS, T. M. et al. *The Tomb of Queen Tiyi*. San Francisco, 1990.

DAVIS, T. M. et al. *The Tomb of Thoutmôsis IV*. London, 1904.

DAVIS, W. V. "Tutankhamun's Razor–box: A Problem in Lexicography." *Journal of Egyptian Archaeology* 63 (1977): 107–111.

Desroches–Noblecourt, C. "La Cueillette du raisin á la fin de l'époque amarnienne." *Journal of Egyptian Archaeology* 54 (1968): 82–88.

Desroches–Noblecourt, C. *Tutankhamon et son temps*. Exhibition catalogue. Paris, 1967.

Desroches–Noblecourt, C. *Tutankhamen. Life and Death of a Pharaoh*. London, 1963.

DIJK, J. van. and M. EATON–KRAUSS. "Tutankhamun and Memphis." *Mitteilungen des Deutschen Archäologischen Instituts, Abteilung Kairo* 42 (1986): 35–41.

DODSON, A. *The Canopic Equipment of the Kings of Egypt*. London, 1994.

DODSON, A. "The Canopic Coffinettes of Tutankhamun and the Identity of Ankhkheperure." In *Egyptian Museum Collections around the World: Studies for the Centennial of the Egyptian Museum, Cairo*, edited by by M. Eldamaty and M. Trad, 275–285. Cairo, 2002.

DRENKHAHN, R. "Eine Umbettung Tutanchamuns." *Mitteilunen des Deutschen Archäologischen Instituts Abteilung Kairo* 39 (1983): 29–38.

DRIOTON, E. "La cryptographie de la chapelle de Toutankhamon." *Journal of Egyptian Archaeology* 35 (1949): 117–122.

E

EATON-KRAUSS, M. *The Sarcophagus in the Tomb of Tutankhamun*. Oxford, 1993.

EATON-KRAUSS, M. "Die Throne Tutankhamuns." *Göttinger Miszellen* 76 (1984): 7–10.

Eaton-Krauss, M. "The Titulary of Tutankhamun." In *Form und Mass: Beiträge zur literatur, Sprache, und Kunst des Alten Ägypten. Festschrift für Gerhard Fecht zum 65. Geburtstag am 6. Februar 1987*, edited by J. Osing and G. Dreyer. Wiesbaden, 1987.
Eaton-Krauss, M. "Tutankhamun at Karnak." *Mitteilungen des Deutschen Archäologischen Instituts Abteilung Kairo* 44 (1988): 1–11.
Eaton-Krauss, M. "Walter Segal's Documentation of CT 51113, the Throne of Princess Sat–Amun." *Journal of Egyptian Archaeology* 75 (1989): 77–88.
Eaton-Krauss, M. and E. Graefe. *The Small Golden Shrine from the Tomb of Tutankhamun*. Oxford, 1985.
Edwards, I. E. S., *Treasures of Tutankhamun*. Exhibition catalog. London, 1972.
Edwards, I. E. S. *Tutankhamun: His Tomb and its Treasures*. New York, 1976.
Edwards, I. E. S. Tutankhamun's Jewelry. New York, 1976.
Edwards, I. E. S. "Zoomorphic Anomalies in Tutankhamun's Treasures." *American Journal of Archaeology* 83 (1979): 205–206.
El-Khouli, A. *Stone Vessels, Pottery and Sealings from the Tomb of Tutankhamun*. Oxford, 1993.
Engelbach, R. "A Hitherto Unknown Statue of King Tut'ankhamûn." *Annales du Service des Antiquités de l'Égypte* 38 (1938): 23–28.
Engelbach, R. "A Hitherto Unknown Statue of King Tut'ankhamûn – Further Remarks." *Annales du Service des Antiquités de l'Égypte* 39 (1939): 195.
Epigraphic Survey. *Reliefs and Inscriptions at Luxor Temple, Volume 1: The Festival Procession of Opet in the Colonnade Hall*. Oriental Institute Publications 112. Chicago: Oriental Institute of the University of Chicago, 1994.

F

Fairman, H. W. "Tutankhamun and the End of the 18th Dynasty." *Antiquity* 46 (1972): 15–18.
Fazzini, R. *Tutankhamun and the African Heritage: A View of Society in the Time of the Boy King*. New York, 1978.
Feucht-Putz, E. *Die Königliche Pektorale*. Bamberg, 1967.
Fischer, C. S. "The Eckley B. Coxe Jr. Egyptian Expedition." *The Museum Journal* 8.4 (1917): 211–237.
Fisher, M. "A New Kingdom Ostracon Found in the Kings' Valley." In *Perspectives on Ancient Egypt: Studies in Honor of Edward Brovarski*, edited by Z. A. Hawass et al., 93 100. Cairo: SCA Press, 2010.
Forbes, D. "Ritual Figures in KV 62." *Amarna Letters* 3 (1994): 110 127.
Fox, P. *Tutankhamun's Treasure*. London, 1961.
Freed, R., Y. Markowitz, and S. D'Auria. *Pharaohs of the Sun*. Boston, 1999.

G

Gabolde, M. "Ay, Toutankhamon et les martelages de la stele de la restoration de Karnak (Cairo CG 34183)." *Bulletin de la Société d'Égyptologie Genève* 11 (1987): 37–81.
Gabolde, M. *D'Ankhenaton à Toutánkhamon. Collection de l'Institut d'Archéologie et d'Histoire de l'Antiquitié* 3. Lyon, 1998.
Gardiner, A. H. "Tutankhamun's Gold Dagger." *Journal of Egyptian Archaeology* 27 (1941): 1.
Gardiner, A. H. "Tutankhamun's Iron Dagger." *Journal of Egyptian Archaeology* 28 (1942): 1
Germer, R. *Flora des pharaonischen Ägypten*. Cairo, 1991.
Germer, R. *Die Pflanzenmaterialien aus dem Grab des Tutanchamun*. Hildesheim, 1959.
Gohary, J. "Nefertiti at Karnak." In *Glimpses of Ancient Egypt: Studies in Honour of H. W. Fairman*, edited by J. Ruffle et al., 30–31. Warminster, 1979.
Griffith Institute. Tutankhamun: The Anatomy of an Excavation. http://www.griffith.ox.ac.uk/tutankhamundiscovery.html
Graefe, E. "The Royal Cache and the Tomb Robberies." In *The Theban Necropolis: Past, Present and Future*, edited by N. Strucwick and J. H. Taylor. London, 2003.
Gunn, B. "Notes on the Aten and His Names." *Journal of Egyptian Archaeology* 9 (1923): 168–176.
Güterbock, H. G. "The Deeds of Suppiluliumas as Told by his Son, Mursili II." *Journal of Cuneiform Studies* 10 (1956): 41–68, 75–98, 107–130.

H

Habachi, L. *Tell Basta*. Cairo, 1957.
Habachi, L. "Unknown or Little Known Monuments of Tutankhamun and of his Viziers." In *Glimpses of Ancient Egypt: Studies in Honour of H. W. Fairman*, edited by J. Ruffle et al, 32–41. Warminster, 1979.
Hall, H. R. H. "Objects of Tutankhamun in the British Museum." *Journal of Egyptian Archaeology* 14 (1928): 74–77.
Harris, J. E. et al. "Mummy of the Elder Lady in the Tomb of Amenhotep II." *Science* 2000 (4346) (9th June 1978): 1149–1151.
Harris, J. R. "Akhenaten or Nefertiti." *Acta Orientalia* 38 (1977): 5–10.
Harris, J. R. "Contributions to the History of the Eighteenth Dynasty 2. Amehotep III. A Terminus for the Co-regency with Akhenaten." *Studien zur Altägyptischen Kultur* 2 (1975): 98–101.
Harris, J. R. "Kiya." *Chronique d'Égypte* 49 (1974): 25–30.
Harris, J. R. "Neferneferuaten." *Göttinger Miszellen* 4 (1973): 15, 17.
Harris, J. R. "Neferneferuaten Regnans." *Acta Orientalia* 36 (1974): 11–21.
Harris J. R. "Nefertiti Rediviva." *Acta Orientalia* 35 (1973): 5–13.
Harrison, R. G. "An Anatomical Examination of the Pharaonic Remains Purported to be Ahenaten." *Journal of Egyptian Archaeology* 52 (1966): 95–119.
Harrison, R. G. "Post Mortem on Two Pharaohs: Was Tutankhamun's Skull Fractured." *Buried History* (1972): 18–21.
Harrison, R. G. "Tutankhamun's Postmortem." *The Lancet* (1973): 259.
Harrison, R. G. and A. G. Abdalla. "The Remains of Tutankhamun." *Antiquity* 46 (1972): 8–14
Harrison, R. G., R. C. Connolly, and A. Abdalla. "Kinship of Smenkhkare and Tutankhamen Demonstrated Serologically." *Nature* 224 (25th October 1969): 325–326.
Harrison, R. G. et al. "A Mummified Foetus from the Tomb of Tutankhamun." *Antiquity* 53 (1979): 19–21.
Hawass, Z. et al. "Completed Tomographic Evaluation of Pharaoh Tutankhamun ca. 1300 BC." *Annales du Service des Antiquités de l'Égypte* 81 (2007).
Hawass, Z. *Curse of the Pharaohs: My Adventures with Mummies*. Washington, D.C.: National Geographic, 2005.
Hawass, Z. "Dancing with the Pharaohs: The New Royal Mummies Hall at the Egyptian Museum, Cairo." *Kmt* 17.1 (2006).
Hawass, Z. "The Discovery of the Mummy of Queen Hatshepsut." *Festschrift for Ola El Aguizy*. Institut Français d'Archéologie Orientale, forthcoming.
Hawass, Z. "Egypt's Hidden Tombs Revealed." *National Geographic Magazine* (September 2002): 32–34.
Hawass, Z. "The Egyptian Expedition in the Valley of the Kings: Excavation Season 2, Part 1, 2008–2009." In *The Proceedings of the 10th International Egyptology Conference, Cyprus* (forthcoming 2013).
Hawass, Z. "The Egyptian Monuments: Problems and Solutions." *International Journal of Cultural Property* 4.1 (1995): 105–117.
Hawass, Z. *The Golden King: The World of Tutankhamun*. Cairo: AUC Press, 2006.
Hawass, Z. *The Great Book of Ancient Egypt: In the Realm of the Pharaohs*. Vercelli, Italy: White Star, 2006.
Hawass, Z. *The Hidden Treasures of the Egyptian Museum: One Hundred Masterpieces from the Centennial Exhibition*. Cairo: AUC Press, 2002.
Hawass, Z. *The Hidden Treasures of the Egyptian Museum: One Hundred Masterpieces from the Centennial Exhibition*. Washington, D.C.: National Geographic, 2002.
Hawass, Z. "King Tut Returns: Tutankhamun and the Golden Age of the Pharaohs." *Kmt* 16.2 (2005).
Hawass, Z. "King Tutankhamun." In *Ancient Egypt at the Cairo Museum*, edited by A. Radwan. Cairo: SCA Press, 2009.
Hawass, Z. *Life in Paradise: The Noble Tombs of Thebes*. London: Thames and Hudson, 2009.
Hawass, Z. "Mother, Wife or Daughter of the Kings." In *Queenship in Egypt: from Hetepheres to Cleopatra*, edited by C. Ziegler. Paris, 2008.
Hawass, Z. et al. "The Mysterious Tunnel of Seti I." *The Valley of the Kings after Howard Carter*. Cairo: SCA Press, 2013.
Hawass, Z. "New Evidence for the Cause of Tutankhamun's Death." Bibliotheca Alexandrina (2011): http://www.bibalex.org/archeology/attachments/lectures/2012012213420493l4.pdf
Hawass, Z. "Newly Discovered Scenes of Tutankhamun from Memphis and Rediscovered Blocks from Heliopolis." In *The Art and Culture of Ancient Egypt: Studies in Honor of Dorothea Arnold*. New York: Metropolitan Mueum of Art, forthcoming.
Hawass Z. "Preliminary Report for the SCA Excavation at the Valley of the Kings: The First Season 2007–2008." In *Thebes and Beyond: Studies in Honour of Kent R. Weeks*, edited by Z. Hawass and S. Ikram. Annales du Service des Antiquités de l'Égypte 41 (Cairo, 2010).
Hawass, Z. "Quest for the Mummy of Hatshepsut: Could She be the Lady in the Attic of the Egyptian Museum, Cairo?" *Kmt* 17.1 (2006).
Hawass, Z. *The Royal Tombs of Egypt: The Art of Thebes Revealed*. De Agostini, Italy, 2006.
Hawass, Z. "The Scientific Search for Hatshepsut's Mummy." *Kmt* 18.3 (2007).
Hawass, Z. *Secrets from the Sand: My Search for Egypt's Past*. New York: H. Abrams, 2004.
Hawass, Z. (ed.). *Silent Images: Women in Pharaonic Egypt*. Cairo: AUC Press, 2010.
Hawass, Z. "A Statue of Thutmose II and the God Amun: Genuine or Fake?" In The Realm of the Pharaohs: Essays in Honor of Tohfa Handoussa, edited by Z. Hawass et al. Annales du Service des Antiquités de l'Égypte Supp. 37. Cairo: SCA Press, 2008.

Hawass, Z. "The Tomb of Tutankhamun's Mother? An 18th Dynasty Chamber in the Valley of the Kings." In *Discovery: Unearthing the New Treasures of Archaeology*, edited by B. Fagan. London: Thames and Hudson, 2007.

Hawass, Z. *Tutankhamun and the Golden Age of the Pharaohs*. Washington, D.C.: National Geographic, 2005.

Hawass, Z. *Tutankhamun from H. Carter to Z. Hawass*. Photos by S. Vanini. Viterbo, Italy: Laboratoriorosso, 2013.

Hawass, Z. *Tutankhamun: The Mystery of the Boy King*. Washington, D.C.: National Geographic, 2009.

Hawass, Z. *Tutankhamun: The Treasures of the Tomb*. London: Thames and Hudson, 2007.

Hawass, Z. "The Unfinished Obelisk Quarry at Aswan." In *Beyond the Horizon: Studies in Egyptian Art, Archaeology and History in Honor of Barry J. Kemp*, edited by S. Ikram and A. Dodson, vol. 2. Cairo, 2009.

Hawass, Z. *The Valley of the Golden Mummies*. New York: Harry Abrams, 2000.

Hawass, Z. "World Heritage Sites in Egypt." In *Egypt Cultural and Natural Heritage*. Barcelona, 2010.

Hawass, Z. et al., "Ancestry and Pathology in Tutankhamun's Family." *Journal of the American Medical Association* 303 (2011).

Hawass, Z., et al. "The Discovery of the Missing Parts of the Statue of Amenhotep III and Queen Tiye at the Egyptian Museum." *Annales du Service des Antiquités de l'Égypte* 58 (2013).

Hawass, Z. et al. "Excavations North-West of Amenhotep III Temple: Season 2010–2011." Annales du Service des Antiquités de l'Égypte, forthcoming.

Hawass, Z. et al. *Tutankhamun: The Golden King and the Great Pharaohs*. Washington, D.C.: National Geographic, 2009.

Hawass, Z. and S. Ikram. *Unearthing the Royal Mummies*. Cairo: AUC Press, forthcoming.

Hawass, Z. and S. Saleem. "Mummified daughters of King Tutankhamun: Archaeological and CT Studies." *The American Journal of Roentgenology* 197.5 (2011): 829–836.

Hawass, Z., A. Wagdy, and O. Abouzeid. "Excavation North-West of Amenhotep III Temple." *Annales du Service des Antiquités de l'Égypte*, forthcoming.

Helck, W. "Kiya." *Mitteilunen des Deutschen Archäologischen Instituts Abteilung Kairo* 40 (1984): 159–167.

Hepper, F. N. *Pharaoh's Flowers: Plants of Tutankhamun's Tomb*. London, 1990.

Hickmann, H. *Instruments de Musique*. Cairo, 1949.

Houlihan, P. F. and S. M. Goodman. "Comments on the Identification of Birds Depicted on Tutankhamun's Embossed Gold Fan." *Journal of the Society of the Study of Egyptian Antiquities* 914 (August 1978): 219–225.

Hoving, T. *Tutankhamun: The Untold Story*. New York, 1978.

Hornung, E. et al. *The Quest for Immortality: Treasures of Ancient Egypt*. Washington, 2002.

Hummel, S. "Tut-ench-Amun auf dem Leoparden." *Asiatische Studien* 23–24 (1974–1975): 65–67.

I

Ikram, S. and Dodson, A. *The Mummy in Ancient Egypt: Equipping the Dead for Eternity*. London, 1998.

J

James, T. G. H. *Howard Carter: The Path to Tutankhamun*. Cairo, 2001.

James, T. G. H., and T. Hoving. *Tutankhamun: The Eternal Splendour of the Boy Pharaoh*. Vercelli, 2000.

Jequier, G. "Apropos de grands lits de Toutankhamon." *Recueil de travaux relatifs à la philology et à l'archéologie égyptienne et Assyriennes* 49 (1923): 205–210.

Johnson, W. R. "Akhenaten in Nubia." In *Ancient Nubia: African Kingdoms on the Nile*, edited by M. M. Fischer et al., 92–93. Cairo: AUC Press, 2012.

Johnson, W. R. "Amenhotep III and Amarna: Some New Considerations." *Journal of Egyptian Archaeology* 82 (1996): 65–82.

Johnson, W. R. "Amenhotep III's 'Deification' Style." *Kmt* 2.2 (1991), 23.

Johnson, W. R. 1991. "The Dazzling Sun Disk: Iconographic Evidence that Amenhotep III Reigned as the Aten Personified." *Kmt* 2.2 (1991): 14–23, 60–63, 65 66.

Johnson, W. R. "The Deified Amenhotep III as the Living Re-Horakhty: Stylistic and Iconographic Considerations." In *Sesto Congresso internazionale di egittologia: atti I*, 231–236. Turin, Italy: International Association of Egyptologists

Johnson, W. R. "Honorific Figures of Amenhotep III in the Luxor Temple Colonnade Hall." In *For His Ka: Essays Offered in Memory of Klaus Baer*, edited by D. P. Silverman, 133–144. Chicago: Oriental Institute and University of Chicago Press.

Johnson, W. R. "Monuments and Monumental Art under Amenhotep III: Evolution and Meaning." In *Amenhotep III: Perspectives on His Reign*, edited by D. B. O'Connor and E. H. Cline, 63–94. Ann Arbor: University of Michigan Press, 1998.

Johnson, W. R. "A Sandstone Relief of Tutankhamun in the Liverpool Museum from the Luxor Temple Colonnade Hall." In *Causing His Name to Live: Studies in Egyptian Epigraphy and History in Memory of William J. Murnane*, edited by P. J. Brand and L. Cooper,125–128. Leiden; Brill, 2009.

Johnson, W. R. "Tutankhamen–Period Battle Narratives at Luxor." *Kmt* 20.4 (2009): 20–33.

Johnson, W. R. and P. Lacovara. "A Composite Statue of Amenhotep III in the Cairo Museum." In *Egyptian Museum Collections around the World: Studies for the Centennial of the Egyptian Musuem, Cairo*, edited by by M. Eldamaty and M. Trad, 591–594. Cairo, 2002.

Johnson, W. R., P. Lacovara, and N. Reeves. "A Composite Statue Element in the Museum of Fine Arts, Boston." *Revue d'Égyptologie* 47 (1996): 173–179.

Jones, D. *Model Boats from the Tomb of Tutankhamun*. Oxford, 1990.

de Jong, A. "Feline Deities." In *The Oxford Encyclopedia of Ancient Egypt*, edited by D. Redford, vol. 1. Oxford, 2001.

K

Kamal, M. "Fouilles du Service des Antiquités á Tell el-Marna en 1934." *Annales du Service des Antiquités de l'Égypte* 35 (1935): 193–196.

Kamal, M. "Some Fragments from Shawabti-Figures of Akhenaten in the Egyptian Museum." *Annales du Service des Antiquités de l'Égypte* 39 (1939): 381–382.

Keating, R. "Blowing Tutankhamun's Trumpet." The Listener 877/2246 (13 April 1972): 479–480.

Kemp, B. J. et al. *Amarna Reports 1*. London, 1984.

Kessler, D. "Zu den Jagdszenen auf dem kleinen goldenen Tutanchamun schrein." *Göttinger Miszellen* 90 (1986): 35–44.

Khouly, A. el, and G. T. Martin. *Excavations in the Royal Necropolis at El Amarna*. Cairo, 1987.

Killen, G. Ancient *Egyptian Furniture Vol. 1: 4000–1300 BC*. Warminster, 1980.

Killen, G. *Ancient Egyptian Furniture Vol. 2: Boxes, Chests and Footstools*. Warminster, 1994.

Kirby, P. R. "The Trumpets of Tutankh-Amen and their Successors." *Journal of the Royal Anthropological Institute of Great Britain and Ireland* 77 (1947): 33–45.

Kosloff, A. and B. Bryan. *Egypt's Dazzling Sun: Amenhotep III and His World*. Cleveland, 1992.

Krauss, R. "Kija – ursprüngliche Besitzerin der Kanopen aus KV 55." *Mitteilungen des Deutschen Archäologischen Instituts, Abteilung Kairo* 42 (1986): 67–80.

Krauss, R. "Zum archäologischen Befund im thebanischen Konigsgrab Nr. 62." *Mitteilungen der deutschen Orientgesellschaft zu Berlin* 118 (1986): 165–181.

L

Laboury, D. "Mise au point sur l'iconographie de Neferneferouaton, le predecesseur de Toutankhamon." In *Egyptian Museum Collections around the World: Studies for the Centennial of the Egyptian Musuem, Cairo*, edited by M. Eldamaty and M. Trad, 711–722. Cairo, 2002.

Larson, J. "The Heb–Sed Robe and the Ceremonial Robe of Tutankhamun." *Journal of Egyptian Archaeology* 67 (1981): 180–181.

Lawton, J. "The Last Survivor." *Aramco World* 32.6 (November – December 1981): 10–21.

Leek, F. F. "How Old was Tutankhamun." *Journal of Egyptian Archaeology* 63 (1977): 112–115.

Leek, F. F. *The Human Remains from the Tomb of Tutankhamun*. Oxford, 1977.

Legrain, G. "Le grand stèle de Toutankhamanou á Karnak." *Recueil de traveaux relatifs à la philologie et à l'archéologie égyptiennes et assyriennes* 29 (1907).

Legrain, G. "Notes d'inspection XXVIII, le protocole de Toutankhamon." *Annales du Service des Antiquités de l'Égypte* 6 (1905): 192.

Legrain, G. "Notes d'inspection LII. Un duplicate de le grande stele de Toutankhamanou á la grande stele de Toutankhamanou á Karnak." *Annales du Service des Antiquités de l'Égypte* 8 (1907): 256–258.

Legrain, G. "Rapport sur les travaux executes á Karnak du 31 octobre 1902 au 15 mai 1903." *Annales du Service des Antiquités de l'Égypte* 5 (1905): 1–43.

Legrain, G. *Répertoire genealogique du Musée du Caire. Monuments de la XVIIe et la XVIIIe dynastie*. Geneva, 1908.

Legrain, G. *Statues et Statuettes de rois et de particuliers I*. Cairo, 1906.

Leibovitch, J. A. *A Guide to the Treasures of Tutankhamun*. Cairo, 1945.

Lesko, L. H. *King Tut's Wine Cellar*. Berkeley, 1977.

Lichtheim, M. *Ancient Egyptian Literature 1: The Old and Middle Kingdoms*. Berkeley, 1973.

Lichtheim, M. *Ancient Egyptian Literature 2: The New Kingdom*. Berkeley, 1976.

LITTAUER, M. A. and J. H. CROWEL. *Chariots and Related Equipment from the Tomb of Tutankhamun*. Oxford, 1985.

LITTAUER, M. A. and J. H. CROWEL. "Unrecognized Linch Pins from the Tombs of Tutankhamun and Amenophis III: A Reply." *Göttinger Miszellen* 100 (1987): 57–61.

LOEBEN, C. "Abbildungs Konkordanz zwischen der englischen und der deutschen Ausgabe von Carters Tutanchamun-Publikation." *Göttinger Miszellen* 40 (1980): 69–80.

LOEBEN, C. "Ein Bestattung der großen königlichen Gemahlin Nofretete in Amarna? Die Totenfigur der Nofretete." *Mitteilunen des Deutschen Archäologischen Instituts Abteilung Kairo* 42 (1986): 79–107.

LORET, V. "Le tombeau d'Amenophis II et la cachette royale de Biban el Molouk." *Bulletin de l'Institut Français d'Archéologie Orientale* 9 (1899): 98–122.

LUCAS, A. "Notes on Some Objects from the Tomb of Tutankhamun." *Annales du Service des Antiquités de l'Égypte* 41 (1942): 135–147.

LUCAS, A. "Notes on Some of the Objects from the Tomb of Tutankhamun." *Annales du Service des Antiquités de l'Égypte* 45 (1947): 133–134.

M

MACDOWELL, A. G. *Village Life in Ancient Egypt. Laundry Lists and Love Songs*. Oxford, 1999.

MACE. A. C. "Work at the Tomb of Tutankhamon." *Egyptian Expedition 1922–1923/Bulletin of the Metropolitan Museum of Art* (December 1923 Part II): 5–11.

MALEK, J. *The Treasures of Tutankhamun*. London: Andre Deutsch 2006 and 2012.

MALLAKH, K. EL, and A. C. BRACKMAN. *The Gold of Tutankhamen*. New York, 1978.

MANNICHE, L. *Ancient Egyptian Musical Instruments*. Munich, 1975.

MANNICHE, L. "The Body Colours of Gods and Man in Inlaid Jewellery and Related Objects from the Tomb of Tutankhamun." *Acta Orientalia* 43 (1982): 5–12.

MANNICHE, L. *Musical Instruments from the Tomb of Tutankhamun*. Oxford, 1975.

MANNICHE, L. "The So-called Scenes of Daily Life in the Private Tombs of the Eighteenth Dynasty: An Overview." In *The Theban Necropolis: Past, Present and Future*, edited by N. Strudwick and J. H. Taylor, 40–45. London: 2003.

MANNICHE, L. "The Wife of Bata." *Göttinger Miszellen* 18 (1975): 33–35.

MARIETTE, A. *Notice des Principaux Monumetns exposés dans les galleries provisoires du Musée d' antiquités égyptiennes de S. A. Le Vice-Roi á Boulaq*. Alexandria, 1868.

MARTIN, G. *The Hidden Tombs of Memphis*. London, 1990.

MARTIN, G. The *Memphite Tomb of Horemheb, Commander-in-Chief of Tutankhamun I*. London, 1990.

MARTIN, G. *The Royal Tomb at el-Amarna I: The Objects*. London, 1974.

MARTIN, G. *The Royal Tomb at El-Amarna II*. London, 1989.

MCDOWELL, A. G. *Jurisdiction in the Workmen's Community of Deir el-Medina*. Leiden, 1990.

MCLEOD, W. *Composite Bows from the Tomb of Tutankhamun*. Oxford, 1970.

McLeod, W. *Self Bows and Other Archery Tackle from the Tomb of Tutankhamun*. Oxford, 1982.

MELTZER, E. S. "The Parentage of Tutankhamun and Smenkhkare." *Journal of Egyptian Archaeology* 64 (1978): 134–135.

METROPOLITAN MUSEUM OF ART. *Treasures of Tutankhamun at the Metropolitan Museum of Art*. New York, 1978.

METROPOLITAN MUSEUM OF ART. *Wonderful Things: The Discovery of Tutankhamun's Tomb*. New York, 1976.

MONTAGU, J. "One of Tutankhamun's Trumpets." *Journal of Egyptian Archaeology* 64 (1978): 133–134.

MORKOT, R. "Nakhtmin, the Supposed Viceroy of Ay." *Wepwawet* 1 (1985): 4.

MÜLLER, H. W. et al. *Nofretete–Echnaton*. Mainz, 1976.

MURNANE, W. J. *Ancient Egyptian Coregencies*. Chicago, 1977.

MURNANE, W. J. "Tutankhamun on the Eighth Pylon at Karnak." *Varia Aegyptiaca* 1 (1985): 59–68.

MURRAY, H. and M. NUTTALL. *A Handlist to Howard Carter's Catalogue of Objects in Tutankhamun's Tomb*. Oxford, 1963.

N

NEWBERRY, P. *Funerary Statues and Model Sarcophagi*: Vol. 2 and 3. Cairo, 1930–1957.

NOLTE, B. Die *Glasgefässe im Alten Ägypten*. Munch, 1968.

O

OCKINGA, B. *A Tomb from the Reign of Tutankhamun at Akhmim*. Australian Center for Egyptology Reports 10. Warminster, 1997.

OSBORN, D. J. "Corrections and Identifications of the Alabaster Ibexes in Tutankhamun's Treasures." *Journal of Egyptian Archaeology* 73 (1987): 243–244.

P

PECK, W. H. "The Discoverer of the Tomb of Tutankhamun and the Detroit Institute of the Arts." *Journal of the Society of the Study of Egyptian Antiquities* 11 (1981): 65–67.

PEET, T. E., L. Woolley, et al. *The City of Akhenaton I* (London, 1923).

PENDLEBURY, J. D. S. *The City of Akhenaten Part III: The Central City and the Official Quarters*. London, 1951.

PENDLEBURY, J. D. S. "Preliminary Report of the Excavations at Tell el–Amarnah, 1932–33." *Journal of Egyptian Archaeology* 19 (1933): 113–118.

PENDLEBURY, J. D. S. *Tell el–Amarna*. London, 1935.

PEREPELKIN, G. *Keie i Semenekhkare* (Moscow, 1979).

PEREPELKIN, G. *The Secret of the Gold Coffin* (Moscow, 1978).

PETRIE, W. M. F. *Kahun, Gurab, and Hawara*. London, 1890.

PETRIE, W. M. F. *Tell el Amarna*. London, 1894.

PFISTER, R. "Les textiles du tombeau de Toutankhamon." *Revue des Arts Asiatiques* 11 (1937): 208–218.

PIANKOFF, A. *Les chapelles de Tout-ankh-Amon*. Cairo, 1952.

PIANKOFF, A. *The Shrines of Tut-Ankh-Amon*. New York, 1955.

PIOTROVSKY, B. B. et al., *Sokrovishcha grobnitsy Tutankhamona*. Exhibition catalog. Moscow, 1973–1974.

PODGÓRSKI, T. "The Position of Tutankhamun's Feathered Corselet against Iconographic Sources." In *Fifth International Congress of Egyptologists, Abstracts of Papers*, 220. Cairo, 1988.

Q

QUIBELL, J. "A Tomb at Haweret el Gurob." *Annales du Service des Antiquités de l'Égypte* 2 (1902): 141–143.

R

RATIÉ, S. "Quelques problemes soulevés pour la persecution de Toutankhamon." *Hommages à François Doumas*, vol. 2, 545–548. Montpellier, 1986).

RAY, J. D. "The Parentage of Tutankhamun." *Antiquity* 49/113 (March 1975): 45–47.

RAY, J. D. Review article of D. B. Redford, Akhenaten, the Heretic King. *Göttinger Miszellen* 86 (1985): 81–93.

REDFORD, D. B. *Akhenaten, the Heretic King*. Princeton, 1984.

REDFORD, D. B. *History and Chronology of the Eighteenth Dynasty of Egypt: Seven Studies*. Toronto, 1967.

REDFORD, D. B. "Once again, the Filiation of Tutankhamun." *Journal of the Society of the Study of Egyptian Antiquities* 9/3 (June 1979): 111–115.

REED, C. A. and D. J. OSBORN. "Taxonomic transgressions in Tutankhamun's Treasures." *American Journal of Archaeology* 82 (1978): 273–283.

REEVES, C. N. "On the Miniature Mask from the Tutankhamun Embalming Cache." *Bulletin de la Société d'Égyptologie Genève* 8 (1983): 81–83.

REEVES, C. N. "Tutankhamun and His Papyri." *Göttinger Miszellen* 88 (1985): 39–45.

REEVES, C. N. Valley *of the Kings: The Decline of a Royal Necropolis*. London, 1990.

REEVES, N. *Ancient Egypt: The Great Discoveries: A Year-by-Year Chronicle*. London, 2000.

Reeves, N. *Ancient Egypt at Highclere Castle*. Highclere, 1989.

REEVES, N. *The Complete Tutankhamun*. London, 1990.

REEVES, N. "A Further Occurrence of Nefertiti as Hmt nswt." *Göttinger Miszellen* 30 (1978): 61–69.

REEVES, N. "New Light on Kiya from Texts in the British Museum." *Journal of Egyptian Archaeology* 74 (1988): 91–101.

REEVES, N. *Tutankhamun Pocket Guide*. London, 1987.

REEVES, N. "Tuthmosis IV as 'Great–Grandfather' of Tutankhamun." *Göttinger Miszellen* 56 (1982): 65–69.

Reeves, N. and R. H. Wilkinson. *The Complete Valley of the Kings*. London, 1998.

RIESTERER, P. *Das Ägyptische Museum Kairo II. Grabschatz des Tut–ench–Amun*. 3 Auflage. Cairo, 1972.

RITNER, R. K. "Unrecognized Decorated Linch Pins from the Tomb of Tutankhamon and Amenhotep III." *Göttinger Miszellen* 74 (1986): 53–56.

ROBINS, G. "Isis, Nephthys, Selket, and Neith Represented on the Sarcophagus of Tutankhamun and in Four Free.standing Statues found in KV 62." *Göttinger Miszellen* 72 (1984): 21–25.

ROBINS, G. *Musical Instruments from the Tomb of Tutankhamun*. Oxford, 1976.

ROBINS, G. "The Proportions of Figures in the Decoration of the Tombs of Tutankhmaun (KV 62) and Ay (KV 23)." *Göttinger Miszellen* 72 (1984): 27–32.

ROBINS, G. "Two Statues from the Tomb of Tutankhamun." *Göttinger Miszellen* 71 (1984): 47–50.

ROMER, J. *Valley of the Kings*. London, 1981.

ROSS, E. D. *The Art of Egypt through the Ages*. London, 1931.

Roth, A. M. and C. Roehrig. "Magical Bricks and the Bricks of Birth." *Journal of Egyptian Archaeology* 33 (2002): 120–139.

Rowe, A. "Inscriptions on the Model Coffin Containing the Lock of Hair of Queen Tiye." *Annales du Service des Antiquités de l'Égypte* 40 (1940–1941): 623–627.

S

Saad, R. "Fragments d'un monument de Toutankhamon retrouvés dans le IVe pylone de Karnak." *Karnak V 1970–1972*, 93–109. Cairo, 1975.

Saleem, S. N. and Z. Hawass. „Variability in Brain Treatment During Mummification of Royal Egyptians Dated to the 18th–20th Dynasties: Archaeologic and MDCT Study." *American Journal of Radiology*, forthcoming.

Saleh, M. and H. Sourouzian, H. *The Egyptian Museum, Cairo: Official Catalogue*. Mainz, 1986.

Samson, J. *Amarna, City of Akhenaten: Nefertiti as Pharaoh*. Warminster, 1978.

Schaden, O. J. *The God's Father Ay*. PhD dissertation, University of Minnesota. University Microfilms, 1978.

Schlogl, H. A. *Echnaton – Tutanchamun: Fakten und Texte*. Weisbaden, 1983.

Schneider, H. D. *Shabtis: An Introdution to the History of Ancient Egyptian Funerary Statuettes with a Catalogue of the Collection of Shabtis in the National Museum of Antiquities at Leiden*. 2 vols. Leiden, 1977.

Schorsch, D. "Precious-Metal Polychromy in Egypt in the Time of Tutankhamun." *Journal of Egyptian Archaeology* 87 (2001): 63–71.

Schulman, A. R. "Ankhesenamun, Nefretity, and the Amka Affair." *Journal of the American Research Center in Egypt* 15 (1978): 43–48.

Schulman, A. R. "The Berlin 'Trauerrelief' (No. 12411) and Some Officials of Tutankhamun and Ay." *Journal of the American Research Center in Egypt* 4 (1965): 55–68.

Schulman, A. R. "Excursus on the Military Officer Nakhtmin." *Journal of the American Research Center in Egypt* 3 (1964): 124–126.

Schulman, A. R. "Some Observations on the Military Background of the Amarna Period." *Journal of the American Research Center in Egypt* 3 (1964): 51–69.

Seele, K. C. "King Ay and the Close of the Amarna Age." *Journal of Near Eastern Studies* 14 (1955): 168–180.

Seton-Williams, M. V. *Tutankhamun der Pharao, das Grab, der Goldschatz*. Frankfurt, 1980.

Settgast, J. et al. *Tutanchamun*. Berlin exhibition catalog. Mainz, 1980. (Similar catalogs were prepared for Cologne, Hamburg, Hanover, and Munich.)

Silverman, D. P. "Cryptographic Writing in the Tomb of Tutankhamun." *Studien zur Altägyptischen Kultur* 8 (1980): 233–236.

Silverman, D. P. "The Curse of the Pharaohs." *Expedition* 29.2 (1987): 56–63.

Silverman, D. P. *Fifty Wonders of Tutankhamun*. New York, 1978.

Silverman, D. P. *Masterpieces of Tutankhamun*. New York, 1978.

Simpson, W. K. "The Head of a Statue of Tutankhamun in the Metropolitan Museum." *Journal of Egyptian Archaeology* 41 (1955): 112–114.

Smith. B. W., D. B. Redford, et. al. *The Akhenaten Temple Project I*. Warminster, 1976.

Smith, G. E. *Tutankhamen and the Discovery of His Tomb by the Late Earl of Carnarvon and Mr Howard Carter*. London, 1923.

Smith, J. L. *Tombs, Temples, and Ancient Art*. Edited by C. L. Smith. Norman, 1956.

Spiegelberg, W. "Zu dem Grabfunde des Tutenchamun." *Orientalistische Literaturzeitung* 3 (1925): 140–144.

Spiegelberg, W. "Die Grabkammer des Tutenchamun." *Annales du Service des Antiquités de l'Égypte* 38 (1938): 641–667.

Spiegelberg, W. "Zu dem Jagdbildern des Tutanchamun." *Orientalistische Literaturzeitung* 28 (1938): 569–571.

T

Tait, W. J. *Game–boxes and Accessories from the Tomb of Tutankhamun*. Oxford, 1982.

Tawfik, S. "Aton Studies 3. Back again to Nefer–nefru–Aton." *Mitteilunen des Deutschen Archäologischen Instituts Abteilung Kairo* 31 (1975): 159–168.

Tawfik, S. "Tutanchamuns Grab: Provisorium oder Kuntsvolles Novum?" In *Quaerentes Scientiam. Festgabe für Wolfhart Westendorf zu seinem 70. Geburtstag*, edited by H. Behlmer, vol. 2, 1131–1139. Göttingen, 1984.

Thibault, J. "La masque d'or de Toutankhamon radiographié." *Photo-ciné-revue* (May 1968): 216–217.

Thomas, E. "The Four Niches and Amuletic Figures in Theban Royal Tombs." *Journal of the American Research Center in Egypt* 3 (1965): 71–78.

Tiradritti, F. *The Treasures of the Egyptian Museum*. Vercelli, 1999.

V

Vandenberg, P. *The Curse of the Pharaohs*. New York, 1975.

Vandersleyen, C. "L'iconographie de Tutankhamon et les effigies provenant de sa tombe." *Bulletin de la Société d'Égyptologie Genève* 9-10 (1984–1985): 309–321.

Vandersleyen, C. "Pourquoi a ete creusée la tombe de Toutankhamun." In *Studia Paulo Naster Oblata*, edited by J. J. Quaegebeur, vol. 2, 263–268. Louvain, 1982.

Vandersleyen C. "Quelques enigmas éclaircies à propos de la tombe de Toutankhamon." *Bulletin de la Société d'Égyptologie Genève* 8 (1983): 97–99.

Vergote, J. *Toutankhamon dans les archives Hittites*. Istanbul, 1961.

Vilimkova, M. "Pectoralien in Form von Tutanchamûns erstem Namen nb-xprw-ra und ihre Varianten." *Annals of the Náprstek Museum* 9 (1980): 163–169.

W

Wallert, I. Der verzierte Löffel. *Seine Formgeschichte und Verwendungim alten Ägyptien*. Cairo, 1967.

Weeks, K. R. *The illustrated Guide To Luxor: Tombs, Temples, and Museums*. Vercelli: White Star, 2005.

Weeks, K. R. *KV 5: A Preliminary Report on the Excavation of the Tomb of the Sons of Rameses II in the Valley of the Kings*. Cairo: AUC Press, 2002.

Weeks, K. R. *The Lost Tomb*. New York: William Morrow, 1998.

Weeks, K. R. (ed.) *The Treasures of the Valley of the Kings: Tombs and Temples of the Theban West Bank in Luxor*. Cairo: AUC Press, 2002.

Weigall, A. *The Life and Times of Achenaton, Pharaoh of Egypt*. London, 1922.

Weigall, A. *Tutankhamon and Other Essays*. New York, 1924.

Westendorf, W. "Bermerkungen zur 'Kammer de Wiedergeburt' im Tutanchamungrab." *Zeitschrift für ägyptische Sprache und Altertumskunde* 94 (1967): 1939–150.

Wiese, A. and A. Brodbeck (eds.). *Tutankhamun: The Golden Beyond*. Basel, 2004.

Wijngaarden, W. D. van. "Objects of Tutankhamun in the Rijksmuseum of Antiquities at Leiden." *Journal of Egyptian Archaeology* 22 (1936): 1–2.

Wildung, D. and G. Grimm. *Gütter und Pharaonen*. Mainz, 1978.

Wilkinson, A. *Ancient Egyptian Jewellery*. London, 1971.

Wilkinson, A. "Evidence for Osirian Rituals in the Tomb of Tutankhamun." In *Pharaonic Egypt: The Bible and Christianity*, edited by S. I Groll, 328–340. Jerusalem, 1985.

Wilkinson, A. "Jewelry for a Procession in the Bed Chamber in the Tomb of Tutankhamun." *Bulletin de l'Institut Français d'Archéologie Orientale* 84 (1984): 335–345.

Williams, M. O. "At the Tomb of Tutankhamen." *National Geographic Magazine* (May 1923): 461–508.

Winlock, H. E. *Materials Used in the Embalming of King Tût-'ankh-Amun*. New York, 1941.

Winlock, H. E. *The Treasures of Three Egyptian Princesses*. New York, 1948.

Winlock, H. E. *Tutankhamun's Funeral*. Introduction and Appendix by Dorothea Arnold. New York, 2010.

Wood, R. W. "The Purple Gold of Tutankhamun." *Journal of Egyptian Archaeology* 20 (1934): 62–65.

Wynne, B. *Behind the Mask of Tutankhamen*. London, 1972.

Z

Zabkar, V. "Correlation of the Transformation Spells of the Book of the Dead and the Amulets of Tutankhamun's Mummy." In *Mélanges offerts à Jean Vercoutter*, edited by F. Geus and F. Thill, 375–388. Paris, 1985.

Ziegler, C. (ed.). *The Pharaohs*. Milan, 2002.

INDEX

A

Aanen 24
Abbott and Costello Meet the Mummy 222
Abdel Aziz, Sabri 155
Abdel Badea, Mohamed 199
Abdel Fatah, Sherief 156
Abdel Kader, Mohamed 250
Abdel Rahman, Hani 155, 165
Abdel Rasoul 62, 186
Abdel Rasoul family 174, 182, 186
Abdel Rasoul, Hussein 62
Abdel Rasoul, Sheikh Ali 62, 89, 186
Abdel Shakour, Moustafa 187
Abou el Dahab, Atef 242
Abou Zied, Omar 206
Abusir 19, 32, 35
Abydos 21, 22, 45, 56, 61
Adam, Shihata 246
Adamson, Richard 61
Adze 97, 228, 229, 235
Aegean 87
Aegean influence 73, 146
Aegyptische Nachrichten 251
Afghanistan 145
Afifi, Mahmoud 217
Afnet 73
Africa 72, 79, 131
afterlife 9, 19, 41, 45, 46, 47, 48, 52, 71, 72, 80, 85, 96, 97, 111, 120, 128, 130, 134, 135, 142, 143, 157
afterlife, democratization of 56, 57, 143, 155, 162
Agricultural Museum (Cairo) 239
Ahhotep I 21
Ahmed, Amal 165
Ahmose (king) 21, 22, 156, 186, 249
Ahmose (queen) 22
Ahmose-Nefertari 21, 22
akh 41
Akhenaten (see also: Amenhotep IV) 9, 15, 26, 27, 28, 29, 30, 31, 33, 34, 46, 47, 58, 68, 77, 79, 81, 86, 103, 104, 106, 120, 153, 162, 163, 164, 166, 167, 169, 170, 171, 175, 183, 197, 206, 209, 237, 249
Akhenaten Museum 206
Akhetaten 27, 28, 162, 163
Akhmim 34, 224
alabaster (see: calcite) 21, 29, 42, 65, 69, 70, 71, 77, 80, 83, 87, 89, 90, 91, 98, 101, 104, 110, 114, 115, 116, 121, 128, 135, 136, 148, 157, 182, 204, 205, 206, 226, 227, 228, 230, 231, 233, 235, 236, 237, 238
al-Asfar, Ali 181
Alcott, Louisa May 214
Alexander the Great 65
Allen, James 29
Allied Control Council 252
alloy, copper 72, 103
almonds 157
Aly Gamal Edlin 156
Amarna 26, 27, 28, 30, 31, 32, 47, 58, 68, 69, 79, 96, 146, 162, 163, 164, 166, 183, 197, 206, 224, 249, 251, 252,
Amarna letters 28
Amarna Period 9, 28, 30, 34, 52, 58, 68, 77, 79, 81, 83, 93, 156, 162, 167, 175, 183, 207,
Amarna Period, artistic conventions 96, 120,
Amarna Royal Tombs Project 29, 170, 191
Amarna style 34, 35,
amazonite 103
Amduat (see also, *Imy Duat*, *Book of What is in the Netherworld*) 34, 49, 52, 53, 93, 97
Amenhotep called Huy 35
Amenhotep I 15, 22
Amenhotep II 23, 53, 185, 198
Amenhotep III 15, 23, 24, 25,32, 35, 68, 77, 124, 125, 146, 154,162, 163, 164, 166, 167, 169, 197, 199, 204, 205, 206, 236, 237
Amenhotep IV (see also: Akhenaten) 15, 25, 26, 162
Amenmesse, tomb of 181
Amennakht, tomb of 190
Amer, Hany 165
Amherst, Lord 58
Ammut 41, 74, 75
Amonherkhepershef, tomb of 168
Amonherkhepeshef 178
amphora 135, 195, 235
amphora, Canaanite 198
amphora, double 135, 235
amulet 43, 79, 137, 142, 149, 150, 151, 195, 230, 231, 232,238
amulet, Anubis 150, 232
amulet, *djed* 151, 228, 232, 233, 237, 238
amulet, double uraeus 149
amulet, gold 137, 150
amulet, heart 137, 238
amulet, Horus 79, 80, 150, 232
amulet, human-headed uraeus 149, 232
amulet, *khepesh* 137, 238
amulet, papyrus 150
amulet, scimitar 137, 238
amulet, Thoth 150, 232
amulet, vulture 149, 232
amulet, *wadj* 150, 232, 232
Amun 19, 21, 22, 23, 25, 26, 27, 31, 32, 33, 35, 46, 57, 71, 76, 86, 90, 185, 206, 207, 208, 241
Amun, God's Wife of 21, 22
Amun-Re 31, 53, 76, 90, 148, 183
Ancient DNA Laboratory (Cairo) 165
androgenous 27
animals, wild 120, 132, 159
ankh 23, 71, 89, 95, 97, 113, 118, 122, 135, 178, 179, 206, 229, 233, 238
Ankhesenamun 29, 30, 31, 32, 36, 37, 81, 83, 85, 89, 136, 164, 166, 169, 170, 175, 183, 197, 224
Ankhesenamun, embalming cache of 183
Ankhesenpaaten 30, 162, 163
Ankhhaf 65
Ankhkheperure Neferneferuaten 68
Ankhkheperure/Ankhetkheperure/Ankh(et)kheperure 29, 68, 110, 111, 120, 143, 162, 163
Annexe 68, 85, 119, 127, 128, 130, 134, 137, 138, 150, 230, 235
Antechamber 48, 63, 68, 69, 71, 72, 79, 85, 87, 88, 89, 91, 96, 101, 128, 130, 134, 145, 227
Antiquities Department 61, 186, 187,
Antiquities Service 58, 63, 64, 65, 68, 70, 88, 89, 92, 93, 98, 142, 216
Anubis 41, 42, 43, 50, 57, 90, 97, 104, 119, 143, 150, 179, 183, 195, 214, 232
Anubis amulet 150, 232
Anubis fetish 90, 231
Anubis shrine 104, 105, 112, 214, 233
Anubis, as a ram 180
Apis bull 32
Apophis 52, 53
appliqué, leopard head 70, 77
Artatama 24, 249
Archaeological Museum of South Tyrol (Italy) 156
architecture 18, 48, 179, 187,
army 23, 33, 70, 90, 137, 146
Arnold, Dorothea 7, 242
arrow 23, 32, 33, 58, 70, 146, 158, 159, 228, 229, 231, 235, 236, 237, 240, 241, 243
artist 23, 27, 30, 35, 58, 91, 96, 97, 98, 103, 114, 116, 189, 199, 207, 250
artistic convention 120, 167
Arts and Exhibitions International 223, 247
Ashmunein 30, 163, 243
astronomical instrument 163
atef crown 22, 178, 241
Aten 26, 27, 29, 30, 31, 83, 93, 162, 167, 183
Aten, Dazzling 25, 26,
Aten, Great Hymn to the 26,
Aten, temples of 27, 28
Atlanta (USA) 223, 248
Attorney General (Egypt) 217
Atum 53, 76, 108, 122, 137, 234
autosomal DNA 167
Avaris 20, 21
ax, model 197
Ay 15, 24, 26, 77, 97, 128, 163, 183, 197, 224, 243
Ay, tomb of (Amarna) 26
Ay, tomb of (Thebes) 197, 224
Ayrton, Edward 47, 58, 68, 198

B

ba 41, 44, 53, 126, 143
baboon 34, 41, 49, 97, 114, 206, 207, 208
Bahariya Oasis 60, 65, 217
Bak 27
Baketaten 164
Ball, Markus 165
bandages 42, 43, 90, 106, 126, 142, 143, 144, 154,182, 228, 240
banquet, funerary 47
barge, ceremonial 139
bark 139
barley 31, 124, 240
barque, day- 52,
barque, lunar 114,
barque, night- 52,
barque, solar 52, 97, 138
basket 71, 88, 89, 112, 113, 128, 148, 195, 226, 227, 229, 230, 231, 235, 236, 237, 240, 241
basket, *heb* 95
basket, *neb* 72,95, 112, 131, 148
battle 20, 33, 70, 76, 79, 120, 137, 146, 148,
BBC 90
beads 77, 101, 103, 124, 143, 147, 148, 153, 154, 157, 227, 229, 232, 233, 236, 240, 242
beard 86, 98, 103, 122, 205, 207
bed 60, 65, 74, 81, 156, 182, 183, 229
bed, Ammut 74, 75, 85 , 230
bed, cow 74, 81, 228,
bed, lion 74, 227
bed, ritual 72, 74, 81
bed, with lion legs 81, 241
beef 157
Belzoni, Giovanni Battista 170, 186
benben 45, 137
Benedite, Georges 215
Beni Hasan 58
Bent'anta, tomb of 180
benu 137
Berlin (Germany) 9, 246, 251
Berlin Museum (Germany) 250, 252
Bes 77, 87, 133, 136, 230
Bes, head of 91
Bes-head disks 87
bier 98, 126, 220, 231, 234
Biga 35
black cumin 157
black spots on walls of KV 62 211
black, as color of resurrection 73, 95, 113, 124
Blessed Fields 41
blinkers 87, 230
Blome, Peter 246
blood type 154
blue crown 30, 79, 89, 95, 97, 113, 128
boat 29, 52, 96, 97, 114, 127, 136, 138, 179, 189, 209
boat in tank 136, 237
boat, calcite 136, 237
boat, model 127, 138, 233, 234, 235, 236, 237, 241
bone 47, 153, 154, 156, 158, 166, 169, 170, 180, 182, 197, 198, 224, 226, 231, 240, 241
Book of Gates 52, 53
Book of the Dead (see also, *Chapters of Coming Forth by Day*) 34, 49, 53, 93, 106, 128, 150, 214, 252
Book of What is in the Netherworld (see also, *Amduat*, *Imy Duat*) 49
boomerang 146, 235, 237, 238, 240
Boraik, Mansour 7, 216
Borchardt, Ludwig 250, 251, 252
Bourse Egyptienne, La 252
bow 70, 139, 146, 158, 228, 230, 231, 234, 235, 237, 240, 241
box 13, 57, 68, 70, 72, 76, 77, 80, 104, 110, 112, 114, 116, 124, 126, 130, 155, 157, 170, 226, 228, 229, 233, 234–238, 240, 24, 243, 246, 250
box, canopic 65, 110, 233
box, cartouche 72, 95, 106, 113, 116, 227, 235, 238
box, cosmetic 78, 95, 231
box, ivory 79, 80, 227, 228, 231
box, ring 79, 80, 228
bracelet 116, 145, 151, 232, 233, 237, 238, 240, 242
bracelet, amuletic 145, 232
brain, removal of 42, 169
bread 157, 229, 238
Breasted, James Henry 60, 61
Brigham Young University 165
broad collar 76, 85, 103, 113, 144, 206, 207, 242
Brock, Lyla Pinch 191
bronze 70, 71, 73, 76, 79, 80, 90, 98, 120, 122, 124, 182, 209, 226, 227, 228, 229, 234, 235, 237, 238, 240, 241, 250
brush holder 119, 233
Brussels Museum (Belgium) 91
bull 77, 91, 127
bull, Apis 32
bureaucracy 18
Burial Chamber 35, 37, 47, 49, 52, 53, 58, 61, 63, 64, 68, 73, 88, 89, 90, 92, 96, 97, 98, 104, 152, 155, 170, 185, 186, 187, 189, 214, 216, 227, 231, 232, 242
burials, intrusive 180
burnisher, papyrus 119, 233
Burton, Harry 48, 58, 60, 61, 62, 63, 69, 70, 88, 104, 130, 142, 154, 156, 168, 174, 214, 215, 216, 264
Burton, James 175, 178, 179
Bush, George W. 223
bust of Nefertiti 27, 250, 251
Byblos 19

C

cache, embalming 181, 183
cache, mummy 13, 174, 182
Cairo 7, 9, 13, 18, 19, 63, 65, 69, 89, 92, 93, 94, 155, 174, 185, 186, 199, 214, 216, 225, 239, 240, 242, 245, 246, 247, 252, 264
Cairo University 165, 168, 211, 240, 245
calcite (= Egyptian alabaster) 65, 69, 70, 71, 77, 80, 83, 87, 89, 90, 91, 98, 101, 104, 110, 114, 115, 116, 121, 128, 135, 136, 148, 157, 182, 204, 205, 206, 226, 227, 228, 230, 231, 233, 235, 236, 237, 238
Callendar, Arthur 61
Camel 223
Campbell, Thomas 7, 242
canary 217
cancer 22, 217
canine 104, 146
canopic box 65, 110, 233
canopic canopy 108
canopic chest 108, 111, 233
canopic coffinette 110, 111
canopic jar 29, 110, 179, 180, 198
canopic shrine 104, 110, 112, 246
canopic stoppers 198
canopy, canopic 108
Capart, Jean 89
Capart, M. 91
captive, Nubian 78, 229
Carlos Museum, Michael C. (USA) 223
Carnarvon estate 64
Carnarvon, Earl of 58, 62
Carnarvon, Lady 64
Carnarvon, Lord 58, 60, 61, 63, 68, 69, 85, 89, 214, 215, 223
carnelian 83, 95, 103, 106, 107, 112, 113, 114, 115, 116, 117, 119, 143, 144, 147, 153, 228, 232
Carter, Howard 9, 13, 37, 57, 58, 60, 69, 163, 174, 175, 181, 186, 187, 191, 210, 211, 215, 223, 241, 242
cartonnage 47
cartouche 25, 47, 72, 79, 83, 90, 95, 105, 111, 116, 118, 131, 135, 143, 145, 146, 148, 178, 183, 195, 197, 221, 241
cartouche box 72, 95, 106, 113, 116, 227, 235, 238
cartouche fan 94
cedar 72, 131, 229, 245
cenotaph 180
cenotaph for family of Rameses II 180
Central Hospital Bolzano (Italy) 165
ceremony, Opening of the Mouth 44, 71, 72, 91, 137
chair 30, 73, 83, 88, 89, 229
chair, child's 73, 227
chair, wooden 131, 235
chalcedony 114, 147, 233
Chamber, Burial 35, 37, 47, 49, 52, 53, 58, 61, 63, 64, 68, 73, 88, 89, 90, 92, 96, 97, 98, 104, 152, 155, 170, 185, 186, 187, 189, 214, 216, 227, 231, 232, 242
Chanel, Coco 169
chaos 21, 32, 45, 53, 70, 77, 78, 90, 91, 120, 137, 138
chapel, tomb 44
Chapters of Coming Forth by Day (see also, *Book of the Dead*) 49, 75
chariot 23, 32, 34, 35, 58, 76, 77, 86, 87, 94, 157, 159, 228, 229, 230, 234, 240
chariot, ceremonial 87
chariot, fittings 58, 87
charioteer 34
Cheops 214
chest, canopic 108, 111, 233
chest, long-legged 131
chest, painted 70, 71, 76, 229
chest, portable 72
chest, traveling 72
chest, wooden 126, 237
Chicago 220, 222, 223, 244, 246, 247
Chicago Tribune 223
chickpeas 157
Chile 168
Chinchorro culture 168
Cleopatra 222
cloison/cloisonné 146, 147
cloth 58, 71, 73, 79, 80, 170, 179, 180, 182, 227, 228, 229, 240
clothing 44, 48, 70, 73, 86, 116, 131, 181, 217
club foot 158
CNN 210
cobra 62, 83, 100, 101, 105, 113, 114, 115, 135, 144, 148, 149, 153, 217, 231
cobra goddess 18, 77, 100, 149
cocculus 157
Coffin A 183
Coffin F 182
Coffin Texts 49
coffin, first 100, 124
coffin, inner 234

coffin, miniature (see also: coffinette) 125, 234
coffin, outer 64, 98, 100, 101
coffin, second 100, 101, 162, 231
coffin, third 101, 125, 142, 211
coffinette (see also, coffin, miniature) 111, 182
coffinette, canopic 110, 111
coffins, nest of miniature 125
collar 47, 77, 104, 144, 182, 206, 228, 232
collar, broad 76, 85, 103, 113, 144, 206, 227, 242
collar, faience 77, 227, 232
collar, falcon 144
collar, gold 27, 101
collar, *shebyu* 27, 101
collar, Two Ladies 144
collar, *wesekh* 144
colossal statue 25, 27, 205
Colossi of Memnon 204
conservation 61, 64, 93, 100, 155, 205, 209, 225, 240, 247
conservator 61, 89, 93
container, cosmetic 78, 95, 228
container, duck/goose 95, 228
container, ivory 78, 228
contract between Carnarvon and the *Times* of London 215
copper 58, 80, 90, 91, 197
copper alloy 72, 103
coregency 22, 25, 28, 162, 163
coregent 22, 47, 162
Corelli, Marie 214
coriander 157, 240
cornflower 98
corselet 76, 80, 85, 86, 94, 113, 228, 229
cosmetic container 78, 95, 228
cosmetic jar 91, 231
cosmetics 33
cosmos 21, 40, 85
counterpoise (see also, counter-weight) 114, 115, 144, 147, 148, 233
counterweight (see also, counter-poise) 113
court, royal 31, 34, 197
court, royal, relocation of 162
courtiers 31, 34, 47
cow 25, 46, 74, 81, 179, 241
creation 27, 30, 45, 57, 68, 74, 134, 166, 167, 175
crescent, lunar 114
crocodile 74, 75
crook 31, 98, 100, 101, 113, 116, 117, 124, 143, 228, 233
Cross, Stephen 191
crown 18, 19, 25, 29, 31, 44, 79, 83, 86, 128, 136, 179, 207, 209, 241, 250
crown, *atef* 22, 178,241
crown, blue 30, 79, 89, 95, 97, 113, 128
crown, red 18, 94, 105, 114, 121, 148, 205, 209
crown, white 18, 94, 105, 114, 122, 124, 128, 148
crystal 70, 71, 107
CT scan 13, 42, 154, 156, 157, 158, 159, 167, 169, 170
CT scanner 13, 154, 166, 216, 217
cup 58, 71, 83, 89, 227
cup, drinking 71
cup, lotus 69, 71
cups, pottery 226
curse 9, 214, 215, 216, 217, 222, 223
Curse of the Pharaohs, The 215

D

dagger 146, 231
dagger, ceremonial 146
Daily Show, The 223
Dakhleh Oasis 168
dates 76, 83, 178, 183, 185, 210
Davies, Norman de Garis 29
Davis, Theodore 47, 57, 58, 68, 175, 198
de Montebello, Philippe 242
death 21, 26, 27, 28, 37, 39, 40, 41, 47, 49, 65, 73, 78, 100, 146, 148, 153, 154, 156, 157, 158, 159, 163, 167, 169, 170, 175, 198, 214,215, 225
deformity, genetic 169
deification of the king 25
deification of the queen 25
Deir el-Bahri 186, 210, 246
Deir el-Bahri, mummy cache of 174, 182
Delta 18, 20, 32, 144, 150, 183
Derry, Douglas 142, 153, 154, 157, 163, 168, 169, 224, 240
desert 32, 40, 42, 46, 52, 56, 65, 70, 91, 94, 132, 138, 151, 159, 215, 216, 217, 225
Desert, Eastern 33, 58, 124
Deutsche Orient-Gesellschaft 252
diadem 153, 154, 232
diet 157
diorite 204
diplomacy 30
Discovery Channel 165, 169
Discovery Times Square 223, 242, 247
disease 27, 113, 121, 155, 156, 158, 167
disk, lunar 114, 145, 148
disk, solar (= Aten) 25, 26, 30, 72, 74, 81, 94, 105, 112, 113, 114, 121, 147, 148, 162, 178
disks, Bes-head 87
division of finds 57, 251
Djahy 33
djed 122, 88, 105, 148, 151, 214, 231, 232, 233
djed amulet 151, 228, 232, 233, 237, 238
Djedefre 19
Djeser-Kheperure Smenkhkare 29
Djoser 45
DNA 7, 9, 13, 158, 165, 166, 167, 169, 170, 171, 224
DNA, autosomal 166, 167
DNA, mitochondrial 166
DNA, nuclear 166
dog 70, 91, 94, 214, 238
donkey 61, 62
drink 41, 48, 128, 157
Duamutef 108, 123, 234
Duat 49, 52
duck 116, 228
dwarf 77, 136
Dynasty, 1st 18, 56
Dynasty, 2nd 42
Dynasty, 3rd 18, 45, 53
Dynasty, 4th 19, 70
Dynasty, 5th 19, 49
Dynasty, 6th 14, 49
Dynasty, 11th 58
Dynasty, 12th 18, 19
Dynasty, 13th 20
Dynasty, 18th 15, 21, 22, 23, 24, 25, 26, 27, 28, 29, 30, 34, 36, 41, 44, 47, 53, 57, 58, 79, 162, 166, 175, 178, 183, 184, 185, 186, 191, 197, 198, 207, 214, 224
Dynasty, 19th 15, 41, 42, 43, 49, 50, 51, 53, 56, 58, 178, 180, 181, 249
Dynasty, 20th 15, 52, 56, 57, 175
Dynasty, 21st 57, 185

E

EAO (= Egyptian Antiquities Organization) 245, 246
Earl of Carnarvon 58, 62
earrings 116
ebony 68, 69, 72, 73, 78, 80, 81, 85, 98, 100, 116, 122, 131, 226, 227, 228, 229, 230, 231, 233,235, 237
education 210
Egarter, Edward 156
Egypt, Lower 18, 31, 57, 79, 80, 94, 98, 105, 114, 120, 131, 138, 148, 149, 150, 158, 205, 206, 209
Egypt, Upper 18, 19, 20, 31, 58, 79, 80, 92, 94, 98, 105, 108, 114, 120, 122, 124, 131, 138, 144, 148, 149, 186, 227
Egyptian Antiquities Organization (= EAO) 223, 245, 246, 250
Egyptian Antiquities Service 63, 65
Egyptian Mummy Project 7, 22, 154, 224
Egyptian Museum (Cairo) 7, 9, 13, 18, 20, 21, 22, 23, 24, 26, 27,28, 29, 30, 32, 35, 41, 42, 57, 63, 65, 77, 89, 91, 92, 93, 96, 104, 155, 162, 164, 65, 167, 170, 185,187, 199, 203, 209, 217, 222, 225, 239, 240, 242, 245, 246, 248
El Damaty, Mamdouh 247
El Gasab, Gamal 187
El Kab 35
El Leithy, Ahmed 184, 190
El Marsam Hotel 174, 186
El Orabi, Fouad 223, 246
el Sadik, Wafaa 248
El Sawy, Abdel Monem 223
El-Awady, Tarek 187, 189
Elder Lady 164, 166, 167, 171
electrum 32, 148, 151, 237
elephant tusk 79
Elephantine 32
Élisabeth, Queen of Belgium 89
Elleithy, Hisham 165
Eloquent Peasant, Tale of the 19
el-Sheikh, Essam 156
embalmer 42, 43, 104, 142, 143, 144, 146, 150, 156, 157, 165, 166, 168, 169
embalming 43, 104, 143, 150, 154, 156, 157, 168, 169, 182
embalming cache 183
embalming workshop 42
Emory University (USA) 223
enemies 19, 21, 25, 28, 33, 52, 53, 77, 87, 139, 245
Entrance Corridor 44, 68, 69, 226
epiphyses 153, 156
eternity 72, 80, 88, 95, 111, 113, 114, 115, 116, 118, 143, 148
ethmoid bone 42
Euphrates River 22
European Union 211, 225
Evelyn, Lady (= Herbert, Evelyn) 69, 88, 89
Exelon Company 223
external trappings 143
eye 26, 32, 43, 44, 65, 69, 70, 71, 74, 78, 98, 100, 101, 103, 104, 114, 115, 123, 147, 148, 153, 154, 198, 205, 206, 207, 223, 252
Eye of Horus (see also, *Wedjat*) 74, 87, 98, 148

F

Faculty of Medicine (Alexandria) 142
Faculty of Medicine (Cairo University) 165, 168, 240
faience 58, 68, 77, 78, 80, 83, 84, 87, 88, 98, 100, 101,103, 116, 122, 128, 135, 137, 151, 153, 179, 189, 197, 222, 226, 227, 228, 229, 230, 232, 233, 235, 236, 237, 238
Faiyum 19, 33
falcon 103, 116, 124, 126, 132, 144, 145, 147
falcon collar 144
falcon pendant 147
falcon, Gemehsu 124, 234
falcon, Soped 124, 234
family, royal 9, 21, 22, 26, 27, 28, 29, 30, 47, 162, 250
fan 30, 35, 94, 164, 178, 179, 223, 231, 233, 235, 237, 242
fan, cartouche 94
fan, ostrich hunt 76, 94, 231
fan-bearer 70, 94
Faras 35
Farouk, King 77
Fateen, Mohamed 165
Fathalla, Dina 165
Feast, Beautiful F. of the Valley 31
feast, funerary 44, 58, 182, 183, 242
feather 35, 41, 76, 104, 137, 146, 229, 240
feather of truth 75
feldspar 106, 107, 115, 145, 145, 148, 150, 226
femur 157
fenugreek 157
Festival of Opet 31, 33, 243
festival, *sed* 28, 113
fetish, Anubis 90, 231
fetus 126, 168, 169, 170, 171, 234
Field Museum of Natural History (Chicago) 223, 246, 247
Fields, Blessed 41
figure, funerary (see also, *shabti*) 34
figure, glass 79, 228
figure, ritual 86, 122, 123
figure, royal 79
figures of deities 22, 97, 104, 105, 108, 119, 120, 121, 124, 178, 209, 214, 232, 233, 234, 240
finger stalls 152
First Intermediate Period 14, 19, 41, 49, 128,
fittings, chariot 58, 87
flail 31, 128, 98, 100, 101, 113, 116, 117, 124, 128, 143, 233
Fletcher, Joanne 169
flint 197, 238
flood 18, 43, 57, 70, 170, 178, 189, 191, 211, 214, 216
flood, structure to control 190
flowers 30, 32, 47, 69, 71, 100, 101, 148, 159, 182
foes 70, 139, 228
food in Tutankhamun's tomb 157
foot/feet 32, 68, 70, 81, 91, 98, 116, 127, 152, 153, 156, 158, 159, 170, 185, 220, 229, 243
Foote Hall, Lindsley 61
footrest 73, 84, 227, 229, 235, 236, 237
footstool 230
foreign foes 19, 29, 91
foreigners in Egypt 20, 21, 25,27, 28, 70, 101
fortifications 19
Fouad, King of Egypt 133, 252
foundation deposit 57, 197, 224, 226
Fox Theater 223
fracture 157, 159
frankincense 43
fruit 68, 116, 72, 157, 158, 226, 227, 228, 229, 233, 237, 238, 240, 241
funeral 43, 44, 57, 74, 79, 81, 96, 101, 120, 182, 220
funerary feast 44, 58, 182, 183, 242
funerary figure (see also, *shabti*) 34
funerary figure, king upon a bier 126
funerary temple of Amenhotep III 199, 204
funerary temple of Hatshepsut 210
funerary temple of Rameses III 199
furniture 31, 57, 65, 74, 81, 130, 151, 195

G

Gaballah, Fawzi 165
Gad, Yahia 165
game 30, 48, 64, 134, 226, 228, 235, 237
game board 30, 116, 134, 235, 237
Garcia, Terry 247
garden 27, 30, 32
Gardiner, Alan H. 60, 61, 112
garland 98, 100, 101, 135, 144, 231
garlic 72, 157, 227
gazelle 70
Geb 41, 108, 122, 234
Gemehsu 124, 234
General Hospital of Bolzano (Italy) 156
German Oriental Society 252
Germany 165, 246, 247, 250, 251, 252
germinating Osiris figure 124, 234
gesso 68, 73, 84, 86, 92, 98, 104, 108, 116, 119, 125, 131, 226, 227, 229, 230, 240
Getty Conservation Institute 210, 211, 239
Giza 13, 18, 22, 23, 24, 32, 45, 60, 61, 70, 190, 225, 243, 246, 247
Glass 43, 68, 70, 71, 72, 74, 76, 79, 83, 87, 91, 94, 95, 98, 100, 101, 103, 105, 106, 107, 108, 111–126, 128, 133, 136, 137, 143–148, 153, 155, 164, 179, 195, 226, 227, 231, 237, 228, 242
goat 81, 157, 186, 195,
god, creator 26, 76, 78, 85, 90, 108, 121, 122, 137, 182
god, hawk-headed 179
god, universal 26
God's Father 34
God's Wife of Amun 21, 22
goddess, cobra 18, 77, 100, 149
goddess, lioness 25, 74, 113
goddess, vulture 77, 94, 100,124, 149
gold 28, 32, 35, 37, 43, 44, 48, 57, 58, 65, 68, 69, 71, 72, 73, 76, 77, 79, 80, 81, 83, 85-88, 90, 91, 94, 95, 96, 98, 100, 101, 103, 104–107, 111–119, 121, 124, 125, 131, 133, 136, 137, 139, 142–153, 164, 198, 209, 210, 222, 226–238, 241–243
gold mines 20, 21
gold of honor 77
Golden Horus 31, 131
Golden Mask 37, 73, 101, 103, 116, 117, 220, 222, 231, 239, 245
Golden Shrine, Small 32, 158, 159, 220
golden shrines 37, 52, 76, 81, 85, 215, 229
golden throne 69, 73, 83, 85, 245,
goldsmith 19
good god 94, 120, 121, 145, 146, 148, 150
goose/geese 81, 157, 228, 231
Gostner, Paul 156, 165
Gould, Jay 215
governor 19, 35, 210, 217
GPR survey (= ground-penetrating radar survey) 191
Grand Egyptian Museum 13, 93, 225, 240, 247, 250
granite 19, 23, 24, 25, 91, 98, 128, 162, 206, 207, 208
Grant, Cary 222
grapes 157
grave 42, 44
Great Flood 74
Great House (shrine) 92
Great Litany of Re 53
Great One of Magic 149
Great Royal Wife 28, 29, 49, 125, 164
Great Sphinx 23, 32, 73
grewia 157
ground-penetrating radar survey (= GPR) 191
guardian statue 73, 88, 227
Güterbock, Hans Gustav 250, 252
gypsum 98, 178

H

hair 43, 167, 168, 170, 230, 238
hair, lock of 125, 164, 167, 234
hall, pillared 47, 178, 179, 180
Hamdi, Salah Bey 142
Hamed, Aiman 187
Hanna, Morcos Bey 64, 98, 216
Hauser, Walter 61
Hapy 108
harem 13, 28, 33
Hari, Robert 170
harpooner 120
harpooner, figure of Tutankhamun as 220, 233
Harris, James E. 154, 169
Harrison, R. G. 154, 156
Har-sa-Iset 123
Hasan, Naglaa 165
Hathor 23, 25, 46, 69, 81, 97, 118, 121, 151, 178, 179, 180, 233, 241
Hatshepsut 13, 15, 22, 23, 29, 47, 56, 57, 58, 210, 246
Hawass, Zahi 7, 9, 13, 33, 42, 47, 181, 251
He Who is in the Bandages 90
head of Bes 91
head of Nefertem 86
headrest 70, 81, 131, 133, 227, 241
headrest, glass 133
headrest, ivory 133
headrest, with Bes 133
headrest, with Shu 133
healing 25, 121, 204
health 33, 65, 85, 89, 113, 148 155, 156, 158, 159, 182
heart 13, 35, 41, 43, 75, 104, 106, 147, 216, 233
heart amulet 137, 238
heart spell 106
heb basket 95
Heh 71, 89, 95, 113, 114, 115, 116, 118, 148
heirlooms 37, 77
Heliopolis 27, 31, 94, 206
Heliopolis, Southern (= Thebes) 31
Hennuttaneb 164
Henutwadjbu 183
heqa scepter 116, 117, 241
Heqanefer 35
Herbert, Aubrey 215
Herbert, Evelyn (= Lady Evelyn) 61
Herbert, George (see also, Carnarvon, Earl of, Carnarvon, Lord) 58
Herbert, Jean Margaret 62
Herodotus 158
heron 137, 233, 238
Herwer 123
heset vase 137, 236, 238
Hetepheres 158
Hetepheres, tomb of 65
hide (animal) 81, 132, 236
hieratic 79, 189, 226, 235, 238
hieroglyphs 116, 143, 149, 178, 221
Highclere Castle 60, 61, 214, 242
Hill, Marsha 242
hippopotamus 74, 75, 120, 138, 204
Hittite prince 37, 183
Hittites 28, 29, 33, 37, 250
Hittites, letter to 29
Hodgkin's disease 65
holder, brush 119, 233
honey 157
Horakhety (nur Re-Horakhety) 26, 92, 114, 124, 145, 206
Horemakhet 23, 32

Horemheb 15, 29, 31, 33, 34, 36, 37, 48, 58, 70, 77, 170, 243
horizon 23, 27, 31, 43, 74, 112, 133
horse 58, 70, 77, 87, 157, 229
Horus 18, 23, 31, 49, 50, 73, 74, 79, 103, 113, 120, 124, 126, 131, 144, 148, 150, 178, 206, 233, 234
Horus amulet 79, 80, 150, 232
Horus the Behedite 106
Horus the Child 79, 80
Horus the Great 123
Horus, Eye of (see also: *Wedjat*) 74, 87, 98, 148
Horus, son of Isis 44, 123, 150, 179, 206
Hosni, Farouk 216, 246
Hoving, Thomas 222, 223, 245
hunting 32, 35, 47, 70, 76, 85, 87, 91, 138, 146, 159, 225, 227, 237
Huri 198
huts, workmen's 60, 191, 194, 197
Huy 35
Huya, tomb of 28
Hyksos 20, 21
Hymn, Great H. to the Aten 26

I

I Was a Teenage Mummy 222
Ibex 91, 136, 237
Ibis 41, 114, 150, 232
Ibrahiem, Saed 187
Ihy 121, 233, 234
Imhotep 45
imiut 90
Imsety 108, 233
Imy Duat (see also, *Amduat*, *Book of What is in the Netherworld*) 49
incense 35, 72, 178, 227
incest, royal 167
incision (mummification) 42, 168, 169
Indus Valley 145
Ineni 56, 57
infection 63, 78, 156, 159, 214, 217
inlay 32, 71, 76, 94, 98, 100, 101, 103: 108, 112, 116, 135, 139, 143, 145, 147, 148, 150, 151, 226, 228,29, 231, 232, 235, 236
Institute for Mummies and the Iceman (Italy) 165
Institute of Human Genetics, University of Tubingen (Germany) 165, 166
intestines 43, 104, 108
inundation 40
Iny 183
Ipy 35
iron 69, 77, 146, 232, 234
Iset C 164, 167
Isis 41, 43, 44, 88, 92, 93, 97, 98, 101,105, 106, 108, 115, 149, 183, 233, 234, 249
Isis-Mehtet 74
Iskander, Zaki 154
Ismail, Somaia 165
iteru 52
Iusaas 76
ivory 68, 72-74, 78-81, 91, 116, 118,119, 133, 134, 136, 220, 226-231, 233, 235, 237, 238, 240

J

jackal 41, 57, 90, 104, 123, 146, 150, 214
jar, canopic 29, 110, 179, 180, 198
jar, cosmetic 91, 231
jar, wine 72, 157, 183, 231, 235-237, 240
jewelry 19, 43, 57, 64, 69, 73, 85,86, 104, 112, 113, 116, 136, 142, 144, 147, 149, 153, 157, 226, 233, 239
Johnson, Ray 7, 33, 158, 183, 208
Jones, Ernest Harold 58
Journal of the American Medical Association 170
jubilee 28, 89
judges, divine 41
judgment after death 41, 75
jujubes 157
juniper berries 157

K

ka 41, 71, 73, 86, 97, 113, 143, 178
Kamose 21
Kampp, Friederike 35
Karnak 21-23, 26, 27, 31, 33
Kashu 49
Kasr El Aini Hospital (Cairo) 168, 240
Kawa 35
Kerma 22
Khaemwaset, tomb of 57
Khafre 32, 70
Khairat, Rabab 165
khat 73, 98, 129, 153, 227
kheker 206
kheper 72, 112
kheperu 112
khepesh 137
khepesh amulet 137, 238
Khepri 49, 52, 95, 97, 206
Kheruef, tomb of 164
Khnum 35, 180
Khodary, El Taieb Mohamed 199, 206
Khonsu 27, 31, 33
Khufu 19, 45, 65
king 9, 13, 18, 19, 21-23, 25-37, 41, 43, 45-49, 52, 53, 56-58, 62, 64, 65, 68-73, 75-80, 83, 85, 86, 89, 91, 92, 94-98, 100, 101, 103-106, 108, 110, 111, 113, 114, 116-118, 120, 121, 124-127, 131, 132, 134, 137, 138, 143, 145, 146, 148, 150, 153-159, 162-164, 166, 167, 170, 178, 179, 183, 187, 189, 195, 204-209, 217, 220, 224, 225, 252
King Tutankhamun Family Project 162, 167
king, divine nature of 25, 131, 132, 144
king, female 162
king's daughter of his body 162, 170
king's son of his body 163
Kingdom, Middle 14, 19, 43, 45, 46, 49, 56, 58, 98, 128
Kingdom, New 15, 21, 41, 42, 46,49, 53, 56, 70, 76, 86, 117, 127, 128, 135, 137, 166, 170, 175, 182
Kingdom, Old 14, 18, 19, 26, 41, 42, 45, 53, 56, 65, 72, 128, 158
kit, scribal 119
Kiya 29
Kom el-Hitan 25, 199, 204, 205, 206
Kotb, Abdel Hamied 155
KV "C" 191, 195
KV 4 60, 104, 241
KV 5 13, 175, 176, 178, 179, 180
KV 7 180, 189, 190
KV 8 190
KV 9 60
KV 10 181, 249
KV 15 104, 142, 215
KV 17 50, 51, 186, 187
KV 20 47, 57
KV 21 166, 170, 171, 175, 224
KV 22 47, 197
KV 23 34, 36, 37, 47, 197
KV 24 197
KV 25 197
KV 27 175
KV 28 175
KV 29 184
KV 31 175, 249
KV 32 185
KV 33 175
KV 34 47
KV 35 164, 169, 170, 182, 198, 224
KV 36 57
KV 40 184
KV 41 175
KV 43 57
KV 46 47, 164, 171, 183
KV 48 175, 198
KV 49 198
KV 51 198
KV 52 198
KV 53 13, 175, 198
KV 54 47, 58, 175, 182, 183, 242
KV 55 28, 29, 58, 68, 104, 164, 182, 183, 249
KV 55 mummy 28, 153, 154, 163, 164, 166, 167, 171
KV 60 13, 22
KV 62 37, 47, 68, 163, 164, 171, 174, 183, 226, 239, 241
KV 63 13, 181, 182, 183, 185, 191
KV 64 13, 184, 185
KV35EL mummy 166, 167, 171
KV35YL mummy 166, 167, 171
kyphoscoliosis 158

L

Lacau, Pierre 63, 64, 88, 142
Lach, Mark 223
Lacovara, Peter 223
Lady of the West 180
lamp 76, 89, 217
lamp, calcite 89
lapis lazuli 32, 44, 103, 111, 112, 114, 115, 116, 133, 143, 145, 147, 148, 150, 228, 232, 238, 241
law 63
Learning Resource Center, Kasr Al Ainy Faculty of Medicine, Cairo University 165
leather 76, 81, 86, 139, 152, 229, 230, 233, 237, 238
Lebanon 72, 131
Lefébvre, Gustave 250, 251, 252
legumes 157
lentils 157
leopard 71, 97, 120, 209, 227, 228
leopard, Tutankhamun on a 209, 234
Lepsius, Karl Richard 175
letter to the Hittites 29
letters 28, 220, 223
letters, Amarna 27, 28
Levant 19-21, 23, 33, 70, 145
LI 220, 245
Libre Belgique, Le 252
Libya 19, 22
Lichtheim, Miriam 26
lily/lilies 79, 80, 138, 146
Lilyquist, Christine 245
limestone 18, 20-22, 26-29, 33,60, 68, 121, 128, 163, 179, 195, 199, 227, 229, 241, 250, 251
linen 42, 43, 47, 58, 64, 68, 81, 83, 86, 89, 92, 98, 100, 101, 104, 110, 112, 119, 120, 124-127, 133, 142, 143, 147, 149, 152-154, 156, 168, 169, 182, 198, 227-229, 231-233, 236, 237, 240-242
lion 74, 77, 81, 91, 98, 132, 136, 231, 237
lioness 121
Lisht 18, 19
literature 19
liver 13, 43, 104, 108
London *Times* 214
looting of the Egyptian Museum 210
Lord of the Mummy Wrappings 104
Los Angeles 220, 222, 223, 244, 245, 246, 247
Los Angeles County Museum (= LA County Museum) 223, 244, 246, 247
Los Angeles *Times* 223
"Lost in a Pyramid, or the Mummy's Curse" 214
lotus 18, 68, 69, 77, 85, 90, 91, 118, 135, 136, 144, 148, 180, 220
Louden, Jane Webb 214
Lucas, Alfred 60, 61, 65, 70, 93, 142, 154
lunar barque 114
lunar crescent 114
lunar disk 114, 145, 148
lungs 43, 104, 108, 131
Luxor 9, 22, 26, 33, 57, 58, 61, 65, 68, 70, 89, 155, 163, 164, 174, 181, 185, 186, 210, 215-217, 225, 241, 243
Luxor Museum 7, 19, 22, 23, 35, 240, 241
Luxor, west bank of 23, 33, 37, 56, 62, 199, 210, 214, 241, 243

M

maat 21, 75, 78, 104, 137
Maat 41, 49, 92, 93, 113, 178
mace 69, 73, 91, 97
Mace, Arthur 60, 61, 70, 88, 89
mace, ceremonial 91
magical brick 214
Mahdy, Mohammed 215
Maia 13, 30
Maia, tomb of 30, 31, 243
Maiherpri 57
makeup 118, 159
malaria 158, 159
Malqata 33, 174, 186
Mandjet 52
mandrake 116, 237
mannequin 86
Marfan syndrome 27, 162, 167
Mariette, Auguste 199
marriage, royal 24, 25, 30
marsh 30, 47, 95
Martin, Geoffrey 170, 191
Martin, Steve 220
mask 43, 47, 58, 103, 104, 142, 143, 153, 157, 210, 221, 222
Mask, Golden 37, 73, 101, 103, 116, 117, 220, 222, 231, 239, 245
Massachusetts Institute of Technology 61
mastaba 45
Maya 34, 126, 128
Maya, tomb of 31, 34, 243
medical papyri 158
Medinet el-Ghurob 28
Medinet Habu 199
Mehit-weret 74
Meketaten 29, 164
Memnon, Colossi of 204
Memphis 13, 18, 19, 27, 30-34, 90, 113, 122, 159, 163, 170, 178, 225
men/mun 116
Menkaret 121, 209, 234
Mentuhotep II 58
mercenaries 21, 83
Merenptah, tomb of 190, 195
Meretseger 149, 175, 198
Meritaten 28, 29, 68, 119, 164, 233
Meritaten-the-Younger 28
Merton, Arthur 63
Meryet 34
Meryetamun, tomb of 180
Meryre, tomb of 29
Mesektet 52
Mesopotamia 145
Metropolitan Museum of Art 7, 47, 58, 61, 63, 69, 70, 220, 222, 242, 245, 246
Middle Egypt 27
Middle Kingdom 14, 19, 43, 45, 46, 49, 56, 58, 98, 128
military 23, 32-36, 63, 77, 90
Min 24, 33, 58
Minister of Culture 216, 223, 245, 246, 252
Minister of Public Works 98, 216
Minister of State for Antiquities 9, 209
Ministry of Culture 250
Ministry of Public Works 64, 89
Ministry of State for Antiquities 184
Minya 190, 206
mirror 79, 118, 153
mirror case 118, 233
Miserendino, Tom 247
Mistress of Turquoise 151
Mit Rahina 18, 19
Mitanni 27, 24, 28, 33, 146, 249
mitochondrial DNA 166
model 76, 86, 119, 138, 139, 197, 228, 229, 230, 233, 234, 238
model ax 197
Mokhtar, Gamal 223, 245, 246
Monroe, Marilyn 169
Montu 132
Morsches, Richard 245
mosquito 63, 214
mosquito bite 214
mound, primeval 45, 56
mourners 44, 98, 182
mtDNA 166, 167, 170
mud brick 20, 32, 45, 214, 233
mummies, unidentified 162
mummification 41-43, 47, 48, 58, 74, 90, 96, 108, 143, 154, 156, 166, 169, 180, 182, 183, 242
mummy 317a 168, 169, 171
mummy 317b 168, 169, 171
mummy bands 143, 231
mummy cache 13
mummy KV21A 170, 224
mummy KV21B 170, 224
mummy KV35EL 166, 167, 171
mummy KV35YL 166, 167, 171
Mummy!, The, Or, a Tale of the Twenty-Second Century 214
mummy, Akhenaten 29, 163, 164, 167, 171
mummy, Amenhotep III 167, 171
mummy, Ankhesenamun 166, 169
mummy, Elder Lady 164, 166, 167, 171
mummy, fetus 164, 166, 168, 169, 171, 234, 240
mummy, KV 55 28, 153, 154, 163, 164, 166, 167, 171
mummy, Mutnodjmet 168, 170
mummy, Nefertiti 166, 169, 170
mummy, Smenkhkare 166, 167
mummy, Tiye 164, 166, 167, 171, 182
mummy, Tjuya 58, 154, 164, 166, 167, 171
mummy, Tutankhamun 142, 149, 155-158, 166, 169, 171, 216
mummy, Yuya 58, 154, 164, 166, 167, 171
mummy/mummies 13, 20, 22, 27, 28, 42, 43, 47, 53, 57, 58, 64,65, 71, 72, 74, 89, 91, 96-98, 101, 103, 106, 117, 121-124, 128, 139,142-147, 149-159, 162-170, 174, 182, 185, 186, 198, 209, 214-217, 222, 224, 239
murder 13, 24, 148, 154
Murray, Helen 226
Mut 27, 31, 33, 149
Mutemwia 24, 249
Mutnodjmet 168, 170, 224
muu-dancers 44
myrrh 43

N

Naga el Deir 61
Nakhtefmut 185
Nakhtmin 34, 128
names, royal 47, 68, 131, 163, 238
Narmer Palette 18, 152
National Geographic Society 154, 247
National Research Center (Cairo) 165
natron 43, 47, 182
Near East 77
neb basket 72, 95,112,131,148
Nebetiah 164, 167
Nebkheperure (= prenomen of Tutankhamun) 31, 71, 72, 79, 94, 95, 112, 113, 115, 120, 145, 146, 148, 150, 183, 233, 241
necklace 62, 77, 79, 85, 114, 115, 124, 135, 147, 148, 226-229, 231, 233
necropolis, Memphite 30
necropolis, royal 13, 34, 57, 126, 174
necropolis, Theban 46, 149, 174, 198, 239
nefer 135
Neferneferuaten 26, 29, 68
Neferneferuaten-the-Younger 29
Neferneferure 29
Nefertem 27, 64, 68, 118, 121
Nefertem, king as 220, 226, 245
Nefertiti 26, 27, 28, 29, 37, 120, 162, 164, 166, 167, 169, 170, 175, 183, 224, 252
Nefertiti, bust of 27, 250, 251
Nefertiti, disappearance of 28
Nefertum-Hor-Heken 178
Neferure 22
Nehemesbastet 185
Nehes 49
Neith 98, 108, 223
Nekhbet 18,77, 100, 101, 111, 124, 144, 148, 149
nekhekh 117
nemes 73, 100, 101, 103, 110, 124, 129, 199, 206, 227
nemset ewer 80
nemset vase 137, 236
nemset vessel 77
Nephthys 43, 44, 98, 101, 105, 106, 106, 108, 233, 234
netherworld 41, 48, 49, 52, 53, 73, 75, 90, 93, 97, 119, 120, 122, 134, 146, 157, 180, 187
Neues Museum 251
New Kingdom 15, 21, 41, 42, 46, 49, 53, 56, 70, 76, 86, 117, 127, 128, 135, 137, 166, 170, 175, 182
New Orleans 220, 222, 246
New Orleans Museum of Art 220, 246
New York 69, 175, 220, 222, 223, 242, 244-247
Newberry, Percy 58, 61
Newman, Walter 246
Newsday 220, 245
niche 179-181, 232
night 34, 47, 52, 68, 71, 73, 74, 88, 89, 120, 124, 150, 174, 175, 223
night, hours of 49, 52, 97
Nile River 18, 40
Nile Valley 18, 144
Nine Bows 139
Nixon, Richard 245
nomarch 19
Norman, John 247
Nour El Din, Abdel Halim 165
Nubia 19, 21, 22, 25, 27, 35, 37, 78
Nubia, viceroy of 22, 35
Nubian 20-22, 32, 35, 70, 83, 132, 139, 228, 229

Nubian captive 78, 229
Nubian wig 83, 94
nuclear DNA 166
Numhauser, Andre 247
Nun 43
nurse 183
nurse, royal 183
Nut 41, 92, 97, 105, 107, 108, 111, 122, 124, 143, 223
Nuttall, Mary 226
ny-ny 97

O

obelisk 22, 208
obsidian 21, 98, 101, 103, 104, 114, 119–122, 124, 153
Ockinga, Boyo 34
oil 30, 57, 76, 83, 85, 89, 130, 157, 226
ointment 78
Old Kingdom 14, 18, 19, 26, 41, 42, 45, 53, 56, 65, 72, 128, 158
olive leaves 98, 100
Om Kalthoum 169
Opening of the Mouth 37, 97
Opening of the Mouth ceremony 44, 71, 72, 91, 137
Opet, Festival of 31, 33, 243
order, cosmic 21, 41, 85, 92, 137
organs, internal 28, 36, 42
Oriental Institute 61, 163, 244
ornament, hawk (from chariot) 230
Osiris 19, 21, 22, 23, 30, 41, 44, 49, 52, 53, 72, 73, 75, 79, 88, 92, 93, 97, 98, 101, 104-106, 123, 126, 144, 148, 150, 151, 179, 180, 187, 214, 232, 233
Osiris, germinating O. figure 124, 234
Osiris, Judgment Hall of 41
Osiris, the 168, 183, 215
ostracon/ostraca 195, 196, 198
ostrich 35, 41, 70, 72, 76, 94, 124, 137, 148, 227, 233
ox 231, 233, 235

P

paint 96, 103, 116, 195, 227
Painted Chest 70, 71, 76
paintings, wall 96, 211
palace 27, 28, 30, 31, 32, 33, 45, 86, 225
palace, Memphis 31, 32
palace, of Amenhotep III (Malqata) 174
Palace of the North (shrine) 93
Palace, North (Amarna) 28
Palace, North Riverside (Amarna) 28
palette (roof of mouth), cleft 156
palette (scribal) 119, 233, 238
palette (scribal) of Nemser 152
palette (scribal), model 119
palette, scribal 119
pall 64, 89, 92, 101, 231, 240, 241
palm rib 71, 76, 80, 115, 231
Panakht 35
Papworth, Mark 170
papyrus 18, 47, 56, 69, 73, 80, 81, 85, 96, 114, 119, 120, 138, 139, 150, 152, 159, 227–230, 233, 236
papyrus amulet 150
papyrus burnisher 119, 233
P apyrus Ebers 158
Parenefer 35
Parke-Bernet Galleries 223
Parliament, Egyptian 246
Paser 56, 57
Pawera 56, 57
peas 157
pectoral 76, 105, 106, 112, 113, 114, 148, 157, 229, 231, 233
pectoral, with scarab 106, 107, 233
pectorals, inlaid 143, 232
pedigree, Tutankhamun's 170
pelvis 153
pendant 112, 114, 115, 124, 137, 147, 150, 226, 227, 232, 233
pendant, coronation 76, 113, 114
pendant, falcon 147
pendant, name 112
pendant, *Wedjat*-eye 148, 232
penis 153, 154, 157
Pentu 35
per wer (shrine) 92, 108
perfume 68, 121
Permanent Committee 181, 184, 185
persea 157, 231, 233, 240
pet 94, 111
Petrie, William Flinders 58
Philadelphia 223, 244, 247
photograph 47, 60, 62, 154, 157, 174, 181, 184, 210, 215, 223, 226, 250, 264
photographer 61, 70, 104, 211
pillows 182
pins 98, 100, 101
pit 54
Place of Eternity 34
plants 18, 23, 30, 40, 53, 114, 73, 91, 124, 131
plaque, openwork 77
plaques 77, 88, 144, 220, 226, 231
plaster 28, 42, 47, 71, 98, 178, 179, 195, 226–229, 250, 251
pneumonia 214, 215
Pococke, Richard 175
poles, carrying 72, 104
police 56, 88, 185, 209, 210, 220, 221,
police report 220
polymorphic regions 166
pomegranate 220, 227, 236
pond 30
poppy/poppies 116
portable chest 72
Portchester, Lord 214
potsherds 68, 182, 226, 231
pottery 47, 58, 62, 108, 119, 128, 135, 182, 185, 189, 195, 197, 205, 224, 226, 227, 229, 230, 231, 235, 237, 241
poultry 157
Predynastic Period 91, 92, 127, 135
pregnancies 36
priest 24, 31, 34, 43, 44, 48, 52, 57, 58, 69, 70, 71, 104, 166, 170, 179, 180, 182, 183
priest, high 24, 29, 35, 57, 162,
priest, *sem* 97
priestess 29, 81
prime minister of Egypt 250, 251
prince 23, 29, 37, 162, 178, 179, 180, 215, 224
prince, crown 33
prince, Hittite 37, 183
princess 21, 25, 28, 29, 30, 164, 185, 215, 250, 251
prisoner 91, 139
procession, funeral 44, 79
protectorate 63
Prussian Cultural Heritage Foundation 250, 251
Ptah 27, 32, 35, 76, 90, 113, 121, 122, 136, 178, 233, 234
Ptahemhaty 35
Ptah-Sokar-Osiris 108
Public Works Department (Egypt) 64
pulses 157
Pusch, Casten M. 165, 166
pylon 22, 31, 70, 104, 105, 205, 233
Pyramid Texts 49 53, 93
Pyramid, Great 45, 65, 246
Pyramid, Step 45
pyramids 13, 18, 19, 45, 46, 56, 190, 225, 247

Q

Qadesh 33
Qebehsenuef 108
quarry, Year 16 inscription at 28
quartz 103–105, 116,
quartzite 27, 63, 98, 205, 229, 235, 243
queen 13, 21, 22, 27, 29, 30, 37, 47, 56, 65, 81, 83, 85, 89, 134, 149, 159, 162, 163, 166–170, 175, 183, 195, 199, 224, 250
queen in kingly role 22, 29
Quibell, James 57, 58, 63
Qurn, el- 46, 56
Qurna, village of 210
Qurna 62, 210
QV 55 168
QV 66 41, 49
QV 68 180
QV 71 180

R

Rameses (son of Rameses II) 178
Rameses I 53
Rameses II (Rameses the Great) 48, 62, 90, 146, 175, 178, 179, 180, 186, 195
Rameses II, tomb of 178, 180, 189, 190
Rameses III 13, 57, 168, 199,
Rameses IV 52, 249
Rameses VI 60, 174, 249
Rameses X 57
Rameses XI 249
Rameses XI, tomb of 60, 68, 104, 241
rays, solar/of the Aten 26, 29, 30
Re 72, 79, 90, 94, 112, 121, 124, 137, 144, 148, 183
Re, Son of 79
rebirth 40, 53, 68, 71, 74, 95, 106, 112, 124, 136, 175
Reeves, Nicholas 29, 163, 191, 198
regent 21, 22
Re-Horakhety 26, 92, 114, 124, 145, 206
Reisner, George Andrew 65
Re-Khepri 73
religion 23, 25, 27, 30, 31, 39, 40, 162, 175
religion, change in 31,
religion, restoration of 163
replica of Nefertari's tomb 225
replica of Tutankhamun's tomb 211, 225
resin 68, 91, 103, 108, 120, 121, 124, 126, 142, 145, 153, 157, 182, 226, 227, 231, 232, 237, 240
rest house 32, 52, 62, 70, 225, 243, 245, 246
rest house, Howard Carter's 210, 211, 214, 225
rest house, tourist 191, 195
restoration 189, 199, 209, 211
resurrection 41, 44, 53, 68, 73–75, 85, 112, 113, 151
Revolution (Egyptian) 9, 184, 185, 209, 210, 217, 224, 252
ribs 156, 157, 231
ring 37, 80, 114, 115, 145, 146, 226, 227, 230, 242
ring box 79, 80, 228
ring, resin 145
ring, scarab 145
rings, triple 145
rishi pattern 98, 100, 101, 111
ritual figures 122, 123
ritual, religious 21, 41, 43, 44, 97, 105, 197
Road, Royal 27
robbery, tomb 56, 57
robe 70, 71, 80, 86, 227, 228, 235
rock crystal 146
Rockefeller, David 242
Roheim, Afifi 190
Romer, John 57, 225, 241
room alpha 164
Rowe, John 223
royal nurse 57, 183
Royal Tomb (Amarna) 29, 164
Royer, Charles 220
Rudder 127, 138
Rühli, Frank J. 156
Ryan, Donald 170

S

Sadat, Anwar 245, 246
Sadek, Abdel Aziz 246
safflower 157
sa 136
sail 127, 138
Saleh, Mohamed 165, 217
sandal 58, 70, 139, 152, 157, 227–230, 232, 233, 235–238, 240, 241
sandals, gold 152, 233
sandals, with enemy figures 139
Saqqara 13, 30, 33, 45, 47, 49, 58, 170, 243
Saqqara, North 18
sarcophagus 48, 52, 58, 63, 64, 65, 89, 93, 95, 98, 99, 100, 101,142, 153, 155, 157, 195, 211, 216, 231, 239, 242
SCA (= Supreme Council of Antiquities) 246, 247, 252
scales 41, 104, 146
scarab 34, 37, 49, 52, 62, 68, 72, 79, 80, 95, 97, 106, 112, 114–116, 145, 148, 206, 208, 226, 228, 229, 232, 233
scarab, commemorative 25
Schaden, Otto 7, 181–183
Schäfer, Heinrich 252
Schiaparelli, Ernesto 168
Schist 233
scimitar 237, 238
scimitar amulet 137, 238
scoliosis 154, 156, 169
scorpion 198, 246
scribal kit 119
scribal palette 119, 233, 238
scribal palette, of Meritaten 119, 233
scribe 41, 74
sculptor 27, 250
seal of the royal necropolis 226
seal/sealing 35, 37, 56, 57, 58, 61, 68, 88, 89, 93, 112, 120, 126, 131, 164, 181–183, 209, 214, 217, 226–228, 231, 233, 236, 241
Seattle (USA) 220, 222, 244, 246, 248
Seba 35
Sobekemsaf 57
Second Intermediate Period 15, 20, 32, 87
Secretary of State (United States) 252
sed festival 28, 113
sed shrine 89
Sedinga 25
Sekhmet 27, 76, 113, 121, 233, 234
Sekhmet, as goddess of healing 25, 113, 204
Sekhmet, statues of 25
Selim, Ashraf 156, 165
sem priest 97
sema-tawy 131
Sened 122, 234
senet 134
Senmut 22, 23
Sennedjem 34, 224
Sennedjem, tomb of 34
Senwosret III 19
Sepulchral Chamber (= Burial Chamber) 88
Seqenenre Tao 20, 21
Serapeum 32
serekh 113
sesame 157
Setepenre 29
Seth 41, 44, 90, 120, 148, 204
Seti I, tomb of 13, 50, 51, 175, 186, 225
Seti I, tunnel of 13, 186
Seti II, tomb of 89, 104, 142, 215
sexual imagery 85
shabti 34, 48, 126, 128, 129, 179, 189, 195, 209, 226, 229, 233–238, 241
Shafik, Mervat 156
Sharif, Omar 223
She Who Loves Silence 175
Shebl, Yasser 216
shebyu collar 27, 101
sheep 157
Sheikh Ali 186, 187, 189
Sheikh Nagdy 174, 175
shen 72, 80, 95, 11, 114, 115, 116, 118, 131, 143, 148
Shepheard Hotel 214
shield 132, 235–237
Shipwrecked Sailor, Tale of the 19
Shonet el Zibieb 56
short tandem repeat (= STR) 166
shrine 28, 37, 48, 53, 61, 63, 69, 85, 88, 89, 92–94, 96, 98, 104,105, 108, 120, 122, 136, 231, 233, 234, 239, 240, 241, 242
shrine, Anubis 104, 105, 112, 214, 233
shrine, canopic 104, 110, 112, 246
shrine, golden 37, 52, 76, 81, 85, 215, 229
shrine, second 89, 91, 92, 93, 95, 231
shrine, *sed* 89
Shrine, Small Golden 32, 158, 159, 220
shroud, mummy 53, 98, 142,
Shu 26, 122, 133, 148, 182, 234
Siemens Ltd 154
silver 32, 68, 71, 83, 85, 87, 90, 91, 95, 98, 100, 106-107, 110, 113, 114, 118, 124, 143, 148, 209, 220, 231, 236, 238, 242
Simon, James 252
Sinai 151, 225
songstress of Amun 185
Sinuhe, Story of 19
sistrum/sistra 80, 81, 121
Sitamun 47, 164, 167, 249
Skeletons 168
skiff 120, 138
skull 42, 122, 153, 154, 156, 168-170, 179, 198
sledge 44, 85, 96, 104, 108, 110, 120, 227, 233
small golden shrine 32, 158, 159, 220
Smenkhkare 15, 29, 31, 100, 162, 164, 167, 226, 249
smiting scene 29, 32, 243
Soeib, Ahmed 155
Sohag 13, 34, 243
soil 21, 73, 124, 187
Sokar (god) 52, 178
solar barque 52, 97, 138
solar court 208
solar disk (= Aten) 25, 26, 30, 72, 74, 81, 94, 105, 112, 113, 114, 121, 147, 148, 162, 178
soldier 28, 70
Soleb 25, 163
solstice, summer 31
solstice, winter 31
Son of Re 79
Sons of Horus 36, 111, 123, 143
Sopdet 43
Sopdu 124
Soped 124
Soped falcon 124, 234
Sothis 43
Sourouzian, Hourig 204, 205
Southern Heliopolis 31
sphinx 25, 87, 132, 204, 206, 222
Sphinx, Great 23, 32, 73
sphinx, king as a 127, 132
sphinx, queen as a 204
spinal dysraphism 169
spine 151, 154, 156–158, 167, 169, 170
Sprengel's deformity 169
Stadelmann, Rainer 204, 205
staff 63, 69, 73, 78, 91, 97, 158, 228, 229, 231, 235–237
staff, with figure of king 91
staff, with Nubian captive 78
stairway 47, 61, 68, 189, 226
stalls, finger 152
stalls, toe 152, 157
stand, vase 80, 228
State Department (USA) 245
statue of Amenhotep III and Queen Tiye (colossal) 24, 203
statue, colossal 25, 27, 205
statue, cult 32
statue, guardian 88, 227
statue, sphinx 241
Statues, Guardian 73
statues, servant 48
stela of Nehmesbastet 185
Stela, Restoration 32, 33, 225
sternum 156
Stewart, John 223
stick 78, 80, 91, 158, 159, 182, 228–231, 237
stomach 13, 43, 104, 108, 123
stone 32, 43, 44, 45, 58, 61, 62, 65, 68, 72, 84, 88, 91, 98, 100, 103, 112, 118, 119, 128, 145, 147, 150, 155, 179, 181, 188, 189, 195, 197, 199, 205, 206, 217, 226–229, 238, 250
stone, semiprecious 74, 76, 83, 98, 100, 101, 112, 113
stool 81, 228–230, 235–237
stool, dummy folding 81
stoppers, canopic 198
STR (= short tandem repeat) 166
Strouhal, Eugen 170
style, Amarna 34, 35
sun 19, 26, 31, 34, 40, 42, 47, 49, 52, 53, 68, 69, 73, 74, 75, 85, 92, 95, 97, 100, 114, 115, 118, 123, 133, 142, 144, 148, 175, 206, 233
sun disk 62, 87, 95, 105, 106, 145
Suppiluliumas 29
Supreme Council of Antiquities (= SCA) 184, 210, 246
Supreme Council of Antiquities, Secretary General of 9, 154, 165, 246, 250, 251, 252
Susie 214
swamp 138
sword 137, 146, 237
sycomore fig 157
Syria 22, 28, 70, 73, 87, 137

T

tadpole 71, 80, 95, 115, 118
Tadukhepa 164
Taemwadjsi 35
Taftaf 210
Tahrir Square 13, 209, 210, 225, 239
Tata 122, 234
Tatanen 122, 234
Taweret 249
Taylor, Elizabeth 222
Tefnut 26, 122, 182
temple 18, 19, 21, 22, 23, 26–28, 31–33, 57, 58, 70, 86, 104, 105, 163, 199, 205, 206, 208, 232
temple of millions of years 47
temple, construction of 23, 24
Temple, Great T. of the Aten 27
temple, mortuary/funerary 25, 47, 56, 62, 199, 204, 210
Temple, Small T. of the Aten 27/28
temples, Aten 27, 28
tenon 98, 100, 101, 240
terrorists 246
textile 65, 71, 77, 228, 229, 240
textile, fragment 71, 242
Texts, Coffin 49
Texts, Pyramid 49, 53, 93
texts, religious 53
texts, sacred 47
The Mummy, The 214, 222
Theban Mapping Project 175, 180, 198
Theban necropolis 46, 149, 174, 198, 239
Thebes 19, 20, 21, 23, 27, 28, 31–35, 37, 41–44, 46, 47, 49, 52, 53, 57, 71, 79, 132, 144, 174, 182, 241
thieves 44, 45, 57, 71, 76, 83, 118, 131, 135
Thinis 35
Third Intermediate Period 15, 182
Thomas, Elizabeth 175
Thoth 41, 49, 114, 119, 145, 148, 233
Thoth amulet 150, 232
Throne, Golden 69, 73, 83, 85, 245
throw stick 80, 85, 146, 228, 235, 238
Thutmose (sculptor) 250
Thutmose I 15, 22, 30, 31, 32, 56, 57, 249
Thutmose II 15, 22, 42, 225, 249
Thutmose III 15, 22, 23, 33, 37, 42, 47, 48, 53, 68, 77, 146, 183, 186, 235, 237, 243, 249
Thutmose IV 15, 23, 24, 57, 163, 197, 249
Times of London 63
Times of London, contract with 215
Tiye 24, 25, 27, 29, 47, 125, 154, 162, 164, 167, 169, 170, 171, 182, 196, 203, 204, 224, 237, 249
Tiye, at Amarna 28
Tjaru 183
tjet knot 88
Tjuya 24, 34, 47, 58, 61, 145, 158, 162, 164, 166, 167, 183, 209
toe stalls 152
tomb of Amenhotep I 175
tomb of Amenhotep II 58, 166, 198
tomb of Amenhotep III 47, 197, 223
tomb of Amenmesse 181
tomb of Ay 197, 224
tomb of Bent'anta 180
tomb of Horemheb at Memphis 34, 41, 47, 52, 53, 58, 168, 182
tomb of Huy 25, 37, 210, 243
tomb of Kheruef 164
tomb of Merenptah 190, 195
tomb of Meryetamun 180
tomb of Nefartari, replica of 211, 225
tomb of Nefertari 41, 49, 211, 225
tomb of Queen Tiaa 185
tomb of Rameses II 178, 180, 189, 190
tomb of Rameses VIII 175, 190
tomb of Seti I 13, 50, 51, 175, 186, 225
tomb of Seti II 89, 104, 142, 215
tomb of the sons of Rameses II 175, 176, 180
tomb of Thutmose I 47, 56
tomb of Thutmose III 47, 53
tomb of Tutankhamun 9, 13, 56, 58, 174, 175, 181, 191, 214, 215, 225, 242
tomb of Yuya and Tjuya 47, 61, 154, 183
tomb, private 47, 57, 58
tomb, replica of 211, 225
Tomb, Royal (Amarna) 29, 164
Tomb builders 47, 190
Toot Uncommons 220
tooth/teeth 13, 153, 156, 169
torch holder 76, 227
torso of Tutankhamun 86, 229
tourists 58, 155, 175, 210, 211, 216, 225, 246
tours of artifacts from the tomb 13, 244, 245, 246
tours of artifacts from the tomb, ban on 246
trade 19, 135, 145
trappings, mummy 143
traveling chest 72
Treasures of Tutankhamun exhibit 222
Treasury 62, 68, 76, 87, 104, 108, 120, 124, 127, 128, 214, 215, 224, 233
trolley 210
true of voice 73, 120, 121
trumpet 90, 209, 228
trumpet, gold 90, 231
trumpet, silver 90, 231
trumpet, wooden core of 90
truth 41, 57, 69, 75, 89, 92, 104, 113, 217, 224
TT 162 (= Theban Tomb 162) 35
TT 192 (= Theban Tomb 192) 164
tunnel of Seti I 13, 186
Turkey 28
turquoise 32, 106, 112, 114, 115, 116, 133, 143, 151, 154, 222
Tutankhamun 7, 9, 13, 15, 18, 28, 29, 30–35, 37, 47, 53, 57, 58, 64, 65, 68, 70, 71, 73, 76, 77, 78, 79, 81, 83, 85, 86, 87, 90, 97, 98, 100, 101, 103, 105, 110, 111, 114, 116, 120, 124, 125, 128, 132, 139, 151, 154, 157, 158, 163, 169, 183, 208, 209, 210, 216, 217, 220, 221, 222, 223
Tutankhamun and the Golden Age of the Pharaohs exhibit 223, 242, 246–248
Tutankhamun as child 95, 116, 131
Tutankhamun restores religion 163
Tutankhamun, battles of 33, 70, 146
Tutankhamun, blood type of 154
Tutankhamun, children of 164, 224
Tutankhamun, coronation of 30, 32, 72, 91, 116
Tutankhamun, death of 37, 47, 146, 156, 159, 167, 225
Tutankhamun, embalming cache of 183
Tutankhamun, family of 9, 13, 161, 162, 166, 170, 224
Tutankhamun, father of 9, 79, 153, 154, 159, 163, 164, 166, 167
Tutankhamun, figure of 126, 234
Tutankhamun, funeral of 96
Tutankhamun, harem of 35, 164
Tutankhamun, health of 156, 159
Tutankhamun, height of 153, 156
Tutankhamun, heir of 36, 37
Tutankhamun, hunting 32, 35,70, 146, 159, 225
Tutankhamun, monuments of 243
Tutankhamun, mother of 167
Tutankhamun, mummy of 142, 149, 155-158, 166, 169, 171, 216
Tutankhamun, murder of 154
Tutankhamun, names of 241
Tutankhamun, officials of 35
Tutankhamun, pedigree of 171
Tutankhamun, tomb of 9, 13, 56, 58, 174, 175, 181, 191, 214, 215, 225, 242
Tutankhamun, tutor of 13, 34, 224
Tutankhamun, weak/disabled 158, 159
Tutankhamun, wet nurse of 13, 30
Tutankhamun, wife of 30, 164, 166
Tutankhaten 29, 30, 31, 37, 71, 72, 83, 117, 162, 163
Tutankhuaten 30, 162, 163
Tutmania 13, 63, 220, 222, 223
twenty squares 134
Two Ladies 31
Two Ladies collar 144

U

Umm el-Qaab 56
UNESCO 222, 246, 251
Unguent 80, 101, 130, 135, 136, 142, 166, 235, 236, 237
unification of Egypt 18, 80
Union of the Two Lands 18, 131
University of Basel 184, 185
University of Chicago 33, 61, 157, 163, 246
University of Liverpool 154
University of Memphis 181
University of Michigan 154
University of Pennsylvania 186
University of Tubingen 165, 166
University of Zurich 156
Untold Story of Tutankhamun, The 222
uraeus/uraei 30, 86, 98, 100,103, 114, 116, 148, 149, 153, 207, 209, 232
uraeus amulet 149
uraeus, double 149
uraeus, flexible 153
uraeus, human-headed 149, 232
USAID 199, 211
Userhat 190
Usermont 35

V

Valley of Re 52
Valley of the Golden Mummies 60, 62, 65, 217
Valley of the Kings 9, 13, 23, 24, 28, 28, 34, 36, 31, 46, 47, 50, 51, 52, 53, 56, 57, 58, 60, 63, 68, 77,89, 96, 155, 164, 170, 174, 175, 176, 179, 181, 82, 184, 185, 186, 190, 191,194, 195, 196, 187, 198, 210, 211, 216, 223, 225, 239, 247
Valley of the Kings Foundation 221
Valley of the Kings, non-royal burial in 56, 57, 143, 155, 162
Valley of the Monkeys 13, 17, 37, 46, 197, 224
Valley of the Queens 41, 44, 46,49, 50, 56, 168, 210, 225
Valley Temple of Khafre 243
Vandenberg, Philipp 215
Vase 69, 77, 80, 135, 137, 226,227, 228, 230, 235, 235, 236,237, 238
vase stand 80, 228
vase, calcite 69, 80, 135, 226,227, 228, 230, 231, 235, 236, 237, 238
vase, long-necked 135
vase, faience 135, 137, 227, 228, 235, 238
vase, *heset* 137, 236, 238
vase, *nemset* 77
vase, ovoid 80
vase, unguent 135, 136 235, 236
vessel 37, 80, 130, 135, 136, 137, 235, 236, 237
vessel, bell-shaped 135, 236
vessel, calcite 37
vessel, faience 80
vessel, lion-shaped 136
vessel, *nemset* 137, 236
vessel, ritual 80
vessel, unguent 80, 130, 135, 136, 235, 236, 237
viceroy of Nubia 22, 35
vizier 35, 44, 45, 57, 65, 97, 190, 253
vulture 18, 77, 98, 100, 03, 105,114, 144, 146, 149, 153, 220, 231, 232, 233
vulture amulet 232
vulture goddess 77, 94, 100, 124, 149

W

wadi 28, 197, 198
Wadi, Great Royal (Amarna) 28
Wadj 150, 232, 233
Wadjet 18, 77, 100, 110, 111, 144,148, 149, 233
Wagdy, Adel Ghaffar 199, 206
walking stick 78, 158, 228, 290
wall paintings 30, 88, 97, 97, 104, 178, 179, 180, 181, 182, 211
wall paintings, Burial Chamber 49, 88, 96, 97, 211
Wallach, Amei 220, 245
war helmet 113
warfare 87
was 114, 122, 131, 231, 238
Wasef, Sally 165
Washington, DC 220, 223, 244, 246, 248
Water 43, 45, 52, 68, 71, 72, 77, 97, 137, 138, 181, 190, 186, 199, 206, 211
Waterboy 61
watermelon 157
Waziri, Moustafa 216
weapons 28, 31, 34, 70, 90, 137, 146, 235, 237
weben 137
wedjat 74, 87, 98, 104, 148,
wedjat-eye pendant 74, 87, 98, 104, 148, 232
Weeks, Kent 175
Weigall, Arthur 58
well shaft, ritual 47
Wenennefer 13
Werethekau (goddess) 149
Wernes 52
Wesekh 144
west 9, 19, 23, 27, 46, 97, 108, 179, 180, 197, 246
West Valley 197
Wet nurse 13, 30, 31, 162, 248
White Wall 18
Wife, Great Royal 28, 29, 49, 125, 164
wig, Nubian 83, 94
wig, tripartite 122, 129, 206
Wildung, Dietrich 250
window of appearances 27, 57
wine 43, 68, 71, 130, 158, 183, 221, 228
Winlock, H. E. 47, 57, 58, 68
Wishing Cup 69, 71
wood 13, 21, 30, 35, 41, 42, 43, 57, 64, 65, 68, 69, 70–74, 76, 78, 80, 81, 83–94, 98,100, 101, 104, 108, 116–128, 131, 132, 133, 138,139, 155, 157, 158, 162, 163, 164, 182, 183, 185, 198, 226–235, 237, 238
workmen 60, 61, 62, 74, 89, 96, 101, 187, 189, 190, 191, 194, 195, 197
World Monument Fund 210
World War I 63
World War II 65, 252

X

X-ray 9, 103, 169, 154, 156

Y

Y chromosome 166, 167
Year 16 inscription (Akhenaten) 28, 169
Younger Lady 224
Yuti 27
Yuya 24, 34, 41, 47, 58, 61, 154, 158, 162, 164, 166, 167, 171, 209
Yuya and Tjuya, tomb of 47, 61, 154, 183

Z

Zaghlul, Saad 64
Zink, Albert 165

DISCOVERING TUTANKHAMUN
–
FROM HOWARD CARTER TO DNA

by Zahi Hawass

First published in 2013 by
The American University in Cairo Press
113 Sharia Kasr el Aini, Cairo, Egypt
420 Fifth Avenue, New York, NY 10018
www.aucpress.com

in cooperation with Semmel Concerts GmbH

Exclusive distribution outside Egypt and North America by
I.B.Tauris & Co Ltd., 6 Salem Road, London, W2 4BU

Dar el Kutub No. 14518/13
ISBN 978 977 416 637 2

Dar el Kutub Cataloging-in-Publication Data

Hawass, Zahi
Discovering Tutankhamun: From Howard Carter to DNA /
Zahi Hawass.
Cairo: The American University in Cairo Press, 2013.

p.cm.
ISBN 978 977 416 637 2
1. Tutankhamun, King of Egypt
2. Tutankhamun, King of Egypt—Tomb
3. Egypt, Antiquities
932.014092

1 2 3 4 5   17 16 15 14 13

Written by
Zahi Hawass

Designed by
Fuhrer Visuelle Gestaltung OG, Vienna
Aleksandra Fuhrer
www.zehnbeispiele.com

Cover Illustration by
Dewynters PLC, London
www.dewynters.com

Photographs by
Harry Burton from The Griffith Institute Archive, University of Oxford
Sandro Vannini, Viterbo
Photo Archive Zahi Hawass

Photo Editor
Sandro Vannini, Viterbo
Tarek El Awady, Cairo

Foreword by
Jaromir Malek, Oxford

Editorial Consultant
Noreen Doyle, Tucson

Copyedited by
Ingrid Blom-Böer, Cologne
Alison Flint Steiner, Vienna

Project Management by
Christoph Scholz, Bayreuth
Oliver Rosenwald, Bayreuth

Printed in Germany by Himmer AG, Augsburg

The American University in Cairo Press
Cairo   New York